Conserving Migratory Birds

Edited by

T. SALATHÉ

WWF

Published with financial support from the
World Wide Fund for Nature

ICBP Technical Publication No. 12

Cover illustration: The Barn Swallow (*Hirundo rustica*), drawn by
Norman Arlott.

**A catalogue record for this book is available from the
British Library**

ISBN 0-946888-20-5
ISSN 0277-1330

Published by the International Council for Bird Preservation,
Cambridge, U.K.

Camera-ready text prepared for publication by Regina Pfaff and
Irene Hughes, ICBP.

Printed and bound by Page Bros. (Norwich) Ltd, Norfolk, U.K.

INTERNATIONAL COUNCIL FOR BIRD PRESERVATION

The International Council for Bird Preservation (ICBP), founded in 1922, is a global federation of 350 member organizations and representatives in 111 countries. Its aim is to save the world's birds and their habitats. Through this, it is also working towards the sustainable use of natural resources and the preservation of the diversity and quality of all life on earth.

ICBP pursues three main activities:

   * **Research** – Scientific information on the status and conservation needs of birds and their habitats is collected, analysed and disseminated. This is used to identify priority areas for action and forms the basis for the field programme and the determination of policy.

   * **Advocacy and Policy** – ICBP makes recommendations and seeks to influence policies, where they concern birds and their habitats, at a regional, national and international level, from a sound scientific and independent base.

   * **Field Projects** – A coherent programme of projects is targeted at carefully identified priority species, areas or habitats, involving direct action (species and habitat management) and indirect action (education, training, legislation). Currently, over 60 projects are in progress.

The work of ICBP is coordinated by a team of professional staff at the world headquarters in Cambridge, U.K. ICBP also has an executive office in Washington D.C., U.S.A. ICBP publishes the results of its work as a series of Technical Publications, Monographs and Study Reports. Technical Publications provide up-to-date and in-depth treatment of major bird conservation issues; Monographs give comprehensive information on specific or regional issues relating to bird conservation, and Study Reports present the results of certain field, research or investigative projects.

Three membership schemes (World Bird Club, Rare Bird Club and World Environment Partnership) allow individuals and corporations to support the work of ICBP. Its quarterly publication, *World Birdwatch*, is sent to all members.

ICBP, 32 Cambridge Road, Girton, Cambridge CB3 0PJ, U.K.
U.K. Charity No. 286211

CONTENTS

PART III: CONSERVING MIGRATORY BIRDS

CASE STUDIES

REGIONAL OVERVIEWS

FOREWORD

by Christoph Imboden
Director-General, ICBP

Ever since its founding days ICBP has used the example of migratory birds to advocate that nature conservation requires international cooperation. Today, in a world saturated with news about global environmental issues, nobody questions this concept any more, but in 1922 it was the prudent and pioneering mind only that recognized the need and promoted the idea.

The present level of cooperation between nations in assessing and solving environmental problems is generally encouraging. It is the result of a significant increase in environmental awareness during the past two decades throughout the world. ICBP can likewise point, with some pride, to many projects and programmes addressing the mutual interests and concerns of various nations, bringing together people from different continents and different cultures to find solutions to problems that cannot be resolved by any one country on its own. The migratory birds programme in Europe, for example, has certainly been a key catalyst in bringing not only conservationists of different nations together, but in getting governments to adopt joint strategies for protecting a form of wildlife that does not recognize national boundaries and continental divides.

The increasing international solidarity and partnership in conservation is, of course, rooted in the growing recognition of worldwide ecological and socio-economic interdependences. Environmental problems are generally not just the result of a local action, but originate from a complex web of causes and effects interlinking the natural world with the socio-economic systems of human society form local to global levels. However, are international conservation activities in reality paying enough attention to the true implications of these global and transdisciplinary connections that we now recognize as lying at the heart of most environmental issues? Do we indeed fully understand them?

Despite the new environmental internationalism I believe we are still far from addressing the real issues – that is, the causes of the problems rather than the symptoms only. The latter are easier to deal with; they can be addressed on technical level, mainly requiring the investment of money. Much international conservation cooperation still functions on the basis of developed countries, through government or NGO agencies, providing financial support for technological cures in less developed countries.

To tackle the underlying causes – unsustainable use of resources, poverty, north–south divide, third world debt, population growth – requires a different form of cooperation: indeed, it demands a commitment to truly joint action, targeted towards ultimate factors such as the world's global exchange economy which, directly or indirectly, is the driving force behind most environmental problems.

How should this affect conservation programmes for migratory birds? In the Americas as well as in Europe/Africa there is more and more evidence today that land-use practices in wintering areas are an important factor influencing population levels of migratory birds. The "technological" solution is to initiate programmes to establish protected areas (such as wetland reserves on the African coast) for resting and wintering migrants. To get to the *causes*, international cooperation should be more vigorously directed towards the development of trade policies that give all partners the best chance of establishing truly sustainable agricultural practices in their region. Nobody has yet, unfortunately, assessed in detail how the new international GATT treaties will affect land-use practices and the conservation of critical ecosystems (for residential and migratory species) in all parts of the world, north and south.

Looking at the general conservation situation of migratory birds it is interesting to note that only a small number of them fall into the category of globally threatened species. Despite their annual journeys, exposing them to additional hazards that non-migrants do not face, relatively few migratory species have fallen to such critically low numbers that they must be considered globally endangered.

A listing in the international Red Data Book should, however, not be the only criterion for becoming concerned about the status of a species. Investigations in North America and Europe suggest that there is hardly a migratory species that, during the past 20 years, has not declined in numbers. This slow erosion of the abundance (and distribution range) of numerous "common" or widespread species throughout the world is a hitherto greatly neglected aspect of the loss of global biodiversity. In addition to the 11 per cent of bird species considered globally threatened I believe that as many as 60 per cent of the world's birds are undergoing some form of decline in abundance and/or distribution. If it is happening with regard to the birds, there is no reason to assume that the status of other animal and plant species is not being eroded in a similar fashion.

This problem needs to be studied urgently and systematically. Since they are well researched and better documented that any other class of animals or plants, the birds offer our best hope to shed some light quickly on this neglected, and possibly very serious, dimension of biodiversity loss. Migratory birds might be particularly valuable and suitable indicators for this task since local monitoring programmes, at breeding and migration sites, are already in progress in many countries. To maximize the usefulness of such programmes for conservation purposes a high degree of international cooperation is needed. These programmes should be standardized and coordinated centrally by a body such as ICBP so that comparative analyses, covering the entire world, can easily be made and the problem be assessed globally and objectively.

I am delighted that, at last, ICBP now has in its technical publication series a volume about the flagship *migratory birds* and would like to thank all the authors for their contributions and the editor, Tobias Salathé, for his persevering work.

EDITOR'S PREFACE

by Tobias Salathé
Migratory Birds Programme Coordinator, ICBP

Migratory birds, which regularly cover long distances between their breeding and wintering areas, have always been of concern to conservationists: indeed it was the wish to promote agreements between governments on their protection from human over-exploitation that led to the foundation of ICBP in 1922. This concern subsequently grew, particularly in Europe, to such a degree that a specific conservation programme for migrants of the West Palearctic–African flyways was started in 1976.

PART I of this book summarizes this development and the underlying reasons for it. After 12 years of conservation activities under this programme, it was felt timely to review its activities, critically assess its achievements and propose future strategies. To this end a one-day workshop was held during the 17th Conference of the ICBP European Continental Section on 20 May 1989 at the Çucurova University of Adana in Turkey, with financial support from the World Wide Fund for Nature (WWF). Papers 1, 6, 7, 9, 10, 11, 19, 22, and 23 represent the proceedings of most of the revised contributions to this workshop. Although the contents of this publication are therefore necessarily biased towards the problems of the West Palearctic–African flyways, every effort has been made to include also relevant contributions relating to the American and Asian–Australasian flyways.

PART II provides an overview of the problems facing migratory birds. Although habitat loss and degradation (e.g. through pollution by pesticide side effects) are by far the main causes for concern, some regional accounts of the scale of human persecution at migration bottlenecks are included here, as this is a specific threat to migratory birds.

PART III highlights selected conservation activities in an exemplary way. The authors of these contributions, although often directly involved in the implementation of the projects they describe, are still best qualified, due to their intimacy with the problems they have had to overcome, to assess the merits and failures of the projects and to present the lessons to be learnt. This part of the book is completed by regional reviews of the American and Asian–Australasian flyways (papers 15 to 18).

PART IV provides the views on how to move forwards of experts from international conservation organizations equally concerned about migratory birds. Specific emphasis is placed on international law, which is often so crucial for the protection of those birds that are the common responsibility of many nations. The Forward Plan for the ICBP Migratory Birds Programme in the West Palearctic–African flyways concludes the volume.

This book is not a scientific treatise on the ecology of migrants. Comprehensive overviews have been published for the Palearctic–African flyways (Schütz *et al.* 1971; Moreau 1972) and the Americas (Keast & Morton 1980), and recent symposia (1989 on the ecology and conservation of Neotropical migrant landbirds at Woods Hole, U.S.A.; and 1991 on the ecology and conservation of Palearctic–African migrants at Norwich, U.K.) are likely to summarize further results of scientific field studies. This volume differs from others in the ICBP Technical Publications series in that it is intended to demonstrate specific problems and approaches to solving them, rather than to provide a comprehensive discussion of the issues, species, habitats or sites concerned. Conservation of migratory birds has become such a vast and complex subject that it could hardly be dealt with adequately in one volume. In addition, readers of these contributions will soon realize that migratory birds not only deserve attention in their own right but also act as "flagships" for wider conservation issues, especially the need for an international as opposed to a national focus.

I am thankful to all the authors who freely gave their time and expertise to contribute to this volume. In the United States, Kim Young did a great job in finding and liaising with the authors of the American contributions. Noritaka Ichida suggested authors for the Asian contributions. George Archibald, Susie Biber-Klemm, Nigel Collar, Nonie Coulthard, Pat Dugan, Curt Freese, Adam Gretton, Richard Grimmett, Christoph Imboden, Tony Juniper, Cyrille de Klemm, Miriam Langeveld, Gernant Magnin, Eugene Morton, Mike Moser, Duncan Parish, Mike Parr, Mike Rands, Goetz Rheinwald, Chandler Robbins, Derek Scott, Stan Senner, Shunji Usui, Nigel Varty, Martha van der Voort and David Wells critically reviewed typescripts and made helpful comments. Martyn Bramwell prepared the revised texts for publication. At ICBP, Irene Hughes and Regina Pfaff were essential in producing the camera-ready copy for this book. I would like to thank them all for the pleasure it was working together.

REFERENCES

KEAST, A. & MORTON, E. S., eds. (1980) *Migrant birds in the Neotropics: ecology, behavior, distribution and conservation.* Washington, D.C.: Smithsonian Institution.

MOREAU, R. E. (1972) *The Palearctic–African bird migration systems.* London and New York: Academic Press.

SCHÜTZ, E., BERTHOLD, P., GWINNER, E. & OELKE, H. (1971) *Grundriss der Vogelzugskunde.* Berlin and Hamburg: Paul Parey.

PART I
WHY MIGRATORY BIRDS?

The first part of this volume provides the reader with information about why, since its foundation, ICBP has been concerned about migratory birds. It summarizes the reasons for this concern and the history of international agreements for the protection of migrants, and recapitulates how a specific programme was set up in Europe to help the migratory summer visitors of this continent during their transits of the Mediterranean and their winter sojourns in Africa. This background information is necessary to explain the regional bias of this volume towards the West Palearctic–African flyways: a bias that arises from purely historical factors.

T. Salathé

THE ICBP MIGRATORY BIRDS CONSERVATION PROGRAMME

TOBIAS SALATHÉ

*International Council for Bird Preservation, 32 Cambridge Road,
Girton, Cambridge CB3 0PJ, U.K.*

ABSTRACT

A brief historical overview is given of the growth of concern for international conservation efforts for migratory birds, and the specific conservation programme for the West Palearctic–African flyways currently being pursued by the ICBP Secretariat with support from specific committees and agencies in several European countries. Major results of the ICBP Migratory Birds Conservation Programme are reviewed. The paper gives an overview of the aims, approaches and constraints of activities undertaken during a dozen years, refers to the assessments of specific projects of the Migratory Birds Conservation Programme provided in other papers in this volume, and lists the reasons for ICBP to continue to address specifically the problems of migratory birds, not only for their own sake but also within the broader perspectives of the conservation and sustainable use of natural resources.

INTRODUCTION

Twice a year, with the changing of the seasons, occurs the phenomenon of bird migration which has fascinated man for thousands of years. The fact that it is such a common strategy among birds indicates that it must be a successful adaptation. Yet it also makes migrants one of the most difficult groups in which to detect significant threats or changes in population size. Their mobility and their tendency to concentrate in very large numbers on the breeding grounds, during migration and in their wintering quarters, make migratory birds particularly attractive to human interest and care, but also extremely susceptible to changes in the environment and fluctuations in the level of human exploitation or persecution.

Bird migration is a different phenomenon at either end of the intercontinental flyways. People living in northern latitudes are familiar with the disappearance of many migrant species during autumn and enjoy their return to the breeding grounds in spring, when passerines fill the air with an increasingly diverse dawn chorus. Quite differently, people living at lower latitudes close to strategic stop-over sites on main flyways or in regions of winter concentrations experience a sudden abundance of all kinds of feathered visitors and exploit the abundant resource for sport and subsistence. So there is a gain, cultural or economic, to be made by everyone from migratory birds.

With the increasing understanding of the scientific facts of bird migration and the growing knowledge about the migration patterns and flyways of different groups of migrants, concern about their fate grew among ornithologists. Increasingly, news of the disappearance and decline of populations furthered the belief that numbers of migratory birds are declining and added to the concern about human killing of migratory birds at bottleneck areas along the flyways. Dedicated conservationists realized at the beginning of the century that problems of declining populations of migrants are of international concern, and that therefore only an international approach and coordinated action would be appropriate.

HISTORICAL DEVELOPMENT

In 1902, delegates from 12 European countries signed the (mainly utilitarian) Convention for the Protection of Birds useful to Agriculture, which regulated the killing, capturing and trading of some 150 species, most of them migratory. This early intergovernmental agreement was soon followed by other conventions and bilateral treaties (*Table 1*). Boardman (1981) and Lyster (1985) give a useful overview of the development of international law which plays such a particular role in the protection of migratory birds. Also, many of the case studies and more general papers in this volume will point out the importance of particular legal agreements. But migratory birds did not only spur the advancement of wildlife conservation laws: they were also the catalyst for the creation of the first truly international conservation organization, the International Council for Bird Preservation (ICBP). It was the will to protect vulnerable migratory species that led to the creation of ICBP in 1922 by American and British ornithologists. ICBP and its constituent national member organizations were leading forces behind further developments in favour of migratory birds protection.

Among ornithologists in central Europe, concern about the fate of "their" migrant summer visitors during migration and wintering in the Mediterranean and Africa grew to such a degree that in 1976 the European Committee for the Prevention of Mass Destruction of Migratory Birds was formed by ICBP. Naturally, the committee's main aim was to bring to an end the mass catching and destruction of migratory birds in the Mediterranean. A coordinator was appointed to elaborate international and national priorities and to help a number of educational projects in Mediterranean countries with money raised by supporting committees in the Netherlands and the U.K., later also in Denmark, Switzerland and the Federal Republic of Germany. What started in the Netherlands with a focus on the indiscriminate killing of migrants in the Mediterranean (Woldhek 1980) grew with the years to a more broadly oriented conservation programme. Thus a symposium on "Problems and Prospects of Migratory Birds in Africa" (MacDonald & Goriup 1985) was held in 1983 at the 14th Conference of ICBP's European Continental Section in Rochefort (France). The ICBP Secretariat drafted for this occasion a plan for a "Campaign for the Conservation of Migratory Birds", and the programme of the European committee, originally run from the headquarters of the Dutch Society for the Protection of Birds, was widened in its scope to include African problems, transferred to the ICBP Secretariat, and guided by a newly named "ICBP Migratory Birds Committee".

Table 1: Chronological list of international agreements of relevance for migratory bird conservation.

Treaties	Established
Species-oriented treaties	
Convention on the Protection of Birds Useful to Agriculture ("1902 Convention"; 12 European States)	1902
Convention on the Protection of Migratory Birds ("1916 Convention"; Canada and U.S.A.)	1916
Convention on the Protection of Migratory Birds and Game Mammals ("1936 Convention"; Mexico and U.S.A.)	1936
International Convention on the Protection of Birds ("1950 Convention"; European States)	1950
Benelux Convention on the Hunting and Protection of Birds ("Benelux Convention"; Belgium, Netherlands and Luxembourg)	1970
Convention on the Protection of Migratory Birds and Birds in Danger of Extinction and their Environment ("1972 Convention"; Japan and U.S.A.)	1972
Convention on the Protection of Migratory Birds and Birds Under Threat of Extinction and on the Means of Protecting Them ("1973 Convention"; U.S.S.R. and Japan)	1973
Agreement on the Protection of Migratory Birds and Birds in Danger of Extinction and their Environment ("1974 Convention"; Japan and Australia)	1974
Convention Concerning the Conservation of Migratory Birds and their Environment ("1976 Convention"; U.S.S.R. and U.S.A.)	1976
Directive of the Council of the European Economic Community on the Conservation of Wild Birds ("Birds Directive"; 12 EC Member States)	1979
Regional conventions	
Convention on Nature Protection and Wildlife Preservation in the Western Hemisphere ("Western Hemisphere Convention"; administered by OAS)	1940
African Convention on the Conservation of Nature and Natural Resources ("African Convention"; administered by OAU)	1968
Convention on the Conservation of European Wildlife and Natural Habitats ("Berne Convention"; administered by the Council of Europe)	1979
ASEAN Agreement on the Conservation of Nature and Natural Resources	1985
Convention for Protection and Development of the Natural Resources and Environment of the South Pacific Region	1985
Global conventions	
Convention on Wetlands of International Importance Especially as Waterfowl Habitat ("Ramsar Convention"; administered by IUCN)	1971

(*continued*)

Table 1: Continued

Treaties	Established
Global conventions (*continued*)	
Convention Concerning the Protection of the World Cultural and Natural Heritage ("World Heritage Convention"; administered by UNESCO)	1972
Convention on International Trade in Endangered Species of Wild Fauna and Flora ("CITES" or "Washington Convention"; administered by a central Secretariat and national Authorities of the Member States)	1973
Convention on the Conservation of Migratory Species of Wild Animals ("CMS" or "Bonn Convention"; administered by UNEP)	1979

After Lyster 1985 and U.S. Congress OTA 1987.

Acronyms used: ASEAN = Association of South East-Asian Nations; IUCN = International Union for Conservation of Nature and Natural Resources; OAS = Organization of American States; OAU = Organization of African Unity; UNEP = United Nations Environment Programme; UNESCO = United Nations Educational, Scientific and Cultural Organization.

THE ICBP MIGRATORY BIRDS CONSERVATION PROGRAMME

All these developments were strongly helped by the joint preparation of a "Programme for the Conservation of Migratory Birds" by IUCN (The World Conservation Union), IWRB (the International Waterfowl and Wetlands Research Bureau), WWF (the World Wide Fund for Nature) and ICBP (cf. Anonymous 1984). This document provided the basis for a major fundraising campaign in 1984 by the Swiss national sections of WWF and ICBP to support a set of jointly developed conservation projects. The programme covered such varied issues as the development of species management plans for international legal instruments (cf. Goriup & Schulz, this volume), the development of institutional capacities (cf. Sultana and Yazgan, this volume) and data bases (cf. Moser, this volume), and specific conservation problems like those related to wetlands (cf. Coulthard, this volume) and to pollution through pesticide use (e.g. Mullié *et al.*, this volume). Thereby, the foundations for an integrated conservation programme were laid, and the partner organizations took responsibility for their respective projects. For ICBP this meant that its original concerns about migratory birds were recognized by its major international sister organizations, and that additional funding sources became available for these specific projects through the fundraising campaign in Switzerland. Naturally ICBP remained the organization mostly concerned with field projects for the specific conservation of migratory birds, and has continued to pursue the programme ever since.

Objectives
With the establishment of an ICBP Action Plan for the years 1986-1990 at the XIX ICBP World Conference in Kingston (Canada) in 1986, the conservation of migratory birds was included in ICBP's global priorities, and during the subsequent years the "ICBP Migratory Birds Conservation Programme" was fully integrated

into the overall ICBP Conservation Programme. The programme has since been active in ICBP's five major areas of operation:

Data gathering and analysis: to monitor the conservation status of important bird areas, to detect population trends of selected migratory bird species and establish the ecological basis behind changes detected on migration and at their wintering areas, and to monitor the effects of the mass killing of migratory birds in some countries.

Education and training: to increase public and government awareness of the need to conserve migratory birds, to provide training in habitat management, scientific monitoring of populations, sustainable wildlife utilization and environmental education for technical staff in developing countries, and to make available and promote the wide dissemination of simple educational materials.

Species and habitat management: to identify important bird areas requiring priority conservation measures by establishing or expanding existing protected areas, to provide advice and assistance with the drawing up and implementation of management plans for such areas, and to assist with the development of regional management plans for threatened migratory species.

Network building: to develop a network of organizations and individuals promoting the conservation of birds and their habitats at local, national, regional and international levels and to foster the formation of organizations devoted to the study and conservation of birds in countries and regions where none exist yet.

International cooperation: to advise governments on appropriate national wildlife legislation, to promote the signing and ratification of relevant international wildlife conventions, and to lobby for the rigorous enforcement of existing national and international wildlife legislation.

For many years the funds raised by national committees through regular public campaigns formed the only source of finances for the programme, and only more recently has the ICBP Secretariat been able to find financial support for specific projects from governmental sources and aid agencies. It is therefore not surprising that the majority of the projects in the early years consisted of very limited but specific support for local groups, such as the provision of educational materials (leaflets, posters, stickers, films, slide-show equipment, etc.), the short-term remuneration of lobbyists, guides and reserve wardens for specific tasks, the training of conservation and education officers, or the provision of office equipment to local and national bird protection societies in their earliest days of establishment. A general analysis of the programme's activities (*Table 2*) shows that the number of projects undertaken over a specific period of time has not changed drastically during the 12 years since 1978. But in line with the developments mentioned above, the regional emphasis which was focusing mainly on southern Europe and the Mediterranean shifted somewhat towards countries in northern Africa and the Middle East, and projects have become more international, comprehensive and expensive.

Due to these circumstances the ICBP Migratory Birds Conservation Programme has focused mainly on educational and training aspects (more than 50 per cent of all funds spent), followed by species and habitat management, data gathering and

Table 2: General characteristics of migratory birds conservation projects carried out by the European Committee for the Prevention of Mass Destruction of Migratory Birds (*Period I*) and the ICBP Migratory Birds Conservation Programme (*Period II:* after the Rochefort Conference, including the joint campaign with IUCN, IWRB and WWF; *Period III:* after inclusion of the Programme into ICBP's Action Plan 1986-1989).

	Period I 1978-1983	Period II 1983-1986	Period III 1987-1989
Number of projects undertaken (projects undertaken per year)	69 (12.9)	47 (14.5)	43 (14.3)
Average GBP[1] spent per project	1,300	2,500	14,700
Number of countries covered[2]	12	15	17

Top four countries with largest number of projects (in brackets):

	Malta (19)	Italy (8)	International (11)
	Spain (13)	Cyprus (5)	Turkey (5)
	Italy (11)	International (4)	Cyprus (4)
	Turkey & France (5)	Turkey & Malta (3)	Egypt (3)

Notes: 1 Great Britain Pound Sterling; 2 Including international projects as an additional category.

analysis, and the strengthening of local conservation organizations, plus the promotion of conservation legislation. Rands (1987) analysed the programme's activities between 1978 and 1986 in detail. A similar breakdown will not be repeated here, but a few of the main activities deserve further mention. A feeling that more data on the threats and problems facing migratory birds were needed to assess their situation better and prepare recommendations for improvement has prevailed since the start of the programme. Consequently, several comprehensive reports were produced. Bijlsma's study on bottleneck areas for migratory birds in the Mediterranean region (1987) was a follow-up study to Woldhek's assessment of bird killing in the Mediterranean (1980). Grimmett and Jones's inventory of Important Bird Areas in Europe (1989) lists all stop-over and wintering sites important for migrants in Europe, and the results of a questionnaire sent out to many correspondents in Europe and Africa provided a review of the problems affecting Palearctic migratory birds in Africa (Grimmett 1987). Thus ICBP's programme department was increasingly able to base the choice of its priorities for field projects on reliable scientific data and assessments by regional specialists. Many data on migratory waterbirds in the Mediterranean and West Africa were collected by the Dutch Working Group for International Wader and Waterfowl Research (e.g. WIWO 1989), and in a similar way the Centre for Environmental Studies at the University of Leiden produced overviews of the importance of Sahel wetlands for Palearctic migrants (in prep.) and on the likely changes to wetlands the many hydrological development projects in West Africa are going to create (van Ketel *et al.* 1987). Most recently, the ICBP Migratory Birds Conservation Programme was able to collaborate more closely with the Commission of the European Communities (Directorate-General XI for Environment, Consumer Protection and Nuclear Safety) by preparing an overview of conservation priorities for European migrants (Biber & Salathé 1990).

Conservation education
In addition to many one-off activities in support of local educational projects, the ICBP Migratory Birds Conservation Programme has created educational materials

which have been distributed in several countries. A wallchart depicting the main migratory bird flyways between Europe and Africa was produced in ten languages (English, French, German, Portuguese, Spanish, Italian, Romanian, Greek, Turkish and Arabic), and nearly 50,000 copies have so far been distributed in about 25 countries. The back of this wallchart provides detailed information about bird migration, important stop-over and wintering areas in Europe and Africa, threats to migratory birds, and the aims of international conventions and conservation organizations. Whilst this poster was warmly welcomed in many black African countries where it served as a first entry point for ICBP, subsequent experience showed that such a poster is not likely to have a lasting impact as long as it does not form part of a wider educational campaign. The large amount of information packed onto both sides of the poster needs careful explanation by a teacher in order for the target audience (mainly school children) to understand the message correctly. Among the lessons learnt during the distribution of this poster was the importance of recognizing that international educational tools must be adapted to each country's specific needs. Therefore the most recent Arabic versions of the chart were prepared separately in Morocco and Egypt by national wildlife education experts to form, together with other materials, an integral part of comprehensive education programmes for school children and the general public. Even though it is often easier to produce the colour separations (or even print the coloured parts) in Europe, as much as possible of the preparation and production process should be done in the country concerned. This is the best way to ensure that national education officers consider the materials as their own tools and consequently they will be inclined to disseminate them widely.

These experiences also apply to other international educational tools prepared under this programme, particularly the *Mediterranean Bird Book*. Right from the start the European Committee developed the idea of producing a pragmatic booklet on birds for countries where no ornithological field guides exist. This handy publication of about 40 pages was to be distributed widely among school teachers and children. The concept of the book was to show the most characteristic birds in full colour (96 species) accompanied by a short introduction, in black-and-white, to the biology of birds, the main threats they face, and how to observe them. To date such a booklet has been produced for nine countries in 13 different languages: Portugal, Morocco (French; Arabic version in preparation), Yugoslavia (Serbo-Croat, Slovenian, Serbian and Hungarian; Macedonian and Albanian versions in preparation), Greece, Turkey, Lebanon (Arabic, French/English), Jordan (Arabic), Egypt (Arabic) and Sudan (Arabic). The booklet proved most successful in those countries where it became an integral part of wildlife education. In Portugal the Ministry of Education provided the possibility for a large print run; the Turkish Society for the Protection of Nature (DHKD) reproduced the booklet in various forms (cf. Yazgan, this volume), and the Egyptian Wildlife Service produced different work booklets on related themes in black-and-white for wide distribution to school children during conservation education classes. At the time of writing, the artist Robin Reckitt has painted vignettes depicting nearly 230 different bird species and subspecies in their typical Mediterranean or African habitats. Additional interest in using them has recently been expressed in Cyprus, Tunisia, Malta, Cape Verde, Senegal and other countries. A set of postcards using the book's artwork of typical birds has been produced in Egypt by a commercial publisher. These postcards are now promoting the conservation education project of ICBP and the Egyptian Wildlife Service and providing some royalties for it.

A third type of educational material produced for the ICBP Migratory Birds Conservation Programme consisted of audio-visual slide shows and a short video film on "The Miracle of Migration", initially produced in six languages (English, French, Italian, Greek, Turkish and Arabic) and so far distributed, shown and broadcast in nearly 20 countries. ICBP itself never had the technical expertise and capacity to produce such materials and had to rely heavily on the support of professionals through collaboration with the International Centre for Conservation Education (ICCE) and the London-based Media Natura media charity.

Species and habitat management
In the field of species management, the ICBP Migratory Birds Conservation Programme was particularly active in drawing up a conservation management plan for the White Stork (*Ciconia ciconia*) based on the results of an international symposium in Walsrode (F.R.G.) in 1985 (Rheinwald *et al.* 1989). This species, unlike many others, enjoys an intimate bond with man and serves therefore as a test case on how efficient a single-species management plan, which has to cover nearly 60 range states with different economies, cultures and political constraints, can possibly be (cf. Goriup & Schulz, this volume). Similar preparations for species action plans, although on a much smaller scale, are under way for Lesser Kestrel (*Falco naumanni*) (Biber 1990), Corncrake (*Crex crex*) (Sothmann 1991) and Slender-billed Curlew (*Numenius tenuirostris*) (Gretton 1991).

Habitat and site management projects normally require the presence of specialists in the field, and due to the funding constraints on the programme, its efforts and merits in this field have so far been rather limited. An assessment of the importance of the coastal wetlands of Liberia for wintering waterbirds was undertaken by Gatter (1988), and a similar study in the coastal zone of Guinea is currently under way and will provide the national authorities with recommendations on where and how to set up nature reserves (Altenburg & van der Kamp 1991). Management recommendations and advice have been provided through the programme for sites in Yugoslavia (Kopački Rit), Turkey (Ereğli Marshes, Lake Gala), Malta (cf. Sultana, this volume), Egypt (Lake Bardawil) and Morocco (Merja Zerga, Sidi Boughaba lake). Out of these, the involvement in wetland conservation in Morocco has been the most active: it included the holding of a training course on wetland ecology and management for reserve managers of the regional authorities, and (most recently) the preparation of a brochure and teachers' pack on wetland conservation, together with the Society for the Protection of Animals in North Africa (and Société Protectrice des Animaux, Rabat).

International cooperation
From the beginning, one of the aims of the programme was to further international treaties, such as the Convention on the Conservation of Migratory Species (Bonn Convention) and the Convention on Wetlands of International Importance especially as Waterfowl Habitat (Ramsar Convention). In the fields of species and habitat management, collaborations with the bureaux of these conventions, the Commission of the European Communities, and IUCN's and WWF's field programmes, have proved to be most useful.

Network building
A cornerstone of the programme is the initial support provided to local conservation organizations. Sultana and Yazgan assess the merits of these aspects for NGOs in Malta and Turkey in separate papers in this volume. Support for the Italian League for the Protection of Birds (LIPU), the French association MIGRANS (which is wardening crucial bottleneck areas to gather data on migrants

and prevent illegal shooting), and the Egyptian Wildlife Service (a governmental organization), and the creation of the Egyptian Wildlife Society (a non-governmental organization), are also worth mentioning.

WHY FOCUS ON MIGRATORY BIRDS ?

This brief overview shows that the ICBP Migratory Birds Conservation Programme does not only focus on migratory birds in their own right, but also uses them as flagships for wider conservation problems which are encountered along the West Palearctic–African flyways. Some fundamental issues which make migratory birds (as a category) particularly suitable as foci for conservation campaigns have indeed been addressed by the programme's activities, as outlined below:

— Migratory birds, because of their popular appeal and conspicuousness (mass concentrations, high visibility, dawn chorus), are ideal for introducing the general public to the value, importance and beauty of wildlife and the need for nature conservation in general. In this capacity they provide an excellent fundraising potential for conservation projects.
— Migrants form a link between countries, and in doing so emphasise the need for international cooperation (as opposed to a national focus) for effective conservation (cf. Ntiamoa-Baidu, this volume).
— Migrant birds often link wealthy developed nations, where many migratory species breed and in which conservation organizations are well established, with less developed countries, where the majority of migrants spend the winter and where conservation movements and the practices of sustainable development are in their infancy. They are thus particularly useful for promoting the concept of wealthy nations providing finance and expertise to poorer countries for the conservation of shared resources.
— Migrants may act as sensitive environmental indicators and early warning systems (as, for example, did the Whitethroat (*Sylvia communis*) and Sand Martin (*Riparia riparia*), whose population decline made conservationists in Europe aware of the intercontinental consequences of the extreme drought conditions in the winter quarters of these species in the Sahel; cf. Goriup & Schulz, this volume).

Turning back to the (long-distance) migratory species themselves, the specific concerns of the ICBP Migratory Birds Conservation Programme for the West Palearctic–African flyways will be placed in the context of ICBP's global bird conservation priorities. According to recent ICBP research (Collar & Andrew 1988) most of the globally threatened species (11 per cent of the world's bird species) occur in tropical forests or on oceanic islands (*Table 3*). Despite the fact that migratory birds are subject to more potential perils, most of the highly threatened species are non-migratory. Migrants generally have larger populations, a larger distribution range and *r*-selected reproductive strategies, all adaptations geared to coping with the unpredictable ecological conditions long-distance migrants regularly have to face along their intercontinental journeys, and which reduce their risk of becoming globally threatened. However, migratory birds face serious hazards from degradation of many habitats along their migratory routes, and from hunting and other forms of direct persecution, as well as pesticide contamination (cf. contributions in PART II of this volume).

12 T. Salathé

Table 3: Top 15 geopolitical units holding important numbers of threatened bird species and threatened endemics according to Collar & Andrew 1988.

Geopolitical unit	Threatened bird species	Threatened endemics
Indonesia	126	91
Brazil	121	68
China	81	18
Peru	71	27
Colombia	70	32
India	62	11
Argentina	56	4
Ecuador	51	7
Philippines	42	34
Thailand	39	2
U.S.S.R.	38	0
Myanmar	37	2
Paraguay	36	0
Australia	34	33
Viet Nam	34	8

In the context of the programme for the West Palearctic–African flyways the European countries each hold only a few (0-15) globally threatened species. Together they account for 29 species (<3 per cent of all globally threatened species) out of which only seven are long-distance migrants (*Figure 1*), namely the Lesser White-fronted Goose (*Anser erythropus*), Red-breasted Goose (*Branta ruficollis*), Lesser Kestrel (*Falco naumanni*), Corncrake, Sociable Plover (*Chettusia gregaria*), Slender-billed Curlew and Aquatic Warbler (*Acrocephalus paludicola*). Although research into the problems of some of these species is under way, the single-species approach clearly can not be the most efficient way of dealing with conservation problems for the Migratory Birds Conservation Programme. The most numerous and conspicuous West Palearctic long-distance migrants are waterfowl, waders, terns, larks, swallows, warblers, and many others whose appeal is due to their colourful plumage (e.g. Hoopoe (*Upupa epops*)), evocative song (e.g. European Cuckoo (*Cuculus canorus*) and Golden Oriole (*Oriolus oriolus*)) or particular behaviour (e.g. shrikes). It is therefore obvious that the ICBP Migratory Birds Conservation Programme has rather to focus on conservation problems at key sites, where large numbers of birds of these groups gather to breed, to refuel during migration or to winter. For those that do not congregate, but instead disperse, like most passerines, the habitat approach is likely to be most useful, i.e. to promote the wise human exploitation of the natural resources of important breeding, resting and wintering habitats (i.e. forests, grasslands and wetlands in European breeding areas; scrubland, maquis and wetlands in the Mediterranean; and grasslands, savannas and wetlands in African wintering zones).

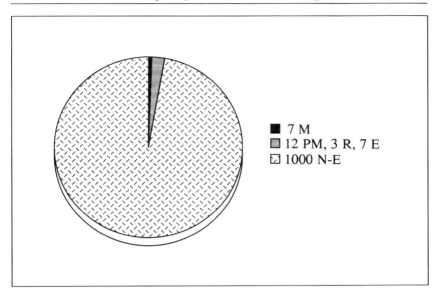

■ 7 M
▨ 12 PM, 3 R, 7 E
▨ 1000 N-E

Figure 1: The number of globally threatened birds in Europe (*after* Grimmett & Jones 1989) in relation to the total number of globally threatened species. M = European migrants; PM = European partial migrants; R = European residents; E = European endemics; N-E = non-European threatened species.

CONCLUSION

Above all, migratory birds are the common property and responsibility of many nations, and are therefore extremely valuable in establishing bonds of interest between countries. The Arctic Tern (*Sterna paradisaea*), for example, takes the whole world as its habitat. Migrating over the oceans, the industrially polluted North Sea coast is only a few dozen hours' flying time from the burning shanty towns of West Africa and the pristine Antarctic waters threatened by oil slicks and overfishing. This bird therefore requires conservation at a succession of sites, ideally through the centralized coordination of the activities of different interest groups; and this work is valuable not only for its own sake, but also for the educational and institutional value it brings to southern countries, often establishing major connections through which many other kinds of conservation can follow. Although migrants are in most cases not species threatened by immediate extinction, many of them already show serious population declines (e.g. Berthold *et al.* 1986 for the West Palearctic; Terborgh 1989 for the Nearctic) and thus serve as valuable indicators of environmental degradation and as a popular focus for conservation projects addressing the underlying causes. We are only just beginning to understand these global connections. Perhaps we can start by taking a lesson from the migratory birds. They acknowledge no borders: it is a principle we should make our own.

ACKNOWLEDGEMENTS

I would like to thank Christoph Imboden and Mike Rands for valuable comments on the first draft of this article.

REFERENCES

ALTENBURG, W. & VAN DER KAMP, J. (1991) *Ornithological importance of coastal wetlands in Guinea*. Cambridge, U.K.: International Council for Bird Preservation (Stud. Rep. 47).

ANONYMOUS. (1984) A programme for the conservation of migratory birds. Report prepared for WWF-Switzerland by IUCN, ICBP, IWRB. Gland.

BERTHOLD, P., FLIEGE, G., QUERNER, U. & WINKLER, H. (1986) Die Bestandsentwicklung von Kleinvögeln in Mitteleuropa: Analyse von Fangzahlen. *J. Orn.* 127: 397-438.

BIBER, J.-P. (1990) *The conservation of western Lesser Kestrel populations*. Cambridge, U.K.: International Council for Bird Preservation (Stud. Rep. 41).

BIBER, J.-P. & SALATHÉ, T. (1990) Conservation priorities for migratory birds of the European Community. Commission of the European Community (DG XI). Final Report (B/6610/62/88).

BIJLSMA, R. G. (1987) *Bottleneck areas for migratory birds in the Mediterranean Region.* Cambridge, U.K.: International Council for Bird Preservation (Stud. Rep. 18).

BOARDMAN, R. (1981) *International organization and the conservation of nature*. London: Macmillan Press.

COLLAR, N. J. & ANDREW, P. (1988) *Birds to watch: the ICBP world checklist of threatened birds*. Cambridge, U.K.: International Council for Bird Preservation (Techn. Publ. 8).

GATTER, W. (1988) *The coastal wetlands of Liberia: their importance for wintering waterbirds*. Cambridge, U.K.: International Council for Bird Preservation (Stud. Rep. 26).

GRETTON, A. (1991) The ecology and conservation of the Slender-billed Curlew *Numenius tenuirostris*. Cambridge, U.K.: International Council for Bird Preservation (Monogr. 6).

GRIMMETT, R. F. A. (1987) *A review of the problems affecting Palearctic migratory birds in Africa.* Cambridge, U.K.: International Council for Bird Preservation (Stud. Rep. 22).

GRIMMETT, R. F. A. & JONES, T. A. (1989) *Important bird areas in Europe.* Cambridge, U.K.: International Council for Bird Preservation (Techn. Publ. 9).

VAN KETEL, A., MARCHAND, M. & RODENBURG, W. F. (1987) Revue d'Afrique occidentale: aperçu détaillé des projets d'aménagement hydrologique et description de leurs incidences sur les zones humides. *Rapport EDWIN* 1. Leiden.

LYSTER, S. (1985) *International wildlife law.* Cambridge: Grotius Publications.

MacDONALD, A. & GORIUP, P. (1985) Migratory birds: problems and prospects in Africa. Report of the 14th Conference of the European Continental Section of ICBP, Cambridge, 1983.

RANDS, M. (1987) The ICBP migratory birds programme: a strategy for future priorities and projects. Unpubl. report.

RHEINWALD, G., OGDEN, J. & SCHULZ, H., eds. (1989) Weißstorch – White Stork. *Proceedings 1st Internat. Stork Conserv. Symposium.* Schriftenreihe des Dachverbandes Deutscher Avifaunisten 10. Braunschweig.

SOTHMANN, L., ed. (1991) Biologie, Status und Schutz des Wachtelkönigs. Sonderheft. Vogelwelt 112/1-2.

TERBORGH, J. (1989) *Where have all the birds gone?* Princeton, New Jersey: Princeton University Press.

U.S. CONGRESS OFFICE OF TECHNOLOGY ASSESSMENT. (1987) *Technologies to maintain biological diversity.* Washington, D.C.: U.S. Government Printing Office (OTA-F-330).

WIWO. (1989) *Forward Plan 1989-1993.* Zeist: Foundation Working Group for International Wader and Waterfowl Research.

WOLDHEK, S. (1980) *Bird killing in the Mediterranean.* Second edition. Zeist: European Committee for the Prevention of Mass Destruction of Migratory Birds.

PART II
PROBLEMS FACING MIGRATORY BIRDS

PART II of this volume is intended as a reminder of the need for concern about migratory birds. The threats they are facing are manifold, and interrelated in a complex manner with other environmental problems: thus it is difficult to single out specific threats to migrants. Nevertheless, a preliminary attempt has been made to provide a global overview of the problems either common to or specific to the major intercontinental flyways. It reveals that our knowledge is still very patchy and far too limited. More large-scale research addressing directly the relevant conservation problems is needed to provide us with clear guidelines for the conservation of many declining migrant bird populations.

A selection of case studies which provide basic information on some of the questions raised are also presented in this part. Although limited in scope and size, the study on pesticide impacts on wintering birds in West Africa, of which Mullié *et al.* report the main results, is probably still the first and only one of its kind. Magnin summarizes current knowledge on large-scale persecution of migrants in the Mediterranean. His picture is still incomplete, providing eloquent proof of the large gaps that exist in the availability of the detailed data required to plan concrete conservation measures. But some important studies are now under way or planned, and it is to be hoped that the financial means to carry them out can be found. Hutt's assessment of similar problems in the Caribbean reminds the reader that the negative impacts of migratory bird shooting are not restricted to the Mediterranean. Parish & Howes (1990) have recently presented a similar account for hunting activities in the Asian–Australasian flyways.

Most recently a symposium on the "Management of Waterfowl Populations" organized by the International Waterfowl and Wetlands Research Bureau (IWRB), has addressed similar questions in relation to the conservation of migratory gamebirds. The proceedings (Matthews 1990) contain some relevant new information. But the debate on hunting impact on migratory bird populations is far from closed: much remains to be done, and unless there is a functioning population-monitoring programme, providing the necessary data with which to set up population management plans for different flyways, we shall not be sure what proportion of the decline of a given species is being caused by human taking. Meltofte (1990) has recently reiterated a few of the pertinent questions.

T. Salathé

REFERENCES

MATTHEWS, G. V. T., ed. (1990) *Managing waterfowl populations.*   Slimbridge: International Waterfowl and Wetlands Research Bureau (Spec. Publ. 12).

MELTOFTE, H. (1990) Is a hunting harvest a "wise use" of wetlands: the need for critical research. P. 154 in G. V. T. Matthews, ed. *Managing waterfowl populations.* Slimbridge: International Waterfowl and Wetlands Research Bureau (Spec. Publ. 12).

PARISH, D. & HOWES, J. R. (1990) Waterbird hunting and management in S.E. Asia. Pp. 128-131 in G. V. T. Matthews, ed. *Managing waterfowl populations.*   Slimbridge: International Waterfowl and Wetlands Research Bureau (Spec. Publ. 12).

THREATS TO MIGRATORY BIRDS

JEAN-PIERRE BIBER[1] & TOBIAS SALATHÉ[2]

1 *Bureau NATCONS, Steinengraben 2, CH-4051 Basel, Switzerland*
2 *International Council for Bird Preservation, 32 Cambridge Road, Girton, Cambridge CB3 0PJ, U.K.*

ABSTRACT

The paper provides an introduction to the physiological requirements of migratory birds, their main intercontinental flyways, the natural risks and human-induced threats to which they are exposed, and the most endangered and declining species. It is intended as a preliminary overview of the conservation problems related to migratory birds and as a guide to the problems, the literature and the following contributions to this volume.

INTRODUCTION

This contribution aims to provide an overview of the specific threats to which migratory birds are exposed. It enumerates the natural risks and hazards encountered during their often extremely long journeys, and further details the additional human-induced threats they face. These added threats are increasingly of importance to a number of migrants that must now be considered globally threatened, and to an even larger number of migrants that have shown marked population declines during the most recent decades. We try to present a balanced view, referring to important results of current research, although we feel that this article can present only a very preliminary contribution towards a global review of the state of migratory birds. Nevertheless, it became increasingly apparent during the writing of this paper, that basic large-scale research is urgently needed to provide data and solutions to the conservation problems responsible for the widespread population decline of migratory birds. Some recommendations to this end are given throughout the text.

Birds considered in this contribution are species or populations that migrate between often very distant breeding and wintering grounds, at predictable times each year and in response to seasonal fluctuations in the ecological conditions within their range. By leaving their breeding and wintering areas respectively they are on the one hand avoiding the high mortality rates resident counterparts are likely to suffer during severe climatic conditions (cold, drought or rainy seasons) with reduced food availability, and on the other hand exposing themselves to specific hazards during migration. Cold and wet weather conditions prevent soaring birds from moving, while smaller species will be prevented from migrating at all by strong headwinds or be blown off track over continents and oceans far away from their normal routes. A mountain range may become an impassable obstacle during bad weather conditions, and may trap many migrants. Feeders on aerial insects may be prevented from essential food intake during cold weather.

Smaller migrants may have a further hazard to face: birds of prey such as the Eleonora's Falcon (*Falco eleonorae*) or Sooty Falcon (*F. concolor*) specialize in exploiting concentrations of migrants, and time their breeding seasons to profit from maximum autumn passerine migration as a food source for their young (Walter 1979). It is estimated that about 4,500 pairs of Eleonora's Falcon breed on the migration routes of Palearctic passerines, and that, together with their young, they consume five to ten million migratory birds each autumn (Mead 1983).

Migratory birds have to cope with intra- and interspecific competition in ways rather different from those of residents. The latter can start to secure a breeding territory early in spring, or even during winter, while migrants can do so only after arriving in their breeding area immediately prior to the start of reproductive activities. Similarly, when reaching their winter quarters in autumn, migrants have to compete with local residents and other migrants already present in the same area (Greenberg 1986). Recent ecological field work showed that in many cases migrants are not floaters with flexibility in their choice of habitat, but have to set up and defend winter territories in order to secure sufficient food supplies (Rappole & Warner 1980; Lynch *et al.* 1985; Morton *et al.* 1987; Rappole *et al.* 1989; Winkler *et al.* 1990; Lopez & Greenberg 1990). Furthermore, in defending winter territories in a particular habitat, migrants become exposed to the same threats of habitat loss that local residents face (Rappole & Morton 1985). On the other hand, competition in the northern breeding areas for low resource levels during (northern) winter is substantially reduced with the disappearance of the migrants. Thus migration can definitely be seen as an adaptive strategy which would not have persisted without a clear selective advantage (Ketterson & Nolan 1983; Cox 1985; Lundberg 1988). There is still academic debate over the question of whether or not long-distance migrants have merely evolved from historically tropical species that were able to exploit niches in temperate breeding areas – the prevailing view in the Americas (Keast & Morton 1985) – or if breeders of the temperate zone have merely to escape deteriorating ecological conditions by migrating to lower latitudes. This is the preferred explanation for the Palearctic–African flyways (Moreau 1972) the pattern of which has evolved since the last ice-ages. The greater mobility and more pronounced adaptability of migrants, as opposed to residents, makes it more difficult to assess their conservation status and to identify relevant threats, and it is harder to estimate accurately their population size and dynamics and to establish interdependence with habitat variables.

Like all wildlife, migratory birds are exposed to ever-increasing threats of human origin. Their habitats are modified or destroyed through agriculture, forestry, fishing, recreation, water management, urbanization, industrialization, transport facilities and building works. The fact that many migrants concentrate during migration at specific sites, and follow fixed flyways, makes them even more vulnerable to ecological alterations at key sites. Combined with the problem of direct human persecution, these may result in disastrous impacts.

Before assessing these threats to migrants it is useful to review some of the specific metabolic patterns of, and constraints on, migrating birds which may make them more vulnerable to human-induced disturbances than other, non-migratory birds.

THE STRESS OF MIGRATION

The seasonal movements of migratory birds are controlled by internal circannual rhythms which steer all important annual events in most species investigated so far (Berthold 1988). Evidence suggests that the migratory direction is also inherited (Berthold 1977, 1984), and even a seasonal shift in the migratory direction can be endogenously programmed (Gwinner & Wiltschko 1978).

Many species spend most of the year on migration leaving only a short time period for reproduction and moult. Some species arrive at their breeding places in the Northern Hemisphere only in May or June and leave again two to three months later. In this short period they have not only, like residents, to establish a territory, find a mate (although certain species do this already during migration), build a nest, lay and incubate a clutch, raise young, and eventually start moult, but also to store sufficient energy reserves for the journey. Certain species, ducks and geese, but also some waders (e.g. Northern Lapwing, *Vanellus vanellus*) and passerines (e.g. European Starlings, *Sturnus vulgaris*) undertake an additional moult-migration not related to the flyway towards their winter quarters. Many ducks move to places where they can safely moult their flight feathers simultaneously, resulting in a short time during which they are unable to fly.

Long-distance migrants, which often undertake intercontinental journeys, need to build up sufficient energy resources to be able to fly over large inhospitable areas with no or only scarce food resources and shelter. They may have to cross ecological barriers of several hundred kilometres, such as the Mediterranean, the Sahara, the Caribbean or the western Pacific. Lipids, stocked mainly subcutaneously in the body of migrants, provide this necessary source of energy. The principal mechanism for fat deposition is an active increase in feeding time and food intake. Deposit fat is synthesized from carbohydrates, mainly in the liver (Berthold 1975). Migratory fat deposition is correlated with the distances that must be covered. Hummingbirds and small passerines that cross important ecological barriers deposit on average 30-47 per cent of their lean weight (the maximum being slightly over 50 per cent), while fat deposits in short- and medium-distance migrants average only about 13-25 per cent (Berthold 1975). Many birds begin migration with low to moderate fat reserves which they increase during migration reaching a maximum level before undertaking long non-stop flights (Odum *et al.* 1961). Completion of fat deposition in small passerines may require only four to ten days, with a fattening rate of about 0.1 to 1.5 g/day. This allows the birds to restore depleted fat reserves rapidly at stop-over sites during migration.

In larger birds, the relative amount of fat reserves is considerably less than in smaller ones for thermodynamic reasons. Large waders do not exceed about 20 per cent of their lean weight even prior to long non-stop flights (Berthold 1975). These large birds are able to cross huge ecological barriers with only half the proportion of deposit fat carried by passerines (Schaefer 1968). The weight of huge fat reserves might even prevent larger birds from flying at the speed that would give them maximum range (Pennycuick 1969).

Besides storing fat reserves, water and temperature regulation play an important role in the metabolic physiology of migratory birds. It has been shown that water loss through respiration and through the skin during flight considerably exceeds the metabolic water production. It is not yet clear what effect dehydration in migratory birds could have in limiting flight range, but it has been suggested that high-altitude flights (Berthold 1975) and nocturnal migration (Dorka 1966) help to reduce excessive water loss and hyperthermy. Nocturnal migration could also be a behavioural adaptation allowing more time for foraging during daytime or protecting migrants from predators hunting during daytime. Other behavioural patterns of migratory birds which have been observed in several species, like the reduction of total daytime activity, the disappearance of the late afternoon peak of activity and the appearance of a characteristic pause in the evening, can also be interpreted as energy saving (Berthold 1975).

Recent observations suggest that quite a number of passerines do not cross the Sahara in non-stop flight (Bairlein 1988ab) but make stop-overs within the desert. The main purpose of these halts might simply be to rest in a shady place which does not necessarily provide the birds with food. Bairlein studied body mass and subcutaneous fat deposition in European migrants at a stop-over site north of the Sahara, in northern Algeria. He found that trans-Saharan migrants showed pronounced migratory fattening during their stop-over periods, whereas birds wintering in the western Mediterranean did not. His data support the assumption that many trans-Saharan migrants not only cross the Sahara in stages, but also spend significant time between the sea and the desert in the Mediterranean *maquis* to build up necessary fat deposits. The strategic importance of the conservation of such stop-over sites for long-distance migrants has not yet been duly recognized. Often migrants reach an ecological barrier without having enough energy reserves to cross it in non-stop flight. Less than 20 per cent of Quails (*Coturnix coturnix*) caught in autumn in the northern Sinai had the required amount of fat to reach their wintering grounds without additional food (Zuckerbrot *et al.* 1980). Biebach (1985) made similar findings with passerines caught in oases in the Sahara.

It is largely unknown what percentage of the migrants do actually accomplish their journey, which may be several thousand kilometres each way (10,000 km for many species, and up to 19,000 km or more for some waders and the Arctic Tern (*Sterna paradisea*)). Additional losses linked to climatic conditions, predators, competition and scarce resources encountered during migration would be counterbalanced by different density-dependent survival rates for residents and migrants as long as migration remains an evolutionary stable strategy. But the recent decline of many populations of migratory birds (cf. below) shows that such a balance may now be seriously jeopardized by human-induced factors. Bird migration remains an ecological theme of extreme complexity (Morton 1980; Lövei 1989). Deliberately we have not even touched upon the manifold problems of orientation and navigation during migration, which *per se* may impose further stress on the metabolism of a migrating bird.

THE MAIN INTERCONTINENTAL FLYWAYS

An important part of the bird migration phenomenon involves movements between continents. The study of migration patterns during this century led to the discovery of a number of relatively narrow flyways used by a large number of long-distance migrants. Because of the concentrations of birds on these flyways they are of special conservation concern. Many smaller species, however, migrate over wide fronts without following particular flyways (Schüz 1971).   Moreau (1972), Curry-Lindahl (1981, 1982) and Mead (1983) give a good idea of the main flyways, which are simplified in *Figure 1* of chapter 20 (p. 347) An equally important, but unfortunately much less investigated part of the bird migration phenomenon involves within-continent and altitudinal movements of short-distance and partial migrants. The lack of adequate research and the consequent limitation of our understanding of these patterns in South America, Africa, South and South-East Asia is a particular drawback to improving the conservation status of many species and their habitats. Unfortunately so far, most ornithologists have tended to focus almost exclusively on long-distance migrants breeding in the northern continents.

On the European continent, migration southwards and south-westwards after the breeding season occurs on a wide front in many species. Siberian birds (e.g. ducks or thrushes) start flying westwards to Europe and then partly follow a SSW route. Important concentrations occur during autumn migration and throughout winter on the northern coast of the Mediterranean, in wetland and *maquis* habitats with abundant food resources. Some species fly straight across the sea, while others make stop-overs on Mediterranean islands. Soaring species such as storks, pelicans and many raptors have to choose narrow sea crossings at the Straits of Gibraltar and Messina or cross the eastern Mediterranean over the Bosphorus and along the Levant coast. Birds following the western Mediterranean flyway cross the western Sahara and tend to winter in western Africa, mainly in the Sahel countries (Moreau 1973), some going as far south as Angola. Birds using the eastern Mediterranean flyway cross the eastern Sahara, many of them following the Nile valley or the Red Sea coast and the Rift Valley. These birds winter mainly in eastern and southern Africa. In some species (e.g. Whitethroat (*Sylvia communis*) and White Stork (*Ciconia ciconia*), eastern European populations take the eastern flyway and western populations the western flyway. In addition to these relatively well known movements between the West Palearctic and Africa, many breeding birds from Siberia and Central Asia (up to 120° East and further) also migrate to south-eastern Africa (Moreau 1972), although information on their flyways is as yet much more scanty.

In the Western Hemisphere there are four important flyways used by birds breeding in North America and wintering mainly in Central America, with some species moving as far as Tierra del Fuego at the southern tip of South America. The most eastern, the Atlantic Flyway, follows the east coast of North America south to Florida, and is about 500 km wide. Many ducks and geese coming from Greenland and Canada follow this flyway. Birds breeding in Canada and Alaska use the Mississippi Flyway with its many wetlands on which some eight million ducks, geese, swans and coots spend the winter. This flyway seems also to be the main route for North American migrants that travel further south to Central and northern South America. The Central Flyway runs east of the Rocky Mountains to the coastal wetlands of Texas and Louisiana. Birds breeding in northern Alaska, the Yukon region and the prairies of Canada and the U.S.A. use this flyway to reach the Gulf of Mexico and Central America. The most western route, the Pacific Flyway, leads birds which breed mainly in north-western North America along the Rocky Mountains and the east coast of the Pacific southwards to Central America (Curry-Lindahl 1982; Morrison & Myers 1989).

The Wheatear (*Oenanthe oenanthe*) is one of the most spectacular migrants: its breeding range extends from eastern Canada and Greenland through Eurasia to Alaska. All these birds winter in Africa. Among the waders, terns and seabirds, there are several species with similarly extraordinary migration routes. The Arctic Tern (*Sterna paradisea*) breeds north of the Arctic Circle and winters in the Antarctic pack ice. Several Holarctic breeding birds spend the winter in the South Pacific (e.g. Bristle-thighed Curlew (*Numenius tahitiensis*) and Lesser Golden Plover (*Pluvialis dominica*)) and South Atlantic (e.g. Great Shearwater (*Puffinus gravis*)).

The Asian and Asian–Australasian migration systems are less well known. Important wintering areas of Palearctic birds in Asia lie south of the Caspian Sea, on the Indian subcontinent, in Japan and in the Asian tropics. The deserts of

Central Asia and the Himalayas form ecological barriers of similar importance to the Mediterranean Sea and Sahara. Some species migrate west of the central Asian mountains, others on the eastern side. But a large number cross the Himalayas over a wide front. Many species seem to follow the eastern and western coasts of India, wintering eventually in Sri Lanka. Others breeding in Central Asia fly through continental South-East Asia to the Andaman Islands and the western Indonesian islands. Important flyways follow the Asian Pacific coast, through eastern Indonesia and the Philippines to Australia (Curry-Lindahl 1982; McClure 1984; Lane & Parish, this volume).

HUMAN-INDUCED THREATS

Habitat destruction

Recent global overviews of the principal threats to birdlife (Diamond *et al.* 1987; Collar & Andrew 1988; Rands 1989) revealed clearly that the alteration and destruction of natural and semi-natural habitats are *the* major threats. They affect migratory birds in nearly every place they visit in the course of their annual cycle, except possibly in the Arctic breeding grounds. Two aspects have to be considered, namely the general large-scale alteration and reduction of particular habitat types (for which general conservation measures need to be applied) and the destruction of specific sites (requiring site-specific conservation measures).

General large-scale destruction of habitat types. In densely populated and industrialized Europe the breeding habitats of migratory birds that are disappearing are open or semi-open areas (wet and dry grassland, heath and moorland, open woodland, non-intensively used farmland, wasteland) and wetlands (marshes, bogs, riverine forests, open waters and their borderlines). Forest birds are not yet threatened as much by general habitat modification and destruction as the wetland species and birds of natural grasslands, but air pollution (acid rain) is destroying North American and European forests at an alarming rate.

In Europe the main risks stem from the general trend towards intensified land use for agriculture and forestry, i.e. the afforestation of heathland and open woodland, and/or their conversion into cultivated land; the drainage of riverine forests and their conversion into economically more profitable timber plantations; the conversion of unused wasteland into agricultural land, and the drainage of marshes, peat bogs and wet meadows into intensively cultivated arable land (e.g. Baldock 1990). Many natural and semi-natural habitats are lost through housing and industrial developments and the construction of roads. Diversifying habitat features such as hedgerows, woodlots, single trees, bushes and traditional orchards are disappearing rapidly, to be replaced by intensively farmed monocultures, dwarf fruit trees, vines, or livestock forage. Since livestock are increasingly kept in stables and fed with imported fodder, meadows and open woodland traditionally used for grazing are disappearing. Additionally, the loss of high-quality arable land to building developments in densely populated areas has the consequence of increasing the intensification of agriculture on the remaining land. Lakes and rivers are threatened by eutrophication, drainage or the destruction of natural shorelines. The heavy human recreational pressure on diverse lakeside habitats very often results in the destruction of reedbeds (already weakened by water eutrophication) and other natural shoreline vegetation zones (Biber & Salathé 1990).

Figure 1:   Complete drainage for irrigation purposes of a small wetland breeding habitat used by over ten breeding migratory species.   In a resolution on the occasion of its 17th Conference in 1989 in Adana, Turkey, the ICBP European Continental Section urged all countries concerned "to avoid the destruction of small wetland patches which are cumulatively of ecological importance". *(Photo*: T. Salathé)

Similar developments are taking place in industrialized and densely populated areas in Asia, Australasia and America.   In North America, the problems are similar to those in Europe and the U.S.S.R. (Neave 1983; Zoltai 1983; Goodman 1983).   The fragmentation of large boreal forests has been identified as a factor affecting migrants in a particular way (Morton & Greenberg 1989; Terborgh 1989; Askins *et al.* 1990).   The opening up of large boreal forest tracts has led to the disappearance of some species which only inhabit large tracts of forests (e.g. Worm-eating Warbler (*Helmitheros vermivorus*)).   It has also created much more forest edge, the preferred habitat of nest-parasitizing cowbirds (*Molothrus* sp.) and mammalian and avian nest-predators.   The negative impact of predators and parasites is assumed to be involved in the decline of many populations of Nearctic long-distance migrants in recent times (Morse 1989).   Forest fragmentation and environmental changes around urban and suburban forest reserves, where long-term studies have been undertaken, have consistently revealed severe population declines in many species of forest-dwelling Nearctic migrants during the past 30-40 years. Such examples demonstrate the complex ecological consequences that human-induced habitat changes can have on species communities of that area. Problems linked with intensification of agricultural exploitation are affecting the habitats of a number of waterfowl and shorebird species migrating in the U.S. plains areas.   The wetlands of the U.S. have been dramatically altered and reduced with devastating effects on some migrants' populations (USFWS 1988; USEPA 1989).

In the southern wintering areas of Holarctic long-distance migrants, habitat destruction is no less of a conservation problem.   Many of the Nearctic migrants winter in various primary and secondary habitats in Central America, where they are affected by large-scale habitat alterations (wetland drainage, landslides at cleared forest slopes) and deforestation (Terborgh 1980, 1989; Askins *et al.* 1990). Although the effect on migrant populations of habitat alterations in the wintering areas has been somewhat disputed by Hutto (1988) there is growing concern that a combination of forest fragmentation in North America and deforestation in Central America is the most important factor responsible for the decline of many Nearctic migrants (Symposium on the Ecology and Conservation of Neotropical Migrant Landbirds, Woods Hole, Mass. 1989).

Recent extreme drought conditions in Africa are thought to have contributed substantially to the decline of many Palearctic migrants wintering in the savanna and steppe zone of the Sahel (Berthold 1973). Although such large-scale climatic events could be considered to fall outside the scope of human-induced threats, it has to be borne in mind that, besides the probable link between regional droughts and global consequences of air pollution with greenhouse gases (global warming), at a local scale drought effects are compounded by increasing human pressure on fragile arid habitats, such as over-grazing, over-use of firewood, burning of the remaining vegetation, drainage of wetlands, and over-fishing. All these human habitat alterations have negative consequences for migrants (Svensson 1985; Roux & Jarry 1984; van der Linden 1988; Thiollay 1989).

Wetland drainage is probably one of the most important and certainly the most evident human-induced threat in many regions of North America, Europe and Africa. Large grants are still being paid in some countries for the drainage of wetlands for agricultural development. Uncontrolled disposal of industrial and domestic waste is resulting in pollution and deterioration of natural habitats often of crucial importance for migrants (USDI 1988; Dugan 1990). In a survey conducted by ICBP, on the problems affecting Palearctic migratory birds in Africa (Grimmett 1987), water management programmes (canalization of rivers, dam construction, control of flooding and drainage) have been found to have an important, and in some areas even dramatic, impact on habitats used by Palearctic migrants. They fundamentally alter the annual flooding patterns over large areas in the Senegal, Inner Niger, and Nile valleys, the Lake Chad basin and other areas (van Ketel *et al.* 1987). According to the planned water regulation works, about 40 per cent of the Sahelian floodplain area is doomed to disappear. This may well create man-made drought conditions over large parts of the Sahel through the consequences of related climatic alterations. Natural temporary wetlands are increasingly replaced by irrigated rice fields (van der Linden 1988). While this could seem beneficial for wintering Palearctic waterbirds, the pesticides used in these cultures are creating new problems (cf. Mullié, this volume). Far-reaching ecological consequences of water management schemes for Palearctic migrants have been mentioned by correspondents for more than half of the 39 African countries involved in the questionnaire survey (Grimmett 1987).

Threats to specific sites. Lists of important sites for migratory birds exist for most of the continents, although to varying degrees of specificity. Recently compiled large-scale inventories of wetlands can provide a first approach. Such inventories have been published for the West Palearctic (Carp 1980; Scott 1980), the Neotropics (Scott & Carbonell 1986; Morrison & Ross 1989), and Asia (Scott 1989). Inventories for the U.S.A. and Canada are nearly completed, those for Africa, Oceania and Australia are under way; and it is hoped to close the remaining gap in global coverage with a future inventory for the Middle East (IWRB *in litt.*). Most of the wetlands listed are important stop-over sites not only for waterbirds but also for many migrant landbirds which refuel in natural habitats surrounding the water surfaces (shrub and grassland, etc.).

For Africa a list of zones of special interest for the conservation of migratory birds of the European Community was compiled by Ledant *et al.* (1986). It includes many wetlands, but also steppe, savanna, mountain and tropical forest areas, and gives information on the risks affecting these sites. Many oases in the Sahara desert are important, though information on individual sites is still scarce. Grimmett's (1987) analysis of the continent-wide questionnaire lists a series of threatened areas, mostly wetlands, in 19 African countries.

A list of "Important Bird Areas in Europe" (Grimmett & Jones 1989) contains 2,444 sites in 32 countries. Many of these are wetlands of international importance as stop-over and wintering sites for waterbirds (according to the numerical criteria of the Ramsar Convention). Langeveld & Grimmett (1990) have provided a shadow list of 1,097 wetlands for future listing under the Ramsar Convention. Some sites are known as bottleneck areas for migrants en route to and from Africa; others cover a great variety of habitats.

Conclusion. This short overview of the problems of habitat destruction and alteration facing migratory birds shows that the analysis of continuing habitat loss is still very limited. Habitat destruction has to be stopped urgently where it most affects the diversity of life. To be successful, this has to be complemented by further research to list the distribution and to monitor the evolution of habitats under pressure from human developments, and by socio-economic and legal studies which will reveal how best to use natural and semi-natural habitats and their resources in a sustainable way. Continent-wide and global data to support political action for habitat conservation are still too rare in most parts of the industrialized world, and are completely missing in most developing countries.

Hunting and human persecution

Migratory bird trapping and hunting has been practised for generations (reports from Egypt date back to 4000BC), but the reasons for hunting have changed profoundly in many regions, and methods have become much more efficient, especially with the wide use of shotguns and synthetic fibre nets which allow easy and plentiful catching. Subsistence hunting of migratory birds is now of reduced importance as explained by several authors in Diamond & Filion (1987), while recreational (i.e. sport) hunting becomes increasingly of socio-economic value (Diamond & Filion 1987; SEIS 1988), in both industrialized and developing countries which are increasingly visited by foreign hunting tours. Unfortunately, the lack of scientific data for most of the species impedes an assessment of the impact of human persecution of migrants on their population dynamics. However, a recent continent-wide mortality analysis of recoveries of ringed European migrants showed a significant decrease in survival for Eurasian Robin (*Erithacus rubecula*) and Song Thrush (*Turdus philomelos*) (the two species for which sufficient data and time were available to carry out a detailed analysis) with increased shooting and trapping pressure. Thus the mortality resulting from the taking of birds from these populations contributes to the overall mortality and is at least partially additive and not fully compensated for in the absence of human taking by other population-density-dependent mortality factors. After studies in North America on Mallard (*Anas plathyrhynchos*) (Anderson & Burnham 1976) this is the first study to suggest additive mortality as a result of hunting of passerine migrants (Tucker *et al.* 1990). This is an important contribution to the understanding of the impact that hunting and other forms of direct human persecution have on many declining migrants. As we are all aware, numerous sad stories have proved that humans are able to hunt migratory birds to extinction (North American Passenger Pigeon (*Ectopistes migratorius*), Greenway 1967) or close to it (Whooping Crane (*Grus americana*), Doughty 1989; Eskimo and Slender-billed Curlews (*Numenius borealis* and *N. tenuirostris*), Gollop *et al.* 1986; Gretton 1991).

A particular problem for many migrants is the still widely occurring, mostly illegal, and indiscriminate hunting and trapping of millions of shorebirds and landbirds, mostly passerines but also colourful species (mainly Coraciiformes) and raptors (Falconiformes), in specific regions of the Old and New World. The accounts by Magnin and Hutt in this volume and by Parish & Howes (1990) give an impression of its extent and peculiarities. Numerous methods are employed for catching such birds, many of which are unselective. Such human persecution tends to focus on bottleneck areas (islands, land bridges and mountain passes) where migrants concentrate in large numbers and are particularly vulnerable to hunters (e.g. Bijlsma 1987).

In the absence of an adequate understanding of the relationship between direct human persecution and the population dynamics of many declining migrants, a risk-aversive management strategy should be applied, which puts the burden of proof that hunting does not contribute to the population decline of an exploited migrant upon the hunters, calls for a population monitoring system for all species open to hunting, and installs ecologically safe hunting regulations and their enforcement in all regions concerned (see Biber & Salathé 1990 for a more detailed account).

Loss of food resources

The depletion of food resources in the breeding, migrating and wintering areas due to increased use of pesticides in agriculture is an important cause of decline in many migratory birds. Particularly affected are insectivorous species of agricultural land, which feed on large insects (beetles, crickets, grasshoppers, etc.), such as the declining Lesser Kestrel (*Falco naumanni*) (Biber 1990), Eurasian Hoopoe (*Upupa epops*), and Red-backed Shrike (*Lanius collurio*). Nevertheless, data to document the widespread decline of animal (mainly insect) and vegetarian (mainly seed) food resources of migrants is scarce and scattered, and only few attempts have yet been made to analyse the subsequent effects on bird populations (e.g. Potts 1986, although for a resident – the Grey Partridge (*Perdix perdix*)). Clearly an analytical overview to address the priority problems and to suggest practical solutions is urgently needed. The widespread loss of food resources may turn out to be a much more important threat to migrants than indiscriminate killing by hunters.

Poisoning by biochemicals

Pesticide poisoning has been an important cause of decline for many raptors (Ratcliffe 1980; Ellenberg 1981; Risebrough 1989). When the use of DDT and its derivates was banned, and after the use of PCBs was drastically reduced in many parts of the world, the situation improved somewhat (Meyburg & Chancellor 1989). Recently, rodenticides have caused the death of raptors in some regions of Europe (Jacquat 1982), highlighting the lasting potential of harmful side-effects inherent even in legal pesticides. Pesticide poisoning in the African winter quarters or during migration has been thought to be an important cause of decline for insectivorous passerines breeding in Europe (Berthold 1973). The use of dieldrin in the tsetse fly control programmes in Africa caused particularly high avian mortalities (Wilson 1972). Risebrough (1986) concluded that the major negative pesticide side-effects occur in developing countries, where application restrictions are inappropriate or not enforced, and where ecological side-effects are largely undocumented, while in the North the ecological consequences of pesticides have decreased in recent years, mainly through the efforts of conservationists lobbying for stricter regulations and tighter controls. Still, much work is needed to improve the impact assessment of hazardous pesticides (AEDG 1989).

Lead poisoning due to the ingestion of used lead shot (disposed of by hunters at high densities in key hunting areas) by many waterbirds during foraging (to serve as grit in the gizzard) is now known to be an important cause of disease and mortality (Pain 1990; Moser, this volume). Clearly lead shot needs to be replaced by safer materials worldwide.

Physical obstacles in the migratory flyways
Electric power lines obstructing the flight paths of large soaring birds may cause significant mortality, mainly among young and inexperienced individuals. Thus an important proportion of the local Dalmatian Pelican (*Pelecanus crispus*) population was killed by flying into a power line located between their roosting island and their feeding grounds at Porto-Lago in northern Greece, a major wintering ground for the species (Crivelli *et al.* 1988). This line was later dismantled thanks to the efforts of the Hellenic Ornithological Society. Fiedler & Wissner (1980) and Stolt *et al.* (1986) provide many suggestions for reducing the dangers of power lines to soaring migrants. In a similar way lighthouses, transmitter towers and other constructions may locally present lethal obstacles to thousands of migrants, and even function as a deadly attraction (like the powerful beams of lighthouses during the night; Mead 1983). At several (mainly military) airfields, collisions between large migrants and aircrafts are a serious hazard to man and material (Blokpoel 1976): where threatened species are involved, the problem can become of conservation concern.

Human disturbance
Human disturbance may pose a significant problem to migrants (mainly geese, ducks and waders) concentrating in large numbers in one place for feeding or roosting. Disturbance provoked by hunting and various recreational activities (bathing, surfing, boating, walking, jogging, birdwatching, etc.) puts substantial stress on the time- and energy-budget of the many individuals concerned, and this can significantly lower their chances of survival (e.g. Meile 1991).

THE MOST THREATENED MIGRANTS

The most recent overview of all globally threatened bird species (Collar & Andrew 1988) lists 1,029 species. Only 106 of these species (10.3 per cent) fall in the category of long-distance (often intercontinental) migrants (*Table 1*). This is a general sign that migrants are, in evolutionary terms, more adaptable than highly specialized endemics and residents, and therefore better equipped to cope with rapidly changing ecological conditions (as has been shown experimentally for a partial migrant by Berthold *et al.* 1990). On the other hand it becomes apparent that the great majority of globally threatened migrants are birds depending on wetlands (41 per cent). This shows that the global loss of natural wetlands has attained a level at which it clearly affects entire groups of vertebrate communities (e.g. six out of nine migratory species of cranes are globally threatened). Some

Table 1: Globally threatened bird species of which at least some populations are regular (often long-distance) migrants (according to Collar & Andrew 1988 and N. Collar, pers. comm.).

Raptors (7 species)
Milvus milvus
Haliaeetus leucoryphus
Haliaeetus albicilla
Haliaeetus pelagicus

Accipiter poliogaster
Aquila heliaca
Falco naumanni

Other landbirds (29 species)
Otis tarda
Tetrax tetrax
Chlamydotis undulata
Sypheotides indica
Columba punicea
Neophema chrysogaster
Apus acuticauda
Phibalura flavirostris
Yetapa risoria
Pitta nympha

Pseudochelidon sirintarae (?)
Tachycineta cyaneoviridis
Hirundo perdita (?)
Anthus chacoensis
Erithacus ruficeps
Erithacus obscurus
Turdus fischeri
Turdus feae
Acrocephalus paludicola
Acrocephalus sorghophilus

Megalurus pryeri
Rhinomyias brunneata
Emberiza sulphurata
Sporophila palustris (?)
Vermivora bachmanii
Dendroica chrysoparia
Dendroica kirtlandii
Vireo atricapillus
Oriolus mellianus

Seabirds (27 species)
Diomedea amsterdamensis
Diomedea albatrus
Pterodroma aterrima
Pterodroma hasitata
Pterodroma cahow
Pterodroma becki
Pterodroma magentae
Pterodroma feae
Pterodroma madeirae

Pterodroma phaeopygia
Pterodroma cooki
Pterodroma axillaris
Pterodroma defillippiana
Pterodroma pycrofti
Pterodroma macgillivrayi
Procellaria westlandica
Puffinus creatopus
Puffinus heinrothi

Puffinus newelli
Puffinus auricularis
Oceanodroma macrodactyla
Oceanodroma markhami
Oceanodroma hornbyi
Pelecanoides garnoti
Sula abbotti
Synthliboramphus wumizusume

Wetland birds (43 species)
Pelecanus philippensis
Pelecanus crispus
Phalacrocorax pygmeus
Gorsagius goisagi
Egretta eulophotes
Mycteria cinerea
Ciconia boyciana
Leptopilos javanicus (?)
Leptopilos dubius (?)
Platalea minor
Phoenicoparrus andinus
Phoenicoparrus jamesi
Anser erythropus
Branta ruficollis
Chloephaga rubidiceps

Tadorna cristata (?)
Anas formosa
Marmaronetta angustirostris
Aythya baeri
Mergus squamatus
Oxyura leucocephala
Grus nigricollis
Grus monacha
Grus japonensis
Grus americana
Grus vipio
Grus leucogeranus
Crex crex
Coturnicops exquisitus
Chettusia gregaria

Charadrius melodus
Numenius borealis
Numenius tahitiensis
Numenius tenuirostris
Tringa guttifer
Gallinago nemoricola
Limnodromus semipalmatus
Eurynorhynchus semipalmatus
Larus audouinii
Larus relictus
Larus saundersi
Sterna balaenarum
Sterna bernsteini

of the globally threatened wetland species are part of groups (waterfowl and waders) that are regularly exploited by hunters. Careful evaluation of the respective influences on population dynamics of habitat loss vs hunting impact is therefore required for species like the Lesser White-fronted Goose (*Anser erythropus*), Red-breasted Goose (*Branta ruficollis*), Eskimo Curlew and Slender-billed Curlew, while other long-lived species with a slow generation turnover may suffer from poaching mortality (e.g. Dalmatian Pelican (*Pelecanus crispus*)). The seabirds present another significant group (26 per cent) of globally threatened migrants. Due to their specific biology, spending most of their lifetime migrating long distances over the open sea but being tied to very distinct terrestrial places for breeding, they need specific conservation measures which have recently been addressed by ICBP (Croxall *et al.* 1984; Croxall 1991). However, as recently detailed by Johnson & Stattersfield (1990) and emanating by deduction from the information contained in *Table 1*, it becomes evident that island endemics and tropical bird species with a restricted range present a much greater conservation urgency in terms of the number of species concerned than the restricted number of globally threatened migrants.

There is however, no reason why conservationists should only be concerned once a species has become globally threatened, i.e. is in danger of extinction (Senner 1988). Migratory birds serve as valuable indicators of environmental change in their breeding, migration and wintering habitats. To date we know the results of extensive long-term monitoring programmes and recent surveys of different categories of migrants in large parts of North America and Europe (and more scattered in other regions) which have revealed widespread declines of many long-distance migrants (Robbins *et al.* 1986; Davidson & Pienkowski 1987; Pashley & Martin 1988; Boyd & Pirot 1989; Howe *et al.* 1989; Terborgh 1989; Berthold *et al.* 1986). The overall population trends are negative in many species. The United States Fish and Wildlife Service identified 30 species (7 per cent) of 407 migratory nongame (i.e. neither game nor endangered and threatened species) of management concern because of documented or apparent population declines, small or restricted populations, or dependence on restricted or vulnerable habitats (USFWS 1987). Out of 42 flyway-populations of North American waterfowl, 5 (12 per cent) have recently shown population declines, while 16 have shown no change and 18 populations (geese and swans) have shown population increases due to management measures (USDI-Environment Canada 1986). For the West Palearctic and Sahelian Africa, Pirot *et al.* (1989) report 11 (18 per cent) decreasing populations of waterfowl (and Coot *Fulica atra*) while 18 were stable, 22 insufficiently known, and 10 increasing. For the East Atlantic wader migration flyway Smit & Piersma (1989) report 3 (21 per cent) decreasing wader species, 1 insufficiently known, and 10 increasing species (although for nine of them the increase in population size seems only to be the result of more complete counts). An analysis of long-term trapping efforts at three ringing stations in central Europe by Berthold *et al.* (1986) revealed that 26 (70 per cent) of the 37 passerine migrants investigated showed negative population trends. Clearly continent-wide monitoring has to be maintained and better standardized in order to provide sufficient and reliable data supporting species and habitat management measures.

CONCLUSION

A few fundamental points are apparent. Migratory birds, although often very conspicuous and attracting much (consumptive and non-consumptive) interest (cf. Salathé, this volume), are still a group of species for which population sizes, trends, distribution, ecology and conservation needs are in many cases insufficiently known. This represents the first major handicap in preparing recovery plans. Due to their mobility and complex ecology, deriving from the fact that these birds cyclically frequent different biogeographical areas and geopolitical units, conservation plans have further to cope with a multitude of ecological and political problems, and this represents the second major handicap for targetting conservation actions. Even a single-species-specific approach has to take into account the complex pattern of ecological, legal, economic and social factors influencing the habitats or sites a particular species depends upon during its annual cycle.   Such factors complicate straightforward conservation approaches to a substantial degree.   Conservation programmes that address whole groups of migratory birds, specific habitats, or key sites are therefore more likely to be efficient and to help in a lasting way.   Special emphasis must be put on coordinated activities along the main flyways.   All essential parts of the network of breeding, stop-over and wintering areas of threatened populations have to be recognized and preserved as an entity to allow the survival of migratory species. (An example of such a conservation approach is given by Hunter *et al.* in this volume for shorebirds, which gather in conspicuous groups at key sites that are relatively easy to identify in comparison with discrete migrant landbirds that disperse widely.)   Migrants are in urgent need of coordinated efforts.   Their conservation is valuable not only for its own sake, but also for the educational and institutional value it can bring to all range states, often by establishing major connections through which many other kinds of conservation can follow.

ACKNOWLEDGEMENTS

The senior author acknowledges support from the Natural History Museum in Berne, Switzerland.   Both authors would like to thank Nigel Collar, Christoph Imboden, Mike Rands and Martha van der Voort for having made constructive remarks on earlier versions of this paper.

REFERENCES

AVIAN EFFECTS DIALOG GROUP. (1989) *Pesticides and birds: improving impact assessment.* Washington, D.C.: Conservation Foundation Report.

ANDERSON, D. R. & BURNHAM, K. P. (1976) *Population ecology of the mallard, Vol. VI: The effect of exploitation on survival.* Washington, D.C.: U.S. Fish and Wildlife Service (Resrce. Publ. 128).

ASKINS, R. A., LYNCH, J. F. & GREENBERG, R. (1990) Population declines in migratory birds in eastern North America. *Current Orn.* 7: 1-58.

BAIRLEIN, F. (1988a) Herbstlicher Durchzug, Körpergewichte und Fettdeposition von Zugvögeln in einem Rastgebiet in Nordalgerien. *Vogelwarte* 34: 237-248.

BAIRLEIN, F. (1988b) How do migratory songbirds cross the Sahara? *Trends Ecol. Evol.* 3: 191-194.

BALDOCK D. (1990) Agriculture and habitat loss in Europe. Gland, Switzerland: WWF International (C.A.P. Discus. Pap. no. 3).

BERTHOLD, P. (1973) Über starken Rückgang der Dorngrasmücke *Sylvia communis* und anderer Singvogelarten im westlichen Europa. *J. Orn.* 114: 348-360.

BERTHOLD, P. (1975) Migration: control and metabolic physiology. In D. S. Farner & J. R. King, eds. *Avian Biol.* 5: 77-128.

BERTHOLD, P. (1977) Endogene Steuerung des Vogelzuges. *Vogelwarte* 29, Sonderheft: 4-15.

BERTHOLD, P. (1984) The endogenous control of bird migration: a survey of experimental evidence. *Bird Study* 31: 19-27.

BERTHOLD, P. (1988) The biology of the genus Sylvia – a model and a challenge for Afro-European cooperation. *Tauraco* 1: 3-28.

BERTHOLD, P., FLIEGE, G., QUERNER, U. & WINKLER, H. (1986) Die Bestandsentwicklung von Kleinvögeln in Mitteleuropa: Analyse von Fangzahlen. *J. Orn.* 127: 397-438.

BERTHOLD, P., MOHR, G. & QUERNER, U. (1990) Steuerung und potentielle Evolutionsgeschwindigkeit des obligaten Teilzieherverhaltens: Ergebnisse eines Zweiweg-Selektionsexperiments mit der Mönchsgrasmücke. *J. Orn.* **131**: 33-46.

BIBBY, C. J. & GREEN, R. E. (1981) Autumn migration strategy of Reed and Sedge Warblers. *Ornis Scand.* **12**: 1-12.

BIBER, J.-P. (1990) *The conservation of Western Lesser Kestrel populations.* Cambridge, U.K.: International Council for Bird Preservation (Stud. Rep. 41).

BIBER, J.-P. & SALATHÉ, T. (1990) Conservation priorities for migratory birds of the European Community. Commission of the European Community (DG XI). Final Rep. (B/6610/62/88).

BIEBACH, H. (1985) Sahara stopover in migratory flycatcher: fat and food affect the time program. *Experientia* **41**: 695-697.

BIJLSMA, R. G. (1987) *Bottleneck areas for migratory birds in the Mediterranean region.* Cambridge, U.K.: International Council for Bird Preservation (Stud. Rep. 18).

BLOKPOEL, H. (1976) *Bird hazards to aircraft.* Canadian Wildlife Service. Minister of Supply and Services Canada.

BOYD, H. & PIROT, J.-Y., eds. (1989) *Flyways and reserve networks for waterbirds.* Slimbridge, U.K.: International Waterfowl and Wetlands Research Bureau (Spec. Publ. 9).

CARP, E. (1980) *Directory of wetlands of international importance in the Western Palearctic.* Nairobi: United Nations Environment Programme; Gland: International Union for the Conservation of Nature and Natural Resources.

COLLAR, N. J. & ANDREW, P. (1988) *Birds to watch: the ICBP world checklist of threatened birds.* Cambridge, U.K.: International Council for Bird Preservation (Techn. Publ. 8).

COX, G. W. (1985) The evolution of avian migration systems between temperate and tropical regions of the New World. *Amer. Naturalist* **126**: 451-474.

CRIVELLI, A. J., JERRENTRUP, H. & MITCHEV, T. (1988) Electric power lines: a cause of mortality in *Pelecanus crispus* Bruch, a world endangered bird species, in Porto-Lagos, Greece. *Colon. Waterbirds* **11**: 301-305.

CROXALL, J. P., ed. (1991) *Seabird status and conservation: a supplement.* Cambridge, U.K.: International Council for Bird Preservation (Techn. Publ. 11).

CROXALL, J. P., EVANS, P. G. H. & SCHREIBER, R. W., eds. (1984) *Status and conservation of the world's seabirds.* Cambridge, U.K.: International Council for Bird Preservation (Techn. Publ. 2).

CURRY-LINDAHL, K. (1981) *Bird migration in Africa. Movements between six continents.* Vols. 1 and 2. London: Academic Press.

CURRY-LINDAHL, K. (1982) *Das grosse Buch vom Vogelzug.* Berlin: Paul Parey.

DAVIDSON, N. C. & PIENKOWSKI, M. W., eds. (1987) *The conservation of international flyway populations of waders.* Slimbridge, U.K.: Wader Study Goup (Bull. 49, Suppl.)/ International Waterfowl and Wetlands Research Bureau (Spec. Publ. 7).

DELGADO B. F. S. (1985) Present situation of the forest birds of Panama. Pp. 77-93 in A. W. Diamond & T. E. Lovejoy, eds. *Conservation of tropical forest birds.* Cambridge: U.K.: International Council for Bird Preservation (Techn. Publ. 4).

DIAMOND, A. W., SCHREIBER, R. L., ATTENBOROUGH, D. & PRESTT, I. (1987) *Save the birds.* Cambridge, U.K.: Cambridge University Press.

DIAMOND, A. W. & FILION, F. L. (1987) *The value of birds.* Cambridge: U.K.: International Council for Bird Preservation (Techn. Publ. 6).

DORKA, V. (1966) Das jahres- und tageszeitliche Zugmuster von Kurz- und Langstreckenziehern nach Beobachtungen auf den Alpenpässen Cou/Bretolet. *Orn. Beob.* **63**: 165-223.

DOUGHTY, R. W. (1989) *Return of the Whooping Crane.* Austin: University of Texas Press.

DUGAN, P. J. (1990) *Wetland conservation: a review of current issues and required action.* Gland: International Union for the Conservation of Nature and Natural Resources.

ELLENBERG, H., ed. (1981) Greifvögel und Pestizide: Versuch einer Bilanz für Mitteleuropa. *Ökologie der Vögel* **3**: Sonderheft.

FIEDLER, G. & WISSNER, A. (1980) Freileitungen als tödliche Gefahr für Störche. *Ökologie der Vögel* **2**, Sonderheft: 59-110.

GOLLOP, J. B., BARRY, T. W. & IVERSEN, E. H. (1986) *Eskimo Curlew: a vanishing species?* Regina: Saskatchewan Natural History Society (Spec. Publ. 17).

GOODMAN, A. S. (1983) Habitat conservation in northern Canada. Pp. 51-53 in H. Boyd, ed. *First western hemisphere waterfowl and waterbird symposium.*

GREENBERG, R. (1986) Competition in migrant birds in the nonbreeding season. *Current Orn.* 3: 281-308.

GREENWAY, J. C. (1967) *Extinct and vanishing birds of the world.* New York: Dover Publications.

GRETTON, A. (1991) The ecology and conservation of the Slender-billed Curlew *Numenius tenuirostris.* Cambridge, U.K.: International Council for Bird Preservation (Monogr. 6).

GRIMMETT, R. F. A. (1987) *A review of the problems affecting Palearctic migratory birds in Africa.* Cambridge, U.K.: International Council for Bird Preservation (Stud. Rep. 22).

GRIMMETT, R. F. A. & JONES, T. A. (1989) *Important bird areas in Europe.* Cambridge, U.K.: International Council for Bird Preservation (Techn. Publ. 9).

GWINNER, E. & WILTSCHKO, W. (1978) Endogenously controlled changes in migratory direction of the Garden Warbler *Sylvia borin. J. comp. Physiol.* 125: 267-273.

HOWE, M. A., GEISSLER, P. H. & HARRINGTON, B. A. (1989) Population trends of North American shorebirds based on the international shorebird survey. *Biol. Conserv.* 49: 185-199.

HUTTO, R. L. (1988) Is tropical deforestation responsible for the reported declines in neotropical migrant populations? *Amer. Birds* 42: 375-379.

JACQUAT, M. S. (1982) Remarques sur l'utilisation de l'ARVICOSTOP pour lutter contre les pullulations du Campagnol terrestre et sur ses conséquences pour la faune. *Nos Oiseaux* 36: 397-400.

JOHNSON, T. H. & STATTERSFIELD, A. J. (1990) A global review of island endemic birds. *Ibis* 132: 167-180.

KEAST, A. & MORTON, E. S., eds. (1980) *Migrant birds in the Neotropics: ecology, behavior, distribution, and conservation.* Washington, D.C.: Smithsonian Institution.

VAN KETEL, A., MARCHAND, M. & RODENBURG, W. F. (1987) Revue d'Afrique occidentale: aperçu détaillé des projets d'aménagement hydrologique et description de leurs incidences sur les zones humides. *Rapport EDWIN* 1. Leiden.

KETTERSON, E. D. & NOLAN, V. (1983) The evolution of differential bird migration. *Current Orn.* 1: 357-402.

LANGEVELD, M. J. & GRIMMETT, R. F. A. (1990) *Important bird areas in Europe: wetlands for the shadow list of Ramsar sites.* Cambridge: U.K.: International Council for Bird Preservation; Slimbridge, U.K.: International Waterfowl and Wetlands Research Bureau.

LEDANT, J.-P., ROUX, F., JARRY, G., GAMMELL, A., SMIT, C., BAIRLEIN, F. & WILLE, H. (1986) Aperçu des zones de grand intérêt pour la conservation des espèces d'oiseaux migrateurs de la Communauté en Afrique. Rapport final (U/84/129). Luxembourg: Commission des Communautés Européennes.

VAN DER LINDEN, J. (1988) The importance of Sahel wetlands for Palearctic migratory birds. Draft report to ICBP, Cambridge, U.K.

LOPEZ, A. & GREENBERG, R. (1990) Sexual segregation by habitat in migratory warblers in Quintana Roo, Mexico. *Auk* 107: 539-543.

LÖVEI, G. L. (1989) Passerine migration between the Palearctic and Africa. *Current Orn.* 6: 143-174.

LUNDBERG, P. (1988) The evolution of partial migration in birds. *Trends Ecol. Evol.* 3: 172-175.

LYNCH, J. F., MORTON, E. S. & VAN DER VOORT, M. E. (1985) Habitat segregation between the sexes of wintering Hooded Warblers *Wilsonia citrina. Auk* 102: 714-721.

McCLURE, H. E. (1974) *Migration and survival of the birds of Asia.* Bangkok, Thailand: U.S. Army Medical Component, SEATO Medical Project.

MEAD, C. (1983) *Bird Migration.* Country Life Books. Rushden, U.K.: The Hamlyn Publishing Group.

MEILE, P. (1991) Die Bedeutung der "Gemeinschaftlichen Wasserjagd" für überwinternde Wasservögel am Ermatinger Becken. *Orn. Beob.* 88: 27-56.

MEYBURG, B. U. & CHANCELLOR, R. D., eds. (1989) *Raptors in the modern world.* Berlin, London and Paris: World Working Group on Birds of Prey and Owls.

MOREAU, R. E. (1972) *The Palearctic–African bird migration systems.* London and New York: Academic Press.

MOREAU, R. E. (1973) The Sahel zone as an environment for Palearctic migrants. *Ibis* **115**: 413-417.
MORRISON, R. I. G. & MYERS, J. P. (1989) Shorebird flyways in the New World. Pp. 85-96 in H. Boyd & J.-Y. Pirot, eds. *Flyways and reserve networks for waterbirds.* Slimbridge, U.K.: International Waterfowl and Wetlands Research Bureau (Spec. Publ. 9).
MORRISON, R. I. G. & ROSS, R. K. (1989) *Atlas of Nearctic shorebirds on the coast of South America, Vols. 1 and 2.* Canadian Wildlife Service (Spec. Publ.).
MORSE, D. H. (1989) *American warblers.* Cambridge, Mass.: Harvard University Press.
MORTON, E. S. (1980) The importance of migrant birds to the advancement of evolutionary theory. Pp. 557-560 in A. Keast & E. S. Morton, eds. *Migrant birds in the Neotropics: ecology, behavior, distribution, and conservation.* Washington, D.C.: Smithsonian Institution Press.
MORTON, E. S. & GREENBERG, R. (1989) The outlook for migratory songbirds: "future shock" for birders. *Amer. Birds* **43**: 178-183.
MORTON, E. S., LYNCH, J. F., YOUNG, K. & MEHLHOP, P. (1987) Do male Hooded Warblers exclude females from nonbreeding territories in tropical forests? *Auk* **104**: 133-134.
NEAVE, D. J. (1983) Waterfowl and wetlands: problems and programs in Alberta. Pp. 8-12 in H. Boyd, ed. *First western hemisphere waterfowl and waterbird symposium.* Ottawa: Canadian Wildlife Service; Slimbridge, U.K.: International Waterfowl and Wetlands Research Bureau.
ODUM, E. P., CONNELL, C. E. & STODDARD, H. L. (1961) Flight energy and estimated flight ranges in some migratory birds. *Auk* **78**: 515-527.
PAIN, D. (1990) Lead poisoning in waterfowl: a review. Pp. 172-181 in G. V. T. Matthews, ed. *Managing waterfowl populations.* Slimbridge, U.K.: International Waterfowl and Wetlands Research Bureau (Spec. Publ. 12).
PARISH, D. (1989) Population estimates of waterbirds using the East Asian/Australasian flyway. Pp. 8-13 in H. Boyd & J.-Y. Pirot, eds. *Flyways and reserve networks for waterbirds.* Slimbridge, U.K.: International Waterfowl and Wetlands Research Bureau (Spec. Publ. 9).
PASHLEY, D. N. & MARTIN, R. P. (1988) The contribution of Christmas bird counts to knowledge of the winter distribution of migratory warblers in the Neotropics. *Amer. Birds* **42**: 1164-1176.
PENNYCUICK, C. J. (1969) The mechanics of bird migration. *Ibis* **111**: 525-556.
PIROT, J.-Y., LAURSEN, K., MADSEN, J. & MONVAL, J. Y. (1989) Population estimates of swans, geese, ducks, and Eurasian Coot *Fulica atra* in the Western Palearctic and Sahelian Africa. Pp. 14-23 in H. Boyd & J.-Y. Pirot, eds. *Flyways and reserve networks for waterbirds.* Slimbridge, U.K.: International Waterfowl and Wetlands Research Bureau (Spec. Publ. 9).
POTTS, G. R. (1986) *The partridge: pesticides, predation and conservation.* London: Collins.
RANDS, M. R. W. (1989) Conserving threatened birds: an overview of the species and the threats with some roles for population studies. *Berichte Dt. Sektion Internat. Rat Vogelschutz* **28**: 101-112.
RAPPOLE, J. H. & MORTON, E. S. (1985) Effects of habitat alteration on a tropical avian forest community. Pp. 1013-1021 in P. A. Buckley, M. S. Foster, E. S. Morton, R. S. Ridgely & F. G. Buckley, eds. *Neotropical ornithology.* Washington, D.C.: American Ornithologists' Union (Orn. Monogr. 36).
RAPPOLE, J. H., RAMOS, M. A. & WINKLER, K. (1989) Wintering Wood Thrush movements and mortality in southern Veracruz. *Auk* **106**: 402-410.
RAPPOLE, J. H. & WARNER, D. W. (1980) Ecological aspects of migrant bird behaviour in Veracruz, Mexico. Pp. 353-393 in A. Keast & E. S. Morton, eds. *Migrant birds in the Neotropics: ecology, behavior, distribution, and conservation.* Washington, D.C.: Smithsonian Institution Press.
RATCLIFFE, D. A. (1980) *The Peregrine Falcon.* Calton, U.K.: Poyser.
RISEBROUGH, R. W. (1986) Pesticides and bird populations. *Current Orn.* 3: 397-427.
RISEBROUGH, R. W. (1989) Toxic chemicals and birds of prey: discussions at Eilat in 1987. Pp. 515-525 in B. U. Meyburg & R. D. Chancellor, eds. *Raptors in the modern world.* Berlin, London and Paris: World Working Group on Birds of Prey and Owls.

ROBBINS, C. S., BYSTRAK, D. & GEISSLER, P. H. (1986) *The breeding bird survey: its first fifteen years, 1965-1979.* Washington, D.C.: U.S. Dept of the Interior, Fish and Wildlife Service (Resrce. Publ. 157).

ROUX, F. & JARRY, G. (1984) Numbers, composition and distribution of populations of Anatidae wintering in West Africa. *Wildfowl* **35**: 48-60.

SCHAEFER, G. W. (1968) Energy requirement of migratory flight. *Ibis* **110**: 413-414.

SCHÜTZ, E., BERTHOLD, P., GWINNER, E. & OELKE, H. (1971) *Grundriss der Vogelzugskunde.* Berlin and Hamburg: Paul Parey.

SCOTT, D. A. (1980) *A preliminary inventory of wetlands of international importance for waterfowl in West Europe and Northwest Africa.* Slimbridge, U.K.: International Waterfowl and Wetlands Research Bureau (Spec. Publ. 2).

SCOTT, D. A., ed. (1989) *A directory of Asian wetlands.* Cambridge, U.K. and Gland: International Union for the Conservation of Nature and Natural Resources.

SCOTT, D. A. & CARBONELL, M. (1986) *A directory of Neotropical wetlands.* Cambridge, U.K.: International Union for the Conservation of Nature and Natural Resources; Slimbridge, U.K.: International Waterfowl and Wetlands Research Bureau.

SEIS. (1988) *Issuance of annual regulations permitting the sport hunting of migratory birds.* U.S. Dept of the Interior, Fish and Wildlife Service. Final Supplemental Environmental Impact Statement.

SENNER, S. E. (1988) Saving birds while they are still common: an historical perspective. *Endangered Species Update* **5**: 1-4.

SMIT, C. J. & PIERSMA, T. (1989) Numbers, midwinter distribution, and migration of wader populations using the East Atlantic flyway. Pp. 24-63 in H. Boyd & J.-Y. Pirot, eds. *Flyways and reserve networks for waterbirds.* Slimbridge, U.K.: International Waterfowl and Wetlands Research Bureau (Spec. Publ. 9).

STOLT, B. O., FRANSSON, T., ÅKESSON, S. & SÄLLSTRÖM, B. (1986) *Transmission lines and bird mortality.* Stockholm: Naturhistoriska Riksmusset.

SVENSSON, S.E. (1985) Effects of changes in tropical environments on the North European avifauna. *Ornis Fennica* **62**: 56-63.

TERBORGH, J. (1980) The conservation status of Neotropical migrants. Pp. 21-30 in A. Keast & E. S. Morton, eds. *Migrant birds in the Neotropics: ecology, behavior, distribution, and conservation.* Washington, D.C.: Smithsonian Institution Press.

TERBORGH, J. (1989) *Where have all the birds gone?* Princeton, New Jersey: Princeton University Press.

THIOLLAY, J. M. (1989) Distribution and ecology of Palearctic birds of prey wintering in West and Central Africa. Pp. 95-107 in B.U. Meyburg & R. D. Chancellor, eds. (1989) *Raptors in the modern world.* Berlin, London and Paris: World Working Group on Birds of Prey and Owls.

TUCKER, G. M., McCULLOCH, M. N. & BAILLIE, S. R. (1990) *Review of the importance of losses incurred to migratory birds during migration.* Tring, U.K.: British Trust for Ornithology (Resrch. Rep. 58).

U.S. DEPT OF THE INTERIOR, FISH AND WILDLIFE SERVICE. (1988) The impact of federal programs on wetlands, Vol. 1: the lower Mississippi alluvial plain and the prairie pothole region. Report to Congress by the Secretary of the Interior, Washington, D.C.

U.S. DEPT OF THE INTERIOR, FISH AND WILDLIFE SERVICE AND ENVIRONMENT CANADA. (1986) *North American Waterfowl Management Plan: a strategy for cooperation.* Canadian Wildlife Service.

U.S. ENVIRONMENTAL PROTECTION AGENCY. (1989) *Prairie basin wetlands of the Dakotas.* Dept of the Interior (Biol. Rep. 857.28). Cooperative Publications.

U.S. FISH AND WILDLIFE SERVICE. (1987) *Migratory nongame birds of management concern in the United States: the 1987 list.* Washington, D.C.: Office of Migratory Bird Management.

U.S. FISH AND WILDLIFE SERVICE. (1988) *Concept plan for waterfowl habitat protection, prairie potholes and parklands, U.S. portion.* Dept of the Interior.

WALTER, H. (1979) *Eleonora's Falcon, adaptation to prey and habitat in a social raptor.* Chicago: University of Chicago Press.

WILSON, V. J. (1972) Observations on the effect of dieldrin on wildlife during tsetse fly *Glossina morsitans* control operations in eastern Zambia. *Arnoldia* (Rhodesia) **5**: 1-12.

WINKLER, K., RAPPOLE, J. H. & RAMOS, M. A. (1990) Population dynamics of the wood thrush in southern Veracruz, Mexico. *Condor* **92**: 444-460.

ZOLTAI, S. C. (1983) An overview of the wetlands of Canada. Pp. 45-49 in H. Boyd ed. *First western hemisphere waterfowl and waterbird symposium.* Ottawa: Canadian Wildlife Service; Slimbridge, U.K.: International Waterfowl and Wetlands Research Bureau.

ZUCKERBROT, Y. D., SAFRIEL, U. & PAZ, U. (1980) Autumn migration of Quail *Coturnix coturnix* at the North coast of the Sinai peninsula. *Ibis* **122**: 1-14.

ICBP Technical Publication No. 12, 1991

THE IMPACT OF PESTICIDES ON PALEARCTIC MIGRATORY BIRDS IN THE WESTERN SAHEL

WIM C. MULLIÉ[1], PETER J. VERWEY[1], ALBERT G. BERENDS[1],
JAMES W. EVERTS[1], FATOU SÈNE[2] & JAN H. KOEMAN[1]

1 *Department of Toxicology, Wageningen Agricultural University,
P.O. Box 8129, 6700 EV Wageningen, Netherlands*
2 *Institut des Sciences de l'Environnement, Université Cheikh Anta Diop,
Dakar, Sénégal*

ABSTRACT

The main objective of the present study was to assess the possible impact of the use of pesticides on Palearctic migratory birds wintering in the Senegal River delta covering an area of 3,700 km^2 and originally consisting of flood plains, marshes, permanent lakes and river branches. Land use development projects have turned large parts of the area into agricultural plots. Of the two major lakes of the delta only Lac de Guiers, which serves as a water reservoir for the capital (Dakar), is still intact. Lac Rkiz on the Mauritanian side of the river now has an artificial inundation regime and is partly used for agricultural purposes.

The use of pesticides in west-Sahelian countries has been reviewed, and related to habitat use by Palearctic migrants. Irrigated rice was found to be an important crop in this respect, and Senegal appeared to be the main user of pesticides in irrigated rice in the region.

Three taxa were selected for intensive studies: Ardeidae, Charadriiformes and *Motacilla flava*. These birds were censused in rice-fields and at the same time a number of biotic and abiotic variables were measured. The results show markedly low bird densities, especially for Charadriiformes, in fields that were treated with pesticides, compared to untreated fields. It was also demonstrated that the attractiveness of rice-fields for the birds concerned depends on the vegetation structure, the presence of uncovered area, the water depth and the biomass of aquatic macrofauna. The most commonly used insecticide in rice, carbofuran, was found to be hazardous to wildlife.

If the present development policy for the Senegal River basin remains unchanged, pesticide input may increase considerably, which will further reduce the carrying capacity of irrigated rice-fields as a habitat for Palearctic migrants. We therefore recommend that attempts should be made to increase the surface area of nature reserves, and of unsprayed buffer areas in the delta, and that more selective insect control methods than the use of carbofuran should be developed. A study on Integrated Pest Management in rice crops is also strongly recommended.

GENERAL INTRODUCTION

It is becoming increasingly recognized by conservation-oriented individuals and groups that special efforts are required to safeguard the future survival of migratory bird populations, especially species that migrate over long distances. Migratory bird species are subject to many threats, both by natural factors and by various human activities.

The present study was undertaken at the request of ICBP and sponsored by World Wide Fund for Nature (WWF) and the Netherlands' Ministry of Housing, Physical Planning and Environment. The main objective of the study was to make an assessment of the possible impact the use of pesticides might have on Palearctic migratory birds wintering in the delta of the Senegal River, which forms the natural boundary between Senegal and Mauritania.

There is a general feeling that the use of pesticides in Africa may represent a meaningful threat to many Palearctic migrants (and intra-African migrants and resident species as well), although there are few data to substantiate this allegation. Dead specimens of migratory birds have been recorded in connection with high dose-rate applications of dieldrin and endosulfan in tsetse control operations in Nigeria (Koeman *et al.* 1971, 1978). It is also claimed that locust and bird control campaigns have caused casualties among an array of species of migratory birds (Thiollay, Roux, pers. comm.; Curry-Lindahl 1981; see also Balk & Koeman 1984). Furthermore, there is circumstantial evidence that insecticides and rodenticides are at least in part responsible for the decline of resident bird populations in Egypt (Mullié & Meininger 1985).

Birds can be affected in a number of ways. First by direct contact with the chemicals, secondly through secondary poisoning (feeding on contaminated food) and thirdly by starvation because their food resource is eliminated.

An accurate analysis of pesticide hazards with regard to these birds is extremely difficult, if not beyond our present research capabilities. Clear-cut conclusions can only be drawn when it can be demonstrated that the decline of a population follows from a disturbance of a birth/mortality ratio caused by exposure of individuals and/or habitat to pesticides. There are very few well-documented cases where such causal relationships can be proven adequately. A well-known example is the impaired reproduction induced by DDE in certain species of waterbirds and birds of prey (e.g. Henny 1975; Anderson *et al.* 1975). In the sixties the population of the Sandwich Tern (*Sterna sandvicensis*), a Palearctic migrant which winters in Africa, showed a dramatic decline in north-western Europe. A detailed analysis of the situation revealed that the decline was not related to factors operating during migration or in winter territories. The decline was caused by excessive mortality in chicks and juveniles, killed by chlorinated hydrocarbon insecticides (cyclodiene type) released from a factory. In this case a causal relationship between the presence of a pollutant and the decline of a population could be established (Koeman & van Genderen 1972).

However, at present the various factors mentioned earlier, which affect or which may affect migratory birds, generally act simultaneously, and no single one of these has so far been proved to be much more important than any other. Birds are killed by hunting; substantial parts of their habitat are affected by a variety of land use developments, including pesticide applications, while there are also natural phenomena (e.g. climate) to contend with. An appropriate assessment of the relative importance of all these impact factors with regard to population changes in migratory birds would require a research effort by far exceeding the research input that has been realized so far. Therefore, for the time being one can only rely upon case studies which deal with fragments of the problem. The present study forms an example of such a fragmentary approach:

– To identify pesticide inputs in the western Sahel, especially in the Senegal River delta, and with special emphasis on rice-fields.

- To investigate plant protection measures and cultural methods in rice-fields in relation to the presence of birds.
- To estimate future hazards from pesticide use in agriculture in the western Sahel in relation to river basin development.
- To make recommendations for sustainable development.

The regional developments in vector control in the western Sahel will not be dealt with in detail in this publication. The (possible) side-effects of pesticide applications in vector control and public health protection have been reviewed recently (Balk & Koeman 1984; Dejoux 1988; van der Valk & Koeman 1988). The reader is referred to these publications for additional information.

THE PRESENT USE OF PESTICIDES IN AGRICULTURE IN THE WESTERN SAHEL

The western Sahel is defined here as Mauritania (south of 18°N), Senegal, Gambia, Guinea-Bissau, Mali (south of 18°N) and Burkina Faso. The use of pesticides in agriculture is reviewed country-wise. Based on the information available, Senegal appears to be the main user. This paper will, therefore, present data from this country in more detail.

Senegal

General. The Société de Promotion Industrielle et Agricole (SPIA) and the Societé d'Engrais et de Produits Chimiques (SSEPC) produce, formulate and sell pesticides. Together they control 75-90 per cent of the pesticide market in Senegal, which in 1983 was estimated to be 3-3.5 x 10^6 kg. The SPIA has a 60-70 per cent share of this market. However 1 x 10^6 kg has been exported. The SSEPC, with an estimated 25-30 per cent market share, sells c.125 different pesticides, of which HCH, malathion and endosulfan are the most important, followed by fenitrothion, oxydiazon, dimethoate and paraquat. *Figure 1* shows pesticide distribution in Senegal. The proportion of the different crops treated with pesticides, as estimated by the Direction de Protection des Végétaux, together with the cost of the chemicals, is given in *Table 1*.

Senegal delta. A number of pesticides are used in the Senegal delta, including insecticides (mainly carbofuran), fungicides and herbicides (mainly propanil). Over the past few decades the use of pesticides has shown an upward trend (Morel, Voisin, pers. comm.) which is a logical consequence of the changes in land use and agricultural practice in general.

Pesticides are supplied through two different channels. Most of the rice areas are exploited under the auspices of SAED (Société Nationale d'Aménagement et d'Exploitation du Delta du Fleuve Sénégal). Until 1987 this organization acted as an extension service to the farmers and also supplied equipment and materials, including seed, fertilizers and pesticides. Pesticides are mainly used against diseases and stem borers in rice.

Large-scale applications also occur in the sugar cane plantations managed by the Compagnie Sucrière Sénégalaise (CSS). It is important to mention the use of dieldrin. This compound is applied by CSS for the treatment of cuttings immediately after planting. After examination of dieldrin residues in soil, sediments and piscivorous birds, Mullié *et al.* (1989) concluded that the present selective application of dieldrin probably does not represent a serious threat to the

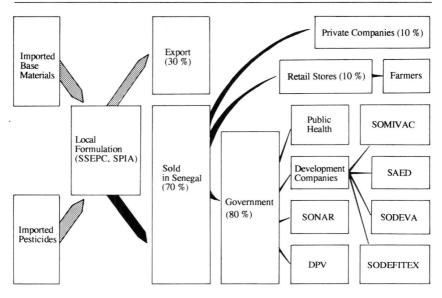

Figure 1: Structure of the pesticide market in Senegal.

local environment. However, clearing of containers and disposal of waste or surplus deserves full attention. This remains a potential source of future contamination. Since dieldrin production has ceased, the compound will probably be replaced by other control methods in future years.

In tomato cultures, mainly insecticides (monocrotophos and carbofuran) and fungicides (captafol, polyram and maneb) are used (Everts & Koeman 1984).

Table 1: Marketing of pesticides by the Societé de Promotion Industrielle et Agricole (SPIA) in 1983.

Product	Quantity (tonnes)	Product	Quantity (litres)
HCH	1,248	Cypermethrin	131,000
Propoxur 1%	512	Cypermethrin/dimethoate	430,000
Methyl-parathion	203	Fenitrothion ULV	21,000
Pirimiphos-methyl	77	Chlorpyriphos	12,000
Diazinon 3%	67	Other (dieldrin, aldrin,	
Heptachlor 20%	n/a	lindane, parathion,	
Thiram 24%	10.5	endosulfan, propanil,	
Other (malathion, etc.)	11.5	EDB, paraquat)	36,000
Total	2,529		630,000

Source: DPV rapport sur SPIA, Dakar, juin 1984.

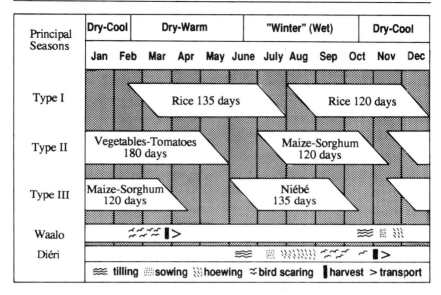

Figure 2:   Crop calendar for the main crops in the Senegal valley and delta.
(*After* van Lavieren & van Wetten 1988.)

Senegal valley. In the Senegal valley two types of agriculture are traditionally practiced. The first, recession agriculture after the annual flood, is practised in the "Walo", the clayish soils bordering the river. The total flooded area varies between 80,000 and 180,000 ha with 32,000-90,000 ha harvested, the main product being sorghum (van Lavieren & van Wetten 1989).

The second type of agriculture is practised in the "Diéri", the area immediately bordering the flood plain. Here, agriculture is entirely rain-fed and the main crops are millet, beans (niébe), maize, melons and ground-nuts (van Lavieren & van Wetten 1988; W. C. Mullié, pers. obs.). The crop calendar for the main crops in the Senegal delta and valley is given in *Figure 2*.

Pesticides are used both in Walo and Diéri cultures. In 1982, 2,000 ha of traditional cultures in the Dagana region were treated with 52 tons of HCH, and in the Kanel region between Matam and Bakel 3,000 ha, being 25 per cent of the cultivated area, was treated with pesticides (Everts & Koeman 1984). HCH and propoxur are the most commonly used compounds.

Casamance. In 1981, only 3,000 ha of rain-fed rice in the Lower Casamance were treated with pesticides (Germain & Thiam 1983), this being less than five per cent of the total area cultivated. For health reasons, the SAED is hesitant to introduce herbicides since women exclusively do the field work (Everts & Koeman 1984). Several herbicides and insecticides have been tested, however, for future use in the Casamance such as oxadiazon, propanil-bentazon, propanil-benthiocarb, butralin and fluorodifen (ISRA 1984).

Cotton fields in the Upper Casamance, with a total surface area of 46,000 ha (FAO 1985), are treated at 10-15-day intervals, predominantly with pyrethroids: deltamethrin (16 g/ha) and cypermethrin (40 g/ha). In addition, in 1983/84

SODEFITEX (1984) treated approximately 20 per cent of the cotton area with herbicides, mainly cotodon (dipropetryn + metolachlor)-paraquat.

Pesticide use by SOMIVAC in 1982 in the Casamance accounted for 8,400 kg of fungicides, 10,845 kg of HCH, 3,697 l of thimul 35 (endosulfan), and 898 l of preforan (fluorodifen) (SOMIVAC 1983).

Cap Vert and Louga region. In the Cap Vert there is irregular use of thimul 35, fenvalerate, cyper- and deltamethrin, acephate, chlorpyriphos-ethyl, diazinon and dimethoate. Rather small quantities of HCH, DDT, maneb and monocrotophos are used (Evert & Koeman 1984). On the 1,121,000 ha of ground-nuts between St-Louis and The Gambia, the most commonly used pesticides are HCH, propoxur (15 kg/ha) and thimul 35 against Coleoptera and Orthoptera; dieldrin against *Amsacta* and Coleoptera; and cypermethrin. Locally, carbofuran and various seed dressings are applied. Side-effects of thimul 35 on horses and sheep have been reported after treatment of fallow land (Everts & Koeman 1984). Effects on birds have not been reported.

Mauritania
Little information is available from Mauritania, since the SONADER (Société National de Développement Rural, Mauritania) does not keep records. Van Lavieren & van Wetten (1989) mention fenitrothion, "capnecryrox" (active ingredient unknown; probably misspelt) and lindane being used in the Mauritanian part of the Senegal delta. At least some of these products are purchased in Senegal. However, the present use of pesticides on rice in Mauritania appears to be less than in Senegal (L. P. van Lavieren, EUROCONSULT, pers. comm.).

The Gambia
Of the total surface area of 23,900 ha of rice, only 500-1,100 ha are actually treated with pesticides (M. Schellekens, EUROCONSULT, pers. comm.).

Guinea-Bissau
In rice land in Guinea-Bissau, representing up to 56 per cent of the total arable land (FAO 1985), there is probably no pesticide input of any importance (J. van der Kamp, pers. comm.).

Mali
Mali has major irrigation schemes for rice production, totalling 137,900 ha. At least on the 37,000 ha managed by the Office du Niger (O.N.) and approximately 13,000 ha of "illegal" rice-fields bordering the O.N. scheme north of Markala, there are no pesticide inputs (van Dongen & Genet 1986; P. van Blom, pers. comm.).

Pesticide use in rice-fields in Mali has only been mentioned for the Boucle du Niger and the Aval de Bourem, both in eastern Mali (Ledant 1987). In 1982/1983, field trials with dimecron (phosphamidon) at 250 g a.i./ha were performed in irrigated rice in two areas of the O.N. at Kolongo and Kokry (Doumbia *et al.* 1983). Pesticides sold by the Société Malienne d'Engrais et de Produits Chimiques at Bamako included predominantly lindane and some dieldrin, carbofuran 5 per cent, methyl parathion and DDT (M. Thauront, ICBP France, *in litt.*).

Pesticides are probably mainly used in cotton production in south-east Mali. A summary of cotton production and related pesticide use in some west Sahelian countries is given in *Table 2*. No information is available on the compounds actually used in Mali.

Table 2: Summary of surface areas cultivated with cotton, and related insecticide use in Senegal, Mali and Burkina Faso.

Country		1982/1983	1983/1984
Senegal			
Cotton	ha	42,018	33,353
Insecticides	l	663,434	431,135
Insecticides/ha	l/ha	15.8	12.9
Mali			
Cotton	ha	97,868	104,459
Insecticides	l	1,045,000	1,000,000
Insecticides/ha	l/ha	10.7	9.6
Burkina Faso			
Cotton	ha	71,970	76,790
Insecticides	l	475,000	475,000
Insecticides/ha	l/ha	6.6	6.2

After Catrisse (1985).

Between 1962 and 1968 Laferrère (1983) found that two species of roller, the Abyssinian Roller (*Coracias abyssinica*) and the Rufous-crowned Roller (*C. naevius*) disappeared from south-east Mali after the extension of cotton cultivation in this region and following pesticide treatments against "punaise des capsules". On several occasions after these treatments, individuals of Abyssinian Roller were found paralysed. A similar development was observed in Egypt where Cattle Egret (*Bubulcus ibis*), Black Kite (*Milvus migrans*), Black-shouldered Kite (*Elanus caeruleus*) and Pied Kingfisher (*Ceryle rudis*) completely disappeared or reached very low population densities in the main cotton-growing areas in the 1970s, with some recent recovery, particularly of Black-shouldered Kite (Mullié & Meininger 1985; Mullié 1989). Although there is no proof, this decline might have resulted from intensified pesticide treatments in cotton. In a study in Chad in 1968-1969 Everaarts *et al.* (1971) demonstrated bird mortality in cotton cultures after endrin and dieldrin applications, while insectivorous species were already becoming scarce in cotton-growing areas.

Burkina Faso

Except for public health and vector control, there is little use of pesticides in Burkina Faso, and the use of pesticides in (irrigated) rice is thought to be of little importance. According to CILLS (1986) chemical treatment of irrigated rice will be further investigated in 1988-1991 in two pilot studies of 1,200 ha in the Kou Valley and 320 ha at Karfiguella. Apparently this will include the greater part of Burkina's c.2,000 ha of irrigated area (FAO 1985).

Compared with Senegal and Mali, Burkina Faso appears to have the lowest pesticide input per hectare in cotton production. However, caution is required in comparisons of the potential risk since apart from Senegal no information is available on the compounds actually used.

In a previous study, endosulfan applications in tsetse control field trials caused fish mortality (Baldry *et al.* 1981). Deltamethrin and permethrin applications severely affected populations of the shrimps *Caridina africana* and *Macrobrachium raridens* and terrestrial invertebrate populations in the study area. However, no

Table 3: Number of birds (*Quelea quelea, Passer luteus, Ploceus* sp.) killed in 1980 by OCLALAV in the western Sahel.

Country	Avicides	Quantity	Number of birds killed
Senegal	Phosdrin	49.5 l	15.05 x 10⁶
Mauritania	Parathion 25%	417 l	
Mali (west)	Toritox	50 l	
	Explosives	13,397 kg	
Mali	Parathion 25%	7,385 l	42.1 x 10⁶
Burkina Faso	Parathion 95%	415 l	
	Fenthion	1,600 l	
	Explosives	1,725 kg	

Source: OCLALAV 1981.

effects on survival or population fluctuations of insectivorous birds were noticed (Everts *et al.* 1978; Takken *et al.* 1978).

AGRO-CHEMICALS USED FOR BIRD, GRASSHOPPER AND LOCUST CONTROL

Although avicides, acridicides and locusticides which are in general not applied directly to arable land are beyond the scope of the present study, they may pose severe (temporary) restrictions on the use of the habitats where these compounds are used. In a harsh environment, with food being the limiting factor, this may be a factor of importance for Palearctic species wintering in the western Sahel. Therefore these inputs will be mentioned briefly.

Chemical control of birds

Locally, granivorous passerines can cause considerable damage to crops. The Organisation Commune de Lutte Antiacridienne et de Lutte Antiaviaire (OCLALAV) has been responsible for protecting crops from bird damage in the Sahel region for the past few decades. In 1988 its tasks were taken over by the national plant protection services (DPV).

Control agents are pesticides (parathion, fenthion; in the past also phosdrin) and explosives. Target organisms are granivorous passerines, mainly Quelea (*Quelea quelea*), Golden Sparrow (*Passer luteus*) and weavers (*Ploceus* sp.) (Ward 1972; Drees 1980). Bird control is localized to night roosts or breeding areas of the target species. Night roosts, particularly when present in reeds or *Typha* marshes, are generally shared with Palearctic non-target species like Sand Martin (*Riparia riparia*) and Yellow Wagtail (*Motacilla flava*) (e.g. Ledant 1987). In addition ducks, waders, rails, gallinules and several warblers use these habitats permanently. *Table 3* gives an impression of the number of birds killed in 1980.

Several authors have stressed that side-effects occur on a regular basis, but a general overview is not available. Ducks, Black-tailed Godwit (*Limosa limosa*), Ruff (*Philomachus pugnax*) (Roux 1976), Sand Martin, herons, cormorants, Yellow Wagtails and kingfishers have been mentioned as casualties. Moreover, all fish, amphibians, reptiles, birds and mammals killed or debilitated by avicides attract storks, herons, and certain birds of prey (e.g. Leuthold & Leuthold 1972), which could give rise to secondary poisoning. Casualties of 200 White Storks (Nikolaus

1981) and over 500 small Palearctic migrants in nine species, apart from Afro-tropical species (Elmalik, *In* Schulz 1988), have been documented for treatment of Quelea colonies with fenthion ("Queletox"). Thiollay, who has considerable experience with birds of prey in West Africa, even states (*In* Schulz 1988) that in his opinion chemical bird control is one of the main causes of the decline of bird of prey populations in West Africa; furthermore he cites a Quelea control operation which was not effective as far as *Quelea* was concerned, but killed almost all other birds on the site (pers. comm.).

Further documented evidence is provided by Thomsett (1987) who claimed that the populations of seven species of birds of prey on the north-western slopes of Mt Kenya were almost entirely wiped out by a *Quelea* eradication scheme with fenthion in June 1984. In addition, many hundreds of other bird species were found to have died after spraying, while recovery of raptor populations to pre-spray levels did not occur within the next two years (Thomsett 1987).

Severe mortality of non-target bird fauna after treatment with fenthion was also documented for South Africa (Tarboton 1987; Colahan & Ferreira 1989) and Botswana (Simmons 1987). Subsequently, the Directorate of Resource Conservation of the South African Department of Agricultural Economics and Marketing has discontinued the spraying of reedbed roosts and other roosts associated with open water (Allan 1989).

Meanwhile an in-depth study has been performed on the side-effects of fenthion for bird control in Kenya (Bruggers *et al.* 1989). The results of this study clearly demonstrate that the use of fenthion is extremely hazardous for non-target species and that predatory and insectivorous birds were exposed to potentially harmful residues.

In 1980 OCLALAV (1981) performed field trials in The Gambia and the Senegal delta with furadan (carbofuran) 75 per cent as an avicide. Field dosages of 1.9-7.5 kg a.i./ha on limited surface areas of rice-fields produced "résultats ... très encourageants". Thus carbofuran was recommended for further use, also in counter season cultures. This development is particularly alarming, since it is now a well-established fact that field dosages of 0.5-1.0 kg a.i./ha in rice-fields give rise to dramatic effects on many non-target organisms. The use of this chemical is hazardous for wildlife, and it severely reduces the carrying capacity of irrigated rice for birds, including waders, and other insectivorous organisms (Mullié *et al.* 1991).

There is a recent development to replace avicides – at least partially – with repellents, such as methiocarb (Ruelle & Bruggers 1979; Hamza *et al.* 1982) and frightening agents, such as avitrol (Shefte *et al.* 1982). Methiocarb is thought to repel birds by causing an illness-induced conditioned aversion (Rogers 1974, 1978).

Between 1980 and 1985, bird control activities in the Senegal River basin in Senegal were rather limited (Everts *et al.* 1985). However, since 1985 there have been regular bird control operations between Richard Toll and Kaskas. Dead or debilitated birds were not removed after spraying, and they attracted large numbers of predators and scavengers (J. Betlem, pers. comm.). In December 1987 a roost of Quelea in the classified forest of N'Galoué, near Podor, was treated by the DPV. In the days following treatment a number of Jackals (*Canis aureus*), Black Kites, Kestrels (*Falco tinnunculus*) (Betlem 1988), and owls (J. Betlem, pers. comm.) were found poisoned in a wide area around the roost. The DPV is also planning bird control activity in 1990 in the sugar cane area of Richard Toll (pers. comm.).

According to Meinzingen *et al.* (1989) it seems unlikely that Quelea control is having much impact on non-target species populations, despite spectacular numbers of casualties sometimes reported. Compared to agricultural spraying practice, the

Table 4: Pesticides used for locust control in the western Sahel in 1986 in aerial applications.

Product		Senegal	Mali	Gambia	Mauritania	Burkina Faso
	ha	1,159,800	484,000	247,710	193,100	211,140
Chlorpyriphos-ethyl	l	5,000	-	-	-	-
Diazinon	l	40,000	56,400	9,400	10,500	17,000
Fenitr. + fenvaler.	l	20,000	-	-	-	-
Idem (solid)	kg	100	-	-	-	-
Fenitrothion[1]	tonne	1,945	-	-	-	-
Fenitrothion[2]	l	287,320	235,025	41,870	37,500	59,780
Fenvalerate	l	-	-	-	4,000	-
HCH 25	tonne	-	514	-	-	-
Malathion ULV 960	l	212,500	10,000	71,070	10,000	-
Propoxur 1% PP	tonne	700	-	-	-	147
Propoxur 2% PP	tonne	-	-	-	640	40

After T. Rachadi (*In* Duranton *et al.* 1987), FAO (1986), and U.S. Congress (1990).

Notes: 1 Fenitrothion sachets 200G 2% + idem 2.5% PP + idem 3% PP combined; 2 Fenitrothion ULV 500 + idem ULV 960/1,000 + idem 500 CE combined.

amount of Quelea spraying being carried out reputedly is small. However, we tend to disagree with this view because spraying of avicides at high dose rates is certainly not comparable with the use of agricultural pesticides at dose rates intended to *avoid* casualties among non-target fauna.

The attraction of Quelea concentrations for an array of non-target species, often scavengers and predators, places grave responsibilities on the bird control agency. The use of fenthion (Queletox) is detrimental to many non-target species.

Grasshopper and locust control

In *Table 4*, pesticides used in 1986 for the control of the Senegalese Grasshopper (*Oedaleus senegalensis*) and to some extent the Desert Locust (*Schistocerca gregaria*) in the western Sahel are summarized. The total area covered was 2,158,750 ha. In addition, 500,393 ha were treated through ground control (U.S. Congress 1990). Pesticides used for ground control operations are incompletely included in *Table 4*. In 1987, pesticide input was less than in 1986 after the decrease in Senegalese Grasshopper populations. However, starting from 1988, agro-chemical input has increased considerably after Desert Locust populations exploded. In 1989 there were no major outbreaks of Desert Locust in the western Sahel. However, locally, Senegalese Grasshopper populations increased rapidly and were treated with insecticides. The main reason for this rapid recovery of Senegalese Grasshopper populations was thought to be the decline in egg parasite populations as a side-effect of previous chemical treatment.

Relatively small areas were treated with dieldrin against immatures. In 1980, in Mali, 11,165 ha were treated at an application rate of maximally 55 g a.i./ha (OCLALAV 1981). In addition to the amounts given in *Table 4*, in 1986 40,000 ha were treated with dieldrin and fenitrothion. According to the FAO, dieldrin application of up to 75 g/ha is thought to be without risk for terrestrial vertebrates (van der Valk 1988). The present policy of FAO, however, is to abandon the use of dieldrin completely, and to intensify the development of other control methods for immatures, such as insect growth regulators. At least since 1988/1989 no dieldrin has been used for locust and grasshopper control (H. van der Valk, FAO pers. comm.).

At present, very little is known about the side-effects of megascale locust or grasshopper control operations. Older information is often anecdotal, and based on circumstantial evidence or second-hand information. Most information concerns the White Stork (*Ciconia ciconia*). The only classic studies on side-effects of locust control operations on White Storks did not show major effects of the use of BHC (HCH). However, the possibility of side-effects of other insecticides like dieldrin and DNOC was considered to be likely (Vesey-FitzGerald 1959; Schwitulla 1962; Milstein 1964, 1965).

Thiollay (pers. comm.) has seen thousands of storks destroyed after locust control, but other ornithologists remark that there is no proof that this was due to the pesticide used (dieldrin) (Morel, Roux, pers. comm.; Curry-Lindahl 1981). Schüz (1955) mentions stork mortality after locust control in Morocco and Algeria, but here also there is only circumstantial evidence. It was suggested that the disappearance of migratory locusts due to chemical control since the fifties led to a substantial decline in the number of storks (Dallinga & Schoenmakers 1984; Schulz 1988), but see Goriup & Schulz (this volume).

Locust control is reported to be detrimental also to certain birds of prey such as Montagu's Harrier (*Circus pygargus*) and Red-footed Falcon (*Falco vespertinus*), some herons in Mali (e.g. Cattle Egret), bustards (after dieldrin application; J.- M. Thiollay, *in litt.*), shrikes, rollers, bee-eaters, and incidentally warblers like Whitethroat (*Sylvia communis*). The Montagu's Harrier is an avid locust consumer with c.95 per cent of 150 pellets collected near Mbour, Senegal 1988/1989, consisting of Orthoptera (F. Baillon, pers. comm.).

According to Thiollay (1986; 1989), the raptor species in which a marked decline has been reported, both on their European breeding grounds and on their spring migration in Tunisia and in West Africa, are Montagu's and Pallid Harrier (*Circus macrourus*), Red-footed Falcon and Lesser Kestrel (*Falco naumanni*), all predators of locusts in the dry Savannah belt.

A poorly coordinated action against Desert Locust at Mbour, Senegal, early February 1989 and involving five independently operating American, Canadian and Senegalese aerial and ground spray teams (!), resulted in a heavy overdosing with fenitrothion and malathion and subsequently a massive kill of birds at the ORSTOM Ornithological Station (F. Baillon, pers. comm.). On the roads within the 56 ha station 62 birds of 15 species were found, among which 26 Red-beaked Hornbills (*Tockus erythrorhynchus*), three Hoopoes (*Epupa epops*), two Redshanks (*Tringa totanus*) and one Tawny Eagle (*Aquila rapax*). A casual relationship between spraying and mortality could be confirmed by analysis of brain cholinesterase (ChE) activity (kindly performed by B. Niane & M. Ciss, Dakar University) in a Hoopoe collected and put at W. C. Mullié's disposal. This activity was only 22 per cent of ChE activity in control Hoopoes (Keith & Mullié 1990) and as such indicative for poisoning by a ChE inhibitor.

Recent field trials in 12-ha plots near Nara, Mali, with four different insecticides, did not produce direct mortality in birds. In plots treated with chlorpyrifos (171 g/ha), however, there was a significant reduction in bird numbers after treatment, which might be attributed to the effect of treatment (Dynamac 1988a). A comparable study in the Tokar delta of Sudan, with six insecticides tested in 100-ha plots, neither produced direct mortality, nor statistically significant change in numbers of birds present (Dynamac 1988b). Another study in Wadi Diib, Salala, north-eastern Sudan, with eight insecticides tested, did not detect enzymatic or microsomal changes in birds (Müller 1988a, 1988b). The results from these studies have only limited value, since the design does not meet the minimum requirements for field studies of this kind.

The only study available to date, which was sufficiently large to account for "border effects" and to cover possible side-effects on birds, invertebrates and key soil processes, is a pilot study to the environmental effects of chemical grasshopper and locust control in northern Senegal (Everts 1990). Field work on birds in this study (Keith & Mullié 1990; Mullié & Keith 1991) revealed statistically significant effects of fenitrothion (485 and 825 g a.i./ha) and chlorpyrifos (270 and 387 g a.i./ha) on the following species or species groups: the sum of 21 most common species (numbers), the sum of 71 regular species (numbers), Singing Bush-Lark (*Mirafra javanica*; numbers, territoriality, breeding performance, food, weight), Buffalo Weaver (*Bubalornis albirostris*; breeding performance, probably numbers), Blue-naped Mousebird (*Urocolius macrourus*; numbers), Abyssinian Roller (numbers) and Hoopoe (probably numbers). In addition to these secondary effects, up to 13 per cent of the total population of birds inhabiting sprayed plots were killed by the high dose treatments (approximately twice the dose recommended for Desert Locust control), as was demonstrated by inhibition of brain cholinesterase activity (Keith & Mullié 1990). Overdosing regularly occurs under operational conditions (information FAO) as is also demonstrated by the example of Mbour (above).

Appraisal

With respect to scale, regularity, and types of pesticides used, irrigated rice is important. Although the quantities used per hectare are lower than in several other crops, notably cotton, the cultivation of irrigated rice in or bordering wetlands of high conservation value introduces potential hazards. Therefore, the remainder will deal with irrigated rice.

HABITAT USE BY PALEARCTIC BIRDS
IN THE WESTERN SAHEL

The habitat use of Palearctic birds migrating through or staging in the western Sahel is still imperfectly known. The best-studied group, the waterbirds, are generally confined to wetland habitats. Areas of international importance for these species are the Senegal delta in Senegal and Mauritania, the inner delta of the Niger in Mali and the rice-fields and intertidal mudflats of Guinea-Bissau. The presence of vast areas of muddy or inundated rice-fields is of particular importance, since these offer – within certain limits – an important feeding habitat for a range of species. The study of Altenburg and van der Kamp (1985) clearly shows that in Senegal, The Gambia and Guinea-Bissau, significant numbers of Palearctic and Ethiopian waterfowl winter in wet rice-fields, with Guinea-Bissau being of particular importance.

Table 5 summarizes information on the present surface areas cultivated with rice in the western Sahel, together with information on pesticide use. Although Senegal is not the main rice producer, it uses most pesticides in its (irrigated) rice-fields.

The Senegal delta is situated between 15°50' and 16°40'N, and 15°40' and 16°40'W, on the border of Mauritania and Senegal (*Figure 3*). Downstream from Richard Toll the delta covers an area of 3,700 km², divided into a Mauritanian section of about 1,300 km² and a Senegalese section of about 2,400 km². The

Table 5: Present rice cultivation and pesticide use in the western Sahel (mid-1980s).

Area	Type of culture (ha)			
	Irrigated	Marsh (rain-fed)	Inundated	Total
Mauritania				
Senegal delta	5,000++	-	-	5,000[1]
Senegal				
Senegal valley	5,800++	-	-	5,800[2]
Senegal delta	10,500++	-	-	10,500[2]
Siné Saloum	-	1,750	-	1,750[3]
Casamance	500++	65,900+	-	66,400[3]
Gambia	1,100++	22,800	-	23,900[3]
Guinea-Bissau	-	107,000	-	107,000[3]
Mali				
Niger delta	137,900*	-	120,000[4]	257,900
Burkina Faso	2,000*	-	?	30,000[1]

Key: ++   pesticides used on entire cultivated area.
    +   pesticides used on less than 5% of cultivated area.
    *   pesticide use only in experimental plots.

Sources: 1 FAO 1985; 2 Plan Directeur 1988; 3 Altenburg & van der Kamp 1985; 4 Breman *et al.* 1987 (quoted *In* Rodenburg *et al.* 1988).

delta originally consisted of large flood-plains which were flooded temporarily each year, freshwater ponds and watercourses, as well as brackish marshes. South of Richard Toll there was an open connection between the Senegal River and a large freshwater lake, Lac de Guiers. Ever since 1903, large-scale land use development projects have changed the landscape. Dikes were built alongside the Senegal River, particularly since the early 1960s, and complex irrigation systems have been created (*Figure 3*). As a consequence, large parts of the flood-plains are not flooded any more, apart from the sites that were turned into agricultural plots (especially rice and sugar cane). A total surface area of 800 km^2 of periodic aquatic habitat was lost, not only to irrigation but also to desertification (Roux 1976). Total areas cultivated with rice and sugar cane account for 10,500 ha and 7,000 ha respectively, being more than 80 per cent of the total irrigated area in the Senegalese part of the delta. On the remaining 4,000 ha, other crops such as tomatoes are being cultivated.

Some marshes and smaller lakes were saved and have been included in the Djoudj National Park (c.120 km^2). A former bird sanctuary, the Ndiael depression (160 km^2), has dried out due to land use developments. Lac de Guiers is largely intact. It is connected, however, to the vast irrigation complex from which it receives drainwater, and to the Senegal River (by a large canal), although it is controlled by a sluice gate. During the wet season and shortly afterwards there are many smaller ponds and depressions in the delta. As the delta is situated in the Sahel zone with an annual rainfall varying from 0 to 350 mm, these ponds dry out within one to three months of the rains stopping.

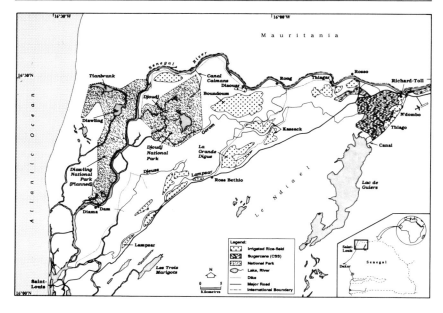

Figure 3: Map of the Senegal delta.

The other major lake in the delta area used to be Lac Rkiz in southern Mauritania. However, due to reclamation for agricultural development, and to recent drought, it has lost most of its significance. Currently it is better described as a "temporarily and artificially inundated depression" than as a "lake" (van Wetten *et al.* 1989).

The studies of Tréca (1975) and Altenburg & van der Kamp (1986) show the importance of inundated rice-fields, particularly as a habitat for ducks and waders, with Ruff (10,000-20,000) and Wood Sandpiper (*T. glareola*) (5,000-10,000) being the most numerous species. They allow for the division given in *Table 6*.

The relative importance of rice-fields for several species increases during and after harvest. In particular the numbers of Black-tailed Godwit and Ruff may increase considerably. On 15 December 1980, for instance, 15,000-20,000 Ruffs were counted in a 1,800-ha complex of rice-fields north-east of Ross-Bethio, in and near the périmètre "La Grande Digue" (Poorter *et al.* 1982; J. van der Kamp, pers. comm.).

The Wood Sandpiper is one of the commonest waders, and almost completely confined to wet rice-fields (Poorter *et al.* 1982; Altenburg & van der Kamp 1986). The statement of Roux (1959) that the Wood Sandpiper was the commonest species but one, after Ruff, in the period before the major reclamation efforts had started, implies that the species may have partially adapted to the loss of flood-plains.

The Black-tailed Godwit declined in numbers significantly in the Senegal delta: from over 100,000 in the late 1950s, to 20,000 in the 1970s, and down to 10,000 in the 1980s (Altenburg & van der Kamp 1985) due to the loss of flood-plain habitat due to the construction of dikes, and drought over the past twenty years. This population now relies heavily upon rice-fields during late season (Tréca

Table 6: Estimated presence of waterbirds in rice-fields, expressed as percentage of total number present in the Senegal delta. Based on figures presented by Treca (1975) for July-November 1973, and by Altenburg and van der Kamp (1986) for October 1983.

Percentage of number in Senegal delta present in rice-fields		
0-30%	31-70%	70-100%
Phalacrocorax africanus	*Egretta alba/intermedia*	*Charadrius dubius*
Egretta garzetta	*Circus aeruginosus*	*Tringa nebularia*
Ardea cinerea	*Charadrius hiaticula*	*Tringa stagnatilis*
Ardea purpurea	*Actitis hypoleucos*	*Tringa glareola*
Plegadis falcinellus	*Gallinago gallinago*	*Tringa ochropus*
Circus pygargus	*Philomachus pugnax*	*Tringa erythropus*
Calidris alpina	*Limosa limosa*	*Calidris minuta*
Anas querquedula	*Himantopus himantopus*	*Chlidonias* sp.
Anas acuta		
Ethiopian ducks		
hundreds	10,000-25,000	10,000-25,000

1984). In years with below-average rainfall, when few naturally inundated wetlands are available, inundated rice-fields may be of particular importance.

Although the surface area of rice in the Senegal valley and delta is less than five per cent of the total rice area in the western Sahel, approximately 70 per cent of all pesticides used on rice are used in this region. Therefore it seemed relevant to concentrate our study on this habitat in the Senegal delta because: (1) the habitat is of significance to many different bird species; (2) pesticide input can be quantified and its side-effects studied; and (3) major land-use changes are to be expected in the entire flood-plain area (Drijver & Marchand 1985).

BIRDS OF THE RICE-FIELDS OF THE SENEGAL DELTA AND THE EFFECTS OF CULTURAL PRACTICES

At the time of our field study the main wetlands of the delta region were the areas irrigated for rice cultivation. Rainfall had been below average for the third year in succession. A bird census was made in these fields, and some fields were selected for additional studies. Detailed accounts of the methods used, and the results, can be found in ICBP Study Report No. 36.

Sixty-three bird species were recorded in rice-fields. Ruff and Sand Martin were the most abundant Palearctic migrants. The Cattle Egret was the most abundant Afro-tropical species. The highest number of birds was found at Thiagar, a poorly drained and cultivated area. This is the only area where no efforts were made by farmers to chase weavers away.

The Cattle Egret was observed in groups of 10 to 20 individuals on both dry and wet fields. The highest numbers were counted just after the harvesting of the rice. The solitary Squacco Heron (*Ardeola ralloides*) was found regularly in rice-fields, along the canals and in drainage areas. Marsh Harriers (*Circus aeruginosus*) and Black Kites were abundant, while Black-shouldered Kites were observed regularly. Kestrels arrived in the area only after the harvest.

Charadriiformes were most commonly observed on wet soils. Wood Sandpipers were very common, both in small groups or solitarily. After the harvest, Ruffs were seen in the fields in large numbers. The less common Snipe (*Gallinago gallinago*) was mainly confined to muddy sites covered by vegetation. The very common Yellow Wagtail was observed along rice-fields, near canals and in drainage areas. As far as the Charadriiformes are concerned, treated fields attracted very low numbers as compared to untreated ones. Only the Cattle Egret was seen more in treated than in untreated fields.

The variables which describe the structure of the vegetation are crop height and percentage open space. In the treated fields the percentage open space was generally lower than in the untreated ones. Weeds were more prominent in untreated than in treated fields.

The pesticides used in these fields were propanil, weedone (2,4-D) and furadan (carbofuran). Propanil is most widely used as a post-emergence herbicide at about 2 kg a.i./ha. Carbofuran is applied in granular formulation (furadan 3G) by hand against rice-borers at about 600 g a.i./ha. The mean application rates were lower than the advised ones. Weedone was used in one field at 1.200 g a.i./ha.

Fertilizers are applied as top dressing and as basal dressing. For top dressing NPK 18.46.08 was used in 13 fields and urea was applied in 17 fields as a basal dressing. No correlation could be demonstrated between the use of fertilizers and bird numbers, or with any of the other variables. The use of pesticides, however, is significantly related to differences in the ecosystem and henceforth to its attractiveness for birds.

In most treated fields a lower biomass of aquatic fauna was found than in the control. The difference was most remarkable in a field that had been treated twice with carbofuran, shortly before the observations were made. The farmers who had carried out the application reported mortality in frogs and fish. Of the three bird taxa analysed, Charadriiformes showed the highest correlation with biomass of aquatic macroinvertebrates.

Because of the observed low biomass in fields treated with carbofuran, and the acute effects reported by farmers, carbofuran applications were studied in more detail. The study dealt with the acute toxicity of irrigation water in treated fields and the effects of the treatments on macro-invertebrate populations in an experimental set-up. The results of this study are published elsewhere (Mullié *et al.* 1991), but it is relevant to quote some of the major conclusions.

It was found that numbers of Hydrometridae, Hydrocorisae, Amphibicorisae, Diptera, Odonata and Ephemeroptera were severely reduced after treatment. Their numbers remained significantly lower than those in control plots until 30-40 days after treatment. Total biomass of macro-invertebrates was still lower than that of the control 50 days after treatment. Side-effects were also observed in frogs and birds: twenty unidentified weavers and one White Wagtail (*Motacilla alba*) died.

CONCLUSIONS

The following main conclusion can be drawn. The diminished value of the treated rice-field habitats is related to a complex of factors, including:

(a) the use of pesticides;
(b) crop height;
(c) biomass (abundance and density of food organisms);
(d) the availability of open space (uncovered areas within the rice-fields which appear to attract birds); and
(e) the presence of weeds.

These factors are interlinked in various ways, e.g. the vegetation structure is markedly affected by weed control measures, and biomass of macro-invertebrates is lower in plots treated with pesticides, notably carbofuran.

The special study of carbofuran showed that biomass of macro-invertebrates remains significantly reduced at least until 50 days after treatment. Particularly when multiple treatments per season are applied, this may adversely affect the carrying capacity of these habitats for waders and other insectivorous birds. Therefore, well-managed rice-fields do not appear to be an alternative for naturally inundated wetlands.

POSSIBLE ECOTOXICOLOGICAL CONSEQUENCES
OF RIVER BASIN DEVELOPMENT

Senegal delta

In order to reduce Senegal's dependence on food imports, the Organisation pour la Mise en Valeur de la Vallée du Fleuve Sénégal (OMVS) has developed an ambitious plan for the Senegal River basin. The basis for future agricultural development is the construction of two dams, one at Diama, north of St Louis (completed in 1986), and one at Manantali, in the Bafing tributary, 90 km south-east of Bafoulabé, Mali (completed in 1988). Furthermore, a dike will be constructed along the right bank of the Senegal River in Mauritania (started in 1988), in order to allow for reclamation in the Mauritanian part of the Senegal delta (*Figure 4*). It is not known if the recent political conflicts between Senegal and Mauritania will influence the execution of these plans.

The completion of these constructions will:

– Stop the intrusion of salt water from the sea during the dry season.
– Allow for a gradual replacement of the traditional Walo "culture de décrue" with irrigated crops, mainly rice, in double culture (culture de contre-saison).
– Regulate discharges of the Senegal River, make the river navigable throughout the year, and create a freshwater lake upstream from Diama.

If the present policy remains unchanged, pesticide input may increase considerably, as predicted in the OMVS (n.d.) final report. For birds using the Senegal delta and valley, this may have several consequences:

– Within the next decade the "Walo" culture, well adapted to the local environment and the traditions of the human population, will be completely replaced by irrigated agriculture. A number of measures have been proposed to reduce the possible side-effects of future pesticide applications in the Senegal delta (see below).
– It is obvious from the results of the present study that rice-fields treated with pesticides are far less attractive to migratory birds (especially Charadriiformes and Yellow Wagtail) than untreated fields. A further intensification and better management of irrigated agriculture therefore may limit the significance of rice-fields as a feeding habitat. The bird species mentioned in the second and right column of *Table 6* are particularly at risk.
– The most hazardous pesticide application identified in the present study is carbofuran (furadan). Use of an alternative, i.e. diazinon, may also have adverse environmental effects (Mullié *et al.* 1991). Increased use of either carbofuran or diazinon therefore represents a hazard to aquatic and bird wildlife in these areas.

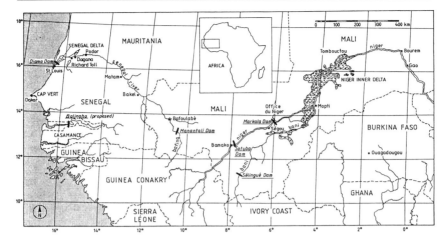

Figure 4: Map showing the major river basin development projects in the western Sahel, and key to localities mentioned in the text.

– Serious impact, either direct or indirect, has to be envisaged in connection with the large-scale treatment of drains with herbicides (e.g. paraquat, diuron), and run-off of fish-toxic insecticides like endosulfan. Incidental fish-kills have already been reported.

In order to limit the potential hazards from pesticide use, a central drain (émissaire) has been planned for the drainage of 35,310 ha (out of 66,240 ha) of delta irrigations. To prevent contamination of Lake Diama, this émissaire will be connected to the Senegal River downstream from Diama (Plan Directeur, 1988). For the drainage of the largest périmètre of Boundoum, actually 4,263 ha (*Figure 3*), a temporary solution has been proposed of constructing a siphon under the Gorom to drain in a depression down from Boundoum until the émissaire is in operation (van Lavieren & van Wetten 1988). Even when the émissaire is operational, considerable areas will drain directly into the Senegal River.

The future control of pesticide use will be difficult or even impossible. Since 1987 the SAED has no longer been responsible for distribution of pesticides to the farmers. The farmers now have to deal with commercial suppliers through the Caisse Nationale de Crédit Agricole Sénégalais (CNCAS). This may result in a decrease in pesticide use and a shift to cheaper compounds. The cheaper pesticides are generally the most environmentally hazardous compounds.

Further development of the Senegal River basin using irrigated agriculture may increase the incidence of pests. An increase in murid rodent populations, locally reaching pest levels in some périmètres, has already been observed since 1977. Anti-coagulant rodenticides, such as chlorophacinone, coumachlor and coumafuryl have been introduced meanwhile (Plan Directeur 1988).

Tréca (1975, 1984, pers. comm.) suggested that the introduction of out-of-season rice production may encourage extensive damage by Black-tailed Godwit, Ruff and several species of ducks, since sowing coincides with the presence of large concentrations of these rice-eating species. (See also crop calendar, *Figure 2*).

The Direction de Protection des Végétaux and the Direction de l'Environnement in Senegal are currently preparing legislation on pesticides. This will be a major leap forward and it will facilitate control on banned or restricted products. However, as long as Mauritania does not have comparable legislation the actual use in the delta may be influenced by border crossing trade, especially now SAED's control has ceased. This trade, however, is probably much reduced because of closure of the border between Senegal and Mauritania in 1989.

The Gambia and the Casamance

The Organisation pour la Mise en Valeur du Fleuve Gambie (OMVG) has well-advanced plans for damming the river at Balingho, approximately 128 km from the mouth of the river (*Figure 4*). The barrage will prevent saline intrusion up-river and will create a freshwater reservoir of 33,000 ha. Funding is now being sought for its construction (Grimmett 1987). It is not known whether the plans cover the development of irrigated agriculture, which may cause problems identical to those mentioned for the OMVS scheme in Senegal. A dam was built in a tributary of the Casamance River in 1982 (Wolff 1986). Pesticide run-off by means of drains into the reservoir may be a potential threat.

Mali

Presently four dams exist in the upstream part of the Niger: Sélingué, Markala, Sotuba and Karamsasso (*Figure 4*). Eleven other dams in the Niger or its tributaries are planned or currently under study (Drijver & Marchand 1985). The lack of capital to rehabilitate the presently degraded or insufficiently developed infrastructure and to bring an additional 360,000 ha of irrigable land into production is a serious constraint for further development (USAID 1986). Based on the present pesticide input in irrigated rice in Mali, and the apparently delayed development, pesticide problems appear to be less urgent than in the Senegal delta.

Reduction of pesticide use in rice

The FAO had a major success in Indonesia by introducing Integrated Pest Management (IPM) in commercial rice-fields. This method emphasized (FAO 1988):

- Growing a healthy rice crop.
- Conserving the natural predators found in every rice-field.
- Using resistant varieties if locally acceptable.
- Using insecticides only when needed, based on the balance of field populations of pests and predators.

A presidential instruction of 1986 banned the use of 57 registered brands of broad-spectrum insecticides on rice. This was done explicitly on the ecological grounds that these products destroyed natural enemy control and induced destructive Brown Planthopper outbreaks. Within two years of the start of the IPM national strategy, the number of pesticide applications dropped from 4.5 to 0.44 per season, while farmers' yields rose from 6.1 to 7.4 tons per hectare (FAO, 1988).

Although the cultural history of irrigated rice cultivation in Senegal as well as the pest species involved (rice stem borers) differs from the Indonesian situation, it might be rewarding to investigate the possibilities for IPM in rice in Senegal. This could be a step forward in reducing future hazards from pesticide use.

RECOMMENDATIONS

It is recommended:

1. That attempts should be made to increase the surface area of nature reserves in the Senegal River delta, because substantially altered irrigated areas – as has been shown in the present study – do not provide suitable habitats for (migratory) birds. Therefore the management of the Djoudj National Parc and the projected Diawling reserve in Mauritania with related wetlands will become crucial to preserve the carrying capacity of the Senegal delta for (Palearctic) birds. They should be managed to ensure both feeding and roosting habitats. At the present moment birds leave the protected areas to use agricultural land because there are no adequate feeding areas within the national parks.

2. That herbicide use in drains and irrigation channels should be avoided as much as possible. Adverse side-effects on the biotic component of these channels and connected water systems might be expected. Mechanical clearing of weeds is a good alternative.

3. That an integrated pest control programme should be developed. The present study shows that several insecticides, notably carbofuran, have strong adverse environmental effects. Efforts should be made to identify insecticides or other control methods that are more selective with regard to non-target organisms. The establishment of unsprayed buffer zones in the irrigated areas should be considered.

4. That pesticide input in irrigated rice production should be reviewed critically, in the light of an economic analysis of an integrated programme in comparison with current practices. The broader issues of the value of traditional agriculture versus modern irrigation should also be considered. A detailed analysis of this fundamental issue may provide the best argument for environmentally sensitive practices in the long term.

ACKNOWLEDGEMENTS

We are indebted to the following organizations for their help and support: Ministère de la Recherche Scientifique et Technique du Sénégal, Ministère d'Agriculture, Direction de Protection des Végétaux du Sénégal, the Royal Dutch Embassy of Dakar, Société d'Aménagements et d'Exploitation de Terre du Delta (SAED) and the Office de la Recherche Scientifique et Technique Outre-Mer (ORSTOM).

We wish to thank the Compagnie Sucrière Sénégalaise (CSS) for the opportunity of working on their plantation and also the Institut Sénégalais de Recherches Agricoles for providing free housing.

We are grateful to Mr G. J. Morel (ORSTOM, Richard Toll) and Mr T. Diop (ISRA, Richard Toll) for their valuable advice. Mr M. Schellekens and Mr L. P. van Lavieren, both Euroconsult, Arnhem, kindly allowed us to extract information from the "Plan Directeur" when it was still in the draft stage. Mr P. van Blom, Eefde, informed us about the management of irrigated rice by the Office du Niger in Mali.

Finally we wish to thank Mr A. T. Bâ (Directeur ISE) for his cooperation, A. Samb (ISE, Dakar) and Mr B. Diagne (Ex-OCLALAV, Richard Toll) for their support in the field. P. P. Vincke, B. Tréca and P. Dugan commented on the manuscript, and E. E. Khounganian kindly drew the map of *Figure 3*. They are gratefully acknowledged.

REFERENCES

ALLAN, D. (1989) Poisoning of Red-billed Queleas in South Africa. *Gabar* **4(2)**: 2-3.

ALTENBURG, W. & VAN DER KAMP, J. (1985) Importance des zones humides de la Mauritanie du sud, du Sénégal, de la Gambie et de la Guinée-Bissau pour la Barge à Queue Noire (*Limosa l. limosa*). Leersum: *RIN contributions to research on management of natural resources* 1985-1.

ALTENBURG, W. & VAN DER KAMP, J. (1986) Oiseaux d'eau dans les zones humides de la Mauritanie du Sud, du Sénégal et de la Guinée-Bissau; Octobre-décembre 1983. Leersum: *RIN contributions to research on management of natural resources* 1986-1.

ANDERSON, D. W., JEHL, J. R., RISEBROUGH, R. W., WOODS, L. A., DEWEESE, L. R. & EDGECOMB, W. G. (1975) Brown Pelicans: Improved Reproduction on the Southern Californian Coast. *Science* **190**: 806-608.

BALDRY, D. A. T., EVERTS, J., ROMAN B., BOON VON OCHSSEE, G. A. & LAVEISSIERE, C. (1981) The experimental application of insecticides from a helicopter for the control of riverine populations of *Glossina tachinoides* in West Africa. Part VIII: The effects of two spray applications of OMS-570 (endosulfan) and of OMS-1998 (decamethrin) on *G. tachinoides* and on non-target organisms in Upper Volta. *Trop. Pest Mgmt.* **27**: 83-110.

BALK, F. & KOEMAN, J. H. (1984) *Future hazards from pesticide use.* Gland: International Union for the Conservation of Nature and Natural Resources (Commission on Ecology Papers no. 6).

BETLEM, J. (1988) Slecht winterhalfjaar voor trekvogels in West-Afrika. *Vogeljaar* **36**: 166-167.

BREMAN, H. & TRAORE, N. *et al.* (1987) *Analyse des conditions de l'élevage et propositions de politiques et de programmes en Mali.* Report for Club du Sahel. Wageningen: CABO. [Quoted in Rodenburg *et al.* 1988.]

BRUGGERS, R. L., JAEGER, M. M., KEITH, J. O., HEGDAL, P. L., BOURASSA, J. B., LATIGO, A. A. & GILLIS, J. N. (1989) Impact of fenthion on non-target birds during Quelea control in Kenya. *Wildl. Soc. Bull.* **17**: 149-160.

CATRISSE, B. (1985) Le coton dans 10 pays d'Afrique francophone. *Afrique Agriculture* **117**: 12-23.

CEC. (1985) *Evaluation of the Community's Environmental Research programmes 1976-1983.* G. Fülgraff *et al.* Commission of the European Communities (Rep. no. 4).

CILLS. (1986) Protection des végétaux (1988-1991). Document de projet Burkina Faso. Comité interétats de lutte contre la sécheresse dans le Sahel.

COLAHAN, B. D. & FERREIRA, N. A. (1989) Steppe Buzzards poisoned in the course of *Quelea* spraying in the Orange Free State, South Africa. *Gabar* **4(2)**: 17.

CURRY-LINDAHL, K. (1981) *Bird migration in Africa. Movements between six continents.* Vols. 1 and 2. London: Academic Press.

DALLINGA, H. & SCHOENMAKERS, M. (1984) *Populatieveranderingen bij de Ooievaar Ciconia ciconia ciconia in de periode 1850-1975.* Zeist: Nederlandse Vereniging tot Bescherming van Vogels.

DEJOUX, C. (1988) *La pollution des eaux continentales Africaines.* Paris: Editions de l'ORSTOM (Coll. Trav. Docs. no. 213).

VAN DONGEN, L. & GENET, W. (1986) *De semi-extensieve rijstteelt binnen het Office du Niger, Mali.* Wageningen: Vakgroep weg- en waterbouwkunde en irrigatie.

DOUMBIA, Y. O., SIDIBE, B., TOURE, K. & BONZI, M. S. (1983) *Cellule défense des cultures projet lutte intégrée Mali. Résultats campagnes 1982-1983. Entomologie.* Bamako: Ministère de l'agriculture de Mali (Document no. 6).

DREES, E. M. (1980) *Bird pests in agriculture in West Africa and their control.* Wageningen: Department of nature conservation. [Internal report LH/nr. 544.]

DRIJVER, C. A. & MARCHAND, M. (1985) *Taming the floods: environmental aspects of floodplain development in Africa.* Leiden: Leiden University, Centre for Environmental Studies.

DURANTON, J.-F., LAUNOIS, M., LAUNOIS-LUONG, M. H. LECOQ, M. & RACHADI, T. (1987) *Guide antiacridien du Sahel.* Paris/Montpellier: CIRAD/PRIFAS.

DYNAMAC. (1988a) *Results of the Mali pesticide testing trials against the Senegalese Grasshopper.* Rockville: Dynamac Corporation.

DYNAMAC. (1988b) *Results of the locust pesticide testing trials in Sudan.* Rockville: Dynamac Corporation/Consortium for International Crop Protection.

EVERAARTS, J. M., KOEMAN, J. H. & BRADER, L. (1971) Contribution a l'étude des effets suré quelques elements de la faune sauvage des insecticides organo-chlores utilisés au Chad en culture cotonière. *Cot. Fib. Trop.* **26**: 385-394.

EVERTS, J. W., BOON VON OCHSSEE, G. A., PAK, G. A. & KOEMAN, J. H. (1978) *Report on the side-effects of experimental insecticide spraying by helicopter against* Glossina *spp. in Upper Volta.* Wageningen: Agricultural University, Dept. of Toxicology.

EVERTS, J. W. & KOEMAN, J. H. (1984) *L'effet des pesticides sur l'environnement au Sahel. Rapport de deux missions écotoxicologiques.* Wageningen: Université Agronomique, Section de Toxicologie.

EVERTS, J. W., NEERING, K. E. & KOEMAN, J. H. (1985) *Etudes phytopharmaceutiques et écologiques dans les pays du Sahel. Le Sénégal.* Wageningen: Université Agronomique, Section de Toxicologie.

FAO. (1985) *FAO production yearbook 1984, Vol. 38.* Roma: Food and Agriculture Organization of the United Nations (Statistics Ser. no. 61).

FAO. (1986) *Reports of the joint FAO/Donor missions to review the 1986 Grasshopper campaign in the Sahel and in the Sudan.* Rome: Food and Agriculture Organization of the United Nations.

FAO. (1988) *Integrated Pest Management in rice in Indonesia.* Jakarta: Food and Agriculture Organization of the United Nations.

GERMAIN, P. & THIAM, A. (1983) Les pesticides au Sénégal: une menace? *ENDA série études et recherches* no. 83-83.

GRIMMETT, R. F. A. (1987) *A review of the problems affecting Palearctic migratory birds in Africa.* Cambridge, U.K.: International Council for Bird Preservation (Stud. Rep. 22).

HAMZA, M., ALI, B., EL HAIG, I., BOHL, W., BESSER, J., DE GRAZIO, J. & BRUGGERS, R. L. (1982) Evaluating the bird repellency of methiocarb. *Malimbus* **4**: 33-41.

HENNY, C. J. (1975) *Research, management and status of the Osprey in North America.* Vienna: World Conference on Birds of Prey. Pp. 199-222.

ISRA. (1984) *Département de recherches sur les productions végétales. Rapport annuel 1983.* Dakar: Ministère de la recherche scientifique et technique.

KEITH, J. O. & MULLIÉ, W. C. (1990) Birds. Pp. 235-270 in J. W. Everts, ed. *Environmental effects of chemical locust and grasshopper control: a pilot study.* Rome: Food and Agriculture Organization of the United Nations.

KOEMAN, J. H., DEN BOER, W. M. J., FEITH, A. F., DE IONGH, H. H., SPLIETHOFF, P. C., NA'ISA, B. K. & SPIELBERGER, U. (1978) Three years observation on side-effects of helicopter applications of insecticide to exterminate *Glossina* species in Nigeria. *Environ. Pollut.* **15**: 31-59.

KOEMAN, J. H. & VAN GENDEREN, H. (1972) Tissue levels in animals and effects caused by chlorinated hydrocarbon insecticides, chlorinated biphenyls and mercury in the marine environment along the Netherland's coast. Pp. 428-435 in *Marine pollution and sea life.* Surrey: Fishing News (Books) Ltd.

KOEMAN, J. H., RIJKSEN, H. D., SMIES, M., NA'ISA, B. K. & MACLENNAN, K. J. R. (1971) Faunal changes in a swamp habitat in Nigeria sprayed with insecticide to exterminate *Glossina. Neth. J. Zool.* **21**: 443-463.

LAFERRÈRE, M. (1983) A propos de l'action des pesticides sur la faune en Afrique. *Aves* **20**: 173-175.

VAN LAVIEREN, B. & VAN WETTEN, J. C. J. (1988) *Profil de l'environnement de la vallée du Fleuve Sénégal.* Arnhem: Euroconsult/RIN-Texel (draft edition).

LEDANT, J.-P., ed. (1987) *Aperçu des zones de grand intérêt pour la conservation des espèces d'oiseaux migrateurs de la Communauté en Afrique.* Rapport final. Luxembourg: Commission des Communautés Européennes.

LEUTHOLD, W. & LEUTHOLD, B. (1972) Blutschnabelweber (*Quelea quelea*) als Beute von Greif- und Stelzvögeln. *Vogelwarte* **26**: 352-354.

MEINZINGEN, W. W., BASHIR, E. A., PARKER, J. D., HECKEL, J.-U. & ELLIOTT, C. C. H. (1989) Lethal control of Quelea. Pp. 293-316 in R. L. Bruggers & C. C. H. Elliott, eds. *Quelea quelea Africa's bird pest.* Oxford: Oxford University Press.

MILSTEIN, P. LE SUEUR. (1964) Preliminary observations of White Storks feeding on poisoned Brown Locusts. Proc. 2nd. Pan-African Orn. Congr. *Ostrich Supp.*: 197-215.

MILSTEIN, P. LE SUEUR. (1965) Über BHC-vergiftete Heuschrecken als Nahrung des Weissstorchs in Südafrika. *Vogelwarte* **23**: 117-121.

MÜLLER, P. (1988a) *Ökotoxikologische Wirkungen von chlorierten Kohlenwasserstoffen. Phosphorsäureestern, Carbamaten und Pyrethroiden im nordöstlichen Sudan.* Saarbrücken: Institut für Biogeographie der Universität des Saarlandes.

MÜLLER, P. (1988b) Ecotoxicological effects of chlorinated hydrocarbons, phosphoric esters, carbamates and pyrethroids on ecosystems in north-east Sudan. *Report of the meeting on the use and hazards of dieldrin in desert locust control.* Rome: Food and Agriculture Organization of the United Nations (Annex III: 11-13).

MULLIÉ W. C. (1989) Responses of birds to changing environments. Pp. 96-110 in S. M. Goodman & P. L. Meininger, eds. *The birds of Egypt.* Oxford: Oxford University Press.

MULLIÉ, W. C. & KEITH, J. O. (1991) Notes on the breeding biology, food and weight of the Singing Bush-Lark *Mirafra javanica* in northern Senegal. *Malimbus* (in press).

MULLIÉ, W. C. & MEININGER, P. L. (1985) The decline of bird of prey populations in Egypt. Pp. 61-82 in I. Newton & R. D. Chancellor, eds. *Conservation studies on raptors.* Cambridge, U.K.: International Council for Bird Preservation (Techn. Publ. 5).

MULLIÉ, W. C., VERWEY, P. J., BERENDS, A. G., EVERTS, J. W., SÈNE, F. & KOEMAN, J. H. (1989) *The impact of pesticides on Palearctic migratory birds in the Western Sahel, with special reference to the Senegal River delta.* Cambridge, U.K.: International Council for Bird Preservation (Stud. Rep. 36).

MULLIÉ, W. C., VERWEY, P. J., BERENDS, A. G., SÈNE, F., KOEMAN, J. H. & EVERTS, J. W. (1991) The impact of furadan 3G (carbofuran) applications on aquatic macro-invertebrates in irrigated rice in Senegal. *Arch. Environ. Contam. Toxicol.* **20**: 177-182.

NIKOLAUS, G. (1981) Gift für Queleas – Todesfalle für Weissstörche. *Wir und die Vögel.* **13**(3): 16.

OCLALAV. (1981) Comité technique. Pp. 323. Dakar: Organisation Commune de Lutte Antiacridienne et de Lutte Antiaviaire.

OMVS. (n.d.) Rapport final de Synthèse: Evaluation des effets sur l'environnement d'aménagement prévus dans le bassin du Fleuve Sénégal. Organisation pour la Mise en Valeur de la Vallée du Fleuve Sénégal.

PLAN DIRECTEUR DE DÉVELOPPEMENT INTEGRÉ POUR LA RIVE GAUCHE DE LA VALLÉE DU FLEUVE SÉNÉGAL. (1988) Gersar/Cacg, Euroconsult, Sir Alexander Gibb and Partners, Soned-Afrique. Dakar: Ministère du plan et de la coopération/PNUD/BIRD [édition provisoire].

POORTER, E. P. R., VAN DER KAMP EN J. JONKER. (1982) *Verslag van de Lepelaar expeditie naar de Senegaldelta in de winter 1980-1981.* Lelystad: Ministerie van Verkeer en Waterstaat, Rijksdienst voor de IJsselmeerpolders. Werkdocument 1982-199 Abw.

RODENBURG, W. F., DRIJVER, C. A. & FISELIER, J. (1988) *Sahel Wetlands 2020: changing development policies or losing the best of Sahelian resources.* Leiden: Leiden University, Centre for Environmental Studies [draft].

ROGERS, J. G. (1974) Responses of caged Red-winged Blackbirds to two types of repellents. *J. Wildl. Mgmt.* **38**: 418-423.

ROGERS, J. G. (1978) Some characteristics of conditioned aversion in Red-winged Blackbirds. *Auk* **95**: 362-369.

ROUX, F. (1959) Quelques données sur les anatidés et charadriidés paléarctiques hivernant dans la basse vallée du Sénégal et sur leur écologie. *La Terre et la Vie* **106**: 315-321.

ROUX, F. (1976) The status of wetlands in the west African Sahel: their value for waterfowl and their future. Pp. 272-287 in M. Smart, ed. *Proc. Intern. Conf. Wetl. Waterfowl.* Heiligenhafen, 1974.

RUELLE, P. & BRUGGERS, R. L. (1979) *Evaluating bird protection to mechanically sown rice seed treated with methiocarb at Nianga, Senegal, West Africa.* Am. Soc. for testing of Mat. Vertebrate Pest Control and Management Materials, ASTM STP 680, Beck, J. R., ed.: pp. 211-216.

SCHULZ, H. (1988) *Weissstorchzug. Ökologie, Gefährdung und Schutz des Weissstorchs in Afrika und Nahost.* Weikersheim: Verlag Josef Margraf.

SCHÜZ, E. (1955) Störche und andere Vögel als Heuschreckenvertilger in Afrika. *Vogelwarte* **18**: 93-95.

SCHWITULLA, H. (1962) Heuschreckenbekämpfung und Störche. *Gesunde Pflanzen* **14**: 70-71.

SHEFTE, N., BRUGGERS, R. L. & SCHAFER, E. W. (1982) Repellency and toxicity of three bird control chemicals to four species of African grain-eating birds. *J. Wildl. Mgmt.* **46**: 453-457.

SIMMONS, R. (1987) Poison spraying to continue. *Gabar* **2**: 39.

SODEFITEX. (1983) *Rapport d'activités campagne 1982/1983.*

SODEFITEX. (1984) *Rapport d'activités campagne 1983/1984.*

SOMIVAC. (1983) *Rapport annuel d'activités 1982/1983.*

SPSSX INFORMATION ANALYSIS SYSTEM, RELEASE 2.1. (1986) *SPSSx User's Guide.* Second edition. New York.

TARBOTON, W. (1987) Red-billed Quelea spraying in South Africa. *Gabar* **2**: 38-39.

TAKKEN, W., BALK, F., JANSEN, R. C. & KOEMAN, J. H. (1978) The experimental application of insecticides from a helicopter for the control of riverine populations of *Glossina tachinoides* in West Africa. VI. Observations on side effects. *PANS* **24**: 455-466.

THIOLLAY, J.-M. (1986) The situation of raptors overwintering in West Africa. *Gabar* **1**: 31.

THIOLLAY, J.-M. (1989) Distribution and ecology of Palearctic birds of prey wintering in West and Central Africa. Pp. 95-107 in B.U. Meyburg & R. D. Chancellor, eds. (1989) *Raptors in the modern world.* Berlin, London and Paris: World Working Group on Birds of Prey and Owls.

THOMSETT, S. (1987) Raptor deaths as a result of poisoning Quelea in Kenya. *Gabar* **2**: 33-38.

TRÉCA, B. (1975) Les oiseaux d'eau et la riziculture dans le delta du Sénégal. *L'Oiseau et R.F.O.* **45**: 259-265.

TRÉCA, B. (1984) La Barge à queue noire (*Limosa limosa*) dans le delta du Sénégal: régime alimentaire, données biométriques, importance économique. *L'Oiseau et R.F.O.* **54**: 247-262.

USAID. (1986) The potential for investment in irrigated agriculture in Mali. Annex. B.

U.S. CONGRESS, OFFICE OF TECHNOLOGY ASSESSMENT (1990) *A plague of locusts – special report.* OTA-F-450. Washington, D.C.: U.S. Government Printing Office.

VAN DER VALK, H. C. H. G. (1988) *Environmental impact of dieldrin applications in locust control. A hazard assessment.* Rome: Food and Agriculture Organization of the United Nations, working paper (Dieldrin Meeting, 21 October 1988).

VAN DER VALK, H. C. H. G. & KOEMAN, J. H. (1988) *Ecological impact of pesticide use in developing countries.* The Hague: Ministry of Housing, Physical Planning and Environment.

VESEY-FITZGERALD, D. F. (1959) Locust control operations and their possible effect on the population of the White Stork *Ciconia ciconia. The Ostrich* **30**: 65-68.

WARD, P. (1972) *Manuel des techniques utilisées dans la recherche sur les Queleas.* Rome: Food and Agriculture Organization of the United Nations, document de travail (AGP: RAF/67/587).

VAN WETTEN, J., MBARÉ, C. O., BINSBERGEN, M. & VAN SPANJE, T. (1989) Zones humides du sud de la Mauritanie. Leersum: RIN contributions to research on management of natural resources 1990-91.

WOLFF, W. J. (1986) *De effecten op het milieu van natte civieltechnische werken, vervuiling en toerisme in kustgebieden van ontwikkelingslanden. In:* Commissie Ecologie en Ontwikkelingssamenwerking. Documentatie bij het advies Milieu en Ontwikkelingssamenwerking uitgebracht aan de Minister van Ontwikkelingssamenwerking.

HUNTING AND PERSECUTION OF MIGRATORY BIRDS IN THE MEDITERRANEAN REGION

GERNANT MAGNIN

P.O. Box 41173, 9701 CD Groningen, Netherlands

ABSTRACT

The shooting and trapping of migratory birds in the Mediterranean region have been practised for a very long time. Probably around 1,000 million birds are killed annually (including probably some 100,000 raptors) by 9-10 million shooters and an additional 1 million trappers. In the countries north of the Mediterranean Sea, hunting consists mainly of "sport hunting"; in some other countries in the Middle East and North Africa, shooting and trapping of migratory birds for sale in local markets is still practised mainly by local hunters.

A large number of different hunting techniques are discussed in this chapter, and case studies from Turkey, Cyprus and Egypt explain some local customs in detail. The main effects of hunting are discussed, and it is recommended that detailed studies are carried out to determine the exact annual toll per species and per country.

INTRODUCTION

Every year a large number of migratory birds are shot and trapped in the Mediterranean countries. Only in recent years has the magnitude of the annual culling of migrating species become better understood, and it is likely that up to 1,000 million birds are killed each year. Considering the decline in many migratory bird species due to loss of habitat in their breeding and/or wintering grounds, it seems vital to determine the backgrounds and dimensions of this hunting pleasure and its possible impact on individual species.

In this paper a general picture of migratory bird hunting in the Mediterranean basin will be provided. In most of the area covered there is also extensive shooting of wintering waterfowl. Hunting of waterfowl sometimes overlaps with the hunting of other migrant birds, but is not discussed in this paper (see Moser, this volume).

The hunting of migratory birds is an old practice in the countries surrounding the Mediterranean. The netting of huge numbers of migrating Quail (*Coturnix coturnix*) in Egypt has been described since the Old Kingdom (c.2650-2150BC). Throughout the centuries people in the Mediterranean region have profited from the millions of birds that migrate through the area on their way to their wintering grounds in Africa or to their breeding grounds in Europe. Hunting of birds was carried out mainly by subsistence hunters or by countrymen to complement the daily menu, and as a pastime by people of the more privileged classes. In recent years, in most countries, hunting has been carried out principally as a pastime, and this is generally referred to now as "sport hunting".

LEGISLATION

Hunting legislation varies from country to country. Of the 18 Mediterranean countries, five are bound by the EC Wild Birds Directive, seven are party to the Berne Convention, seven have signed the Bonn Convention and 11 are party to the Ramsar Convention. All these conventions include important provisions dealing with hunting practices, but contracting parties can, in some cases, make reservations, for example regarding the list of protected species (see Biber-Klemm, this volume).

Enforcement
It is important to realize that what is generally referred to as the *mass slaughter of migrants in the Mediterranean*, i.e. the killing of raptors, egrets, etc. and huge numbers of songbirds, is in many instances already illegal according to the existing hunting laws of the individual countries. The killing of millions of songbirds in Cyprus every year on lime-sticks is principally illegal as lime-sticks are by law a prohibited method for bird trapping. The killing every year of thousands of raptors in north-east Turkey is similarly illegal as according to Turkish hunting laws all birds of prey are protected. In practically all Mediterranean countries, birds of prey, herons, flamingoes, pelicans, etc. are protected. In addition, some countries have a *bag-limit system* that should prevent the killing of excessively large numbers of birds. Yet, considering the traditional "mass slaughter" as known from many places, it is obvious that current legal obligations are neither followed by the hunters nor enforced by the authorities. The state of affairs in many countries will not improve even if they are bound by international conventions that regulate hunting practices. Basically, only a change in mentality can save bird lives, and such a change can be expected in the long term only if attempts are made to educate hunters, would-be hunters and authorities: in the short term, international legal obligations are a useful tool by which to oblige the relevant authorities to implement hunting legislation.

HUNTERS AND TRAPPERS

"Hunters" in this respect refers only to people who hunt birds by the use of a shotgun; "trappers" refers to people who persecute birds by any other means.

Hunters
The actual number of hunters per country is almost impossible to determine correctly. In some countries reliable figures are provided by hunting organizations or by the government, but in many countries numbers provided refer only to the number of licensed shotgun owners or hunting-licence holders, and these cannot be regarded as being a true representation of the total number of hunters, i.e. people who go out to shoot birds on a regular basis. Considering that there are often large numbers of people without any licence, and the fact that the activity of hunters varies greatly, it is preferable not to give too much weight to a certain number of "hunters" per country. For example, Italy has an estimated 2.2 million

Table 1: Estimated numbers of shotgun hunters in the Mediterranean countries. *After* Woldhek (1980); Magnin (1986, 1987, 1989); ICBP-EC Working Group (1983); Bertelsen & Simonsen (1989); Lambertini & Tallone (1990).

Portugal	c.200,000	Syria	unknown
Spain	c.1,000,000	Lebanon	150,000– 500,000
France	c.2,000,000	Jordan	1,000
Italy	c.2,200,000	Israel	5,500
Malta	13,700	Egypt	"thousands"
Yugoslavia	c.300,000	Libya	unknown
Greece	c.300,000	Tunisia	c.8,000
Turkey	c.3,000,000–4,000,000	Algeria	unknown
Cyprus (only southern part)	c.40,000	Morocco	30,000

people who own a shotgun (Cassola 1979; Lambertini & Tallone 1990) and Turkey has 3 to 4 million people with a shotgun (Magnin 1989); yet, I am reluctant to compare these figures with regards to hunting activity, given considerable differences in mentality and practical conditions, for example the amount of ammunition spent per hunter. But, being aware of these problems, the figures quoted for the number of people with a shotgun, and the total population per country, do provide us with an indication of the power of the hunting lobbies. Countries with large numbers of shotgun owners often manufacture guns, gunpowder and cartridges locally, and this produces powerful lobbies. In addition, in countries where hunting is a widely practised pastime and thus a socially well established phenomenon, many politicians are hunters themselves or have close relatives who are hunters, resulting sometimes in great difficulties in achieving better legislation or enforcement. This factor is apparent, for example, in Malta, where after 25 years of intensive campaigning the indiscriminate and illegal killing of raptors in Buskett Gardens (the only woodland area on Malta, and the size of only a few football fields) was still not halted by the authorities.

In all, in the area covered in this chapter, 9-10 million hunters are active. In addition, probably up to 1 million people are engaged in the trapping business.

Women play virtually no part in the field of hunting. In most countries the minimum age for obtaining a shotgun and hunting licence is 18. Typically, hunting or the use of a shotgun stands for virility and masculinity, and young boys growing up in an environment of shotguns, without being offered any alternatives, are normally eager to become hunters themselves as quickly as possible. The self-perpetuation of hunting through family and social ties has been noted, amongst others, by Peterle (*In* Cassola 1979). It is even justifiable to say that family and social ties today are the prime factors perpetuating hunting since "new" hunters are hardly brought forth any more as the traditional incentive for hunting, the acquisition of food, is no longer valid. Indeed, personally I have very rarely met a hunter from a non-hunting family. In addition there are many families, especially in the cities, of which the sons are not interested in hunting and will eventually not take up their fathers' places in the field. So, strictly, there should be a net reduction in the number of hunters, were it not that, for the time being, the rapid population growth and increasing amount of spare time in some countries cause a net increase in hunting activity. But in countries where both these factors have stabilized and where nature awareness is increasing, the trend for the number of hunters is expected to be negative.

Rough estimation of total number of birds killed. Obviously a very large number of migratory birds are taken yearly in the Mediterranean region. Considering that there are 9-10 million hunters and an additional 1 million trappers, probably up to 1,000 millions birds are killed annually. This number includes probably some 100,000 raptors, and many millions are almost certainly either protected species or species hunted illegally.

Motives. Throughout the area, but especially in the more industrialized countries, widespread social welfare, the generally wide availability of motor transport, and greatly increased spare time have led to an increase in several forms of outdoor recreation, and in some countries this has included a marked increase in hunting. Instead of the explanations that "hunters manage wildlife" or "hunting is a deep-rooted, natural, human instinct", it is now often heard that hunting is merely an escape into the countryside in pursuit of a "return to nature", like other people trying to achieve this by going for walks or riding off-road vehicles. Also carrying a weapon (and shooting a bird) is for many men a way to compensate for loss of personal physical strength. The experience is that the so-called "cowboys", those who attach greatest value to the "image" side of carrying a weapon, are not really hunters in the true sense of the word and in general they are held in low esteem by genuine traditional hunters.   Many of the "cruelty cases", described by correspondents in order to mobilize public opinion, are committed by these "cowboys".   Classical, though not very common, scenes include shooting at butterflies, cats, dogs and people, and cutting the legs and wings off live birds.
More commonly practised is the shooting of birds of prey, pelicans, and other large and conspicuous birds that are not "game" by any means. Although in a few countries these birds are shot for taxidermy, generally they are killed solely to impress other people. In most instances the killing of these birds is not committed by single hunters, but by hunters acting as a group. The psychological motives underlying the misconduct of the "cowboy" type of hunter are beyond the scope of this paper, and it should be made clear that this behaviour is exhibited by only a small minority of the hunters.   However, it is fully understandable that the misbehaviour of a few affects the prestige of many, and that those few are a disgrace to the "sport of hunting".
The argument that hunters are "managing wildlife populations" is hardly valid for migratory bird persecution as there is generally no (or only very restricted) knowledge available concerning the status, distribution and migration of the populations concerned, making accurate "management" virtually impossible. Compared to central and northern Europe there exist only a few breeding and release programmes for resident gamebirds (*Alectoris* sp.) which could be considered "population management" in the Mediterranean.

TRAPPERS

Trappers are considerably fewer in number than shotgun hunters. Based on Woldhek (1980) and personal data, the total number of trappers in the Mediterranean area probably does not exceed one million, with trapping being concentrated in Portugal, Spain, southern France, northern Italy, Malta, Cyprus and Egypt. A large number of trappers practise trapping only irregularly. Yet, the total number of birds killed annually is substantial, as catches per trapper are much higher than those per shooter. In Cyprus, annual catches per trapper often exceed 3,000 birds, in Spain snare trappers catch up to 4,200 thrushes per year, and in Malta some 15,000 trappers catch over 3 million birds per year. Typically, trapping is carried out by people who cannot afford a shotgun, although (e.g. in Italy and Malta) trapping is also carried out by the well-to-do. Boys are often very actively engaged in trapping business. Egg-collecting has been reported from some countries, but is most probably not substantial anywhere. However, Goodman & Meininger (1989) state that egg-collecting from seabird colonies in Egypt is considered a threat.

TRADE

Many parties have an interest in hunting activities and might constitute strong lobbies. Restaurant keepers, canning factories, taxidermists and weapon and ammunition manufacturers in some countries lobby against large-scale education programmes as they have an interest in maintaining the largest possible number of hunters. Others recognize their responsibility and support governments, hunting clubs and conservation organizations in their efforts to control hunting.

Trade in dead and live (migratory) birds occurs on both local and international scale. Local bird markets are familiar sights in France, Italy and Egypt, where cage-birds and dead gamebirds are sold. Despite local legislation, these markets often openly offer protected species. Goodman & Meininger (1989) list the estimated average numbers of waterbirds offered for sale in the Port Said market in Egypt: the list included 125-150 Little Egrets (*Egretta garzetta*), 25 Purple Herons (*Ardea purpurea*), 7,000 Little Stints (*Calidris minuta*), 10,000 Dunlins (*C. alpina*), 1,250-1,350 Ruff (*Philomachus pugnax*) and 60-70 Little Terns (*Sterna albifrons*), mainly obtained during the migration season. In Cyprus, 12 pickled *Sylvia* warblers in a jar are typically sold for 10 CYP (c.21 USD). In Malta, Greenfinches (*Carduelis chloris*) that are good songsters can fetch up to 30 MTL (c.90 USD). Taxidermy is extremely popular in Malta, and considering the large number of birds mounted the annual turnover of the taxidermy industry must amount to many thousands of Maltese Lira. In France there is a lively commerce in thrush pâté, obtained from shot or trapped migratory and wintering thrushes.

The annual turnover of weapons and ammunition is almost impossible to estimate, but considering some 10 million hunters (equalling 10 million guns), if each was fired 200 times per year some 2,000 million x 30 grammes = 60,000 tonnes of lead would be discharged into the Mediterranean area each year. Obviously the ammunition industry has a large market, and considerable political influence.

International trade in birds takes place on a vast scale. In Spain, official figures for 1982, 1983 and 1984 show total exports of 352,868, 726,562 and 573,088 migrant songbirds respectively, mainly to France and Italy, but the actual numbers were probably much higher (Munoz-Cobo 1985). However, due to new and more strictly enforced international legislation, it seems that the international trade is now largely on the decline.

METHODS

Many different methods of shooting and trapping migrant birds are used in the Mediterranean region. Some commonly used techniques are briefly reviewed here.

Shooting
Shooting is often carried out whilst walking in the countryside, with or without a dog to flush the birds. More often, in the case of migratory birds, hunters use

hides in which to wait concealed for the birds to come within range. Hides vary from simple natural hides such as trees or bushes, to high man-made towers that are positioned at vantage points and may be used for tens of years or longer. In places (common in Malta) migratory birds (including raptors) are shot from high-powered inflatable boats which can outpace any flying bird. Though generally strictly forbidden (and also considered as highly unsporting by genuine hunters) the use of these and other speed-boats may be on the increase in many Mediterranean countries.

Hunters employ a wide variety of techniques to lure migrating birds to their hides. Much used is the fluttering decoy, a live dove or other bird tethered to a stick that moves up and down when the hunter pulls a rope, inducing the bird to flap its wings. Sometimes fluttering decoys are tethered to a large spinning wheel that is controlled by the hunter. Widely used, and available in hundreds of different versions, are whistles and other devices that aim to imitate birds' flight calls and attempt to seduce overflying birds to halt their journey and land. Whistles are made from metal or from natural materials, like the Golden Plover (*Pluvialis apricaris*) whistle used in Malta, which is made from Giant Reed (*Arundo donax*). Shooters in Malta employ a device locally called *alwettiera* that is used to attract migrating Skylarks (*Alauda arvensis*). An elongated pyramid-shaped wooden block, covered with small pieces of mirror, is fixed horizontally on a vertical rod which is pushed into the ground. The wooden block rotates when the hunter, some 20 m away in cover, pulls a rope, and the reflecting sunlight attracts the skylarks towards what seems to be a pool of water.

Trapping

The trapping of migratory birds is carried out in many different ways. If the birds trapped are intended to be eaten they are killed immediately after capture, but many birds are caught to serve as decoys for future trapping, or to be kept as "pets". It is impossible to review all the different trapping methods here, but commonly used are nets that resemble the mist-nets used by bird ringers. Birds are either lured to the net by decoys or chased into the net. In south-east France, huge vertically placed nets are positioned in narrow mountain passes, and doves (Columbidae) are chased into them by people waving flags, throwing stones and shouting.

Very commonly used throughout the Mediterranean region are different kinds of clap-nets to which migrating birds are lured either by decoys or by using bait. Hunters wait concealed until the birds are underneath the net, and then pull a rope after which the net falls and covers the birds. In Malta, typical finch-trapping sites measure 15 x 7 m, and to attract birds the trappers use, on average, 40 birds placed in cages around the site, plus some fluttering decoys. Two large nets, stretched flat on the ground, are operated by the trapper from his hide. By pulling a rope, the trapper makes the nets rise, and then fall down quickly, one overlapping the other. Finch species typically trapped this way are Chaffinch (*Fringilla coelebs*), Goldfinch (*Carduelis carduelis*), Siskin (*C. spinus*), Greenfinch (*C. chloris*), Linnet (*C. cannabina*), and Serin (*Serinus serinus*).

Wire cage-traps, widely used in the Mediterranean countries, work automatically and typically consist of a centre compartment, in which the decoy bird is kept supplied with food and water, and two catching compartments, one on each side of the decoy compartment. The catching compartments are baited with seeds, and the wild bird is caught when it settles on a perch, automatically releasing the flap door of the trap. In Malta, wire cage-traps are employed chiefly to trap Hawfinches (*Coccothraustes coccothraustes*) and Robins (*Erithacus rubecula*).

In Spain, migrating or wintering thrushes (*Turdus* sp.) are trapped in strong wire-spring traps (baited with ants) that kill the caught bird instantaneously. In France, *"lecques"* or *"tendelles"* are stone traps that crush the bird as it looks for food underneath. "Snares" have been reported from most countries and are the most widely accepted method of catching birds without the use of bait. Originally snares were made of horse-hair but this is now increasingly replaced by nylon. In Spain, snare-trappers have been reported using 720 snares per trapper at a time, catching 4,200 thrushes per trapper per year.

Widely used throughout the area are lime-sticks, wooden rods coated with a sticky substance (often, as in Cyprus, made from the fruit of the Assyrian Plum (*Cordia myxa*). Birds that alight on a lime-stick immediately become fixed by the glue. A method that is probably very rare in the Mediterranean but reported from Turkey is the procurement of birds by throwing wooden clubs at them. Boys in Egypt have been reported to kill even small birds like Lesser Whitethroat (*Sylvia curruca*) by throwing stones. On the Black Sea coast of Turkey, local people go out during rainy nights in September and simply catch by hand the exhausted Quail that hide in the tea fields.

CASE STUDIES

Turkey

In north-east Turkey, roughly in the coastal region east from Rize up to the Russian border, local people have practised for centuries the trapping of migratory Sparrowhawks. The Sparrowhawks were originally intended to be used for the hawking of migratory Quail. Recent detailed investigations, as published in ICBP Study Report No. 34 (Magnin 1989) describe how small village boys put soapy water in holes in the ground in order to catch a Mole Cricket (*Gryllotalpa vulgaris*), which is then put in a special cage-trap. The Mole Crickets serve as bait to attract migrating Red-backed Shrikes (*Lanius collurio*) which are caught during August, the peak migration period. The trapped birds, mainly juveniles, are tied to sticks (c.1 m long) and provided with small leather caps covering both eyes (*Figure 1*). The Sparrowhawk trapper waits concealed in a hide and lures migrating Sparrowhawks to a triangular net by inducing the Red-backed Shrike to flutter behind the net. The main trapping season is during September. Trapped Sparrowhawks are taken home, fitted with a bell, and are accustomed to human presence and touch within a few days. If Sparrowhawks are intended (and found suitable) for Quail hawking, a simple training programme lasting a few days follows. Hawking is carried out mainly in tea and corn fields in the coastal strip especially after a rainy night when migrating Quail are forced to break their journey. The ICBP Study Report gives ample proof that, in contrast with common belief, the catching of Quail is not at all a matter of livelihood for the local people (although it may have been in the past). It also shows that only a small number of Sparrowhawk owners bother to train the birds for hawking, and that most of the Sparrowhawks are merely kept as pets during September and October. Trade in Sparrowhawks plays a minor role, and typically the birds are released during October. An estimated 4,000 trappers catch several tens of thousands of migratory Sparrowhawks each year in the region, of which probably some ten thousand die as a consequence of diseases and the fact that release takes place too late for the birds to proceed with migration. In addition, some 15,000 migratory raptors including Lesser-spotted Eagles (*Aquila pomerina*), Short-toed Eagles (*Circaetus gallicus*), Honey Buzzards (*Pernis apivorus*) and Levant Sparrowhawks (*Accipiter*

Figure 1: Blindfolded Red-backed Shrike serving as a lure for Sparrowhawks (*Accipiter nisus*) in north-east Turkey. (*Photo*: G. Magnin)

brevipes), are shot or trapped and fed to the Red-backed Shrikes, which are strict meat-eaters. Also the Red-backed Shrikes are released too late to proceed with migration, and it is presumed that all (circa) 9,000 birds succumb in the course of the winter.

Cyprus

The old custom of trapping migratory songbirds by the use of lime-sticks is described in detail by Magnin (1987). Especially on the south-east tip of Cyprus, in the Paralimni area, people cut 75 cm-long Pomegranate (*Punica granata*) branches and coat them with a sticky substance made by mixing the fruits of the Assyrian Plum (*Cordia myxa*) with honey (*Figure 2*). An extra long lime-stick, used to trap migrating Bee-eaters (*Merops apiaster*), is not used any more as numbers moving through Cyprus have allegedly declined seriously in recent years. During the early morning hours, the lime-sticks are placed in shrubs or vineyards and newly arrived migrating passerines, especially Blackcaps (*Sylvia atricapilla*) are driven towards them by people shouting and throwing stones. Individual limers use some 150 lime-sticks on average. Some 122 bird species have been recorded trapped on lime-sticks, including Little Bittern (*Ixobrychus minutus*), Pallid Harrier (*Circus macrourus*), Scops Owl (*Otus scops*), Great-spotted Cuckoo (*Clamator glandarius*) and Kingfisher (*Alcedo atthis*), but the majority of the trapped birds are migratory *Sylvia* warblers, with the most numerous single species being the Blackcap. The main liming season is the period September-November, but inland trapping of thrushes (*Turdus* sp.) occurs throughout the winter months. During spring, liming is practised on a small scale. Mist-nets were introduced in the late 1960s and rapidly became common. They were considered more efficient than lime-sticks, but were subject to considerable criticism from conservationists and the general public due to the indiscriminate nature of the trapping. Also, hunters turned

Figure 2: An elderly Cypriot bird limer going out to place his lime-sticks to catch warblers and other passerines. (*Photo:* G. Magnin)

against the large-scale use of mist-nets after the cover of a hunting magazine had pictured a Chukar (*Alectoris chukar*), the main game species in Cyprus, dangling in a mist-net; and from 1984 onwards police started acting against the use of mist-nets (which were, and are, like lime-sticks, prohibited according to Cypriot law). Still, during 1986 investigations, mist-nets were found regularly. Both mist-nets and lime-sticks are often employed in a passive way; that is, they are put out at the beginning of the season and checked once a day or less often. The result is that large numbers of trapped birds die slowly in the nets or on the sticks. Those that are collected are plucked and served by the dozen, either grilled or pickled. The export of pickled passerines, locally called *Ambelopoulia* hardly occurs any more and the catching of birds is thought to be for no-one a matter of livelihood. The total number of birds caught during 1986 approached 2.2 million.

Figure 3: A Nightingale (*Luscinia megarhynchos*) glued on a lime-stick.
(*Photo:* G. Magnin)

Egypt

The trapping of migrating Quail has long been a tradition in Egypt. Between 1906 and 1913 the numbers of Quail exported from the country ranged from one to two million, but in recent years annual catches probably have not exceeded several hundreds of thousands (Goodman & Meininger 1989). All along the Egyptian Mediterranean coast Quail are being trapped, mainly during September. "Trammel-nets", described by the Greek historian Diodorus (first century BC), are most commonly used and consist of two panels, a small mesh net stretched in front of a net of larger mesh, the whole unit being generally 4 m high and 16 m long. In September 1980 an estimated 61 km of the 130-km shoreline between Baltim and Port Said was spanned by nets.

Another common method of catching is locally called *munsaab*. The trap usually consists of a bunch of tall sea-shore grass (*Ammophila arenaria*), arranged in a tent-like structure with the entrance facing south and a piece of fishing net closing off the seaward opening. Thousands of *munsaab* are operated in autumn, especially in the area west of Alexandria.

As spring migratory movements of Quail are more diffuse than in autumn, other methods are also used to secure Quail, including a technique that is probably the same as that depicted in the tomb of Mereruka (c.2325BC). A fine-mesh net is held horizontally by four men and drawn at night over a growing crop where birds are suspected to be resting. Apart from Quail, in Egypt migratory passerines are also secured in large numbers by the use of lime-sticks, air rifles, shotguns and nets. There is a lively trade in dead and live birds. All birds are intended for human consumption.

PROBLEMS RELATED TO THE HUNTING OF MIGRATORY BIRDS

The direct and side effects of legal hunting can be categorized as follows (after Berndt & Winkel 1976):

1.   Hunting as a mortality factor

Additive hunting mortality is the foremost impact of hunting on bird populations. Recent studies in North America have shown that hunting mortality is very likely to be additive (vs compensatory) for declining and small populations (SEIS 1988; Moser, this volume). Excessive hunting was responsible for the regional extinction of large birds such as vultures, eagles, and Eagle Owls (*Bubo bubo*) in the Mediterranean. In addition to the birds bagged by hunters, many individuals are crippled by lead shot but not retrieved.

2.   Hunting as a selective factor on populations

Selective killing (e.g. of only males) unbalances the natural optimal population structure. Unbalanced sex and age ratios may seriously disturb populations and finally result in declining numbers.

3.   Hunting as a selective factor on communities

Excessive hunting of one species may have interspecific negative effects. Classical examples include the removal of Sparrowhawks, resulting in a booming population of Tree Sparrows (*Passer montanus*) that drives out other hole-nest breeders in a forest, and the killing of Goshawks (*Accipiter gentilis*) resulting in an increase of Crows (*Corvus corone*) that produces increased nest larceny and declining numbers of Lapwings (*Vanellus vanellus*).

4.   Hunting as a threat to look-alike species

Through accidents and mistakes, hunting leads to the decline of populations of protected species. Well known is the shooting of the Lesser White-fronted Goose (*Anser erythropus*), a species protected almost everywhere but frequently mistaken for the White-fronted Goose (*A. albifrons*). The nearly extinct Slender-billed Curlew (*Numenius tenuirostris*) is suffering from hunting losses as it is almost undistinguishable in the field from the Common Curlew (*N. arquata*), which is still shot legally in several regions.

5.   Hunting as a disturbance factor

This is probably the most serious side-effect of hunting, both legal and illegal. Shots not only kill the target bird but also scare hundreds or even thousands of other birds in the same area, so that they subsequently disperse over a large area. At small wetlands, birds may even leave the area completely during days of heavy hunting pressure. If this occurs at a place that is crucial as a stop-over site for waders, for example, it might well be that many birds will fail to reach the next stop-over site due to exhaustion provoked by the hunting disturbance. Birds of prey that migrate south through Italy and North Africa often arrive at Malta, half-way point of the sea-crossing, in the afternoon, too late to continue to Tunisia. The main roosting place for birds of prey is Buskett Gardens, the largest afforested area on Malta although it is only the size of a few football fields. Virtually no raptor is allowed to roost in the trees of Buskett Gardens due to the intensive hunting pressure, and unknown numbers of birds are forced to continue their migration in the dark or in bad physical conditions. In the long term, birds tend generally to avoid man and inhabited areas, finally resulting in further habitat loss.

CONCLUSIONS

In Europe, a majority of all migratory bird species have suffered a decline in numbers during this century as shown by Bijlsma (1987) and Berthold (1986). The main reason for this is probably the loss of habitat at breeding and wintering sites, but shooting and trapping may have contributed considerably to the decline. It is therefore recommended that detailed studies be carried out as a matter of urgency to measure the impact of hunting mortality on different populations of migratory species.

In order to curb large-scale illegal hunting practices, recommended conservation action includes: education of youngsters, hunters and authorities; promoting enforcement of existing wildlife legislation; promoting ratification of international conventions relevant to bird conservation; and supporting bird/wildlife tourism.

Sincere hunters and hunters' associations should be involved more in conservation programmes in order to safeguard their game for the future, and to curb the unnecessary killing of raptors, pelicans, herons and other protected species.

REFERENCES

BERNDT, R. & WINKEL, W. (1976) Vogelwelt und Jagd. *Ber. Dt. Sektion Int. Rat. Vogelschutz no.* **16**: 82-88.

BERTELSEN, J. & SIMONSEN, N. H. (1989) Documentation on Bird Hunting and the Conservation Status of the Species Involved. Situation in 1986. Denmark: Ministry of the Environment. Revised edition December 1989.

BERTHOLD, P., FLIEGE, G., QUERNER, U. & WINKLER, H. (1986) Die Bestandsentwicklung von Kleinvögeln in Mitteleuropa: Analyse von Fangzahlen. *J. Orn.* **127**: 397-438.

BIJLSMA, R. G. (1987) *Bottleneck areas for migratory birds in the Mediterranean region.* Cambridge, U.K.: International Council for Bird Preservation (Stud. Rep. 18).

BRAAKHEKKE, W. G. (1983) *Hunting wild birds: laws and practices in 8 EEC member states.* Zeist: ICPB-EC Working Group.

CASSOLA, F. (1979) Shooting in Italy: the present situation and future perspectives. *Biol. Conserv.* **12**: 85-105.

GOODMAN, S. M. & MEININGER, P. L. (1989) *The birds of Egypt.* Oxford: Oxford University Press.

LAMBERTINI, M. & TALLONE, G. (1990) *Bird killing in Italy.* Parma: Lega Italiana per la Protezione degli Uccelli (Report).

MAGNIN, G. (1986) *An assessment of illegal shooting and catching of birds in Malta.* Cambridge, U.K.: International Council for Bird Preservation (Stud. Rep. 13).

MAGNIN, G. (1987) *An account of the illegal catching and shooting of birds in Cyprus during 1986.* Cambridge, U.K.: International Council for Bird Preservation (Stud. Rep. 21).

MAGNIN, G. (1989) *Falconry and hunting in Turkey during 1987.* Cambridge, U.K.: International Council for Bird Preservation (Stud. Rep. 34).

MUNOZ-COBO, J. (1985) *Trapping of small birds and thrushes in the province of Jaen (southern Spain).* Spain: CODA.

SEIS. (1988) *Issuance of annual regulations permitting the sport hunting of migratory birds.* U.S. Dept of the Interior, Fish and Wildlife Service. Final Supplemental Environmental Impact Statement.

SEPANSO. (1982) *Chasses traditionnelles des oiseaux migrateurs dans le sud-ouest de la France.* France: SEPANSO.

SULTANA, J. & GAUCI, C. (1982) *A new guide to the birds of Malta.* Valetta: Malta Ornithological Society.

WOLDHEK, S. (1980) *Bird killing in the Mediterranean.* Second edition. Zeist: European Committee for the Prevention of Mass Destruction of Migratory Birds.

ICBP Technical Publication No. 12, 1991

SHOOTING OF MIGRATING SHOREBIRDS IN BARBADOS

MAURICE B. HUTT

4a Pavilion Court, Hastings, Christ Church, Barbados, West Indies

ABSTRACT

The small island of Barbados, the most easterly of the Lesser Antilles, situated 150 km east of St Vincent, is favourably placed geographically to serve as a way-station for thousands of migrant shorebirds undertaking long flights south and south-east from North American breeding areas to South American winter quarters. During the fall migration, from early July to mid-October, large numbers of these birds are shot each year in a number of mostly artificial shooting swamps by a small number of hunters (probably fewer than 100). This annual slaughter, little known outside Barbados, is arousing growing opposition amongst members of the Barbadian public.

The methods and techniques used to decoy the passing flocks are described, with a short history of the shooting from 1902 to the 1980s, with figures for the numbers of birds of different species shot and a review of those shorebird species that are the principal quarry of the hunters.

The failure of attempted conservation efforts is reported, particularly the refusal of the Barbados National Trust to support the cause of bird protection. Although committed by a resolution agreed to at the Trust's AGM in 1980 to campaign for the inclusion of all migrant shorebird species in a new, revised schedule to the existing 1907 Wild Birds' Protection Act, sufficient pressure has still not been placed on the government to end this annual slaughter.

A list of all migrant shorebird species is given, along with a brief note of four possible wildlife refuges for these birds.

INTRODUCTION

In recent years, much publicity has been given to campaigns against the annual slaughter of many western Palearctic migrants in a number of Mediterranean countries. There has been strong focus on the small island of Malta, where the killing of migrant birds is a way of life.

But for a hundred persons willing to support campaigns to stop the massacre in Portugal, Spain, France, Italy, Greece and Turkey, how many have even heard of the continued annual slaughter of thousands of migrating shorebirds from North America in a small West Indian island not much larger than Malta, with a population not much less?

These shorebirds, of more than a dozen species, mostly nesting in Canada on the far northern tundra, undergo long-distance migrations south and south-east to winter quarters in various regions of South America (Bent 1927, 1929). In Canada and in transit through the U.S.A. these birds are fully protected by law, but when they arrive in Barbados, weary after traversing varying distances of open sea, they are blasted out of existence by waiting gunners.

Some 70-75 per cent of the estimated 15,000–20,000 shorebirds killed each year belong to two species with large populations, the Lesser Yellowlegs (*Tringa flavipes*) and the Pectoral Sandpiper (*Calidris melanotos*), while another 10-12 per cent are American Golden Plovers (*Pluvialis dominica*) (classification according to Hayman *et al.* 1986). But as all birds, except the small *Calidris* sandpipers – the Least, Semipalmated, Western and White-rumped (*C. minutilla, C. pusilla, C. mauri* and *C. fuscicollis*), the Spotted Sandpiper (*Actitis macularia*) and the Semipalmated Plover (*Charadrius semipalmatus*) are shot, regardless of species identity, when they fly into man-made artificial swamps, it has happened that members of endangered species have also been killed. The most notable example was the shooting, on 4 September 1963, at Fosters swamp in St Lucy, of an Eskimo Curlew (*Numenius borealis*), a species on the verge of extinction (specimen in the Hutt Collection at the Philadelphia Academy of Sciences).

BARBADOS: GENERAL NATURAL HISTORY

Barbados in the West Indies is a small island, 34 km north to south, 22 km east to west at the widest point, of relatively low relief, with hills rising to 338 m in the form of a raised plateau (*Figure 1*). It is situated about 150 km east of the Lesser Antillean island arc, equidistant from the islands of St Vincent, due west, and St Lucia, due west-north-west. With an area of 430 km² and a population of more than 250,000 persons, it is one of the most densely populated islands in the world, with an average density of 581 p/km².

In geological terms Barbados is very young. Six-sevenths of the island are covered with a blanket of raised coral limestone terraces, at least ten in number, successive coral reef tracts varying in age from the youngest, just above sea level, at 60,000 years B.P. to the uppermost at just over 300 m at c.1,000,000 years B.P. This coral rock capping is extensively fissured with a series of irregular longitudinal cuts up to 30 m deep and 100 m wide known locally as 'gullies'. The other one-seventh of the surface consists of a semi-circular erosional bowl adjoining part of the north-east coast, with irregular relief in the form of heavily eroded Tertiary rocks, and one small river system.

The climate is tropical, but as a result of the cooling effects of the prevailing east-north-east trade wind, temperatures rarely exceed 32°C. The average annual rainfall varies from about 1,150 mm on the coast to 1,900 mm in the hills, falling mostly during the rainy season from June to November.

Settled from Britain from 1627 onwards, by about 1665 practically all of the original forest cover had been destroyed to make way for sugar cane plantations which replaced the subsistence smallholdings producing low-grade tobacco and cotton for export. By that date the island, uninhabited in 1627, had a population of about 20,000 white settlers from Britain and about the same number of black slaves brought in from various regions of West Africa to work on the sugar cane plantations. Continuous cultivation of sugar cane remained the normal pattern of agriculture for more than three centuries from 1665; only in the 1980s has the acreage under cane shown a marked decline.

Only a few small residual areas of woodland survive, notably the 20-ha Turner's Hall Wood in St Andrew's parish, sited on a steep hill slope. In this relict

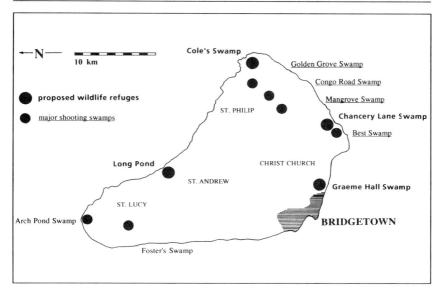

Figure 1: The island of Barbados (located 13°2'N, 59°30'W) showing the location of major shooting swamps and sites of wildlife refuges required.

woodland, just over 110 plant species survive, including over 30 trees, about 20 shrubs and a handful of lianas. It is a debased fragment of the original tropical mesophytic forest, of which other remnants survive as undercliff woods on the exposed eastern slopes below the 4.8-km-long Hackleton's Cliff inland escarpment system in St Joseph and St John (Gooding 1974).

Of a total of about 700 plant species, more than 150 are introduced naturalized species, many of them weeds of cane-fields.

THE BREEDING BIRDS

The relative geographical isolation of Barbados and its limited range of habitats contribute to the small number of breeding species, as does the brief period of its geological history (Bond 1954). There are no mountains and so no montane forest; no lakes, no rivers flowing all the year round, no estuary with saltings and mudflats and no real marshland. Endless fields of sugar cane, until recently covering about 35 per cent of the total surface area, hold no birds except a small finch, the Black-faced Grassquit (*Tiaris bicolor*).

The sole breeding seabird is Audubon's Shearwater (*Puffinus lherminieri*), of which a few pairs nest in a coral rock stack close inshore off the north coast, in St Lucy's parish. The two resident species of heron and egret are the wide-ranging Green-backed Heron (*Butorides striatus* ssp. *virescens*) and the Cattle Egret (*Bubulcus ibis*) which began nesting in Graeme Hall swamp in Christ Church in 1972, increasing rapidly in numbers to 10,000+ by 1989.

There are no breeding anatids, no resident raptors and no nesting shorebirds. The endemic race, *barbadensis*, of the wide-ranging Common Moorhen (*Gallinula chloropus*) is much reduced in numbers by habitat destruction, down to c.30 pairs.

Very abundant are the small Common Ground Dove (*Columbina passerina*) and the medium-sized Zenaida Dove (*Zenaida aurita*), while the large Red-necked Pigeon (*Columba squamosa*), very rare in 1954, has increased markedly since about 1970, partly as a result of deliberate introductions.

The White-tailed Nightjar (*Caprimulgus cayennensis*) probably breeds in small numbers, but no eggs or nestlings have been found. The two resident hummingbirds, both common, are the small, straight-billed Antillean Crested Hummingbird (*Orthorhynchus cristatus*) and the larger, curve-billed, Green-throated Carib (*Eulampis holosericeus*). The two resident tyrant flycatchers are the common, conspicuous, Grey Kingbird (*Tyrannus dominicensis*) and the smaller, retiring, less numerous Caribbean Elaenia (*Elaenia martinica*).

The handsome, large Caribbean Martin (*Progne dominicensis*) nests in small numbers in buildings in Bridgetown, the capital, and sparingly on both seacliffs and inland crags. The birds are absent from the island from November to late February, migrating south to South America. The 23-cm Scaly-breasted Thrasher (*Margarops fuscus*) barely survives in the wilder, remoter parts of the island, in a few of the more inaccessible gullies, but the 17-cm Black-whiskered Vireo (*Vireo altiloquus*) is widespread in surviving woodland tracts and in gardens with clumps of thickly-foliaged trees, especially *Ficus* spp.

The endemic nominate race of the Yellow Warbler (*Dendroica petechia*) has declined in range and numbers over the years. Its preferred habitat is mangrove, both the Red Mangrove (*Rhizophora mangle*) confined to Graeme Hall swamp in Christ Church, situated just inland from the south coast 5 km east of Bridgetown, and the White Mangrove (*Laguncularia racemosa*) growing commonly in Graeme Hall swamp and in a few limited locations along the west coast. The Graeme Hall swamp is the stronghold of the species, with 12-15 pairs; the total population may be 35-40 pairs. Brood parasitism by the numerous Shiny Cowbird (*Molothrus bonariensis*), and habitat loss through tourist development along the west coast, have contributed to the low population level of this endangered endemic race of a species widely distributed through North and Central America, the Caribbean islands and northern South America.

The attractive small black and yellow Bananaquit (*Coereba flaveola*) is common and confiding, as is the highly gregarious Caribbean Grackle (*Quiscalus lugubris*) the common host of the Shiny Cowbird, the latter now widespread over most of the island. The Grassland Yellowfinch (*Sicalis luteola*), introduced probably about 1900 (Bond 1955), reached a population peak about 1955, declining in numbers rapidly from about 1965. Numerous sugar cane fires spreading into Sour Grass pastures where the birds nested, and later, predation of nestlings by Cattle Egrets, may account for the decline in numbers. Both the Lesser Antillean Bullfinch (*Loxigilla noctis barbadensis*) and the Black-faced Grassquit are common in most habitats.

Barbados, geographically isolated, geologically young, densely populated, with a limited range of habitats and with only c.25 breeding species, contrasts markedly with the neighbouring much older, volcanic, mountainous islands; both St Lucia and St Vincent, the two nearest islands to westward, have c.50 breeding species each, with a number of endemic species.

SHOOTING OF MIGRATORY SHOREBIRDS

Hunting techniques

The somewhat isolated position of Barbados makes it a favoured location for the occurrence, in varying numbers, of a considerable range of North American migrant shorebird species. These birds are transients through the island during the mid-July to late-October fall migration season, flocks and individuals en route from northern North American breeding areas to South American winter quarters. A majority of the birds on passage belong to species representing the family Scolopacidae, and are far-flying, long-distance migrants which, in the absence of coastal saltmarsh and mudflats, are attracted to the relatively small areas of surface water available.

Numbers of these transient shorebirds are shot each year in what are known locally as 'shooting swamps', which are carefully designed to offer major attractions to tired migrants seeking resting and feeding grounds on an island almost completely lacking coastal mudflats and either salt or freshwater marshes suitable for their needs. These artificial swamps vary in size, the larger ones having up to 2 ha of open water contained in a series of embanked enclosures formed with bulldozers and known as 'trays', with shallow water suited to shorebird needs, especially those of the most commonly shot species, the Lesser Yellowlegs.

Every possible device and strategem is employed by the shooting men who own and operate the swamps to decoy passing flocks, smaller parties and single birds down to the 'trays', where the gunners wait, concealed from view in the shelter of a wooden shooting hut. Special flat mudbanks of limited size, known as 'alighting land', are constructed within easy shotgun range of the shooting hut. Live birds of all the species habitually shot are kept in wired enclosures close to the hut, so that they will 'mark' flocks approaching and passing overhead by uttering repeated calls. These birds are usually individuals slightly wounded by shotgun pellets which have subsequently recovered. A few are birds trapped at the cages.

To supplement the calls of the caged birds, most of the gunners use skilfully made whistles cut to imitate the calls of a particular species, usually those of the Lesser Yellowlegs, locally called the 'Longleg', which make up a little over half of all birds shot. Other whistles imitate the calls of the American Golden Plover, known locally in breeding plumage as the 'Black-breast Plover', for which specially prepared short grass areas are maintained close to the shooting hut in the larger swamps.

Since about 1960, such whistled calls have been supplemented by the use of amplified tape recordings of the calls of approaching flocks, broadcast through loudspeakers placed on top of the hut. These tapes are switched on when the live birds 'mark', or when the gunners spot such flocks, some of which, especially plover flocks, may be flying at heights of 450-500 m. In addition, artificial decoys made of wood, metal and plastic, painted to imitate the various species to be decoyed, are extensively used.

Historical development of shooting techniques

Between the two World Wars, and up to the 1950s, shooting swamps were small, the water sometimes drying out during the somewhat erratic rainy season extending from June to early December. In default of adequate rainfall, trays could be filled with water pumped up by means of unreliable wind-driven 'fan mills'. 'No water, no birds' was axiomatic.

Up to the 1950s, double-barrelled shotguns were used to kill the migrant shorebirds, and there did survive among many of the older gunners a tradition and code of sportsmanship by which, normally, only flying shots were taken. Even that code was forgotten on days of big flights, when the pressure to achieve a large score for the swamp, in order to get ahead of other, rival swamps, tended to become paramount.

In the 1960s came the adoption of the new pump-action and automatic shotguns, able to fire six cartridges with machinegun-like rapidity. With this new development came a new, callous, intensely competitive spirit, especially among the younger gunners, but including several of the older, more senior men who owned some of the larger swamps. This new attitude quickly replaced the older, more restrained sporting attitudes. Bird flocks, decoyed into the swamp, were allowed to alight on the special mudbanks close to the hut. On a given signal all the gunners present, often up to half a dozen at the larger swamps on good 'flight days', fired simultaneously at the densely crowded birds. The object was to kill all the birds that could be decoyed into the swamp, and it was considered a matter of much regret, almost a disgrace, if any got away.

This drastic change in attitude led to the enlargement of the bigger swamps, some owned by wealthy individuals, others by syndicates. Larger areas of water were impounded by bulldozing more 'trays'; large, powerful diesel-electric pumps were installed at several of the large swamps to keep the water levels constant and every effort was made to maximize the effectiveness of the methods used to call down passing flocks. Intense rivalry developed between the ten or so top shooting swamps to have the largest score of birds shot for the day, the week, and above all for the three months of the official shooting season, 15 July to 15 October. A number of swamps installed telephones and it became customary to call up rival swamps during the morning to ascertain their current scores.

In the nineteenth century a law had been passed by the Legislature prohibiting any shooting on Sundays, and this had been adhered to for many years, even if Sunday produced a notable shorebird passage. But in the early 1960s this law was 'reinterpreted' by a lawyer who was himself a keen shooting man. Henceforward the law was ignored by most of the gunners. No action was taken by the authorities, probably because the Premier, who became the first Prime Minister when Barbados achieved independence within the Commonwealth in 1966, was himself a keen shooting man.

The number of shooting swamps reached a high point in the 1960s, when more than 20 were being operated, chiefly in the parishes of St Lucy, in the north of the island, and in Christ Church and St Philip, in the south and east respectively, with a few in other parishes, including St Michael in the south-west. Of these, about ten were major establishments. The big swamps had an average membership of five to six gunners, who shared the operating expenses, with others turning up on big flight days. Such swamps were, and still are, normally manned each day of the shooting season from dawn until about noon, the time of day when most birds fly, especially from August through to early October. If a flight was being sustained at midday, some gunners would stay on until darkness fell. In a number of the larger swamps, members not present that morning were notified by telephone around 9.00-10.00 am if a heavy flight was in progress, so they could take time off work to go to the swamp and join in the shooting.

The standard ambition at any swamp was to have 'a hundred day', with over 100 individuals of all shootable species killed. By the early 1960s the ambition was to achieve 'two-hundred days' and more. The old record for one day's shooting at any swamp stood at 522 birds killed at the old Rockley swamp in Christ Church, later a nine-hole golf course, now a large tourist hotel complex. This was broken in the early 1970s when over 700 birds were shot in one day at the Friendship swamp in St Lucy.

NUMBERS OF BIRDS SHOT

A number of scores of shooting swamps available over varying periods give valuable information on the numbers of birds shot and the seasonal variations. They are analysed in the remainder of this paper.

The Chancery Lane swamp in eastern Christ Church adjoins the south-east coast of the island where the coastal configuration funnels flocks moving southwards over Inch Marlowe Point out to sea, bringing about a concentration of flylines. It is a saltmarsh complex of c.20 ha lying just inland of a sand-dune area well covered with coastal scrub, and a low oblique coral limestone escarpment. In the July-November rainy season it accumulates shallow surface water, making it attractive to many shorebirds. Close to the south is an area of open Sour Grass pasture attractive to the American Golden Plover. From around 1960, housing has been built on the north and west sides in increasing densities, but before that date almost no houses existed. Since the Second World War, when an airstrip was built close to the northern side of the swamp area, increasing airport usage by numbers of wide-bodied jets has produced an increasing disturbance factor, as has tourist developments to both north and south.

The Chancery Lane swamp scores of birds shot for the years 1902-1921 inclusive total 30,376, an annual average of 1,518. Variations were very marked, attributable to differences in rainfall and the passage of cyclonic weather, and to the extent to which shooters were present day by day during the mid-July to mid-October shooting season.

For the period of 20 years, the total number of Lesser Yellowlegs shot, 16,371, made up 54 per cent of all birds killed, but this proportion varied annually between 38 per cent and 78 per cent. Pectoral Sandpipers were accounting on average for 33 per cent (29-53 per cent) or 10,073 birds shot. A good passage of both species was needed to produce high totals. During these years, American Golden Plovers were scarce, totalling only 1,066 (3.5 per cent of all birds shot), a very different pattern from that of the 1950s and 1960s when the species had recovered from the heavy shooting pressure in North America in earlier decades (*Figure 2*). Greater Yellowlegs totalled 1,583 (5.3 per cent). Stilt Sandpipers (*Micropalma himantopus*) and Short-billed Dowitchers (*Limnodromus griseus*) were not scored separately, being included in a 'Various' column. Ruddy Turnstones (*Arenaria interpres*) were listed in a separate column: as Chancery Lane is a coastal swamp, the birds occur quite commonly there.

A notable Christ Church swamp was situated at Rockley, a few hundred metres inland from the south coast in an area of c.4 ha of flat grassy pasture, an artificial swamp well designed and maintained by the owner. The coastal zone between the open pastureland and the coast was much built up from the 1920s on, and further encroachment of built-up areas brought about the closing down of the swamp in 1947. By that time a nine-hole golf course had been set up on part of the pastureland.

Detailed scores for the Rockley swamp, kept by Charles Manning and his son, the late Eric Manning, cover the years 1921 to 1947. Rockley Swamp was the leading swamp, in numbers of birds shot, during the earlier years, but declined rapidly after 1939. The run of scores from 1921 to 1939 only are analysed. During

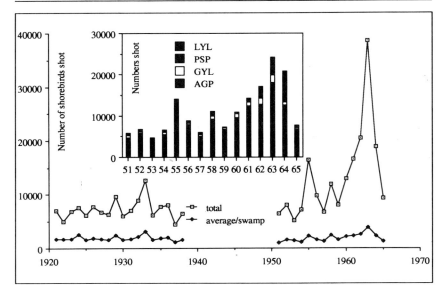

Figure 2: Annual shorebird shooting scores for the period 1921-1938 (four swamps) and 1951-1965 (varying number of four to ten swamps). The scores for the four most commonly shot species are given for the period 1951-1965. LYL = Lesser Yellowlegs (*Tringa flavipes*); PSP = Pectoral Sandpiper (*Calidris melanotos*); GYL = Greater Yellowlegs (*Tringa melanoleuca*); AGP = American Golden Plover (*Pluvialis dominicana*).

this period of 19 years inclusive, a total of 57,284 birds were shot and recorded, giving the high annual average of 3,014 ranging from 2,463 in thedrought year 1934 following a year with notable hurricanes, to a maximum of 4,980. Lesser Yellowlegs shot totalled 28,996 birds (51 per cent), followed by Pectoral Sandpipers which totalled 18,198 (32 per cent). Good Pectoral flights in late September and early October were hoped for by the shooting men to boost the scores accumulated from modest Lesser Yellowlegs flights in the period 15 August to 15 September, the peak period for the movement of this species through the island.

American Golden Plovers shot over the period totalled 3,107 (5.4 per cent).

Shooting patterns after the war
The closing down of the successful Rockley swamp in Christ Church was partly compensated for by the development of Phinney's Hill, in St Philip, from 1932, by the neighbouring Golden Grove swamp, and by the gradual establishment of a successful shooting swamp at Fosters, in St Lucy. For the five-year period 1946-1950, the total number of birds shot for which records are available was 31,244, an average per annum of 6,248 per annum.

The next five-year period, 1951-1955, produced a total of 43,875 birds killed, an average per annum of 8,775. Much of this increase came from the massive score of 16,393 for 1955, a total to which weather-affected flights contributed a good deal.

Of the 1955 record score, the Lesser Yellowlegs shot numbered 8,907 (54 per cent), a total second only to that of the great hurricane year, 1933, which yielded 9,056. The Pectoral Sandpiper score, at 4,086, was slightly more than the 3,935 of 1933, making up 25 per cent. A marked increase was seen in the number of American Golden Plovers shot, numbering from 534 to 965 in the years 1946-1950, reflecting the recovery in the breeding population in North America. The total for the period 1956-1960 was 49,553 with an annual average of 9,911 birds shot. The appreciably higher average of birds shot was attributable to the extension and improvement of several of the larger swamps, with the installation of better pumps, the more regular manning of several swamps, the increasing use of pump-action and automatic shotguns and the growth of competition between the leading swamps. The year 1960 produced the highest score with 12,986 birds shot: 1958 was a close second with 11,990.

The early sixties
During the five-year period 1961-1965, the average number of birds shot per annum in the major swamps, which had climbed rather slowly from around 7,275 in the years from 1921 to 1938 and had risen to just under 10,000 in 1956-1960, doubled to the enormous figure of 20,000 (*Figure 2*). This massive increase was attributable to a number of factors.

Some of older swamps were much altered. The Golden Grove swamp was completely resited on a low hill about 600 m south of the old location. Fosters swamp was much extended with improved water pumping facilities, emerging as a tremendous draw for birds coming into the island from the north-west, probably on passage from the Vieux Fort swamp complex in south-west St Lucia, studied by the author in 1955-1956. A completely new swamp was established at Mangrove, near Six Cross Roads in St Philip, with ample surface water, proving to be very much 'in the line' of birds on passage overland through the eastern part of the island, and a rival to Golden Grove and neighbouring Phinney's Hill swamps. The old-established Chancery Lane was more efficiently managed, while Best Swamp, between Chancery Lane and Inch Marlowe, emerged as a major shooting swamp.

Of this massive five-year total of 103,717 birds shot, no fewer than 38,514 were killed in the peak year, 1963. (If an estimate is included for birds shot in swamps for which no formal records are available, the 1963 total for the whole island would probably exceed 46,000.)

Although several of the flights for 1963 were plainly affected by weather patterns, the greatest sustained flight ever known in the island, which lasted from 23-29 August and produced a total of 7,687 birds shot in the major swamps, was not obviously produced by bad weather in the vicinity of the island. *Figure 3* summarizes the three major flights in 1963. The great flight of 23-29 August was primarily a migration of Lesser Yellowlegs. The three days of 2-4 September were primarily a plover flight, while the last period 30 September-2 October is a good example of a flight of Pectoral Sandpipers.

After 1963
The very heavy flights of 1963 encouraged swamp owners to undertake more extensions and improvements. A large new swamp was created at Friendship in St Lucy, on the site of a traditional 'plover pasture'. But the two following seasons, especially 1965, were disappointing to the shooting fraternity while costs were rising rapidly.

In various swamps, new 'trays' were added, shooting huts were resited in more favourable locations within the swamp complex and more members were recruited to share the additional expense. Competition among the major swamps was greatly

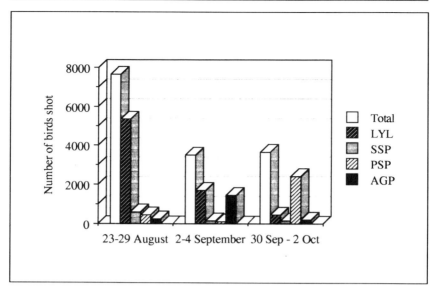

Figure 3: Total shooting scores and scores of selected species shot during the exceptionally large flights of the 1963 migrating season. LYL = Lesser Yellowlegs (*Tringa flavipes*); SSP = Stilt Sandpiper (*Calidris himantopus*); PSP = Pectoral Sandpiper (*Calidris melanotos*); AGP = American Golden Plover (*Pluvialis dominicana*).

intensified, and all remaining scruples about shooting birds on the ground, known as 'ground bouncing', were abandoned. While no subsequent year produced quite the same combination of favourable factors for the gunners, in the later 1960s and in the 1970s totals shot each year stayed in the 15,000 to 20,000 range, and each of the three or four leading swamps reckoned to score 4,000 birds per annum. However, swamp operating costs have escalated, from the cost of shotgun cartridges to water pumping expenses, and a number of the older swamp owners have died, leaving no successors. Graeme Hall swamp complex, once with a 30-ha mosaic of mangrove and sedge, the foremost wetland of Barbados, ceased to operate as a shooting swamp after 1970. Increased housing to the west and north-west has also affected adversely the pattern of migrant shorebird flights to the swamp.

To sum up the current situation, five large shooting swamps are still operating; Golden Grove, Congo Road and Mangrove in St Philip, Fosters in St Lucy, and Best swamp in Christ Church. Hunters in each of these swamps aspire to kill up to 4,000 and more birds each shooting season. A figure of 15,000 to 20,000 birds killed per annum is realistic, most birds being shot by about 50 men who are financial partners in one of the major swamps, gunners invited for a day's shooting, and casual gunners – mostly young men who take a day off work when birds are flying.

MIGRANT SHOREBIRD SPECIES SHOT IN BARBADOS

The bird most commonly shot is the Lesser Yellowlegs, which makes up about half of all birds shot. These birds commonly arrive in small flocks of 10-15 individuals, but in heavy weather may occur in flocks of 50 plus, and exceptionally 200 plus. They occur from mid-July through to late September, first arrivals being the adults, followed later in the season by immatures – known to the gunners as 'second flight Longlegs'. Birds of this species decoy easily to the swamps and tend to alight in close company on the special 'alighting land' mudbanks. The immature birds are easy prey, decoying readily, to be blown up on the ground in patterns of slaughter highly offensive to any person of sensibility and concern for wildlife. It is unusual for large numbers to occur after about 15 September in a normal year.

Often flying in mixed flocks with the Lesser Yellowlegs is the smaller, Stilt Sandpiper, known in Barbados as the 'Cue' from the single 'whu' flight call. These birds are almost always seen in non-breeding plumage.

The larger Greater Yellowlegs (*Tringa melanoleuca*), known locally as the 'Pica' or 'Piker', makes up about 7-8 per cent of birds shot. They usually fly in flocks of less than a dozen individuals, but sometimes up to twenty birds; in heavy weather they may occur in large mixed flocks with Lesser Yellowlegs, Stilt Sandpipers, Short-billed Dowitchers (*Limnodromus griseus*) and Pectoral Sandpipers, known locally as the 'Chirp', from its harsh, reedy 'churk' flight call. Pectoral Sandpipers are common fall transients in Barbados, occurring as single individuals, small parties and flocks, the latter usually of no more than about 25 birds, but sometimes larger. This species makes up, on average, about 25 per cent of all birds shot.

Pectoral Sandpiper flights are particularly dependent on weather patterns, the birds occurring in varying numbers all through the three-month mid-July to mid-October shooting season. As with most species of migrant shorebirds in Barbados, the adult birds pass through first, followed later by the birds of the year. In some years, if there is heavy weather during the first two weeks of October, there may be extensive flights of immature Pectorals, known as 'October Chirp'. During a heavy flight there may be flocks of 10-25 birds coming into a swamp, such as Best swamp, every 15-20 minutes for some hours after dawn, pitching down in a compact mass, often forward on their breasts, while they are shot at by the gunners. In the absence of heavy weather at the critical migration time, there may be virtually no passage of these 'October Chirp'. The birds probably pass well out in the Atlantic to the east of the island. The slightly smaller (200-210 mm) Sanderling (*Calidris alba*), known in Barbados as the 'Sandy Snipe', is found along sandy beaches, and in one or two coastal swamps.

A shorebird species shot regularly in varying numbers, especially in the coastal swamps, is the Short-billed Dowitcher, known in Barbados as the 'Duckleg'. The birds usually arrive as single individuals or in small parties of up to 5-10, only rarely in flocks.

Other large shorebirds occurring in Barbados in small numbers, and which are regularly shot, are the American race of Whimbrel, or Hudsonian Curlew (*Numenius phaeopus hudsonicus*), named 'Crookbill' in Barbados from its decurved bill, and the Willet (*Catoptrophorus semipalmatus*), known misleadingly as the 'White-tailed Curlew'. Whimbrels occur chiefly as single birds and in small parties of up to half a dozen birds. While they may be observed at any time during the migration season, my records over more than thirty years indicate the peak passage period to be 10-19 September, thus substantiating the traditional designation by the gunners of 12 September as 'Crookbill Day'. The birds occur chiefly at swamps near the coast. Willets occur uncommonly, usually fairly early in the season, in July-August, mostly at coastal swamps but also inland.

The Hudsonian Godwit (*Limosa haemastica*) occurs uncommonly at the southeastern tip of the island, from which birds take off on the c.480-km over-ocean flight to northern South America. Godwits are seen only during or just after heavy weather; normally the flyline is well out in the Atlantic to the east of Barbados.

The Ruddy Turnstone (*Arenaria interpres*) is a regular fall transient, flying in small parties of up to half a dozen individuals, and alighting chiefly in the coastal swamps.

Apart from the Scolopacids, one species of the plover family, Charadriidae, is a prime target of the Barbadian gunners, and that is the handsome American Golden Plover (*Pluvialis dominica*), known in Barbados as the 'Black-breast Plover' in adult plumage, and as the 'Grey-breast Plover' in winter dress and for birds of the year. This species is even more subject to variations in occurrence patterns and numbers than the Pectoral Sandpiper, particularly the immatures. The period from 25 August to 20 September is the time of the plover passage, while single adults may occur from about 10 August.

The long-distance over-ocean flight from Nova Scotia to northern South America of c.3,860 km passes well to the east of Barbados, but some flocks pass over the island even in fine weather, with the east-north-east trade wind blowing. Flocks of 50-75 birds, and sometimes up to 200 plus birds, can be observed flying straight over the island at heights of 460-615 m, chiefly from the parishes of St Philip and eastern Christ Church in the south-east parts of the island.

Heavy weather resulting from the passage in a westerly to north-westerly direction of tropical depressions, some of them incipient hurricanes, will force the plover flocks westwards to Barbados, and bring them down on to the open grassy pastures and freshly ploughed ground. After really severe weather conditions which coincide with the 25 days peak of the plover migration, with strong winds and torrential tropical rain (up to 150 mm in 12 hours and more), there may be hundreds of plover scattered in flocks over much of the island, including the playing fields of Harrison College, not far from the centre of Bridgetown, the capital. As the passage period lasts for no more than three to four weeks, in the absence of low pressure tropical easterly waves, relatively few plover will be shot, while in other years with suitable weather conditions, large numbers may be killed.

A few Black-bellied Plover (*Pluvialis squatarola*), known in Barbados as 'Squealer Plover' or 'Loggerhead Plover', are shot in coastal swamps, always as single birds. The balance of birds shot include such uncommon if fairly regular transients as Wilson's Phalarope (*Phalaropus tricolor*), Buff-breasted Sandpiper (*Tryngites subruficollis*) and Killdeer (*Charadrius vociferus*). A few Solitary Sandpipers (*Tringa solitaria*), known as 'Blackbacks', are shot, as is the American race of Snipe (*Gallinago gallinago delicata*), mostly in October and in November, after the official shooting season is over. A few of these birds may winter in Graeme Hall and Chancery Lane swamps.

A shorebird of great appeal is the finely streaked and chevroned Upland Sandpiper (*Bertramia longicauda*), known as the 'Cotton Tree Plover', which occurs as single birds, small parties and flocks of up to 15 individuals. Single birds fly over at heights of 90-150 m, uttering at regular intervals the far-carrying 'kip-ip-ip' call. Very early dates are 4 August 1942 and 8 August 1927, but 15-20 August covers most early occurrences, the bulk of the passage taking place in September, with stragglers in October (19 October 1957 was a late date, and 20 November 1964 exceptionally late). Fortunately the bird prefers dry grassland to muddy swamp margins, and does not respond to decoy whistling, but the gunners pursue them on rough grassland.

In heavy weather a few Red Knot (*Calidris canutus*) may occur – mostly at coastal swamps, and mainly during the last week of August and the first two weeks of September.

POSSIBLE CONSERVATION MEASURES

In Barbados the Wild Birds' Protection Act dates from 1907, with a very short schedule including only a handful of local breeding species considered to be beneficial to agriculture, and the attractive regular winter resident Parulid Warbler, the American Redstart (*Setophaga ruticilla*), locally known as the 'Christmas Bird'.

As a founder member of the Council of the Barbados National Trust, established in 1961, I drew up a revised schedule to the act in 1976, in which I included 46 species of resident, transient and winter resident bird species. I did include four shorebird species, as a very modest first instalment (as I hoped) of protection for the group. These were the Buff-breasted Sandpiper (*Tryngites subruficollis*), a rare visitor to coastal pastures, many of which are being built over for housing; the Ruff (*Philomachus pugnax*), a transatlantic migrant which occurs regularly in small numbers; the uncommon Hudsonian Godwit and the Upland Sandpiper.

I did not include in the proposed new schedule any of the shorebirds normally shot in some numbers, being well aware that if this was done, the amendment to the act would have been voted down in the Legislature. The shooting men are a small but influential lobby, many of them wealthy, able and willing to exert a great deal of behind-the-scenes pressure in many fields. Nevertheless, the new schedule was accepted by the Legislature and became law in 1977; but the protection afforded the four rare shorebird species remains a dead letter, with no attempt made to enforce it.

Further efforts for bird protection

In 1980, when a vice-president of the Barbados National Trust, I succeeded in carrying at the Annual General Meeting a resolution in favour of placing all the shorebird species known to visit Barbados on a proposed new revised schedule to the Wild Birds' Protection Act. This thus became the official policy of the National Trust.

I campaigned for an end to the annual slaughter in my two weekly columns in the local newspaper, *The Barbados Advocate*. One, entitled 'The Need for Conservation', was published from 1975 on; the other, 'Barbadian Nature Diary', from 1977 (Hutt 1979, 1986). Unfortunately, the powerful hunters' lobby succeeded in terminating these columns, and after 1981 the National Trust executive tacitly abandoned any attempt to press the cause of bird protection on the government. In response to this situation, in 1983 I founded a pressure group, the Barbados Wildlife Protection Association, to campaign for the total abolition of bird shooting in the island. Barbados is the only island in the English-speaking Caribbean where migrant shorebirds are shot systematically. All the shorebird species habitually shot on the island receive total protection at all seasons both in Canada and in the U.S.A., where they breed in various habitats from Arctic tundra to muskeg swamps.

RECOMMENDATIONS FOR THE FUTURE

A simple amendment to the existing Wild Birds' Protection Act of 1907, bringing in a new schedule of totally protected species listing all the species of migrant shorebirds which have been recorded in Barbados, including common, uncommon, rare species and vagrants, so as to leave no loophole, would suffice. Once such a revised schedule to the act, listing the species included in the Appendix below, is accepted by the Legislature and effectively and consistently enforced, Barbados could take its place as a community willing to join those nations of the world which do more than pay mere lip service to the need for effective conservation measures.

The next step
Wildlife Refuges, established primarily to preserve all birdlife – resident species, winter visitors and transients – should be set up at the following locations (cf. Hutt *In* Scott & Carbonell 1986):

1. Graeme Hall Swamp in Christ Church: c.31 ha.
2. Chancery Lane Swamp in Christ Church: c.20 ha.
3. Long Pond in St Andrew: c.20 ha.
4. Cole's Swamp in St Philip: c.8 ha.

ACKNOWLEDGEMENTS

I wish to acknowledge the receipt of information from the score books of various shooting swamps in Barbados from the owners, and in particular to the following deceased persons: Theo Alleyne, B. Bradshaw, J. Egan, Eric Manning, Geoffrey Manning, C. G. Massiah, Sir Grey Massiah, Dr Hallam Massiah, Clarence Skinner.

APPENDIX
(to be included in a revised schedule to the
Wild Birds' Protection Act, 1907)

Haematopus palliatus	American Oystercatcher
Himantopus himantopus	Black-necked Stilt
Recurvirostra americana	American Avocet
Pluvialis dominica	American Golden Plover; Black-breast Plover; Grey-breast Plover
Pluvialis squatarola	Black-bellied Plover; Squealer Plover; Loggerhead Plover
Charadrius semipalmatus	Semipalmated Plover; Ringneck Plover
Charadrius wilsonia	Wilson's Plover; Thick-billed Plover
Charadrius vociferus	Killdeer
Charadrius melodus	Piping Plover
Charadrius alexandrinus	Snowy Plover
Charadrius collaris	Collared Plover
Limosa haemastica	Hudsonian Godwit
Numenius borealis	Eskimo Curlew; Chittering Curlew
Numenius phaeopus	Whimbrel; Hudsonian Curlew; Crookbill
Bartramia longicauda	Upland Sandpiper; Cotton Tree Plover
Tringa melanoleuca	Greater Yellowlegs; Pica; Piker
Tringa flavipes	Lesser Yellowlegs; Longleg
Tringa solitaria	Solitary Sandpiper; Blackback
Catoptrophorus semipalmatus	Willet; White-tailed Curlew
Actitis macularia	Spotted Sandpiper; Wag
Arenaria interpres	Ruddy Turnstone; Sandy Plover; Redleg
Phalaropus tricolor	Wilson's Phalarope
Gallinago gallinago	Common Snipe

Limnodromus griseus	Short-billed Dowitcher; Duckleg
Limnodromus scolopaceus	Long-billed Dowitcher; Duckleg
Calidris canutus	Red Knot; Rock Plover; Silverwing
Calidris alba	Sanderling; Sandy Snipe
Calidris pusilla	Semipalmated Sandpiper; Nit
Calidris mauri	Western Sandpiper; Nit
Calidris minutilla	Least Sandpiper; Nit
Calidris fuscicollis	White-rumped Sandpiper; Grey Nit
Calidris bairdii	Baird's Sandpiper
Calidris melanotos	Pectoral Sandpiper; Chirp
Micropalama himantopus	Stilt Sandpiper; Cue
Tryngites subruficollis	Buff-breasted Sandpiper
Philomachus pugnax	Ruff; Reeve (female)

REFERENCES

AMERICAN ORNITHOLOGISTS' UNION. (1983) *Check-list of North American birds.* Sixth edition. Lawrence, Kansas: Allen Press.

BENT, A. C. (1927 and 1929). *Life histories of North American shorebirds*: Parts 1 and 2.

BOND, J. (1954) *Check-list of birds of the West Indies.* Acad. Sci Phil. with numerous Supplements over more than 30 years.

GOODING, E. G. B. (1974) *The plant communities of Barbados.* Gov. Print.

HAYMAN, P., MARCHANT, J. & PRATER, T. (1986) *Shorebirds.* London: Croom Helm.

HUTT, M. B. (1979) *Barbadian nature diary.* Halifax, Nova Scotia: Layne Co.

HUTT, M. B. (1986) *A naturalist's year in Barbados.* Bedford, Nova Scotia: Layne Co.

SCOTT, D. A. & CARBONELL, M. (1986) *A directory of Neotropical wetlands.* Cambridge, U.K.: International Union for the Conservation of Nature and Natural Resources; Slimbridge, U.K.: International Waterfowl and Wetlands Research Bureau.

PART III
CONSERVING MIGRATORY BIRDS

This part is not a review of migratory species and their problems, nor a series of guidelines on how such problems can be solved. Instead it presents a number of case studies which have been selected to illustrate comprehensive approaches to solving the conservation problems of migratory birds. Criteria for inclusion were (1) the importance that conservation activities and their implications have within a given project, as opposed to the relative importance of pure data-gathering and research; (2) the aim of approaching complex conservation problems in a long-term and comprehensive way, as opposed to using narrowly focused one-off activities; and (3) the provision of experience gained while implementing field projects over several years, as opposed to new concepts arising directly from the drawing board. The case studies represent a very varied selection, and cannot provide a general recipe for how to carry out successful projects. However, some lessons can be learnt, and hopefully the projects presented here may serve as examples to advance conservation activities in regions and flyways other than the ones reported here.

PART III starts with a classical species-oriented approach – the conservation and management of the White Stork (*Ciconia ciconia*), a species which, of all the wild birds, has one of the most intimate bonds with humankind. Nevertheless, the contribution by Goriup & Schulz emphasizes clearly the legal and administrative complexities that must be overcome if the species and its habitats are to be saved. Thauront & Fofana provide insight into the value of this species as a focus for conservation education in rural communities in its African winter quarters. Crivelli *et al.* stress that sound conservation action must rely on good scientific data, and on analysis of the species' ecology. Although their contribution summarizes state-of-the-art knowledge on Palearctic pelicans, much of our understanding is still based on diffuse data and gross estimates. The two following contributions by Yazgan and Sultana take the species-oriented approach a step further, by showing where it may lead if taken up by active groups dedicated to campaigning and lobbying for greater awareness and concern for the protection of species and their habitats. In common with the contribution by Hutt (in PART II), they summarize the experiences of the first generation of dedicated conservationists acting in an intellectual environment in which an acceptance of indiscriminate and unrestricted use of natural resources still seems to be the overwhelming attitude. Their contributions also exemplify how international support (technical and financial) during the initial years of newly-established conservation groups can help achieve essential goals. The following contributions by Ntiamoa-Baidu and Coulthard assess how efficient "flagship species" can be in generating support for conservation projects conceived in the "bird-loving" North, how they serve as an entry point for conservation activities in rural Africa, and how the projects are perceived by local people living in the migrants' winter habitats. Both contributions stress the need to develop species-oriented activities within integrated management projects that also take into account the socio-economic context of rapidly developing human communities exploiting natural resources upon which the migrant birds also depend.

From the Asian flyways Higuchi and Severinghaus report on additional species-oriented activities, and here the affinities between the problems affecting different intercontinental flyways immediately become apparent. There are certainly other migrants for which specific conservation programmes have been established, and for some of them overviews have recently been published (e.g. Trumpeter Swan (*Cygnus buccinator*), Banko 1980; Eskimo Curlew (*Numenius borealis*), Gollop *et al.* 1986; Bachman's Warbler (*Vermivora bachmanii*), Hamel 1987; various cranes (*Grus* spp.), Archibald & Pasquier 1987; Kirtland's Warbler (*Dendroica kirtlandii*), Anonymous 1989; Whooping Crane (*Grus americana*), Doughty 1989; Scarlet Ibis (*Eudocimus ruber*), Frederick *et al.* 1990). Others are expected shortly, and yet others may well have been overlooked by the editor of this volume as the examples published here were selected also to provide ideas that go beyond the species level and address conservation issues of wider concern.

The contributions by Howe, Rappole and Lane & Parish close PART III with regional overviews of the American and Asian–Australasian flyways. The authors stress the need for sufficient and accurate research into the species' ecology in both the breeding and wintering areas, in order to lay a firm base upon which to build a legislative structure and prepare field actions to protect the species and their habitats. They provide concrete recommendations for key habitats and sites upon which migrants depend. An increasingly successful initiative creating an intercontinental network of reserves linking breeding, stop-over and wintering sites along the flyways of American waders is presented by Hunter *et al.* as an example which might well be taken up in other parts of the world.

T. Salathé

REFERENCES

ANONYMOUS. (1989) *At the crossroads – extinction or survival?* Kirtland's Warbler Symposium 1989. U.S. Forest Service, Huron-Manistree National Forests.
ARCHIBALD, G. W. & PASQUIER, R. F., eds. (1987) *Proceedings of the 1983 international crane workshop.* Baraboo: International Crane Foundation.
BANKO, W. E. (1980) *The Trumpeter Swan.* Lincoln and London: University of Nebraska Press.

DOUGHTY, R. W. (1989) *Return of the Whooping Crane.* Austin: University of Texas Press.

FREDERICK, P. C., MORALES, G., SPAANS, A. L. & LUTHIN, C. S. (1990) *The Scarlet Ibis: status, conservation and recent research.* Slimbridge, U.K.: International Waterfowl and Wetlands Research Bureau (Spec. Publ. 11).

GOLLOP, J. B., BARRY, T. W. & IVERSEN, E. H. (1986) *Eskimo Curlew: a vanishing species?* Regina: Saskatchewan Natural History Society (Spec. Publ. 17).

HAMEL, P. B. (1986) *Bachmann's Warbler: a species in peril.* Washington, D.C.: Smithsonian Institution.

CONSERVATION MANAGEMENT OF THE WHITE STORK: AN INTERNATIONAL NEED AND OPPORTUNITY

PAUL D. GORIUP[1] & HOLGER SCHULZ[2,3]

1 *The Nature Conservation Bureau, 36 Kingfisher Court, Hambridge Road, Newbury RG14 5SJ, U.K.*
2 *WWF-Germany, Hedderichstrasse 110, 6000 Frankfurt/Main, F.R.G.*
3 *present address: National Wildlife Research Centre, P.O. Box 1086, Taif, Saudi Arabia*

Even the Stork in the heavens
Knows her times;
And the Turtle Dove, Swallow and Crane
Keep the time of their coming
Jeremiah 8, vii

ABSTRACT

The White Stork population inhabiting Europe, Africa and Asia Minor has long been held in high esteem by the people in most countries in which it occurs. As commensals of man, White Storks visiting Europe to breed during the summer enjoyed a long period of expansion while forested habitats were cleared for pasture and crops. During this century, however, their numbers have declined with increasing speed in the west of their breeding range, and there are signs of this process spreading eastwards. Moreover, in the last few decades, White Storks have faced mounting pressures on their habitats and food supply in their principal winter quarters in Africa.

Consequently, the White Stork has been included in Appendix II of the Bonn Convention. This means that the opportunity now exists for the species to be safeguarded by implementing a series of integrated measures covered by an Agreement. These measures depend for their success on international cooperation. This paper explores the current situation of the White Stork and proposes a number of national and international conservation actions that could be incorporated in such an Agreement.

INTRODUCTION

Of the large migratory birds breeding in Europe and wintering in Africa, the White Stork is surely one of the most spectacular. It has certainly long featured in the art and folklore of rural communities where it is welcomed as a harbinger of spring (and babies), and as a useful predator of agricultural pests. Given these attributes, it is astonishing that the White Stork has been allowed to suffer such a huge decline almost throughout its range over the last hundred years that today only internationally-coordinated measures will save it from further diminution and local extinctions.

The entry into force of the Bonn Convention on the Conservation of Migratory Species of Wild Animals in 1983 has afforded the much-needed legal framework within which conservation action for the White Stork can be planned and implemented throughout its range. At the First Conference of the Parties to the Bonn Convention (Bonn, 1983), the White Stork was identified as both a priority for attention, and an excellent model for developing international Agreements incorporating detailed management plans: few species have been so well documented as the White Stork. Consequently, in 1986, the Commission of the European Community contracted ICBP to review the available information and compile a report containing the elements necessary for such a management plan. The report was submitted to the EC in 1988: the following paper includes the substance of that report, up-dated where appropriate. The full Agreement is under development and it is expected to be discussed at the Third Conference of the Parties in 1991.

BIOLOGY OF THE WHITE STORK: A REVIEW

The vast majority of White Storks belong to the nominate subspecies *Ciconia ciconia ciconia*; a second much smaller population, *C. c. asiatica*, breeds in central Soviet Asia and winters in the Indian subcontinent (Cramp & Simmons 1977). The endangered Eastern White Stork (*C. boyciana*) is very closely related but is now generally regarded as a separate species (Collar & Andrew 1988). This paper deals only with the nominate subspecies in the main part of its range (*Table 1*). Also excluded are the small (mostly non-migratory) feral populations that have been established in Switzerland, Belgium, the Netherlands, France and West Germany (Rheinwald *et al.* 1989).

In Europe and the Mediterranean basin, White Storks are immediately recognizable by their large size (standing over 1 m high, with a wingspan of 155-165 cm), striking white body with black on the flight feathers, and long red bill and legs. The most similar bird in Africa is the resident Yellow-billed Stork (*Mycteria ibis*), but this bird is smaller, has red on the forehead and, as its name indicates, has a yellow bill. Fortunately, the conservation prospects for the White Stork are greatly favoured by its size, handsome appearance and great familiarity and respect among most of the human populations with whom it shares much of its habitat.

Distribution
As a long-distance migrant, the nominate White Stork has been recorded in practically all European, African, Arabian and west Asian countries at some time (Rheinwald *et al.* 1989; Schulz 1988). However, the principal Range States are those listed in *Table 1*. The bulk of the breeding population (up to 120,000 pairs) occurs in continental Europe (including Turkey), although a significant proportion (up to 16,350 pairs) breeds in North Africa (chiefly Morocco). Some birds breed in Israel (up to 50 pairs), while 5-10 pairs breed at the extreme tip of South Africa. Further east, Iran supports up to 2,350 pairs (about 2 per cent of the total) and

small breeding populations may still exist in Syria and Iraq, but no recent information is available from these countries.

Status

According to the international census carried out by E. Schüz on behalf of ICBP in 1984 (see below), and other recently available information, the current population of the nominate White Stork does not exceed some 130,000 breeding pairs and, including immature non-breeding birds over-summering in Africa and fledged young of the year, over 500,000 individuals in total in July (*Table 1*). There may in fact be more birds than have been detected so far in their breeding grounds since censuses of migratory birds suggest a total of nearly 500,000 birds passing through Israel alone (Leshem, in prep.; Horin 1989).

Fossil storks have been found in North America, as far apart as Florida and California. These finds suggest that the stork once had a much wider distribution than today, and the fact that wide expanses of suitable habitat in the Old World are unoccupied by storks is perhaps indicative of a species in long-term decline (Gooders 1969). Considerable information on the relative status of the White Stork in Europe during recent times is available from various accounts dating back to the early seventeenth century, regional censuses dating from the nineteenth century and finally regular international counts begun in 1934 (Schüz 1936; Dallinga & Schoenmakers 1989). Across the breeding range as a whole, the numbers of White Storks have fluctuated widely, with periods of steep decline followed by rapid increases and phases of relative stability. The population level today is falling and is under half of what it was 40 years ago, matching other low points during the previous two centuries. The crucial differences in the current situation, however, are that there has been a marked regional shift in population distribution and abundance, the decline has lasted for an unusually long period and is spreading in extent, and the prospects for natural recovery seem poor.

North-western Europe has suffered the worst effects (*Table 2*). The number of White Storks of the eastern subpopulation (i.e. those breeding east of about 11°E and north of about 52°N (see **Movements**, below) occurring in the European Community, Switzerland and Sweden has declined by at least 12,500 breeding pairs since 1900. This represents a loss of 80 per cent of those nesting in the region and over 10 per cent of the whole subpopulation. White Storks of the smaller, western subpopulation have declined even more severely in the region (becoming almost confined to the Iberian peninsula) with corresponding decreases of migratory birds noted in the winter quarters of West Africa. During the last 100 years, White Storks have become extinct as breeding birds in Belgium (1985), Switzerland (1949) and Sweden (1954), while only a handful remain in Denmark, France and the Netherlands (Rheinwald *et al.* 1989). Six times as many storks have been lost from Spain as from the whole of the rest of Western Europe.

The populations of White Storks in the East European region have hardly fared any better. Although storks are still found in good numbers in many countries, heavy declines of up to 50 per cent have been recorded since the 1960s. Current populations in Poland, Slovak SR, Hungary, Austria and Latvia SSR are relatively stable, but their prospects are not good; those in Romania, Bulgaria, Yugoslavia, Greece, Turkey and the Russian SSR are in slow continuous decline; only in the Czech SR and Estonian SSR has a significant increase taken place since 1934, growing from 194 to 652 pairs and from 318 to 1,378 pairs respectively, by 1984.

Since 1973, a few pairs of White Storks have bred in Israel where irrigated farmland now provides good feeding opportunities (Raviv 1989).

Table 1: Indicative population status of the White Stork (*C. c. ciconia*) in Range States with recommendations for appropriate conservation actions. (*Principal sources:* Rheinwald *et al.* 1989; Schulz 1988.)

Country/Region	Breeding no. birds (census)[1]	Non-breeding & juvenile birds (estimated)[2]	Birds in winter	Birds on passage[3]	Recommended Range State conservation actions
EASTERN POPULATION					
Albania	<100	<80	-	-	PSM
Austria	630	440	-	low 1000s?	HC,LRE,OCM,PSM
Botswana	-	-	low 1000s?	low 1000s?	HC,PCA,PSM
Bulgaria	10,840	9,800	-	166-227,000	HC,LRE,OCM,PSM
Czechoslovakia	3,340	3,250	-	high 1000s	HC,LRE,OCM,PSM
Egypt	-	low 100s	low 100s	<400,000	LRE,PSM,TSP
Ethiopia[4]	-	-	low 100s	low 100s	PSM
German Dem. Rep.[12]	5,550	4,000	-	low 100s	HC,LRE,PSM
Hungary	9,380	8,160	-	low 10,000s	HC,LRE,OCM,PSM
Iraq	?	?	-	low 100s	PSM
Iran	4,700	4,000	low 100s	low 1000s	HC,LRE,PSM,TSP
Israel[5]	<100	<100	2-4,000	<500,000	HC,LRE,OCM,PCA,PSM
Jordan[6]	-	rare	<100	<500,000	HC,LRE,PCA,PSM
Kenya[6]	-	low 100s	low 1000s	high 1000s	HC,LRE,PCA,PSM
Lebanon	-	<100	<100	<400,000	LRE,PA,TSP
Lesotho	-	<100	500-1,000	low 100s	HC,LRE,PA,PSM
Malawi	-	-	low 100s	low 1000s	HC,LRE,PSM
Moçambique	-	-	low 1000s	high 1000s?	HC,LRE,PSM
Namibia	-	<100	low 100s	low 100s	PSM,TSP
Oman	-	-	low 100s	low 100s	HC,LRE,PA,PCA,PSM
Poland	61,000	54,000	-	?	HC,LRE,PSM
Romania	2,300	2,465	-	<370,000	HC,LRE,PSM
Saudi Arabia	-	-	low 100s	low 100s	LRE,PA,PSM
Southern Africa[6,7]	<10	low 100s	25-200,000	-	HC,LRE,OCM,PCA,PSM
Soviet Union	>85,000	>80,000	-	-	HC,LRE,OCM,PCA[8],PSM
Armenian SSR	?	?			
Azerbaijan SSR	?	?	?	20-24,000	
Byelorussian SSR	<20,000	<15,000	-		
Estonian SSR	2,760	2,430			
Georgian SSR	?	?			
Latvian SSR	12,500	10,700			
Lithuanian SSR	13,500	11,500			
Moldavian SSR	?	?			
Russian SFSR	5,360	4,500	-		
Ukrainian SSR	30,000	25,000	-		
Sudan	-	-	low 1000s	<400,000	HC,LRE,PA,PCA,PSM,TSP
Syria	?	?	?	<400,000	LRE,PA,HC,TSP
Tanzania	-	5,000	100,000	high 1000s	LRE,PCA,PSM
Turkey	>18,000	>15,000	low 100s	<370,000	HC,LRE,PA,PSM
Uganda	-	-	rare	high 1000s	LRE,PSM
Yemen Arab Republic	-	-	1000	low 100s	HC,LRE,PA,PSM
Yugoslavia	6,000	5,400	-	-	HC,LRE,OCM,PSM
Zaire	-	-	rare	low 100s	PSM
Zambia	-	<100	low 1000s	high 1000s	HC,LRE,PCA,PSM
Zimbabwe[6]	-	low 100s	high 1000s	high 1000s	HC,LRE,PCA,PSM
WEST EUROPE/NORTH-WEST AFRICA POPULATION					
Algeria	<4,000	3,000	-	low 100s	HC,LRE,PSM
Benin	-	-	100-200	-	LRE,TSP
Burkina Faso	-	-	100-200	-	LRE,TSP
Chad	-	-	low 100s	low 100s	LRE,PA,PSM,TSP
Cameroon	-	-	low 1000s	low 100s	HC,LRE,PCA,PSM
Ghana	-	-	100-200	-	LRE,TSP
Ivory Coast	-	-	rare	rare	TSP
Libya	-	-	rare	rare	TSP
Mali	-	?	many 1000s	many 1000s	HC,LRE,PA,PCA,PSM,TSP
Mauritania	-	-	a few 1000s?	many 1000s	HC,LRE,PA,PSM,TSP
Morocco	28,000	22,000	low 100s	30-35,000	HC,LRE,PCA,PSM,TSP,PCA
Niger	-	-	low 100s	low 1000s	HC,PA,PCA,PSM,TSP
Nigeria	-	-	low 100s	-	HC,LRE,PA,TSP
Senegal & Gambia	-	-	low 100s	rare	HC,LRE,PA,TSP
Tunisia	660	300	rare	low 100s	HC,LRE,PCA,PSM

(continued)

Table 1: Continued

Country/Region	Breeding no. birds (census)[1]	Non-breeding & juvenile birds (estimated)[2]	Birds in winter	Birds on passage[3]	Recommended Range State conservation actions
THE EUROPEAN COMMUNITY[9]					HC,HR,LRE,OCM,PA,PCA[8],PSM
Western population	<17,000	<14,500	low 1000s	<31,500	
Eastern population	<3,200	<3,000	?	high 10,000s	
Denmark	<24	<20	-	-	HC,HR,LRE,PSM
France	26	40	rare	low 100s	HC,HR,LRE,PSM
Aquitaine	4	8			
Basse Normandie	4	7			
Champagne-Ardenne	2	2			
Pays de la Loire	2	3			
Poitou Charentes	10	16			
Rhône-Alpes	4	4			
German Fed. Rep.	<1,270	<1,200	rare	-	HC,HR,LRE,OCM,PA,PCA[8],PSM
Baden-Württemberg[10]	20				
Bayern[11]	138	120			
Bremen[11]	6	12			
Hamburg[11]	16	16			
Hessen[10]	8	8			
Niedersachsen[11]	572	550			
Nordrhein-Westfalen[10]	10	10			
Schleswig-Holstein[11]	500	450			
Greece	<2,000	<1,900	?	many 10,000s	HC,LRE,PSM,TSP
Ipiros	200	?			
Kentriki Ellas	<50	?			
Makedonia	1,200	950			
Nissoi	10	?			
Peloponnissos	<50	?			
Thessalia	160	?			
Thraki	350	285			
Netherlands	4	?	-	-	HC,HR,LRE,PSM
Portugal	<3,066	<2,450	<100	-	HC,LRE,PSM
Alentejo	2,420	1,850			
Algarve	100	100			
Centro	266	210			
Lisboa e Tejo	204	240			
Norte	66	50			
Spain	>13,500	7-12,000	low 1000s	low 100s	HC,LRE,PSM
Andalucía	1,332	655			
Aragón	290	192			
Castilla-La Mancha	1,050	393			
Castilla y León	4,086	2,255			
Cantabria	52	25			
Cataluña	38	24			
Extremadura	6,044	3,727			
Foral de Navarra	82	87			
Galicia	8	12			
La Rioja	92	45			
Madrid	430	207			
Pais Vasco	2	2			
United Kingdom					
Gibraltar	-	-	-	<31,500	PCA[8],PSM

Notes: Range States in bold lettering are Parties to the Bonn Convention as of May 1991.

1 Breeding population data from census counts in 1984, or published reports not earlier than 1975; 2 Estimates of non-breeding and progeny production are based on calculations from 1984 census results and productivity data; 3 Figures for autumn migration, excluding local breeding birds that migrate; 4 Much increased numbers during locust outbreak years; 5 Birds follow the Jordan river valley, the border between the countries; 6 Wintering population size depends on abundance of food, especially army worms or locusts: stork numbers may rise to many tens of thousands, reaching hundreds of thousands, during infestation years; 7 Republic of South Africa, Swaziland and Transkei; 8 Applies principally to foreign aid projects in Africa; 9 Data excludes birds derived from captive stock and those in the former German Democratic Republic; 10 Most storks follow the eastern migration route, a few the western route; 11 These storks chiefly follow the eastern migration route; 12 From 1990, this population covered by EC membership of the Bonn Convention; HC = Habitat Conservation; HR = Habitat Restoration and Recreation; LRE = Legislative Review and Enforcement; OCM = Overhead Cable Management; PA = Public Awareness; PCA = Pesticide Application Assessment; PSM = Population Survey and Monitoring; TSP = Trapping, Shooting and Poisoning Controls.

Table 2: Decline of the White Stork in western Europe: numbers of breeding pairs in 1934 and 1984.

Country	1934	1984	% loss
Sweden	12	Extinct	100
Denmark	859	19	97
Netherlands	273	8	97
German FR	4,557	668	85
France	150	13	93
Switzerland	10	Extinct	100
Spain	14,500	6,750	74
Portugal	5,500	1,533	72
Total	25,849	8,991	65

Movements

At the end of the breeding season, most White Storks fly south to spend the northern winter in Africa (Creutz 1988; Schulz 1988). Because of their large size, White Storks prefer to conserve energy during migration by practising soaring rather than flapping flight. Suitable thermals in which to gain height occur only over land so the birds tend to avoid crossing wide expanses of water. Thus, to reach Africa they generally follow one of two main routes that carry them round either side of the Mediterranean Sea (*Figure 1*). To the west, birds cross between the continents at the Straits of Gibraltar, while to the east (used by the great majority of birds), they pass over the Bosphorus. Relatively few birds cross the Mediterranean by other routes: down the Italian coast to Tunisia or perhaps over the Greek islands to Crete and Egypt, or across Cyprus to the Middle East. Much farther to the east is another route, rather poorly known, that leads to Arabia and the Indian subcontinent (Gallagher 1989). The return migration in the spring follows fairly closely the routes used in the autumn, but is generally more westerly (for example, few spring migrants pass through Oman), less use is made of coastlines and the passage time is much quicker.

The western migration. The western route is used by the 30,000 or so White Storks breeding in Portugal, Spain, France and south-west Germany. The so-called 'migratory divide' from the eastern route runs up from the foothills of the Alps broadly along longitude 11°E to Harz and then (in former times when birds still bred in this area) west to Osnabrück and southern IJsselmeer. There is, however, quite a wide corridor of overlap along this line, so the former Swiss population and the extant one of western Germany, for example, could go either way (Dallinga & Schoenmakers 1989; Schüz 1962).

Starting from mid-July and continuing until the end of August, White Storks cross the Straits of Gibraltar to Morocco, arriving around Tangier. They move on down a relatively narrow path between the coast and the Atlas Mountains, and are joined by local Moroccan birds. At about latitude 30°N (Agadir), the route swings inland, heading south-east to Tindouf in Algeria. Here, they meet more birds coming from western Algeria, before crossing the Mauritanian Sahara to reach their wintering quarters in the west and central Sudano-Sahel zone savannas (Schulz 1988).

There no longer seems to be any major areas of regular concentration (if indeed these ever existed) in the Sudano-Sahel zone (Schulz 1988), though parties of White Storks, never more than one or two thousand, may congregate where locust

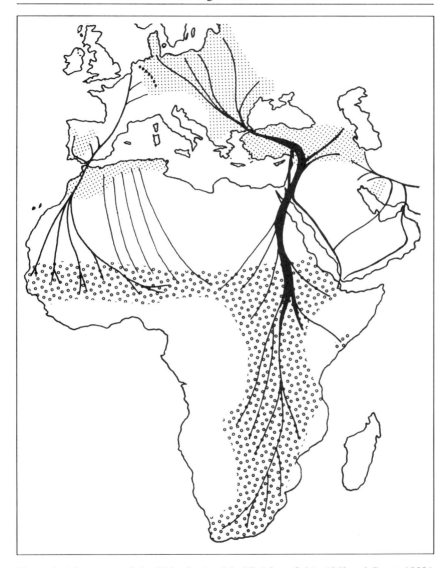

Figure 1: Movements of the White Stork. (Modified from Schüz 1962 and Creutz 1988.)

outbreaks occur. However, the current pattern of winter distribution seems to be one of wide dispersal from the west coast river estuaries of Mauritania and Senegal east through Mali and Niger to the fringes of Lake Chad in Nigeria (Walsh 1989). Such a huge area could easily absorb the few tens of thousands of storks involved without them having to concentrate in large flocks. Nevertheless, it is likely that certain wetland areas of the west and central Sudano-Sahel zone do play a vital role in maintaining numbers now, and may certainly do so in the future. They are: the Senegal and Siné-Saloum river deltas (Senegal), the inundation zone of the

Niger River (Mali) and the floodplain of the Komadugu Gana River near Nguru (Nigeria).

A few thousand birds spend the winter at various points along the migration route in southern Iberia, Morocco and Mauritania. The populations breeding in eastern Algeria and Tunisia apparently fly directly south across the desert via a chain of hills and oases to Mali and Niger.

The primary eastern migration. To the east of the migration divide mentioned above, White Storks move south-east and south towards the Bosphorus and Dardanelles of Turkey where they cross the narrow channel between Europe and Asia. If the birds are delayed by bad weather, they can congregate in enormous flocks numbering tens of thousands. The peak passage period is around mid-August and a total of up to 370,000 birds pass through this funnel.

The White Storks reaching Turkey from north and central Europe must cross Bulgaria and, to a great extent, Romania as well. However, it is not clear whether this part of the journey is done non-stop or whether certain areas serve as resting places. There are observations of 135,000 or more storks moving along the Black Sea coast of Bulgaria (Grimmett & Jones 1989) but no information exists as to the possible crucial importance for migrating storks of wetlands near the coast of the Moldavian SSR or the Danube delta in Romania. According to IUCN (1987), between 20,000 and 24,000 White Storks winter in the Kirov Bays area of the south-western Caspian Sea (140 km south of Baku): whether these are locally breeding birds or migrants from the west is not known.

Once in Turkey, the White Storks cross the broad expanses of the Anatolian steppes where ample resting places are afforded by the many wetlands present in the region. Joined by local White Storks that swell the number of migratory birds to nearly 400,000, they head south-east to the Göksu delta near Adana (Kasparek & Kiliç 1989), there crossing the Gulf of Iskenderun into Syria where they turn south following the coast and Asi (Orontes) river valley. The White Storks continue to follow the east Mediterranean coastal belt through Lebanon, Israel and Jordan (as far inland as the Azraq oasis) to Eilat on the Gulf of Aqaba or across the Sinai to Tur on the Gulf of Suez. Some birds may stop briefly in the irrigated areas of Israel, but the bulk seem to make this part of the journey without pause (the transit of Israel takes five to eight hours), probably resting mainly in the Sinai. The entry to Africa is made by crossing the Gulf of Suez to reach the Nile valley at the Qina bend (26°N) in Egypt (Schulz 1988).

The few White Storks breeding in southern Greece either move east to cross the Marmora Sea directly or via the Bosphorus (Kasparek & Kiliç 1989) or may possibly head south exploiting the thermals generated by islands as far as Crete, and then crossing the Mediterranean Sea to Egypt. Such birds might account for some of those noted wintering in the Nile delta.

The large parties of White Storks that arrive in Egypt only rest in the country: most do not seem to feed or drink there. Rather, as soon as possible, they proceed south along the Nile to Lake Nasser, across the Nubian Desert and into Sudan to regain the Nile at Abu Hamed (19°N) (Schulz 1988). From there on, the migration becomes more leisurely, with White Storks spending many weeks feeding in the Sudanian savanna as they move gradually south to the main wintering grounds in eastern and southern Africa. The speed of this movement, and the degree to which the majority of birds go south, depends on the availability of suitable feeding areas, and in particular the occurrence of infestations of insects such as army worms and locusts (Schulz 1988). The most important resting areas in Sudan occur in the region bounded by Wad Madani, Gedaref and Sennar (south-east of Khartoum) with the greatest concentrations near the Rahad irrigation scheme. Here, nearly all the storks using the eastern migration route may remain for some time between mid-September and the end of October. Other concentrations are found near Naurariya (40 km south-west of Sennar) and in the Butana region near Manaqil (Schulz 1988).

The main path southwards for the White Stork, after Sudan, follows the eastern side of the Nile to Lake Victoria, although the birds fan out to the west (to Zaire) and even farther east (to the coast of Ethiopia) if conditions are favourable. Thus, the border area between Uganda and Kenya services the birds until they enter Tanzania, arguably the first consistently important wintering range state. In Tanzania, the main feeding area appears to be the Serengeti National Park and its environs: in January 1987 over 100,000 birds were present in the area, attracted by an outbreak of army worms (Schulz 1988). In years of low insect abundance, the White Storks proceed southwards, keeping mainly to the west of Lake Malawi and following the Luangwa valley in Zambia (a noted stop-over point is the South Luangwa National Park), into Zimbabwe and then into South Africa; rather few birds winter in Malawi, Moçambique, Zambia or Botswana (Schulz 1988).

While in Zimbabwe, White Storks are widely distributed, favouring agricultural areas (Rockingham-Gill & Mundy 1989). A substantial proportion of the White Stork population may eventually reach South Africa by the time of peak concentration in January. In years when feeding conditions in East Africa are poor, up to 200,000 birds can be found in South Africa; even in relatively good years further north, 20,000-25,000 birds will occur in the country. The most important wintering areas in South Africa are along the Limpopo River (north Transvaal), west Natal, the Vaals-Harts irrigation area near Kimberley and other irrigated areas in Cape Province (Schulz 1988).

The secondary eastern migration. The relatively small proportion of White Storks that breed in the extreme east of the range have a different pattern of migration from that described above. At the present time, not much is known of their precise movements and most analyses rely on conjecture. The birds involved are those breeding in the Soviet Republics of Armenia and Azerbaijan, in Iran and any that remain in Iraq. They appear to fly south-east towards the Persian Gulf, skirting the Zagros Mountains perhaps as far as the saline sebkahs around Hamune e Jaz Murran and the coast near Bandar Abas in Iran. Here, some birds (2,000 at most) turn south, crossing the Straits of Hormuz to the United Arab Emirates and Oman, and then follow the coast (or sometimes fly across Saudi Arabia: 70 have been recorded over Riyadh: A. Stagg, pers. comm.) through Yemen where they either winter, spread north along the Tihama into Saudi Arabia, or continue to Djibouti and Ethiopia by crossing the Bab el Mandeb straits. A few (low hundreds at most) apparently continue east along the Makran coast to the Indus delta in Pakistan (T. Roberts, pers. comm.) or the wetlands of Gujarat in India (Majumdar 1989). The majority of these storks, however, spend the winter in Iran itself (before the Gulf Wars, mainly in the Shatt al Arab wetlands). Observations of White Storks crossing Afghanistan, moving through northern Pakistan and entering India probably concern the eastern race *C. c. asiatica*.

Habitat

In its breeding quarters, the White Stork occupies a fairly wide range of open habitat types in the vicinity of fresh water, where foraging by walking slowly along and grabbing surface-living prey is possible (Cramp & Simmons 1977). Thus, storks use sites from wetland margins and riverine parkland forest to moist meadows, paddyfields and irrigated croplands, arable fields and pastures (such as the *dehesa* of Iberia). These sites are often close to or intimately associated with human settlements (on passage, even rubbish tips may be visited) and traditional farming practices such as creating herb-rich meadows for stock grazing and hay production have proved beneficial for storks. Thick, tall vegetation such as scrub and reedbeds is not favoured. Nesting sites are usually situated on elevated, sunny positions like cliff ledges, tree-tops, roofs, church spires, hay stacks and pylons. The birds avoid regions that are damp or frost-prone, so their altitudinal range varies from sea level up to 2,500 m in Morocco and 2,000 m in Armenia, but only up to a limit of about 500 m in central Europe.

Similar selection criteria apply in the wintering quarters (Schulz 1988). In Sudan, for example, habitat choice seems to be influenced by the availability of water (where birds tend to congregate to pass the midday, drinking and keeping cool), vegetation height (fairly low) and composition (i.e. somewhere between dry steppe and *Acacia* parkland), and food abundance. White Storks often gather at recent grass-fire sites to take advantage of the rich pickings of burned insects and other small animals. As in the breeding grounds, agricultural areas (particularly lucerne (*Medicago sativa*) crops) are used, and in some places (e.g. Israel, Zimbabwe and South Africa) are almost exclusively selected. An unusual White Stork locality (for Africa) occurs in Lesotho where some 500-1,000 birds regularly winter (and a few immatures remain for the summer) around Latseng-la-Letsie, a lake at an altitude of over 2,250 m in the Drakensberg Mountains (P. Osborne, pers. comm.). The habitat used here comprises small, steep-sided damp valleys close to intensively cultivated valley floors and terraces.

Diet and feeding

The White Stork feeds exclusively on animal matter, with no significant difference between the sexes or between adults and immatures (Cramp & Simmons 1977). It takes a very wide variety of food in its diet, including small mammals (especially voles (*Microtus* spp.) during plague years), eggs, fledglings and small birds, reptiles, amphibians, fish and invertebrates according to the opportunities afforded. Pellets of regurgitated indigestible material are produced (easily found around nest sites) and these can provide a good indication of what food is being taken in any particular situation.

During the breeding season, birds are now rarely seen to congregate in feeding parties where they may have done so in the past. During the migration and winter periods, however, huge aggregations can assemble where outbreaks of insects occur. Thus, flocks of 50,000-100,000 or more birds have been found in a relatively small area, feeding intensively on pests such as locusts (e.g. *Locusta migratoria* and *Schistocerca gregaria*), army worms (*Spodoptera exempta* (Lepidoptera)) and Lucerne Moth (*Colias electo*) caterpillars (Dallinga & Schoenmakers 1989; Schulz 1988).

White Storks may well depend upon these outbreaks not merely to survive the winter, but also to accumulate enough fat for the spring migration and a successful breeding season in the following year: if no outbreaks occur in East Africa, the birds have to keep moving further south to find food, meaning a longer, more arduous return journey. A study of the feeding efficiency of White Storks in Sudan (Schulz 1988) revealed that even when locusts were abundant, much more time and energy had to be expended to catch them than is required to obtain food in Europe. In Sudan, the storks had to work continuously for most of the day to obtain their food requirement whereas in West Germany storks foraged for periods lasting only 20-120 minutes, with long breaks for resting and preening. A lack of insect outbreaks in West Africa is even more serious as the White Storks wintering there have nowhere else to go.

Breeding

White Storks arrive back on their breeding grounds in the early spring, the exact timing depending on latitude, migratory route followed and wintering and migratory conditions prevailing in Africa (Cramp & Simmons 1977; Lack 1966). Thus, arrival begins in late January or early February in Morocco, and may continue as late as early June in the north of the range. In general, birds in the western population begin nesting from March to April, while the eastern population start their season some 10-20 days later, from April to May. This staggered arrival is constant and can be used to distinguish which birds belong to which population in the overlap zone of central Europe. The commencement of breeding in any given region is a vital factor in determining the success of that breeding season: the later it starts, the fewer young are produced (see **Population dynamics**, below).

Males generally arrive about a week before females, taking up possession of nests which they defend from occupation by other males. The first female to arrive at the nest is usually accepted and a monogamous, seasonal pair-bond is formed. The most obvious interaction between male and female is a noisy and spectacular bill-clattering display. The same pair may nest together over more than one season, probably from being attracted to the same nest site rather than to the particular partner.

Nest sites are usually well removed from each other, although colonies of up to 30 pairs occur in some areas, especially in Iberia. The nest is situated in a sunny, elevated position, on a tree, cliff-ledge or man-made structure. It is built from branches and sticks with a daub of earth and dung, and lined with twigs and grass, and in urban areas, materials such as paper and rags. The nest averages 1-2 m in height and 80-150 cm across, but old nests that are added to each year can reach 2.5 m in height and weigh around 2 tonnes. Nest sites can remain in use for considerable periods – one known to exist in 1549 was still being occupied in 1930 – but a new nest can be constructed in as little as eight days.

The clutch size varies from two to six eggs, with four being the most usual number laid. Replacement clutches are rare and there is only one brood. The incubation period is 33-34 days, with sitting shared by both sexes. The eggs hatch asynchronously and both parents care for and feed the young, but the smallest of the brood often starve: the number of young successfully fledged is normally between two and three. Sometimes, an adult may kill and eat a nestling (so-called *chronism*), or throw it out of the nest, if it appears weak. The young leave the nest at 58-64 days of age and become independent 7-20 days thereafter, when they leave the nesting area.

Quite a large proportion of nests (around 30 per cent) may be occupied by birds that do not lay eggs. These are often sub-adult birds prospecting future sites: if food availability is good, they may return the following year to breed, otherwise they tend to move elsewhere. Thus, less favourable areas are utilized only when the best habitats are fully occupied. The age of first breeding varies between three and six years (rarely two or seven years), with four years being the most usual. As would be expected, first breeders are not as successful as more experienced birds in producing young so that the overall productivity in a breeding season rarely exceeds an average of two fledged birds per pair that laid eggs. In central Europe, about 60 per cent of maturing White Storks return to breed within 25 km of their natal area and 80 per cent within 50 km of it; only about 1 per cent of them breed more than 500 km from their natal area.

Population dynamics

Long series of reproductive data are available for some White Stork populations, notably in Oldenburg (Lower Saxony, F.R.G.) and Alsace (France) (Lack 1966;

Kanyamibwa *et al.* 1990). These data indicate that the average annual reproductive production varies between 1.5 and 3.1 young per nesting pair (2.6 to 3.3 young per pair that raised at least one young). The degree of breeding success is closely associated with the date of return of the storks to their nests: the later the arrival, the less successful the breeding season. In some years (*Störungsjahre*), as many as 70 per cent of storks may fail to raise any young at all. However, within the range recorded above, the level of annual reproductive production in any one year has no significant effect on (i.e. is not correlated with) the number of breeding birds four or five years later, when the young of that year start to breed.

According to Lack (1966), the clear implication of these findings is that, under natural conditions, the population size of the White Stork is regulated by factors other than average reproductive success alone. Probably the most important natural control is that exerted by climatic conditions in the wintering grounds and hence the availability of food (especially the occurrence of locust outbreaks) which in turn determines the rate of mortality in the population. From ringing returns, the White Stork does in fact appear to suffer a relatively high mortality rate for a bird of its size: between 27 and 39 per cent per year.

A subsequent exhaustive study undertaken by Dallinga & Schoenmakers (1989), and a re-examination of the Alsatian data by Kanyamibwa *et al.* (1990), sought to establish whether or not there was a link between stork numbers and feeding conditions in Africa. It was shown for the western subpopulation that there is a definite relationship between the winter discharges of the Senegal and Niger rivers (as a measure of rainfall in the western Sudano-Sahel zone), the occurrence of locust outbreaks (at least prior to control programmes in recent times), and the date of arrival of birds in their breeding grounds. In years of higher discharge, there is a greater likelihood of an abundance of locust and other insects, and the storks return earlier, resulting in increased productivity. (Preliminary evidence from the 1989 breeding season in Spain suggests that nesting success was unusually high: locust infestations in Africa during 1987-1989 have been the largest since the mid-1960s – see below.) In years of low river discharge, the birds are more stressed by food shortages but are prevented from moving elsewhere by the belt of forest to the south. The failure of rains is further exacerbated by the fact that the birds arrive towards the end of the rainy season, when the vegetation is beginning to die back. Consequently, many die and the remainder return late to the breeding grounds. Apart from rainfall levels, however, Kanyamibwa *et al.* (1990) suggest that other (unknown) causes have also contributed to the decline of the Alsatian stork population since 1961.

A similar relationship exists for the eastern subpopulation, but other factors are also involved, making the situation more complex. For example, the birds arrive at the onset of the rainy season in East Africa when other abundant food sources (e.g. army worm plagues) may be present even if locust swarms are not. On the other hand, the vegetation is generally taller and foraging therefore more difficult – hence the attractiveness of burnt areas. Moreover, there is a larger area available to them to move around in search of food, not only spatially but also qualitatively since favourable foraging land in the form of alfalfa crops has become more widespread. However, the farther south the birds have to move, the more they are likely to suffer higher mortality (but so far probably not so high as to cause a long-term decline in the subpopulation as a whole), and the later they arrive back on their breeding grounds.

It seems, therefore, that the decline of the western subpopulation of the White Stork can best be explained by a combination of the increasingly frequent droughts in West Africa and the Sudano-Sahel zone accompanied by unfavourable wetland development (e.g. for rice, cotton and sugar production) and locust control programmes. Of course, loss of breeding habitat has also played a part, but many still suitable areas, particularly in France (Schierer 1966), remain unoccupied. By contrast, since the current decline of the eastern subpopulation is confined mainly to north-west Europe, while remaining stable or even increasing on the eastern flank of its range, its status is more likely to be affected by the absolute loss of suitable breeding grounds from intensive land-use practices than by abnormal pressures in its wintering area or during migration (see below). As intensive land use spreads eastwards following recent political changes and land privatization in former COMECON countries, the decline of the White Stork population there can be expected to follow in its wake.

THREATS TO THE WHITE STORK

The previous section has demonstrated that the declines observed in the western and eastern subpopulations of the White Stork cannot be attributed solely to natural causes such as depressed breeding success from climatic change or disease. Rather, it appears that each subpopulation is suffering adverse effects in both the breeding and wintering quarters, but in different measures, and thus consequences, on the population level. Thus, the western birds are most affected by the conditions currently prevailing in the wintering area of West Africa and the Sudano-Sahel zone, while the eastern birds currently are more vulnerable to being squeezed out of their breeding range by intensive land-use practices. The western birds suffer the most since they find no respite in either western Africa or the western European breeding grounds, whereas the eastern birds have the opportunity to compensate for poor breeding success by enjoying better survival rates in eastern and southern Africa during the winter. Although these generalizations may serve to set the immediate management priorities in the Range States concerned, there is no room for complacency in any part of the White Storks' range.

The natural causes of White Stork mortality have been described: the principal factor is the amount of rainfall and thus the habitat and feeding conditions prevailing during the winter. The following account describes the various sources of abnormal impacts on the population, and their relative importance. A simplified diagram of the life-cycle of the White Stork is shown in *Figure 2*.

Loss of breeding habitat

Since the early 1950s, agricultural development in Europe has proceeded at an unprecedented rate, especially in Member States of the EC (Molenaar 1983). Land-use intensification has resulted in the drainage of wet meadows and mechanized ploughing of rough pastures to sow fertilized crops or swards of more productive varieties of grasses such as Italian Rye-grass (*Lolium perenne*) for cattle fodder. These wet meadows and rough pastures were the habitats most favoured by White Storks for catching their food. The new vegetation, often cut and recultivated at regular intervals, was no longer suitable for prey species such as the mice, voles, frogs and grasshoppers that were formerly present in great numbers. Subadult storks returning to old nest sites found that food availability was no longer sufficient to support breeding, and they moved elsewhere. Pairs that carried on breeding in traditional sites that had been 'improved' for agriculture suffered much reduced reproductive success. Nesting birds became increasingly confined to agriculturally marginal areas, especially uncultivable river valleys.

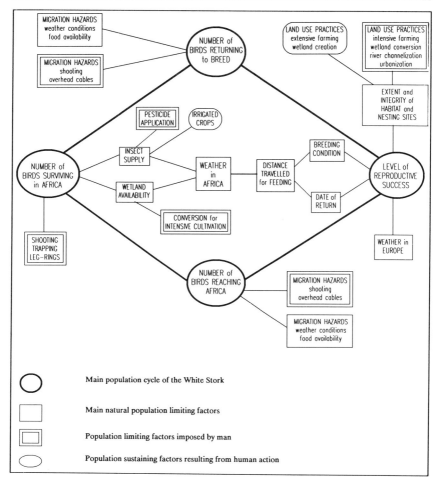

Figure 2: Diagram of the life-cycle and main factors affecting the status of the White Stork. The western subpopulation suffers most in the wintering grounds (left-hand side of chart) while the eastern subpopulation is affected more by impacts in the breeding range (right-hand side of chart). For full details refer to text. Based on Lack (1966); Schulz (1988); and Dallinga & Schoenmakers (1989).

Western Germany and Croatia compared. White Stork populations in western Germany have declined dramatically. The number of breeding pairs decreased from 2,500 in 1958 to around 500 in 1989 – a decrease of 80 per cent in only 30 years. If this trend continues, the White Stork population of western Germany will certainly disappear during the next few decades.

The last localities for White Storks in the region are in the flood-plains of large rivers and in marshes and wet grasslands. Areas not subject to regular flooding do not attract White Storks even if their water-tables are relatively high. In most areas, floods are now prevented by dams, embankments, pumping stations and river canalization schemes: suitable habitats for storks are rapidly diminishing and this loss is the single most important cause of the decline of White Storks in western Germany.

The huge impact of habitat destruction on the White Stork populations of central Europe can be amply demonstrated by comparing population dynamics data from Lower Saxony (where most of the remaining western German White Storks now breed) with that from 'optimum' habitat like the River Sava inundation zone in Croatia, Yugoslavia. Here, extensive areas of grassland are regularly flooded (and can be used only for pasture), while large patches may be under water throughout the year. Hence, the biomass of invertebrates and, in particular, amphibians, is very high and provides an abundant source of food for White Storks.

During the breeding season, flocks of up to 400 birds can be seen feeding in the Sava region (Schulz, pers. obs.). In the small villages situated along the Sava flood-plain, up to 50 pairs of White Storks nest. In 1987, the average number of chicks per nest was 2.83, while in Lower Saxony the average was 1.19; as many as six young were fledged from several Croatian nests – a figure hardly ever matched in central Europe (Schneider 1988). Considering only the nests that were successful in 1987, the number of fledged young was 3.36 per nest, compared with only 2.22 in Lower Saxony.

Recent investigations into the reasons behind such a distinct difference in the reproductive success of the two White Stork populations revealed that:

- In the Sava flood-plain, good foraging grounds lie only some hundreds of metres to a few kilometres from the birds' nests, whereas in Lower Saxony the feeding areas are often many kilometres away from the nest.
- Food in the Sava flood-plain is abundant: in some areas storks were seen to catch up to ten tadpoles where they stood, and chicks were seen refusing food because they were not hungry. This is in stark contrast with Lower Saxony where storks have to invest much effort and time in finding enough food to feed their young.
- The parts of the Sava flood-plain used for feeding by White Storks have a variable topography, providing water levels from 0 up to 50 cm depth throughout the year, so food is available even during dry periods. In Lower Saxony, most grassland areas are uniformly flat and well-drained, so no wet patches are left in the summer.
- The White Stork foraging area in the Sava flood-plain extends over more than 150 km^2, but 'suitable' foraging areas in Lower Saxony rarely exceed a few hectares.

The above comparison clearly demonstrates that habitat quality is paramount: even the best stork habitats in western Germany come nowhere near the conditions found in a really suitable habitat. The future implications for the remaining White Stork populations in more recent members of the EC (Greece, Spain and Portugal) are obvious unless adequate habitat protection measures are taken. Within the range of the eastern subpopulations, there appears to be a high probability of recolonization where suitable habitats can be recreated. Within the range of the existing western subpopulation, suitable habitats in France, Switzerland and southern Holland, even if currently unoccupied, must be protected to allow recolonization should conditions in West Africa ameliorate, whether by climatic change or human intervention or both.

Loss of nest sites

A related threat is loss and destruction of nest sites. New buildings in rural areas often have roofs that cannot support stork nests, while nests on structures such as pylons, trees or church spires are destroyed during maintenance work. Although perhaps not a major impact on the population as a whole, these losses can often be avoided, or made good simply by erecting platforms (Creutz, 1988) and replacing the nests (some 2,500 such platforms have been placed on pylons in Hungary). Special efforts in this regard should be made where traditional sites will be affected, particularly in regions experiencing declines.

Habitat loss in the winter quarters

Damage to, and deterioration of, wintering areas has been most severe in West Africa as a result of the prolonged Sudano-Sahelian drought and the various water control schemes carried out on the Senegal and Niger rivers (Dallinga & Schoenmakers 1989; Walsh 1989). Most irrigation schemes not only reduce the amount of moist natural grassland available in the winter after the rains have ended, but also serve heavily insecticide-dosed crops such as cotton, rice or sugar, none of which attracts storks in any numbers because little insect food is available. In addition, frequent droughts have resulted in extensive tracts of new desert resulting from overgrazing of stock to support an increasing human population, substantially reducing the area of the Sudano-Sahel savannas to which the storks are confined and which they must use for feeding. At present, the Sahara Desert is advancing southwards at the rate of up to 15 km per year. The White Storks of the western subpopulation are consequently under great pressure from these impacts and it only needs relatively small additional problems with food supply (e.g. from locust control, see below) or loss of breeding habitat, to precipitate a heavy decline in numbers.

Although drought has affected northern parts of the East African wintering grounds (chiefly Sudan), the effects have been mitigated somewhat by the expansion of irrigated alfalfa crops where, in contrast to the west, birds can obtain food such as Lucerne Moth caterpillars. Moreover, the birds can keep moving much farther south in search of food, to the tip of the continent if necessary, without encountering obstacles like forest belts.

Locust control programmes

The wintering quarters of both subpopulations of the White Stork largely coincide with areas often affected by plagues of locusts, in particular the African Migratory Locust (*Locusta migratoria*), the Brown Locust (*Locustana pardalina*), the Red Locust (*Nomadacris septemfasciata*) and the Desert Locust (*Schistocerca gregaria*) (Dallinga & Schoenmakers 1989; Schulz 1988). These insects live as solitary grasshoppers until favourable conditions such as high rainfall cause a massive increase in population size. Then, they grow bigger wings and longer legs, become gregarious and migrate over large distances (up to 200 km a day) before pausing to breed again (sometimes 5,000 km from the original outbreak location). Swarms can be huge, covering an area of 120 km by 25 km and containing 150,000 million individuals that destroy 300,000 tonnes of vegetation a day. It is hardly surprising, therefore, that since the 1940s, the locust swarms have been brought under ever tighter control through the use of insecticides, especially of dieldrin from the 1950s until its prohibition in the early 1980s. The last serious outbreaks of locusts occurred during 1962-1963, although with good rainfall in Sudan and other parts of the Sahel from 1985 to 1988, large outbreaks have since occurred across the Sahel, North Africa and into Arabia.

White Storks have frequently been witnessed accumulating at locust plagues, sometimes in flocks of over 150,000 birds. Such numbers of birds have the potential to clear locusts from some 140 ha per day, making them a very useful agent of control in some localized areas. However, they can make no impact on vast swarms. On the other hand, the inhibition of locust plagues limits an important source of food for White Storks, especially in the west where locust numbers tended to remain high without much fluctuation from year to year. It is significant that the onset of the steady decline of the western subpopulation of White Storks breeding in France and south-west Germany began in 1961, just as large locust swarms were eradicated from West Africa (Dallinga & Schoenmakers 1989).

Hunting

The shooting and trapping of White Storks during their migration and in their winter quarters have attracted a lot of attention and have often been identified as major factors in the decline of the population. Certainly, hunting is the major cause of mortality reported in ringing returns, but these data are heavily biased towards recoveries made by the hunters themselves.

Intensive hunting occurs principally in Syria and Lebanon, affecting the eastern subpopulation as it migrates to and from Africa (Schulz 1988). Rough estimates suggest that the number of White Storks shot each year as they pass through Syria and Lebanon is 4,000-6,000, with a further 2,000-3,000 killed in other areas of the wintering quarters. This represents about 1-2 per cent of the eastern subpopulation, but in view of the high natural mortality of the species (27-39 per cent; see **Population dynamics**, above) this is hardly significant.

The western subpopulation suffers comparable hunting pressure only in Mali where many hundreds, perhaps up to a few thousands of storks are killed each year in the Niger inundation zone (Thauront 1989). A few hundreds are also killed annually in northern Nigeria. Again, this mortality is not significant for the population as a whole, but it could affect certain local groups that breed and winter together.

In general, it seems that hunting at current levels is not as important a factor as the previous impacts. However, if the population of White Storks continues to decline, the number of birds killed will rise as a proportion of the population and could contribute to local extinctions. Therefore, steps should be taken to control hunting before this stage is reached.

Ringing

White Storks regulate their body temperatures in hot climates by defecating on their legs: the evaporation of the moisture from the faeces helps to cool the blood, but builds up layers of dry uric acid several millimetres thick. Such deposits can form a hard layer around and underneath any leg-ring that has been fitted to the bird, especially if it is fitted to the tibiotarsus (i.e. the upper leg), constricting the flow of blood and preventing the bird from bending its leg. The level of mortality caused by this method of marking birds could be significant: in some European countries nearly 70 per cent of offspring are leg-ringed, and an estimated 5 per cent of these young birds (i.e. 3 per cent of annual production of young) per year die from ring-related ailments (Schulz 1987). Many others clearly suffer great distress so methods of monitoring White Stork movements (such as satellite telemetry or patagial wing-tags) should be used instead. This recommendation does not apply to the feral birds that winter wholly in Europe: they should continue to be leg-ringed.

Overhead cables

In some Range States (e.g. Austria, Spain, GDR, Israel), the proliferation of pylons and overhead cables has caused concern because storks collide with them, especially during poor weather or when young leave nests built on the pylons themselves. Collisions can result in electrocution as well as physical damage if the wires are close together. This is not usually a serious cause of mortality, but can be locally significant (Fiedler & Wissner 1986): since it can be easily avoided by marking certain stretches of the cables with coloured bollards and by making nests on the pylons safer, this ought to be done.

Ingestion of synthetic chemicals

To what degree White Storks suffer from chemical contamination as a result of consuming insects, birds and rodents treated with organophosphate and organochlorine pesticides has not been established. Direct effects have been reported only rarely, most frequently from Israel where parties of birds have died after taking mice killed with rodenticides applied to alfalfa crops. It is possible that accumulations of pesticides in their body-fat may affect the breeding performance or migratory ability of White Storks, but no data are available about the toxicology of the various compounds involved with respect to the stork, and current evidence suggests that any effects would in any case affect relatively few birds in small areas (Büthe *et al.* 1989). However, this matter deserves further research and measures need to be taken to prevent gratuitous or careless spraying of pesticides by providing better expertise and training in control programmes.

Perhaps more important than pesticide application in Africa has been the high levels of polychlorinated biphenyls (PCBs) recorded in the carcasses of birds collected in Israel and in addled eggs collected in Germany and Holland (Büthe *et al.* 1989; Schulz 1988). These chemicals, produced by the combustion of plastics and other waste materials from the electronics industry, are known to severely reduce avian breeding success. Thus, the accumulation of PCBs in Europe seems to pose a greater threat to White Storks than pesticides ingested in Africa. This matter requires urgent investigation and appropriate action.

COVERAGE BY EXISTING INTERNATIONAL LAW

The implementation of the provisions of an eventual governing Agreement for the conservation of the White Stork can be considerably enhanced by linking them to specific requirements of existing domestic and, in particular, international legislation. Nearly all Range States have afforded formal protection to the White Stork as a species, prohibiting its killing or other forms of disturbance. However, much still remains to be done in respect of habitats in the breeding and wintering quarters and along the main migration paths. This deficiency can best be redressed by adhering to the major international conventions that apply to the White Stork and thus complementing any future Agreement under the Bonn Convention itself. More details of the legislation listed below are given elsewhere in this volume, and in Lyster (1985).

Bonn Convention on the Conservation of Migratory Species of Wild Animals

It should be noted that Parties to the governing Agreement need not necessarily be Parties to the Bonn Convention itself. Clearly, any Range State in this situation should consider full accession to the Bonn Convention in order to participate fully in its overall operation through the Standing Committee and Scientific Council.

Ramsar Convention on Wetlands of International Importance Especially as Waterfowl Habitat

There are no appendices of threatened species in the Ramsar Convention. Internationally important wetlands are identified according to criteria established by the Parties, most recently reviewed at the Regina Conference in 1987. In the present context, wetland sites of vital importance for White Storks could be designated according to the criterion *"A wetland should be considered internationally important if it supports an appreciable assemblage of rare, vulnerable or endangered species or subspecies of plant or animal, or an appreciable number of individuals of any one or more of these species"*. At the present time, no Ramsar sites have been declared for their importance as stork habitats, but a number of potential areas could be readily identified especially certain stretches of European riverine habitat (e.g. of the Danube, Rhine, Ebro, Charente, Nestos, Sava and Drava).

Berne Convention on the Conservation of European Wildlife and Natural Habitats

The White Stork is included in Appendix II of the Berne Convention. This qualifies it for special legislative and administrative measures to protect its habitat, with special regard for the maintenance of habitats. Moreover, as a migratory species, the White Stork attracts coverage not only in its European breeding grounds, but also during migration and in its winter quarters. Parties to the Berne Convention (which include the important Range States of Turkey and Senegal) are thus encouraged to take coordinated conservation initiatives outside those areas within their jurisdiction, for example by sponsoring exchange, training and research of workers from other countries and by ameliorating the environmental impacts of development aid schemes.

African Convention on the Conservation of Nature and Natural Resources

The White Stork is included in Class A of the African Convention, affording it strict protection from killing or capture. The Convention also provides for the establishment of conservation areas, and in Article VII calls on Parties to *"manage aquatic environments whether in fresh, brackish or coastal water, with a view to minimizing deleterious effects of any water and land-use practice which might adversely affect aquatic habitats"*. A number of existing protected areas in Africa (e.g. the Serengeti National Park and associated areas in Tanzania and the Luangwa National Park in Zambia) are important for storks, but the coverage needs to be extended.

European Community Directive on the Conservation of Wild Birds

The White Stork is included in Annex I of the Birds Directive. This confers special protection status on the bird and its habitat, including breeding, resting and wintering sites (especially wetlands) within the European Community. Important areas should be designated as *Special Protection Areas* where conservation of the White Stork has a higher priority than development or recreational uses. In contrast with the previous conventions, however, there is an enforcement agency, namely the European Commission, that can take Member States before the European Court if they fail to meet their obligations under the Birds Directive.

Table 3: List of Important Bird Areas in the EC where significant numbers of White Storks occur (Grimmett & Jones 1989). *Note:* Protection of these sites can only be one part of a conservation programme for the White Stork since it is a widely dispersed species.

Federal Republic Germany
Sorge Niederung
Donau-Tal
Aisch-Regnitz-Grund
Dümmersee
Drömling
Aller-Niederung

Greece
Evros Delta Nature Reserve
Nestos Delta
Limni Kerkinitis
Artzan Marshes
Lakes Volvi and Langada
Limni Cheimaditis/Zazari
Limni Mikra Prespa National Park
Limni Orestiada-Kastoria
Ori Timfi/Smolikas National Park
Ekvoles Kalamas
Limni Limnopoula
Ekvoli/Stena Acherondas
Amvrakikos Kolpos
Limnothalassa Mesolonghion
Limnothalassa Kalogria
Kolpos Kallonis
Pangion Oros
Limni Agras

Portugal
Tejo Estuary
Sado Estuary Nature Reserve
Guadiana River
Rio Formosa
Algarve coast
Castro-Marim Nature Reserve
Castro Verde
Elvas
Moura-Safara
Evora

Spain
Doñana National Park
Embalse del Ebro
Río Moros
Riofrío-Segovia
Valle y Sierra de Alcudia
Sierra de los Canalizos
Sierra de Chorito National Park
El Pardo-Viñuelas
Cortados del Jarama
Llanos de Oropesa
Valle del Tiétar
Embalse de Alcántara
Campo Arañuelo
Embalse de Valdecañas
Embalse de Puerto Peña
Sierra de Montánchez
Trujillo-Torrecillas de la Tiesa
Llanos entre Cáceres y Trujillo
Embalse de Salor
Aldea del Cano
Cáceres-Malpartida-Arroyo de la Luz
Brozas-Membrío
Siruela-Agudo
Granja de Torre Hermosa-Llerena
Mérida-Embalses de Montijo y Prosperina
Volongo
Cheles-Villanueva del Fresno-Barcarrota
Medina-Sidonia
Tarifa

Yet, even this most powerful of conservation tools has failed to halt the decline of the White Stork in the European Community. A large part of the reason is that the birds breed over large areas that are often prime agricultural land, with nests widely dispersed. It is therefore difficult to establish the *Special Protection Areas* that they need, but a small number do exist, either fully designated or with candidate status as proposed by ICBP (*Table 3*). However, there are provisions under Article 3 whereby habitat can be restored, and as agricultural land comes out of production to reduce farm surpluses, opportunities may arise to encourage storks to recolonize some parts of their former range. Special attention should be paid to the progress made by Turkey in joining the European Community as this Range State holds an important breeding population of White Storks, and hosts the most important migration path to Africa.

PROPOSALS FOR INTERNATIONALLY COORDINATED CONSERVATION ACTIONS

The following conservation actions can be implemented successfully only by international cooperation and coordination. This implies the establishment or designation of a coordinating centre, either within an existing organization such as a government wildlife research agency or ICBP, or the founding of a new body specifically charged with coordinating White Stork research and conservation.

Biological research

The population dynamics and breeding ecology of the White Stork have been studied in depth. However, many other basic aspects of its biology have not been described and thus their implications for the bird's conservation remain unknown. These gaps in knowledge span a wide variety of topics that can best be addressed by an internationally coordinated research programme. Such a programme ought to include at least the following studies:

- Feeding ecology in passage and wintering areas.
- Migration energetics to determine food requirements and staging post frequency.
- Movements and habitat use in the passage and wintering areas through use of satellite tracking and remote sensing.
- Impact of pesticide applications on mortality rates.
- Importance of habitat substitutes such as alfalfa crops for supporting migratory and wintering birds.
- Importance of subadult populations oversummering in Africa (especially Tanzania) in overall population dynamics.

The coordinating body should promote projects to investigate those aspects of the biology of the White Stork that have a direct bearing on its conservation. The results of these investigations should be published as widely as possible.

Documentation centres

Effective conservation of the White Stork depends on the availability of information to, among others, politicians, managers, researchers and journalists. This implies that all relevant information should be deposited in one or more easily accessible repositories. All Range State and internationally compiled material should be copied to each of the centres concerned.

The coordinating body should nominate at least two White Stork Documentation Centres, one in Europe and one in Africa.

International censuses

The first international White Stork breeding census, covering north-west and central Europe, was organized by Ernst Schüz in 1934. Since then, there have been three more international censuses, also initiated by Schüz and covering even wider areas of the range, in 1958, 1974 and 1982. Furthermore, there have been more regular, though more recent, counts at key points along the migration routes, such as Gibraltar, the Bosphorus and in Israel. These counts have provided a unique and invaluable set of baseline data from which the recent steep decline in the population was detected and against which the effectiveness of international conservation measures can be evaluated. The coordinating body should ensure that these international censuses are continued and that parts of the breeding range previously omitted (especially in the Far East) are included.

The coordinating body should organize a census of breeding White Storks throughout their range at intervals of not more than ten years. The census should as far as possible within each Range State territory record the following parameters:

- Number of nests occupied by a pair.
- Number of pairs that laid eggs, and the clutch size.
- Number of eggs that hatched in each nest.
- Number of young fledged from each nest.

In addition, notes should be kept of incidents such as predation, weather conditions and any other important observations affecting breeding success. The annual migration counts should also be maintained as a cross-check on the breeding censuses, and to provide a more continuous data set. However, analysis of migrating birds is fraught with difficulty because of the number of variables that can affect the counts (weather, observer bias, time of day, etc.).

Pathological research and monitoring

In many parts of its range, the White Stork is reduced to fragmented populations of small size. It is possible that these birds may be more vulnerable to extinction from causes such as increased parasite load, disease or exposure to toxic chemicals even if other environmental factors remain favourable. The bodies and eggs of White Storks from Europe and the Middle East have been shown to contain high levels of polychlorinated biphenyls (PCBs). These residues are produced by poor disposal of wastes, chiefly from the electronics industry, and could play a major part in reducing breeding success and migratory fitness. However, very little is known about these aspects of White Stork conservation. The coordinating body should therefore institute a monitoring and *post-mortem* programme to determine the cause of death of birds found dead and to analyse the chemical pollution load in various organs, tissues and eggs. Any evidence that certain causes of mortality are significant should be taken into account in conducting other conservation activities.

The coordinating body should:

1. Nominate a White Stork pathological laboratory where whole bodies or samples and eggs can be sent for *post-mortem* analysis.
2. Install pollution monitoring equipment in stork breeding areas close to industrial zones to obtain baseline data on pollution loads.

Register of Experts

As conservation action gathers momentum, more and more people will become involved in the work, and the demands for expert assistance will increase. Thus, the coordinating body should ensure that appropriate expertise can be consulted at short notice.

The coordinating body should establish and maintain a Register of Experts covering all aspects of implementing stork conservation measures.

Conservation management and research training programmes

The conservation of the White Stork will be hampered because of the lack of trained personnel in many parts of its range. Shortages of ecologists, management planners and public awareness specialists are particularly acute. The coordinating body should ensure that selected personnel from Range States where these skills are not available can receive appropriate tuition. It should be made a condition of providing the training that the personnel are then deployed for at least three years in the field for which they have been prepared.

The coordinating body should establish a cooperative programme between Range States to share the resources and transfer the skills needed to implement stork conservation measures.

PROPOSALS FOR RANGE STATE CONSERVATION ACTIONS

Habitat conservation

The habitat types favoured by White Storks for breeding, migration resting places and overwintering largely coincide with landforms highly suitable for farming development, whether for cereal or cash crops, paddyfields or grazing pastures. In the breeding areas, as agricultural methods become more and more intensive, White Storks become increasingly less able to adapt to the changes caused. In particular, the drainage of wet meadows, conversion of rough pasture to monocultural swards or non-rotational crops, canalization and deepening of river courses and application of pesticides affect food supply and foraging ability. These factors drive maturing birds to other areas in search of suitable nesting sites, and lead to reduced breeding success in the established adult population. Within a few years a severe decline begins.

Along the migration routes and in the wintering areas, the effects of agricultural development can be positive or negative. Certain crops, especially alfalfa (*Medicago sativa*) can be helpful as they do not grow very high, are not rain-dependent in occurrence since they are irrigated, and often support relatively high populations of insects such as Lucerne Moth (*Colias electo*) caterpillars that the storks can feed on. The main danger is that the lucerne crops may be treated with highly toxic rodenticides to control mice: the storks take the dead mice and can also succumb to the poison. On the other hand, cash crops like cotton or sugar, or rice paddies, are usually heavily treated with pesticides and so are not only devoid of insects, but also replace natural wetland areas where storks once foraged and could keep cool during the midday heat.

Since the White Stork is a species that generally lives widely dispersed throughout the year, whether breeding or wintering (the population is highly concentrated only during the spring and autumn migration), site-based conservation measures cannot provide the sole solution to the problems facing the species. However, where significant groups of birds do occur regularly, site protection and management policies should be carried out. Such congregations of White Storks include the breeding colonies found in Iberia and other parts of the range in the east, major stop-over sites in Spain, Morocco, Egypt and Sudan, and wintering areas of the western subpopulation in Portugal, Spain, Morocco, Mauritania, Senegal, Mali and Niger.

The purposes of this measure are to institute a system of site protection and management for those places (especially wetlands) where White Storks regularly congregate and to encourage the integration of stork conservation with farming development.

Within their overall land-use planning policies, Range States should carry out actions such as those listed below in order to conserve White Storks:

1. Identify all sites where a significant number of the White Storks occur regularly, whether as breeding, passage or wintering birds.
2. All sites identified above should be accorded strict protection from habitat loss or degradation according to the provisions of national and, where appropriate,

international legislation. Site protection may be zoned, according to size and local circumstances of traditional land use, into core and buffer areas.

3. Prepare White Stork management plans for all protected sites according to accepted international standards e.g. those established by the International Union for the Conservation of Nature and Natural Resources (IUCN).

4. Where full site protection for existing breeding areas is impractical, ensure that these areas are not brought under any more intensive farming than is already being practised.

5. Where White Storks breed widely dispersed, develop large-scale stork management zones where agricultural practice ranges from neutral to positive for stork conservation. (In the European Community, these zones could be designated as *Environmentally Sensitive Areas* or "set-aside" areas, with land-holders receiving management grant-aid under the Agricultural Structures Directive.)

6. Identify and designate as controlled areas regularly used stop-over or wintering sites on agricultural land and ensure that they are not converted for more intensive or harmful agricultural uses (e.g. cash crops).

7. Ensure that pesticides are not applied to any agricultural area while significant numbers of storks are present, if necessary by means of temporary banning orders. Provision should be made for compensating any proven damage to the crops.

8. Where appropriate, identify and include wetlands of international importance for White Storks in the Ramsar List.

9. Carry out detailed assessments of the ecological implications of wetland development projects, whether financed by national or overseas aid budgets with a view to avoiding deterioration of habitat availability for White Storks.

Habitat restoration and recreation

The most important single reason for the decline of the eastern subpopulation of the White Stork is destruction and deterioration of its breeding habitat. These impacts have been especially severe in the north-west of its range where agricultural policies have encouraged drainage and conversion to intensive monocultures of the same lowland pastures and meadows that White Storks depend on for their own food and for feeding their young. In western Germany, at least, measures like erecting nesting platforms, marking overhead power cables, preventing shooting and initiating educational campaigns are of secondary importance. As a way of increasing public awareness of the plight of the White Stork, it has been declared the 'National Bird' of Germany. Several voluntary bodies have been working for many years to slow the storks' decline, among them the former Deutscher Bund für Vogelschutz (now Naturschutzbund Deutschland), Bund für Umwelt- und Naturschutz in Deutschland (BUND) and WWF-Germany. However, habitat management for storks requires periodic flooding of meadows as well as other operations that counter high-productivity agriculture. In an intensively farmed region like western Germany, these practices are not generally welcomed, so only minor successes have been achieved.

Creating small ponds to improve food availability, especially of amphibians, has been a major conservation activity for many years in western Germany. In several 'White Stork regions', small areas of a few hectares were declared protected and could be used only for extensive agriculture. Government-sponsored set-aside schemes were also implemented, although these were often developed without regard for the real needs of White Storks. Moreover, as the Croatian studies mentioned previously indicate, these operations were carried out on far too small a scale. Even in Bergenhusen, a community dubbed the 'German White Stork village' where there were still ten nesting pairs of storks in 1987, no habitat management works beyond some cosmetic exercises have been carried out. Like elsewhere, effort has been chiefly directed at maintaining nest sites, ringing fledglings, providing food in dry summers, and running a stork hospital and breeding centre.

Captive breeding and reintroduction is increasingly being employed as a method of saving White Storks in western Germany, irrespective of the fact that practically no suitable habitat is available for the released birds, and notwithstanding all the attendant problems and considerable recurring costs of maintaining captive stock. Meanwhile, what habitat remains deteriorates further, and wild birds find it harder and harder to feed their young. In spring 1989, a large proportion of the nestlings at Bergenhusen died during a cold spell because of their weakness from lack of food.

Saving, and perhaps enlarging, the western German and other European White Stork populations essentially means one thing: establishing grasslands extending over several hundred hectares, especially in regions where White Storks still breed, where the water-table can be elevated to be at or very close to the ground surface (around Bergenhusen this can be simply achieved by reducing the pumping rate and damming drainage channels). Detailed plans for doing just this in several places have been drawn up, and opportunities to implement them may now be at hand as the EC, and the German Government itself, seek ways to reduce agricultural production. The first steps towards an efficient White Stork conservation programme are now being taken. In Bavaria, the state government and voluntary organizations have jointly prepared an inventory of important White Stork habitats, and assisted by grants from the EC, the Bavarian government has started to buy, restore and manage some of these sites. In Lower Saxony, the state government is promoting a large project to purchase White Stork habitats along the Aller River. Voluntary organizations are seeking support for a large conservation scheme, including habitat management, at Bergenhusen, and here tourism and public interest is being used to help generate the substantial funds required. The relative strength of the population in the east and the inherent dispersive ability of the White Stork gives a good chance for encouraging recolonization in the north-west providing the few remaining areas of occupied habitat can be extended and large new areas of habitat established.

The aim of this measure is therefore to create a sufficient number of suitable breeding sites so that storks can move easily from one to the other. This would mean that sites should initially be situated in and along the entire length of major river flood-plains, for example, the Rhine, Rhône and Danube, thus forming site corridors from which expansion to other areas can take place later. The proximity of sites along the flood-plain corridor should be compatible with local ecological conditions and the dispersal ability and habitat requirements of the White Stork. Similarly, within the recent range of the western subpopulation of the White Stork, river site corridors could be established along the Charente, Loire and Ems to encourage recolonization. In this context it is interesting to note that the State of Florida, U.S.A., is preparing to spend 150 million USD on restoring the natural flow of the Kissimmee River as a way of reducing the river's pollution load and improving fish stocks (*The Economist*, 9 December 1989). Moreover, WWF is initiating a campaign to restore river flood-plains (Braakhekke & Vera 1990).

Range States should identify suitable recolonization areas along river corridors where storks currently breed or recently bred and bring them under management agreements with the landowners. These agreements should prohibit potentially damaging operations to the site and specify those activities that may need to be undertaken to restore its quality, such as:

– Recreating a mosaic of native grassland and meadow habitats.
– Retention or creation and maintenance of ditches, ponds, lakes and other wetland types and their associated fauna.

Legislative review and enforcement

The White Stork can be effectively conserved only if there are appropriate laws in place to deter people from wantonly killing or disturbing the birds, or destroying their habitats. In most Range States there already exists national legislation affording at least nominal protection for individuals of the species. In addition, a number of Range States are contracting parties to international instruments apart from the Bonn Convention itself that cover the bird and/or its habitat, namely:

– The African Convention on the Conservation of Nature and Natural Resources.
– The Ramsar Convention on Wetlands of International Importance especially as Waterfowl Habitat.
– The Berne Convention on the Conservation of European Wildlife and Natural Habitats.
– The European Council Directive on the Conservation of Wild Birds.

The aim of this measure is to facilitate implementation of a governing Agreement under the Bonn Convention by complementing it with the provisions of existing national and international laws.

Range States should carry out the following activities:

1. Review the coverage of domestic legislation to ensure that the White Stork is protected from persecution and that threatened habitats can be safeguarded.
2. Review the extent to which domestic legislation and its implementation meet the requirements of the international instruments listed above with respect to the White Stork, where the Range State is also a contracting party to those instruments. Any deficiencies revealed should be corrected.
3. Eligible Range States that are not already contracting parties to the appropriate international instruments listed above should consider accession to them and then carry out the review mentioned in (2) above.
4. Range states that are not contracted to the Bonn Convention should seriously consider acceding to it.

Public awareness

Throughout the greater part of its breeding range, the White Stork is a visitor that nests in close proximity to man. The birds' arrival each spring coincides with a natural increase in human birth-rate, and the White Stork has become a widely welcomed traditional symbol of fertility. It is one of the most well-known birds in Europe and is accorded almost universal respect and protection.

However, the White Stork is not so specially recognized elsewhere on its migration route or in its wintering quarters. Therefore it is more difficult to elicit support among and participation of local people in these countries for the conservation measures that the White Stork requires.

The purpose of this measure is to generate and distribute information in various forms that will explain the overall aims of the White Stork Management Agreement, and in particular the specific activities being proposed that may affect the interests of local people. A good example of this sort of work is the distribution of posters in West Africa by ICBP-France (Terrasse 1986).

Range States should augment any field or other conservation activities relating to the White Stork with a programme of public awareness and communication designed to suit the particular circumstances of the project concerned.

Overhead cable management

The White Stork is vulnerable to colliding with overhead cables while taking off or landing, especially when alarmed or during bad weather. Young birds may kill themselves as they leave a nest constructed on a pylon. On the other hand, the erection of pylons may provide nesting sites in areas where suitable sites are scarce. This can be helpful but also attracts the White Storks towards danger.

The purpose of this measure is to minimize if not eliminate the hazards posed to White Storks by overhead cables. Where White Storks regularly occur as breeding, passage or wintering birds in the vicinity of existing or planned overhead cables, Range States should carry out one or more of the activities listed below:

1. Where mortality of White Storks is particularly severe, arrange for the cables to be buried.
2. Where occasional mortality of White Storks occurs, arrange for the overhead cables to be clearly marked with bollards or some similar device and for the wire spacing to be wide enough to prevent electrocution.
3. Where White Storks use pylons for nesting, ensure that young leaving the nest are shielded from falling on to the overhead cables.
4. Where nests exist on pylons, ensure that they are not disturbed or destroyed by routine maintenance which should be deferred to the non-breeding season.

Pest control assessment

The application of pesticides to control rodents, birds, locusts, army worms and other crop pests can pose a lethal hazard for White Storks during migration and in their wintering quarters. Reports from some parts of the birds' range indicate that hundreds of storks can die after eating the carcasses of pests soon after application of chemical control agents (mainly organophosphate or organochlorine compounds). It is also possible that insidious long-term effects can occur as the chemicals accumulate in the fatty tissue of the bird, causing death when the fats are metabolized during periods of high activity, e.g. during migration or while feeding young.

The impact of chemical control agents on White Storks is compounded by the fact that some (e.g. carbamat and dieldrin on locusts, fenitrothion on army worms and fenthion on queleas) are often applied by subcontractors to aid programmes, who may carry out the work irrespective of its need or efficacy. Thus, temporary and local abundances of grasshoppers of non-migratory species may be sprayed even though they do not pose any significant agricultural threat. Quelea flocks change their roosting places frequently: by the time a control team arrives, the vast majority of birds may already have moved away, yet the full dose of chemical is applied as contracted, leaving highly poisonous carcasses on the ground which may be eaten by storks, or even picked up by local people.

The purpose of this measure is to reduce the actual or potential mortality caused to White Storks by pest control programmes. In areas where significant numbers of White Storks regularly occur, Range States should endeavour to improve the standards of their pest control programmes, whether financed directly or from overseas aid, by regularly and on a case-by-case basis assessing their need and efficacy. This implies carrying out at least the following activities:

1. Ensuring that pest control programmes financed by overseas aid agencies of Range States are subject to the same conditions and safeguards as those conducted domestically.
2. Including a biologist trained in pest identification and ecology as an integral member of pest control teams and taking due account of his/her advice about the necessity of control in a specific instance.
3. Ensuring that subcontractors are well trained in the application of the specific chemicals being applied and that dose rates are not exceeded or excess chemicals dumped.
4. Carrying out post-application surveys to monitor the effects of application on the target as well as non-target species.

Population survey and monitoring

Despite the fact that the White Stork has been and continues to be one of the most intensively studied bird species in the world, nearly all the information available refers to the breeding range. The biology and ecology of the White Stork is poorly known elsewhere, during migration and in its wintering areas. This large gap in knowledge needs to be plugged if a future Agreement is to have maximum effect. Moreover, the constantly changing situation in the breeding range, which will itself be affected by the very implementation of these guidelines, has to be carefully documented and analysed.

The purpose of this measure is to maintain adequate and up-to-date coverage of the ecology, population dynamics and distribution of the White Stork within Range States (*Figure 3*). Range States should carry out at least the activities listed below in order to obtain basic information regarding the status, distribution and ecology of the White Stork within their territories.

1. Prepare maps of all existing or recently occupied areas used for breeding, resting or wintering, with details of number of birds involved. Such maps to be updated at least every five years.
2. Record and evaluate the importance of habitats used for various activities such as feeding, resting and nesting.
3. Record and evaluate the causes of mortality to White Storks.
4. Record and relay to the appropriate authority (or White Stork coordinating body) details of any leg-rings or other marks observed or found on storks.
5. In the breeding areas, conduct annual surveys of nests in at least two key areas, and record the following parameters:

   – Dates of arrival of first and last pairs at nest.
   – Total number of suitable nests present in the area.
   – Number of new nests built.
   – Number of old and new nests occupied by a pair.
   – Number of pairs that laid eggs, and clutch size.
   – Number of eggs that hatched in each old or new nest.
   – Number of young fledged from each old or new nest.

In addition, notes should be kept of incidents such as predation, weather conditions and any other important observations affecting breeding success.

Trapping, hunting and poisoning controls

The White Stork is subject to mortality from direct human persecution and indirectly from other human activities aimed at killing larger carnivores such as foxes and jackals. Hunting is most prevalent in Syria and Lebanon where several thousand birds are shot each year during the migration periods. Much of this

Figure 3: Little is known of the movements, habitat use and feeding ecology of storks on their wintering grounds, here in Kenya. (*Photo:* P. Goriup)

killing is simply for target practice. In the Sahel region, particularly in Niger and Nigeria, thousands of wintering storks are trapped using snares set around wetlands. These birds are sold for food. In some parts of the breeding andwintering range, poison bait is put out to kill larger carnivores: storks may eat the bait instead.

The purpose of this measure is to prevent this unnecessary and harmful level of mortality in the White Stork population. Range States should ensure that their legislation prohibits any killing of White Storks by any method whatsoever. Incidental killing of White Storks by careless laying of poison baits or similar methods should also be subject to penalties.

ACKNOWLEDGEMENTS

The research carried out during the preparation of this paper was originally supported by a grant from the Commission of the European Community. Compilation and translations of German texts were undertaken by Eve Imboden. The authors are most grateful for the expert advice and material support from the staff of ICBP, DBV and WWF-Germany. The text of this paper has benefited from the constructive comments made by Goetz Rheinwald, Judith Johnson, Richard Grimmett and Tobias Salathé.

REFERENCES

BRAAKHEKKE, W. G. & VERA, F. (1990) Floodplain conservation in Europe: what chances? *WWF Reports*, December 1989/January 1990.

VON BÜTHE, A., HEIDEMANN, A. PETERAT, B. &. TERNES, W. (1989) Schadstoffbelastung des Weissstorchs *Ciconia ciconia* durch Schwermetalle, persistente pestizide und industriechemikalien. Pp. 415-422 in G. Rheinwald, J. Ogden & H. Schulz, eds. *Proceedings 1st International Stork Conservation Symposium.* Schriftenreihe des Dachverbandes Deutscher Avifaunisten 10. Braunschweig.

COLLAR, N. J. & ANDREW, P. (1988) *Birds to watch: the ICBP world checklist of threatened birds.* Cambridge, U.K.: International Council for Bird Preservation (Techn. Publ. 8).

CRAMP, S. & SIMMONS, K. E. L. (eds.) (1977) *The birds of the Western Palearctic,* Vol. 1. Oxford.

CREUTZ, G. (1988) *Der Weissstorch.* Wittenberg Lutherstadt: A. Ziemen.

DALLINGA, J. H. & SCHOENMAKERS, S. (1989) Population changes of the White Stork since the 1850s in relation to food resources. Pp. 231-262 in G. Rheinwald, J. Ogden & H. Schulz, eds. *Proceedings 1st International Stork Conservation Symposium.* Schriftenreihe des Dachverbandes Deutscher Avifaunisten 10. Braunschweig.

FIEDLER, G. & WISSNER, A. (1966) Freileitungen als tödliche Gefahr für Weissstörche. *Beih. Veröff. Naturschutz Landschaftspflege Bad. Württ.* **43**: 257-270.

GALLAGHER, M. D. (1989) The White Stork in Oman, eastern Arabia. Pp. 327-330 in G. Rheinwald, J. Ogden & H. Schulz, eds. *Proceedings 1st International Stork Conservation Symposium.* Schriftenreihe des Dachverbandes Deutscher Avifaunisten 10. Braunschweig.

GOODERS, J. E., ed. (1969) *Birds of the world* **1**: 149-152.

GRIMMETT, R. F. A. & JONES, T. A. (1989) *Important bird areas in Europe.* Cambridge, U.K.: International Council for Bird Preservation (Techn. Publ. 9).

HORIN, O. (1989) Survey of White Stork migration: Israel, spring 1984. Pp. 307-316 in G. Rheinwald, J. Ogden & H. Schulz, eds. *Proceedings 1st International Stork Conservation Symposium.* Schriftenreihe des Dachverbandes Deutscher Avifaunisten 10. Braunschweig.

IUCN. (1987) *Directory of wetlands of international importance.* Cambridge, U.K.: International Union for the Conservation of Nature and Natural Resources.

KANYAMIBWA, S., SCHIERER, A., PRADEL, R. & LEBRETON, J. D. (1990) Changes in the adult annual survival rates in a western European population of the White Stork *Ciconia ciconia. Ibis* **132**: 27-35.

KASPAREK, M. & KILIÇ, A. (1989) Zum Zug des Weissstorchs durch die Türkei. Pp. 297-306 in G. Rheinwald, J. Ogden & H. Schulz, eds. *Proceedings 1st International Stork Conservation Symposium.* Schriftenreihe des Dachverbandes Deutscher Avifaunisten 10. Braunschweig.

LACK, D. (1966) *Population studies in birds.* Oxford: Clarendon.

LYSTER, S. (1985) *International wildlife law.* Cambridge: Grotius Publications.

MAJUMDAR, N. (1989) Past and present wintering distribution of the White Stork in India and suggestions for its conservation. Pp. 373-378 in G. Rheinwald, J. Ogden & H. Schulz, eds. *Proceedings 1st International Stork Conservation Symposium.* Schriftenreihe des Dachverbandes Deutscher Avifaunisten 10. Braunschweig.

MOLENAAR, J. G. (1983) Agriculture and its effects on birdlife in Europe. Pp. 13-36 in *Agriculture and birdlife in Europe.* Report of the 13th Conference of the European Continental Section of ICBP, Doorn, Netherlands, 27-30 November, 1981. Cambridge: U.K.: International Council for Bird Preservation.

RAVIV, M. (1989) Ring recoveries of the White Stork in Israel and Sinai, 1909-1982. Pp. 317-324 in G. Rheinwald, J. Ogden & H. Schulz, eds. *Proceedings 1st International Stork Conservation Symposium.* Schriftenreihe des Dachverbandes Deutscher Avifaunisten 10. Braunschweig.

RHEINWALD, G., OGDEN, J. & SCHULZ, H., eds. (1989) Weissstorch – White Stork. *Proceedings 1st International Stork Conservation Symposium.* Schriftenreihe des Dachverbandes Deutscher Avifaunisten 10. Braunschweig.

ROCKINGHAM-GILL, D. V. & MUNDY, P. J. (1989) Status and distribution of the White Stork in Zimbabwe. Pp. 361-364 in G. Rheinwald, J. Ogden & H. Schulz, eds. *Proceedings 1st International Stork Conservation Symposium.* Schriftenreihe des Dachverbandes Deutscher Avifaunisten 10. Braunschweig.

SCHIERER, A. (1986) Vierzig Jahre Weissstorch-Forschung und Schutz im Elsass. *Beih. Veröff. Naturschutz Landschaftspflege Bad. Württ.* **43**: 329-341.

SCHNEIDER, M. (1988) Periodisch überschwemmtes Dauergrünland ermöglicht optimalen Bruterfolg des Weissstorches in der Save-Stromaue. *Vogelwarte* **34**: 164-173.

SCHULZ, H. (1987) Thermoregulatorisches Beinkoten des Weissstorchs (*Ciconia ciconia*). Analyse des Verhaltens und seiner Bedeutung für Verluste bei beringten Störchen im afrikanischen Winterquartier. *Vogelwarte* **34**: 107-117.

SCHULZ, H. (1988) *Weissstorchzug. Ökologie, Gefährdung und Schutz des Weissstorchs in Afrika und Nahost. WWF-Umweltforschung* 3. Weikerscheim: Josef Margraf.

SCHÜZ, E. (1936) Internationale Bestandsaufnahme am Weissen Storch 1934. *Orn. Mber.* **44**: 33-41.

SCHÜZ, E. (1962) Über die nordwestliche Zugscheide des Weissen Storchs. *Vogelwarte* **21**: 269-290.

TERRASSE, M. (1986) Projet d'éducation pour la Cicogne Blanche en Afrique Occidentale. *Beih. Veröff. Naturschutz Landschaftspflege Bad. Württ.* **43**: 343-346.

THAURONT, M. (1989) Donneés sur la distribution et les conditions d'hivernage de la Cicogne Blanche *Ciconia ciconia* au Mali. Report to the 17th Conference of the European Continental Section of ICBP, Adana, Turkey, 15-20 May 1989.

WALSH, J. F. (1989) Wetlands of the moist-savanna region of West Africa, and their importance to migratory White Storks *Ciconia ciconia*. Pp. 271-280 in G. Rheinwald, J. Ogden & H. Schulz, eds. *Proceedings 1st International Stork Conservation Symposium.* Schriftenreihe des Dachverbandes Deutscher Avifaunisten 10. Braunschweig.

EDUCATIONAL PROJECTS FOR THE CONSERVATION OF MIGRATORY BIRDS IN THE INNER DELTA OF THE NIGER (MALI)

MARC THAURONT[1] & BOUBA FOFANA[2]

1 *ICBP-France, 29 rue du Mont-Valérien, 92210 Saint-Cloud, France*
2 *Association Malienne pour la Protection des Oiseaux, B.P. 91, Mopti, Mali*

ABSTRACT

The inner delta of the Niger is, with its 30,000 km², one of the most important wetlands of the western Sahel. It is located in Mali, at the confluence of the rivers Bani and Niger The 20,000 km² flooded each year provide a rich source of natural resources for this area: pasture land, fishing and important arable land. The flood-plains and lakes are the winter habitat of about 350 different species of birds numbering several million individuals during the winter period. However, drought, large dams and irrigation systems, and poaching are greatly affecting the region.

Confronted with this problem, the Malian Government, the IUCN and WWF decided in 1984 to start a conservation project for the delta. Against this background an environmental education package for schools, entitled WALIA, was instituted. At the same time, the French Section of the ICBP under the Migratory Birds Programme initiated, in 1985, an educational project on the conservation of migratory birds and their habitats, using the White Stork (*Ciconia ciconia*) as a primary example.

This paper describes the essence of the two projects and the methods used by each party, and also stresses the importance of their cooperation with each other. Some aspects of the evaluation are presented in order that lessons may be learnt for the future.

INTRODUCTION

Although a large part of Mali is located in the Sahara desert, the diversity of the natural habitats of this country is fairly important. The area includes savannas and dry Sudanian forests (in the south), as well as sandy plateaus and cliffs (Dogon country), and important flood-plains.

The inner delta of the Niger is therefore, with its area of 30,000 km², one of the most important wetlands of the western Sahel. It is located at the confluence of the Bani and the Niger, rising in the Fouta Djallon (Guinea) where annual rainfall exceeds 1,800 mm. The evolution of the river courses and the important annual floods have, over the centuries, created a very dense network of wetlands where branches of the rivers, lakes, ponds and flood-plains succeed alternately (*Figure 1*).

129

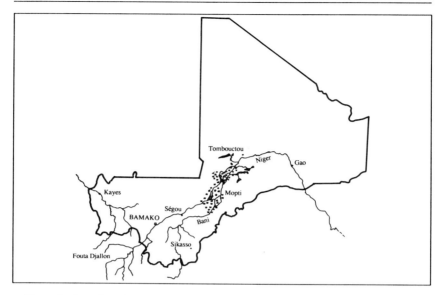

Figure 1: Location of the main wetlands of the inner river delta of the Niger in Mali.

EXCEPTIONAL NATURAL RESOURCES

The area of 20,000 km² flooded every year constitutes a remarkable natural resource for this region.   The productivity of the meadows (composed predominantly of "Bourgou" (*Echinocloa stagnina*) is five to ten times higher than in the rest of the Sahelian area. Therefore, pressures caused by human activities such as fishing, livestock raising, agriculture and hunting for food, though traditional, are heavier in the delta.

During an average year, the delta produces 100,000 tons of rice and sugar cane and 100,000 tons of fish, and feeds 1 million cattle and 2 million goats and sheep. It therefore constitutes a vital centre for the country's economy, with 20 per cent of the Malian cattle and with fishing representing 8 per cent of the total value of the country's exports.

The wildlife shows similar impressive numbers – over 130 species of fish, numerous mammals (manatees, hippopotamus, wart-hogs ...) and a particularly rich avifauna. Indeed, the flood-plains and the lakes shelter 350 bird species, 31 per cent being of Palearctic origin (Drijver & Marchand 1985). During the winter season several million birds use the delta, including very large populations of Garganey (*Anas querquedula*), Pintail (*Anas acuta*), Marsh Terns (*Chlidonias* spp.), Ruff (*Philomachus pugnax*) and Yellow Wagtails (*Motacilla flava*) (Jarry & Roux 1987; J. Trotignon & J. Skinner, pers. comm.).

CONSEQUENCES OF THE DROUGHT AND CONSERVATION OF THE DELTA

The conservation of this area is as vital for the economy of Mali as for the survival of the birds. However, the delta has been facing regular droughts since 1969 (with peaks in 1972-1973 and 1984/1985/1986, G. Jarry pers. comm.) and these have broken up the ecological balance of the area. The vegetation cover has been affected both by water shortage and over-grazing, and by the felling of trees by local populations. Above all, the absence of any regeneration, due to grazing by goats, poses a serious threat to the few existing forests. Many ponds and lakes are now dry, and the impact of flood control by means of hydraulic installations (dams of Markala and Selingue; irrigation system of the Niger Office) is not precisely known. The loss of productivity caused by these factors has also created other problems directly affecting the fauna. Thus, poaching is a common problem, despite a hunting ban imposed by the Malian authorities since 1978. Hunting represents a traditional activity which plays an important role in the structure of Malian society. The populations of many species of mammal and bird, such as the African Darter (*Anhinga rufa*), have decreased dramatically because of poaching and drought.

In view of these problems, the Malian Government, IUCN and WWF decided in 1984 to join forces in an attempt to improve the management of the environment, and a conservation project for the delta was consequently set up. Its objective is to help Mali to define a management guide for this region which would serve as a model for integrated utilization of the natural resources of the country.

The main objective of the first phase of the project has been a better understanding of the delta itself, on socio-economic and ethnological criteria as well as at the biological level. One of the methods used has been the development of a dialogue with the local populations with a view to proposing realistic measures to overcome, in the future, problems linked to the viability and perennial character of the natural diversity and productivity of the area.

As well as taking these steps, it appeared necessary from the start to do some groundwork in order to increase the awareness of the local populations. It was, therefore, with this perspective in mind that WALIA – an environmental education project for schools – was started. At the same time, and within the framework of the Migratory Birds Programme, the French Section of ICBP initiated in 1985 a conservation project for the White Stork (*Ciconia ciconia*) in West Africa where hunting still constitutes the major cause of regression for this species. The delta being one of the regions where this problem seems most acute (according to ringing records – Thauront & Duquet 1991), we decided to conduct a long-term project in this area. The ornithological value of the delta and the problems facing the area persuaded us not to restrict the project to the White Stork but to develop an educational project on the conservation of Palearctic and Afrotropical migratory birds and their habitats. An agreement has been signed with IUCN, and joint visits have been organized with WALIA in the schools of the Fifth District of Mali, which includes the Niger inner delta.

WALIA: AN EDUCATIONAL ENVIRONMENTAL MAGAZINE

The project team has produced a magazine aimed at the 4,000 secondary school children in the area of Mopti. It is entitled *WALIA*, the name of Abdim's Stork (*Ciconia abdimii*) in peuhl. This bird is believed to be a good-luck symbol and it announces the return of the rainy season. The objective of the magazine is to help the children to better understand and protect the environment in which they live. It acts as a forum for exchanges of ideas, thoughts and long-term interventions.

In a first phase, the activities of WALIA were limited to the production of the magazine and to its distribution in the schools through an education team. Its task was to explain the articles to the children and to test their understanding of the magazine. Various topics were covered by the magazine, such as the functioning of ecosystems, health hygiene and knowledge of the flora and fauna, but it also included educational games, readers' letters, drawing competitions and the like. Thus a didactical tool, so far missing in the area, was offered to the local schools. It is during this first phase that a team from the ICBP French Section started to collaborate with WALIA, introducing new educational materials such as audio-visual aids and display boards.

WALIA has been in its second phase since the school year 1987/1988. The project has a new objective, which is the involvement of the school children in resource management and sustainable development. That is to say, WALIA wishes to go beyond the production of a magazine in order to encourage a responsible participation of the children based on development activities whilst improving the means and methods of their presentation. WALIA equipped itself with new structures and diversified its activities to cover two main areas: production of educational materials and interactive visits to local schools. The magazine will continue to be the main method, but graphic material (e.g. posters and display boards) and audio-visual aids will also be produced, based on the topics covered in the magazine, the IUCN project results and the school children's suggestions, or other services (Eaux et Forêts). In this way, WALIA will try to adapt its material to a more stimulating type of presentation with the object of making its message more interesting.

This educational programme will have three main objectives:

- To ensure wide circulation of the magazine *WALIA* and to encourage the exchange of ideas with the schools in order to increase interest in the subjects discussed.
- To make schools aware of their own responsibility for organizing the circulation of *WALIA* and for collecting and providing information to be published in the magazine.
- To try to make young people aware of their responsibility concerning environmental issues related to development projects in their country. Groups of pupil volunteers will be tested on the means of increasing awareness of the conservation situation and disseminating information within their community.

ICBP FRENCH SECTION PROJECT

The main objective of the project arranged by the ICBP French Section was to increase awareness of, and stimulate interest in, conservation amongst school children, basing the approach on birdlife. This course was chosen for three reasons. Firstly, the early interest European and North American ornithologists have shown in pioneering conservation efforts. This is further explained by the immense emotional richness in observer obtains in studying birds, creatures easily observed and of great morphological and behavioural diversity, especially in relation to their migration. Lastly, birds are good environmental indicators and therefore very useful elements in the direct approach to solving environmental problems.

That is why the following topics were taken up for our campaign from October 1986 to March 1987:

- Presentation of the great variety of the Malian avifauna.
- Bird biology and ecology.

Figure 2: Display panels on migrants are explained to school children who then have to respond to specific questions in their exercise books. (*Photo*: M. Thauront)

— The phenomena of migration patterns, bird ringing, threats to migratory birds (habitat loss, hunting, etc.).

Malian culture has a strong and pervasive verbal tradition and that is why we have attached so much importance to using educational aids that stimulate interactive dialogue with the pupils and indeed with the rest of the local population as well. Thus we have used display panels, drawings and slide shows, the whole being combined to produce a lively presentation based on a narrative story, games, drawings and direct dialogue with school children.

School visits were divided into two sessions. The first visit was to teach pupils to observe the variety of birdlife that exists. With this in view, display panels presenting four species of Malian bird were used in conjunction with exercise books on the cover of which there were outlines of the same birds. After some explanation, the object of the game-competition was to recognize the birds on the exercise books with the help of the panels, and in this way learn their names. After this, each pupil was invited to colour in the bird on the exercise book with the help of the panels and the pencils we had supplied (*Figure 2*). Lastly, a slide show was given in the evening, often with the whole village in attendance. This event included games, and discussion about what had been seen during the day.

The object of the second visit was to expand the project to portray bird habitat, with a special presentation on migration phenomena. For this, the team consisting of a member of the ICBP French Section, the ICBP Malian representative and an engineer sent by the Malian Eaux and Forêts Department, again used display panels. Here the presentation took a theoretical form, with pupils acting as various characters. One pupil was a 'dougou-dougou' (the Malian name for Garganey, *Anas querquedula*), which was ringed and which was making its way towards Europe, etc. Afterwards, there was a general question time for pupils.

AN EXAMPLE OF UNITED EFFORT

The entire preparation of the project had been improved with the help and collaboration of WALIA at their meetings in both Europe and Mali. In particular, our venue had been announced and prepared in the Magazine *WALIA*. Meetings between the two parties took place to evaluate progress; and from this it emerged that by using instructional aids it had been possible to awaken a greater interest and make a larger impact than otherwise would have been the case. In this way, WALIA was able to benefit from the experience for preparation of its own second phase.

Pupil participation was very good despite the fact that they were rather timid as a result of not being used to this type of instruction (using sophisticated materials and a European approach). In total, nearly 4,000 pupils were contacted, and to this number may be added many parents and children who were not at school but who attended and participated in the audio-visual sessions held in the evenings.

Also, WALIA and ICBP were able to exchange materials. The former accepted responsibility for the petrol and logistical support, and lodging expenses, and the latter bought materials (a canoe and a generator) which were left for the WALIA project when the visits were over.

In this part of Mali, very few organizations use schools for disseminating information. Common presentation of our two activities therefore brought about some identity problems. In fact, whereas WALIA had limited means at the time (e.g. one magazine per several pupils) and above all the team had visited each school only once, the ICBP team arrived with full equipment (display panels, projector, exercise books and pencils for everyone). Thus the activities of ICBP have destabilized the approach used by WALIA by giving the impression that the whole project was concerned solely with birds.

CONFLICT OF TWO DIFFERENT APPROACHES: A LESSON FOR THE FUTURE

As an objective for its magazine, WALIA seeks to have a global approach to environmental issues, covering subjects ranging from natural habitats to social health problems. In this way it supports the project which goes further, dealing also with development aid programmes. The ICBP French Section had, on the other hand, decided to use birds as the main input for introducing conservation problems. But in a developing country faced, in the short term, with crucial problems of management of its natural resources, it is difficult to assess whether the bird-oriented message is satisfactorily put across and whether or not it is providing lasting results for conservation. It seems in the long term difficult to carry on with two parallel projects. The local authorities and population would not benefit fully from two projects, each with a fundamentally different approach. On the other hand, the collaboration brought about at the time of the arrival of the ICBP team in Mali allowed for a significant advance both in the techniques used and in creating greater awareness of conservation problems.

It is obvious that migrating birds will benefit in the long term from the work of WALIA and IUCN, although these projects are concentrated only on one part of the Niger inner delta. The WALIA programme is concentrated only on school children, which represents a small percentage of young people. It would be desirable, for example, to follow up the programme with further audio-visual presentations for whole villages in order to reach a wider public. Other organizations, such as Volontaires du Progrès and the U.S. Peace corps, could also play a role in such activities for local people.

On the other hand, numerous other problems exist in this essential area for bird conservation. In fact, basic knowledge of avian biology is still largely lacking. The impact of large dams and irrigation installations on the evolution of bird habitats is still unclear; the legal status and the management methods of the sites listed under the Ramsar Convention are still vague; and there remains the unresolved question of sustainable levels of hunting by the rural population. It is, therefore, of primary importance to integrate all these elements into the conservation programmes presented to the Malians.

The ICBP French Section is prepared to continue to invest in conserving the Malian migratory birds. However, this investment will depend on the projects that IUCN wishes to develop, the need for collaboration expressed by WALIA, and the extent of the desire for strong action on the part of the new Malian Association for the Protection of Birds.

REFERENCES

CURRY, P. J. & SAYER, J. A. (1979) The inundation zone of the Niger as an environment for Palearctic migrants. *Ibis* **121**: 20-40.

DRIJVER, C. A. & MARCHAND, M. (1985) *Taming the floods: environmental aspects of floodplain development in Africa*. Leiden: Leiden University, Centre for Environmental Studies.

FOFANA, B. (1987) Education and awareness. *World Birdwatch* **9(1)**: 9.

IUCN. (1985) Projet de conservation dans le Delta Intérieur du Niger, rapport semestriel Juillet-Décembre 1984. IUCN/CDC 15 pp. Gland: International Union for the Conservation of Nature and Natural Resources.

LAMARCHE, B. (1980) Liste commentée des oiseaux du Mali. *Malimbus* **2(2)**: 121-158.

JARRY, G. & ROUX, F. (1987) Importance, composition et distribution des populations d'anatidés présentes en hiver dans l'ouest africain tropical. *Rev. Ecol. (Terre Vie)*, suppl. **4**: 205-219.

ROUX, F. (1973) Censuses of Anatidae in the Central delta of the Niger and the Senegal delta, January 1972. *Wildfowl* **24**: 63-80.

THAURONT, M. (1986) Ciconia. *Naturopa* **54**: 9-10.

THAURONT, M. (1987) Mali. *World Birdwatch* **9(1)**: 8-9.

THAURONT, M. & DUQUET, M. (1991) Données sur la distribution et les conditions d'hivernage de la Cigogne blanche *Ciconia ciconia* au Mali. *Alauda* **59**: 101-110.

CONSERVATION AND MANAGEMENT OF PELICANS NESTING IN THE PALEARCTIC

ALAIN J. CRIVELLI[1], GEORGE CATSADORAKIS[2],
HANS JERRENTRUP[3], DIONYSSIA HATZILACOS[4] &
TANYU MICHEV[5]

1 *Station Biologique de la Tour du Valat, le Sambuc, 13200 Arles, France*
2 *Oxia-Prespa, 530 77 Agios Germanos, Greece*
3 *P.O. Box 47, 64200 Hrysoupolis, Greece*
4 *22 Anatolikis Thrakis, Papagos-Athens, Greece*
5 *Bulgarian Academy of Sciences, Research and Coordination Centre
for Preservation and Restoration of the Environment,
Gagarin St 2, 1113 Sofia, Bulgaria*

ABSTRACT

The two species of pelican nesting in the Palearctic, the Great White Pelican (*Pelecanus onocrotalus*) and the Dalmatian Pelican (*Pelecanus crispus*) are now vulnerable throughout their distribution range from south-eastern Europe to China. The Palearctic population of the Great White Pelican is estimated to be between 7,345 and 10,500 breeding pairs nesting in 23-25 breeding sites. The Dalmatian Pelican population is estimated to be between 1,900 and 2,700 breeding pairs nesting in 23-24 breeding sites. New data on the breeding biology of both species are presented. Knowledge on feeding ecology, dispersing, migration and wintering are reviewed. Past and present threats include disturbance, drainage of wetlands, hunting, mortality due to electric power lines, pesticides, tourism and degradation of the quality of wetlands. Conservation and management measures are reviewed and evaluated. Recommendations are made in order to stop the decline in numbers of the two species of pelican breeding in the Palearctic, and to enhance their recovery.

INTRODUCTION

The two species of pelican nesting in the Palearctic, the Great White Pelican (*Pelecanus onocrotalus*) and the Dalmatian Pelican (*Pelecanus crispus*) were originally very widely distributed from Europe to western China (Andrews 1899; Newton 1928; Hatting 1963; Kessler 1978). With the coming of industrialization, with agricultural development and with increasing human population pressure, their distribution ranges have shrunk, the number of breeding sites has declined, and there has been a heavy reduction in the size of the population of both species. During the present century the decline in the population of the two species has steadily worsened to the point where they are now protected species in all the countries in which they occur. In addition, for the last ten years the Dalmatian Pelican has been declared "Vulnerable" on a world scale in the ICBP *Red Data Book* (King 1981).

For some strange reason, these two species were almost completely neglected by conservationists for a long time, and very few scientific studies on their ecology, behaviour and population dynamics were undertaken. Fortunately, the ecology of the two species and the problems of their conservation have been studied in detail since 1983 in Greece, Bulgaria, Yugoslavia, Turkey and Iran (Michev 1981; Crivelli & Vizi 1981; Hatzilacos 1986; Crivelli 1987; Crivelli *et al.* 1988; Crivelli *et al.* 1989, 1991).

The aims of this paper are to give an account of the present status of the two species of pelican breeding in the Palearctic, and to provide new data on their breeding biology, dispersion and wintering and on the factors involved in their present decline. An evaluation of the results of the first experimental management carried out over the last few years on these two species is also described. Finally, concrete proposals are made to ensure better protection and management of the two species, in order to halt their decline and to encourage a revival, so that in the future the two pelican species will no longer figure in the red data lists of endangered species.

RANGE, BIOLOGY, DISTRIBUTION AND POPULATION NUMBERS

Crivelli & Schreiber (1984) reviewed the status of the seven species of pelican found throughout the world. They estimated that there were 15,000-20,000 breeding pairs of the Great White Pelicans in the Palearctic and 530-1,380 breeding pairs of Dalmatian Pelicans in the entire world. Previously Crivelli & Vizi (1981) had described the status of the Dalmatian Pelican in each of the countries within its range. Using our own census data, and recent information obtained from colleagues working in other countries, we have been able to revise our estimates of the number of breeding sites and of the total number of breeding pairs of the two species.

A total of 23-25 breeding sites of the Great White Pelican is recorded for the entire Palearctic, and the number of breeding pairs is estimated between 7,345 and 10,500 (*Table 1*). However, the breeding of large colonies of this species is strongly suspected in Iraq and in Pakistan. Although the numbers of breeding pairs in Greece, Romania and the U.S.S.R. have remained stable over the last five years, those in Turkey have greatly declined. The figures for the number of breeding sites and total number of breeding pairs of the Dalmatian Pelican (*Table 2*) have tended to increase or at least remain stable. However, the results should be interpreted with care, since they are due mainly to: (a) the rediscovery of Dalmatian Pelicans nesting in Albania (Bogliani *et al.* 1986; Lamani, pers. comm.) and (b) high numbers of birds published in the different red data books for endangered species of the U.S.S.R. (Bannikov 1978; Gvozdev 1978; Kolosov 1983 and Borodin 1984). These figures for the number of breeding pairs need confirming, as is also the case for the Albanian figures. Whatever the validity of these figures, it is still true that about two-thirds of the breeding pairs and more than a third of the breeding sites of the Dalmatian Pelican are in the U.S.S.R. This highlights the important responsibility of this country as far as the future of the Dalmatian Pelican is concerned. In the other countries where this species breeds, the populations have remained stable over the last five years, except in Turkey and

Table 1: The remaining breeding grounds of *Pelecanus onocrotalus*, with estimated numbers of breeding pairs.

Country	Number of breeding pairs	Number of breeding grounds
Greece	40-150	1
Iran	235-550	3
Iraq	??	??
Pakistan/India	??	??
Romania	3,000-3,500	1
Turkey	500-1,500?	1
U.S.S.R.	3,070-4,300?	16-18
TOTAL	**7,345-10,500**	**23-25**

Key: ? These estimations are not considered reliable due to a lack of accurate and recent censuses.

?? Suspected breeding.

Table 2: The remaining breeding grounds of *Pelecanus crispus*, with estimated numbers of breeding pairs.

Country	Number of breeding pairs	Number of breeding grounds
Albania	70-100?	1
Bulgaria	70-90	1
China	??	??
Greece	125-210	2
Iran	5-10	1
Iraq	??	??
Mongolia	40-50?	1
Romania	36-115	2
Turkey	70-115?	5
U.S.S.R.	1,500-2,000	7-8
Yugoslavia	10-20	1
TOTAL	**1,926-2,710**	**21-22**

Key: ? These estimations are not considered reliable due to a lack of accurate and recent censuses.

?? Suspected breeding.

in China. In the latter country the last remaining known breeding colony of Dalmatian Pelicans disappeared because of the complete drying out of Lop Lake.

For the two species of pelican in general the data on the status of the populations and on changes of population size are still far from satisfactory. We are still a long way from having reliable annual censuses, which would allow correct assessment of population changes of these two endangered species.

Breeding biology
Up until a few years ago, information on the principal variables in the breeding biology of the Great White and Dalmatian Pelicans was still very limited (Cramp *et al.* 1977; Dementiev & Gladkov 1951). Since 1983, we have carried out

detailed studies on the breeding biology, feeding ecology and population dynamics of the two species of pelican nesting at Lake Mikri Prespa in north-western Greece and on the Dalmatian Pelican on a group of coastal lagoons on the Gulf of Amvrakikos. Only a few of these results have so far been published (Hatzilacos 1986; Crivelli 1987); the rest still being in preparation. For this reason we will present only a general summary of the main variables in the breeding biology of the two pelican species nesting in Greece (*Table 3*). Within each pelican colony the nests are not distributed uniformly but are clustered into breeding units of from one to about fifty nests, separated by areas without nests. Although the average number of nests in each of these breeding units is greater in the Great White Pelican than in the Dalmatian Pelican, over the whole range of total colony sizes, this difference is not significant (ANOVA, P >0.05). Elsewhere, however, colonies of Great White Pelicans can contain as many as several hundred pairs (e.g. in the Danube Delta), whereas the Dalmatian Pelican rarely exceeds 250 pairs. There is also no significant difference in clutch size between the two species. The average laying date for the first egg is, however, significantly different between the species (ANOVA, P <0.001), Great White Pelicans laying a good month later than Dalmatian Pelicans. The breeding success as well as the hatching success of the Dalmatian Pelicans nesting at Prespa is significantly higher than that of the Great White Pelican at the same site (Newman & Keuls, P <0.05), but the breeding success and hatching success of the Dalmatian Pelicans nesting at Amvrakikos are not significantly different from either the Dalmatian or Great White Pelicans at Prespa. In both species the highest mortality occurs at the egg stage (infertile eggs, eggs rolling out of the nest). Dalmatian Pelicans can very easily rear two chick to fledging (Crivelli 1987), but this is very rarely seen in the Great White Pelican (Hatzilacos, unpublished data). During the breeding season, predation on the eggs and chicks is very limited (e.g. from *Pica pica*, *Corvus corone*, *Larus cachinnans*). On the other hand, as for example when the water level drops, breeding units can sometimes be completely wiped out by mammalian predators (e.g. by wild boar at Srebarna, Bulgaria, T. Michev, pers. comm.; and dog, wolf or fox at Mikri Prespa, Greece in 1989, Crivelli & Catsadorakis, unpublished data). With the present state of our knowledge of the population dynamics of pelicans it would appear that the reproductive success of the Dalmatian Pelican should be sufficient to ensure an increase in population size, while the success recorded in the case of the Great White Pelican should be sufficient to at least keep the population stable.

Feeding ecology

Great White and Dalmatian Pelicans are strictly piscivorous, although we have found *Triturus* sp. in the diet of Great White Pelicans nesting at Mikri Prespa (Crivelli & Catsadorakis, unpublished data). The Great White Pelicans nesting on Lake Mikri Prespa hardly ever feed on the Prespa lakes, but fly long distances to their feeding grounds (Crivelli 1984), sometimes more than 100 km from the nesting colony (e.g. Lakes Kastoria, Chimaditis, Kerkini and the Axios Delta; Hatzilacos, in prep.)

The lack of shallow water feeding grounds at the nesting sites explains this behaviour, which has also been frequently observed in this species in Iran and in Africa (Guillet & Crowe 1983; Berry *et al.* 1973; D. Scott, pers. comm.). Such movements represent only a very small energy expenditure for these magnificent soarers. In contrast, the Dalmatian Pelicans feed on the Prespa lakes, except for a few weeks at the beginning of the breeding season when they feed at Lake Kastoria (Crivelli 1987). Unlike the Great White Pelican, which feeds almost entirely in groups (communal fishing), the Dalmatian Pelican feeds alone or in

Table 3: Summary of the reproductive biology of the Dalmatian Pelican and the Great White Pelican nesting at Lake Mikri Prespa, north-western Greece.

Parameters	*Pelecanus crispus*		*Pelecanus onocrotalus*
	Lake Prespa (1984–1989, N = 6)	Amvrakikos Gulf (1984–1989, N = 6)	Lake Prespa (1986–1989, N = 4)
Mean ± SD of number of breeding attempts 1983–1989	**142.8 ± 19.2**	**31.7 ± 7.7**	**102.1 ± 20.6**
(range)	(113 – 165)	(12 – 38)	(71 – 139)
Mean ± SD size of breeding units	**10.6 ± 8.8**	**8.8 ± 6.1**	**13.3 ± 10.5**
(range)	(1 – 51)	(1 – 25)	(1 – 52)
Mean date of the first egg laid	**7th of March**	**2nd of March**	**13th of April**
(range)	(19/2 – 18/3)	(5/2 – 19/3)	(7/4 – 16/4)
Mean ± SD annual clutch size	**1.83 ± 0.07**	**1.80 ± 0.10**	**1.93 ± 0.11**
(range)	(1.76 – 1.94)	(1.60 – 1.92)	(1.84 – 2.10)
Mean ± SD hatching success (%)	**65.3 ± 5.8**	**52.3 ± 15.1**	**41.4 ± 7.7**
(range)	(55.8 – 70.3)	(35.5 – 67.8)	(33.0 – 48.1)
Mean ± SD breeding success (chicks/per breeding attempt)	**1.03 ± 0.17**	**0.86 ± 0.24**	**0.64 ± 0.12**
(range)	(0.76 – 1.20)	(0.58 – 1.16)	(0.52 – 0.83)

small groups of two to three birds (Crivelli & Vizi 1981). The composition of the diet of the two species depends almost entirely on the relative abundance of prey species on the feeding grounds, on their spatial and temporal distribution, and to a lesser extent on the behaviour of the prey species. Up until now, we have never been able to demonstrate any food shortage which could, for example, affect the number of birds breeding, or their reproductive success, at any of the sites we have studied.

Dispersion and migration

One of the differences in the life strategies of the Great White Pelican and the Dalmatian Pelican is that the Great White is a true long-distance migrant, while the other is merely dispersive. However, in Asia, Dalmatian Pelicans do undertake lengthy migrations. It is only recently that the dispersion of the Dalmatian Pelican (Crivelli 1987) and the migratory routes and timing of migration of the Great White Pelican have been studied (Crivelli *et al.* 1991). The most important wetlands used during migration and dispersion have now been identified in many countries, especially in south-eastern Europe (*Table 4*). However, this list cannot be considered exhaustive because there are doubtless many important sites from the Middle East to China which remain unknown. The great majority of these sites do not benefit from any conservation measures, and are subject to intense tourist pressure and a wide range of degradations (eutrophication, destruction of shorelines, pollution, etc.) which could all prevent them from being used by pelicans in the future, thus rendering migratory and dispersal movements all the

Table 4: Sites of importance during the pre- and post-breeding dispersal of Dalmatian and Great White Pelicans nesting in the Palearctic.

Species	Major sites	Secondary sites
Dalmatian Pelican	Lake Kerkini (Greece)	Evros Delta (Greece)
	Porto-Lago coastal area (Greece)	Axios Delta (Greece)
	Lake Kastoria (Greece)	Lake Dojran (Greece-Yugoslavia
	Kalamas Delta (Greece)	Lake Marmara (Turkey)
	Burgas coastal area (Bulgaria)	Camaltı Tuzlası (Turkey)
	Menderes Delta (Turkey)	Bandarabbas (Iran)
	Lake Manyas (Turkey)	
	Euphrates-Tigris Delta (Iraq)?	
	Volga Delta (U.S.S.R.)	
Great White Pelican	Lake Kerkini (Greece)	Porto-Lago coastal area (Greece)
	Lake Kastoria (Greece)	Evros Delta (Greece)
	Burgas coastal area (Bulgaria)	Lake Koronia (Greece)
	Lake Manyas (Turkey)	Lake Veggoritis (Greece)
	Göksu Delta (Turkey)	Lake Eber (Turkey)
	Lake Huleh (Israel)	Lake Akşehir (Turkey)
	Bardawil lagoon (Egypt)	Assuan Reservoir (Egypt)
	Euphrates-Tigris Delta (Iraq)?	Yatata Reservoir (Bulgaria)
	Seistan wetlands (Iran-Afghanistan)	Varnensko Lake (Bulgaria)

Key: ? Areas suspected to be important as stopover sites during dispersal of pelicans, but for which no recent data are available.

more hazardous. It is striking to note how many of these sites are used by both Great White and Dalmatian Pelicans, which shows the extent to which the number of sites suitable for these birds has been reduced.

Wintering sites

The wintering sites of the Dalmatian Pelican in south-east Europe and Turkey are well known (Crivelli & Vizi 1981; Crivelli 1987), and recently this list has been extended to cover the Middle East and Asia (*Table 5*). The study of the changes in winter counts is an effective way of following population trends of a species. In the case of the Dalmatian Pelican such an exercise has only become feasible on a world scale for the years 1987–1989 (*Table 6*); years in which the first winter counts were undertaken in Asia and in the Middle East (Van der Ven 1987, 1988; Scott & Rose 1989). On the other hand, on a more regional scale, comparison of the counts undertaken in Greece and Turkey at the beginning of the 1970s with those of the end of the 1980s, that is 15 years later (*Table 7*), show clearly that the population of this species in this region has declined, and that the decline is closely related to the drop in the number of breeding birds. On a world scale, because of the great differences observed from one year to another (e.g. in Pakistan), it is still too early to draw any definite conclusions, especially as there is no information on the number of Dalmatian Pelicans wintering in Albania and in the delta of the Tigris and Euphrates in Iraq. However, a reasonable estimate of the world wintering population is about 5,500–6,500 individuals.

In the case of the Great White Pelican, the wintering grounds are known only for the asiatic breed population, which winters mainly in Pakistan, in India and in the delta of the Tigris and Euphrates in Iraq (Scott & Carp 1982), with a small number wintering in Iran (*Table 6*). However, the exact wintering grounds of the

Table 5: Sites of importance for the wintering of Dalmatian and Great White Pelicans nesting in the Palearctic.

Species	Major sites	Secondary sites
Dalmatian Pelican	Lake Kerkini (Greece) Porto-Lago coastal area (Greece) Amvrakikos Gulf (Greece) Menderes Delta (Turkey) Caspian Sea shores (Iran) Euphrates-Tigris Delta (Iraq)? Nalsarovar Reservoir (India) Mai Po (Hong Kong) Coastal lagoons (Albania) Turkmena Region (U.S.S.R.)	Evros Delta (Greece) Kalamas Delta (Greece) Göksu Delta (Turkey) Camaltı Tuzlası (Turkey) Lake Manyas (Turkey) Kızılırmak Delta (Turkey) Seistan wetlands (Iran-Afghanistan) Lake Parishan (Iran) Dash Kaur (Pakistan) Gujarat Province (India) Southern Gulf of Kutch (India) Sultanpur Jheels (India)
Great White Pelican	Euphrates-Tigris Delta (Iraq) Indus River Delta (Pakistan) Southern Sudan (Sudan)? Ethiopian wetlands (Ethiopia)? Eastern Saurashtra (India) Great Rann of Kutch (India) Seistan wetlands (Iran-Afghanistan)	Lake Huleh (Israel) Bandarabbas (Iran) Lake Hudero (Pakistan) Rajasthan Province (India) Southern Gulf of Kutch (India) Lake Khijadia (India)

Note: ? Areas suspected to be important for the wintering of pelicans, but for which no recent data are available.

Table 6: Mid-winter counts of Dalmatian and Great White Pelicans in the Palearctic in January 1987, 1988 and 1989.

Wintering grounds	P. crispus 1987	1988	1989	P. onocrotalus 1987	1988	1989
South-eastern Europe						
Albania	?	?	?	-	-	-
Greece[1]	616	577	235	-	9	3
Turkey[2]	233	167	333	5	4	3
Middle East and Asia[3]						
U.S.S.R.[4]	134	98	202	7	140	48
Iran	?	265	752	?	254	101
Iraq	?	?	?	?	?	?
Pakistan	296	2,921	529	280	17,631	25,838
India	49	60	38	2,330	5,940	67
China	21	33	39	-	-	-
Hong Kong	17	33	-	-	-	-
TOTAL	**1,366**	**4,154**	**2,128**	**2,622**	**23,978**	**26,060**

Notes: 1 Hellenic Ornithological Society 1987, 1988; 2 Dijksen, pers. comm.; 3 Van der Ven 1987, 1988; Scott & Rose 1989; 4 Poslavski & Shirekov 1990.

Table 7: Comparison of the numbers of Dalmatian Pelicans wintering in Greece and Turkey in the seventies and in the eighties.

Countries	1971	1973	1986	1987	1988	1989
Greece	598	824	447	616	577	235
Turkey	619	400	182	233	167	333
TOTAL	**1,217**	**1,224**	**629**	**849**	**744**	**568**

other two-thirds of the Palearctic breeding population remain unknown. Crivelli *et al.* (1991) have brought forward a hypothesis that the Great White Pelicans nesting in south-east Europe, Turkey, Iran and the south-west of the Soviet Union probably winter in southern Sudan and/or in Ethiopia. For evident conservation reasons it is important to determine the precise location of these wintering grounds, and to determine if the Palearctic population of the Great White Pelican mixes on the wintering grounds with the local African populations, or if it remains independent.

PAST AND PRESENT THREATS

The decline of the two species of pelican nesting in the Palearctic started a very long time ago, and increased alarmingly in the middle of the last century, mainly due to the drainage of a large number of wetlands containing breeding colonies. This decline has continued up until the present day because of the extension of agriculture into the remotest areas, the continued destruction of colonies by professional fishermen, and the general degradation of wetlands throughout the range of the two species. For example, the excessive use of the rivers draining into the Aral Sea (U.S.S.R.) and Lake Lop (China) for irrigation water has led to the disappearance of all the nesting colonies in these wetlands. In the case of the Aral Sea, a drop in level of 30 m has led to the disappearance of all of the littoral zone, whereas Lake Lop has dried up completely. Decreasing water level due to irrigation and to severe drought in the breeding areas in the 1980s has been an increasing problem for nesting pelicans. Large and stable reed islands, usually surrounded by open water, are therefore connected with the mainland allowing mammalian predators (wolves, jackals, foxes, wild boars and stray dogs) to visit these breeding islands and to destroy the colonies. At Lake Mikri Prespa, at Srebarna Nature Reserve and in the Danube Delta several cases of such predation have been observed resulting in a low breeding success of these colonies. In the 1970s and early 1980s many breeding colonies were repeatedly destroyed by fishermen (e.g. Lake Mikri Prespa, Calmati Tuzlasi Lagoon, the Danube Delta, the Menderes Delta and Lake Skadar), causing either a drop in the number of breeding pairs or complete abandonment of a colony. Finally, the great increase in ornithological tourism and wildlife photography has caused disturbance from time to time in many colonies, generally leading to abandonment of the colony.

All the above causes for decline take place on the breeding grounds, but unfortunately, additional and more serious causes for decline also occur during migration, dispersion and on the wintering grounds. These causes are mainly illegal shooting and to a lesser extent collision with high-tension power lines. These two factors reduce the survival rate of the young and immature birds and drastically reduce the size of the adult population of both species. For example,

Figure 1: Hunter with freshly shot Great White Pelican (*Pelecanus onocrotalus*) in the Göksu Delta, Turkey. The species is protected by law in Turkey. (*Photo:* G. Magnin)

in the case of the Dalmatian Pelican, even with good breeding success, the mortality of all age classes is too high to enable the population to increase, and it just about manages to maintain the present level. Shooting is certainly the most worrying cause of mortality in the pelicans at the moment (*Figure 1*). Both species are equally affected, and two examples will serve as illustrations: one in Greece and one in Turkey. At Lake Kerkini in north-western Greece we have recorded at least 15 Dalmatian Pelicans killed by shooting in 1987 (Crivelli & Jerrentrup, unpublished data). In Turkey, 35 Great White Pelicans (half of which were immatures) were shot between November and December 1987 in the delta of the Göksu (Magnin 1989). Twenty Dalmatian Pelicans have also been shot in the Menderes Delta (Turkey) from October 1988 to June 1989 (Heins & Rösler 1989).

Most of the time, pelicans are shot for "sport", or because they have been accused of taking fish from fish-farms or lakes.

Crivelli *et al.* (1988) have described the negative effects of an electric power line inconveniently situated between the roosting site and feeding grounds of Dalmatian Pelicans wintering at Porto-Lago. Although in this case the problem has been solved by the dismantling of the line, how many other as yet unidentified lines continue to kill pelicans? Recently such a case has been identified and studied, this time on a breeding site: Lake Mikri Prespa. The "natural" mortality of all age classes of Dalmatian Pelican has doubled over the space of four years at this site due to deaths caused by a power line situated between the breeding colony and the main feeding grounds (*Table 8*). At the same site, the deaths caused by collisions with the power line only represent one eighth of the "natural" mortality of the Great White Pelican. The difference between the two species is easily explained by the fact that the Great White Pelican hardly ever feeds at Prespa, and therefore does not have to fly over the power line in question.

Finally, some other less frequent factors also threaten pelican populations. These include egg collectors (eggs of *P. crispus* stolen by German collectors in the Kizilirmak Delta, Turkey; Eames 1989), and the taking of chicks to supply zoos, and even villages – for example in Greece and Cyprus, where villages like to have a pelican as a pet. Great White Pelicans were found regularly for sale on Damietta and Port-Said market in Egypt. These birds were caught during migration (Goodman & Meininger 1989). Lastly, it is not uncommon to find pelicans drowned in the nets of fishermen. Pesticides and heavy metal contamination are other potential threats for pelicans. No-one will forget the dramatic case of the Brown Pelican (*Pelecanus occidentalis*) which almost disappeared from the Californian coasts because of DDT contamination. This problem has only recently been studied in pelicans in Europe (Fossi *et al.* 1984; Crivelli *et al.* 1989). Although a decrease of 12–20 per cent in eggshell thickness of *P. crispus* significantly correlated with DDE concentrations, has been recorded at Lake Prespa (Greece), no impact on reproductive success has been observed. A similar study on *P. onocrotalus* nesting in Greece is currently being undertaken.

The combined effect of all of these causes of mortality contributes to the decline of the two species of pelican breeding in the Palearctic, by reducing the number of breeding, feeding and staging sites, and by seriously decreasing the size of the population.

CONSERVATION AND MANAGEMENT MEASURES

Full or temporary protection of breeding colonies

More than half of the breeding sites of the two species of pelican in the Palearctic benefit from no protection measures. Protection of the breeding sites is absolutely essential to ensure that reproductive success is high: without this no increase in the populations of the two species is possible. The creation of nature reserves in the breeding sites is the ideal solution, since this not only protects the colony during the breeding season, but also provides some measure of safeguard for the wetland habitats on the site. If such a degree of conservation proves impossible, it should still be possible to ensure some protection during the breeding season (March to July) in order to prevent disturbance of the breeding colonies by fishermen, birdwatchers or photographers. In order to ensure such protection the employment of wardens would be required. An experiment along these lines has been carried out at Amvrakikos in western Greece, where a permanent watch was kept by volunteer wardens from the Hellenic Ornithological Society over the lagoon in

Table 8: Mortality of Dalmatian and Great White Pelicans during the breeding season at Lake Mikri Prespa. The flags were set in October 1988.

	Species	N per year	Juvenile[1]	Immature[2]	Adult	Unknown
Electric power lines						
1985	*P. crispus*	3	0	0	1	2
	P. onocrotalus	0	0	0	0	0
1986	*P. crispus*	2	2	0	0	0
	P. onocrotalus	0	0	0	0	0
1987	*P. crispus*	4	2	1	1	0
	P. onocrotalus	1	0	0	1	0
1988	*P. crispus*	5	3	0	2	0
	P. onocrotalus	1	0	0	1	0
TOTAL	***P. crispus***	**14**	**7**	**1**	**4**	**2**
	P. onocrotalus	**2**	**0**	**0**	**2**	**0**
1989	*P. crispus*	0	0	0	0	0
	P. onocrotalus	0	0	0	0	0
Other causes						
1985	*P. crispus*	5	0	2	3	0
	P. onocrotalus[3]	3	1	0	2	0
1986	*P. crispus*	4	1	1	2	0
	P. onocrotalus	3	0	0	3	0
1987	*P. crispus*	1	1	0	0	0
	P. onocrotalus	5	0	0	5	0
1988	*P. crispus*	4	1	0	2	1
	P. onocrotalus	7	0	0	7	0
TOTAL	***P. crispus***	**14**	**3**	**3**	**7**	**1**
	P. onocrotalus	**18**	**1**	**0**	**17**	**0**
1989	*P. crispus*	3	1	1	1	0
	P. onocrotalus	1	0	0	1	0

Notes: 1 Chicks that have just fledged; 2 Birds that are one or two years old; 3 Hatzilacos, unpublished data.

which was situated a breeding colony of Dalmatian Pelicans. Along with the wardening, the volunteers also set up an educational programme, particularly directed towards the fishermen and aiming to explain the protection measures and generally advance the cause of wildlife conservation. Although the results of the educational programme would appear to be positive, those of the wardening are more difficult to evaluate since, although disturbance from tourists, birdwatchers and fishermen was reduced, it was not possible to prevent disturbance caused by local fishermen whenever it occurred.

"Improving" the habitat

Habitat improvement, whether on breeding, staging or wintering grounds, can certainly be an important form of management, provided that it is based on solid scientific knowledge not only of the species concerned, but also of the functioning

Figure 2: Elevated nest platforms provided for Dalmatian Pelicans (*Pelecanus crispus*) at Lake Manyas, Turkey. (*Photo:* A. Crivelli)

of the ecosystem in question. Great care must be taken before undertaking any form of habitat management for birds, particularly in the case of endangered species, since such actions can sometimes turn out to have deleterious consequences for the birds they were intended to help. In the case of pelicans, such management has been carried out mainly at breeding localities, and especially on the nest sites. Several workers have, for various reasons, installed floating rafts in order to provide safer nesting sites for a larger number of pelicans (Volga Delta, U.S.S.R.: Bondarev 1976; Lake Srebarna, Bulgaria: T. Mitchev, pers. comm.; Lake Mikri Prespa: Crivelli & Catsadorakis, unpublished data). All of these activities met with success, although in certain cases the rafts had to be replaced after a few years because of deterioration. A similar experiment has been carried out at Lake Manyas in Turkey since 1967. Here, wooden platforms serving as nest supports for Dalmatian Pelicans were erected at 2-4 m above the water level, around a flooded forest situated in the Kuscenneti National Park (*Figure 2*). The installation of artificial nesting platforms for pelicans is not recommended outside fully protected areas.

Another problem observed at many breeding sites is the degradation or erosion of the breeding islands. Because of severe weather in the winter, or the actions of the birds themselves in the breeding season, the nesting sites deteriorate more or less rapidly until they are no longer fit for nesting, forcing the birds to go elsewhere to find new sites (Crivelli 1987; Crivelli, Catsadorakis & Hatzilacos, in prep.). When the nest sites are situated in reedbeds the birds do not appear to have much trouble in finding new locations, but on coastal lagoons (e.g. Amvrakikos) or on reservoirs (e.g. Manych-Gudilo), the birds sooner or later find that there are no longer any suitable nesting sites. There are only two solutions to this problem: (a) regular reconstruction of the nesting islands before they become too degraded; this requires the construction of a gently sloping shoreline on at least one of the sides of the island so that the chicks can clamber easily ashore or (b) installation of a nylon-encased concrete revetment to make the shoreline stabilization more permanent (Fabriform Revet Mats, U.S.A.), as has been done with success on a breeding island of the American White Pelican (*P. erythrorhynchos*) on a reservoir in Colorado (U.S.A.). The disadvantage of this solution is its cost: 160,000 USD for a surface area of about 0.6 ha.

Electric power lines
Electric power lines have been identified as being a frequent cause of mortality in both species of pelican, on the breeding, staging and wintering grounds (Crivelli *et al.* 1988). The pelicans do not die as a result of electrocution, but from collision with the lines. When such lines are found in the proximity of a nesting colony or an important roost, a regular check for dead birds should be made under the lines. If corpses are found, the electricity company should be contacted immediately so that they can install flags on the wires, or better still so that they can put underground the section of the line responsible for the deaths. Red plastic flags were tested for the first time with pelicans in the spring of 1989 at Lake Mikri Prespa (Crivelli & Catsadorakis, unpublished data). The flags were installed in the autumn of 1988 on a 2-3 km section of line which had killed numerous pelicans (*Table 8*). The first results showed a drastic reduction in the mortality, since no pelican was killed in 1989. However, it was noted that 20-30 per cent of the flags were damaged during the winter and that is therefore necessary to use flags made of a more durable material. Before recommending the use of flags, we would like to continue these tests at Lake Prespa for another year (1990).

Fisheries and fish-farm problems
Both species of pelican are regularly shot by fishermen, on open waters and when they visit fish-farms. They are accused of consuming large quantities of commercially valuable fish. In fish-farms the problem can be effectively resolved by installing a series of horizontal strings spaced at intervals, which prevent the birds from landing. Bird scarers working on bottled gas, and sound recordings of various noises, have proved to have little effect in the medium term and are not recommended. Unlike some other piscivorous birds, pelicans do not compete to any extent with the interests of fishermen, for two reasons: (a) pelicans mostly consume fish with little or no commercial value and because of this play an important role in maintaining the equilibrium of fish communities and (b) they do not wound fish with their beaks as do cormorants (Im & Hafner 1984). Crivelli (1987) estimated that the breeding population of Dalmatian Pelicans at Lake Mikri Prespa consumed on average, between 1984 and 1986, somewhere between 58 and 84 tonnes of commercially non-valuable fish per year. At Amvrakikos, during the breeding season (c.229 days) the nesting Dalmatian Pelicans consumed 13-18 tonnes of fish, of which 90 per cent were eels, a commercially important species. The quantity of eels consumed represented between 8.8 and 12.7 per cent of the quantity of eels caught by fishermen in the four lagoons around the pelican colony. The economic loss was estimated at between 11,600 USD and 17,000 USD.

Shooting
Here the problem is simple: the two species of pelican breeding in the Palearctic are protected in all of the countries in which they breed, transit or winter, and cannot legally be shot for any reason whatsoever. Therefore, if pelicans continue to be killed it is because these laws are not strictly applied, or that there are not enough game wardens to ensure that they are respected. It would be very wise to

establish non-hunting areas on the principal wintering localities in order to reduce the number of birds shot during this period. In the last resort the problem of shooting is one of education and information.

Education
Much remains to be done in this field. Most of the educational campaigns that have been carried out have been designed by biologists, and have been of questionable value. It is time that the wildlife conservation movement understood that educational campaigns should be designed and executed by professional publicists, and not by biologists. This is also true for the design of leaflets, booklets and posters.

RECOMMENDATIONS

- To coordinate scientific research and management programmes on the Dalmatian and Great White Pelicans at international level.
- To convince national and/or local governments to establish permanent or seasonal wildlife reserves on those pelican breeding sites not yet protected.
- To continue scientific research on the two species, particularly in the fields of population dynamics, on the exchange of individuals between colonies, and on wintering.
- To monitor every three years the concentration of pollutants in the eggs, and the eggshell thickness, in both species of pelican.
- To implement and enforce wild bird protection laws.
- To carry out educational campaigns, especially aimed at hunters and fishermen.
- Not to undertake management programmes on pelicans until the relevant problems have been identified and studied scientifically, and after a programme to monitor the effects of management has been planned.
- As long as the size of the two populations does not increase significantly, not to attempt to create any new breeding colonies.

The aims of our work should be to halt the decline in the numbers of the two species of pelican breeding in the Palearctic and to succeed in taking measures that will bring about in the more-or-less long term, an increase in their populations. When the two species disappear from the lists of endangered species, we will then know that we have succeeded, as the Americans and Canadians did with the American White Pelican, and the American with the Brown Pelican.

ACKNOWLEDGEMENTS

The research programme on pelicans has been funded by EC Research Division (DG XII), by the Basler Stiftung für biologische Forschung, by the Foundation Tour du Valat and by WWF-International. We thank warmly D. Vizi, M. Siki, F. Dupont, Th. Nasiridis, M. Malakou and Y. Petridis for their help in the field, and Dr. D. A. Scott for his valuable comments on the manuscript.

REFERENCES

ANDREWS, C. W. (1899) On some remains of birds from the lake-dwelling of Glastonbury, Somersetshire. *Ibis*, Ser. **7**: 351.

BANNIKOV, A. G. (1978) *Red Data Book of the U.S.S.R.: rare and endangered species of animals and plants.* Moscow: Lesnaya Promyshlennost Publishers. (In Russian.)

BARBIERI, F., BOGLIANI, G. & PRIGIONI, C. (1986) Note sull'ornitofauna dell'Albania. *Riv. Ital. Orn., Milano* **56**: 53-66.

BERRY, H. H., STARK, HH. P. & VAN VUUREN, A. S. (1973) White pelicans *Pelecanus onocrotalus* breeding on the Etosha Pan, South West Africa, during 1971. *Madoqua* **7**: 17-31.

BORODIN, A. M. (1984) *Red Data Book of the U.S.S.R.: rare and endangered species of animals and plants.* Second (revised and enlarged) edition. Vol. 1: Animals. Moscow: Lesnaya Promyshlennost Publishers. (In Russian.)

CRAMP, S., ed. (1977) *Handbook of the birds of Europe, the Middle East and North Africa*, Vol. 1. Oxford: Oxford University Press.

CRIVELLI, A. J. (1984) European Pelican populations and their conservation. Proceedings of the EEC Contact Group Meeting on Conservation of Birds, Durham, England, 1983: 123-127.

CRIVELLI, A. J. (1987) The ecology and behaviour of the Dalmatian pelican, *Pelecanus crispus* Bruch: a world endangered species. Final report. Commission of the European Communities, DG XII.

CRIVELLI, A. J., FOCARDI, S., FOSSI, C., LEONZIO, C., MASSI, A. & RENZONI, A. (1989) Trace elements and chlorinated hydrocarbons in eggs of *Pelecanus crispus*: a world endangered bird species nesting at Lake Mikri Prespa, north-western Greece. *Environ. Pollut.* **61**: 135-247.

CRIVELLI, A. J., JERRENTRUP, H. & MITCHEV, T. (1988) Electric power lines: a cause of mortality in *Pelecanus crispus* Bruch, a world endangered bird species in Porto-Lago, Greece. *Colon. Waterbirds* **11**: 301-305.

CRIVELLI, A. J., LESHEM, Y., MICHEV, T. & JERRENTRUP, H. (1991) Where do Palearctic Great White Pelicans (*Pelecanus onocrotalus*) presently overwinter? *Rev. Ecol. (Terre Vie)* **46**: 145-171.

CRIVELLI, A. J. & SCHREIBER, R. W. (1984) Status of Pelecanidae. *Biol. Conserv.* **30**: 147-156.

CRIVELLI, A. J. & VIZI, O. (1981) The Dalmatian Pelican, *Pelecanus crispus* Bruch 1832: a recently world endangered bird species. *Biol. Conserv.* **20**: 297-310.

DEMENTIEV, G. & GLADKOV, N. A. (1951) *Birds of the Soviet Union, 1.* Jerusalem: Israel. Program for Scientific Translations.

EAMES, J. (1989) Selected bird observations from Turkey: spring and summer 1987. *OSME Bull.* **23**: 6-13.

FOSSI, C., FOCARDI, S., LEONZIO, C. & RENZONI, A. (1984) Trace-metals and chlorinated hydrocarbons in birds' eggs from the Delta of the Danube. *Environ. Conserv.* **11**: 345-350.

GOODMAN, S. M. & MEININGER, P. L. (1989) *The birds of Egypt.* Oxford: Oxford University Press.

GUILLET, A AND CROWE, T. M. (1983) Temporal variation in breeding, foraging and bird sanctuary visitation by a southern African population of Great White pelicans *Pelecanus onocrotalus. Biol. Conserv.* **26**: 15-31.

GVOZDEV, E. V. (1978) *Red Data Book of Kazakh SSR: rare and endangered species of animals and plants.* Part 1: Vertebrates. Alma-Ata: Kainar Publishing House.

HATTING, T. (1963) On subfossil finds of Dalmatian pelican (*Pelecanus crispus* Bruch) from Denmark. *Vidensk. Medd. Dansk naturh. Foren.* **125**: 337-351.

HATZILACOS, D. (1986) Preliminary data on the breeding and feeding biology of the White pelican (*Pelecanus onocrotalus*) at Lake Mikri Prespa. *Biologia Gallo–hellenica* **12**: 497-506.

HEINS, J. U. & RÖSLER, S. (1989) Forschungsprojekt Landbewirtschaftung und Naturschutz im Menderes-Delta Südwest Türkei: Zwischenbericht, Gesamthochschule Kassel, 22 pp.

HELLENIC ORNITHOLOGICAL SOCIETY. (1987) Midwinter waterfowl census, Greece: 1987. Duplicated report, Athens, Greece.

HELLENIC ORNITHOLOGICAL SOCIETY. (1988) Midwinter waterfowl census, Greece 1988. Duplicated report, Athens, Greece.

IM, B. H. & HAFNER, H. (1984) Impact des oiseaux piscivores et plus particulièrement du grand cormoran (*Phalacrocorax carbo sinensis*) sur les exploitations piscicoles en Camargue, France. Commission of the European Communities, DG XII.

KESSLER, E. (1978) Nouvelles contributions concernant la présence du genre *Pelecanus* dans l'avifaune sousfossile de Roumanie. *Nymphacea* 6: 181-182.

KING, W. B. (1981) Endangered birds of the world. *The ICBP Bird Red Data Book.* Washington, D.C.: Smithsonian Institution.

KOLOSOV, A. M. (1983) *Red Data Book of the RSFSR: animals.* Moscow: Rossel' khozizdat Publishers. (In Russian.)

MAGNIN, G. (1989) *Falconry and hunting in Turkey during 1987.* Cambridge, U.K.: International Council for Bird Preservation (Stud. Rep. 34).

MITCHEV, T. (1981) The Dalmatian pelican (*Pelecanus crispus*) – Its numbers and population dynamics in the Srebarna Nature Reserve, south Dobrodgea. *Proceedings of the Regional Symposium MAB-UNESCO*, 20-24 October 1980, at Blagoevgrad, Sofia: 516-527. (In Bulgarian with English summary.)

NEWTON, E. T. (1928) Pelican in Yorkshire peat. *Naturalist*: 857: 167-68.

POSLAVSKI, A. N. & SHIREKOV, R. S. (1990) The number and distribution of wintering waterfowl in eastern Turkmena. Symposium on managing waterfowl populations, Astrakhan, U.S.S.R., October 1989. Slimbridge, U.K.: International Waterfowl and Wetlands Research Bureau (Spec. Publ., in press).

SCOTT, D. A. & CARP, E. (1982) A midwinter survey of wetlands in Mesopotamia, Iraq: 1979. *Sandgrouse* 4: 60-76.

SCOTT, D. A. & ROSE, P. M. (1989) *Asian waterfowl census, 1989.* Slimbridge, U.K.: International Waterfowl and Wetlands Research Bureau.

VAN DER VEN, J. (1987) Asian waterfowl 1987. Midwinter bird observations in most Asian countries. IWRB duplicated report, U.K.

VAN DER VEN, J. (1988) Asian waterfowl 1988. Midwinter bird observations in most Asian countries. IWRB duplicated report, U.K.

INCREASING CONSERVATION CONCERN IN TURKEY

NERGIS YAZGAN

Doğal Hayatı Koruma Derneği (DHKD), PK 18, 80810 Bebek-Istanbul, Turkey

ABSTRACT

Turkey is ornithologically one of the most important countries in Europe. Nature awareness of the authorities and the general public is typically bad, and rapid population and economic growth impose serious threats to birds and their habitats. Only in recent years has nature conservation work been carried out by a few NGOs. The DHKD, the Society for the Protection of Nature, is now one of Turkey's leading NGOs, campaigning for the preservation of Turkey's natural resources. This paper describes the history of DHKD and some of its present activities.

THE IMPORTANCE OF TURKEY FOR MIGRATORY BIRDS

Turkey is probably the most important country in Europe as far as biological diversity and population numbers for many plant and animal species are concerned. Its geographical position, at the junction of the Asian, European and African continents, makes Turkey a region of great importance for migratory birds. The country boasts two major flyways for migratory birds: the western flyway is of particular importance for storks since practically the whole European population of White Stork (*Ciconia ciconia*) migrates over Istanbul in autumn and spring. Tens of thousands of raptors follow the same route, and it is assumed that the whole population of the Levant Sparrowhawk (*Accipiter brevipes*) is amongst the migrating raptors. In eastern Turkey, a recently discovered raptor migration route involves maybe over one million raptors, including practically all migrating raptors breeding west of the Urals. Turkey is also of great importance for migrating waders, herons and passerines. Recent detailed research by WIWO (Netherlands) revealed the importance of the Turkish wetlands for migratory waders. Assessment of the data gathered during the annual IWRB Midwinter Waterfowl Counts (Rose *in litt.*; Dijksen & Blomert 1989) shows that the Turkish wetlands contain hundreds of thousands of waterfowl during winter. An alarming development concerns the serious decline in many species, especially in the numbers of wintering dabbling ducks. On average, losses were over 50 per cent, and for Red-crested Pochard (*Netta rufina)* the decline was even 84 per cent in the period 1970-1989. The drop in the number of internationally important sites from 17–12 is an indication of the decreasing value of Turkish wetlands to wintering ducks and Coot (*Fulica atra).*

THE CONSERVATION MOVEMENT IN TURKEY

Turkey has the fastest-rising population growth rate (2.3 per cent in general, and up to 5-6 per cent in cities due to trans-migration) and has been following a "cash crop" liberal economic policy since 1982. All these facts create an immense responsibility, and place constant pressure on all of Turkey's fauna and flora. After 1982 the government adopted the policy that as a developing country Turkey should first develop its economy and then later see what could be done for the environment. In 1983 the Undersecretariat of the Environment was reduced to a General Directorateship. The Ministry of Forestry, which was a strong ministry until then, was absorbed into the Ministry of Agriculture, Forestry and Rural Affairs. Also reduced both in their authority and capacity were the Fisheries and Re-afforestation Departments – all of which contributed very negatively to the state of the environment in Turkey. The Environmental Law, passed in 1983, still cannot be enforced properly because the stipulations and penalties for enforcement are lacking. Today, in 1990, there is still no Ministry for the Environment, but the Undersecretariat for the Environment has been re-established since the end of 1989. Presently, a state minister is responsible for the environment.

In January 1990, for the first time in Turkish conservation history, the government decided to grant financial help to Turkish NGOs that are active in the field of conservation. About 500 million Turkish Pounds will be distributed amongst five NGOs, among them DHKD, according to projects submitted. It is obvious from the emerging environmental awareness of the public at large, and the recent conservation battles that have been waged throughout the country, as well as the lack of enforcement of environmental legislation, that Turkey is heading towards an acute and serious environmental crisis and has to find ways of progressing towards sustainable development.

The first conservation issue that can be well remembered in Turkey are the conservation efforts to save the Northern Bald Ibis (*Geronticus eremita*), an action led by DHKD, with WWF and the Ministry of Forestry, in the period 1975 to the 1980s. Certainly a milestone in Turkish conservation history was the project in 1984 to build a thermic power station in Gökova in southern Turkey – one of the most picturesque and unspoilt coastlines on the southern coast and a World Heritage Site candidate for Turkey. Unfortunately the resistance of the local people and green intellectuals, which emerged as a result of the Gökova incident, were not enough to deter the plans made in Ankara. However, the most important and far-reaching conservation issue ever has been the Dalyan sea turtle project which will be dealt with in more detail later.

HISTORY OF THE DHKD

Founded in 1975, the birth of the society coincides with, or rather marks, the beginning of the conservation movement in Turkey. The first task of the society was to bring the decline of the Bald Ibis population in Birecik to the attention of the general public both within and outside Turkey. As a result, the Bald Ibis became the symbol of DHKD. The "White Stork Count", with participation of the elementary schools in Thrace, and involvement in the Bird Paradise at Manyas (Kuş) Gölü, were the first bird protection activities of DHKD in the period 1975-1980.

The most crucial and now famous conservation battle in Turkey started in 1986 and made DHKD widely known in Turkey as well as abroad. In 1986 the Turkish

Government had decided that it was time to claim a larger share of the tourism market in the Mediterranean, realising that it is one of the last countries still holding an unspoilt and extremely beautiful coastline. In 1986, the construction of a huge hotel complex was started on the Iztuzu beach near Dalyan, on the Turkish south coast. The beach is of major importance as a nesting place for the Loggerhead Sea Turtle (*Caretta caretta*), and the complex wetland system comprising the Koycegiz lake and the reedbeds and marshes between Dalyan and the beach at Iztuzu form a unique combination of different habitats which is no longer encountered anywhere else in the Mediterranean. For its ornithological importance the whole area was put on the list of Important Bird Areas in Turkey. DHKD's intensive campaign eventually lead to the cancellation of the whole project, and the area was properly taken under protection by the Turkish Government in 1988. During 1988 and 1989, DHKD carried out extensive campaigns to educate foreign and Turkish visitors to the area.

The real thrust for DHKD bird conservation work started in 1986 when ICBP decided to "invest" in conservation in Turkey. First the ICBP *Mediterranean Bird Book* was translated and adapted to Turkey. Then, in 1987, ICBP gave a three-year contract to DHKD to get it "off the ground". Until then DHKD had in fact no telephone, no office, nor any secretarial staff. Also important in DHKD's development was WWF's decision to assist the DHKD turtle project in 1987, which support has continued up to the present day in increasing amounts. Today, DHKD has two offices and 13 full-time staff, and has bought most of the necessary office equipment. We now have very good contacts with the press and most of the government ministries. But most important has been the fund-raising and public awareness success of DHKD since 1985, procuring local funding to match foreign funding sources, an activity which is spiralling in increasing amounts every year.

Since January 1989, birdwatchers in DHKD have been united in a special Bird Section that now coordinates the bird conservation work of DHKD. The training and recruitment of new birdwatchers is one of the main aims of this section. The establishment of a successful and active Bird Section has been greatly enhanced by the assistance of the ICBP representative in Turkey. Over the last three years DHKD has been involved in, or has initiated, a number of bird conservation projects which are briefly reviewed below.

In brief, DHKD is one of the handful of NGOs working in the field of conservation and the only action group that can claim two successful campaigns, good relations with the government and a professional full-time staff.

RECENT DHKD CONSERVATION PROJECTS

Göksu Delta
In the Göksu Delta, previously unknown in Turkey for its ornithological importance, DHKD discovered in November 1988, whilst preparing excursions for the ICBP Conference in 1989, that construction of holiday houses had been started in the middle of the delta, acutely threatening the area. Moreover, DHKD research revealed plans for the construction of an airport and a shrimp farm in the Göksu Delta. During the campaign to save the delta, DHKD especially emphasized the fact that the delta is the only breeding place in Turkey of the Purple Gallinule (*Porphyrio porphyrio*). DHKD triggered a great amount of publicity in press and TV and an intensive letter campaign. As a result, the building of the houses was

Figure 1: Children in a Turkish primary school reading the booklet *"Kuşların Dünyası"* about the *"World of Birds"*. (*Photo:* DHKD/G. Magnin)

stopped, the airport was cancelled, and finally the shrimp farm project annulled. In March 1990 the site was declared a Specially Protected Area.

Lake Gala

Lake Gala, a wetland on the Greek/Turkish border, is an important bird area in Turkey, and one plagued by heavy hunting pressure and bad land management, including extensive drainage schemes and uncontrolled use of pesticides. An ICBP-funded project in 1987 and 1988 included the organization of a symposium and the publication of a series of papers on the importance of this area and its conservation problems. As a result, part of the lake was closed for hunting. The Lake Gala area served as a pilot education area where, in January 1990, DHKD Bird Section members started the special distribution programme of the children's bird book *Kuşların Dünyası*, which was printed with financial help from the British and Netherlands Migratory Bird Committees, and the Danish Ornithological Society (*Figure 1*).

Important Bird Areas

The major ICBP project "Important Bird Areas in Europe" resulted for Turkey in a special, extended version in Turkish, highlighting the 79 Turkish IBA sites. The Turkish IBA booklet was distributed amongst relevant authorities throughout the country, and serves in many planning departments as an important reference work. During 1990, with financial aid from the State Ministry responsible for the Environment, 1,000 more copies of the Turkish edition were printed. ICBP and DHKD now have planned a follow-up programme that includes updating the information and bringing these Turkish IBAs to the attention of relevant authorities.

EDUCATION

Education, of course, has always been one of the main components of the work of DHKD, although the large number of people and the vastness of the country makes it very difficult to cover the country to a satisfying extent. Over the years, a large number of leaflets, posters and booklets have been published by DHKD, including many issues on birds and bird protection. Four thousand copies of the Turkish version of the ICBP poster "Flying visitors" were published and distributed. During 1986, 40,000 copies of the Turkish version of the ICBP *Mediterranean Bird Book* were prepared with financial help from Vogelbescherming (Netherlands) and distributed throughout Turkey to all primary schools. Inevitably, a number of books were read only by the school principal and the teachers, but a large number did finally end up in the schools' libraries, being in most instances the first booklet dealing with birds to appear in those libraries. During January and February 1989, 100,000 copies of the same booklet appeared as an insert to the weekly instalments of the children's version of the *Encyclopedia Britannica*, and this large number of copies indeed ended up where we aimed, in the hands of Turkish youngsters. In addition, we used the colour separations of the illustrations of the ICBP *Mediterranean Bird Book* to print two posters, indicating per species whether it was fully or partially protected. A set of these posters was sent to all hunting clubs in Turkey. A twenty-page black-and-white booklet, entitled *Kuşların Dünyası (World of the Birds)* was printed in November 1988, in a print-run of 72,000 copies. This booklet was designed for individual use by pupils in primary schools, and DHKD has distributed over 50,000 copies in a few selected Important Bird Areas in Turkey during 1990. Distribution is carried out in a very extensive manner, with courses for teachers, slide shows and videos for the pupils, etc. Also in 1989, another 10,000 copies of the booklet were reprinted by another conservation organization for distribution in North Cyprus.

During peak migration periods over Istanbul, a "Stork Day" in September and a "Bird of Prey Day" in October were organized by DHKD in order to educate the general public. Both events were organized on the Küçük Çamlica hill in Istanbul, a celebrated place for migration observations, and were well covered in the press and visited by a large number of interested people.

PRIORITIES FOR THE FUTURE

The constantly increasing conservation needs of all plants, animals and habitats in Turkey, as well as the rapid growth in membership and the number of projects undertaken by DHKD, necessitate that the working structure of the DHKD become highly professional, well-organized and geared for long-term planning. Increasing financial support from local sources will soon enable DHKD to employ more professional and qualified people in order to improve its coordination of educational, membership and fundraising activities. The growth in membership should also result in a better coverage of the country, and maybe in the future lead to the establishment of DHKD branches in other big cities. The universities in particular should receive regular visits from DHKD representatives in order to recruit interested people from the student world and to establish contacts with scientists in Turkey. This membership drive will certainly be one of DHKD's main activities for the time being. Although the membership of DHKD has nearly doubled in the last six months due to a lot of attention being given to DHKD and conservation in general, we should be much more active in raising members: only a large membership will give DHKD broad-based support and political influence. Large-scale advertisement campaigns in newspapers have just commenced. Lobbying on all levels will continue for many projects, and "Ankara lobbying" will concentrate especially on the Ramsar Convention, not at present signed by Turkey though Turkey possesses at least 61 wetlands that would meet the Ramsar criteria. DHKD has also started campaigning for Turkey to sign CITES. If DHKD has more qualified experts, we will finally be able to spend time on providing the press, especially magazines and newspapers, with background articles on a number of conservation topics. There is a great demand for information at the moment. The press will also be helpful in issues like the Ramsar and CITES conventions. In compliance with the funding offer of the state ministry, DHKD has drawn up five projects. Bird-related projects are: reprinting of the bird posters, brochures on Ramsar and CITES, small-scale elaboration of a conservation education programme to be later adopted by the Ministry of Education (to be printed as an integral part of the education books), and a DHKD-organized workshop where coordination will be attempted amongst the different NGOs in Turkey.

REFERENCES

DHKD. (1986) *Kuşları Tanıyalım*. Istanbul: Doğal Hayatı Koruma Derneği.
DHKD. (1989) *Kuşların Dünyası*. Istanbul: Doğal Hayatı Koruma Derneği.
DHKD. (1989) *Turkey: a challenge for birdwatchers*. Istanbul: Doğal Hayatı Koruma Derneği.
DIJKSEN, L. J. & BLOMERT, A. M. (1989) *Midwinter waterfowl census in Turkey*. January 1989. Zeist: WIWO.
ERTAN, A., KILIÇ, A. & KASPAREK, M. (1989) *Turkiye'nin Onemli Kus Alanları*. Istanbul: Doğal Hayatı Koruma Derneği.
GRIMMETT, R. F. A. & JONES, T. A. (1989) *Important bird areas in Europe*. Cambridge, U.K.: International Council for Bird Preservation (Techn. Publ. 9).

ICBP Technical Publication No. 12, 1991

MALTA ORNITHOLOGICAL SOCIETY: A BIRD PROTECTION SOCIETY IN A HOSTILE ENVIRONMENT

JOE SULTANA

Malta Ornithological Society, P.O. Box 498
Valletta, Malta

ABSTRACT

Bird-shooting and trapping have always been deep-rooted pastimes, and both are carried out indiscriminately in the Maltese Islands. About eight per cent of the population are either shooters or trappers. Since the Malta Ornithological Society was set up in 1962 by a small group of young people aiming at studying and protecting birds, it has grown to over 2,000 members, 80 per cent of whom are youths. The MOS has been instrumental in the setting up of the first educational reserve, has lobbied for bird-protection laws, published several publications, runs a bird-ringing scheme, coordinates a network of teacher-delegates in schools, and now has an office and a full-time director. MOS has evolved into a four-pier system – protection, study, education and youth. The financial help in the form of grants and loans from ICBP and other organizations for specific projects has been matched by the dedication and voluntary work of the MOS leading group of members. This has proved fruitful. The growth of the MOS has accelerated in the past decade since ICBP set up its migratory birds programme. With support, the MOS was able to execute several projects and activities which resulted in a continuous educational campaign, helping to bring about some change in the attitudes towards birds. Projects and publicity acquired credibility and respect for MOS, but they also triggered off stronger opposition from shooters and trappers, who have a strong lobby. The MOS also served as an encouragement to other NGOs, one of which, "Youths for the Environment" is the offspring of MOS Youths. In spite of all this the problem of shooting and trapping has not decreased. It is recommended that MOS should intensify its educational campaign while the authorities should update and strictly enforce the bird laws.

INTRODUCTION

The annual massive Palearctic-African bird migration dominates the Mediterranean's ornithological year. About one-third of the summer bird population breeding in Europe winters in Africa south of the Sahara. Moreau's (1972) impressive estimate of 5,000 million trans-Saharan migrants, which does not include the waterbirds, is today, due to improved methodology and an increase in census and atlas work, considered to be too conservative (Bijlsma 1987).

The Mediterranean, which in winter also harbours large numbers of European birds, does not provide physically unsurmountable obstacles to migrant birds, were

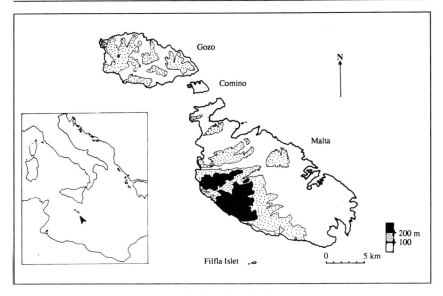

Figure 1: The Maltese Islands.

it not for intensive human interference. For many years there has been large-scale killing and trapping of birds, and hundreds of millions are killed annually in several countries bordering this "inland sea". The magnitude of this killing has been highlighted by Woldhek (1980) and more recently by Bijlsma (1987), the latter dealing mainly with bottleneck areas for soaring birds. In some areas, such as the Maltese Islands, bird-shooting and trapping activities are particularly intensive (Woldhek 1980; Sultana & Gauci 1982; Magnin 1986; Fenech, in press).

GENERAL INFORMATION

The Maltese Islands are situated in the centre of the Mediterranean at approximately 36°N, 14°E (*Figure 1*). The principal islands are Malta (249 km²), Gozo (70 km²) and Comino (2.6 km²). There are also a few smaller islands, of which the most important are Cominotto and Filfla. In spite of their small size and a dense population of some 340,000 people, which results in an intensive and negative human impact on the natural environment, the islands are endowed with a variety of habitat types and a relatively rich flora and fauna. A number of plants (e.g. the Maltese Rock-Centaury (*Palaeocyanus crassifolius*)) and animals (e.g. the Filfla Wall Lizard (*Podarcis filfolensis filfolensis*)) are endemic, and many localities of scientific interest and conservation value are found all over the islands (Schembri *et al.* 1987; Schembri & Sultana 1989). The islands also have five sites in the inventory of *Important Bird Areas in Europe* (Grimmett & Jones 1989).

Although the eastern and south-eastern parts of Malta seem to be one large complex of towns and villages, the western and northern parts, as well as most of Gozo, provide a landscape with terraced hillsides, rocky ridges and fertile valleys, some of which are thick with vegetation. The vegetation is mainly *garigue* with scattered small pockets of *maquis* and only one woodland site (Buskett). Some valley bottoms have standing water for several months after a good rainy season, otherwise marshy habitats are very scarce.

ORNITHOLOGICAL IMPORTANCE

Malta is noteworthy mainly for its breeding seabirds, particularly Storm Petrel (*Hydrobates pelagicus*), Cory's Shearwater (*Calonectris diomedea*) and Levantine Shearwater (*Puffinus puffinus yelkouan*). Otherwise the list of breeding birds, which in all comprises some 18 species, is restricted mostly to a few passerines, which include Short-toed Lark (*Calandrella brachydactyla*), Cetti's Warbler (*Cettia cetti*), Fan-tailed Warbler (*Cisticola juncidis*), Spectacled Warbler (*Sylvia conspicillata*) and Sardinian Warbler (*Sylvia melanocephala*). The rest of the species recorded in the islands are winter visitors (c.50), regular seasonal migrants (c.110) and irregular migrants or vagrants (c.180). These figures reflect the fact that the ornithology of Malta is mainly dominated by the seasonal migration, with birds occurring in highly variable numbers which depend to a large extent on the vagaries of weather (see also DeLucca 1969; Beaman & Galea 1974; Sultana & Gauci 1982).

BIRD-SHOOTING AND TRAPPING

In an area as densely populated as the Maltese Islands, with c.8 per cent of the population being either shooters or trappers, it is to be expected that bird-life is continuously under pressure. Bird-shooting and trapping have always been deep-rooted pastimes and they have always been carried out indiscriminately. This has resulted in the extinction or decline of almost all the larger breeding species, e.g. Jackdaw (*Corvus monedula*), Peregrine (*Falco peregrinus*), Kestrel (*Falco tinnunculus*) and Barn Owl (*Tyto alba*), while the number of migrants killed or trapped runs into hundreds of thousands every year. *Table 1* gives an estimation of the number shot annually of a few selected species (after Sultana & Gauci 1982, and Magnin 1986: both works describe in detail the shooting and trapping carried out in the Maltese Islands).

Shooting is the main conservation hazard and anything the size of a Skylark (*Aluada arvensis*) or larger is shot at. Trapping is mainly confined to finches: Chaffinch (*Fringilla coelebs*), Serin (*Serinus serinus*), Goldfinch (*Carduelis carduelis*), Greenfinch (*C. chloris*), Siskin (*C. spinus*), Linnet (*C. cannabina*) and Hawfinch (*Coccothraustes coccothraustes*)), but Robin (*Erithacus rubecula*) trapping is still very popular, although it has decreased in recent years. The trapping of finches is carried out mainly for caging, while shooting is carried out for fun and for taxidermy. Mounted stuffed birds are very popular for collections as well as for home decorations. Bird-shooting is also carried out at sea from fast motor-powered dinghies and speed-boats, thus intensifying the killing of birds in recent years. Trade in live birds concerns mainly the finches mentioned above.

As in most countries there are legal restrictions against most of the killing and trapping. There are also a number of areas legally declared as bird sanctuaries where all shooting and trapping is prohibited. But the bird laws are neither respected nor properly enforced.

Table 1: Estimation of selected bird species shot annually on the Maltese Islands.

Herons and egrets (*Ardea cinerea, A. purpurea, Egretta garzetta,* *Ardeola ralloides, Nycticorax nycticorax, Ixobrychus minutus*)	3,000 – 5,000
Honey Buzzard (*Pernis apivorus*)	500 – 1,000
Harriers (mostly *Circus aeruginosus*)	500 – 1,000
Falcons (mostly in the following order *Falco tinnunculus, F. subbuteo, F. vespertinus, F. naumanni*)	1,500 – 3,000
Owls (mostly *Otus scops*)	500 – 1,000
Turtle Dove (*Streptopelia turtur*)	100,000 – 200,000
Cuckoo (*Cuculus canorus*), **Bee-eater** (*Merops apiaster*), **Hoopoe** (*Upupa epops*)	2,500 – 5,000
Song Thrush (*Turdus philomelos*)	200,000 – 300,000
Golden Oriole (*Oriolus oriolus*)	4,000 – 7,000

Data by Sultana & Gauci (1982) were based on a number of visits to taxidermists in the late sixties. Magnin's (1986) estimate was based on a survey with several Maltese birdwatchers. Figures by Fenech (in press) are based on recent bags and taxidermists' records and are much higher than previously thought.

MALTA ORNITHOLOGICAL SOCIETY

Foundation

In the midst of this hostile environment for birds, a group of young people decided, in 1962, to set up the Malta Ornithological Society, with the aims of studying and protecting birds and their habitats. Setting up an organization to study birds in Malta was not an unsurmountable task, but forming an organization to protect birds in a country where the killing and trapping of birds was a way of life, was a different matter altogether. The struggle has been an uphill one all the way. The MOS was the first environmental non-governmental organization to be set up in Malta, and to date its membership has grown to over 2,000, with over 80 per cent made up of youths under the age of 24. *Figure 2* shows the rate of growth of the MOS membership.

Main achievements

The achievements of the MOS would not have materialized were it not for the support, both moral and financial, which was received from ICBP and European national organizations such as the RSPB of the United Kingdom, the Vogel Beschmering of the Netherlands, the DBV of the Federal Republic of Germany, the CCPO of Belgium and the former SLKV of Switzerland.

Financial support alone would not have been enough to produce any good results: it needed to be matched with dedication and hardwork from the MOS side. Fortunately this combination was available in Malta and, in fact, seasoned well, with the result that the growth and activities of the MOS accelerated in recent years when financial support was forthcoming. Public relations had to be involved. MOS projects were not only carried out efficiently but were also seen to be carried out. Apart from reaching their objectives, MOS activities created public awareness

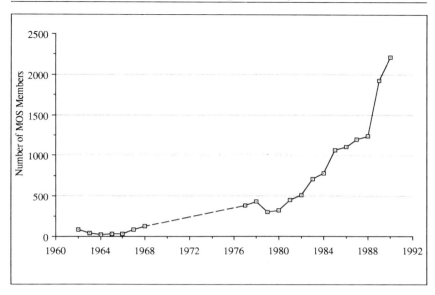

Figure 2: Membership growth of the Malta Ornithological Society.

of the problems, which were being taken for granted or overlooked, and generated interest and funds which could be used for follow-up projects and activities. Well-executed projects and their attendant publicity helped to put MOS on a sound footing, acquiring credibility and respect in the eyes of the authorities and the general public.

The main achievements of the MOS during its first 25 years of existence have been summarized in a special commemorative issue of the MOS magazine *Bird's Eye View* (Doublet 1987). The MOS has been instrumental in the setting up of Malta's first educational nature reserve (*Figure 3*). Ghadira (35°58'N, 14°21'E) was a small, unique, wetland area which until 1978 was rented by the government for the shooting of ducks and other waterbirds. By acquiring funds from overseas, the government was first induced to declare the area a bird sanctuary, and later to give the go-ahead to the MOS to carry out the necessary engineering work to create an improved habitat for birds and to provide educational facilities for visitors.

Work on the reserve started in 1980 and continued during the following three summers. The surface area of the original small pool was enlarged, islands were created, ditches were dug and embankments were constructed surrounding the whole area, while hundreds of trees were planted in appropriate places.

A birdwatching hide and an interpretive centre were also built, and with the posting of a managing warden by the government, groups of young people from schools started to make use of the reserve regularly. The reserve affords sanctuary to many birds during migration, many of which would otherwise be shot in other parts of the islands. But the reserve's main function is educational. Here school children can for the first time watch little waders feeding quietly, unafraid when not molested. Here they can compare the living birds with the lifeless, stuffed effigies in their fathers' collections. Here they can study and observe the elegant Little Egret (*Egretta garzetta*) or the colourful Kingfisher (*Alcedo atthis*) using their

Figure 3: School children visiting Ghadira Nature Reserve. The setting up of this reserve was one of MOS's main achievements. (*Photo*: MOS)

different skills and methods for catching fish which abound in the reserve's brackish water.

The last time that the bird protection regulations were updated, prior to the foundation of the MOS, was in 1937. Since its inception the MOS has lobbied strongly for new bird protection laws, and these were finally issued in 1980. Although leaving much to be desired these regulations can be regarded as a milestone in local bird protection legislation. They introduced for the first time a closed season, limited the number of birds that could be shot or trapped, and updated the list of bird sanctuaries. It is indeed a pity that until now these regulations have very rarely been properly enforced.

The MOS also has various educational and scientific publications to its credit (*Table 2*) and has carried out a continuous educational campaign. In recent years it has started to coordinate a network of teacher delegates in schools to help it in its educational campaigns and to enrol young members.

As can be seen from *Table 2*, MOS has been using printed matter extensively to disseminate information on birds and their conservation as well as to create public awareness. Apart from those listed in *Table 2*, the MOS has published and continues to publish a wide range of leaflets, posters, postcards, handouts, memoranda, reports and car stickers. Funds acquired from the sale of some of the publications were used to subsidize the educational material which was distributed free. Posters with different conservation themes have been regularly printed for distribution in schools and to be exhibited in public places. The popularity of car stickers in Malta has been taken advantage of, and at times the islands were flooded with several different ones all carrying bird conservation messages. Leaflets, posters and stickers were also produced specifically for the various campaigns which the MOS launched from time to time.

Table 2: A selected list of MOS educational and scientific publications.

Bird Studies on Filfla 1970	•	A popular publication to highlight the importance of the islet of Filfla as a breeding station for seabirds.
Il-Merill (26 issues) 1970-1988	•	MOS ornithological journal.
A Guide to the Birds of Malta 1975	•	Annotated checklist.
Bird's Eye View (13 issues) 1977-1990	•	Members' magazine with MOS and local conservation news.
Birds of Prey 1978	•	Educational booklet for schools.
L-Aghsafar 1979	•	Maltese publication with general information on birds and their status in Malta, aimed at the general public. Winner of the Maltese Literary Award 1979.
Breeding Birds 1979	•	Educational booklet for schools.
Il-Ligi Dwar il-Kacca u l-Insib 1981	•	Educational booklet in Maltese defining the bird laws, aimed at shooters and trappers. Distributed free to shooters and trappers through the police licencing office.
A New Guide to the Birds of Malta 1982	•	This publication updated the previous guide, giving past and present status of all birds occurring in Malta, information on the avian environment, distribution of habitats, pattern of migration and ornithological history. Winner of Malta's Literary Award 1982.
Il-Passa ta' l-Aghsafar 1987	•	Educational booklet in Maltese with information on migration for schools.
L-Ghasfur u L-Ambjent Naturali (10 issues) 1983-1989	•	Illustrated magazine for youths on birds and nature in Maltese. Recently renamed 'In-Natura'.

The MOS has also set up a bird-ringing and research scheme with the help of the British Trust for Ornithology (BTO), and has been running this scheme since 1965. In the past decade the MOS has invested heavily in its youth section. The MOS Youths are now a thriving section with their own campaigns, activities and publications. Today's MOS leaders were yesterday's MOS Youths and today's Youths will be tomorrow's leaders. The present strength of the Youths section augurs well for MOS's future. The MOS has also served as an encouragement to other NGOs, one of which "Youths for the Environment", is the offspring of the MOS Youths.

MOS has now evolved into a four tier system – protection, study, education and Youths (*Figure 4*). The credibility which MOS acquired was manifested by the authorities when it was honoured with the issue of an official set of postage stamps to commemorate its 25th Anniversary.

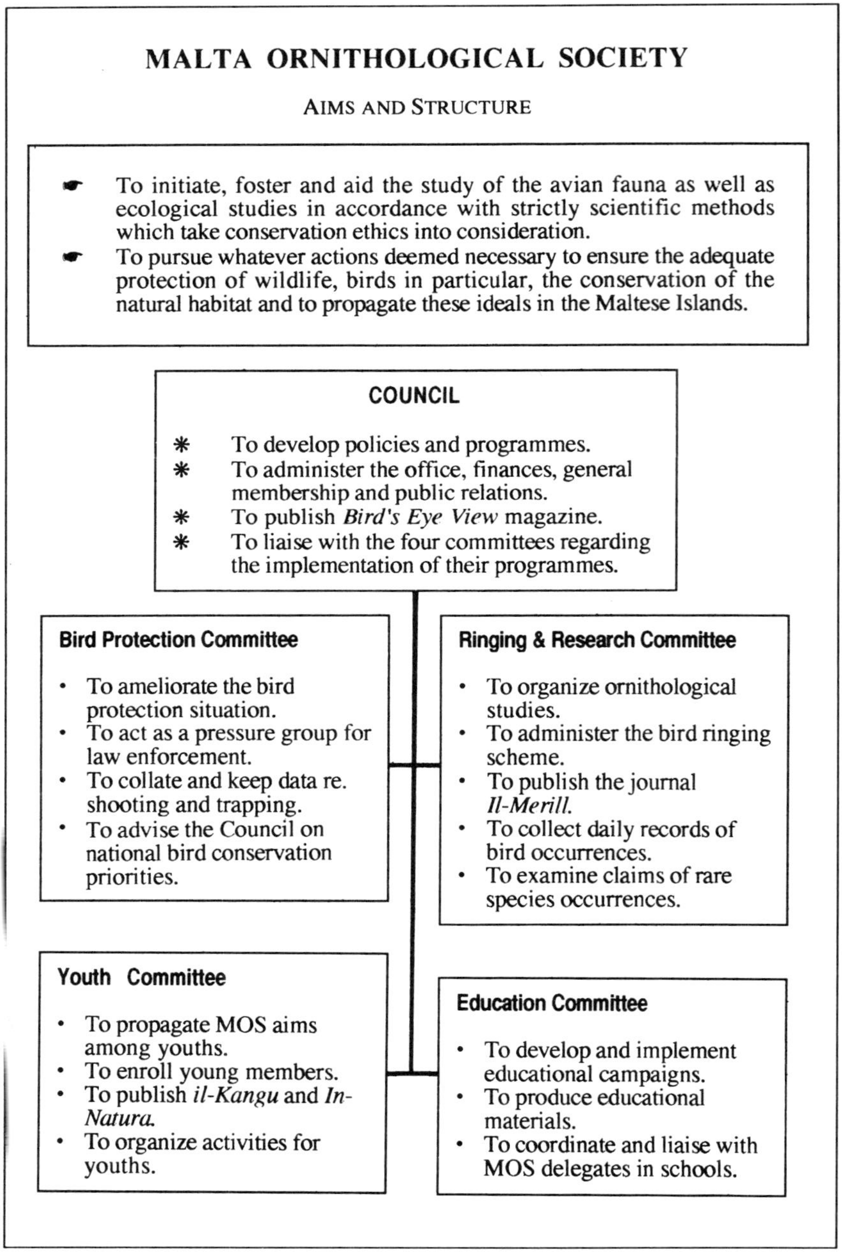

MALTA ORNITHOLOGICAL SOCIETY

AIMS AND STRUCTURE

☞ To initiate, foster and aid the study of the avian fauna as well as ecological studies in accordance with strictly scientific methods which take conservation ethics into consideration.

☞ To pursue whatever actions deemed necessary to ensure the adequate protection of wildlife, birds in particular, the conservation of the natural habitat and to propagate these ideals in the Maltese Islands.

COUNCIL

* To develop policies and programmes.
* To administer the office, finances, general membership and public relations.
* To publish *Bird's Eye View* magazine.
* To liaise with the four committees regarding the implementation of their programmes.

Bird Protection Committee

- To ameliorate the bird protection situation.
- To act as a pressure group for law enforcement.
- To collate and keep data re. shooting and trapping.
- To advise the Council on national bird conservation priorities.

Ringing & Research Committee

- To organize ornithological studies.
- To administer the bird ringing scheme.
- To publish the journal *Il-Merill*.
- To collect daily records of bird occurrences.
- To examine claims of rare species occurrences.

Youth Committee

- To propagate MOS aims among youths.
- To enroll young members.
- To publish *il-Kangu* and *In-Natura*.
- To organize activities for youths.

Education Committee

- To develop and implement educational campaigns.
- To produce educational materials.
- To coordinate and liaise with MOS delegates in schools.

Figure 4: The aims and structure of the MOS.

The increasing amount of work and organization required to carry out all the MOS activities made it essential for MOS to acquire a permanent home. In 1984, a small, old, derelict building was bought with funds that the MOS had raised over the years specifically for such a project. Several members worked incessantly during their spare time to transform it into a decent workplace. Support from ICBP and RSPB helped to furnish this educational centre. The whole place, which is now in regular use, consists mainly of an office, a boardroom, an "infocentre" and a workshop. It is regularly in use for the distribution of material, for the organization of bird conservation plans and for the MOS administration.

Up to the end of 1988, all MOS work had been carried out by council and committee members voluntarily, in their spare time. But with the increasing amount of work, as well as the running of the office, there has been an urgent need to employ a full-time director to manage the MOS education and conservation plans. ICBP's Migratory Birds Programme came to the rescue and the MOS has now employed a full-time director as from January 1989. His main job will be to increase MOS efficiency in its bird protection campaign. His terms of reference also include the raising of funds from local quarters, so that when ICBP's contract is exhausted, MOS will be in a position to continue his employment. Work generates work and the MOS office already seems to have shrunk due to the exigencies of the increasing volume of work.

Current problems

In spite of all the efforts and campaigning against bird killing and trapping the impact of the shooters and trappers has not ameliorated. Although MOS has managed to arouse public awareness of the problems, as well as to acquire the sympathy of the public in general, indiscriminate killing and trapping of birds are still the order of the day. A general improvement in the standard of living, which has taken place in the past 25 years, has meant that more efficient and modern guns could be afforded, while more leisure time was available. The result was that shooting and trapping became more and more intensive.

The growth of the MOS and its credibility triggered off stronger opposition from the shooters and trappers, who rallied together to oppose, at times aggressively, every move of the MOS. When MOS organizes a protest against illegal shooting, the bird-shooters association organizes a counter-protest; and although the authorities and the political parties are generally sympathetic to the conservation cause, the shooters' lobby is still much stronger.

The MOS has been aiming, in recent years, at specific problems, such as the illegal Robin trapping and the shooting of birds of prey, to mention two examples. Thousands of Robins are trapped annually on their arrival in autumn, mainly by the younger generation, and most of these die in captivity after a few days. Due to MOS efforts this practice is now on the decrease. The annual anti-robin-trapping campaign is launched in October to coincide with the arrival of the birds. Street actions, distribution of literature in schools and the use of the mass media are some of the efforts used to counter this problem.

Another priority problem which has been preoccupying MOS is the continual illegal shooting of migrating birds of prey. MOS launches annual campaigns against this practice, urging the authorities to take the necessary action to curb these abuses, and creating more public awareness against bird shooting.

RECOMMENDATIONS

The present situation cannot be improved unless the sympathy towards birds, which has been successfully instilled in the general public over recent years, is not transformed from a lethargic one into a vociferous one, which would plead for bird conservation, thus countering the shooters' strong lobby. This has to be complemented by the updating and enforcing of bird protection laws, for which the authorities' will seems at present to be lacking.

The MOS's dedication in its educational role for bird conservation should be matched officially by the authorities, not only in the form of direct support, but also by making conservation a genuine priority of government, and by working in close cooperation with MOS.

Updating existing laws, which is a prerequisite, becomes futile unless these laws are rigorously enforced. It has been learnt through bitter experience that enacting laws and enforcing them are two different things altogether. The enforcement of bird laws is a *sine qua non* if the present bad situation is to be changed. This could only come about with the setting up of an environmental police section, whose main aim would be to see that the environmental laws are respected and enforced. A memorandum detailing such a proposal has already been sent by the Malta Section of ICBP to the authorities. Until the local conservation lobby is strong enough to put pressure on the authorities to act in this respect, international organizations will continue to have an important role to play here.

ACKNOWLEDGEMENTS

Grateful acknowledgement is due to Tobias Salathé, who commented on a totally different first draft of this contribution and for his useful suggestions to structure the text, which was originally an oral presentation.

REFERENCES

BEAMAN, M. & GALEA, C. (1974) The visible migration of raptors over the Maltese Islands. *Ibis* **116**: 419-431.
BIJLSMA, R. G. (1987) *Bottleneck areas for migratory birds in the Mediterranean region.* Cambridge, U.K.: International Council for Bird Preservation (Stud. Rep. 18).
DELUCCA, C. (1969) Bird migration over the Maltese Islands. *Ibis* **111**: 322-337.
DOUBLET, J. A., ed. (1987) *Bird's eye view.* No. 11 (special 25th anniversary edition). Valetta: Malta Ornithological Society.
FENECH, N. (in press) Fatal flight – a critical study of bird shooting and trapping in the Maltese islands. London: Quiller Press.
GRIMMETT, R. F. A. & JONES, T. A. (1989) *Important bird areas in Europe.* Cambridge, U.K.: International Council for Bird Preservation (Techn. Publ. 9).
MAGNIN, G. (1986) *Assessment of illegal shooting and catching of birds in Malta.* Cambridge, U.K.: International Council for Bird Preservation (Stud. Rep. 13).
MOREAU, R. E. (1972) *The Palearctic–African bird migration systems.* London and New York: Academic Press.
SCHEMBRI, P. J., LANFRANCO, E., FARRUGIA, P., SCHEMBRI, S. & SULTANA, J. (1987) *Localities with conservation value in the Maltese Islands.* Malta: Environment Division, Ministry of Education.
SCHEMBRI, P. J. & SULTANA, J., eds. (1989) *Red data book for the Maltese Islands.* Malta: Department of Information.
SULTANA, J. & GAUCI, C. (1982) *A new guide to the birds of Malta.* Valletta: Malta Ornithological Society.
WOLDHEK, S. (1980) *Bird killing in the Mediterranean.* Second edition. Zeist: European Committee for the Prevention of Mass Destruction of Migratory Birds.

ICBP Technical Publication No. 12, 1991

SPECIES PROTECTION AS A STRATEGY FOR CONSERVATION ACTION IN AFRICA: THE CASE OF THE ROSEATE TERN IN GHANA

YAA NTIAMOA-BAIDU

Zoology Department, University of Ghana, Legon, Accra, Ghana

ABSTRACT

The Save the Seashore Birds Project (SSBP), a joint venture between the International Council for Bird Preservation (ICBP), the Royal Society for the Protection of Birds (RSPB) and the Ghana Government, was established in 1985 as a result of the concern over the rapidly declining populations of the Roseate Tern (*Sterna dougallii*). Using the Roseate Tern as the focal point, the activities of the SSBP have produced results far beyond the initial objective of saving a single species. These include: training of local ornithologists; the identification of important coastal bird habitats; the enacting of laws protecting all terns and selected wetland habitats; increased involvement of scientists in the formulation of environmental and wildlife conservation policies; participation of Ghana in international wildlife conventions; and above all, an increased awareness and concern of the general Ghanaian public for conservation issues and the need to protect wildlife. The achievements of the SSBP clearly demonstrate how concern and action for a single threatened species by international conservation organizations can raise the general status of conservation in countries whose economic situations would otherwise make it impossible to accord any priority to wildlife conservation.

INTRODUCTION

In March 1985, a group of concerned conservationists, scientists and administrators met in Cheltenham, U.K. The group comprised representatives of the International Council for Bird Preservation (ICBP), the Royal Society for the Protection of Birds (RSPB) and the Government of Ghana, as well as invited independent specialists. The concern was over the declining population of the Roseate Tern (*Sterna dougallii*), Britain's rarest breeding seabird. The Irish and British breeding population of this species has declined from some 2,500 pairs to under 500 pairs within the last 20 years (Avery 1987).

The ICBP and RSPB, both conservation organizations working in the interest of birds, were there because they were anxious to save the Roseate Tern and were prepared to make resources available for this purpose. Ghana was invited because her coastal area, which had been identified as an important wintering ground for the Roseate Tern, was also notorious for tern trapping. Ghana recognized the need for wild animal protection, and had the will to initiate appropriate measures. However, faced with numerous more pressing socio-economic responsibilities, Ghana could simply not afford to spend her limited resources on bird protection. The purpose of the meeting, therefore, was to develop international cooperation whereby Ghana, with her will-power and human resources, could use ICBP and RSPB financial and technical resources to save the Roseate Tern.

The Roseate Tern, however, does not move in isolation: therefore the exercise had to include all the other terns that breed in Europe and winter along the Gulf of Guinea coast. Again, these terns share habitat and food resources with other seabirds and shorebirds; and therefore these also had to be taken care of. Thus, even before the project took off, the idea of saving the Roseate Tern had expanded to incorporate all sea- and shorebirds. Hence, with the signing of an agreement between the three bodies (ICBP, RSPB, Ghana Government) in June 1985, the Save the Seashore Birds Project (SSBP) was established, with the aim of protecting both migratory and resident seashore birds and their coastal habitat through research, site protection and education.

This paper reviews the activities and achievements of the SSBP over its first four years, and the effects that these have had on the status of general wildlife conservation in Ghana.

DEVELOPMENT OF LOCAL MANPOWER

Both ICBP and RSPB recognized right from the start that the crucial factors for the success of the project were the involvement of local people both in the decision-making process and implementation, and the availability of trained local manpower. The RSPB therefore made resources available for both formal and informal training of personnel in the U.K. and Ghana. The result is that each member of the team of six persons working for the project has received some form of training, from bird counting to wetlands management and conservation education work.

The RSPB has also supported local training courses. The first one, a three-week international course on Site Management and Species Protection, was held in August 1987 at the University of Ghana. Five West African countries, Ghana, Nigeria, Sierra Leone, Liberia and The Gambia benefited from the course. The 15 participants returned to their homes with a new zeal to promote wetland and bird conservation in their countries.

A second training programme, also held at the University of Ghana, in July 1988, brought together 18 Wildlife Club leaders. The need for this programme arose from the realization that most of the club leaders had limited knowledge of wildlife and often did not know what to do with their clubs. In addition to the training given to the participants on the organization and running of Wildlife Clubs, the workshop also provided a forum for exchange of ideas and generated a lot of interest and enthusiasm among the leaders.

A series of wildlife camps, aimed at increasing knowledge of wild animals and their habitat have also been planned for the club members. The first of such camps was held in December 1988 and was very successful.

CONTRIBUTION TO SCIENTIFIC KNOWLEDGE

An important component of the project's work has been the monitoring of coastal bird populations. Regular surveys are undertaken to assess seashore bird populations in selected key wetland habitats. Through this work it has come to light that the coast of Ghana is not only important for terns, but that it harbours significant shorebird populations. At least nine species of waders – Curlew Sandpiper (*Calidris ferruginea*), Spotted Redshank (*Tringa erythropus*), Greenshank (*T. nebularia*), Little Stint (*C. minuta*), Sanderling (*C. alba*), Ringed Plover (*Charadrius hiaticula*), Grey Plover (*Pluvialis squatarola*), Avocet (*Recurvirostra avosetta*), Whimbrel (*Numenius phaeopus*) occur in internationally important populations (Ntiamoa-Baidu & Grieve 1987; Ntiamoa-Baidu & Hepburn 1988).

A number of coastal wetlands (Keta Lagoon Complex, Songaw Lagoon Complex, Sakumo Lagoon, Densu Delta and Salt Pans Complex, Muni Lagoon) have also been found to be internationally important sites in terms of the species and populations of birds they hold (Ntiamoa-Baidu 1988, in press). Proposals have been submitted for some of these sites to be designated and protected as Ramsar Sites. Boundary demarcation of one of the sites, Sakumo Ramsar Site, is almost completed.

A recent development has been the initiation of a research programme to investigate in more detail the decline of the Roseate Tern and the possible effects on population numbers of mortality factors operating in Ghana. The research, coordinated by RSPB Research Department and part-funded by the European Commission, involves studies of breeding success in all colonies in western Europe and complementary studies on the wintering grounds in Ghana. The work in Ghana, organized through the project, includes a detailed investigation of the trapping of terns along the coastline of Ghana as well as monitoring of the numbers, distribution and movements of roseates and other tern species on the Ghana coast.

NATIONAL CONSERVATION ACTIONS RESULTING FROM SSBP's EFFORTS

One important factor that has contributed to the success of the SSBP is the high degree of interest shown, and the support given, by high-ranking Ghanaian Government officials. This is, to a large extent, due to the fact that the project, through its activities, has gained credibility as a serious conservation organization. The project has been consulted several times on conservation issues in the country; and on each occasion the advice from the project has been taken seriously in government decision-making.

Upon the advice of the project, the Ghana Government has taken several concrete measures which demonstrate its concern for seashore birds and its determination to protect these birds and their wetland habitats. The measures include the ratification of both the Ramsar and Bonn conventions, and the enacting of a law (PNDC Law 1357 of 1 January, 1988) which gives complete protection to all terns in Ghana.

Table 1: Distribution and membership of Wildlife Clubs of Ghana (as at 31 March 1989).

Region	No. of clubs	Membership
Central Region	11	610
Greater Accra Region	9	506
Volta Region	8	470
Eastern Region	2	98
TOTAL	30	1,692

CHANGING ATTITUDES

The impact of the SSBP's activities on the Ghanaian public in respect of creating awareness and promoting interest in conservation issues is probably the project's most important achievement.

This has been made possible through education programmes and public awareness campaigns. Education programmes undertaken include talks, slide and film shows; and the target groups have been mainly school children and coastal communities. Community programmes often attract crowds up to 4,000.

In March 1987, the project launched the Wildlife Clubs of Ghana. At the time of the launching there were only two clubs (both based in schools in Accra and formed as a result of the project's involvement with these schools). *Table 1* gives the present distribution and membership of the Wildlife Clubs. Thirty clubs have been formed in four regions, with a total membership of 1,692 which keeps growing every day. The project's education team pursues a regular programme of school visits, and encourages formation of clubs.

The project supports existing clubs by providing them with education materials. The project has also started producing a club magazine *Nko* ("The Parrots"), aimed at keeping the Ghanaian public informed of conservation issues and promoting exchange of ideas between club members. The clubs themselves generate some funds through membership dues and are able to organize field trips and other activities.

The public awareness activities undertaken include television and radio programmes, production and distribution of publicity materials (pencils, badges, stickers) and special events such as exhibitions and competitions. A short film "Save the Seashore Birds" produced by the project has been highly commended and has been shown several times on Ghana television.

The question often asked is how we know that our education programmes are bearing fruit. Although such results are difficult to quantify, there is some evidence that the Ghanaian public is showing increasing interest and concern for wildlife and environmental conservation issues. The first piece of evidence is provided by the degree of public participation in conservation-related events. In 1986, a national essay competition on wildlife conservation was organized for primary schools. Not a single entry was received. The exercise was repeated early 1989, and as many as 222 entries were received (*Table 2*). An art exhibition on wildlife (the first of its kind) also organized early 1989 recorded 106 entries from 62 participants.

Table 2: Participation in wildlife competitions.

Year	Type of competition	Topic/theme	Category of persons eligible	No. of participants (entries)
1986	Essay	The benefit of conservation of wildlife to Ghana	Elementary school pupils	0
1989	Essay	What wildlife means to me	Elementary school pupils	126
1989	Essay	Conservation for a better future	Students of secondary schools and training colleges	96
1989	Art	Wildlife is our life	Ghanaian artists	62 (106)

A second piece of evidence for the growing public interest in conservation is provided by the great increase in the number of news items, articles and other materials on wildlife and environmental conservation issues reported in the national newspapers. The assumption here is that journalists tend to report on topical issues. A survey of news items reported in *The Daily Graphic* (Ghana's most popular newspaper) over the period 1986-1989, showed a mean of four items on wildlife and related issues per month in 1986, as compared with 30 items per month during the first quarter of this year (*Figure 1*). Articles published ranged from wild animal protection to forestry and environmental issues, including bushfires and desertification.

While we do not by any means claim total credit for this great increase in press interest in conservation-related issues, we believe that the SSBP's activities have contributed immensely to sensitizing the Ghanaian public to the need for wildlife protection and the sustainable use of Ghana's wildlife resources.

LOCAL PEOPLE'S PERCEPTIONS

Experience has shown that conservation projects in Africa can achieve the desired impacts only if the local people can identify themselves and their needs with the projects, and derive concrete benefits from the activities of such projects. Hence, an important factor, which had to be carefully handled to ensure acceptance of the project by the local people, was the people's perceptions and attitudes.

One of the questions I have had to give varied answers to, depending on who is asking the question and where, is "why are we saving seashore birds?". The most simple answer is that seabirds, particularly terns, are useful because they help fishermen locate fish shoals. Very often the simple answer is not satisfactory. In one place I may talk of the importance of coastal lagoons to local communities, stressing the fact that seashore birds form part of the coastal ecosystem, and that destruction of any part of the system upsets the balance. In other places I relate the need for seashore bird protection to the abundance of bushmeat in the past and the present scarcity resulting from over-exploitation. Sometimes the answer focuses on the tourist, recreational, educational and scientific values of seashore birds. It is only on very few occasions that aesthetic value is mentioned: a value which is very important on the European scene but which means very little to the Ghanaian, who sees wildlife primarily as a source of food and/or cash income.

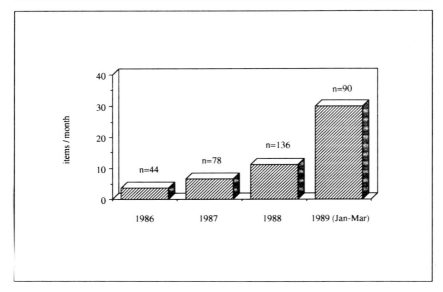

Figure 1: Growth in the number of news items and articles on wildlife and environmental
conservation issues reported in *The Daily Graphic* (1986-1989).

Whether the Roseate Tern becomes extinct or not probably means nothing to the
ordinary Ghanaian.   But the fact that coastal lagoons are over-exploited and
polluted while he is not getting enough fish; the fact that there is scarcity of
bushmeat because of over-exploitation and habitat destruction; the fact that the
river in the village which is the only source of water has dried up because the
watershed has been farmed; all mean a lot to him.   It is all a question of people's
values, attitudes and perceptions; and these are factors which should be seriously
considered in promoting conservation in Africa.

CONCLUSION

The Save the Seashore Birds Project has obviously moved well beyond the initial
aim of protecting a single species – the Roseate Tern.   Although limitations in
resources often make it necessary to have a restricted focus, it is obvious that the
SSBP would not have been so successful if the project's activities had focused
only on the Roseate Tern.   The SSBP's education programmes aim, among other
things, to divert the coastal children's interest in birds from trapping and
destruction to caring and enjoyment. We may or may not succeed in stopping tern
trapping completely, but there is some indication that the rate of trapping has
declined as a result of the project's education activities.   The reduction in tern
trapping may or may not alter the status of the Roseate Tern, since survival of the
species is influenced by a number of factors other than trapping.   Whatever the
outcome, the most important achievement at the end of the day would be the fact
that the SSBP would have succeeded in sensitizing the Ghanaian public to the need
for protection and sustainable utilization of Ghana's wildlife resources.

The results of the current research on the occurrence and rates of tern trapping should allow more specific education actions to be undertaken, directed at eliminating this practice where it occurs. In addition, the research may reveal other factors operating in Ghana which are contributing to the decline of the Roseate Tern, and this may allow more specific conservation actions to be directed at improving the situation and prospects for the species.

The achievements of the SSBP over the four years of its existence clearly demonstrate how the concern and action for a single threatened migratory species by international conservation organizations can promote general conservation action in countries which otherwise could not afford to give wildlife conservation any priority. Both ICBP and RSPB deserve high commendation for the project's achievements and the approach adopted. It is encouraging that the two organizations are expanding their activities in West Africa, and it is hoped that they will draw on the Ghana experience and use bird protection as a means for promoting general conservation action in the region.

REFERENCES

AVERY, M. (1987) Protection of *Sterna dougallii*. Royal Society for the Protection of Birds and Irish Wildbird Conservancy Contract No. 12.05.87.003832.

NTIAMOA-BAIDU, Y. (in press) *Terns in coastal Ghana.*

NTIAMOA-BAIDU, Y. (1988) *Three years of Saving Seashore Birds in Ghana.* Save the Seashore Birds Project Publ. No. 2.

NTIAMOA-BAIDU, Y. & GRIEVE, A. (1987) Palearctic waders in coastal Ghana in 1985/1986. Pp. 76-78 in N. C. Davidson & M. W. Pienkowski, eds. *The conservation of international flyway populations of wader.* Slimbridge, U.K.: Wader Study Goup (Bull. 49, Suppl.)/ International Waterfowl and Wetlands Research Bureau (Spec. Publ. 7).

NTIAMOA-BAIDU, Y. & HEPBURN, I. R. (1988) Wintering waders in coastal Ghana. *RSPB Conserv. Rev.* **2**: 85-88.

ICBP Technical Publication No. 12, 1991

THE HADEJIA-NGURU WETLANDS CONSERVATION PROJECT IN NIGERIA

NONIE D. COULTHARD

*Royal Society for the Protection of Birds,
The Lodge, Sandy, Bedfordshire SG19 2DL, U.K.*

ABSTRACT

The Hadejia-Nguru Wetlands Conservation Project (HNWCP) was established to try to achieve the conservation and sustainable development of a wetland in northern Nigeria which is a wintering area for migrant Palearctic waterfowl and waders. The Hadejia-Nguru Wetlands are threatened by development plans, including dams and large-scale irrigation upstream, which would eliminate or severely reduce the annual flood.

It is argued that annual flooding is essential, not just to maintain a wetland habitat for birds but also to ensure the livelihood of people in the area. The flood supports highly productive traditional systems of flood-recession agriculture and fishing, as well as assuring immediate water supplies and replenishing ground-water reserves.

Some initial problems encountered by the project, and the effectiveness of attempted solutions are discussed. Problems included misconceptions about the project's aims, and difficulties arising from the fact that the project area crosses state boundaries.

Two arguments are raised to counter the criticism that the project area contains lower numbers of migrant waterfowl than other wetlands in the region (notably Lake Chad). One is a fundamental argument about the ways in which conservation projects in Africa can achieve success; the second concerns the need to conserve and monitor all Sahelian wetland sites because of the poorly-understood movements of migrant waterfowl between these sites both within and between European winters.

Dagona Waterfowl Sanctuary is described as an example of action undertaken by the project to demonstrate the effective integration of bird conservation with local human needs.

The conclusion is reached that the conservation of wetland habitats in the Sahel will be achieved only through the involvement of local people and through winning political arguments. Projects such as the HNWCP must demonstrate the effective integration of conservation with small-scale development, and convince decision-makers that this can represent a better alternative to large-scale damming and irrigation schemes – an alternative with long-term, sustainable benefits for both people and birds.

INTRODUCTION

According to World Bank estimates, one in every five or six Africans is a Nigerian, and the population is predicted to grow from the current level of just over 100 million to 529 million (or 500 people per km^2) by the year 2035 (figures quoted in IUCN 1988).

Such a population increase will inevitably result in enormous social pressures and changes and ever-increasing demands by the human population on the country's natural resources. The region of northern Nigeria that is the subject of this paper has already, in recent years, seen rapid increases in population and changes in land-use and agricultural methods (Adams & Hollis 1989). Faced with such a climate of change and human need, it is no easy task to convince people of the importance of conserving migratory birds. At best, conservation may be seen as irrelevant; at worst it may be seen as detrimental to human needs. The task for conservation projects, therefore, is to find ways of reconciling human and conservation needs and to obtain the support and confidence of local people in the actions undertaken by the project.

MIGRATORY BIRDS IN NORTHERN NIGERIA

As one of the larger countries south of the Sahara, Nigeria is a significant area for both the reception and passage of trans-Saharan migrants (Elgood *et al.* 1966). Such Palearctic migrants, which breed in Europe and migrate to spend the northern winter months in Africa, constitute a very important part of Nigeria's avifauna: an estimated 150 (or 18 per cent) of the total list of 800 bird species for Nigeria (Elgood 1981).

Nigeria as a whole may be a particularly important wintering area for certain passerines. For example, Whitethroats (*Sylvia communis*), Wheatears (*Oenanthe oenanthe*) and Yellow Wagtails (*Motacilla flava*) have all been estimated to occur in tens to hundreds of thousands (Elgood *et al.* 1966; Wood 1976). In addition, Nigeria, like other countries bordering the Sahara and containing wetlands of significant size, is of particular importance to migratory Palearctic waterfowl and waders (Ash & Sharland 1986). Regular mid-winter censuses of Palearctic waterfowl in West Africa have revealed three areas of major importance south of the Sahara: the inland delta of the Niger River in Mali, the Senegal River valley and the Lake Chad basin (including the part that falls within Nigeria) (Roux & Jarry 1984; Monval *et al.* 1987).

The Hadejia-Nguru Wetlands lie within the Lake Chad basin and were identified as a specific area of importance to both Palearctic and Afro-tropical water birds (Ash & Sharland 1986). Prior to the establishment of the Hadejia-Nguru Wetlands Conservation Project, however, no detailed counts were carried out in the area.

NORTHERN NIGERIA: PEOPLE AND DEVELOPMENT

Most of northern Nigeria north of a line running west to east at approximately 11 degrees latitude lies within the vegetation zone known as "Sudan savanna". The area is characterized by rainfall of between 500 mm and 1,000 mm per year, which falls almost entirely during the months of May to September, the remaining seven months of the year representing the "dry season" (Elgood 1981). The natural vegetation consists of woodland dominated by trees such as Acacia (*Acacia albida*) and Baobab (*Adansonia digitata*). However, the habitat has been extensively degraded by human activity and livestock grazing, resulting in a landscape now dominated in many areas by grasses and thorn scrub.

The area of interest to the project described consists of the flood-plains of two rivers, the Hadejia and the Jama'are, which flow in a north-easterly direction and combine to form the Yobe River flowing eventually into Lake Chad (*Figure 1*).

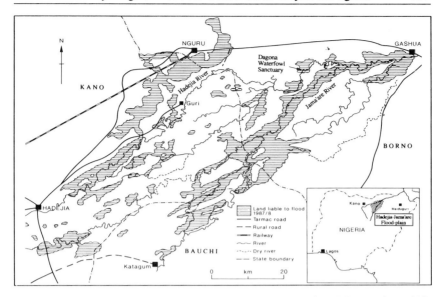

Figure 1:   The Hadejia-Jama'are flood-plain (the 'project area') and its location within Nigeria.

The annual flood in these two rivers spreads out over the surrounding plains from about July onwards, reaching its maximum extent around September, at the end of the rains.   Thereafter, flood-water levels decline until, by June (just before the onset of the next rains), much of the flood-plain area is dry, apart from permanent water-courses and pools in otherwise dry river beds.

Traditional human use of the flood-plain areas reflected these temporal changes in water levels: as the flood rose, people moved away from the vicinity of the rivers, together with their livestock, and cultivated higher ground watered by the rains.   As the flood receded again, people and livestock moved back to cultivate the plains recently fertilized by sediments carried down by the flood.   Important fisheries also depended on the annual cycles of flooding and gradual drying-out, and the Hadejia-Nguru Wetlands were well-known in the past as an area of very high productivity, exporting products including dried or smoked fish and market vegetables to Kano and even as far as Lagos (Adams & Hollis 1989).

The annual flood is also vital in other ways, related to the hydrology of the region.   Apart from acting as an immediate source of water for the wetlands' inhabitants (estimated to number over one million; K. Kimmage, pers. comm.), the flood replenishes ground-water stocks and contributes to the water supply for people who may live tens or hundreds of kilometres from the area actually referred to as "wetlands".

In recent years, however, various development schemes have been devised with a view to eliminating or severely limiting the annual flooding of the rivers in question.   The schemes involve the construction of dams upstream of the Hadejia-Nguru Wetlands, associated with large-scale irrigation to produce commercial crops.   Such schemes ignore the very significant productivity of the wetlands under traditional management, and the fact that local people living within the wetlands will lose their livelihood if the annual flood stops.   Where similar schemes have been implemented elsewhere in northern Nigeria it has quickly become evident that even if the scheme is technically and commercially successful, it is not the local people who benefit (Beckman 1984). Furthermore, such development plans ignore the essential role played by the annual flood in ground-water recharge for the whole region.

The combined effects of drought and upstream impoundment and abstraction of water have reduced water flows into the wetlands and it has been demonstrated that, if all the schemes currently proposed for development on the Hadejia and Jama'are rivers are implemented, there will be no annual flood in the Hadejia-Nguru Wetlands (Adams & Hollis 1989). The project was launched with the aim of combating these threats by finding alternative ways to develop and improve resource use in the area – alternatives which maintain a viable wetland habitat for birds *and* ensure that human exploitation of resources is sustainable in the long-term.

THE HADEJIA-NGURU WETLANDS CONSERVATION PROJECT

The project area in effect encompasses the whole of the combined flood-plains of the Hadejia and Jama'are rivers since the project aims to influence upstream developments to ensure the continued existence of the Hadejia-Nguru Wetlands. The wetlands lie about 200 km east-north-east of Kano city, roughly within a line drawn between the towns of Hadejia, Nguru, Gashua and Katagum, and thus overlap the three northern states of Kano, Borno and Bauchi (*Figure 1*). This whole area covers approximately 5,000 km^2 but much of the land is in fact dry for part or all of the year. In 1987/1988, for example, the maximum area of flood, in September, was estimated at 700 km^2 and the minimum, in June, at 10 km^2 (Benthem, in prep.). Within the area there is a diverse mix of habitats including rice and grass swamps, permanent and temporary marshes, permanent lakes and channels, permanent dry ground and seasonally-flooded plains, the last two categories often extensively cultivated.

The project, initially known as the "Lake Chad Basin Wetland Project – Nigeria" was launched in April 1987 with the signing of a three-year renewable Agreement between the Federal Government of Nigeria, ICBP and The Royal Society for the Protection of Birds (RSPB). The initial aims were stated as follows:

- To explore appropriate land-use options for the water resources of the Hadejia-Nguru Wetlands, to the benefit of wildlife and human communities.
- To monitor wildlife resources, especially Palearctic and intra-African migrants whose movements depend on the seasonal variations in water cover.
- To develop conservation education and public awareness programmes for communities in the area.
- To assist state wildlife departments by training staff both *in situ* and overseas.

The project operates locally through the Nigerian Conservation Foundation (NCF), in collaboration with the ministries responsible for wildlife and natural resources in Bauchi, Borno and Kano states. Funding for the project is provided by RSPB, ICBP, the International Union for the Conservation of Nature and Natural Resources (IUCN), Finnish Aid and the Finnish Association for Nature Protection (FANP), with additional inputs from NCF and the African Wildlife Foundation (AWF).

SOME INITIAL PROJECT PROBLEMS AND
ATTEMPTED SOLUTIONS

Local perceptions of the project

A major problem during the first 18 months of the project was a failure to inform local people (villagers, chiefs and local government) of the aims and intentions of the project. This resulted in basic misconceptions, which ranged from the belief that the project was "another development scheme" involved in dam construction (local workers even offered their services for this purpose), to the idea that the project existed solely to prevent local people capturing wildfowl in order that, when these wildfowl returned to Europe, they could be shot by Europeans.

Part of the reason for the lack of communication was that no one working on the project at this stage was responsible for public awareness and education. Two Nigerians were trained in conservation education techniques in the U.K. but on return to Nigeria did not remain directly attached to the project. There was one expatriate working on the project but his brief was to conduct bird surveys and to map the extent of flooding.

Various recent initiatives have improved the situation considerably. Three Nigerian Project Officers are now attached full-time to the project and one is responsible for a conservation education and awareness campaign, conducted through the organization of local government meetings and visits to villages and communities. The officer gives a slide presentation to illustrate and explain the project's aims and activities. This stresses, in particular, that if the project is successful in helping to conserve the wetland ecosystem as a viable habitat for birds, there will also be a long-term benefit to the resident human population. ICBP migratory birds posters are used to explain the phenomenon of migration and the need for cooperation between countries in the conservation of "shared" birds.

Local game guards from the three states have also been encouraged to explain the project to people in the course of their other activities, in particular to try to ensure that the project is not seen as just a law enforcement agency, preventing people capturing and killing birds. Eighteen game guards from the three states received training in this aspect as well as in bird census techniques on a course run by the project in March 1989 (Smith 1989). This course was extremely popular and further such training will be offered to the state ministries in the future.

It is difficult to evaluate the success of such measures but it appears from the feedback received to date that the project is now better understood locally. Particularly encouraging is the fact that villagers are beginning to ask for help on issues which *are* the project's legitimate concern, such as how to influence those responsible for upstream water management and how to improve agricultural and fisheries production without abandoning traditional methods.

The wide distribution of an explanatory leaflet about the project is helping to inform the general public, both in Nigeria and in other countries, and a similar leaflet in the Hausa and Kanuri languages (produced in Nigeria) should achieve a similar effect locally throughout the flood-plain.

One area which the project does not yet have sufficient resources to tackle is education in schools and the promotion of "Conservation Clubs". Hopefully, the project will become directly involved in this in the future, but for the present its role is to encourage the state ministries of education to undertake conservation education in schools and to assist the ministries in the training of teachers. For example, two week-long education workshops were run for teachers and for Conservation Club leaders in Borno State in March 1988; these were organized in association with the project and funded by AWF (Snelson 1988). Similar initiatives are planned for the other two states.

Project management: ecological ideals versus political realities

Two central problems, relating to project management, were encountered. The first arises from the fact that the project crosses political boundaries, straddling, as it does, three northern states. It makes very sound ecological and hydrological sense to consider the whole flood-plain, or indeed the whole river basin, but there are political consequences.

A number of moves have been made to overcome some of the complexities that have arisen from this situation. Firstly, the project headquarters is situated in Borno State (in Nguru) but the Project Coordinator will be recruited from Kano State. In addition, a management committee on which all three states are represented (in addition to the Federal Department of Forestry) meets every six months to agree on project policy and activities, and regular contacts are maintained between the project and the state ministries throughout the year.

Finally, three Project Officers have been appointed (one from each state), and the management committee was unanimous in agreeing that these officers, although reporting to their respective state ministries, should be assigned responsibilities relating to the whole flood-plain. At the time of writing (early 1990) one officer deals with conservation education and public awareness, one with research and planning, and one with resource utilization and management, across the whole project area.

The second, and related, problem concerned the provision of suitable technical support to the project. This was resolved by the appointment of an expatriate Technical Adviser, part of whose brief was to assist in the identification of suitable Nigerian candidates for the post of Project Coordinator and to provide counterpart training for the coordinator once appointed.

The adviser has played the central role, to date, in supporting the Project Officers and reporting to the management committee and has also been responsible for all project administration in the field. The adviser will continue to play these roles, pending the appointment of the coordinator. During this time, training of Nigerian staff will continue to receive a very high priority, in order to assure the long-term future of the project. Input from outside consultants and tutors will be used where necessary, but the aim will be to establish a core of trained Nigerian conservationists capable of carrying out project activities in the future.

THE PROJECT APPROACH AND SOME SPECIFIC CONSERVATION ACTIONS

"Too few birds"?

At the European end, there has been some criticism of the project for concentrating on an area which may not support particularly large numbers of Palearctic migrants. This criticism, however, ignores both biological and political realities. The area known as the "Hadejia-Nguru Wetlands" was known to support important populations of migrant and resident water birds (Ash & Sharland 1986) but until the project was launched, no detailed counts of waterfowl were undertaken within the flood-plain. (Preliminary reports from the area suggested higher numbers than have been found subsequently during project surveys.) However, the criticism raises (and can be countered by) two important arguments: firstly, a fundamental point about how conservation projects in Africa can achieve success, and secondly, the almost certain inter-dependence of Palearctic waterfowl wintering sites throughout the Sahel.

Success of conservation projects in Africa

Although, clearly, the interest of RSPB and ICBP in initiating a project such as the Hadejia-Nguru Wetlands Conservation Project in Nigeria, is to achieve the conservation of migratory and resident bird species, the ways in which this is achieved may not be straightforward, and various political factors inevitably come into play.

For example, on purely ornithological and conservation grounds, it could be argued that the major priority in the area is to initiate a project on Lake Chad. However, the political complexities of a project which would have to be agreed and administered by four independent countries (Cameroon, Chad, Niger and Nigeria) currently make this an unrealistic proposition and the chances of a successful conservation outcome very low.

The aim of the Hadejia-Nguru Wetlands Conservation Project is to achieve a successful conservation outcome in *one* region of *one* country (northern Nigeria) where there is a realistic chance of success. The primary objective is to save a particular wetland and its birds from destruction or degradation. However, through education and awareness programmes and the demonstration of effective and practical integration of human and wildlife needs in the exploitation of wetland resources, it is hoped that the conservation benefits will spread even more widely than this, helping to encourage positive attitudes to conservation elsewhere in Nigeria and even in other countries.

Although specific conservation actions such as legislation or site protection may be appropriate in some circumstances, in the long-term successful conservation, in Africa as elsewhere, depends on changing peoples' attitudes through education and raising awareness of the issues.

Interdependence of wetland wintering sites

There is growing evidence that Palearctic ducks move between different wetland wintering sites in the Sahel between years and possibly also within a single European winter. An analysis of aerial counts organized by the International Waterfowl and Wetlands Research Bureau (IWRB), and carried out in 1984, 1985 and 1986 in the three main wintering areas for Palearctic waterfowl in West Africa (the Senegal River basin, the inner delta of the Niger River in Mali and the Lake Chad basin) showed numbers fluctuating by as much as a factor of 15 within the same areas in successive years (Monval *et al.* 1987).

It has been suggested that these changes in numbers are largely a consequence of changes in water levels making some sites unsuitable in some years (either too little water or too much, making water bodies too deep for ducks to feed on) (Roux & Jarry 1984; Monval *et al.* 1987). This hypothesis might well have been strengthened, had counts been carried out in the Lake Chad basin in 1985. Relatively low water levels in the basin that year probably created ideal conditions for very large numbers of Palearctic ducks when conditions in the other two major wintering areas were apparently less suitable. Counts were carried out in Mali and Senegal in 1985, but not in the Lake Chad basin; by comparison with earlier years, over a million Palearctic ducks were "missing" from the totals for West Africa. It seems highly likely that these birds (or a large proportion of them) were wintering in the Lake Chad basin, but there is no independent confirmation of this.

A second point to emerge from the analyses is that certain relatively small wetland sites, for example some desert lakes in Mauritania and parts of the Gambia River basin, may act as "refugia" for wildfowl in years when the traditional major wintering areas are unsuitable due to adverse water levels (Monval *et al.* 1987). The Hadejia-Nguru Wetlands may well act as a similar refugium for waterfowl, particularly due to the proximity of the wetlands to Lake Chad (approximately 300 km as the duck flies) where the water level is known to have fluctuated widely in recent years. Unfortunately, no detailed counts were carried out in the wetlands in the years for which the above analyses were conducted, but in the winters of 1987/1988 and 1988/1989 total numbers of Palearctic duck counted in the wetlands were 26,400 and 10,800 respectively (Stowe 1988; Benthem 1991). Results from a January 1990 survey confirm the large fluctuations in numbers between years. Both the numbers of Palearctic duck (43,500) and total wildfowl numbers (58,000) were the highest yet recorded during regular surveys (Stowe & Coulthard 1990).

There is a definite need for repeated and continuing monitoring of waterfowl populations throughout West Africa, especially in years when water conditions in the major river basins vary, in order to elucidate the interdependence of these sites for wintering Palearctic (and Afro-tropical) waterfowl and the relative importance of sites according to prevailing water levels.

The Hadejia-Nguru Wetlands Conservation Project will aim to contribute to this data-gathering, ideally by organizing aerial counts of the wetlands (for compatibility with aerial counts conducted elsewhere) and by contributing to IWRB's West African database and any further West African counts coordinated by IWRB. The project is also promoting more detailed research on the feeding and other requirements of wintering Palearctic ducks and waders in the wetlands, in association with local universities and their students.

Dagona Waterfowl Sanctuary

One of the project activities currently receiving high priority is the attempt to establish a series of sites within the flood-plain at which specific conservation activities are carried out. The intention is to demonstrate how good conservation practices can be integrated with local human needs.

The first of these sites to be established was the Dagona Waterfowl Sanctuary, 28 km east of Nguru in Borno State (*Figure 1*). The area is a Site of Special Conservation Interest under Borno state legislation, and is one of five sites throughout the flood-plain identified as being of particular importance for both Palearctic and Afro-tropical water birds (Benthem 1988; Benthem 1991). The site consists of a permanent water body: an oxbow lake on the Hadejia River. The maximum area of the lake, following replenishment by the annual flood (i.e. around September) is approximately 150 ha: this declines to as little as 15 ha by the end of the dry season in June (Benthem 1988).

In January 1988 the maximum count of Palearctic duck on the oxbow lake was nearly 3,000 (mainly Pintail (*Anas acuta*) numbering 1,960, and Garganey (*A. querquedula*) at 840: Stowe 1988). The lake also holds significant numbers of Afro-tropical ducks and geese at certain times of the year, e.g. 1,200 Spur-winged Geese (*Plectropterus gambensis*) and 900 Knob-billed Geese (*Sarkidiornis melanota*) in July 1989 (M. Dyer, pers. comm.). The oxbow lake serves a variety of other functions. In addition to waterfowl habitat it is an important source of fish for nearby Dagona village and a water supply for livestock.

Following designation of the site as a waterfowl sanctuary during the visit by HRH the Duke of Edinburgh to the project area in February 1989, various conservation activities have been initiated at the site, designed to minimize any conflict between the needs of the people of Dagona village and the birdlife. A fisheries consultant contracted by the project made general recommendations for management of fisheries throughout the flood-plain and specific recommendations for certain sites, including Dagona (IUCN, in prep.). Some recommendations are extremely simple: for example, allowing cattle access to drink only at certain points around the oxbow lake to prevent muddying and destruction of aquatic vegetation. This should improve water conditions for the fish and also benefit the birdlife.

Other conservation activities are more complex and require careful integration with the activities and needs of the local community. In the case of Dagona, this process is greatly facilitated by the fact that the villagers are proud of their waterfowl sanctuary and have requested help from the project to protect it. The project and the Borno State Ministry of Animal and Forest Resources (MAFR) have already helped Dagona village to fence part of the peninsula enclosed by the oxbow to protect it from livestock and to re-plant it with native tree species to enrich the habitat.

The project is also helping with a scheme to construct an artificial fish-pond for the village, which should improve the year-round supply of fish for the population of Dagona as well as relieving some of the fishing pressure (and associated disturbance to birds) on the waterfowl sanctuary. Local fisheries expertise from the Borno State MAFR is being sought in the design of the fish-pond and the choice and management of fish species.

This exercise will be in part experimental but, if successful, is one that could be repeated in similar situations elsewhere in the wetlands. The project intends to help local communities to establish similar "demonstration projects" in a number of sites throughout the flood-plain. The projects are intended to find ways of helping the local community to improve their traditional practices of agriculture, fisheries or livestock husbandry, and to demonstrate the successful and sustainable exploitation of water and water-related resources to other communities.

Conservation education and awareness will have a major role to play at Dagona. It is an ideal site for showing birds to local school children and people from other areas in the wetlands, and there is now a permanent viewing hide (erected for the visit of HRH the Duke of Edinburgh). The aim of such visits will be to explain to people the phenomenon of migration, where the Palearctic ducks go to during the rainy season and why countries should cooperate in their conservation.

CONCLUSIONS: PLANS AND GOALS FOR THE FUTURE

This paper has outlined some of the problems experienced by the Hadejia-Nguru Wetlands Conservation Project in its early days, and some attempted solutions. It was inevitable that there would be initial problems, especially given the political, social and ecological complexity of the area in which the project operates. However, there have been some notable achievements, and the project now has a much greater sense of identity and direction of purpose than it had initially. Following an essential preliminary period involving mainly research and investigation of various kinds, the project will now move forward to consolidate this through implementing some of the recommendations made by consultants and achieving practical conservation actions on the ground.

In addition to "demonstration projects" as described above and continuing research, education, awareness and training activities, another aspect is considered to be of vital importance to the future of the project: this can be described as "influencing decision-makers".

Influencing decision-makers
The success or failure of the Hadejia-Nguru Wetlands Conservation Project may depend ultimately on its ability or inability to influence political decisions

concerning water use and development within the Hadejia-Jama'are flood-plain. If political decisions are taken to implement upstream dams and irrigation schemes, the Hadejia-Nguru Wetlands may be totally destroyed, with very serious consequences for both the people and the birds dependent on this wetland ecosystem.

It is thus crucially important for the project to bring to the attention of these decision-makers research findings which show the importance of annual flooding to the hydrology of the whole region and the survival of its human and wildlife populations. Decision-makers must be convinced that viable alternatives to large-scale dams exist, and that resource use within the wetlands can and should be developed in ways that are sustainable in the long term.

From discussions at the annual Project Advisory Committee meeting, to which all organizations with an interest in water use and management within the project area are invited, there appears to be a consensus among professionals in northern Nigeria about the need for a single (preferably federal) body to oversee water use, planning and management across the whole Hadejia-Jama'are river basin.

The Project will seek to influence the decision-making process where it can, by presenting these views and research findings to relevant state and federal ministries in Nigeria and, where possible, influencing international funding organizations to try to ensure that funds are used to achieve sustainable development not destruction of the wetlands. One advantage of a collaborative international project such as this lies in the benefits that can be gained through shared expertise and combined effort. Through links with other wetland conservation projects in West Africa, and collaboration between the international conservation organizations involved, efforts must be made to try to influence national and international attitudes towards development of wetland resources in northern Nigeria and other Sahelian countries. Projects such as the Hadejia-Nguru Wetlands Conservation Project must demonstrate the effective integration of conservation with small-scale development, and convince decision-makers that this represents a better, sustainable alternative to large-scale dams and irrigation. The conservation of migratory birds dependent on wetlands in the region will depend ultimately on winning this political argument.

ACKNOWLEDGEMENTS

I would like to thank all the staff of the Hadejia-Nguru Wetlands Conservation Project and all the local people in the wetlands whose support and cooperation are essential to the success of the project. Alison Blackwell, Patrick Dugan, Mike Dyer, Tobias Salathé and Tim Stowe all helped to improve the manuscript by commenting on various drafts, and Kevin Kimmage drew the figure.

REFERENCES

ADAMS, W. M. & HOLLIS, G. E. (1989) Hydrology and sustainable resource development of a Sahelian floodplain wetland. Unpubl. report.

ASH, J. S. & SHARLAND, R. E. (1986) *Nigeria: assessment of bird conservation priorities.* Cambridge, U.K.: International Council for Bird Preservation (Stud. Rep. 11).

BECKMAN, B. (1984) Bakolori: Peasants versus State and Industry in Nigeria. Pp. 140-155 in E. Goldsmith & N. Hildyard, eds. *The social and environmental effects of large dams.* Vol. 2. Wadebridge Ecological Centre, U.K.

BENTHEM, W. (1988)   Most important sites for Palearctic waterfowl and waders and recommended key areas in the Hadejia-Nguru Wetlands. Unpubl. draft report to RSPB.

BENTHEM, W. (1991) Flood mapping and waterbird census in the Hadejia-Nguru Wetlands, northern Nigeria, in January-March 1989. Unpubl. final report to RSPB.

ELGOOD, J. H. (1981) *The birds of Nigeria: an annotated check-list.* London: British Ornithologists' Union (Check-list 4).

ELGOOD, J. H., SHARLAND, R. E. & WARD, P. (1966) Palearctic migrants in Nigeria. *Ibis* **108**: 84-116.

IUCN. (in prep.) Combined consultants' report on fisheries, hydrology and sustainable resource development in the Hadejia-Nguru Wetlands. Gland: International Union for the Conservation of Nature and Natural Resources.

IUCN. (1988) Nigeria. Conservation of Biological Diversity. (Briefing document prepared by the World Conservation Monitoring Centre). Cambridge, U.K.: International Union for the Conservation of Nature and Natural Resources.

MONVAL, J.-Y., PIROT, J.-Y. & SMART, M. (1987) *Recensements d'Anatidés et de foulques hivernant en Afrique du nord et de l'ouest: Janvier 1984, 1985 et 1986.* Slimbridge, U.K.: International Waterfowl and Wetlands Research Bureau.

ROUX, F. & JARRY, G. (1984) Numbers, composition and distribution of populations of Anatidae wintering in West Africa. *Wildfowl* **35**: 48-60.

SMITH, K. G. (1989) Hadejia-Nguru Wetlands Conservation Project. Report on Game Guards Training Course 12-22 March 1989. Unpubl. report to RSPB.

SNELSON, D. (1988) Report of visit to Nigeria 12-27 March 1988. Unpubl. AWF report.

STOWE, T. J. (1988) Waterbird survey: Hadejia-Nguru Wetlands, Nigeria, 10 January – 7 February 1988. Unpubl. report to RSPB.

STOWE, T. J. & COULTHARD, N. D. (1990) The conservation of a Nigerian wetland: the Hadejia-Nguru Wetlands Conservation Project. Pp.80-85 in *RSPB Conservation Review 1990,* 4. Sandy, U.K.: The Royal Society for the Protection of Birds.

WOOD, B. (1976) The biology of Yellow Wagtails *Motacilla flava* L. overwintering in Nigeria. Aberdeen: University of Aberdeen. Unpubl. Ph.D. thesis.

ICBP Technical Publication No. 12, 1991

COOPERATIVE WORK ON CRANE MIGRATION FROM JAPAN TO THE U.S.S.R. THROUGH KOREA AND CHINA

HIROYOSHI HIGUCHI

Research Center, Wild Bird Society of Japan, 2-24-5 Higahsi, Shibuya-ku, Tokyo 150, Japan

ABSTRACT

About 10,000 Hooded and White-naped Cranes (*Grus monacha* and *G. vipio*) migrate down to Izumi, southern Japan, to winter. The number of wintering cranes has been increasing from year to year, and the increase of the population, associated with artificial feeding, causes damage to agricultural products such as wheat and beans. Banding studies showed that some of the cranes migrate to and from the Bikin River Basin and Hingan Reserve in eastern U.S.S.R., and the Zhalung Nature Reserve in north-eastern China. Aerial studies showed that the cranes go along the west coast of Kyushu in Japan in spring and arrive at the mouth of the Nakutongan River, near Pusan, Korea, about nine and a half hours after leaving Izumi. International symposia were held, and it was proposed that dispersing the cranes to other areas in Japan and Korea would be an important way of improving relations between people and the cranes. It is apparent that international cooperation is needed and that it would be effective in studying and conserving the cranes migrating through different countries.

INTRODUCTION

In the winter of 1988/1989, some 8,000 Hooded Cranes (*Grus monacha*) and 1,600 White-naped Cranes (*G. vipio*) wintered at Izumi in Kyushu, the southern part of Japan. These two species breed in the wetlands of Siberia and the northern part of China, and winter in Japan and southern China. Since almost all the populations of Hooded Cranes winter in Japan, the protection of the wintering site of these cranes is extremely important. The Wild Bird Society of Japan (WBSJ) and other organizations and workers have been studying the ecology and status of these cranes to promote their conservation.

During the course of the study, the WBSJ has cooperated with scientists and conservationists in South Korea, North Korea, China and the U.S.S.R. Some cooperative work has been developed over the last ten years, and now further cooperation is developing. This is a review paper on the cooperative activities as well as on the ecology and conservation of the cranes.

IZUMI, THE MOST IMPORTANT SITE FOR CRANES WINTERING IN JAPAN

Location and conservation measures

The Izumi Plain, the wintering site of the cranes, is located in southern Kyushu, Japan (32°0'-32°8'N, 130°15'-130°23'E). It faces the Yatsushiro Sea on one side and low hills on the other side. Some 2,500 ha of paddyfields are developed, and the cranes feed there. Of the 2,500 ha, 51 ha were designated a Natural Monument in 1921. People are prevented from entering the area in winter, and 1.5 ha within the area is used by the cranes as a communal roost. There is an artificial feeding site in the 51 ha area. A total of 250 ha (including the 51 ha area) were further designated a Special Monument in 1952.

Only the 1.5 ha area for roosting is owned by the local government: the rest is private land. Every year the local government rents the 51 ha area from the owner, for the cranes, from the time of harvesting rice to early spring.

Crane species wintering at Izumi

The main species are the Hooded and White-naped Cranes (*Grus monacha* and *G. vipio*). Thousands of these cranes come to the area every winter. The Common Crane (*G. grus*) is rare, and fewer than ten individuals of the species visit the area most years. The Sandhill, Japanese, Siberian and Demoiselle Cranes (*G. canadensis, G. japonensis, G. leucogeranus* and *Anthropoides virgo*) are irregular species, and a few individuals of these species are occasionally found (WWFJ 1985).

Ecology of the wintering cranes

In autumn, the cranes arrive at Izumi in mid-October (Ohsako 1987). The number of cranes increases rapidly in November and is stable from December to February (Ohsako 1987).

Most of the cranes spend the daytime at the feeding site and the neighbouring areas (Nishikantaku, Higashikantaku and Kohama) which are adjacent to the roost. About 8-20 per cent of the Hooded Cranes and 4-6 per cent of the White-naped Cranes fly out in the early morning and stay in the surrounding areas (except the feeding site and the neighbouring areas) during the daytime (Abe *et al.* 1988; Ohsako 1989). All cranes gather in the communal roost at night.

In Hooded Cranes, both solitary birds (about 1-2 per cent) and flocks (98-99 per cent) are found outside the feeding site during the daytime (Ohsako 1989). The flock size ranges from two to more than a hundred. The sizes of flocks with fewer than ten birds, in order of frequency, are three (36.1 per cent), two (16.9 per cent), four (14.5 per cent), six (3.6 per cent), five (2.4 per cent), eight (1.2 per cent), and nine (1.2 per cent), based on the data of December 1980. Probably the two-bird flocks consisting of adults are pairs, and three-bird flocks with one juvenile and four-bird flocks with two juveniles are families. Large-size flocks consist of solitary immature birds, solitary adults, pairs and families. The majority of White-naped Cranes in the surrounding areas are pairs with and without families (Abe *et al.* 1988). In the winter of 1985/1986, 4 per cent of the small groups were pairs, 66 per cent included one juvenile, and 30 per cent included two juveniles.

Pairs and families of Hooded and White-naped Cranes defend territories outside the feeding sites (Ohsako 1989; Yanagisawa 1989). The territories are defended by both sexes, but the male takes the active role in direct attacks on intruders (Ohsako 1989). The size of Hooded Crane territories is estimated to be 5–6 ha (Ohsako 1989). The mate of a pair does not change from year to year unless the

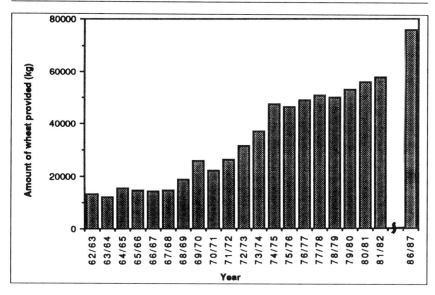

Figure 1: The weight of wheat provided for cranes in recent years. (Data from Ohsako (1987) and Yanagisawa (1989).)

mate dies. The same pair tends to occupy the same site as a territory from year to year.

About 90 per cent of Hooded and White-naped Cranes living in the surrounding area spend the daytime in harvested paddyfields (Yanagisawa 1989). The other cranes stay in wheat and vegetable fields, or in unused paddyfields. A large amount of wheat and a small amount of fish are provided for the cranes at the feeding site. Outside that site the cranes feed on the seeds and tubers of grass and rice, insects, mussels, shrimps and small fish (WWFJ 1985; Hagiwara 1988).

The cranes leave for their breeding grounds in mid-March.

Conservation activities and conservation issues

The wintering population of the cranes was around 500 in the 1920s (WWFJ 1985). Owing to the efforts of local people, such as providing food and safety, the population increased to about 4,000 in 1940 (Hooded, 3,500; White-naped, 500), but the social confusion after World War II reduced the number to only 300 (Hooded, 200-300; White-naped, 20-30); and again local people and the government began to work for the conservation of the cranes. Artificial feeding on a large scale was initiated in the winter of 1962/1963, when 13,410 kg of wheat was provided (*Figure 1*). The population of cranes increased rapidly with the large-scale artificial feeding (*Figure 2*). There is a positive correlation between availability of food and rate of increase of crane population in the following year (*Figure 3*).

The increase in the crane population produced several problems. A serious one is the damage caused to agricultural products such as beans and wheat. It was reported from the local agricultural committee that the damaged area and the extent of damage were respectively about 350 ha and 45 million yen in each year from 1977 to 1979 (WWFJ 1985). To avoid such damage, the government provided

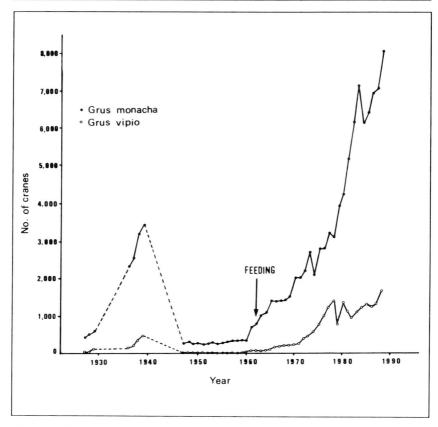

Figure 2: The number of cranes that wintered at Izumi in Kyushu 1927-1989. (From Ohsako (1987) and further data.)

more food to keep the cranes within the 51 ha protected area. In response to this, the cranes began to remain all day at the protected area, and thousands of cranes now live in the 51 ha area (*Figure 4*).

The concentration has also been accelerated by the management of the land surrounding the protected area. This includes readjustment of arable land, making many vinyl plastic houses for green vegetables, and setting nets and strings to repel cranes. Such concentration could be very dangerous for the cranes. Once they get some infectious disease, the whole population of the wintering cranes could face the danger of extinction. The food provided also attracts many ducks, which damage wheat and seaweed in the surrounding area.

There are troublesome problems also in the 51 ha protected area. The rent of the 51 ha area is decided by negotiation between the land owners and the government, and there are big differences in the rent proposed. For example, in the winter of 1980-1981, the rent per 10 a proposed by the owners was 30,000 yen and that by the government was 12,000 yen. Eventually, the rent for the year was set at 13,500 yen (WWFJ 1985), but such a situation leaves the people dissatisfied.

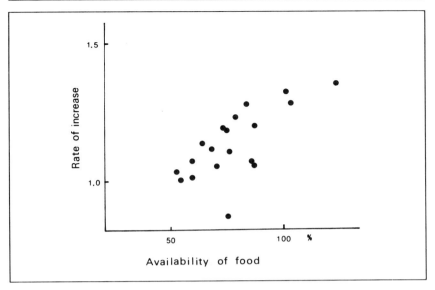

Figure 3: The rate of increase in the number of cranes and relationship between the availability of food in the previous year. Availability of food was calculated by dividing the total amount of food given to cranes in each season by the total amount of food needed for the survival of cranes in each season, multiplied by 100 (Ohsako 1987).

There are several ways of improving the relationship between the local people and the cranes (mostly based on WWFJ 1985). First, important sites for crane life, such as the 51 ha area, should be purchased by the government, whether local or central. If purchase of the important present sites is difficult, alternative sites may be found nearby within Izumi. Making new feeding and roosting sites there, for example, should not be difficult.

Second, some of the cranes wintering at Izumi should be dispersed to other areas. The proposed areas are Ohkuchi, Hishikari and Mannose-gawa in Kagoshima Pref., Aso in Kumamoto Pref., and Nakamura in Kochi Pref. These areas are visited by some cranes every year. Some special techniques may be needed to disperse the cranes there, but the most important method is to reduce the amount of food given at Izumi and to increase the amount and safety at other areas.

Third, conservation biologists and farmers must cooperate to find appropriate methods to reduce the crane damage to agricultural products. Plastic tapes and strings have been set to keep the cranes away from crops. These are sometimes effective; sometimes not. Since the extent of the damage is related to the number of cranes wintering at a location, dispersing cranes is also important in this respect. It is known that the damage was not noticeable when the number of cranes was less than 3,000.

Fourth, a research centre for the cranes is needed. Various kinds of data on the ecology and conservation of the cranes would be collected there, and population estimation and management would be studied by professional biologists.

Finally, laws related to the conservation of the cranes need to be unified. At present the lands the cranes inhabit are managed under the Agricultural Land Law,

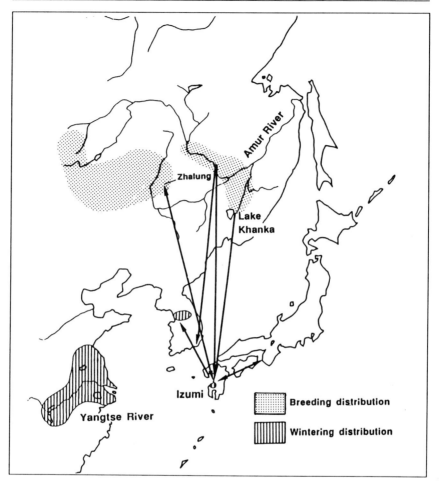

Figure 4: Migration routes of White-naped Cranes (*Grus vipio*) based on ringing data (Ozaki 1988).

matters on the natural monument are controlled by the Law for the Protection of Cultural Properties, and the designation of the wildlife protection areas comes under the Wildlife Protection and Hunting Law. Under such a complicated system of laws, it is very difficult to proceed with effective conservation activities.

THE MIGRATION OF CRANES BETWEEN JAPAN AND THE CONTINENT

Banding project

The Yamashina Institute for Ornithology and the WBSJ sent numbered plastic bands to scientists in China and the U.S.S.R. to study the migration of cranes

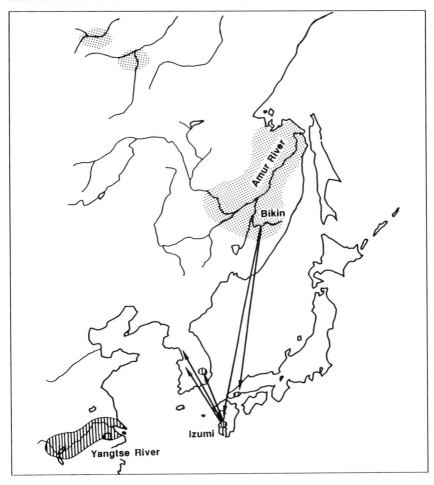

Figure 5: Migration routes of Hooded Cranes (*Grus monacha*) based on ringing data (Ozaki 1988); shading as in *Figure 4*.

between those countries and Japan. This project has been successful, and valuable data have been accumulated (*Figures 5* and *6*). Some examples are listed below.

White-naped Cranes: *J-17 (male) and J-18 (female).* This pair was banded at Izumi on 25 January 1984. They were found in the Zhalung Nature Reserve in northern China in March 1984, and male J-17 was observed on 27 March 1986 at the same place. In June 1987, a chick of J-17 was banded in Zhalung by Mr K. Ozaki of the Yamashina Institute, and it was found at Izumi on 4 December 1987.

Hooded Cranes: *A-50,51,52,53.* These were banded in the Bikin River Basin in the U.S.S.R. on 20-24 July 1985 by Dr Y. V. Shivaev of the U.S.S.R. Academy of Sciences, and were found at Izumi on 20 October 1985.

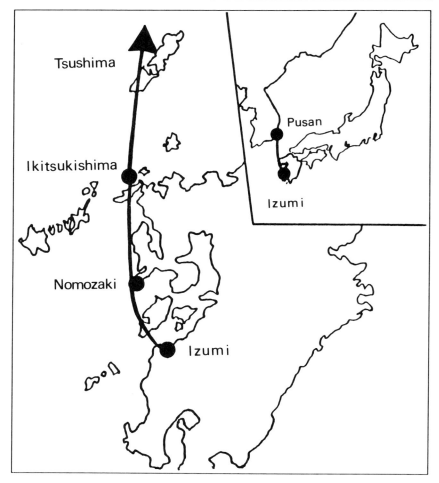

Figure 6: Migration route of Hooded and White-naped Cranes between Japan and Korea as revealed by an aerial study using a motor glider.

White-naped Cranes: *A-18 and A-19.* These were banded in the Hingan Reserve in July 1984 by Dr V. A. Andronov of the U.S.S.R. Academy of Sciences, and found at Izumi in the winter of 1984/1985.

White-naped Cranes: *057 and 060.* These were banded in the Hingan Reserve on 22 July 1984 by Dr S. M. Smirenskii of the U.S.S.R. Academy of Sciences, and were found at Izumi in the winter of 1984/1985.

Aerial study project
A motor glider was used to study the migration route from Izumi, Japan to Pusan, South Korea. That was conducted on 8 March 1987 and 5-9 March 1989. The preliminary study in 1987 was successful, but in 1989 when the weather was not

good we could not fly into Korea, though the migration route within Japan was studied. This aerial study was performed in connection with ground studies. The number of ground study stations was 30 in 1987 and 20 in 1989 in Japan, and 13 in both years in Korea.

Some results obtained were as follows:

1. The cranes migrated along the west coast of Kyushu in Japan. The cranes raised their migrating height by circling in three areas of Kyushu; Kasayama (close to Izumi), Nomozaki and Ikitukishima. The distances between Kasayama and Nomozaki and between Nomozaki and Ikitukishima are almost the same.
2. It took about nine and a half hours for cranes to travel from Izumi to the mouth of the Nakutongan River, near Pusan, Korea.
3. The speed of the migration was 40-50 km/h.
4. The height of the migration was 300-800 m in 1987 and 300-2,000 m in 1989.
5. In 1987, when the weather was fine, the cranes used an ascending current to gain altitude, and then embarked on the migration to the north.
6. The motor glider did not disturb the migrating cranes.

The Argos project

Besides the banding project, the WBSJ has been developing radio transmitters for migratory bird studies in cooperation with the Nippon Telegraph and Telephone Corporation and Dr Masaki Soma of Tokai University. This is a system to study the migration routes of birds using a satellite, NOA.

The transmitters weigh 40-80 grams. The transmitters were successfully used to satellite track Whistling Swans (*Cygnus columbianus*) migrating from Japan to the U.S.S.R. in the spring of 1990 (Higuchi *et al.* in press), and will be attached to the cranes at Izumi in the spring of 1991.

COOPERATION WITH OTHER COUNTRIES

International cooperation is essential if we are to study and conserve the cranes migrating through different countries. However, for many years it was difficult for political and other reasons for biologists and conservationists in the Far East countries to cooperate with each other. The situation is now becoming better, and some cooperative work has started. However, it is just the beginning. The most important need at present is to exchange information on the ecology and conservation of cranes and other birds. The following are brief summaries of cooperative work related to cranes currently being carried out with South Korea, North Korea, China and the U.S.S.R.

South Korea

Joint ground and aerial study for crane migration. A cooperative research project was conducted with the Bird Study groups of six universities of Korea during 9-22 May 1988. Ground observations were made at six areas under the supervision of Dr Kim Tapttuck and Dr Woo Han-Chung. Unfortunately, no big flocks of migrating cranes were observed, but it was a very good trial to study migrating cranes in cooperation with many ornithologists. Joint aerial study has already been mentioned in an earlier section. This was conducted in cooperation with Dr P. Won and other Korean scientists, and some valuable data on crane migration between the two countries were obtained.

Symposium on crane conservation. On 27 February 1988, a crane symposium was held at Izumi in cooperation with Dr Pyong-Oh Won of Korea. The topics included the wintering cranes of South Korea and their conservation (P. Won); the ecology of Hooded Cranes wintering at Taite (Jo Sam-Rae); the present state and conservation of cranes wintering in Japan (Satoshi Nishida); banding studies of cranes in Japan (Kiyoaki Ozaki); and a study of crane migration using the Argos system (Masaki Soma).

Conservation measures in both countries were also discussed, and a feeding programme in South Korea was proposed to disperse the cranes wintering in Japan. The feeding programme is summarized as follows. In Korea, during the autumn migration, cranes stay for a month at Tegu, north of Pusan. However, they fly down to Japan in mid-winter. The reason they do not stay through the winter in Korea may be a scarcity of food in the field. Therefore, if enough food is provided, it may be possible to create viable wintering sites for cranes in Korea.

Proposal for a migratory bird treaty between Korea and Japan. In 1987, the WBSJ contacted the Korean Government, and discussed the possibility of having a migratory bird treaty between Korea and Japan. The Korean Government was interested, and it was discussed again in 1988. The Japanese Government also showed an interest, and a petition by the Nagasaki chapter of the WBSJ to promote this treaty was approved by the Nagasaki and Fukuoka prefectural governments in 1988.

North Korea

Bird conservation symposium. On 24 January 1987, the WBSJ invited Mr Pak Uil, Vice-Chairman of the Institute of Zoology of Pyong Yan, North Korea, and two other scientists, to hold a bird conservation symposium in Tokyo. This was the first direct contact with North Korean scientists since World War II. Much important information was exchanged at the symposium. The topics included the present state of cranes in North Korea (Pak Uil); the migration route of cranes between Japan and Korea (Makoto Kamogawa); the status and conservation of some threatened species in North Korea (Chung Jang Ryol); and bird banding projects in Japan (Masashi Yoshii). It was agreed that cooperative work is greatly needed to study and conserve threatened species in both countries. The proceedings, entitled *"Endangered Bird Species in the Korean Peninsula"* were published by the Natural History Museum of the Korean University in Tokyo and the WBSJ in 1987.

Crane migration study. In March 1987, the migration was studied in North Korea, and the WBSJ received the results. It was estimated that about 820 White-naped and 690 Hooded Cranes passed through two areas in North Korea, and that 10-20 days were required for the cranes to travel to the areas after leaving Izumi. The joint fieldwork for the crane migration is now under discussion, and it is expected to be done in the spring of 1991.

China

Establishment of communications. From 20 May to 3 June 1983, three specialists of the WBSJ were invited by the Ministry of Forestry of China to the Zhalung Nature Reserve to observe the breeding status of the Japanese and White-naped Cranes. The next year, 1984, the WBSJ invited three ornithologists from China to observe the wintering cranes at Izumi.

Bird banding workshop. Under the auspices of the migratory bird treaty between China and Japan, a formal meeting was held on 6-7 June 1985 in Tokyo. Some Chinese authorities were invited, and several projects on research and conservation were approved between the Chinese Government and Japanese NGOs. Taking films of some threatened species of China and their habitats is one of the projects. However, because of unexpected problems, most of the projects have not been realized, and only the banding was promoted.

The first banding workshop was carried out in China during 5-19 October 1985. The Yamashina Institute and the WBSJ sent four Japanese specialists there with the aid of the National Bird Banding Centre of China. Since then the workshop has been conducted each year to exchange information and banding techniques.

Symposium on crane conservation. On 27 February 1988, a crane symposium was held at Izumi. The topics included the introduction of crane studies in China (Yao-kuang Tan); migratory birds and their conservation in Kuwanto Province, China (Wei-ping Liao); the present state and conservation of cranes wintering in Japan (Satoshi Nishida); and a study of crane migration using the Argos system (Masaki Soma). It was agreed that more information is needed to conserve the cranes in both countries and that various kinds of cooperative work are needed to achieve these aims.

Joint fieldwork in the Panching wetland in June 1989. In Liaoning, there is the huge Panching wetland, possibly the biggest in Asia. This is the southern limit of the breeding distribution of Japanese Cranes. In December 1987, the WBSJ invited three specialists of the Ornithological Research Centre of Liaoning, and in return five Japanese specialists visited there in October 1988. Through this exchange, Chinese specialists suggested promoting a joint field study to collect information on the avifauna of this wetland. The wetland is important enough to be protected under the Ramsar Convention. Therefore, information on the avifauna is greatly needed. The first joint field study was conducted in June 1989. Species composition and habitat characteristics of some important species were investigated. It was estimated that four or five pairs of Japanese Cranes breed in this wetland.

The U.S.S.R.

Because most of the winter visitors to Japan breed in the Far East of the U.S.S.R., the exchange of information and specialists between the two areas is essential for the conservation of the birds there. One of the important species breeding in the eastern U.S.S.R. is the Hooded Crane. The WBSJ has been in contact with the U.S.S.R. Academy of Sciences for several years, and reached an agreement in March 1988 for a joint field study of Hooded Cranes at the breeding ground. As this joint study was successful, the U.S.S.R. Academy of Sciences and the WBSJ agreed to promote further studies on the threatened species of the Far East of the U.S.S.R.

Joint field study of Hooded Cranes. From 6 May to 3 June 1988, a field study on the breeding ecology of Hooded Cranes was carried out with the aid of the Japan Cultural Association (Fujimaki *et al.* 1989). The study area, Zumeinaya Mari, is in the middle of the Bikin River, 200 km south of Havarovsk. This wetland is 10 km long and 3 km wide, and is surrounded by forests. Marshes with forest patches are typical breeding habitat of Hooded Cranes in this area. The research group found one nest with two eggs on 13 May, observed the breeding behaviour of the pair, and took films. This nest is the tenth one of Hooded Cranes ever found. However, it was recognized that the peak of the breeding season had already passed.

This area is very important as a breeding site of Hooded Cranes, but is not yet designated a protection area. The necessity to protect this wetland was discussed during the study period.

Bird conservation symposium. On 4 February 1989, a bird conservation symposium was held in Tokyo. Dr V. Khrabryi and Dr She En Sen of the Zoological Institute of the U.S.S.R. Academy of Sciences were invited. The topics included the status and conservation of some threatened species in the eastern U.S.S.R. (V. Khrabryi); a history of avian studies in the U.S.S.R. (She En Sen); the wintering ecology of White-tailed Eagles (*Haliaeetus albicilla*) and Steller's Sea-Eagles (*H. pelagicus*) in Japan (Yuzo Fujimaki); and the origin and development of the avifauna of Japan (Hiroyoshi Higuchi). Information on threatened species of the Far East was exchanged, and it was agreed to promote cooperative fieldwork. A field study of Stellar's Sea-Eagles was conducted in June and July 1989 (Hanawa *et al.* 1989).

FUTURE WORK

We have received valuable information on crane migration and conservation during the course of these cooperative projects with many scientists of East Asia. However, we must collect much more information on the same and related subjects from now on. Future studies will include the following topics: the true extent of the breeding and wintering distribution of each species; migration routes and resting areas of the cranes; habitat characteristics of the breeding and wintering areas; population dynamics and population management; and the creation of new wintering or breeding grounds. International cooperation will be needed to accomplish any of these objectives.

The habitats of the cranes are rapidly disappearing. Specifying and protecting important areas are urgent matters. Recommendations from many countries should help to accomplish this. We hope the friendship and cooperative relationships that were made during the crane studies will continue to work well in the future.

ACKNOWLEDGEMENTS

I thank N. Ichida, S. Hanawa, Y. Ohsako and N. Yanagisawa for valuable information on the cranes, and L. Adams for reviewing the draft. The WBSJ would like to extend sincere thanks to all the people who kindly supported and are supporting our crane studies; particular P. Won, K. Tapttuck, W. Han-Chung, and J. Sam-Rae (South Korea), Pak. Uil, C. J. Ryol (North Korea), Y. Tan, W. Liao (China), V. Khrabryi, S. Ensen, Y. V. Shivaev, V. A. Andronov, S. M. Smirenskii (U.S.S.R.), M. Soma, M. Yoshii, K. Ozaki, S. Matano, M. Kamogawa, T. Nishida, C. Katsura, K. Shimoike, F. Mizoguchi (Japan).

REFERENCES

ABE, N., UCHIDA, Y., YANAGISAWA, N., FUJIMURA, J. & FUJII, T. (1988) Studies of the cranes in Izumi, Kagoshima, Japan. 5. Daytime-dispersion, population and family-size in *G. monacha* and *G. vipio* in 1985-1986. *Rep. Inst. Nat. Stud.* **19**: 7-19. (In Japanese with English summary.)

FUJIMAKI, Y., HANAWA, S., OZAKI, K., YUNOKI, O., NISHIJIMA, F., KHRABRYI, V. M., STARIKOV, Y. B. & SHIBAEV, Y. B. (1989) Breeding status of the Hooded Cranes *Grus monacha* along the Bikin River in the Far East of the U.S.S.R. *Strix* **8**: 199-217.

HAGIWARA, S. (1988) Studies of the cranes in Izumi, Kagoshima, Japan, 13. Wild plants for winter foods in *Grus monacha* and *G. vipio* in Izumi, Japan. *Rep. Inst. Nat. Stud.* **19**: 83-97. (In Japanese.)

HANAWA, S., YUNOKI, O., YAMADA, M., KHRABRYI, V. M., SOKOLOV, E. P., FOKIN, S. I. & MASTEROV, V. B. (1989) Breeding status of the Steller's Sea Eagles *Haliaeetus pelagicus* on the lake Udyl in the Far East of the U.S.S.R. *Strix* **8**: 219-232.

HIGUCHI, H., SATO, F., MATSUI, S., SOMA, M. & KANMURI, N. (in press) Satellite tracking of the migration routes of Whistling Swans *Cygnus columbianus*. *J. Yamashina Institute for Ornithology*.

OHSAKO, Y. (1987) Effects of artificial feeding on cranes wintering in Izumi and Akune, Kyushu, Japan. Pp. 89-98 in G. W. Archibald & R. F. Pasquier, eds. *Proceedings of the 1983 International Crane Workshop*. Baraboo: International Crane Foundation.

OHSAKO, Y. (1989) Flock organization, dispersion and territorial behaviour of wintering Hooded Cranes *Grus monacha* in Izumi and Akune, Kyushu. *Jap. J. Orn.* **38**: 15-29.

OZAKI, K. (1988) Migratory routes of birds shown by banding (Hyosikichosa de wakatta tori no watariruuto). *Dobutsu to Dobutsuen* **40**: 464-467. (In Japanese.)

SONOBE, K. & IZAWA, N., eds. (1987) *Endangered bird species in the Korean Peninsula.* Tokyo: Korean University and Wild Bird Society of Japan, Tokyo.

YANAGISAWA, N. (1989) *The day the cranes migrate (Tsuru No Wataru Hi).* Tokyo: Chikuma-shobo. (In Japanese.)

WWFJ. (1985) Basic research on the conservation and management of Hooded and White-naped Cranes in Izumi, Japan. World Wildlife Fund Japan (Resrch. Rep. 8). (In Japanese.)

THE STATUS AND CONSERVATION OF GREY-FACED BUZZARD-EAGLES AND BROWN SHRIKES MIGRATING THROUGH TAIWAN

LUCIA LIU SEVERINGHAUS

Institute of Zoology, Academia Sinica, Taipei, Taiwan, Republic of China

ABSTRACT

The Grey-faced Buzzard-Eagle (*Butastur indicus*) and the Brown Shrike (*Lanius cristatus*) migrate through Taiwan in concentration in certain localities. They have been hunted traditionally in such places, and high hunting pressure may be the most serious threat to their survival en route. Concentrated efforts aimed at the conservation of these two species began in 1980 and have made them flagship species of wildlife conservation in Taiwan.

This paper attempts to synthesize current knowledge on their migration routes and status in Taiwan, drawing broadly on unpublished data and local records. The history of their harvest is traced back to the earliest information available. The hunting pressure and the market conditions of different times are compared. This is followed by (1) a documentation of all the conservation programmes tried; (2) an evaluation of these programmes, especially where their effectiveness was low; and (3) suggestions for the improvement of current programmes. Several new programmes, including some that require international cooperation, are also proposed.

INTRODUCTION

Migratory species comprise 158 (38 per cent) of the 413 species of birds recorded to date from Taiwan. Among these the Grey-faced Buzzard-Eagle (*Butastur indicus*) and the Brown Shrike (*Lanius cristatus*) are the most well-known. Their fame came as a result of concentrated efforts at their conservation against a localized tradition of heavy exploitation. The promotion of their conservation in 1979-1980 brought together the first informal coalition of environmentalists, NGOs and some relevant government agencies. This cooperative spirit towards conservation goals among different segments of society has lasted to the present.

Conservation efforts concerning both the Brown Shrike and the Grey-faced Buzzard-Eagle have been focused on the southern tip of Taiwan, the HengChun Peninsula (*Figure 1*). The location and topography of this peninsula are the factors that make it significant for migratory birds. There, the mountains of the Central Mountain Range descend into undulating hills before flattening out in the KenTing region. The narrow peninsula is the closest point of land to the Philippines and acts as a natural funnel for migratory birds passing southward.

Figure 1: East Asia with Taiwan and the HengChun Peninsula at its southern end.

Taiwan's weather is influenced by that of the nearby China mainland. From October to April, cold north-eastern winds sweep across the island. The central mountains in southern Taiwan are mostly below 2,000 m in elevation, low enough to allow the winds to blow with great force over and down the west side. Gusts up to 20 m/sec are frequent in the hilly central regions of the HengChun Peninsula. Winds may last only a few hours, or continue for several days to half a month.

It is during the lull in these winds that the Brown Shrikes and the Grey-faced Buzzard-Eagles arrive on their autumn migration, and it is the large numbers and concentrations of these birds that provide the opportunity and incentive for the local people to hunt them.

In the last ten years, much money and effort have gone into the conservation of these two species. Many developmental changes have also taken place in Taiwan in this period of time. In this chapter I will first present current information about the status and migration patterns of these two flagship species, the hunting pressure they are under and early conservation efforts. Then I will discuss the conservation programme of the national park offices in the last eight years, evaluate the effects of these programmes and propose actions for the future.

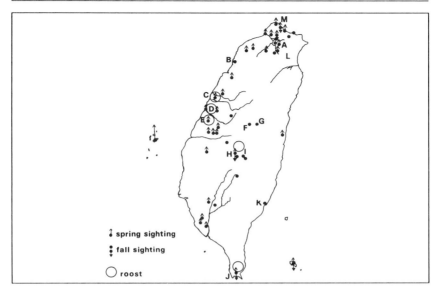

Figure 2: Location of sightings of Grey-faced Buzzard-Eagles. Only at four sites have migrating buzzard-eagles been seen in both spring and autumn. Sites names are: A=Taipei area; B=KuLiao; C=TiehChan Mountain; D=TaTu area; E=PaKua Mountain; F=Meifeng; G=TsuiFeng; H=Ali Shan; I=Yu Shan; J=KenTing; K=TaiTung; K=ILan; M=ChinShan.

THE GREY-FACED BUZZARD-EAGLE

The Grey-faced Buzzard-Eagle breeds in Japan, Korea, Manchuria and the Khaborovsk region of eastern Siberia (McClure 1974; Japan Wild Bird Society 1982; Cheng 1987). The winter range of this species encompasses southern China, South-East Asia, the Philippines, Celebes and New Guinea (McClure 1974). There are apparently two populations. The Japanese population passes through the RyuKyu Islands and Taiwan to winter in the Philippines (McClure 1974). The other population probably winters in South China, South-East Asia and New Guinea (McClure 1974; King *et al.* 1984). The migration route of this population is not yet clear.

Migration routes
Since 1965 it has been known that in October large numbers of Grey-faced Buzzard-Eagles stop overnight in the hills near ManChou village on the HengChun Peninsula before heading south to the Philippines (S. R. Severinghaus, pers. comm.). The Migratory Animal Pathological Survey (MAPS) bird banding team suspected that they entered north-eastern Taiwan from the RyuKyus and moved south along the east coast until reaching the HengChun area.

In order to understand their migration routes within Taiwan, I compiled and mapped all the sighting records of recent years (*Figure 2*), using data from Taipei Wild Bird Society, Taichung Bird Club, Kaohsiung Bird Club, The bird clubs of TamChiang, Tunghai and ChungHsing Universities, and scattered observations of other individuals. Autumn sightings have been recorded in the hilly areas around Taipei city. The species has also been seen passing southward in the high

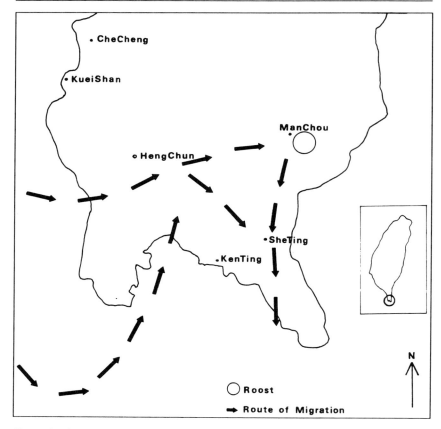

Figure 3: Generalized migration routes of Grey-faced Buzzard-Eagles in October. (Data from Liang (1989) and Lin Wen-hung (pers. comm.).)

mountains near TsuiFeng and MeiFeng (Tasi Mu-chi, pers. comm.) and near YuShan and Ali Shan (Sha 1986, 1988, 1989). The birds followed major river valleys, rising to cross 2,500-metre-high mountain passes.

The distribution pattern of autumn sightings suggests that this species generally follows the mountainous north-south spine of the island down to HengChun Peninsula and from there over the Bashi Channel to the Philippines. Autumn migration apparently does not follow the east coast as previously suspected.

North-flying buzzard-eagles have been sighted in many places on the western plains (*Figure 2*), but the only known place of concentration is in the Tatu-Pakua area in central Taiwan.

The autumn migration of Grey-faced Buzzard-Eagles is more prominent than the spring migration. It is a common sight to see dozens of buzzard-eagles in the air, going to roost or heading south. During northward migration, the birds are more scattered.

Roosts

As buzzard-eagles fly over Taiwan, many stop overnight in wooded areas in foothills or mountain valleys (*Figure 2*). Often the same general roosting area is used repeatedly over the years.

Usually birds arriving after 15:00 h at a given roosting place stop for the night (Lin Wen-hung, pers. comm.). At KenTing, birds in a wide area including those moving over water were seen to circle back into land to roost in the ManChou area (*Figure 3*). If the weather is bad they usually remain at the roosting area until the weather changes (Lin & Lin 1986). Grey-faced Buzzard-Eagles are known to fly from 33 to 280 km a day (McClure 1974). The length of Taiwan is roughly 300 km, and it is very likely that all birds passing over Taiwan roost at least once and that there are many roosting sites in the mountains not yet known.

Migration season and bird numbers

Most of the sightings in September are of single birds or very small flocks. The duration of buzzard-eagle migration usually lasts through October, and the peak of autumn migration at KenTing (the only place regularly manned by observers) is often around 10 October (*Figure 4*).

The data collected by the Conservation Club of National ChungHsing University show that in spring the main flocks pass through central Taiwan between the middle and end of March. This confirms the reports of experienced local hunters who state that the buzzard-eagles usually pass through in concentrations within five days of the vernal equinox (Tsai 1988).

Comparing the total number of buzzard-eagles passing over PaKua Mountain every 30 minutes for 8 days in March 1989, it is apparent that more birds passed over around noon than at other times of the day (*Figure 5*). Buzzard-eagles usually take off from roosts very early in the morning if the weather is not too bad. The noon peak at PaKua Mountain may reflect the distance between PaKua and the birds' previous night's roost, or perhaps the local wind pattern near PaKua somehow delayed birds that otherwise would have passed over earlier.

For the KenTing area, the number of birds over ManChou village was counted every hour in October 1984 (*Figure 6*). Although no records were kept between 10:00 and 15:00 h, the picture is clearly different from that at PaKua Mountain. The number of birds peaked early in the day, dropping to a low level after 07:00 h, and then peaked again by mid-afternoon when birds preparing to roost accumulated. This pattern of variation in bird numbers at ManChou probably represents its closeness to the nearest night roost.

Status and utilization

There is no official record of how long people have been hunting buzzard-eagles. Some say it has been at least one hundred years at ManChou (Chang 1980). The villagers at PaKua Mountain claim they have been trapping eagles for generations.

Traditionally ManChou villagers hunted eagles for food. They believed that a bird that can fly such distances must be endowed with special stamina, and that those who ate it could gain its strength (Lin & Lin 1986). Eagles were also hunted for sport (Chang 1980). After Japan started enforcing strict hunting regulations in the 1970s, many Japanese merchants started to buy from Taiwan the raptor specimens that were still highly popular in the Japanese market (Chang 1980; Lin & Lin 1986). From then until the early 1980s, buzzard-eagles were hunted for the specimen trade (ChunShen 1979). The birds that were caught were always killed, cleaned and preserved locally to be made into specimens in Japan in the future (Chang 1980). Since Japan prohibited the import of raptor specimens in the 1980s

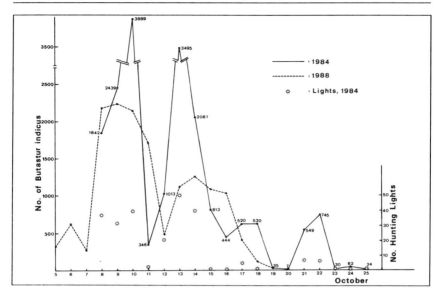

Figure 4: The number of Grey-faced Buzzard-Eagles arriving at ManChou during October, and its relationship to the number of hunting lights seen in 1984. (*After:* Lin & Lin 1986 and Chin *et al.* 1989.)

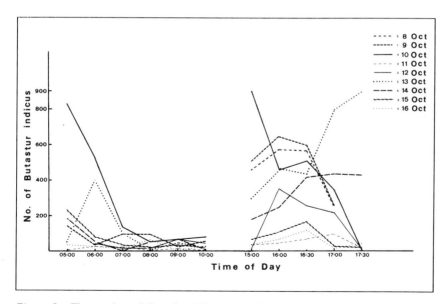

Figure 5: The number of Grey-faced Buzzard-Eagles passing over PaKua Mountain in March 1989 at different times of the day. (Data from the Conservation Club of ChungHsing University.)

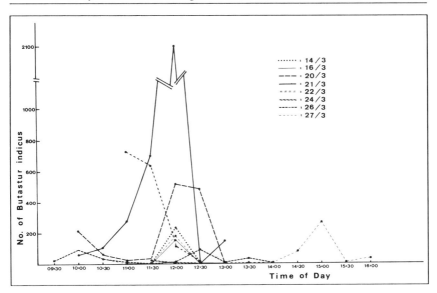

Figure 6: The number of Grey-faced Buzzard-Eagles passing over ManChou in October 1984 at different times of the day. (Data from Lin & Lin (1986).)

as a result of the conservation efforts of the Wild Bird Society of Japan, hunting for the specimen trade has decreased. Now, live-caught birds are no longer killed as the current market price for live birds is twice that for dead birds. The live buzzard-eagles are mostly sold to raptor fanciers: the dead ones are still stuffed and mounted.

Trapping and hunting methods

Grey-faced Buzzard-Eagles are never hunted on the wing, but are usually trapped with tall foot snares or hunted with lights and weapons in the roosts at night. Around the roosting sites at PaKua Mountain in early Marsh, people put up simple bamboo snares that stick out above the trees on wooden mountain slopes. When the birds come down to roost, many land on these snares and get caught. In the ManChou area every October, local hunters watch where the birds are landing to roost in the afternoon. Later they stun and shoot the roosting birds between 19:00 and 22:00 h (Lin & Lin 1986).

The efficiency of the hunters increased greatly with the availability of long-lasting automobile or motorcycle batteries and powerful headlights which freed the hunters' hands in the 1960s. A cross-bow arrangement was the common weapon of the late 1960s (S. R. Severinghaus, pers. comm.). Later, hunters started using dart guns which were effective up to 20 m. This weapon has a sharp hooked point attached to the tip of a thin bamboo stick, powered by a piece of strong rubber fastened on to a wooden gunstock (Chang 1980). Because this weapon is easily and cheaply made, easy to use and quiet when fired, it is still the most common weapon for eagle hunting (Lin & Lin 1986). Air guns are also popular now because they are light in weight and relatively quiet when fired. Fortunately gun control regulations in Taiwan prevented more guns from becoming widely

Table 1: Hunting pressure and market value of the Grey-faced Buzzard-Eagle through the years.

Year	Number of hunters	Number of lights	Number of birds caught	Price (TWD)	Source
1978	–	many	7,000	100	1
1979	–	–	–	170	1
1980	–	–	–	450	1
1983	86	–	994+	–	2
1984	27	50	75	100	2
1987	63+	–	230	–	3
1988	47+	–	271	350	3
1989	70	50	–	live 300 dead 150	4

Sources: 1 Chang 1980; 2 Lin & Lin 1986; 3 Ching *et al.* 1989; 4 Liang Ming-huang, pers. comm.

Key: + Minimum number
            TWD New Taiwan Dollar (25 TWD = 1 USD in 1989)

available (Lin & Lin 1986). With advanced lighting and weapons, a good shooter could take 70-80 eagles in a night (Chang 1980).

Hunting pressure

"Hawks returning from the south – ten thousand come, nine thousand die" goes an old saying of the PaKua Mountain area (Tsai 1988). In the ManChou area, local elders claimed that Grey-faced Buzzard-Eagles used to be so abundant that they could be captured very easily in quantities so large that they had to be carried home on ox-carts. Local people also admitted that the numbers of buzzard-eagles decreased drastically in the late 1970s (Chang 1980). During the peak hunting years in the 1970s, there were so many hunters' lights in the hills that the woods lit up like a prosperous town (Lin & Lin 1986).

The level of buzzard-eagle hunting was reduced in the early 1980s, but a small proportion of the villagers continued to hunt right up until the present (Ching *et al.* 1989). The number of hunting lights counted every night at 20.00 h in October 1984 was proportional to the number of birds present in the area (*Figure 4*).

Table 1 summarizes the hunting pressure on Grey-faced Buzzard-Eagles during the last decade. Data are largely based on questionnaire surveys. The number of hunters who admitted hunting during 1984 seems to be too low (50 lights were seen during one night) and must be taken as indications only. Nevertheless there has been a distinct decrease in the number of eagles caught.

The specimen dealers that crowded the KenTing area every October paid 120-170 TWD for an eagle skin in 1977, and up to 450 TWD (18 USD) in 1981 (Chang 1980). About 30,000 buzzard-eagle skins were shipped to Japan in 1978-1979 (Liang 1988). In March 1989 a trapper at PaKua Mountain sold his eagles to stores at 300 TWD (12 USD) each. A shop in the nearby village had 20 live Grey-faced Buzzard-Eagles for sale in a small cage, each one costing 600 TWD. Unfortunately we do not have reliable data to detect possible population trends. Only systematic and long-term monitoring can provide these data in the future.

A brief conservation history

Advocacy for wildlife conservation before 1960 fell on deaf ears with almost all Taiwanese people in all sectors of society. Japanese dealers shipped numerous bird specimens from Taiwan during their occupation of the island (Hachisuka and Udagawa 1950). Although the MAPS bird banding team knew that ManChou villagers hunted buzzard-eagles in 1965, the team banded only a few dozen birds in the late 1960s. The extent of buzzard-eagle hunting was not known, and it was not a major concern between 1965 and 1969. In the 1960s, the bird trade at tourist spots was rampant. In July 1967 alone the souvenir shops at SunMoon Lake had 1,979 bird specimens of 143 species, of which about eight per cent were raptors. Most stuffed specimens were sold to Japanese in the 1960s (Severinghaus, 1970).

A three-year total hunting ban for Taiwan was initiated in 1972. This was the first action the government took towards the management of its wildlife resources. It curbed the specimen trade at tourist spots, and drove a portion of the business underground. The ban was extended twice (1975-1978, 1978-1981) until it was eventually forgotten by both the law enforcement agencies and the wildlife-consuming public.

The first report of the desperate plight of the Grey-faced Buzzard Eagle – and one that lit the fire for its conservation – was a documentation of the hunting event of October 1978, published in *Echo* magazine (ChunSheng 1979). Many people, including well-known freelance writers and journalists, contacted *Echo* magazine hoping to witness the annual eagle-hunting ritual and to help the birds. The publicity made the villagers at ManChou feel hostile towards visitors. The president of Taipei Bird Club was asked to coordinate a meeting between the hunters of ManChou and the concerned individuals from the rest of the island. This effort coincided with inquiries from Japan about the uncontrolled specimen business. In August 1978 the Director of the Wild Bird Society of Japan came to Taiwan and interviewed specimen dealers in Puli and WuLai. His report was subsequently published in *Tori*, blaming the Japanese merchants for providing the incentive for large-scale slaughtering of raptors (Wu 1980). The Animal Protection Society sponsored a seminar at KenTing on 13 October 1979 and invited hunters, businessmen, scholars, administrators, writers, the news media and representatives from all the bird clubs to discuss the hunting and conservation of Grey-faced Buzzard-Eagles (Ma 1980). This meeting caught the attention of the news media and officially launched the migratory bird protection programme in Taiwan. Since 10 October is the national day of the Republic of China, and since Grey-faced Buzzard-Eagles often arrive at KenTing around this time, some people called it the National Day Bird. The news media picked up on this and the National Day Bird became widely known.

In October 1980, bird club members went to KenTing again to promote Grey-faced Buzzard-Eagle conservation. They found that ManChou High School had already decorated the school with various wildlife protection posters in response to the previous year's conservation effort (Liang 1988). However, migratory bird hunting continued.

In 1981 the Construction and Planning Administration (CPA) was established in the Ministry of the Interior and was placed under the directorship of a dedicated conservationist. This administration was entrusted with the responsibility of setting up the national parks system in Taiwan, and KenTing was the first park to be planned. From 1981 to the present, the National Parks Department and later KenTing National Park headquarters devoted a significant amount of funds and attention to the promotion of migratory bird protection.

THE BROWN SHRIKE

The Brown Shrike is a common Old World migrant. Four subspecies winter in South-East Asia and breed in Japan, Korea, North-east China and Siberia (McClure 1974). Its breeding season is from mid-April to mid-September, and it usually arrives at its breeding range already paired (Fu *et al.* 1984). In Taiwan, it is both a winter resident and transient species.

Which routes the Brown Shrikes take on their way to Taiwan is unknown. During the MAPS programme, more than 35,000 Brown Shrikes were banded in the HungChun area. None of these was recovered on its breeding range in Korea or Japan; therefore, it is most likely that the population of Brown Shrikes coming through Taiwan in the autumn breeds in China (McClure 1974). Many banding recoveries indicate that shrikes also go from the HengChun Peninsula in Taiwan to the Philippines.

Observations show that Brown Shrikes have been seen during every month of the year (*Figure 7*). They occur all over Taiwan from sea level to 2,300 m high in the mountains (*Figure 8*). In September, however, they are more concentrated in the HengChun area and more easily caught because of local habitat conditions. Judging by the diverse plumage patterns seen, it is possible that several subspecies pass through or winter in Taiwan, but very few of the distinctly coloured subspecies that breed in Japan come to Taiwan.

Every year the first shrike appears on 17 or 18 August on Tunghai University campus, while in HengChun they arrive around 8-9 September or "White Dew", a special date in the Chinese agricultural calendar. Thus, the shrikes are called "white dew birds" by some local people. The transients remain on Tunghai campus for only one or two days (own data). Overwintering Brown Shrikes show strong site tenacity to their winter territories. Wintering individuals start disappearing gradually from campus by late March, and territories that become vacant in March and April are often temporarily occupied by spring transients. Chiu (1986) claimed that transient shrikes also maintained territories.

Trapping history

In the 1960s, the local people claimed they had been trapping shrikes for over 100 years (Severinghaus 1972), or for at least seven generations (Yen 1980). However, the habitat of HengChun Peninsula was very different 100 years ago, covered mostly by tropical coastal forest and virgin broadleaf forest (Chen 1985; Nung 1989).

The landscape of the HengChun Peninsula was changed drastically between 1908 and 1913, when the Japanese Government started planting Range Grass (*Panicum maximum*) (Huang Chia, pers. comm.) and Sisal (*Agave rigida*) in large areas (Billings 1987). Shrike trapping in the HengChun Peninsula, therefore, probably only started after 1910.

Trapping methods

Shrikes have traditionally been caught with bamboo foot traps made by the local villagers. Many children assist their fathers in shrike trapping and in this way they learn the skills of making and setting the traps which have been passed down in the HengChun area for generations (Severinghaus 1972). The traps are especially efficient in the HengChun area because there are large tracts of dry open fields, and the slopes of foothills are covered mostly with low bushes, Pandanas (*Pandanus odoratissimus*), and short sisal plants (one of the major crops of the region from the mid-1910s to the mid-1970s). Shrikes prefer perching on a high

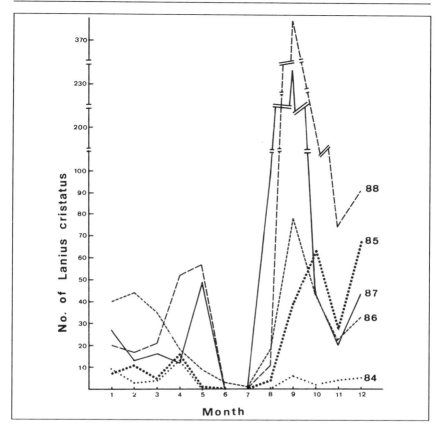

Figure 7:   The number of Brown Shrikes seen in different months of the years 1984-1988.
(Data from the Wild Bird Society of the Republic of China.)

and exposed place. Thus, two to three-metre-tall shrike traps that protrude above the surrounding vegetation are favoured perches.

After setting their traps, the villagers either rest in the shade or go on with their daily tasks in nearby fields. When they hear the harsh screaming of a trapped shrike, they go to the trap and quickly remove the bird, break its lower jaw to prevent being pinched by its strong hooked beak, reset the trap in a few seconds and go back to whatever they were doing until the next bird is caught. Most trappers (51.1 per cent) set traps before or after work, 14.6 per cent of the villagers trap shrikes during their workday, while 5.3 per cent of them devote whole days to trapping (Chiu 1986). These full-day trappers are akin to professional trappers.

The hills around HengChun used to be saturated with traps, each only five to ten metres away from the next one. The MAPS bird banding team estimated that 53.5 per cent of the shrikes migrating through the area were caught on average in the two trapping sites censused near HengChun, and the total number of birds sold to the banding team and sold in restaurants at HengChun was 12,157 in 1967 (Severinghaus 1968). Trappers were found in all the townships of HengChun

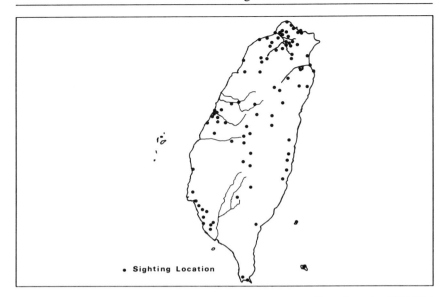

Figure 8: Sighting locations of the Brown Shrike in Taiwan. (Data from the Wild Bird Society of the Republic of China and the bird clubs of Taichung, Kaohsiung, ChungHsing University, Tunghai University and TamKiang University.)

Peninsula, and up to one-third of all households may be engaged in this activity (Severinghaus 1968; Chiu 1986; M. Thelin, unpubl.).

The fate of the trapped shrikes

In 1984 when Chiu did his survey, 33 per cent of the people caught shrikes to eat, 20 per cent gave shrikes to relatives and friends, and 47 per cent sold them to restaurants or merchants.

The market value of Brown Shrikes has increased through the years (*Table 2*). However, the current price of a barbecued shrike converted to 1967 Taiwan dollar values is only 9.67 TWD compared to 3.00 TWD 22 years ago. The major increase has occurred in the quantity of birds sold. In the late 1960s, the clients for barbecued shrikes were local villagers; only a few were sold to PintTung City. Now 2.8 million tourists visit KenTing National Park every year (more than 200,000 every September and October). Potential buyers for barbecued shrikes outnumber by several times the population of the entire HengChun Peninsula (79,580 persons in 1984). Now the vendors in FengKang, CheCheng and HengChun not only sell shrikes during the September-October migration season, but also sell barbecued wintering shrikes and birds of other species all year round, especially during holidays when tourists crowd into the KenTing area. The birds they sell during the non-shrike season are primarily wild doves, domestic quails and some Styan's Bulbuls (*Pycnonotus taivanus*). Where they get the supply of wild birds is not yet known.

Table 2: Hunting pressure and market value of the Brown Shrike through the years.

Year	Number of hunters	Number of traps	Price (TWD)	Barbecued	Number of vendors	Total	Source
1965	–	–	–	–	–	b. 1,349	1
1966	–	–	–	–	–	b. 8,784	1
1967	69*	2,023	1.5	3.0	8	s. 8,695	1
						b. 3,462	
1968	–	–	1.5	3.0	–	–	2
1979	–	–	–	10.0	–	–	3
1980	–	–	3.0	10.0	–	150/vendor	4
1981	–	–	3–6	12.5	–	–	5
1984	824	4,886	–	–	40	s.10,000	3,6
1985	–	3,812	–	–	–	–	3
1986	–	5,745	–	–	–	–	3
1987	–	11,109	–	–	–	–	3
1989	–	–	–	25.0	39	–	7

Sources: 1 Severinghaus 1968; 2 Severinghaus, pers. obs.; 3 Liang 1988; 4 Yen 1980;
5 HanHan & Ma 1983; 6 Chiu 1986; 7 Liang pers. comm.

Key: * data only cover SanChiaoLi area.
b number of shrikes banded.
s number of shrikes sold.

Conservation efforts

The bird banding team of Tunghai University was informed of shrikes for sale at
restaurants in HengChun by Dr T. C. Maa of the Bishop Museum in September
1964. Shrike banding started in 1965 after the team located some trappers. In the
next four years, the banding team banded shrikes, tried to estimate their population,
and surveyed the restaurants and vendors to monitor the scale of shrike
consumption.   The first two articles about the Brown Shrikes in Taiwan
(Severinghaus 1970, 1972) aimed to tell the outside world about the story of this
species.

No one has monitored the population trend of shrikes over the years anywhere
on Taiwan. Nevertheless, the MAPS bird banding team learned from the villagers
that the number of traps they used varied directly with the perceived abundance of
shrikes each year (Severinghaus 1968). Yet despite this, by 1984 some 68 per cent
of the 3,185 local people surveyed thought the population size of the Brown Shrike
had been decreasing; 21 per cent of the people did not know; and only 11 per cent
considered the population size not decreasing (Chiu 1986).

The current concern for Brown Shrikes was started in 1980 by bird club
members who went to KenTing to watch migratory hawks (Liang 1988). They
discovered numerous shrike traps near HengChun and many vendors selling
barbecued shrikes at FengKang. The news media gave shrike trapping and selling
very broad coverage that year. This aroused widespread concern and triggered the
involvement of many conservation-minded people. The publicity in 1980 led to
the most focused effort ever at Brown Shrike conservation, in the form of public
education in 1981, just before the shrikes arrived. This effort was spearheaded by
two well-known writers and by the Construction and Planning Administration, and
was assisted by numerous other individuals and organizations. Some school clubs,

such as the bird club of PingTung Agricultural College, conducted their own programmes for bird protection. These education programmes were aimed at stopping the shrike trapping and persuading people not to eat the birds. The target groups of the education programmes were local villagers, students and tourists (Ma 1981). Diverse techniques were used to reach the public, including slide presentations, lectures, and radio shows involving a young girl acting out the experience of a Brown Shrike being caught and a man impersonating a Grey-faced Buzzard-Eagle (HanHan 1981). Posters with bird protection messages were plastered on walls in public places and face-to-face discussions were organized with villagers at neighbourhood meetings (Liang 1988). The National Parks Department also had 14,000 bookmarks printed with photos of Brown Shrikes, Grey-faced Buzzard-Eagles, or scenery of the KenTing area and these were given to children and tourists as souvenirs and to appeal to their sense of aesthetics (Ma 1981).

The news media of Taiwan jumped into the migratory bird protection campaign with great enthusiasm, and without doubt they made the plight of migratory birds a very important issue in 1981. As a result, folk singers decided to hold a special concert on 14 January 1982 with environment as its theme to welcome in the New Year. Altogether nine songs premiered, including "The Migratory Birds", "The Egrets", "Flying Birds", and "The Grey-faced Buzzard-Eagle". Two of the nine songs were accompanied with dances, two with mime and four with slides. The production was supported by bird clubs, *Echo* magazine, dancers, actors and actresses, the National Parks Department and scholars of ecology and conservation (HanHan 1982).

Starting in 1981, a number of writers began producing articles about the environment and conservation. An anthology titled *We have only one earth* won the Golden Urn Award of 1982. This volume contained many articles about the environment written by HanHan and Ma IKung, among which several dealt with Grey-faced Buzzard-Eagles and Brown Shrikes. HsinTai's book *The revenge of the earth* won the best reportive writing award of 1983. These writers not only became dedicated conservationists themselves after they had become familiar with ecological principles, but their writings also touched and educated a great many people, even if the effects of such education were not immediately apparent. With the cooperation of the Taipei Bird Club, the Provincial Museum of Taiwan put on a two-month photo exhibition, starting in September 1982, under the theme of "Protecting Wild Birds". This show toured the major cities of Taiwan afterwards (Liang 1989).

In 1983 the KenTing office of the Tourism Bureau tried to deter people from eating barbecued shrikes by demonstrating that the shrikes had many internal parasites, including nematodes (*Hamatospiculum cylindricum*) in the head and neck region. Some people were scared off eating shrikes, but others simply decided that if they did not eat the head or neck, they would not be bothered by the parasites.

EFFORTS OF THE NATIONAL PARKS OFFICES

Because KenTing was designated in 1981 to be the first national park, the migratory bird protection programme became a major responsibility of the National Parks Department of the Construction and Planning Administration from then on. Not including research grants, more than five million Taiwan dollars have been spent on public education and law enforcement programmes. Liang (1988) has compiled a thorough documentation of all the national park conservation programmes over the years. He also produced a thoughtful evaluation of the implementation and accomplishments of these programmes from the perspective of a member of the KenTing National Park staff.

The national parks offices prepared and displayed many posters in public places every year. Bookmarks, pamphlets, maps, rulers and other school materials were made and given to students and visitors. Each contained some conservation or migratory bird protection message, trying to remind people that birds are beautiful, that birds have important ecological values, and that trapping migratory birds to eat is cruel. Exhibits of paintings, photographs and picture books on the scenery and birds found in the KenTing area were organized. The goals were to show the local people the beauty and value of the natural resources around them, hoping that their appreciation and love of nature would eventually replace their desire to exploit.

Park staff attended meetings between elected village leaders and their constituents. At these meetings, park staff gave slide shows and talked about bird protection, briefed the local people about the national park and about the National Park Law and other regulations. Park staff also invited the villagers to express their views on the park and on bird protection measures.

KenTing National Park persuaded local schools to teach the students the Migratory Bird song and funded singing competitions within each school and then between schools. Financial assistance was also given to temples at festival time to hold singing competitions of this song. A chorus group was formed with park staff to perform this song. Many lectures, public talks and slide shows have been given by the nature interpreters of KenTing National Park, bird club members, scholars and well-known writers and artists. The content of the talks were usually centred on nature appreciation, bird ecology and stories about birds, and they advocated resource protection within the park.

KenTing National Park contracted the making of a video tape about the Brown Shrike and the Grey-faced Buzzard-Eagle. Free copies of this tape were made and given to all the local primary and middle schools.

Bird club people were invited during October to watch migratory raptors and do raptor counts. They were also invited to participate in the New Year's bird census.

The Taichung Bird Club was contracted to provide bird specimens for permanent exhibits in the visitor centre about the bird resources of KenTing National Park. The Taipei Wild Bird Society was contracted to write a field guide for birds found in KenTing National Park. Local children were taken on bird-watching tours by nature interpreters of the park to learn to appreciate wild birds, and to enjoy them without harming them. At the same time, ecology workshops for teachers of local schools were offered to provide training for potential conservation educators. The KenTing National Park Administration prohibited all the franchise stores within the park from selling wildlife specimens, meat or barbecued birds, and park police and local police patrolled the countryside during September and October to stop shrike trapping and eagle hunting. They confiscated shrike traps and eagle hunting equipment, and anyone caught trapping or hunting could be fined or jailed. The fine could be as high as 15,000 TWD (about 550 USD).

KenTing National Park also contracted scientists, local teachers and bird clubs to conduct important research and survey projects concerning migratory bird protection. These projects provided the information base for action.

EVALUATION OF THE PROGRAMMES

In a culture that has traditionally considered exploiting and consuming wildlife a birthright, the promotion of wildlife conservation is an extremely difficult job.

It has been almost ten years since the beginning of the conservation movement, and in that time the public has changed from being totally ignorant about migratory birds to knowing and even caring about Grey-faced Buzzard-Eagles and Brown Shrikes. Nevertheless, it is difficult to evaluate the extent to which the migratory birds conservation programmes have been successful. The three surveys conducted in recent years (Chiu 1986; Lin & Lin 1986; Ching et al. 1989) give glimpses of the public's attitudes, even though, as pointed out earlier, answers to some questions in these surveys were unreliable. For specifics concerning national park programmes and the opinions of the national park staff, Liang's reports (1988, 1989) are the most important sources. Based on these reports, I will evaluate the public's attitude in detail (especially where the existing programmes have failed), identify areas that need further effort and suggest future possibilities for action.

More than 50 per cent of the people interviewed supported the no-hunting policy of the national park. Only a small number of local people (47 persons) hunted buzzard-eagles in 1988 and less than 20 per cent of the hunters actually opposed the no-hunting regulations. Among high school children, only 11 per cent were involved in eagle hunting in 1988. There is no information on how many people continue to trap shrikes, but among the 20 food stalls I surveyed in December 1989, shrikes constituted roughly one-third of the total barbecued birds for sale. This proportion of course could be different during the peak season for shrikes. But at least it demonstrates that customers are willing to accept birds other than shrikes.

The decrease in buzzard-eagle hunting was attributed to the enforcement of hunting regulations by local police starting in 1982, and the prohibition of the export of raptor specimens by the government of the Republic of China. No doubt the depressed stuffed specimen market in Japan also contributed to the stopping of specimen smuggling and decreased hunting, because otherwise dealers could continue to smuggle the skins into Japan as reported by Chang (1980).

Overall, the number of people who hunt buzzard-eagles in the last few years may have remained at around 50. According to the most recent survey (Ching et al. 1989), 26 among those who claimed to have hunted eagles in 1987 stopped hunting in 1988, but 10 new hunters joined.

Between 55 and 59 per cent of the local people interviewed in 1984 and 1988 agreed that there should be no hunting of migratory birds inside KenTing National Park. The number of people opposed to this regulation was 13-14 per cent in 1983, 19-21 per cent in 1984, and decreased to 8.5 per cent (25 persons) in 1988. Only 9 of the 25 persons actually hunted. Among the remaining 47 persons who hunted in 1988, 30 per cent (14) agreed that there should be no hunting in the park, and 51 per cent (24) expressed no opinion. At ManChou High School, 11 per cent of the 406 students hunted shrikes or eagles. Ninety-two per cent of these students knew that hunting/trapping was illegal, having heard from their families, their teachers or from other people, or by having seen the educational and promotional materials. But for those students who hunted, only 37 per cent felt uncomfortable when doing it, knowing that they should not hunt and that they could get caught and penalized. About 12 per cent of the 406 students interviewed did not support the migratory bird hunting ban. This number is about the same as the number of students who hunted.

These statistics demonstrate that only a small proportion of the local population hunts. But most of today's hunters do not care whether there is a hunting prohibition. Ching et al. (1989) explained that this was because most hunters only hunted eagles as a sport. Those who expressed opposition to this regulation were the few professional hunters whose livelihood was seriously affected by it.

I think these numbers demonstrate clearly that law enforcement has not been effective enough. Recreational hunters violate the regulation at will, regardless of whether their livelihood is affected. Even 62.3 per cent of the student hunters who knew about the no-hunting regulation did not hesitate to violate the law.

Law enforcement has been the weakest link in the migratory bird conservation programme. It is a difficult job to catch poachers under the best conditions: the limited number of police in the HengChun area and within the park make it even more difficult. Eagle poachers could simply turn off their lights and sneak away in the dark. Shrike trappers have learned to move their traps to locations hidden from the roads so police in patrol cars cannot spot them. Many poachers now pluck and prepare the birds in the hills so it is more difficult to find evidence with which to prosecute them. In addition, many poachers have moved off KenTing National Park, and are poaching on areas other than park land where the law was very lax until June 1989.

Furthermore, most policemen traditionally held the same view towards wildlife as the general public. To have effective law enforcement it is essential that the police be won over first. Unfortunately, park policemen who have the sole right to enforce the law within national parks are not members of the park staff. They are regular police rotated to serve in the parks. The rotation scheme places a continuous demand on park staff to "persuade" the new policemen about the significance of conservation. The police force being separate but equal in authority to the park staff, it is also a very delicate matter for the park staff to "educate" the police. In addition, political, cultural and personal factors all contribute to the uneven enforcement of the law (Liang 1988, 1989). New police chiefs tend to demand strict performance for a short period of time. Hunters who have important connections can get by with minimal fines. The ambition and campaign considerations of local political figures, the rivalry between individuals, personality problems and the division of funds all become part of the total picture. Many police feel they are busy enough managing people problems without worrying about bird problems. They do not feel that stopping poachers is part of their duty, and want to be rewarded financially by the national park office for their accomplishments.

Tourists constitute the other part of the problem that needs to be overcome for successful conservation. Many people in other parts of Taiwan have heard about the Grey-faced Buzzard-Eagles and the Brown Shrikes. When they visit the KenTing area, they often try these barbecued birds out of curiosity. Many are vaguely aware of the migratory bird conservation activities of KenTing National Park, but most of them have not linked their barbecued-shrike-eating and eagle-buying behaviour with the meaning of these programmes. A survey of tourists' attitudes towards bird conservation is needed to fully understand the situation.

The existing education programme needs to be improved. School children in the ManChou area did not enjoy all the educational programmes equally (Ching *et al.* 1989). They liked activities that were fun, not restricting, and placed little demand for effort on them. In decreasing order of preference, the activities are: (1) bird-watching trips; (2) film/video viewing; (3) seeing exhibits; (4) decorating their classrooms; (5) singing competitions; and (6) listening to talks or lectures. A great majority of them liked the souvenirs given to them during education programmes, including postcards, bookmarks, stickers, rulers, and clipboards. The largest number of students (26.7 per cent) claim that they learned about migratory birds protection from bird-watching trips. Viewing films (19.6 per cent) and exhibits (12.6 per cent) also ranked high. Twelve per cent of them obtained the information from messages printed on the souvenirs. Singing competitions, classroom lectures and posters all ranked fairly low in effectiveness.

Suggestions for improvement of current programmes

1. The police have to be convinced that enforcing the law concerning wildlife is also a regular part of their job, not extra work. Their rewards should come internally as merit points, promotional opportunities, or other types of credit for good performance within the police system, but not from the national parks system. With the promulgation of the new Wildlife Conservation Law, law enforcement should be slightly easier than before. This new law gives police the right to regulate wildlife hunting and trading outside national parks and reserves.
2. KenTing National Park should form a united task force for migratory bird conservation. All the divisions in the park administration should participate and cooperate with the Conservation or Education Division, and support the programmes in whatever way possible.
3. Education programmes used repeatedly tend to lose effectiveness quickly. A general evaluation and overhaul of the content of existing programmes should be carried out, and new programmes created. KenTing National Park is currently limited in personnel, time and material with which to devise new programmes annually. The teachers and principals of local schools have participated in education programmes before, but these people, like the park personnel, tend to be already overloaded with other responsibilities: they cannot devote all their time to writing conservation education curricula or to creating programmes. It would be worth contracting the design of these education programmes out to a successful promotion company with a proven record of selling products or effecting attitude changes.
4. Competitions for the singing of the Migratory Bird song should be stopped, since most students are bored by it. When appropriate, it is possible to have a chorus group give performances of this and other conservation songs as part of a larger conservation programme.
5. More effort is needed to reach the tourists and shop-keepers.

FUTURE POSSIBILITIES

KenTing National Park has jurisdiction over the management of the park, and is the highest level government agency in the area. Thus, the following suggestions are made with KenTing National Park headquarters as the principle government agency responsible for migratory bird conservation in the region. Needless to say, cooperation of the local administrative offices and the police system are essential to the overall success of any of these programmes.

On education and promotion

1. Contract a well-known dramatist to write a play about either the Brown Shrike or the Grey-faced Buzzard-Eagle. Invite a drama group, or a local school, to put this play on at KenTing, and have it video-taped to be aired on television. It would be best if popular actors and actresses could be talked into accepting parts in this play along with local children.
2. Obtain the cooperation of poultry research groups to cultivate better-tasting quails cheaply, so that vendors can be persuaded to switch from selling wild birds to selling barbecued quail.
3. Hold a local festival during the migration season, and provide visitors with opportunities to watch bird migration, see conservation education programmes, and be judges in a barbecue competition. For the latter, all the local vendors

should be invited to join the competition, but using only domestic quail, other poultry or meat, and vegetables. Winners of the competition should be given a prize which can be displayed. The publicity of winning such a prize should be a major business incentive to local chefs. A demonstration should be set up about conservation laws and why wild birds should be left alone. Information on the nutritional value, toxic accumulation and other health-related factors of wild bird and domestic fowl should also be displayed prominently.
4. Get sociologists and economists involved in the conservation programmes. A study of the local people's needs, their economic status, and their feelings towards market incentives should help experts design better educational and promotional programmes.
5. Invite travel agents to run annual tours during the migration season to promote the public's awareness of bird migration.

On law enforcement
1. Hire hunters as guides for eagle-watching trips. Providing the hunters with alternative ways of using the eagles for profit is definitely worth trying.
2. Ask the central police headquarters to submit plans on how they are going to implement the National Park Law and the Wildlife Conservation Law. Try to convince the police to take some initiative. This may change their attitudes from passively not wanting to do what the park wants them to do, to doing something they plan to do themselves.
3. Hold village leaders responsible, and organize competitions between villages to discover which is the most law-abiding in preventing poaching etc.

INTERNATIONAL COOPERATION

It has long been known that both species are heavily hunted in the Philippines (McClure 1974). During the Second East Asian Bird Protection Conference held in Taiwan in 1983, the representative from RyuKyu showed slides of how Grey-faced Buzzard-Eagles were hunted on RyuKyu Islands. Even if they are hunted in only these three countries, successful conservation programmes in Taiwan alone will not be sufficient to protect the two species. Their migratory nature mandates that international cooperation is essential to the success of their conservation.

The Wild Bird Society of Japan proposed to follow the Grey-faced Buzzard-Eagle flocks down from Korea and Japan to Taiwan and then to the Philippines with a fixed-winged aircraft. The plan was to generate as much publicity in these countries as possible for public education purposes. The officials in Taiwan readily accepted the idea. When this project is ready for action it will no doubt be successful and attract much support for the migratory birds.

Because the Brown Shrike is a common bird it does not attract as much attention and admiration as the Grey-faced Buzzard-Eagle. Nevertheless, its status needs to be monitored internationally. Given the fact that this species demonstrates strong site tenacity on both its breeding and wintering grounds, it is a perfect candidate for an international "adopt-a-bird" programme. I envision this to be a two-step programme. The first steps entails large-scale colour-banding for individual identification purposes. This would make it possible to tell that the bird breeding in A's garden ends up wintering in B's yard. The second step is, through the help of the news media, local bird clubs or conservation organizations, to link up the individuals who share the same bird or birds. Once people know that the birds that come back each year are the same individuals, and that someone at the other end is watching for their safe return, the birds take on a definite personality. People might then become attached to them, and even be proud of the faithful bird visitors that their neighbours or friends are not so lucky to have.

ACKNOWLEDGEMENTS

This paper could not have been completed without the assistance of Dr Sheldon R. Severinghaus, Mr Ming-huang Liang and Mr Chieh-teh Liang. The Wild Bird Society of ROC, the Conservation Club of ChungHsing University, and Dr S. R. Severinghaus gave permission to use their unpublished data. *Echo* magazine, National Parks Department, and KenTing National Park provided reports and reprints. Bird-watchers too numerous to list here generously provided personal observations to help me understand the migration patterns of these two species. To all of them, I am very grateful.

REFERENCES

BILLINGS, B. H. (1987) Sisal development in Taiwan. Pp. 39-77 in *Program for restoration of the HengChun sisal station as a historical monument. Part II.* KenTing National Park (Conserv. Resrch. Rep. no. 39).

CHANG, W. F. (1980) Travellers who don't need visas, the Grey-faced Buzzard-Eagle. *Environ. Sci.* 1: 58-64.

CHEN, Y. F. (1985) *Coastal vegetation of KenTing National Park.* KenTing National Park Headquarters, Construction and Planning Administration, Ministry of the Interior, ROC.

CHENG, T. H. (1987) *A synopsis of the avifauna of China.* Hamburg: Paul Parey.

CHING, C. W., YU, S. T. & CHIANG, C. H. (1989) *A survey of Grey-faced Buzzard-Eagle hunting in ManChou area. Part II.* KenTing National Park.

CHIU, L. Y. (1986) *A preliminary survey of the ecology of and hunting pressure on the Brown Shrike at HengChun region.* KenTing National Park (Conserv. Rep. no. 9).

CHUNSHENG. (1979) Night hunting at ManChou. *Echo magazine* 5: 84-87.

CONSERVATION CLUB OF CHUNGHSING UNIVERSITY. (1988) A study of the northward migration of Grey-faced Buzzard-Eagles passing PaKua Mountain in the spring. Pp. 12-18 in *Annual of Taipei Wild Bird Society.*

HACHISUKA, M. & UDAGAWA, T. (1950) Contributions to the ornithology of Formosa. Part I. *Quarterly J. Taiwan Mus.* 3(4): 187-280.

HANHAN. (1981) Seeing a nest on a southern branch, one should contemplate the route from the north. *United Daily News*, 8 September 1981.

HANHAN. (1982) From "ChaLaKoHan" to "Give Me A Piece of Joyful Land". *United Daily News*, 23 January 1982.

KING, B., WOODCOCK, M. & DICKINSON, E. C. (1984) *A field guide to the birds of South-East Asia.* London: Collins.

LIANG, M. H. (1988) An evaluation of the migratory bird protection program at KenTing National Park and Recommendations. Mimeographed internal report.

LIANG, M. H. (1989) Evaluation of migratory bird protection program in HengChun Peninsula, Taiwan, ROC. Manuscript.

LIEN, H. (1962) *The general history of Taiwan.* Taipei: Taiwan Provincial Government.

LIN, S. S. & LIN, M. H. (1986) *A survey of Grey-faced Buzzard-Eagle hunting in ManChou area.* KenTing National Park (Conserv. Resrch. Rep. no. 10).

LORD MEDWAY. (1970) A ringing study of the migratory Brown Shrike in west Malaysia. *Ibis* 112: 184-198.

MA, I. K. (1980) Who comes to love me? About the bird protection meeting at ManChou on 23 October 1979. *Echo magazine* 7: 100-102.

MA, I. K. (1981) May you rest peacefully in our garden. Pp. 186-198 in HanHan & I. K. Ma (1983) *We have only one earth.* Taipei: ChiuKo Publishing Co.

NATIONAL BIRD BANDING CENTER. (1987) *Chinese Bird Banding Almanac.* LanChou, GanSu: GanSu Science and Technology Press.

NUNGCHIA. (1989) The days of the sisal on HengChun Peninsula. *Agric. Weekly* **15**(30): 14-21.

MCCLURE, H. E. (1974) *Migration and survival of the birds of Asia.* Bangkok, Thailand: U.S. Army Medical Component, SEATO Medical Project.

SEVERINGHAUS, S. R. (1968) The brown shrike (*Lanius cristatus luscionensis*) in Taiwan, 1964-1967. Report presented at 1968 Migratory Animal Pathological Survey Conference, Thailand. Mimeographed.

SEVERINGHAUS, S. R. (1970) Economic aspects of bird conservation in Taiwan. Pp. 156-165 in *IUCN 11th Technical Meeting.* India: New Delhi.

SEVERINGHAUS, S. R. (1972) September delicacy. *Echo, of Things Chinese* **53**: 35-38.

SHA, C. C. (1986) *Fitting shadows and pleasing sounds in the mountains. The bird resources of YuShan National Park.* YuShan National Park.

SHA, C. C. (1988) Notes on bird migration. *Wildbird Soc. of ROC Bull.* **1**(2): 27-34, and **1**(3): 16-25.

SHA, C. C. (1989) Notes on bird migration. *Flying feathers of China* **2**(11): 13-24.

SU, K. A. & LUE, S. C. (1984) *A study of the parasites of the Brown Shrike.* KenTing National Park (Conserv. Resrch. Rep. no. 1).

TSAI, M. H. (1988) Observation of the migration of Grey-faced Buzzard-Eagles. *Yuhina* **42**: 24-26.

WANG, Y. (1985) *The ecological survey on birds at NanZen Ecological Area.* KenTing National Park (Conserv. Resrch. Rep. no. 2).

WILD BIRD SOCIETY OF JAPAN. (1982) *A field guide to the birds of Japan.* Tokyo: Wild Bird Society of Japan.

WU, S. H. (1980) To protect the eagles at ManChou. *Wild Bird* **1**(2): 71-72.

YEN, C. W. (1980) The Brown Shrike. *Environ. Sci.* **1**: 88-92.

FEDERAL RESEARCH ON THE CONSERVATION OF MIGRATORY NONGAME BIRDS IN THE UNITED STATES

MARSHALL A. HOWE[1]

U.S. Fish and Wildlife Service, Patuxent Wildlife Research Center,
Laurel, Maryland 20708, U.S.A.
1 present address: Office of Migratory Bird Management,
U.S. Fish and Wildlife Service, U.S. Dept. of the Interior,
Washington, D.C. 20240, U.S.A.

ABSTRACT

In the United States, the term "nongame birds" applies to all bird species that are neither hunted nor legally endangered or threatened. Although ultimate responsibility for protection of migratory nongame birds lies with the federal government, research and management efforts by the key federal landholding agencies have historically emphasized species of economic importance, game birds and endangered species. In response to various legislative actions between the late 1960s and early 1980s, however, there has been a gradual escalation of research directed towards conservation of migratory nongame birds in these agencies. These studies have focused on two broad objectives (a) development of population sampling and census methods, and (b) identifying habitat requirements of species and species groups and the impacts of habitat changes on populations. The bulk of this research has been conducted by the U.S. Fish and Wildlife Service and the U.S. Forest Service. In this paper, the missions and research structures of these agencies are described briefly, and selected research highlights are discussed at length. Specific examples are development of the Breeding Bird Survey and teasing apart the relative contributions of forest fragmentation on breeding and wintering grounds to declines in populations of Neotropical migrants. Nongame bird research activities in other agencies are also summarized. The cumulative research conducted to date is evaluated in the context of developing a national management strategy to meet future migratory nongame bird conservation needs. Important shortcomings in present federal programmes continue to be insufficient follow-through from research results to direct management action and lack of coordination among agencies with a vested interest in nongame bird conservation. Pending legislation and recent maturation of a comprehensive migratory nongame bird policy in the Fish and Wildlife Service are indications that significant improvements in these areas can be expected.

INTRODUCTION

"Nongame" birds in the United States represent a taxonomically diverse assortment of bird species that cannot be legally hunted and that have not been declared legally "endangered" or "threatened" under the terms of the Endangered Species

Act of 1973 (U.S. Fish and Wildlife Service 1988a). The definition of nongame species has been extended by some state agencies to include endangered and threatened forms. The term "nongame", despite its negative ring, is an appropriate one, as it was popularized to draw attention to the disproportionate emphasis on management of game birds by government wildlife agencies. Further, there is no meaningful biological term applicable to the full spectrum of nongame species.

Today, of approximately 815 species of birds recorded in the United States (U.S.) and its possessions, 58 are game species and 48 (27 of which occur only in Hawaii) are classified as endangered or threatened. Twelve additional species have endangered or threatened races or populations but also have non-endangered representatives in the U.S. (U.S. Fish and Wildlife Service 1986; Gradwohl & Greenberg 1989). Therefore 709 species, 87 per cent of the avifaunal list for the U.S., are nongame birds in the restricted sense. The overwhelming majority of these are migratory birds, which typically cross state or international boundaries as they travel between breeding and wintering grounds. Some 332 species cross the Tropic of Cancer during migration (Rappole *et al.* 1983). Under U.S. law, migratory bird species are under the jurisdiction of the federal government, with the U.S. Fish and Wildlife Service (USFWS) of the Department of the Interior having primary responsibility. Other agencies have secondary responsibilities to meet specific legislative mandates discussed below. The official list of migratory birds protected by federal law under the Migratory Bird Treaty Act of 1918 actually includes many species that are biologically non-migratory. In fact, the only wild species of birds in the United States considered legally non-migratory and relegated solely to the jurisdiction of state agencies are a handful of sedentary game species such as grouse, quail and pheasants. Thus the ultimate responsibility for the protection of all nongame birds rests with the USFWS.

Because the USFWS is relatively small and the scope of wildlife issues so varied and complex, it has been impossible for the agency to address adequately its full range of responsibilities. Activities have necessarily been limited to small subsets of the issues, which have varied over the years as a function of changing public attitudes and economic and political pressures. Earlier in this century, studies of migratory birds by USFWS were guided by the potential economic impacts of birds on American agriculture. In the past several decades most of the resources allocated specifically for migratory birds have been directed to management of migratory waterfowl and, to a lesser extent, other migratory game species. In this effort the USFWS coordinates annual surveys and banding programmes to estimate waterfowl populations, recruitment, survival and harvest rates. It also sets annual hunting regulations for all migratory game birds and provides law enforcement support necessary to enforce migratory bird laws.

With the passage of new environmental and endangered species legislation in the late 1960s and early 1970s, USFWS and other government agencies were required to take on new responsibilities. USFWS developed an extensive programme aimed at protecting and restoring populations of native endangered species and expanded efforts to determine the impacts of environmental contaminants on wildlife. These programmes continue today as priority tasks but address: (1) the needs of a small number of species (endangered and threatened species) or (2) environmental contaminants, just one of many factors potentially affecting populations of a variety of species, particularly those occupying high trophic levels. Similarly, other federal agencies such as the U.S. Forest Service, Bureau of Land Management, and National Park Service have had to develop their own programmes to evaluate the impacts of habitat manipulations on wildlife occurring on their land holdings. In some instances, these requirements have fostered development of fairly extensive research programmes on the habitat requirements of wildlife, including migratory

Table 1:   Statistics on public participation in, and expenditures on, hunting and non-consumptive wildlife-associated recreation (observation, photography, feeding, etc.) in the United States, 1985.[1]

Activity	Participation (millions of people)	Per cent of population over 16 years of age	Expenditures (billions of dollars)
All hunting	16.7	9.0	10.1
Migratory bird hunting only	5.0	2.7	1.1
All non-consumptive recreation	134.7	72.6	14.3
Primary non-consumptive recreation[2]	109.6	59.1	(not available)

1 *Source*: USFWS (1988b); 2 Activities whose primary goal is enjoyment of wildlife.

birds. However, the emphasis has been placed on endangered and game species, the former because of specific legal requirements and the latter to serve the desires of the hunting constituency.

It has been primarily within the past decade that federal and state action with respect to the broad array of "other" migratory birds, the nongame species, has begun to take on focus and direction. A combination of factors is responsible for the recognition of nongame species as a legitimate conservation target.   The Breeding Bird Survey (Robbins *et al.* 1986), one of the few early nongame activities sponsored by the USFWS, is one factor. Discussed in more detail below, the Breeding Bird Survey (BBS) first documented and publicized long-term, nationwide or regional population declines in many species of migratory nongame birds.   This information, in combination with growing awareness of habitat degradation and loss in North America and on the Latin American and Caribbean wintering grounds of many migrants (e.g. Rappole *et al.* 1983; Tiner 1984; Scott & Carbonell 1986), underscored the risk of taking the status of nongame species for granted. At the socio-political level, public opinion surveys conducted by the U.S. Bureau of the Census for the USFWS revealed that public participation in "non-consumptive wildlife-associated recreation" (wildlife observation, photography, feeding, etc.) far exceeded participation in hunting and was economically more significant (*Table 1*).

Beginning in the late 1970s, the USFWS accelerated research efforts to develop and refine population monitoring methods for species inadequately sampled by the BBS and to conduct field studies on habitat requirements of raptors, shorebirds, colonial waterbirds and songbirds. The U.S. Forest Service began placing greater emphasis on studies of bird community structure in relation to forest structure and forest management regimes (e.g. U.S. Forest Service 1975). States began diverting small proportions of wildlife funds provided annually by the federal government (in accordance with the Federal Aid in Wildlife Restoration Act of 1937, *Table 2*) towards management of nongame birds. Many states subsequently developed their own innovative fundraising programmes for nongame bird conservation (Cerulean & Fosburgh 1986; Thompson 1987; Henderson 1988).

Other signs of growing interest in nongame birds in the past decade were the passage of the Fish and Wildlife Conservation Act of 1980 (Nongame Act), specifically authorizing federal aid to states for nongame conservation (to date, no funds have been appropriated to implement this Act), and the development by the USFWS of annotated lists of nongame species with unstable or declining populations (USFWS 1982, 1987). The USFWS also produced a draft of a migratory nongame bird management plan (Shaffer 1983). This document was the first attempt at establishing an official agency policy with respect to nongame bird management and research. Although it was never officially endorsed by the USFWS, it succeeded in heightening awareness of nongame bird issues within the agency and served as a catalyst for recent developments that are revitalizing nongame activities in the USFWS. These are discussed at the conclusion of the paper.

Below, I first present brief descriptions of the key treaties and laws that directly or indirectly define the responsibilities of federal agencies for conservation of migratory nongame birds. This is followed by overviews and selected highlights of nongame bird research accomplishments by federal agency biologists, with emphasis on the USFWS and the U.S. Forest Service. Finally, I provide an evaluation of research progress to date, along with a scenario of likely and desirable initiatives and goals for future research.

STATUTORY AUTHORITIES AND INTERNATIONAL AGREEMENTS

It is likely that few, if any, federal and state nongame programmes would exist were it not for legislative mandates that define the roles and responsibilities of federal agencies. New statutes and amendments to old ones are continually updating and redefining those roles and responsibilities in the light of new knowledge, judicial rulings and public opinion. International treaties and conventions, though not usually legally binding until the passing of implementing legislation, can also exert a powerful influence on agency policy and activity. Various laws and treaties provide the foundation for the recent attention paid by federal agencies to nongame wildlife. Although most are relatively broad in their provisions or vague in their charges to agencies, the cumulative implications are substantial. Given these legal mandates, it becomes possible for environmental lobbying organizations to influence agency actions when the agencies are slow to develop a pro-active position on the issues from within. *Table 2* presents a brief summary of the key treaties and laws that have stimulated federal activity in migratory nongame bird research and management.

RECENT RESEARCH PROGRAMMES OF FEDERAL AGENCIES: GOALS, ORGANIZATION AND SELECTED ACCOMPLISHMENTS

U.S. FISH AND WILDLIFE SERVICE – OVERVIEW

The USFWS is the agency of the U.S. Department of the Interior responsible for managing the nation's fish and wildlife resources. The USFWS ranks third among federal agencies in land holdings, controlling nearly 36 million ha (USFWS 1988c). Of these lands, 97 per cent are managed as National Wildlife Refuges (hereafter "refuges") dedicated to wildlife habitat preservation and management. Although only 13 per cent of refuge lands are located outside Alaska, many of the more than 400 refuges are strategically located along major migration routes and provide stepping stones of protected habitat for migrants and a network of wintering habitats for species that nest at high latitudes. Most refuges contain natural or man-made wetlands managed for the benefit of waterfowl. These wetlands also provide habitat for aquatic nongame species, and many refuges are paying increasing attention to habitat management for nongame birds. Typically, refuges also contain a variety of upland habitats and potentially serve the needs of most species of migratory birds. Although research is not a function of the refuge system, refuges provide outstanding bases for many of the research projects conducted by the USFWS and cooperators.

Migratory bird research by the USFWS is conducted by six wildlife research centres, most with satellite field stations, and by a system of 33 Cooperative Fish and Wildlife Research Units affiliated with major universities around the country. While research conducted by personnel and students at the cooperative units is often geared towards local wildlife management needs of the state in which the university is located, research by the research centres more typically addresses issues of broad regional or national interest, some specifically directed by Congress. Research on migratory nongame birds has been conducted by all the research centres but is presently concentrated at Patuxent Wildlife Research Center (PWRC) in Maryland, the National Ecology Research Center (NERC) in Colorado, and the Alaska Fish and Wildlife Research Center (AFWR) in Alaska. Except for nongame research with a nationwide or international focus, NERC has responsibility for projects west of the Mississippi River, PWRC handles projects east of the Mississippi River, and AFWR deals exclusively with Alaska and its offshore waters.

All migratory nongame bird research in the USFWS relates directly or indirectly to the goal of preventing populations from declining to critical levels. In many cases this means basic research on population dynamics and habitat requirements; in other instances it means experimental or post hoc assessments of environmental impacts on populations. Only a small component of the research effort is species-specific. Rather, most studies address groups of birds with similar ecological requirements (e.g. colonial waterbirds, forest birds) or taxonomic groups (e.g. shorebirds, hawks).

At PWRC, the greatest emphasis has been placed on development of population monitoring and analytical techniques (elaborated below) and on habitat relationships of shorebirds, colonial waterbirds, raptors and songbirds in the eastern United States. In the late 1970s and early 1980s, PWRC biologists pioneered the use of multivariate methods for describing habitat features associated with eastern forest bird species (e.g. Noon & Able 1987; Anderson 1979). An outgrowth of these studies was a series of investigations of the effects of woodlot size on the probability of occurrence of different species (see below). Extensive studies of habitat use patterns by nesting colonial waterbirds and shorebirds have also been conducted through the 1980s (Erwin 1980; Erwin et al. 1981; Howe 1982; Erwin 1983; Spendelow et al. 1989). Erwin (1989) investigated the sensitivity of different species of colonial waterbirds to human intrusion by measuring flushing distances. This study resulted in recommendations to increase the traditional 50 m buffer zone around colonies, as recommended by the National Park Service (Buckley & Buckley 1976), to as much as 200 m for Common Terns (*Sterna hirundo*) in order to minimize disturbance.

At NERC, research on nongame birds has only recently developed into a major programme, and the emphasis has been on the effects of riparian habitat loss and degradation in the arid West on nongame bird communities. Highlights of these studies are presented below. In 1988, with new congressional appropriations for nongame research, NERC began a major initiative to evaluate the significance of

Table 2: Key conventions, treaties and statutory authorities relevant to the development of federal migratory nongame bird programmes.

CONVENTIONS / TREATIES

Convention / Treaty	Year entered into force	Primary federal agency affected[1]	Key provisions	Source
1. Convention for the Protection of Migratory Birds (U.S. – Great Britain)	1916	USFWS	Provides year-round protection for migratory nongame birds and establishes hunting season limits for game birds. Provides list of species groups in each category.	Bean (1977)
2. Convention for the Protection of Migratory Birds and Game Mammals (U.S. – Mexico)	1936	USFWS	Provides protection similar to above and calls for establishment of refuge zones where no hunting can take place.	Bean (1977)
3. Convention on Nature Protection and Wildlife Preservation in the Western Hemisphere (Western Hemisphere Convention)	1940	USFWS	Calls for enactment of domestic wildlife conservation laws, controls on wildlife trade, cooperation in scientific research, and establishment of protected areas by signatory nations.	Bean (1977)
4. Convention for the Protection of Migratory Birds and Birds in Danger of Extinction, and their Habitats (U.S. – Japan)	1972	USFWS	Similar to Great Britain and Mexican Conventions, and sets goals of maintaining optimum numbers of birds. Directs parties to take measures to preserve and enhance environments of protected species, including abatement of pollution and ceasing introduction of exotics to islands.	Bean (1986)

(continued)

Table 2: Continued

CONVENTIONS / TREATIES

Law	Year entered into force	Primary federal agency affected[1]	Key provisions	Source
5. Convention Concerning the Conservation of Migratory Birds and their Environment (U.S. – U.S.S.R.)	1976	USFWS	Similar to above, and directs parties to identify and protect important breeding, wintering, feeding, and moulting areas.	Bean (1986)
6. Convention on Wetlands of International Importance Especially as Waterfowl Habitat (Ramsar Convention)	1986 (U.S. ratification)	USFWS	Encourages designation and protection of wetlands of unusual importance for waterfowl and other waterbirds and encourages wetland research, training, and coordination of wetlands policies among signatory nations.	Bean (1986)

STATUTORY AUTHORITIES

Law	Year entered into force	Primary federal agency affected[1]	Key provisions	Source
1. National Park Service Act	1916	NPS	Directs establishment of national parks for the purpose of conserving scenery, natural and historic objects, and wildlife and leaving them unimpaired for future generations.	Bean (1977)
2. Migratory Bird Treaty Act, as amended	1918	USFWS	Implements the provisions of international treaties (see above) with Great Britain, Mexico, Japan and the U.S.S.R.	Bean (1977)

(continued)

Table 2: Continued

Law	STATUTORY AUTHORITIES			
	Year entered into force	Primary federal agency affected[1]	Key provisions	Source
3. Migratory Bird Conservation Act	1929	USFWS	Establishes a Migratory Bird Conservation Commission to review and approve proposals by the Secretary of the Interior to acquire areas as wildlife refuges.	Bean (1977)
4. Fish and Wildlife Coordination Act	1937	USFWS	Authorizes Secretary of the Interior to assist federal, state, and other agencies in development and protection of wildlife on federal lands and to study effects of pollution. Requires consultation with USFWS and relevant state agency on any water modification project by a federal or federally permitted agency, for the purpose of determining impacts on wildlife.	Bean (1977)
5. Federal Aid in Wildlife Restoration Act (Pittman-Robertson Act)	1937	USFWS	Provides for federal aid to states for wildlife restoration, including research, and an excise tax on sporting arms and ammunition to be used for this purpose. Funding is on a matching basis (75% federal, 25% state). Funds unused by states revert to USFWS and are used to fund migratory bird research and other projects.	Bean (1977)

(continued)

Table 2: Continued

STATUTORY AUTHORITIES

Law	Year entered into force	Primary federal agency affected[1]	Key provisions	Source
6. Multiple-Use Sustained-Yield Act	1960	USFS	Establishes fish and wildlife management as one of several purposes of national forests.	Barton & Fosburgh (1986)
7. National Environmental Policy Act (NEPA)	1969	All agencies	Requires all federal agencies or organizations receiving public funds to make detailed, *a priori* analyses of the potential impacts of all major actions significantly affecting the quality of the human environment. These reports are known as Environmental Impact Statements.	Bean (1977)
8. Endangered Species Conservation Act	1973	USFWS, all agencies	Provides for conservation of threatened and endangered species by federal action and encourages state programmes. Requires *a priori* assessment of the impact of any federal actions on the welfare of endangered species. 1982 amendment implements the provisions of the Western Hemisphere Convention (see above).	Bean (1977, 1986)

(continued)

Table 2: Continued

| Law | STATUTORY AUTHORITIES | | | |
	Year entered into force	Primary federal agency affected[1]	Key provisions	Source
9. National Forest Management Act	1976	USFS	Directs USFS to maintain diversity of plant and animal communities and viable populations of all native vertebrates on national forests and to maintain and improve habitats of management indicator species.	Dickson *et al.* (1984b)
10. Federal Land Policy and Management Act	1976	BLM	Directs BLM to manage lands for multiple use, including wildlife; to designate and protect critical areas for fish and wildlife resources; and to allocate portions of grazing fees for fish and wildlife habitat improvement.	Barton (1986)
11. Forest and Rangeland Renewable Resources Research Act	1978	USFS	Directs USFS to conduct research on endangered and threatened species and on improving fish and wildlife habitat.	Dickson *et al.* (1984b)

(continued)

Table 2: Continued

STATUTORY AUTHORITIES

Law	Year entered into force	Primary federal agency affected[1]	Key provisions	Source
12. Fish and Wildlife Conservation Act (Nongame Act, Forsythe-Chafee act)	1980	USFWS	Provides for federal aid to states on a 75% federal – 25% state basis for conservation of nongame vertebrates and implementation of projects. Up to $5 million of public funds authorized but never appropriated. 1988 amendment (Mitchell amendment) directs the U.S. Department of the Interior to: (a) monitor populations of migratory nongame birds, (b) identify the effects of environmental change and human activity, (c) identify species likely to become endangered, and (d) identify actions needed to prevent endangerment.	Chandler (1986)

1 *Agency abbreviations*: USFWS (U.S. Fish and Wildlife Service), NPS (National Park Service), USFS (U.S. Forest Service), BLM (Bureau of Land Management).

wetland migration stop-overs for shorebirds. This work is focusing on Cheyenne Bottoms, Kansas, a large and partly managed wetland system threatened by diversion of water for agricultural irrigation (Howe 1987). Also planned are studies to ascertain the relative importance of smaller, more transitory wetlands, and whether they are used by a different demographic component of the migrating shorebird population. NERC is also the administrative home of a unit based at the Smithsonian Institution's National Museum of Natural History and responsible for curation of the museum's collection of North American bird specimens and for research on the systematics and distribution of North American birds.

Nongame research at AFWR has been directed primarily at the distribution and ecology of nesting and migrating seabirds and shorebirds. Feeding ecology of seabirds has received particular attention (e.g. Sanger 1987; Vermeer et al. 1987) in relation to offshore oil drilling and loss of birds in commercial gill nets. Long-term studies of the reproduction and population ecology of certain seabird species, particularly the Northern Fulmar (*Fulmarus glacialis*), are also being conducted (e.g. Hatch & Hatch 1988). Investigations of shorebirds include distributional studies (Handel & Dau 1988) and an ongoing study of the status and demography of the Bristle-thighed Curlew (*Numenius tahitiensis*), a rare and little-known species.

The Cooperative Fish and Wildlife Research Units also conduct a wide variety of research on migratory birds, including nongame species, largely through graduate students at the respective universities. Although individually important contributions to our knowledge of migratory nongame birds, these studies are not part of an integrated agency programme and are not treated in this paper.

U.S. FISH AND WILDLIFE SERVICE – SELECTED HIGHLIGHTS
In this section, I elaborate on three areas of USFWS research that illustrate the core of migratory nongame bird programmes at PWRC and NERC: (1) development of population monitoring methods; (2) documenting the effects of forest fragmentation on breeding and wintering birds, and (3) determining the effects of changes in riparian shrub and forest communities on birds in arid western habitats.

Development of population monitoring methods
The ability to monitor population changes over time is a fundamental element of conservation programmes for animals in the wild. If the cause of a potentially threatening population decline can be identified early, restorative measures can be initiated before the species becomes endangered and requires expensive recovery action. This is particularly important and efficient when populations of many species are declining in response to a common environmental stimulus.

The Breeding Bird Survey (BBS), a cooperative venture of the USFWS and Canadian Wildlife Service, was developed during the period of intensive use of the pesticide DDT in North America to provide an index to bird population changes. Unlike the Common Birds Census of Great Britain, in which repeated visits to specific plots are used to map bird territories (Williamson & Homes 1964), the BBS consists of over 1,800 predetermined roadside routes driven once per year during the nesting season by qualified volunteer observers throughout North America (Robbins & Van Velzen 1967). Along each route the observer stops at each of 50 points, 0.8 km apart, and records the number of each species seen or heard during a 3-min period. Each survey is begun 0.5 h after sunrise and lasts approximately 4.5 h. Further details of survey methodology are provided by Robbins & Van Velzen (1967) and Robbins et al. (1986).

A substantial body of research has accumulated as the BBS evolved into the most comprehensive nongame bird monitoring programme in North America. Many of these studies have been associated with the development of effective statistical methods for analysing BBS data to estimate long-term population trends. Traditional methods were unreliable and have been replaced by a new method known as route regression, in which a proportional trend is estimated for each route by using linear regression on a logarithmic scale (Geissler & Noon 1981). These slopes, appropriately weighted, can be combined for routes over any geographic area of interest to produce statistically reliable, regional trend estimates for any species adequately detected by the BBS. Using this method, Robbins *et al.* (1986) produced a summary of population trends of 230 species of North American birds over the first 15 years of the BBS, 1965-1979. In addition to documenting population changes in a number of species (*Figure 1*), this analysis also documented: (a) the short-term impacts of severe winter weather on such species as Carolina Wren (*Thryothorus ludovicianus*) and Tufted Titmouse (*Parus bicolor*); (b) range expansions for species like House Finch (*Carpodacus mexicanus*) and Barn Swallow (*Hirundo rustica*); (c) species-specific density-distribution patterns (*Figure 2*); and (d) continent-wide patterns of avian species richness and diversity. Data on population declines from BBS analyses are now used regularly by the USFWS' Office of Migratory Bird Management to identify species that may require special attention before their populations reach critical levels (USFWS 1987).

Related research has addressed potential sources of bias in BBS methodology. Analyses of the influence of temperature, wind speed, and other weather-related factors (Robbins 1981) were important in the initial development of standardized field methods. Analyses of inter-observer effects revealed biases related to hearing ability and relative experience (Faanes & Bystrak 1981). Because a change of observers on a given route can affect the comparability of survey data among years, a modification of the trend analysis procedure to adjust for observer changes has been developed and is now incorporated in the trend analysis procedure. The USFWS is continuing to conduct research aimed at improving the precision of trend estimates based on the BBS.

Although the BBS stands as a model population monitoring programme, it provides adequate population indices for at most one-third of the North American avifauna. Other species occur too remotely from road systems, have highly clumped distribution patterns, are too nocturnal or secretive, or otherwise do not lend themselves to efficient monitoring by the BBS. Most waterbirds and raptors are examples. For these species, the USFWS has taken a two-pronged approach to improving knowledge of population status: development of new field survey methods and evaluation of existing surveys run by the private sector.

For colonially nesting waterbirds, new field techniques have been developed that both minimize disturbance to nesting birds by the surveyor and produce more reliable estimates of nesting populations in large colonies. Portnoy (1977) developed a method of sampling nests along randomly selected transects perpendicular to the long axis of a nesting colony. Erwin (1981) described another method in which birds flying to and from colonies are censused over a period of hours. Though less reliable than the transect method, the "flight-line" method yields reasonable estimates of nesting populations with minimal effort and no direct disturbance. The USFWS has supported an effort by the Cornell Laboratory of Ornithology to encourage state agencies or other groups surveying waterbird colonies to use standardized inventory methods so that population monitoring will eventually be possible at the national level. The existing national database on these species, the Colonial Bird Register, suffers from inconsistent data-recording methods.

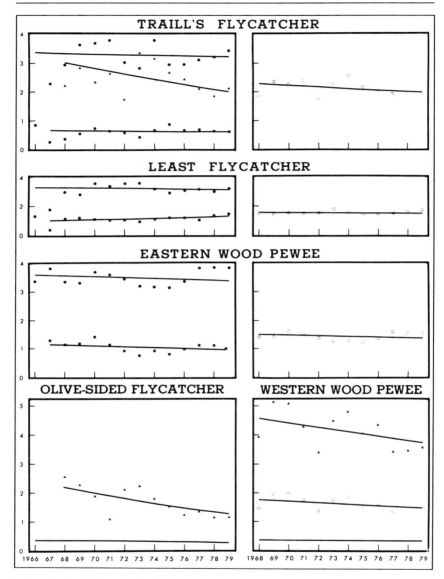

Figure 1: Population trends of five species of migratory flycatchers (Tyrannidae), based on the U.S. Fish and Wildlife Service's Breeding Bird Survey. Numbers on vertical axis represent the mean numbers of birds per route. Open circles = continent-wide trends; solid circles = eastern U.S.; squares = central U.S.; triangles = western U.S. Species: Traill's Flycatcher (*Empidonax traillii* and *E. alnorum*), Least Flycatcher (*E. minimus*), Eastern Wood Pewee (*Contopus virens*), Olive-sided Flycatcher (*C. borealis*), Western Wood Pewee (*C. sordidulus*). (*After* Robbins *et al.* 1986.)

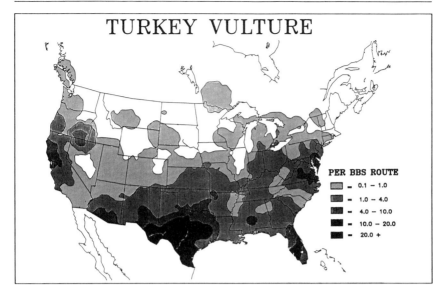

Figure 2: Breeding density-distribution map of the Turkey Vulture (*Cathartes aura*). (*After* U.S. Fish and Wildlife Service's Breeding Bird Survey; courtesy of USFWS).

New techniques for surveying hawk populations, very much needed in view of the ineffectiveness of traditional methods (Fuller & Mosher 1981), are still in the experimental stage. Geissler & Fuller (1986) devised a technique for measuring the proportion of an area occupied by a breeding raptor species in lieu of density estimates or indices of abundance, which are difficult to obtain for raptors. The technique relies on a field estimate of the probability of detection of a raptor, using vocal playback at multiple stopping points along a roadside route surveyed repeatedly. This probability is subsequently used as a correction factor to estimate the area occupied by the species based on surveys conducted only once in similar habitats. A field application of the technique is described by Iverson & Fuller (in press). For national trend estimates, the USFWS is investigating the utility of annual counts of raptors in passage at traditional concentration points.

Research on the applicability of privately operated surveys to population monitoring is perhaps best illustrated by analyses of the National Audubon Society's Christmas Bird Count (CBC) and Manomet Bird Observatory's International Shorebird Survey (ISS). Although these surveys have accumulated large population data sets over many years, they were not originally designed for rigorous monitoring of populations and therefore present a variety of obstacles to statistical analysis. In the CBC, for example, varying numbers of birdwatchers expending varying amounts of effort count all individuals of all species encountered during one winter day within a 12-km radius circle whose centre remains fixed from one year to the next. Butcher *et al.* (in press) compared trend analyses of seven species from BBS data with trend analyses of the same species on their United States wintering grounds from CBC data. Despite the imprecision of CBC methods, six of the seven species showed similar directions and magnitudes of trends for each data set. These results give hope that population trends of many species poorly sampled by the BBS might be ascertained from analysis of CBC data.

The ISS samples shorebird populations several times a year at southbound migration stop-overs, primarily in the eastern United States. Because most species of shorebirds breed and winter in areas lacking easy access, migrating shorebirds offer the best opportunity for population sampling. Recognising the difficulties of extrapolating a sample of migrants to an entire population, biologists at PWRC performed trend analyses on a carefully selected subset of species and survey sites, using the average of the highest three counts during peak migration as the annual measure of population at a site. Of 12 species analysed, two, the Sanderling (*Calidris alba*) and Short-billed Dowitcher (*Limnodromus griseus*), showed statistically probable declines over the period 1972-1983 (Howe *et al.* 1989). Based on these analyses, recommendations have been made for changing the survey design to improve population monitoring capability. Field research is underway to determine how representative population changes at survey sites are of regional changes.

Forest fragmentation research

As in most populated parts of the world, forest area in the United States has not only decreased dramatically at the hand of man, but its configuration has also changed – from one of extensive unbroken tracts to a mosaic of small tracts. This pattern is particularly evident near urban centres. Biologists at PWRC have been studying the effects of forest fragmentation on breeding bird species in eastern deciduous forests since the mid-1970s. Other studies had already documented a direct relationship between forest tract size and bird species richness and in some cases shown that, rather than being a random phenomenon, some species are more sensitive than others to decreasing forest area (see review in Robbins *et al.* 1989). But, until the PWRC studies, the quantitive relationships between forest area and probability of occurrence of different species had not been demonstrated.

These studies were conducted in various forest types in Maryland and adjacent states. Bird populations were sampled at 469 points in 271 forest tracts ranging in size from 0.1 ha to more than 3,000 ha. Logistic regression analyses identified significant relationships between forest area and relative abundance for 38 species of birds. Twenty-six species showed a significant decrease in probability of occurrence as forest area decreased. These species are described as being area-sensitive. Of great interest is the fact that most of the nesting species that are long-distance Neotropical migrants showed low probabilities of occurrence in small tracts. For example, the Northern Parula (*Parula americana*), Black-throated Blue (*Dendroica caerulescens*), Cerulean (*D. cerulea*), Worm-eating (*Helmitheros vermivorus*), Black and White (*Mniotilta varia*), and Canada (*Wilsonia canadensis*) warblers rarely occurred in forest tracts smaller than 100 ha (Robbins *et al.* 1989). By contrast, most sedentary species or short-distance migrants showed either no relationship or an inverse relationship with tract size. Examples of response patterns are shown in *Figure 3*. The strong area-sensitivity of Neotropical migrants may be related to their low reproductive potential (generally single-brooded), combined with elevated levels of predation and/or brood parasitism by Brown-headed Cowbirds (*Molothrus ater*) in small tracts (Wilcove 1985; Andren & Angelstam 1988; Small & Hunter 1988). From a forest management perspective, these studies are critically important because they identify the minimum forest area requirements of those species that tend to succumb to the traditional forest management practice of creating edge habitats.

Robbins and his colleagues have recently extended their studies of forest fragmentation effects on migratory birds to the Neotropical wintering grounds, where deforestation is occurring at an unprecedented pace. Robbins *et al.* (in press) compared bird populations in 18 paired large (>1,000 ha) and small (<50 ha) forest tracts in six countries in Central America, northern South America, and the Caribbean islands. Mist-netting samples were used to supplement point counts at each site. Results of these studies showed that many of the migratory species that are area-sensitive on the breeding grounds use both small fragments and large tracts during winter. Many of the endemic tropical species, particularly the tanagers (Thraupidae), todies (Todidae), and most of the suboscine songbirds appeared to be much more vulnerable to fragmentation than the wintering migrants (Robbins *et al.*, in press). The apparent greater resilience of migrants is encouraging. However, the fact remains that even marginal forest habitat is disappearing rapidly throughout the Neotropics. At present and projected rates, we can expect to witness substantial population declines related directly to winter habitat availability in the very near future.

Fragmentation is just one component of an array of studies being conducted by the USFWS on impacts of land use changes on bird populations. Presently the studies described above are expanding into (a) examining the forest corridor width needed to maintain breeding bird populations and to provide linkages between larger forest tracts, and (b) comparing the impacts on wintering migrants of different agricultural practices in the Neotropics.

Western riparian habitat research

The narrow bands of riparian forest along the flood-plains of rivers and smaller streams in the arid western United States have long been recognized for their importance in perpetuating aquatic and terrestrial wildlife resources. In many areas they represent the only natural forest systems, providing unique breeding habitat for many species of birds and other wildlife, corridors for dispersal, and stop-overs for migrants. Demands for water, timber, grazing land and recreation have imposed intolerable stresses on many of these fragile systems, and the introduction of exotic plant species has further threatened the integrity of natural riparian vegetation (Knopf *et al.* 1988a).

Johnson & Jones (1977) determined that loss of riparian ecosystems in the southwestern states could result in the loss of 47 per cent of the regionally breeding avifauna. Because the problem is one of the most crucial in the West, biologists at NERC are investigating bird community organization and some of the specific impacts of riparian habitat degradation on bird communities. Knopf (1985) inventoried breeding bird communities at six riparian sites along the Platte River between 1,200 m and 2,750 m elevation in Colorado. At all sites, species richness was higher in the riparian zone than in adjacent upland sites. The bird communities were most complex at the lowest elevations and least complex at middle elevations. On the basis of these findings, Knopf (1985) recommended that riparian communities at lower elevations be given highest conservation priority, those at high elevations second priority, and those at mid-elevations lowest priority.

U.S. FOREST SERVICE – OVERVIEW

The U.S. Forest Service (USFS), an agency of the Department of Agriculture, controls 77,000,000 ha of forest and rangeland habitat (Barton & Fosburgh 1986), representing about 26 per cent of federal land holdings in the United States (Bureau of Land Management 1988). These lands are of immense importance for maintaining populations of the nation's forest-dwelling migratory birds. Although the traditional purpose of the National Forest system is to assure continuing availability of commercially harvestable timber, wildlife management goals have

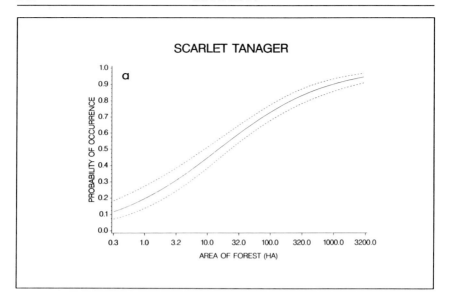

SCARLET TANAGER

a

PROBABILITY OF OCCURRENCE

AREA OF FOREST (HA)

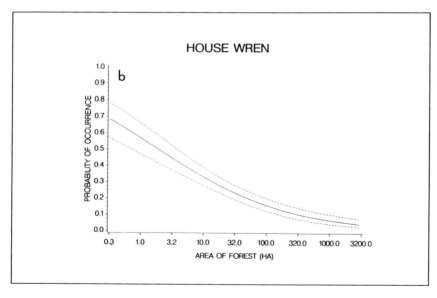

HOUSE WREN

b

PROBABILITY OF OCCURRENCE

AREA OF FOREST (HA)

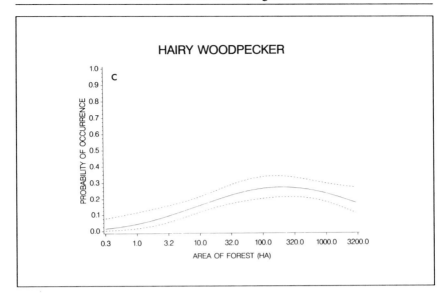

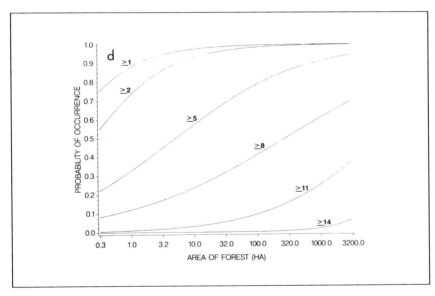

Figure 3: Probability of occurrence of various breeding bird species in eastern deciduous forest as a function of forest area: (a) Scarlet Tanager (*Piranga olivacea*), a migratory forest interior species; (b) House Wren (*Troglodytes aedon*), a migratory edge species; (c) Hairy Woodpecker (*Picoides villosus*), a permanent resident; (d) Probability of detecting at least 1, 2, 5, 8, 11 and 14 species of area-sensitive birds at a random point as a function of forest area. (*After* Robbins *et al.* 1989.)

been increasingly emphasized since the passage of the Multiple-Use Sustained-Yield Act of 1960. The usual goal of managing for game species changed with the language of the National Forest Management Act of 1976, requiring the USFS to provide at least the minimum habitat requirements for maintaining viable populations of all existing native and desirable non-native vertebrate species. This formidable stipulation gave rise to an expansion of investigations into the impacts of forest management practices on nongame bird communities.

The USFS maintains eight regional experimental stations, which are the centres of research in the agency. Research on fish and wildlife habitat relationships at these stations was given a boost by the Forest and Rangeland Renewable Resources Research Act of 1978. Research during the past decade has evolved in accordance with the provisions of this Act, requiring the USFS to conduct research on maintaining and improving fish and wildlife habitat. Dickson *et al.* (1984b) defined four functional areas of nongame research in the USFS: (1) development of new methods and systems of monitoring wildlife; (2) community and habitat response to land management; (3) species-specific studies, and (4) study of the extension and application of ecological concepts to management of wildlife and fish.

Most of the experimental stations have now conducted extensive analyses of habitat relationships of bird communities indigenous to the dominant forest types in their respective areas, e.g. bottomland hardwoods (Dickson 1978), oak-pine and oak-hickory (Evans 1978), spruce-fir (Crawford & Titterington 1979). Many of these studies examine changes in bird communities over time, or differences related to age class of forest stands (Edgerton & Thomas 1978; Dickson *et al.* 1980; Dickson *et al.* 1984a). Some investigators have explored the utility of multivariate statistics for reducing complex combinations of habitat variables to manageable descriptors capable of classifying bird species or species groups according to their habitat requirements (Conner *et al.* 1983a). Several investigators have examined the concept of managing at the level of guilds, groups of species that exploit the same class of environmental resources in a similar way (Root 1967). Verner (1984) concluded that guilds show promise as a means of evaluating habitat quality but that much testing of their applicability is necessary. Because of the subjectivity of assigning bird species to guilds, however, and the great variability shown by species within guilds, the viability of the guild concept for managing forest wildlife has been called into question by other USFS investigators (DeGraaf & Chadwick 1984; Szaro 1986).

Research in the USFS has just begun to address minimal forest area requirements of nongame birds. Traditionally, emphasis in forest management for wildlife has been placed on promoting edge habitats, which often leads to increases in total bird diversity and augments populations of many game birds and mammals. But, as noted above, this practice can have negative impacts on area-sensitive, long-distance migratory birds. The average tract size of 34 ha recommended by Thomas *et al.* (1978) for northwestern coniferous forests seems insufficient, if species-area relationships found in eastern deciduous forests (Robbins *et al.* 1989) apply similarly to coniferous habitats. However, a recent USFS study (Rosenberg & Raphael 1986) failed to find significant area relationships for any bird species, including Neotropical migrants, in Douglas Fir forests in California. More research is needed to establish whether this is a widespread pattern in the West.

The USFS occasionally conducts detailed species-specific studies. Except for the endangered Red-Cockaded Woodpecker (*Picoides borealis*), the nongame species that has received the most attention is the Spotted Owl (*Strix occidentalis*). This species has been the centre of controversy over timber management practices in the Pacific North-west because of its large area requirements in old-growth

(>250 yr) forests dominated by Douglas Fir. Detailed ecological research (e.g. Forsman *et al.* 1984) and legal action culminated in a 1989 proposal by the USFWS to list the northwestern subspecies of the owl as "threatened" under the Endangered Species Act. The results of field and population modelling research on the Spotted Owl, and the implications for forest management, have been thoroughly summarized elsewhere (Forsman & Meslow 1986; Marcot *et al.* 1986; Dawson *et al.* 1987).

U.S. FOREST SERVICE – SELECTED HIGHLIGHTS
In this section I devote special attention to two issues that have been targets of recent USFS research: (1) rigorous testing of bird census methodology, and (2) habitat ecology and management for cavity-nesting species.

Census methodology
The level of precision required in breeding bird survey programmes is a function of the objective of the programme. For monitoring population change at the same location over a period of years, data on absolute densities are not necessary as long as comparable population indices can be obtained by standardized methods. For studies in which breeding bird communities are compared among sites, particularly among habitats, only measures of absolute density assure the necessary comparability. Both types of study play important roles in migratory nongame bird conservation. Jared Verner's series of studies (summarized in Verner 1985) of the effectiveness and limitations of different census methods at the USFS' Pacific South-west Forest and Range Experimental Station in California are the most rigorous evaluations of their kind that have been conducted. Using elegant study designs, he has compared traditional spot-mapping with transect and point-count approaches and examined the influence of potential biases inherent in all methods.

Verner & Ritter (1985, 1988) compared the effectiveness of transects and point counts for determining species richness (number of species), relative abundance, and densities. Variations of both techniques are commonly used in field studies. In transect sampling, the observer counts all birds seen or heard while walking steadily along a predetermined line. In point counts the observer usually moves along a transect to regularly spaced points and counts for a designated time at each point (the Breeding Bird Survey is an example of a specialized variation of the point-count technique). Two important conclusions of these comparisons were that: (a) point counts are more efficient than transect sampling for estimating the species richness of an area, and (b) total counts of individuals give a better approximation of relative abundance of species than frequency of occurrence data. Neither method yields useful estimates of population density. Compared with results from spot-mapping (widely assumed to give the most accurate measure of density), the average error of transect estimates of density was 25 per cent.

In related studies, Verner (1987) examined differences among observers. In utilizing a randomized rotation of three different experienced observers conducting counts at 210 different points, Verner (1987) found a surprising amount of variation among the observers in measures of species richness and total numbers of individuals (the latter ranging from 1915 to 2995). On the basis of these results, Verner (1987) recommended that counts should be repeated by at least three observers to minimize individual bias in detecting birds, if it is not possible for one individual to conduct all censuses for the duration of a study.

The variation in precision Verner and his associates have demonstrated among the many different techniques available has serious implications for the validity and repeatability of surveys. Because monitoring of species populations and

Table 3: Hard snag requirements for nesting and roosting woodpeckers in an Oregon Ponderosa Pine (*Pinus ponderosa*) community.[1]

Species	Minimum snag d.b.h.[2] (cm)	Snags required/100 ha to support various percentages of maximum woodpecker populations:			
		100%	70%	40%	10%
Pileated Woodpecker (*Dryocopus pileatus*)	50.8	32	22	13	3
Williamson's Sapsucker (*Sphyrapicus thyroideus*)	30.5	371	259	148	37
Lewis' Woodpecker (*Melanerpes lewis*)	30.5	249	174	100	25
Northern Flicker (*Colaptes auratus*)	30.5	93	65	37	9
White-headed Woodpecker (*Picoides albolarvatus*)	25.4	558	391	223	56
Hairy Woodpecker (*Picoides villosus*)	25.4	446	312	178	45

1 Adapted from Thomas *et al.* (1979), Table 16; 2 Diameter at breast height.

documentation of bird community composition are such fundamental elements of migratory bird conservation, it is crucial that only rigorously evaluated methods are used and that the highest standards of data collection are maintained.

Cavity-nesting birds

Considerable attention has been paid in the USFS to the impact of forest management on birds that require tree cavities for nesting or roosting (Davis *et al.* 1983). These species, including both excavators like woodpeckers and secondary users like certain owls, wrens, flycatchers and bluebirds, use dead or dying trees (snags), which are typically removed during intensive timber management and opportunistic firewood harvesting (Bull & Partridge 1986). Although most excavators are relatively sedentary, secondary users tend to be migratory. Surveys have shown that fewer snags exist in managed than in unmanaged forests (Cline *et al.* 1980). A body of recent research has focused on the snag requirements of various nongame species and the development of methods for inducing snag formation.

Thomas *et al.* (1979) worked out estimates of snag requirements of various species of woodpecker nesting in the Blue Mountains of Oregon and Washington. For each species, they used information in the literature on tree size requirements and number of cavities required through the annual cycle along with data collected in the field on ratios of suitable snags with cavities to those without to estimate the total number of snags required for each pair. This information was extrapolated to the number of snags required/100 ha to maintain woodpecker populations at incremental percentages of carrying capacity (*Table 3*). These authors estimated that 391 snags/100 ha were necessary to maintain the entire woodpecker community at 70 per cent of potential in a predominantly pine forest.

Because many managed forests contain inadequate numbers of snags to support viable communities of cavity-nesters, it is necessary at times to promote an increase in snag density (Conner *et al.* 1983b; DeGraaf & Shigo 1985). Two recent studies have examined the long-term results of inducing tree death by different methods. The goal of these studies was development of a technique for selective killing of individual trees that is cost-effective in the long term. Conner *et al.* (1983b) found that although herbicide injection and tree girdling both encouraged fungal development and subsequent decay in the heartwood and sapwood of Southern Oaks, the girdling procedure resulted in slower decay. Consequently the resulting snags were available to cavity-nesters for longer periods. Bull & Partridge (1986),, in western Ponderosa Pine forest, conducted a more extensive investigation in which results of six methods were contrasted after a five-year period. Topping trees at 15-25 m with a chainsaw proved far superior to all other methods, in that a much higher percentage of snags remained after five years. Woodpecker foraging was also most frequent in topped trees and least frequent in those treated with herbicide.

Other aspects of snag management for cavity-nesters, including consideration of snag dispersion and length of harvest rotations, continue to be investigated. The incorporation of snag management and methods for improving snag quality and availability in the vast system of National Forests should help perpetuate populations of the 85 species of primary and secondary cavity-nesting birds that occur in the United States.

NONGAME BIRD RESEARCH BY OTHER AGENCIES

Other research efforts on migratory nongame bird conservation are scattered among a handful of other federal agencies. But, in most cases, they constitute a very small component of the agencies' overall activities and are more a result of the expertise of particular staff members than a reflection of clear, programmatic goals. For agencies involved in land management activities requiring impact assessments, the needed research is usually accomplished by contract arrangements with universities or consulting firms or through cooperative agreements with USFWS. Contracted research, though often extensive where environmental impact is involved, is not dealt with here.

The National Park Service (NPS), an agency of the Department of the Interior, ranks fourth among federal agencies in land holdings, controlling about 31,000,000 ha. Unlike most other federal lands, NPS lands are maintained primarily as natural ecosystems for the enjoyment of the public. Consequently, they represent a very important resource for the maintenance of natural bird communities. Land and wildlife management play a relatively minor role. This may account for the fact that NPS employs only about 30 wildlife research biologists and that wildlife research receives only a small fraction of the 2 per cent of the agency's budget that is allocated for research (Wright 1988). Four of the larger National Parks have their own research staffs. The remainder of the research biologists are stationed at Cooperative Park Study Units located at 21 universities around the country. Although these units are analogues of the USFWS' Cooperative Fish and Wildlife Research Units, they differ in that most of the research is conducted within National Parks on subjects relevant to specific National Park interests. Most of the research on migratory nongame birds has focused on reproduction, management, and effects of human disturbance on Atlantic coastal colonial birds (e.g. Buckley & Buckley 1976, 1977), and on reproductive ecology of waterbirds in Everglades National Park, Florida (e.g. Kushlan 1978, 1981). Kushlan's studies of the endangered Wood Stork (*Mycteria americana*) led to significant new concepts of park management with respect to the surrounding landscape and pointed out the irreconcilability of managing for a single species when the ultimate goal of the agency is maintaining natural biological diversity (Kushlan 1979). Another important example of NPS research on nongame birds is Van Riper's elucidation of the role of avian malaria in restricting the ranges and populations of various species of honeycreepers (Drepanididae) in Hawaii (Van Riper *et al.* 1982).

The Bureau of Land Management (BLM), also an agency of the Department of the Interior, controls nearly 122,000,000 ha of land, representing 45.9 per cent of federal land holdings (BLM 1988). Most of this land is open rangeland in the western United States, but also included are 6,600,000 ha of wetlands and 6,200,000 ha of riparian habitat (Barton 1986). Under the terms of the Federal Land Policy and Management Act of 1976 (*Table 2*), BLM is directed to use 50 per cent of its grazing fee receipts for rangeland improvement, including improvement of fish and wildlife habitat. Appropriated funds are also applied to management of fish and wildlife resources, and BLM has a programme goal of ensuring "optimum populations and a natural abundance and diversity of wildlife resources" (BLM 1988). Only a small portion (about 2.8 per cent) of the BLM wildlife and fisheries budget, however, is directed towards wildlife research (Barton 1986).

Raptors have been the primary nongame research target of the BLM. Many studies, mainly oriented towards raptor habitat management and predator-prey relationships, have been conducted over the past two decades (Olendorff *et al.* 1989). Kochert (1987) reviewed the impacts of grazing on habitat and prey resources important to nesting raptors, concluding that more carefully controlled grazing regimes are necessary to minimize impacts on the raptor populations. Steenhof & Kochert (1982) uncovered biases in productivity estimates for nesting raptors and recommended new field and statistical procedures for estimating productivity. Steenhof & Kochert (1988) conducted an extensive analysis of prey selection by three nesting raptor species over ten years of varying prey densities and showed that, although each species had preferred prey, they were able to expand their range of prey selection when preferred items were scarce.

The Smithsonian Institution is a federal scientific agency, partially supported by private funding sources. Strongly museum-oriented, its large scientific staff is employed to conduct basic research in various speciality areas. This stands in contrast to the research of other government agencies, which is typically intended to further the agencies' pragmatic missions. Nonetheless, with increasing concern among many scientists about tropical habitat loss and degradation, the work of some Smithsonian ornithologists has developed a strong conservation bent. For example, Morton (1980) advanced our knowledge of winter requirements of Neotropical migrants by analysing the influence of tropical wet-dry cycles on the evolution of wintering ranges and foraging patterns. Greenberg (1980) developed some intriguing theoretical ideas about migration of Neotropical migrants in relation to their high survivorship and low reproductive rates. His summary of information on productivity and long-term survival (*Table 4*) provides a useful basis for future comparison, as forest fragmentation on both breeding and wintering grounds continues. Based on their cumulative studies, these two authors presented a provocative evaluation of the plight of Neotropical migrants in a recent ICBP column (Morton & Greenberg 1989).

MEETING FUTURE CONSERVATION NEEDS OF MIGRATORY NONGAME BIRDS

Lest the above summary convey the impression that the United States Government is riding the crest of a migratory nongame bird research wave, I should emphasize

Table 4: Productivity and estimated annual adult survival rate requirements to maintain stable populations of selected resident (or short-distance migrant) and long-distance migrant passerine birds.[1]

Species	Fledglings per female	Adult survival rate requirements to maintain population when S_j/S_a=		
		.25	.50	.75[2]
Residents/Short-distance migrants				
Great Tit				
(*Parus major*)	6.0	.57	.50	.31
Black-capped Chickadee				
(*Parus atricapillus*)	5.0	.61	.44	.35
European Blackbird				
(*Turdus merula*)	4.1	.66	.50	.40
Red-winged Blackbird				
(*Agelaius phoeniceus*)	4.2	.65	.49	.39
Song Sparrow				
(*Melospiza melodia*)	6.4	.55	.38	.29
Long-distance migrants				
Acadian Flycatcher				
(*Empidonax virescens*)	3.3	.68	.54	.43
Willow Flycatcher				
(*Empidonax traillii*)	3.2	.69	.55	.44
Willow Flycatcher				
(*Empidonax traillii*)	1.8	.81	.69	.60
Least Flycatcher				
(*Empidonax minimus*)	2.8	.74	.59	.49
Least Flycatcher				
(*Empidonax minimus*)	3.4	.67	.53	.42
Prothonotary Warbler				
(*Protonotaria citrea*)	1.6	.83	.71	.62
Yellow Warbler				
(*Dendroica petechia*)	2.0	.80	.66	.57
Kirtland's Warbler				
(*Dendroica kirtlandii*)	2.2	.79	.64	.55
Prairie Warbler				
(*Dendroica discolor*)	1.1	.88	.77	.69
Ovenbird				
(*Seiurus aurocapillus*)	2.9	.73	.58	.48
Common Yellowthroat				
(*Geothlypis trichas*)	3.2	.69	.55	.44
Wilson's Warbler				
(*Wilsonia pusilla*)	3.0	.72	.57	.47
Yellow-breasted Chat				
(*Icteria virens*)	1.2	.87	.76	.63

1 Adapted from Greenberg (1980); 2 S_j = first year, post-fledging survival rate; S_a = annual adult survival rate. S_j/S_a = believed to be typically 0.25 for resident species.

again that all the activities mentioned are very minor components of agency programmes. Nongame bird conservation continues to take a back seat to traditional issues such as maintaining populations of hunted species, and to issues of a crisis nature, such as the plights of critically endangered species. The overall weakness of federal nongame programmes has come under more and more scrutiny by the conservation community (Senner 1986). Although considerable recent progress has been made, future migratory bird conservation challenges of national and international importance cannot be adequately addressed with the level of federal action typical of recent years.

The problems facing migratory birds in the United States over the next several decades are varied and complex. Habitat degradation continues on many fronts, posing threats to bird species that have managed to survive the already massive landscape changes that have occurred since early settlement. Forests outside designated wilderness areas continue to be fragmented, and old-growth timber has nearly disappeared in National Forests. With natural wet and mesic prairie ecosystems long reduced to remnant patches, advances in irrigation technology are now allowing incursion of agriculture into the remaining arid prairies. Stream channelization, wetland drainage, and water diversion for both agriculture and urban development in the arid west are reducing stream flow-rates and threatening wetlands critical as stop-overs and breeding sites for many migratory aquatic bird species. Beyond national borders the rapid loss of both primary and secondary tropical forest will almost certainly be mirrored by precipitous declines of Neotropical land migrants in the near future (Terborgh 1989).

To deal effectively with the magnitude of internal and external threats to migratory bird populations, more substantial and coordinated federal action will certainly be needed. For agencies whose traditional activities modify the natural landscape (e.g. USFS, BLM), a fuller appreciation of the importance of their lands for migratory birds and stricter regulations interpreting legislative mandates may be necessary. For agencies directly responsible for conserving natural resources (USFWS, NPS) it will require moderate shifts in conservation philosophy and more "hands-on" management. At the federal level, such changes generally occur only when a strong public sentiment for them is evident.

Because the concept of saving species while they are still common (Senner 1988) fails to connote urgency, it has been slow to engender the level of public support necessary to effect changes in public policy. Recent events, however, indicate that heightened public concern about problems facing migratory birds is finally being recognized by government officials. In 1988, for example, Congress passed an amendment to the Nongame Act (see Mitchell Amendment, *Table 2*) that requires the Department of the Interior to conduct specific activities related to the conservation of migratory nongame birds and to report regularly to Congress on actions taken. This is the first time that the Department has received specific legal guidance for activities related to nongame birds other than endangered species.

Since 1987, coordinated action by conservation groups, including ICBP-U.S., has successfully persuaded Congress to appropriate additional funds on an annual basis to the USFWS to enhance its migratory nongame bird management and research programme. In response to these appropriations, the USFWS launched a series of new nongame research projects and prepared a five-year conceptual plan for nongame bird research and management entitled "Nongame Bird Strategies" (USFWS 1988a). Unlike the first such effort (Shaffer 1983), this document was specifically requested by Congress and was made available for public comment. "Nongame Bird Strategies" was warmly welcomed by private conservation interests but received criticism on a variety of grounds. It was widely perceived as being too general, too accommodating to the sometimes competing interests of waterfowl management, and deficient in outlining research priorities.

The USFWS' Office of Migratory Bird Management has recently responded positively to these criticisms by drafting a new version of the plan with input from USFWS research personnel. The draft was issued for public comment in late 1989. It differs from the previous draft in stating more realistic management goals and in charting a clearer course for the research needed before management plans can be implemented. The key research elements of this proposal remain: (a) developing methods for monitoring populations of North American bird species not adequately monitored by existing surveys, and (b) determining the causes of population change.

With respect to monitoring activities under the new plan, the Breeding Bird Survey will continue to function as the primary USFWS programme for monitoring populations of migratory nongame birds. Improvements in BBS methodology will be sought to improve its accuracy and habitat representation. Additional privately operated surveys will be evaluated to determine how effectively they can document long-term changes in populations of species not well sampled by the BBS. These studies will all contribute to an improved ability to detect species with unstable or declining populations. Important new emphases will be on evaluating whether large tracts of federal land can serve as long-term population monitoring sites. By eliminating potential biases associated with roadside surveys, monitoring populations in large, remote tracts may be more effective for detecting responses to more generalized environmental changes such as acidic precipitation or global warming. Studies related to determining the causes of population changes will continue to focus on habitat and land use changes. Attention will be directed to increased use of remote sensing and major land use databases to determine correlations between land use changes and bird populations. Field studies will more thoroughly investigate local effects of habitat fragmentation and agricultural practices.

Perhaps the most important feature of the new plan is a commitment to conservation action to make full use of the results of monitoring and research programmes, with emphasis on habitat evaluation, acquisition and management. The element of follow-through to the habitat management level has been nearly absent in the past, a fundamental feature distinguishing USFWS migratory nongame bird programmes from game bird programmes. The plan proposes such actions as identifying habitats and ecosystems necessary for maintaining populations of sensitive species and determining the degree to which currently protected lands preserve avian diversity. It further recommends that this information be considered in establishing future land acquisition priorities. The plan also encourages deliberate management of USFWS lands for migratory nongame birds, with specific management plans to be developed for declining species.

If the new plan is implemented by USFWS, it will represent an important shift in operating philosophy. It recognizes the importance of population monitoring for all species, and the unique role the federal government can play in monitoring populations nationally. It recognizes that management of habitat for nongame birds and maintaining nongame diversity are important and that National Wildlife Refuges can be an integral part of nongame habitat management programmes. Finally, the document clearly recognizes that migratory bird conservation must be viewed in an international context and encourages international cooperation and technical assistance on migratory bird issues of common interest. Adopting these viewpoints and following through with concrete action would go a long way towards moving the USFWS into a national and international leadership role in nongame bird conservation. The framework of the programme is already in place.

The future of migratory nongame bird research in other federal agencies is somewhat less clear. The NPS is presently giving consideration to launching a programme of migratory bird population monitoring in the National Park system in cooperation with the USFWS. The "Migratory Bird Watch Program" will use long-term monitoring to attempt to document changes in populations of migratory birds in protected areas. Considerable emphasis will also be placed on evaluating the quality, distribution and abundance of critical stop-over habitats within the park system. An important component of this programme will be public education on the importance of having a network of parks throughout the hemisphere, using migratory birds to illustrate the interdependence of parks in different geographic areas (Simons *et al.* 1989). As mentioned above, the USFS continues to conduct research on bird census methods and forest bird communities. It is also initiating a programme to study the ecology of wintering Neotropical migrants in Puerto Rico (J. Wunderle, pers. comm.).

A serious deficiency in all federal programmes, however, is the minimal interaction and sharing of expertise and resources among agencies. A truly national nongame bird conservation programme would benefit greatly from more information-sharing and development of standard methods to address similar problems. The interest of the USFWS, for example, in exploring how federal land holdings can be used in monitoring bird populations and perpetuating natural diversity lends itself naturally to cooperative ventures with other major federal landowners. The land use databases maintained by the USFS have rarely been used in conjunction with bird data (Sheffield 1981) and could be compared, for example, with bird population trend data to look for possible correlative and predictive relationships. Potential exists for cooperation between the USFWS and USFS in designing fragmentation experiments as part of a timber harvest programme. From what we now know of fragmentation effects, the results of such a study could lead to both healthier bird populations and more efficient timber management.

In the long run, effective conservation of migratory nongame birds may well depend upon carefully coordinated conservation policies among the major federal land management agencies. That this has not happened is a reflection of the disparate primary goals of these agencies. Lacking has been a common philosophical thread of sufficient strength to stimulate a cooperative commitment. The conservation concept that may come closest to providing that thread is preservation of biological diversity, a goal that is legally mandated for most of the key agencies but never treated as a primary goal (Office of Technology Assessment 1987). Interest in biodiversity appears to be mounting in many federal agencies. The USFWS, for example, has initiated a pilot study to identify areas high in biodiversity that are not at present under protected status (Scott *et al.* 1987). Recently, an informal interagency dialogue on biodiversity was established for the purpose of identifying common goals and developing policy for managing biodiversity on federal lands. Independently, proposed legislation was introduced in Congress in 1989 that would establish a national policy for conserving biodiversity (National Biological Diversity Conservation and Environmental Research Act) (Blockstein 1989). Among the provisions of this Act would be the establishment of a committee consisting of 12 federal agencies and a scientific advisory board charged with drafting a coordinated national strategy. Any national strategy to preserve biodiversity is certain to encompass many of the objectives of an effective migratory nongame bird conservation programme. Although all of these developments are very recent, and their outcome uncertain, the fact that agencies are now thinking about ways to preserve biodiversity and talking with one another is certainly an encouraging sign for the immediate future of migratory bird conservation in the United States.

REFERENCES

ANDERSON, S. H. (1979) Habitat structure, succession and bird communities. Pp. 9-21 in R. M. DeGraaf & K. E. Evans, eds. *Workshop proceedings: management of north central and northeastern forests for non-game birds.* U.S. Forest Service (Gen. Techn. Rep. NC-51).

ANDRÉN, H. & ANGELSTAM, P. (1988) Elevated predation rates as an edge effect in habitat islands: experimental evidence. *Ecology* 69: 544-547.

BARTON, K. (1986) Wildlife and the Bureau of Land Management. Pp. 497-541 in A. S. Eno, R. L. DiSilvestro & W. J. Chandler, eds. *Audubon Wildlilfe Report 1986.* New York: National Audubon Society.

BARTON, K. & FOSBURGH, W. (1986) The U.S. Forest Service. Pp. 1-156 in A. S. Eno, R. L. DiSilvestro & W. J. Chandler, eds. *Audubon Wildlife Report 1986.* New York: National Audubon Society.

BEAN, M. J. (1977) *The evolution of national wildlife law.* Washington, D.C.: U.S. Council on Environmental Quality.

BEAN, M. J. (1986) International wildlife conservation. Pp. 543-576 in A. S. Eno, R. L. DiSilvestro & W. J. Chandler, eds. *Audubon Wildlife Report 1986.* New York: National Audubon Society.

BLOCKSTEIN, D. E. (1989) Toward a federal plan for biodiversity. *Issues in Sci. and Techn.* V: 63-67.

BUCKLEY, P. A. & BUCKLEY, F. G. (1976) *Guidelines for the protection and management of colonially nesting waterbirds.* Boston: National Park Service.

BUCKLEY, P. A. & BUCKLEY, F. G. (1977) Human encroachment on barrier beaches of the northeastern United States and its impact on coastal birds. Pp. 68-76 in J. H. Noyes & E. H. Zube, eds. *Coastal recreation resources in an urbanizing environment: a monograph.* Amherst: University of Massachusetts.

BULL, E. L. & PARTRIDGE, A. D. (1986) Methods of killing trees for use by cavity nesters. *Wildl. Soc. Bull.* 14: 142-146.

BUREAU OF LAND MANAGEMENT. (1988) Status report – wildlife and fisheries program. Washington, D.C.: Bureau of Land Management.

BUTCHER, G. S., FULLER, M. R., McALLISTER, L. S. & GEISSLER, P. H. (in press) An evaluation of the Christmas Bird Count for monitoring population trends of selected species. *Wildl. Soc. Bull.* 18: 129-134.

CERULEAN, S. & FOSBURGH, W. (1986) State nongame wildlife programs. Pp. 631-656 in A. S. Eno, R. L. DiSilvestro & W. J. Chandler, eds. *Audubon Wildlilfe Report 1986.* New York: National Audubon Society.

CHANDLER, W. J. (1986) Federal grants for state wildlife conservation. Pp. 177-212 in A. S. Eno, R. L. DiSilvestro & W. J. Chandler, eds. *Audubon Wildlilfe Report 1986.* New York: National Audubon Society.

CLINE, S. P., BERG, A. B. & WIGHT, H. M. (1980) Snag characteristics and dynamics in Douglas-fir forests, western Oregon. *J. Wildl. Mgmt.* 44: 773-786.

CONNER, R. N., DICKSON, J. G., LOCKE, B. A. & SEGELQUIST, C. A. (1983a). Vegetation characteristics important to common songbirds in east Texas. *Wilson Bull.* 95: 349-361.

CONNER, R. N., KROLL, J. C. & KULHAVY, D. L. (1983b) The potential of girdled and 2,4-D-injected southern red oaks as woodpecker nesting and foraging sites. *South. J. Appl. Forestry* 7: 125-128.

CRAWFORD, H. S. & TITTERINGTON, R. W. (1979) Effects of silvicultural practices on bird communities in upland spruce-fir stands. Pp. 112-119 in R. M. DeGraaf & K. E. Evans, eds. *Workshop proceedings: management of north central and northeastern forests for non-game birds.* U.S. Forest Service (Gen. Techn. Rep. NC-51).

DAVIS, J. W. , GOODWIN, G. A. & OCKENFELS, R. A., eds. (1983) Snag habitat management: proceedings of the symposium. U.S. Forest Service (Gen. Techn. Rep. RM-99).

DAWSON, W. R., LIGON, D. L., MURPHY J. R., MYERS, J. P., SIMBERLOFF, D. & VERNER, J. (1987) Report of the scientific advisory panel on the spotted owl. *Condor* **89**: 205-229.

DEGRAAF, R. M. & CHADWICK, N. L. (1984) Habitat classification: a comparison using avian species and guilds. *Environ. Mgmt.* **8**: 511-518.

DEGRAAF, R. M. & SHIGO, A. L. (1985) *Managing cavity trees for wildlife in the northeast.* U.S. Forest Service (Gen. Techn. Rep. NE-101).

DICKSON, J. G. (1978) Forest bird communities of the bottomland hardwoods. Pp. 66-73 in R. M. DeGraaf, ed. *Proceedings of the workshop: management of southern forests for nongame birds.* U.S. Forest Service (Gen. Techn. Rep. SE-14).

DICKSON, J. G., CONNER, R. N. & WILLIAMSON, J. H. (1980) Relative abundance of breeding birds in forest stands in the southeast. *South. J. Appl. Forestry* **4**: 174-179.

DICKSON, J. G. CONNER, R. N. & WILLIAMSON, J. H. (1984a) Bird community changes in a young pine plantation in east Texas. *South. J. Appl. Forestry* **8**: 47-51.

DICKSON, J. G., MCILWAIN, J. P. & STORMER, F. A. (1984b) Nongame wildlife management and research in the U.S. Forest Service. Pp. 6-13 in W. C. McComb, ed. *Proceedings of the workshop on management of nongame species and ecological communities.* Lexington: University of Kentucky.

EDGERTON, P. J. & THOMAS, J. W. (1978) Silvicultural options and habitat values in coniferous forests. Pp. 56-65 in R. M. DeGraaf, ed. *Proceedings of the workshop on nongame bird habitat management in the coniferous forests of the western United States.* U.S. Forest Service (Gen. Techn. Rep. PNW-64).

ERWIN, R. M. (1980) Breeding habitat use by colonially nesting waterbirds in two mid-Atlantic U.S. regions under different regimes of human disturbance. *Biol. Conserv.* **18**: 39-51.

ERWIN, R. M. (1981) Censusing wading bird colonies: an update on the "flight-line" count method. *Colon. Waterbirds* **4**: 91-95.

ERWIN, R. M. (1983) Feeding habitats of nesting wading birds: spatial use and social influences. *Auk* **100**: 960-970.

ERWIN, R. M. (1989) Responses to human intruders by birds nesting in colonies: experimental results and management guidelines. *Colon. Waterbirds* **12**: 104-108.

ERWIN, R. M., GALLI, J. & BURGER, J. (1981) Colony site dynamics and habitat use in Atlantic coast seabirds. *Auk* **98**: 550-561.

EVANS, K. E. (1978) Oak–pine and oak–hickory forest bird communities and management options. Pp. 76-89 in R. DeGraaf, ed. *Proceedings of the workshop: management of southern forests for nongame birds.* U.S. Forest Service (Gen. Techn. Rep. SE-14).

FAANES, C. A. & BYSTRAK, D. (1981) The role of observer bias in the North American Breeding Bird Survey. *Stud. Avian Biol.* **6**: 353-359.

FORSMAN, E. & MESLOW, E. C. (1986) The spotted owl. Pp. 743-761 in A. S. Eno, R. L. DiSilvestro & W. J. Chandler, eds. *Audubon Wildlilfe Report 1986.* New York: National Audubon Society.

FORSMAN, E. D., MESLOW, E. C. & WIGHT, H. M. (1984) *Distribution and biology of the spotted owl in Oregon.* Bethesda, MD: The Wildlife Society (Wildl. Monogr. 87).

FULLER, M. R. & MOSHER, J. A. (1981) Methods of detecting and counting raptors: a review. *Stud. Avian Biol.* **6**: 235-246.

GEISSLER, P. H. & FULLER, M. R. (1986) Estimation of the proportion of an area occupied by an animal species. Pp. 533-538 in *Proceedings section on Survey Research Methods.* Chicago: American Statistical Association.

GEISSLER, P. H. & NOON, B. R. (1981) Estimates of avian population trends from the North American Breeding Bird Survey. *Stud. Avian Biol.* **6**: 42-51.

GRADWOHL, J. & GREENBERG, R. (1989) Conserving nongame migratory birds: a strategy for monitoring and research. Pp. 296-329 in W. J. Chandler, ed. *Audubon Wildlife Report 1989/1990.* New York: National Audubon Society.

GREENBERG, R. (1980) Demographic aspects of long-distance migration. Pp. 493-504 in A. Keast & E. S. Morton, eds. *Migrant birds in the Neotropics: ecology, behavior, distribution, and conservation.* Washington, D.C.: Smithsonian Institution Press.

HANDEL, C. M. & DAU, C. P. (1988) Seasonal occurrence of migratory whimbrels and bristle-thighed curlews on the Yukon-Kuskokwim Delta, Alaska. *Condor* **90**: 782-790.

HATCH, S. A. & HATCH, M. A. (1988) Colony attendance and population monitoring of black-legged kittiwakes on the Semidi Islands, Alaska. *Condor* **90**: 613-620.

HENDERSON, C. L. (1988) Nongame bird conservation. *Current Orn.* **5**: 297-312.

HOWE, M. A. (1982) Social organization in a nesting population of eastern willets (*Catoptrophorus semipalmatus*). *Auk* **99**: 88-102.

HOWE, M. A. (1987) Wetlands and waterbird conservation. *Amer. Birds* **41**: 204-209.

HOWE, M. A., GEISSLER, P. H. & HARRINGTON, B. A. (1989) Population trends of North American shorebirds based on the International Shorebird Survey. *Biol. Conserv.* **49**: 185-199.

IVERSON, G. C. & FULLER, M. R. (in press) Woodland nesting raptor survey technique. *Proceedings Midwestern Raptor Management Workshop.*

JOHNSON, R. R. & JONES, D. A., eds. (1977) *Importance, preservation and management of riparian habitat: a symposium.* U.S. Forest Service (Gen. Techn. Rep. RM-43).

KNOPF, F. L. (1985) Significance of riparian vegetation to breeding birds across an altitudinal cline. Pp. 105-111 in R. R. Johnson, C. D. Ziebell, D. R. Patton, P. F. ffolliott & R. H. Hamre, techn. coords., *Riparian ecosystems and their management: reconciling conflicting uses.* U.S. Forest Service (Gen. Techn. Rep. RM-120).

KNOPF, F. L., JOHNSON, R. R., RICH, T., SAMSON, F. B. & SZARO, R. C. (1988) Conservation of riparian ecosystems in the United States. *Wilson Bull.* **100**: 272-284.

KOCHERT, M. N. (1987) Responses of raptors to livestock grazing in the western United States. Pp. 194-203 in B. G. Pendleton, ed. *Proceedings Western Raptor Management Symposium and Workshop.* Washington, D.C.: National Wildlife Federation.

KUSHLAN, J. A. (1978) Feeding ecology of wading birds. *Natn. Audubon Soc. Resrch. Rep.* **7**: 249-297.

KUSHLAN, J. A. (1979) Design and management of continental wildlife reserves: lessons from the Everglades. *Biol. Conserv.* **15**: 281-290.

KUSHLAN, J. A. (1981) Resource use strategies of wading birds. *Wilson Bull.* **93**: 145-163.

MARCOT, B. G., CARRIER, D. & HOLTHAUSEN, R. (1986) The northern spotted owl (*Strix occidentalis caurina*). Pp. 123-145 in B. A. Wilcox, P. F. Brussard & B. G. Marcot, eds. *The management of viable populations: theory, applications, and case studies.* Stanford, Calif.: Stanford University, Center for Conservation Biology.

MORTON, E. S. (1980) Adaptations to seasonal changes by migrant land birds in the Panama Canal Zone. Pp. 437-453 in A. Keast & E. S. Morton, eds. *Migrant birds in the Neotropics: ecology, behavior, distribution, and conservation.* Washington, D.C.: Smithsonian Institution Press.

MORTON, E. S. & GREENBERG, R. (1989) The outlook for migratory songbirds: "future shock" for birders. *Amer. Birds* **43**: 178-183.

NOON, B. R. & ABLE, K. P. (1978) A comparison of avian community structure in the northern and southern Appalachian mountains. Pp. 98-117 in R. DeGraaf, ed. *Proceedings of the workshop: management of southern forests for nongame birds.* U.S. Forest Service (Gen. Techn. Rep. SE-14).

OFFICE OF TECHNOLOGY ASSESSMENT (U.S. CONGRESS). (1987) *Technologies to maintain biological diversity.* Washington, D.C.: U.S. Government Printing Office (OTA-F-330).

OLENDORFF, R. R., BIBLES, D. D., DEAN, M. T., HAUGH, J. R. & KOCHERT, M. N. (1989) Raptor habitat management under the U.S. Bureau of Land Management multiple-use mandate. *Raptor Resrch. Reps.* **8**: 1-80.

PORTNOY, J. W. (1977) *Nesting colonies of seabirds and wading birds – coastal Louisiana, Mississippi, and Alabama.* U.S. Fish and Wildlife Service (FWS/OBS 77/07).

RAPPOLE, J. H., MORTON, E. S., LOVEJOY III, T. E. & RUOS, J. L. (1983) *Nearctic avian migrants in the neotropics.* Washington, D.C.: U.S. Fish and Wildlife Service.

VAN RIPER III, C., VAN RIPER, S. G., GOFF, M. L. & LAIRD, M. (1982) *The impact of malaria on birds in Hawaii Volcanoes National Park.* Manoa, Honolulu: University of Hawaii (Cooperative National Park Resources Studies Unit (Techn. Rep. 47).

ROBBINS, C. S. (1981) Bird activity levels related to weather. *Stud. Avian Biol.* **6**: 301-310.

ROBBINS, C. S., BYSTRAK, D. & GEISSLER, P. H. (1986) *The Breeding Bird Survey: its first fifteen years, 1965-1979.* U.S. Fish and Wildlife Servive (Resrc. Publ. 157).

ROBBINS, C. S., DAWSON, D. K. & DOWELL, B. A. (1989) *Habitat area requirements of breeding forest birds of the Middle Atlantic states.* Bethesda, MD: The Wildlife Society (Wildl. Monogr. 103).

ROBBINS, C. S., DOWELL, B. A., DAWSON, D. K., COATES-ESTRADA, R., COLON, J., ESPINOZA, F. RODRIGUEZ, J., SUTTON, R., VARGAS, T. & WEYER, D. (in press) Comparisons of winter bird populations in extensive neotropical forest and in isolated fragments. Cali, Colombia: Proceedings III Neotropical Ornithological Congress.

ROBBINS, C. S. & VAN VELZEN, W. T. (1967) *The breeding bird survey, 1966.* U.S. Bureau Sport Fish. Wildl. (Spec. Sci. Rep.-Wildlife 102).

ROOT, R. B. (1967) The niche exploitation pattern of the blue-gray gnatcatcher. *Ecol. Monogr.* 37: 317-350.

ROSENBERG, K. V. & RAPHAEL, M. G. (1986) Effects of forest fragmentation on vertebrates in Douglas-fir forests. Pp. 263-272 in J. Verner, M. L. Morrison & C. J. Ralph, eds. *Wildlife 2000: modeling habitat relationships of terrestrial vertebrates.* Madison: University of Wisconsin Press.

SANGER, G. A. (1987) Trophic levels and trophic relationships of seabirds in the Gulf of Alaska. Pp. 229-257 in J. P. Croxall, ed. *Seabirds – feeding ecology and role in marine ecosystems.* Cambridge, U.K.: Cambridge University Press.

SCOTT, D. A. & CARBONELL, M. (1986) *A directory of neotropical wetlands.* Cambridge, U.K.: International Union for the Conservation of Nature and Natural Resources; Slimbridge, U.K.: International Waterfowl and Wetlands Research Bureau.

SCOTT, J. M., CSUTI, B., SMITH, K., ESTES, J. & CAICCO, S. (1987) Beyond endangered species: an integrated conservation strategy for the preservation of biological diversity. *Endangered Species Update* 5: 43-48.

SENNER, S. E. (1986) Federal research on migratory nongame birds: is the United States Fish and Wildlife Service doing its job? *Amer. Birds* 40: 413-417.

SENNER, S. E. (1988) Saving birds while they are still common. *Endangered Species Update* 5: 1-4.

SHAFFER, M. L. (1983) Nongame migratory bird management: the federal role. Washington, D.C.: U.S. Fish and Wildlife Service. Unpubl. draft report.

SHEFFIELD, R. M. (1981) *Multiresource inventories: techniques for evaluating nongame bird habitat.* U.S. Forest Service (Resrch. Rep. SE-218).

SIMONS, T. R., PEINE, J. & CUNNINGHAM, R. (1989) Proposed Migratory Bird Watch Program to encompass research, monitoring, and interpretation. *Park Sci.* 9: 8.

SMALL, M. F. & HUNTER, M. L. (1988) Forest fragmentation and avian nest predation in forested landscapes. *Oecologia* 76: 62-64.

SPENDELOW, J. A., ERWIN, R. M. & WILLIAMS, B. K. (1989) Patterns of species co-occurrence of nesting colonial Ciconiiformes in Atlantic Coast estuarine areas. *Colon. Waterbirds* 12: 51-59.

STEENHOF, K. & KOCHERT, M. N. (1982) An evaluation of methods used to estimate raptor nesting success. *J. Wildl. Mgmt.* 46: 885-893.

STEENHOF, K. & KOCHERT, M. N. (1988) Dietary responses of three raptor species to changing prey densities in a natural environment. *J. Anim. Ecol.* 57: 37-48.

SZARO, R. C. (1986) Guild management: an evaluation of avian guilds as a predictive tool. *Environ. Mgmt.* 10: 681-688.

TERBORGH, J. (1989) *Where have all the birds gone?* Princeton, New Jersey: Princeton University Press.

THOMAS, J. W., ANDERSON, R. G., MASER, C. & BULL, E. L. (1979) Snags. Pp. 60-77 in J. W. Thomas, ed. *Wildlife habitat in managed forests of the Blue Mountains of Oregon and Washington.* United States Department of Agriculture, Forest Service Agricultural (Handbook 553).

THOMAS, J. W., MASER, C. & RODIEK, J. E. (1978) Edges – their interspersion, resulting diversity and its measurements. Pp. 91-100 in R. DeGraaf, ed. *Proceedings of the workshop on nongame bird habitat management in the coniferous forests of the western United States.* U.S. Forest Service (Gen. Techn. Rep. PNW-64).

THOMPSON, B. C. (1987) Attributes and implementation of nongame and endangered species programs in the United States. *Wildl. Soc. Bull.* 15: 210-216.

TINER JR, R. W. (1984) *Wetlands of the United States: current status and recent trends.* Washington, D.C.: U.S. Fish and Wildlife Service, National Wetlands Inventory.

U.S. FISH AND WILDLIFE SERVICE. (1982) Nongame migratory bird species with unstable or decreasing population trends in the United States. Washington, D.C.: Office of Migratory Bird Management. Unpubl. admin. report.

U.S. FISH AND WILDLIFE SERVICE. (1986) *Endangered and threatened wildlife and plants.* Washington, D.C.: Office of Endangered Species.

U.S. FISH AND WILDLIFE SERVICE. (1987) *Migratory nongame birds of management concern in the United States: the 1987 list.* Washington, D.C.: Office of Migratory Bird Management.

U.S. FISH AND WILDLIFE SERVICE. (1988a) *Nongame bird strategies.* Washington, D.C.: Office of Migratory Bird Management.

U.S. FISH AND WILDLIFE SERVICE. (1988b) *1985 national survey of fishing, hunting and wildlife associated recreation.* Washington, D.C.

U.S. FISH AND WILDLIFE SERVICE. (1988c) Annual report of lands under control of the U.S. Fish and Wildlife Service as of September 30, 1988. Washington, D.C.: Division of Realty. Unpubl. report.

U.S. FOREST SERVICE. (1975) *Proceedings of the symposium on management of forest and range habitats for nongame birds.* U.S. Forest Service (Gen. Techn. Rep. WO-1).

VERMEER, K., SEALY, S. G. & SANGER, G. A. (1987) Feeding ecology of Alcidae in the eastern North Pacific Ocean. Pp. 189-227 in J. P. Croxall, ed. *Seabirds–feeding ecology and role in marine ecosystems.* Cambridge, U.K.: Cambridge University Press.

VERNER, J. (1984) The guild concept applied to management of bird populations. *Environ. Mgmt.* **8**: 1-13.

VERNER, J. (1985) Assessment of counting techniques. *Current Orn.* **2**: 247-302.

VERNER, J. (1987) Preliminary results from a system for monitoring trends in bird populations in oak–pine woodlands. *U.S. Forest Serv. Gen. Techn. Rep.* **PSW-100**: 214-222.

VERNER, J. & RITTER, L. V. (1985) A comparison of transects and point counts in oak–pine woodlands of California. *Condor* **87**: 47-68.

VERNER, J. & RITTER, L. V. (1988) A comparison of transects and spot-mapping in oak–pine woodlands in California. *Condor* **90**: 401-419.

WILCOVE, D. S. (1985) Nest predation in forest tracts and the decline of migratory songbirds. *Ecology* **66**: 1211-1214.

WILLIAMSON, K. & HOMES, R. C. (1964) Methods and preliminary results of the Common Birds Census, 1962-1963. *Bird Study* **11**: 240-256.

WRIGHT, R. G. (1988) Wildlife issues in national parks. Pp. 169-196 in W. J. Chandler, ed. *Audubon Wildlife Report 1988/1989.* New York: National Audubon Society.

ICBP Technical Publication No. 12, 1991

MIGRANT BIRDS IN NEOTROPICAL FOREST: A REVIEW FROM A CONSERVATION PERSPECTIVE

JOHN H. RAPPOLE

Conservation and Research Center, National Zoological Park, Smithsonian Institution, Front Royal, Virginia 22630, U.S.A.

ABSTRACT

Early work on the role of European migratory bird species in African tropical communities indicated that migrants were interlopers subsisting on excess resources in marginal habitats where competition with resident species was avoided. This paradigm does not fit the New World avian migration system. Taxonomic and biogeographic data indicate that many Nearctic migrants are not interlopers, but are recently derived from tropical resident species. Nor are they restricted to marginal habitats. One-third of the 332 species of long-distance migrants winter in tropical forest, and many others use pristine habitats of other kinds as integral components of avian tropical communities. Similarly, the habitat needs of transients in *Zugdisposition* (i.e. preparing physiologically for the energy demands of migratory flight) at stopover areas can be quite specific. As habitat degradation throughout the hemisphere increases at an exponential rate, the need for creation of conservation priorities based on our understanding of migrant biology is obvious. Accordingly, the following list is presented: (1) determination of those species at highest risk; (2) determination of key stopover and wintering habitat; and (3) preservation of critical stopover and wintering sites.

INTRODUCTION

Development of an understanding of the conservation needs of migrants in the Neotropics is dependent on knowledge of what the role of the migrant is in tropical communities. Fundamental differences between Euro-African and New World migration patterns have had profound effects on the interpretation of this role by researchers working in the two areas; and as a result, their understanding of the conservation needs for migrants differ as well.

This chapter will serve as a review of concepts of Euro-African and New World migrant biology, and their relationship to migrant conservation. I will summarize information on current conservation problems for migrants that pass through or winter in the northern Neotropics, and will present results of recent studies on population trends of Nearctic migrants. Finally, the chapter will conclude with suggested priorities for conserving migrant birds in the Neotropics.

Table 1: Numbers of migrants from the Holarctic Region wintering in tropical evergreen forest.

Locality	Forest type	Residents	Migrants	Source
Africa – Mt Nimba, Guinea	Equatorial rainforest	150	0	Brosset 1984.
Africa – Nigeria	Equatorial rainforest	?	8	Elgood et al. 1966.
Africa – Gabon	Equatorial rainforest	?	0	Brosset 1968.
Africa – Lamto, Ivory Coast	Equatorial rainforest	113	0	Thiollay 1970a,b.
Africa (different localities)	Equatorial rainforest	?	6	Moreau 1972.
Central America – Panama	Young (>50 years) and old (>100 years) growth wet, lowland forest	131	17	Willis 1980.
Central America – Costa Rica	Lowland rainforest	149	20	Powell & Rappole 1989; Stiles 1976.
Central America – Mexico	Lowland rainforest	120	17	Rappole & Ramos, Annual Report to World Wildlife Fund, 1987; Coates-Estrada et al. 1985.

Note: ? = The actual number of resident species in these forests was not stated; however reported numbers of resident species found at sites in comparable forests is 150-200 species (Colston & Curry-Lindahl 1986; Brown et al. 1982).

DIFFERENCES IN THE NEW WORLD AND EURO-AFRICAN MIGRATION SYSTEMS

New World avian migration systems are dramatically different from Euro-African systems. Thirty-two per cent (107 of 332 species) of Nearctic migrants that winter in the Neotropics are forest-related (Rappole et al. 1983). Wintering migrants comprise 10-15 per cent of forest communities in the northern Neotropics as compared with less than 4 per cent in African forests (Table 1). The Asian migration systems appear to be more similar to those of the New World, with significant percentages of the migrants to southern Asia wintering in evergreen forest (Lekagul 1968; Karr 1976).

The reason for the differences between continental migration systems seems obvious. In contrast to Asia and the New World, there is simply very little forest available in the north or central African tropics or at potential stopover sites. Of Africa's 30.3 million km^2, less than 9 per cent (2.5 million km^2) is potentially rainforest (Keay 1959; Brown et al. 1982), and much of this habitat has been altered or cleared (Colston & Curry-Lindahl 1986). In addition, even historically there has been essentially no evergreen broadleaf forest in Africa located north of 10°N (Keay 1959) (Figure 1). Thus, few species of the African tropical forests

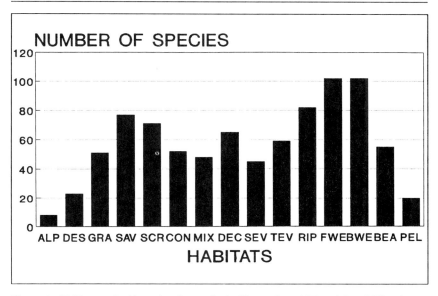

Figure 1: Habitat use by Nearctic migrants in the Neotropics. ALP = alpine; DES = desert-semidesert; GRA = grassland; SAV = savanna; SCR = scrub; CON = coniferous forest; MIX = mixed forest; DEC = deciduous forest; SEV = subtropical evergreen forest; RIP = riparian forest; FWE = freshwater wetlands; BWE = brackish wetlands; BEA = beach; PEL = pelagic, coastal marine.

could take advantage of seasonal resources in the temperate zone, at least in recent times.

This situation is in direct contrast to that which exists in Central America where large blocks of broadleaf, evergreen tropical forest were available in pre-Columbian times north to 23°N (*Figure 2*), and even further along major rivers (Gehlbach *et al.* 1976).

Most landbird migrants of the Euro-African systems inhabit savanna (Moreau 1972; Brown *et al.* 1982; Leisler 1990). Whether or not earlier geologic periods allowed long-distance movements by large numbers of forest-related species in the Euro-African region remains to be deciphered from paleontological evidence.

MIGRANT ECOLOGY IN THE EURO-AFRICAN SYSTEM

The classic study by Morel and Bourlière (1962) of migratory landbirds in the savannas of Senegal is one of the earliest pieces of research to focus on the winter ecology of migratory species. The community that they studied held 66 African species and 31 Palearctic migrants. However, only six of the African species were actually resident on the study site throughout the year. Muscicapids comprised the largest portion of the migrant community (15 species). Morel and Bourlière concluded that migrants composed a drifting population, subsisting on temporarily superabundant resources that could not be completely exploited by resident, sedentary species.

Figure 2: Pristine rainforest in the crater of the Volcan Santa Martha, Tuxtla Mountains, Veracruz, Mexico, where 20 species of Nearctic migrants are regular winter residents.

Subsequently several studies have been presented in support of this concept. Britton (1974) reported that Palearctic migrants wintering in Kenya occupied marginal habitats where they comprised 18-27 per cent of the community as opposed to primary forest where no migrants were observed to be regular members of the community.   Sinclair (1978) found that migrants wintering in *Acacia* savannas of the Serengeti region appeared to be wanderers that were somehow able to track local increases in insect abundance following rains in order to avoid competition with resident species.   Ulfstrand & Alerstam (1977) reported that Palearctic migrants were found almost exclusively in disturbed habitats in Zambia, not in undisturbed woodlands.   Brosset (1968) found that migrants were present only in disturbed areas in Gabon.   He states, "Ecologically, the primary forest appears to be a zoologically saturated biotype, where all the ecological niches are occupied by highly adapted species.   Wherever competition occurs, the migratory species is automatically eliminated" (Brosset 1968).   Gatter & Mattes (1987) report a similar situation in Liberia where numbers of Palearctic migrants have evidently increased substantially with the clearing of equatorial forest.

Leisler (1990) has summarized the current understanding of migrant biology from the Euro-African perspective as follows:

> "There is general agreement that migrants prefer to winter more in semiarid savannas, dry tropical forests (India), grasslands (Africa), riverine habitats (Central America), marginal and disturbed habitats (brushy and forest edges, early forest stages) and habitats modified by man (second growth, farmland parkland, pastures, gardens) than in extensive areas of mature forests especially of wet lowland forests..."

Herrera (1978) formalized this concept of the migrant as a wandering interloper. He states, "...non-resident birds do not really fit into the community of resident ones, but rather superimpose on the latter when enough resources are available to allow survival of extra populations".

MIGRANTS IN THE NEW WORLD SYSTEM

Migrant affinities
Taxonomic and biogeographic information reveals that most Nearctic migrants are derived from tropical resident stock (Mayr 1946; Rappole *et al.* 1983). Forty-eight per cent of all Nearctic species that migrate to the Neotropics are conspecific with Neotropical resident populations, and 78 per cent have Neotropical congeners (Mayr & Short 1970; Rappole *et al.* 1983). These data indicate that migratory species are not interlopers into tropical systems. They are derived from these systems, and partake in long-distance migrations to temperate latitudes presumably to exploit seasonally abundant resources.

Migrant use of tropical forest
Nearly one-third of all migrants to the Neotropics winter in tropical forests (Rappole *et al.* 1983). These species are not restricted to forest edge or disturbed areas, but are found in the most remote, untouched forests remaining in the Western Hemisphere (Rappole *et al.* 1983; Loiselle 1987; Robinson *et al.* 1988; Powell & Rappole, in press). Rappole *et al.* (in press) found 22 species of migrants to be "common" or "uncommon" in the undisturbed 25 km^2, forested interior of the Volcan Santa Martha in the Tuxtla Mountains of southern Veracruz, Mexico.

Powell *et al.* (in press) recorded 20 species of migrants wintering in the undisturbed lowland rainforests of the protected "La Selva" preserve in northern Costa Rica. Among the migrant species found in Costa Rican rainforest is the Eastern Pewee (*Contopus virens*), which is found mainly in openings, either natural (e.g. tree fall, streams) or artificial. In contrast, its closely-related resident congener, the Tropical Pewee (*C. cinereus*) is found chiefly in scrub, pasture hedgerows, and edge; a reverse of the pattern reported for migrant-resident congener pairs in the Euro-African system.

Migrants: foraging niche specialists or generalists?
The breakdown of tropical communities into resident "specialists" and migrant "generalists" that has been proposed for Euro-African communities (Herrera 1978; but see Lack 1986), is not particularly instructive for the Neotropics. As noted above, many tropical forest residents are close relatives of migrants that winter in tropical forest, sharing a variety of morphological and behavioural traits; some indeed are so similar as to be almost identical (*Table 2*).

Furthermore, there are migrant species that exhibit extraordinarily specialized foraging behaviours or morphological characteristics that appear adapted to their tropical, rather than temperate, foraging niche. The Cape May Warbler (*Dendroica tigirna*) forages mainly on insects on the breeding ground (MacArthur 1958). However, its semi-tubular tongue (Gardner 1925) appears to be an adaptation for nectar foraging, a niche it exploits to a considerable extent during migration and on the wintering ground (Kale 1967; Emlen 1973). In addition, Grant (1966), in a study of tarsal length in this species, concluded that in this particular morphological aspect the bird appeared more closely adapted to its wintering habitat than its breeding habitat structure.

The Worm-eating Warbler (*Helmitheros vermivorus*) displays an extremely narrow foraging niche on its wintering grounds in lowland forest of Central

Table 2: Examples of forest-inhabiting, migrant–resident congener pairs that occur in the Neotropics.

Migrant	Resident
Mississippi Kite (*Ictinia mississippiensis*)	Plumbeous Kite[1] (*I. plumbea*)
Sharp-shinned Hawk (*Accipiter striatus*)	Rufous-thighed Hawk[1] (*A. erythronemius*)
Chuck-will's Widow (*Caprimulgus carolinensis*)	Rufous Nightjar[1] (*C. rufus*)
Great-crested Flycatcher (*Myiarchus crinitus*)	Dusky-capped Flycatcher (*M. tuberculifer*)
Yellow-bellied Flycatcher (*Empidonax flaviventris*)	Yellowish Flycatcher (*E. flavescens*)
Swainson's Thrush (*Catharus ustulatus*)	Spotted Nightingale-Thrush (*C. dryas*)
Blue-grey Gnatcatcher (*Polioptila caerulea*)	Tropical Gnatcatcher (*P. plumbea*)
Red-eyed Vireo (*Vireo olivaceus*)	Yellow-green Vireo[1] (*V. flavoviridis*)
Warbling Vireo (*Vireo gilvus*)	Brown-capped Vireo[1] (*V. leucophrys*)
Northern Parula (*Parula americana*)	Tropical Parula[1] (*P. pitiayumi*)

Note: 1 Considered conspecific by some authors (American Ornithologist's Union 1983).

America where it searches for arthropods among dead leaves suspended in vine tangles (Willis 1960; Rappole & Warner 1980). Greenberg (1987a) examined the species both on breeding sites (Maryland, U.S.A.) and wintering sites (Jamaica, Dominican Republic, Belize), and found that this behaviour is mainly associated with wintering sites. On the breeding ground, the birds direct over 75 per cent of their foraging effort towards live foliage. In experiments with hand-raised juvenile birds, individuals demonstrated a distinct preference for the "tropical" foraging mode (i.e. dead leaf search) over the "temperate" mode (live leaf search) (Greenberg 1987b). Two other species of migrants, the Blue-winged Warbler (*Vermivora pinus*) and the Golden-winged Warbler (*V. chrysoptera*), also use this narrow foraging niche during their sojourn on wintering grounds in Central American forests (Morton 1980; Willis 1980; Greenberg 1987a).

The Orchard Oriole (*Icterus spurius*), which feeds mainly on arthropods on its temperate breeding grounds in North America (Roberts 1936), takes a considerable amount of fruit and nectar on the wintering ground (Morton 1980), a behaviour for which its long, split tongue with brushy edges would appear to be a highly specialized adaptation (Morton & Greenberg 1989). The tropical plant that forms a major part of the oriole's winter nectar diet, *Erythrina fusca*, appears adapted to oriole exploitation as well. Its flowers show burnt-orange colour only after being fed upon by the birds. Morton (1979) hypothesized that this colour (which is also the colour of aggressive male Orchard Orioles) served to communicate to the orioles that the nectar had been removed, so that birds would move on to other trees, thus providing adaptive cross-pollination for the plant.

Finally, Moermond & Denslow (1985) point out that among Neotropical frugivores, a group that includes many migrant as well as resident species (Ramos & Warner 1980; Ramos 1988), "The dichotomy of frugivorus birds into specialists and generalists, with only a couple [of] exceptions, is not supported by comparison of diet, behaviour, morphology, or function as dispersers".

Migrants as wanderers

The concept of migrants as homeless "wanderers" during their winter stay in tropical communities that has been proposed for some migrant species in the Euro-African system has only limited application for the Neotropics. Extensive banding studies have documented that individuals of many migrant species remain on a given wintering site throughout the season, and return to the exact same site in subsequent years (see summary of site fidelity data on 50 species of migrants representing 10 different families in Rappole et al. 1983).

Intensive studies using radio tracking with Wood Thrushes (*Hylocichla mustelina*) have found that the majority of these birds spend the winter on defended territories in lowland rainforest (Rappole & Warner 1980; Winker 1989; Rapport et al. 1989). They show intra- and interseasonal fidelity to these territories, returning to the same site year after year. However, a portion of the population, presumably composed primarily of young birds, occupies edge and second-growth habitats from which the birds make sorties into primary forest in evident search for suitable habitat for the establishment of territories. Mortality is much higher among these "floaters" than among the territorial birds. When a "floater" individual finds a suitable site, it establishes a territory and assumes a sedentary mode of existence (Rappole et al. 1989).

It should be noted additionally that the Euro-African literature is by no means unanimous on the subject of the wandering nature of wintering migrants. On the contrary there is a significant number of studies that document the phenomenon of within-season and year-to-year philopatry of migrants to African wintering sites (de Roo & Deheeger 1969; Pearson 1972).

Migrant-resident interaction

The critical piece of evidence that relegates migratory species to a subordinate role in the tropics comes from observation of direct migrant-resident interactions. Leisler (1990) states: "...migrants are usually subordinate to residents and are forced to feed at peripheral or less productive foraging sites...". Leisler's conclusions are based mainly on observations of interactions between Palearctic migrants and African residents in open country of Kenya, where residents are nearly always dominant over migrants (Leisler et al. 1983; Leisler et al., in press). However, there is no evidence in these studies to indicate that the migratory species are (a) excluded from the community or (b) excluded from the use of resources critical to their survival.

Long-term studies in primary forest sites in the Neotropics provide little evidence of migrant-resident interaction as a critical component of community function. Chipley (1976) collected 224 days of observations on migrants and residents in highland forests of the Colombian Andes. He observed 99 interactions, 85 per cent of which were between conspecifics; 7 involved migrants and residents, and migrants were the aggressor in 4 of these. Powell (1977, 1980) spent several years collecting data on the socio-ecology of foraging flocks in the highland forests of Costa Rica in which migrants constitute a small, but stable community component.

He observed a total of 108 interactions during that period, only 3 of which involved a migrant-resident interaction. In two of these instances, the migrant was the aggressor. I collected 700 hours of observations of a tropical avian community in lowland rainforest of southern Veracruz, observing hundreds of interspecific interactions. However, I saw only ten interactions involving migrants. Six of these were between two different migrant species. Other workers in the Neotropics have observed a number of migrant-resident interactions. However, the situations in which interactions were observed normally occurred at resource concentrations: fruiting or flowering plants, ant swarms, garbage dumps, feeders, etc. (Willis 1966; Leck 1972; des Granges & Grant 1980). What these interactions mean in terms of tropical avian community structure and function is not clear, particularly since most of the participants are not obligate dependents on the resource in question. As an example, three of the main species of migrants involved in losing confrontations with antbirds at ant swarms in Willis' (1966) classic account are the Wood Thrush (*Hylocichla mustelina*), the Hooded Warbler (*Wilsonia citrina*) and the Kentucky Warbler (*Oporornis formosus*). A number of long-term studies involving colour-marking, radio-tracking and observation have shown that members of these three migrant species are common winter residents in the wet, lowland forests of Central America, demonstrating both intra- and interseasonal site fidelity to territories on their tropical wintering grounds (Rappole & Warner 1980; Rappole & Morton 1985; Morton *et al.* 1987; Rappole *et al.* 1989). Whatever the significance of the interactions between members of these species and tropical permanent residents, they do not serve to exclude these migrants from tropical primary forest communities.

Migrants as transients in the New World

As mentioned above, the migration problem is somewhat different for the potential tropical migrant attempting to invade the temperate forests of North America, as contrasted with the African migrant. Forest is available over much of the land area that a northbound migrant must traverse in the New World, which is not the case for the Euro-African migrant. However, there are similarities as well. As is the case for many Euro-African migrants, the shortest routes from the tropics to temperate and boreal regions are over extensive expanses of water. For birds from South America, the West Indies, or the Caribbean slope of Central America, a route across the western North Atlantic, Caribbean Sea, or Gulf of Mexico can save hundreds of kilometres. Strong fliers, mostly seabirds and shorebirds, follow a southward course across the western North Atlantic in autumn (*Figure 3*) from the tundra of eastern and central Canada to South America (Cooke 1915; Wetmore 1926). Weather systems tend to move out of the Arctic, east and south, bringing strong northerly tail winds. Several songbirds follow this route as well (Scholander 1955; Rappole *et al.* 1985). Other southward routes for migrants from eastern and central North America involve trans-Caribbean or trans-Gulf flights to tropical wintering grounds (Rappole *et al.* 1985) (*Figure 4, Figure 5*), while birds from western portions of the continent follow a mainly overland route (*Figure 6*).

The spring northward migration routes have a much more westerly swing due to the prevailing easterly and south-easterly winds in the western Atlantic, Caribbean, and Gulf regions, and the probability of encountering strong headwinds at sea from southbound weather systems (Rappole *et al.* 1985). Few individuals, if any, follow the western North Atlantic route in spring. However, many birds do make the spring trans-Gulf crossing despite the risk of storms (Attwater 1982; James 1956; Gauthreaux 1971; Rappole & Blacklock 1985; Rappole *et al.* 1985).

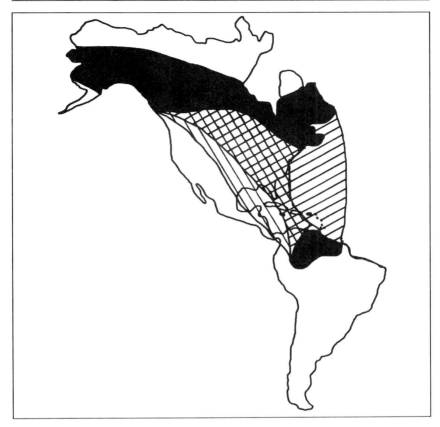

Figure 3: Western North Atlantic Migration Route as followed by the Blackpoll Warbler (*Dendroica striata*). Black = breeding and wintering range, right-to-left hatching (//) = autumn route, left-to-right hatching (\\) = spring route, cross hatching = overlap of spring and autumn routes.

The ecology of transients is a critical and poorly studied field. Work that has been done indicates that transients switch back and forth between two very different physiological states during the course of a migratory journey: Zugstimmung or a "flying" state in which their primary concern is continuation of the migratory flight, and *Zugdisposition* or a "feeding" state during which the bird focuses on rebuilding fat reserves. Behaviour in these two states appears to be radically different. Transients in *Zugstimmung* are gregarious, remaining at a site for only a short time. Their habitat needs are broad since they are not dependent on the resources of the areas in which they stop while in this physiological state. However, birds in *Zugdisposition* are hyperphagic and often aggressively territorial in defense of resources. Their habitat needs can be quite specific (Rappole & Warner 1976).

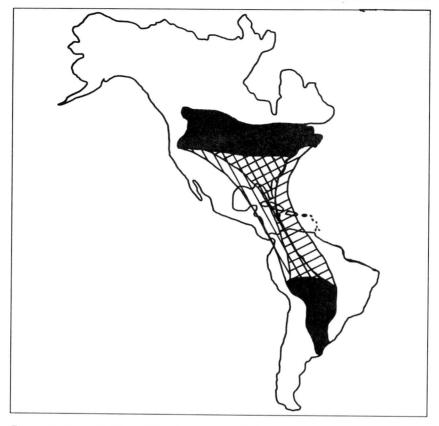

Figure 4:   Trans-Caribbean Migration Route as followed by the Bobolink (*Dolichonyx oryzivorous*); shadings as in *Figure 3.*

CONSERVATION PROBLEMS CONFRONTING MIGRANTS IN THE NEOTROPICS

Available data indicate that migrant species are an integral part of the communities in which they winter, dependent on the resources of those communities. Loss or destruction of those resources through habitat alteration may have the same effect on migrants as on residents. The degree to which migratory species are affected by alteration of tropical habitat is likely to vary naturally from species to species and according to the type of alteration. Indigo Buntings (*Passerina cyanea*), Least Flycatchers (*Empidonax minimus*) and Yellow-breasted Chats (*Icteria virens*) could benefit by conversion of forest to scrub or hedgerow-pasture, while others (e.g. the Wood Thrush *Hylocichla mustelina*, Worm-eating Warbler *Helmitheros vermivorus*, and Black-and-white Warbler *Mniotilta varia*) would disappear (Rappole *et al.*, in press).

The view of migrants as homeless wanderers during the winter period, dependent on temporarily abundant resources in marginal habitats, implies that destruction of forest in the Neotropics should not affect migrants (Hutto 1988). There are studies

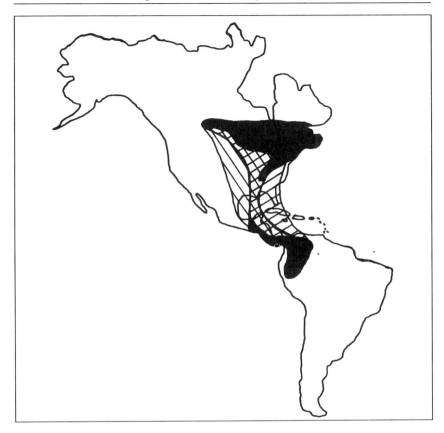

Figure 5: Trans-Gulf Migration Route crossing the Gulf of Mexico as followed by the Blackburnian Warbler (*Dendroica fusca*); shadings as in *Figure 3*.

however, that indicate that migrants are directly affected by such forest destruction. Rappole & Morton (1985) had the unfortunate opportunity to compare the effects of forest disturbances on a tropical avian community in southern Veracruz. When first examined in 1973-1975, this site was a relatively undisturbed, lowland rainforest community (*Figure 1*). We placed 50 nets in a 4.8-ha grid with one net (12 m x 2.6 m, 30 mm mesh) every 50 m on the site, and netted throughout 1973-1974 and 1974-1975. We captured 25.2 forest-dwelling migrants/1,000 net hours and 21.2 forest-dwelling residents/1,000 net hours over these two seasons. On our return to the site in November 1980, we found the study site severely disturbed – 3.2 ha was edge, young second growth or pasture, and only 1.6 ha was still in relatively undisturbed forest. Netting results indicated that forest-related species of both migrants and residents had decreased (16.8 individuals/1,000 net hours and 10.2 individuals/1,000 net hours respectively). Clearly creation of disturbance at this site did not serve to enhance the community of forest-related migrants.

Figure 6: Continental Migration Route as followed by the Wilson's Warbler (*Wilsonia pusilla*); shadings as in *Figure 3*.

Preservation of habitat for transients at stopover sites

Waterfowl managers recognized the need early for preserving wetland stopover sites along the migration route in order to help maintain huntable populations (Chapman *et al.* 1969; Gabucio 1976; Reed 1976). Researchers on shorebirds and cranes also have identified preservation of key stopover sites as critical to conservation of these species.

Protection of stopover sites seems a fairly obvious conservation priority for species with specialized habitat requirements, e.g. freshwater wetlands or broad, rich tidal flats. Requirements for transient songbirds are less obvious, but probably no less critical (Rappole & Warner 1976; Rappole & Warner 1978). As forests disappear in the tropics as well as in isolated riparian sites along the western coast of the Gulf of Mexico, the need for identification and preservation of stopover habitat for transients is likely to increase dramatically over the next decade.

POPULATION TREND STUDIES

Various studies have been done on the population trends of long-distance migrants. These range from studies at specific sites (Briggs & Criswell 1979; Johnston & Winings 1987; Hall 1984; Ambuel & Temple 1982; Askins & Philbrick 1987; Holmes & Sherry 1988) to regional and national summaries (Robbins *et al.* 1986; Holmes & Sherry 1988).

An example is the work of Marshall (1988). Based on censuses conducted in the 1930s in Giant Sequoia (*Sequoia gigantea*) forests and associated riparian habitats of the Sierra Nevada, California, he found an estimated 4 pairs/km^2 of the Olive-sided Flycatcher (*Contopus borealis*) and 12 pairs/km^2 of the Swainson's Thrush (*Catharus ustulatus*). Censuses conducted in 1986 revealed no pairs of either species, despite a lack of obvious deleterious change to their breeding habitats. He concluded that clearing of montane forest on the wintering grounds of these species in El Salvador and other parts of Central America was a possible factor.

Many similar studies have found evidence of long-term declines in migrants on their temperate breeding grounds while Nearctic resident populations in the same areas have remained stable (Morton & Greenberg 1989). Several explanations have been presented for these declines, including: forest fragmentation on the breeding ground (Lynch & Whitcomb 1978; Robbins *et al.* 1989), cowbird parasitism (Wilcove 1985), Dutch Elm disease (Temple & Temple 1976), and secondary forest succession (Holmes & Sherry 1988). The thread that ties these declines together is that most of the declining species are long-distance migrants that breed in forest, stopover in forest and winter in forest in the tropics; and the tropical habitats where these migrants stopover or winter are in the process of being severely altered.

Holmes & Sherry (1988) contend that a conclusion attributing declines of forest-related migrants to wintering ground habitat alteration is inferential (formation of a conclusion based on assumed premises). We argue that such a conclusion is based on induction (reasoning to a general principle based on a set of verifiable observations and experiments): e.g. (1) Wood Thrushes winter on territories in wet, lowland forest in the Neotropics (Willis 1966; Rappole & Warner 1980); (2) there are more Wood Thrushes than space for territories in this habitat type (Rappole & Warner 1980; Winker 1989); (3) Wood Thrushes that do not hold territory in primary forest suffer higher mortality rates than territorial conspecifics (Rappole *et al.* 1989); (4) Wood Thrushes are not found in the pasture and field habitats that are replacing tropical forest (Powell & Rappole, in press); (5) therefore we conclude that overall populations of the Wood Thrush will decline as a result of the conversion of tropical forest to pasture. We do not imply that other factors, acting on migration or on the breeding ground, are not important: however, we do contend that breeding ground factors are not likely to be as universal in their effects as the extensive destruction of wintering or stopover habitat (Ramos 1988).

The Tuxtla Mountains are a microcosm of this situation. Originally, 3,000 km^2 of rain and cloud forest, 50 per cent of the Tuxtlas remained forested in 1960, 33 per cent in 1975, and 15 per cent in 1985 (Rappole *et al.*, in press). The majority of this forest loss was a result of conversion to agricultural fields and pasture. During this period, we estimate that the population of Wood Thrushes (*Hylocichla mustelina*) wintering in the Tuxtlas declined from 112,000 individuals to 34,000, with other forest-related migrants likely to suffer similar declines.

Only three large tracts of wet tropical forest now remain in Mexico, the most important stopover and wintering area for North American migrants: the Tuxtlas, the Uxpanapa and the Lacandon (Ramos & Freese 1987). Similarly, Sader & Joyce (1988), using LANDSAT data, have estimated that of the total amount of tropical forest of all kinds present in Costa Rica in 1940, less than 17 per cent remained as of 1983. El Salvador has been similarly deforested (Marshall 1988). Guatemala, Honduras and Nicaragua still have some large areas of remaining forest, but this situation is changing rapidly as pressures build for uncontrolled development (Myers 1980).

CONSERVATION PRIORITIES

The concept of migrants as members of, and derivatives from, Neotropical communities has a number of interesting theoretical implications concerning their biology, population dynamics and evolution; not to mention its effect on understanding tropical community ecology (Rappole & Warner 1980; Morton 1979, 1980; Rappole et al. 1983). However, the most significant and worrisome aspect of the theory is that it places migrant conservation in the category of a global conservation problem in the nature of atmospheric warming. Local solutions will not work. Instead, an overall conservation strategy must be developed and pursued. The strategy suggested here and discussed below has three main parts:

1. Determination of those species at highest risk.
2. Determination of key stopover and wintering habitat.
3. Determination of critical stopover and wintering sites.

Determination of species at highest risk can be done either directly or indirectly. The direct method involves some assessment of current population size and degree of change in that population over time. In practice, such assessment turns out to be very difficult to obtain until populations have dropped so low as to be obviously in serious danger of extinction. The Breeding Bird Survey of the U.S. Fish and Wildlife Service represents a broad-based attempt to obtain this kind of information on breeding bird population trends in the United States (Robbins et al. 1986). This and similar surveys suffer from a number of methodological problems, not the least of which is the fact that populations are estimated on the basis of singing males. Since unmated males often sing as much or more than paired birds, they introduce a significant unknown and potentially misleading factor that could lead to serious over-estimation of populations (Rappole et al. 1983; Rappole & Waggerman 1986; Morton & Greenberg 1989).

An alternative to extensive surveys is intensive surveys on a number of plots over a wide geographic area representing different habitat types, in which return rates of banded individuals and nesting rates are monitored. However, regardless of the methodology used, years of work are required to separate long-term trends from annual variations due to climate and local food availability (Holmes & Sherry 1988).

As knowledge of the habitat and area requirements of long-distance migrants on their wintering grounds increases, it should be possible to determine population sizes and project declines based on the amounts of remaining and wintering habitat, and their rate of loss, using LANDSAT data (Green et al. 1987; Sader & Joyce 1988; Rappole & Morton, in press; Powell & Rappole, in press) (*Figure 7*). This process will allow conservation organizations to focus resources towards obtaining pieces of critical habitat types to salvage those species in which projected losses indicate serious potential for extinction.

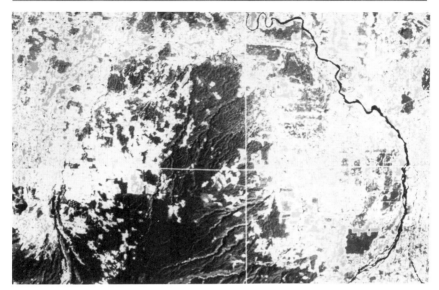

Figure 7: LANDSAT remote sensing photograph classified to show major habitat types of Heredia Province, north-eastern Costa Rica. Dark areas are mostly forest, light areas are cropland and pasture. The Río Sucio is the major river system shown on the right-hand side of the photograph while the central cordillera is in the left centre.

REFERENCES

AMBUEL, B. & TEMPLE, S. A. (1983) Area-dependent changes in the bird communities and vegetation of southern Wisconsin forests. *Ecology* **64**: 1057-1068.

AMERICAN ORNITHOLOGISTS' UNION. (1983) *Check-list of North American birds.* Sixth edition. Lawrence, Kansas: Allen Press.

ASKINS, R. A. & PHILBRICK, M. J. (1987) Effect of changes in regional forest abundance on the decline and recovery of a forest bird community. *Wilson Bull.* **99**: 7-21.

ATTWATER, H. (1892) Warblers destroyed by a "norther". *Auk* **9**: 303.

BRIGGS, S. A. & CRISWELL, J. H. (1979) Gradual silencing of spring in Washington. *Atlantic Nat.* **32**: 19-26.

BRITTON, P. L. (1974) Relative biomass of Ethiopian and Palaearctic passerines in West Kenya habitats. *Bull. Brit. Orn. Club* **94**: 108-113.

BROSSET, A. (1968) Localisation écologique des oiseaux migrateurs dans la forêt équatoriale du Gabon. *Biol. Gabonica* **4**: 211-226.

BROSSET, A. (1984) Oiseaux migrateurs Européens hivernant dans la partie Guinéenne du Mont Nimba. *Alauda* **52**: 81-101.

BROWN, L. H., URBAN, E. K. & NEWMAN, K. (1982) *The birds of Africa, Vol. 1.* New York: Academic Press.

CHAPMAN, J., HENNY, C. & WIGHT, H. (1969). The status, population dynamics and harvest of the dusky Canada Goose. *Wildl. Monogr.* **18**: 1-48.

CHIPLEY, R. M. (1976) The impact of wintering migrant wood warblers on resident insectivorous passerines in a subtropical Colombian oak wood. *Living Bird* **15**: 119-141.

COATES-ESTRADA, R., ESTRADA, A., PASHLEY, D. & BARROW, W. (1985) *Lista de las aves de la Estación de Biología, Los Tuxtlas.* Mexico, D.F.: Instituto de Biología, Dirección General de Publicación, Universidad Nacional Autonoma.

COLSTON, P. R. & CURRY-LINDAHL, K. (1986) *The birds of Mount Nimba, Liberia.*
London: British Museum of Natural History.
COOKE, W. (1915) *Bird migration.* U.S. Department of Agriculture (Div. Biol. Surv. 18).
ELGOOD, J. R., SHARLAND, R. E. & WARD, P. (1966) Palaearctic migrants in Nigeria. *Ibis*
108: 84-116.
EMLEN, J. T. (1973) Territorial aggression in wintering warblers at Bahama agave blossoms.
Wilson Bull. **85**: 71-74.
GABUCIO, M. (1976) Aquatic migratory birds in Mexico. *Trans. N. Amer. Wildl. Nat. Res.
Conf.* **41**: 212-214.
GARDNER, L. L. (1925) The adaptive modifications and the taxonomic value of the tongue
in birds. *Proc. U.S. Natn. Mus.* **67**: 1-49.
GATTER, W. & MATTES, H. (1987) Anpassungen von Schafstelze *Motacilla flava* und
afrikanischen Motacilliden an die Waldzerstörung in Liberia (Westafrika). *Verh. Orn. Ges
Bayern* **24**: 467-477.
GAUTHREAUX JR, S. (1971) A radar and direct visual study of passarine spring migration in
southern Louisiana. *Auk* **88**: 343-365.
GEHLBACK, F. R., DILLON, D. O., HARRELL, H. L., KENNEDY, S. E. & WILSON, K. R. (1976)
Avifauna of the Rio Corona, Tamaulipas, Mexico: Northeastern limit of the tropics. *Auk*
93: 53-65.
DES GRANGES, J. L. & GRANT, P. R. (1980) Migrant hummingbirds' accommodation into
tropical communities. Pp. 395-409 in A. Keast & E. S. Morton, eds. *Migrant birds in the
Neotropics: ecology, behavior, distribution and conservation.* Washington, D.C.:
Smithsonian Institution Press.
GRANT, P. R. (1966) Further information on the relative length of tarsus in land birds. Yale
Peabody Mus. Nat. Hist. *Postilla* **98**: 1-13.
GREEN, K. M., LYNCH, J. F., SIRCAR, J. & GREENBERG, L. S. Z. (1987) LANDSAT remote
sensing to assess habitat for migratory birds in the Yucatan Peninsula, Mexico. *Vida
Silvestre* **1**: 27-38.
GREENBERG, R. (1987a) Seasonal foraging specializations in the worm-eating warbler.
Condor **89**: 158-168.
GREENBERG, R. (1987b) Development of dead leaf foraging in a tropical migrant warbler.
Ecology **68**: 130-141.
HALL, G. A. (1984) Population decline of Neotropical migrants in an Appalachian forest.
Amer. Birds **38**: 14-18.
HERRERA, C. M. (1978) Ecological correlates of residence and non-residence in a
Mediterranean passerine bird community. *J. Anim. Ecol.* **47**: 871-890.
HOLMES, R. T. & SHERRY, T. W. (1988) Assessing population trends of New Hampshire
forest birds: local vs. regional patterns. *Auk* **105**: 756-768.
HUTTO, R. L. (1988) Is tropical deforestation responsible for the reported decline in
neotropical migrant populations? *Amer. Birds* **42**: 375-379.
JAMES, P. (1956) Destruction of warblers on Padre Island, Texas in May, 1951. *Wilson Bull.*
68: 224-227.
JOHNSTON, D. W. & WININGS, D. I. (1987) Natural history of Plummers Island, Maryland.
27. The decline of forest breeding birds on Plummers Island, Maryland and vicinity.
Proc. Biol. Soc. Washington **100**: 762-768.
KALE, H. (1967) Agressive behavior by a migrating Cape May Warbler. *Auk* **84**: 120-121.
KARR, J. R. (1976) On the relative abundance of migrants from the north temperate zone
in tropical habitats. *Wilson Bull.* **88**: 433-458.
KEAY, R. W. J., ed. (1959) *Vegetation map of Africa.* Oxford: Oxford University Press.
LACK, P. C. (1986) Ecological correlates of migrants and residents in a tropical African
savanna. *Ardea* **74**: 111-119.
LECK, C. F. (1972) The impact of some North American migrants at fruiting trees in
Panama. *Auk* **89**: 842-850.
LEISLER, B. (1990) Selection and use of habitat of wintering migrants. Pp. 156-174 in E.
Gwinner, ed. *Bird migration.* Berlin: Springer-Verlag.
LEISLER, B., HEINE, G., DREWS, C. & SIEBENROCK, K. H. (in press) Interspecific aggression
and coexistence between overwintering and local chat-like thrushes in Kenya. *Proc. Pan-
African Orn. Congr.* **7**.

LEISLER, B., HEINE, G & SIEBENROCK K. H. (1983) Einnischung und interspezifische Territorialität überwinternder Steinschmätzer (*Oenanthe isabellina, O. oenanthe, O. pleschanka*) in Kenia. *J. Orn.* **124**: 393-413.

LEKAGUL, B. (1968) *Bird guide of Thailand.* Bangkok, Thailand: Association for the Conservation of Wildlife.

LOISELLE, B. (1987) Migrant abundance in a Costa Rican lowland forest canopy. *J. Trop. Ecol.* **3**: 163-168.

LYNCH, J. F. & WHITCOMB, R. F. (1978) Efects of the insularization of the eastern deciduous forest on avifaunal diversity and turnover. Pp. 461-489 in A. Marmelstein, ed. *Classification, inventory, and evaluation of fish and wildlife habitat.* U.S. Fish and Wildlife Service (Publ. OBS-78176).

MACARTHUR, R. H. (1958) Population ecology of some warblers of northeastern coniferous forests. *Ecology* **39**: 599-619.

MARSHALL, J. T. (1988) Birds lost from a Giant Sequoia forest during fifty years. *Condor* **90**: 359-372.

MAYR, E. (1946) History of North American bird fauna. *Wilson Bull.* **58**: 2-41.

MAYR, E. & SHORT JR, L. L. (1970) Species taxa of North American birds. *Publ. Nuttall Orn. Club* **9**.

MOERMOND, T. C. & DENSLOW, J. S. (1985) Neotropical frugivores: patterns of behavior, morphology, and nutrition, with consequences for fruit selection. *Orn. Monogr.* **36**: 865-897.

MOREAU, R. E. (1972) *The Palearctic–African bird migration systems.* London and New York: Academic Press.

MOREL, G. & BOURLIÈRE, F. (1962) Relations écologiques des avifaunes sédentaires et migratrices dans une savane sahélienne du bas Sénégal. *Terre Vie* **109**: 371-393.

MORTON, E. S. (1979) Effective pollination of *Erythrina fusca* by the Orchard Oriole (*Icterus spurius*): coevolved behavioral manipulation? *Ann. Missouri Botan. Garden* **66**: 482-489.

MORTON, E. S. (1980) Adaptations to seasonal changes by migrant land birds in the Panama Canal Zone. Pp. 437-453 in A. Keast & E. S. Morton, eds. *Migrant birds in the Neotropics: ecology, behavior, distribution and conservation.* Washington, D.C.: Smithsonian Institution Press.

MORTON, E. S. & GREENBERG, R. (1989) The outlook for migratory songbirds: "future shock" for birders. *Amer. Birds* **43**: 178-183.

MORTON, E. S., LYNCH, J. F., YOUNG, K. & MEHLKOP, P. (1987) Do male Hooded Warblers exclude females from nonbreeding territories in tropical forests? *Auk* **104**: 133-134.

MYERS, N. (1980) *Conversion of tropical moist forests.* Natn. Res. Counc., Comm. Res. Priorites Trop. Biol. Washington, D.C.: National Academy of Sciences.

PEARSON, D. J. (1972) The wintering and migration of Palearctic passerines at Kampala, southern Uganda. *Ibis* **114**: 43-60.

POWELL, G. V. N. (1977) Socioecology of mixed species flocks in the Neotropical forest. Davis: University of California (Ph.D. thesis).

POWELL, G. V. N. (1980) Migrant participation in Neotropical mixed species flocks. Pp. 477-483 in A. Keast & E. S. Morton, eds. *Migrant birds in the Neotropics: ecology, behavior, distribution and conservation.* Washington, D.C.: Smithsonian Institution Press.

POWELL, G. V. N., RAPPOLE, J. & SADER, S. (in press) Habitat use by migratory birds wintering in northern Costa Rica. In: D. Johnston & J. Hogan, eds. *Ecology and conservation of Neotropical migrant landbirds.* Massachusetts Audubon Society, Manomet, Massachusetts.

RAMOS, M. A. (1988) Eco-evolutionary aspects of bird movements in the northern Neotropical region. *Proc. Int. Orn. Congr.* **19**: 251-293.

RAMOS, M. A. & FREESE, D. (1987) *World Wildlife Fund country plan program for Mexico.* Washington, D.C.: World Wildlife Fund- U.S.

RAMOS, M. A. & WARNER, D. W. (1980) Analysis of North American subspecies of migrant birds wintering in Los Tuxtlas, southern Veracruz, Mexico. Pp. 173-180 in A. Keast & E. S. Morton, eds. *Migrant birds in the Neotropics: ecology, behavior, distribution and conservation.* Washington, D.C.: Smithsonian Institution Press.

RAPPOLE, J. & BLACKLOCK, G. (1985) *Birds of the Texas coastal bend.* Texas: A&M University Press, College Station.

RAPPOLE, J. & MORTON, E. S. (1985) Effects of habitat alteration on a tropical avian forest community. *Orn. Monogr.* **36**: 1013-1021.

RAPPOLE, J., MORTON, E. S., LOVEJOY III, T. E. & RUOS, J. L. (1983) *Nearctic avian migrants in the Neotropics.* Washington, D.C.: U.S. Fish and Wildlife Service.

RAPPOLE, J., MORTON, E. S. & RAMOS, M. A. (in press) Density, philopatry, and population estimates for songbird migrants wintering in Veracruz. In: D. Johnston & J. Hagan, eds. *Ecology and conservation of Neotropical migrant landbirds.* Massachusetts Audubon Society, Manomet, Massachusetts.

RAPPOLE, J., RAMOS, M., OEHLENSCHLAGER, R., WARNER, D. & BARKAN, C. (1985) Timing of migration and route selection in North American songbirds. *Welder Wildl. Symp.* **1**: 199-214.

RAPPOLE, J., RAMOS, M. A. & WINKER, K. (1989) Wintering Wood Shrush movements and mortality in southern Veracruz. *Auk* **106**: 402-410.

RAPPOLE, J. & WAGGERMAN, G. (1986) Calling males as an index of density for breeding white-winged doves. *Wildl. Soc. Bull.* **14**: 151-155.

RAPPOLE, J. & WARNER, D. (1976) Relationships between behaviour, physiology and weather in avian transients at a migration stopover site. *Oecologia* **26**: 193-212.

RAPPOLE, J. & WARNER, D. (1978) Migratory bird population ecology: conservation implications. *Trans. N. Amer. Wildl. Nat. Res. Conf.* **43**: 235-240.

RAPPOLE J. & WARNER, D. W. (1980) Ecological aspects of migrant bird behavior in Veracruz, Mexico. Pp. 353-393 in A. Keast & E. S. Morton, eds. *Migrant birds in the Neotropics: ecology, behavior, distribution and conservation.* Washington, D.C.: Smithsonian Institution Press.

REED, N. (1976) International cooperation in migratory bird management. *Trans. N. Amer. Wildl. Nat. Res. Conf.* **41**: 223-226.

ROBBINS, C. S., BYSTRAK, D. & GEISSLER, P. H. (1986) *The Breeding Bird Survey: its first fifteen years, 1965-1979.* U.S. Fish and Wildlife Service (Resrce. Publ. 157).

ROBBINS, C. S., DAWSON, D. K. & DOWELL, B. A. (1989) *Habitat area requirements of breeding forest birds of the Middle Atlantic states.* Bethesda, MD: The Wildlife Society (Wildl. Monogr. 103).

ROBERTS, T. S. (1936) *The birds of Minnesota, Vol. 2.* Minneapolis, Minnesota: University of Minnesota Press.

ROBINSON, S., TERBORGH, J. & FITZPATRICK, J. W. (1988) Habitat selection and relative abundance of migrants in southeastern Peru. *Proc. Int. Orn. Congr.* **19**: 2298-2307.

DE ROO, A. & DEHEEGER, J. (1969) Ecology of the Great Reed Warbler (*Acrocephalus arundinaceus*) (L.) wintering in the southern Congo savanna. *Gerfaut* **59**: 260-75.

SADER, S. A. & JOYCE, A. T. (1988) Deforestation rates and trends in Costa Rica, 1940-1983. *Biotropica* **20**: 11-19.

SCHOLANDER, H. (1955) Land birds over the western North Atlantic. *Auk* **72**: 225-239.

SINCLAIR, A. R. E. (1978) Factors affecting the food supply and breeding season of resident birds and movements of Palearctic migrants in a tropical African savanna. *Ibis* **120**: 480-497.

STILES, G. (1976) Checklist of the birds of La Selva and vicinity. University of Costa Rica (mimeographed sheet).

TEMPLE, S. A. & TEMPLE, B. L. (1976) Avian population trends in central New York State, 1935-1973. *Bird-Banding* **47**: 238-257.

THIOLLAY, J. M. (1970a) Le peuplement avien d'une savane préforestière (Lamto, Côte d'Ivoire). Abidjan: Institute of Tropical Ecology, Abidjan University (Ph.D. thesis).

THIOLLAY, J. M. (1970b) Recherches écologiques dans la savane de Lamto (Côte d'Ivoire): Le peuplement avien. *Terre Vie* **24**: 108-144.

ULFSTRAND, S. & ALERSTAM, T. (1977) Bird communities of *Brachystegia* and *Acacia* woodlands in Zambia. *J. Orn.* **118**: 156-174.

WALCOTT, C. F. (1974) Changes in bird life in Cambridge, Massachusetts from 1860 to 1964. *Auk* **91**: 151-160.

WETMORE, A. (1926) *The migrations of birds.* Cambridge, Massachusetts: Harvard University Press.

WILCOVE, D. S. (1985) Nest predation in forest tracts and the decline of migratory songbirds. *Ecology* **66**: 1211-1214.

WILLIS, E. O. (1960) The study of foraging behavior of two species of ant-tanager. *Auk* **77**: 150-170.

WILLIS, E. O. (1966) The role of migrant birds at swarms of army ant. *Living Bird* **5**: 187-231.

WILLIS, E. O. (1980) Ecological roles of migratory and resident birds on Barro Colorado Island, Panama. Pp. 205-225 in A. Keast & E. S. Morton, eds. *Migrant birds in the Neotropics: ecology, behavior, distribution and conservation.*   Washington, D.C.: Smithsonian Institution Press.

WINKER, K. (1989)   Ecology of the Wood Thrush in southern Veracruz, Mexico. Minneapolis: University of Minnesota (M.S. thesis).

ICBP Technical Publication No. 12, 1991

SHOREBIRD AND WETLAND CONSERVATION IN THE WESTERN HEMISPHERE

LAURIE HUNTER[1], PABLO CANEVARI[2],
J. PETER MYERS[3] & LAURA X. PAYNE[2]

1 *The Nature Conservancy, 1815 N. Lynn Street, Arlington, VA 22209, U.S.A.*
2 *WHSRN, c/o Manomet Bird Observatory, P.O. Box 936, Manomet, MA 02345, U.S.A.*
3 *W. Alton Jones Foundation, 232 E. High Street, Charlottesville, VA 22901, U.S.A.*

ABSTRACT

Shorebirds depend upon the continuing viability of critical habitats along their annual migration routes. They concentrate in great numbers in a few essential and irreplaceable locations along these pathways. At times, large proportions of entire populations gather at a single place. These concentrations place enormous numbers of birds at risk from environmental threats. Shorebird habitats are disappearing at an alarming rate and there are suggestions that several species have suffered major declines.

These facts led to the creation of the Western Hemisphere Shorebird Reserve Network (WHSRN) in 1985. The network links sites essential to migratory shorebirds in an innovative international effort for habitat protection.

WHSRN is directed by a council with representatives from South, Central and North America. A secretariat facilitates site inclusion, provides technical assistance to the management authorities of WHSRN sites, and maintains network communications. WHSRN cosponsors workshops in the Neotropics and encourages follow-up activities that support the sustainable use of wetlands and shorebird conservation. To date, nine workshops have been held in seven different Latin American countries with key participation by local organizations.

WHSRN also works to collate information about shorebird numbers, distribution and migratory routes through two different programmes: the International Shorebird Survey (ISS) and the Pan American Shorebird Programme (PASP).

WHSRN's first years have been successful and the network will now tackle follow-up growth and further expansion into new countries. Emphasis will be placed in the Neotropics, where most shorebirds spend more than two-thirds of each year's cycle and where less is known about current trends of wetlands and shorebirds. WHSRN will continue to inform conservationists, biologists and policy-makers throughout the hemisphere about the network; WHSRN recognizes that for any international conservation programme to be successful in the long term, protection efforts must be carried out on both the national and local levels.

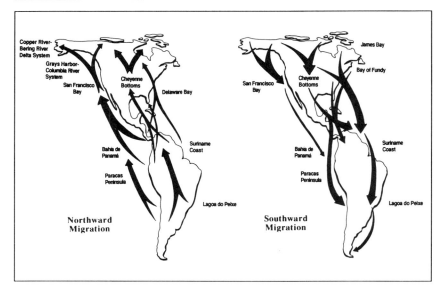

Figure 1: Western Hemisphere shorebird migration routes with major known (southward and northward) staging areas.

INTRODUCTION

The migration of shorebirds is one of the most spectacular and impressive feats in the world of birds. In the Western Hemisphere, millions of shorebirds complete the arduous task of migration every year, some travelling as far as from the northern slope of Alaska to the southern tip of Argentina, often flying non-stop for thousands of miles (Pitelka 1979; Morrison 1984). These birds use very few migration pathways and stop at only a handful of sites along the way to rest and replenish their body fat (Senner 1979; Myers 1986; Myers *et al.* 1987). The rest sites are of vital importance to the shorebirds and are irreplaceable (*Figure 1*). Unfortunately, the birds must compete with humans for many of these sites, which are located along prime coastal beaches and wetlands. It has been a losing battle for the shorebirds, and some populations have decreased significantly over the last two decades.

The Western Hemisphere Shorebird Reserve Network (WHSRN) links these sites, essential to migratory shorebirds, in a voluntary, collaborative effort for habitat protection (Myers *et al.* 1987). WHSRN uses shorebirds as symbols of the intense conservation challenge that wetlands face and of the need for international cooperation in the protection of these areas. Launched in 1985 through the efforts of the World Wildlife Fund, the International Association of Fish and Wildlife Agencies and the Academy of Natural Sciences of Philadelphia, WHSRN brings together wildlife agencies, private conservation groups and other organizations to meet conservation challenges faced by migratory shorebirds and, fundamentally, the habitats in which they live.

The conservation need

Shorebirds depend on the continuing viability of critical habitats along their annual migratory route to provide breeding, stop-over and wintering sites. The birds concentrate in great numbers in a few essential and irreplaceable locations along these pathways. At times, large percentages of entire populations gather at a single place (Myers 1983; Morrison 1984; Senner & Howe 1984). For example:

- Approximately 80 per cent of the world's population of Semipalmated Sandpipers (*Calidris pusilla*) winter along the Suriname coast.
- About 80 per cent of the U.S. East Coast Red Knots (*Calidris canutus*) depend on horseshoe crab eggs in Delaware Bay.
- Nearly 100 per cent of Western Sandpipers (*Calidris mauri*) and Dunlins (*Calidris alpina*) on the Pacific Coast use the Copper River Delta staging site in south-eastern Alaska.
- Approximately 50 per cent of the Arctic shorebirds that pass through the eastern United States during spring will visit one of two staging areas: Cheyenne Bottoms and Delaware Bay.

These concentrations place enormous numbers of birds, even whole populations, at risk from environmental threats and habitat loss. Research conducted over the last 18 years by the Manomet Bird Observatory and the U.S. Fish and Wildlife Service suggests that several species have suffered major declines, exceeding 70 per cent cumulatively. Especially affected are Sanderlings (*Calidris alba*) and Red Knots on the East Coast. These are among the largest declines of common North American bird species reported during the twentieth century (Howe *et al.* 1989).

Many of the wetlands and grasslands essential for shorebirds have been diverted from their natural state for construction, commerce, agriculture and recreation (Senner & Howe 1984; Tiner 1984). Studies from the U.S. Fish and Wildlife Service show that 30-40 per cent of the original U.S. wetlands have been destroyed or reclaimed (Horwitz 1978). Losses in many specific regions within the United States have been much greater. For example, over two-thirds of California's coastal wetlands have now been developed (Speth 1979). By 1938, mosquito-control programmes had affected almost 90 per cent of wetlands between Maine and Virgina (Bourne & Cottam 1950). The system of barrier islands along the coasts of New Jersey and Delaware has largely been given over to densely populated beach resorts. Wetland habitats in Texas and Florida now follow similar paths.

While comparable data from Central and South America on wetland habitat loss are not available, the same general trends prevail. Agriculture encroaches upon coastal saline marshes and grasslands. Human populations expand rapidly into the wetland oases of desert Peru, Chile and Argentina. Widespread, unregulated pesticide and herbicide applications enter soils and waters. New demands for enhanced transportation lead to dredging, filling and other types of wetland destruction. Industrial complexes, airports built on filled mudflats, prawn and shellfish aquaculture, etc. impinge increasingly on critical habitats. These developments all threaten wetlands of immense natural value, natural areas also of significant value to the human environment for their roles in watersheds, as nurseries for fisheries, and as places for enjoyment and recreation.

THE WESTERN HEMISPHERE SHOREBIRD
RESERVE NETWORK

For many shorebird populations, critical sites extend in a chain from Arctic breeding grounds to wintering sites in South America. As with any chain, the system as a whole is only as strong as its weakest link. WHSRN highlights the key roles that particular sites throughout the hemisphere play in maintaining that chain. By joining WHSRN, a site gains explicit acknowledgement of its participation in a hemisphere-wide effort. WHSRN offers support to local wetland conservation initiatives by providing recognition for the importance of member sites in international shorebird migration.

Membership in WHSRN and participation in its projects are wholly voluntary; management authority and priorities remain the prerogative of the land administrator. WHSRN's success depends upon involving those people in wildlife agencies, park systems, governments and private groups that own and manage wetlands. These are the key individuals and organizations whose decisions control the future of wetland habitats.

At the same time, WHSRN enlists the participation of the scientists and conservation groups who are carrying out research on shorebird migration and habitats. Their involvement addresses two essential needs: (1) to examine the roles that different sites play in shorebird migration and thereby identify sites for network participation, and (2) to evaluate management options that can maintain and enhance the value of local wetlands for shorebird migration.

Site acceptance to WHSRN

To be recognized as a WHSRN site, the area must meet biological criteria establishing its importance to shorebirds and must then be nominated by the individuals, organizations or agencies responsible for management of the area. Participation in the network is wholly voluntary both in nomination and in management.

Site membership in WHSRN is compatible with participation in other national or international conservation programmes. For example, the U.S. Fish and Wildlife Service has nominated a long list of National Wildlife Refuges, as has the Instituto Forestal y de Fauna of Peru for several of its National Reserves. Similarly, National Audubon and The Nature Conservancy have both nominated sanctuaries in their systems as WHSRN members.

Biological criteria for site recognition

WHSRN differentiates between several types of sites within the network:

- A *Hemispheric Site* is used by 500,000 or more shorebirds on an annual basis, or supports at least 30 per cent of a flyway population of a given species (*Figure 2*).
- An *International Site* is used by 100,000 or more shorebirds or at least 15 per cent of a flyway population.
- A *Regional Site* is used by 20,000 or more shorebirds or at least five per cent of a flyway population.

An area may be awarded status as an *Endangered Species Reserve* as an alternative designation if it is judged to be of Hemispheric or International Reserve

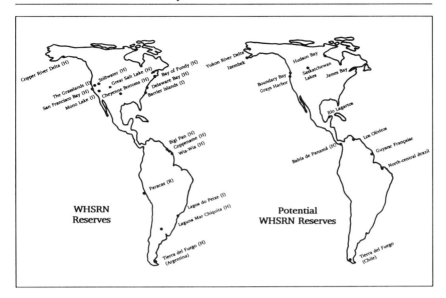

Figure 2: WHSRN reserves (left) and potential reserves (right) with large numbers of shorebirds. Sites must be nominated by the land-owners and accepted by the WHSRN Council. H = Hemisphere sites; I = International sites; R = Regional sites.

status exclusively by virtue of its importance to an endangered or threatened species.

WHSRN encourages sites to "twin" with one or more foreign sites that share birds of the same species linked through particular migration corridors. For example, the Bay of Fundy in Canada is linked with the three coastal reserves in Suriname (Wia-wia Nature Reserve, Coppename Nature Reserve and Bigi Pan Multiple Management Area) because of their importance to the Semipalmated Sandpiper (*Figure 3*).

Levels of participation

Sites once nominated and evaluated for biological appropriateness fall within one of three WHSRN categories:

- *Certified Sites:* The nomination has been ratified by the WHSRN Council. At this point the site joins the network and the sponsoring organization becomes a site designee.
- *Dedicated Sites:* The responsible agency and its government have made a public commitment to manage the site to maintain its importance for migratory shorebirds. This commitment is neither legally binding nor irrevocable but does signal a strong public will to secure protection.
- *Secured Sites:* The site is owned by a wildlife conservation agency, public or private, with a long-term objective for shorebird populations.

WHSRN also encourages shorebird sites to seek participation in the Convention on Wetlands of International Importance (i.e. to become Ramsar sites).

Figure 3: A wall of Semipalmated Sandpipers (*Calidris pusilla*) flying in the Bay of Fundy, Canada. (*Photo:* P. Hicklin)

The WHSRN Council

The WHSRN council exists to stimulate development of the network and to oversee functions related to the network on behalf of the established system. The council provides guidance to WHSRN staff in working with relevant government agencies and land management authorities responsible for important shorebird habitats, reviews nominated sites and ratifies their nomination. It also provides a focal point for disseminating information on shorebirds and their habitats. The WHSRN Council provides a service: neither it nor WHSRN comprise a governing body nor do either lobby for site protection.

The council meets biannually or more frequently as needed. Participants in the council represent a mix of biological and administrative knowledge and members come from countries throughout the Western Hemisphere. The council has a chairperson elected by council members to serve a two-year term of office.

WHSRN staff

WHSRN staff carry out programme activities that further WHSRN's role as a collator and disseminator of biological data and management information about sites important to migratory shorebirds. The staff develop recommendations for the WHSRN Council on the biological eligibility of new network sites and provide technical information to leaders throughout the Americas through special seminars and workshops. The staff also responds to the WHSRN-recognized sites and their management authorities on technical matters that can enhance decision-making capabilities about shorebird conservation management options available for the site.

In addition, the WHSRN staff works with agencies, site managers and experts in shorebird conservation to develop and coordinate research plans for acquiring critical data, as well as developing material for public education related to shorebird and wetland conservation issues, either general to the network as a whole or specific to particular sites.

The staff organizes policy and biology workshops in Central and South America and then works with participants and local networks in developing in-country conservation plans. In addition, WHSRN staff compile and analyse information about critical sites, work with agencies to obtain their designation, and assist agencies, when requested, in developing management plans.

Manomet Bird Observatory (MBO) coordinates the International Shorebird Survey (ISS), to enhance the WHSRN information systems, which include the Pan American Shorebird Program (PASP). The WHSRN staff are employees of MBO. Funding is made possible through generous contributions from charitable and government organizations.

WHSRN workshops

In 1980, the United Nations Education, Scientific and Cultural Organization (UNESCO) and the Ramsar Convention identified wetlands as "the most endangered ecosystem globally". Yet wetland conservation in Central and South America is generally still overlooked today. Shortages of trained personnel, lack of primary information, and inadequate international support for addressing this issue contribute to this situation.

It is very clear that the future of Latin American conservation lies in the hands of Latin Americans. For this reason, WHSRN has developed workshops and training programmes. Two kinds of workshops are offered in each country; one for biologists and one for policy-makers.

Training has two tangible benefits. First, scientists and students develop the biological skills necessary to gather data essential for guiding the network programmes and growth. Second, managers and policy-makers are provided with information and mechanisms addressing the problem of wetlands conservation in each country. For all, education establishes and reinforces commitment by building networks for grassroot support.

WHSRN works in close cooperation with governmental and non-governmental organizations in each country to organize workshops. The preparation of action plans, the provision of grants for needed studies and the designation of national coordinators are all accomplished with primary involvement of people from participating countries.

In Central and South America the problem of conservation of wetlands and shorebirds is not sufficiently known or taken into consideration for various reasons. On the one hand, immediate economic needs and complex political and social situations often push aside important environmental concerns. Furthermore, trained biologists with enough resources to carry out investigations or put energy into conservation issues are few and far between. Much-needed education campaigns suffer from the same problems. Greater international assistance is necessary in order to increase the participation of those people responsible for the well-being of their country's resources.

In 1986-1989, two workshops for policy-makers, directed at politicians and environmental administrators, were conducted in Cordoba Province, Argentina and in Paracas, Peru. In 1989-1990, six workshops for field biologists, including techniques of observation, capture and handling of shorebirds and evaluation of wetlands, were held in Salinas, Ecuador; Punta Rasa, Argentina; La Serena, Chile; Recife, Brazil; Los Olivitos, Venezuela; and Ensenada, Mexico (*Figure 4*). More workshops are planned for the future.

Figure 4: Participating countries in the WHSRN, and places where workshops were held during 1988-1991.

During field workshops, much emphasis is put on research techniques so that participants receive the training that will enable them to conduct their own field studies on shorebirds and wetlands in the future. In the majority of the above-mentioned countries, workshop participants have initiated the formation of a group which conducts research on shorebirds and wetlands and improves information resources in that country. WHSRN provides modest funding to each group (*or local network*) to support the publication and distribution of a locally edited quarterly newsletter and occasional group censuses. The newsletter informs local network members about related activities in their country and, as far as possible, throughout the Neotropics. WHSRN also offers "Grants" (up to 2,000 USD each) for shorebird and wetland research projects in the Neotropics. As a result of WHSRN support, research projects and censuses are currently under way in Argentina, Brazil, Chile and Ecuador, and additional project are being planned in Peru, Venezuela and Mexico.

More than 170 biologists and conservationists have so far participated in the workshops, and over 45 local professors have instructed during them. Furthermore, 26 governmental and non-governmental Neotropical organizations have actively co-organized workshops. This is certainly an example of the strong commitment local organizations have made to WHSRN's training programme. Local organizations have also taken major responsibility for the preparation and publication of informative work manuals used during the workshops. Experts in each country have contributed articles on shorebirds and wetlands and provided important information on local and regional shorebird distribution. Eight different country-specific manuals have been produced so far (in Spanish and Portuguese), as well as a detailed field manual on shorebird handling techniques.

THE INTERNATIONAL SHOREBIRD SURVEY (ISS)

The ISS is a network of over 800 volunteer ornithologists, naturalists and biologists in 23 countries of North, Central and South America. However, over 90 per cent are from the U.S. The network monitors shorebirds' use of wetland areas. Now 18 years in operation, the ISS, founded at MBO, offers a unique and valuable data resource for conservation and research purposes, covering inland and coastal sites.

Data collected cover the distribution and abundance of shorebirds as well as habitat assessments and legal/management profiles of wetlands sites. ISS data have proved immensely useful in identifying site priorities for wetlands conservation action in North America, for expanding basic knowledge about shorebird biology, and in providing the first estimates of long-term population trends across a suite of shorebird species in the U.S. (Howe *et al.* 1989). The ISS network has major gaps, particularly in Central and South America. New efforts are under way to expand coverage through participation of individuals, governmental and non-governmental agencies, and through WHSRN training and other programmes.

THE PAN-AMERICAN SHOREBIRD PROGRAM (PASP)

The biological data that underpin WHSRN planning include not only details of when and where shorebirds use wetland habitats but also of the linkages between critical sites that result from the migrations of specific shorebird populations. These linkages are revealed through intensive banding studies of marked populations, undertaken by biologists at institutions throughout the hemisphere.

PASP acts as a clearing house to maximize collaboration among these many individual studies and also provides equipment and supplies for banding efforts. In its coordinating role, PASP has devised a hemisphere-wide marking scheme to minimize confusion and duplication among different studies. Each country in the Western Hemisphere has a specially designed band, called a flag, which is uniquely colour-coded for the country and informs the observer about the country of origin of the banded bird.

PASP has also developed and distributed PC-based computer software to facilitate data exchange, and has made a limited number of awards of personal computers to upgrade the technical capabilities of investigators in Central and South America. Banding equipment and supplies are regularly awarded to collaborating groups in the Western Hemisphere.

FUTURE DIRECTIONS

WHSRN has had an excellent start in these first few years and is ready to tackle follow-up growth and further expansion into new countries.

In North America, WHSRN will work closely to improve shorebird habitat via management schemes such as the North American Waterfowl Management Plan (NAWMP), a 15-year 1,500 million USD plan to enhance wetlands for waterbirds throughout North America. As part of this effort, a shorebird habitat management manual is being collated and produced by WHSRN, to help integrate traditional management schemes for seasonally flooded wetlands and marsh impoundments, benefiting both shorebirds and waterfowl. In addition, WHSRN will continue to provide technical assistance in research, management, and/or public education to all interested Reserves.

In the Neotropics, where most shorebirds spend more than two-thirds of their life cycle, WHSRN will continue to support research and conservation projects, emphasizing maximum involvement by local organizations involved in the management and conservation of wetlands. More emphasis will be put on bringing sites into the Network and on working with those countries in which initial contacts have been made, where shorebird numbers are high, and where the need for conservation and international assistance is greatest. A joint survey of Southern Latin American wetlands and waterfowl (including shorebirds) will be conducted by the Neotropical Wetlands Program (NWP), a new conservation initiative led by the International Waterfowl and Wetlands Research Bureau (IWRB), Ducks Unlimited (DU), and WHSRN. Local coordinators from Argentina, Chile, Brazil and Uruguay will help organize the census. Finally, workshops will continue to take place, on a regional as well as national scale.

The understanding and commitment of the public in confronting the problems that face shorebirds and wetlands is fundamental to the success of any conservation programme. To this end, WHSRN will continue to inform the conservationists, biologists, policy-makers, and the public throughout the hemisphere about the network and will work to establish a firm basis for future collaboration. WHSRN recognizes and firmly believes that for the network to be successful in the long term and on a hemispheric level, protection efforts must be carried out on the international, national, and local levels.

CHRONICLE OF KEY EVENTS

1985   The International Association of Fish and Wildlife Agencies and the World Wildlife Fund (now World Wide Fund for Nature) become the founding sponsors of the new Western Hemisphere Shorebird Reserve Network.

1986   Delaware Bay is inaugurated as the first Hemispheric Reserve in the network, nominated jointly by the Governors of New Jersey and Delaware, the Hons. Thomas Kean and Michael Castle. Simultaneously, the State of New Jersey and Public Service Electric and Gas Co. establish a fund of $1,000,000 for habitat acquisition along New Jersey's Delaware Bay shore.

The National Forestry and Faunal Institute of Peru nominates the first South American sites for network membership.

1987   Shepody Bay in the Bay of Fundy, Canada, joins with three sites on the coast of Suriname (Wia-wia and Coppename Nature Reserves, and Bigi Pan Multiple Management Area), as twinned Hemispheric Reserves.

National Audubon Society and Manomet Bird Observatory commence collaborative work funded by the J. N. Pew Charitable Trust to further network growth and to undertake training programmes in Central and South America.

U.S. Fish and Wildlife Service Director Frank Dunkle nominates 55 National Wildlife Refuges for membership.

1988   WHSRN holds the first policy training workshops, in Cordoba, Argentina and Paracas, Peru. Minas Basin in the Bay of Fundy, Canada, is dedicated as a second section in the Bay of Fundy Hemispheric Reserve.

Stillwater Wildlife Management Area in Nevada joins WHSRN as a Hemispheric Reserve. Congress appropriates funds to purchase water rights for the wetlands.

1989   Cheyenne Bottoms in Kansas becomes a Hemispheric Reserve. This site is one of the most important inland staging sites for shorebirds in North America.

San Francisco Bay in California becomes a Hemispheric Reserve. Mar Chiquita in Cordoba Province, Argentina becomes a Hemispheric Reserve.

WHSRN holds field training workshops in Salinas, Ecuador; Punta Rasa, Argentina; La Serena, Chile; and Recife, Brazil.

Local networks are formed in Argentina, Chile and Brazil. All three publish newsletters and conduct research nationally.

The Canadian International Development Agency announces a $40,000 grant for work on developing a management plan at the Bigi Pan Multiple Use Area in Suriname.

Two WHSRN computer awards are granted to the Suriname Forest Service and Michel Sallaberry of the Universidad de Chile.

1990 WHSRN holds two field workshops in Los Olivitos, Venezuela and Ensenada, Mexico.

Copper River Delta in Alaska, hosting more than 20 million shorebirds annually, becomes a Hemispheric Reserve.

For more information on WHSRN in the U.S.A., Canada, Mexico, Peru, on the PASP, for technical information, or to receive the newsletter contact: WHSRN, Box 936, Manomet, MA 02345, U.S.A.

For more information on WHSRN in the Neotropical region (excluding Mexico and Peru), contact RHRAP, Monroe 2142, 1428 Capital Federal, Argentina.

REFERENCES

BOURNE, W. S. & COTTAM, C. (1950) *Some biological effects of ditching tidewater marshes.* Washington: U.S. Fish and Wildlife Service (Resrch. Rep. 19).

HORWITZ, E. L. (1978) Our nation's wetlands. Interagency Task Force Report. Washington: U.S. Council on Environmental Quality.

HOWE, M. A., GEISSLER, P. H. & HARRINGTON, B. A. (1989) Population trends of North American shorebirds based on the International Shorebird Survey. *Biol. Conserv.* **49**: 185-199.

MORRISON, R. I. G. (1984) Migration systems of some New World shorebirds. *Behav. Marine Anim.* **6**: 125-202.

MYERS, J. P. (1983) Conservation of migrating shorebirds: Staging areas, geographic bottlenecks and regional movements. *Amer. Birds* **37**: 23-25.

MYERS, J. P. (1986) Sex and gluttony on Delaware Bay. *Nat. Hist.* **95**: 68-77.

MYERS, J. P., MORRISON, R. I. G., ANTAS, P. A., HARRINGTON, B. A., LOVEJOY, T. E., SALLABERRY, M., SENNER, S. E. & TARAK, A. (1987) Conservation strategy for migratory species. *Amer. Sci.* **75**: 19-26.

PITELKA, F. A. (1979) Introduction: The Pacific Coast shorebird scene. *Stud. Avian Biol.* **2**: 1-12.

SENNER, S. E. (1979) An evaluation of the Copper River Delta as a critical habitat for migrating shorebirds. *Stud. Avian Biol.* **2**: 131-145.

SENNER, S. E. & HOWE, M. A. (1984) Conservation of nearctic shorebirds. *Behav. Marine Organ.* **5**: 379-421.

SPETH, J. (1979) Conservation and management of coastal wetlands in California. *Stud. Avian Biol.* **2**: 151-155.

TINER JR, R. W. (1984) *Wetlands of the United States: current status and recent trends.* Washington, D.C.: U.S. Fish and Wildlife Service, National Wetlands Inventory.

A REVIEW OF THE ASIAN–AUSTRALASIAN BIRD MIGRATION SYSTEM

BRETT A. LANE[1] & DUNCAN PARISH[2]

1 *Department of Zoology, University of Melbourne,*
Parkville, Victoria 3052, Australia
2 *Asian Wetland Bureau, Institute for Advanced Studies,*
University of Malaya, 59100 Kuala Lumpur, Malaysia

ABSTRACT

The Asian–Australasian bird migration system is one of the largest and most geographically complex migration systems in the world, yet it is one of the least studied. This paper summarizes briefly what is known about bird migration in the Asian–Australasian region. Particular attention is given to migratory waterbirds, especially the shorebirds, as the most information exists for this group. Where possible, other groups of birds are also discussed. The vast majority of birds in the region migrate from breeding grounds in eastern Siberia, China, Korea and Japan to non-breeding areas in tropical and subtropical parts of the region. A number of species breed and migrate within the tropical parts of the region. A comparatively small number of species breed in Australia and migrate to nearby tropical areas of South-East Asia. Tropical forests and wetlands are particularly important non-breeding habitats for migratory birds, yet these habitats are subject to the greatest threat of destruction from the rapid economic development and extensive exploitation of natural resources now occurring in the region. Hunting is also a significant potential threat to migratory birds in Asia, and the full extent of it is only now being documented. Some examples are presented of management regimes in reserves which illustrate the problems of migratory bird conservation in the region. They demonstrate that a pragmatic approach to the protection of migratory birds can be successful, notwithstanding the high demands being made by human populations on their environment in Asia. General recommendations are made for future research and conservation action in the region.

INTRODUCTION

Geographically, the Asian–Australasian migration system is one of the largest and most complex bird migration systems in the world and, until recently, one of the least studied. It extends from the arctic tundras of Siberia and Alaska, southwards through Asia to the coasts and islands of the eastern Indian and western Pacific oceans, to the southern parts of Australia and to New Zealand.

The Asian mainland is the main breeding area for migratory birds in the region. The large expanses of tundra in northern Siberia provide breeding grounds for large numbers of ducks, geese and shorebirds. Migrant raptors and passerines breed in forest or steppe habitat at lower latitudes in southern Siberia and China. At least four species in the region breed in Alaska. Ducks and geese migrate to Japan, Korea, southern China, Indo-China, Thailand, the Philippines and parts of Indonesia. Shorebirds migrate to South-East Asia, Australia and New Zealand. Passerines and raptors migrate mainly to South-East Asia and Indonesia. Although most breeding areas in Siberia are comparatively intact, with low human population densities, birds come under increasing pressure from hunting and habitat destruction as they move southwards within Asia.

Australia and New Zealand represent the major destinations in the region for many of the migratory shorebirds which breed in the arctic and subarctic parts of the migration system. The islands of the Philippines and Indonesia form important corridors used by shorebirds migrating to Australia, although some fly direct from Japan and China to Australia. Others appear to migrate across vast expanses of the western Pacific Ocean.

A small number of species from a number of groups which breed in Australia migrate to New Guinea and the Lesser Sundas, and at least four species of bird migrate annually between Australia and New Zealand. Many Australian birds are nomadic and sometimes arrive unexpectedly in nearby parts of South-East Asia, New Zealand and the south-west Pacific Islands after exceptional breeding in the inland of the continent after heavy rains.

This paper summarizes briefly the available information on migration routes and staging areas for birds in the region. It is necessarily biased towards migratory waterbirds, especially the shorebirds, as much more data are available for these groups. The sizes of the bird populations involved are considered where data permit. Conservation problems facing migratory birds in the region are also illustrated with a series of examples from Asia and Australia. The final section of this paper reviews progress on migratory bird conservation in the region and makes recommendations for research and conservation measures necessary to improve the survival chances of migratory birds in the region.

BIRD MIGRATION IN THE REGION

This section provides a summary of the sources of information on bird migration in the flyway. This is followed by a brief description of the geography of the flyway as it relates to bird migration, including a brief consideration of migrational barriers and corridors. The final section summarizes what is known about migration routes in the region.

Sources of information

Compared with that on other large migration systems, research in the region has been spasmodic and patchy. Coordinated programmes have been conducted only in the last thirty years. For these reasons, information on the status, populations, migration routes and stop-over areas of migratory birds in the region is incomplete and much remains to be discovered. The sources used here and a brief account of their history are presented below.

Studies on bird migration in the region were initiated in Japan and the Soviet Union in the early part of the 20th century but large-scale studies were not conducted until the 1950s. A small number of national projects to investigate migration have continued since that time, for example in Japan, India and the Soviet Union. Stimulus for studies elsewhere has come primarily from regional initiatives. The main regional programmes to gather information on bird migration in Asia have been the Migratory Animal Pathological Survey (MAPS) (1963-1971), the Interwader Programme (1983-present) and the recently commenced Asian Waterfowl Census (1987-present). MAPS concentrated on large-scale banding (ringing) of migrants and operated in ten countries in East Asia (McClure 1974). Over 1.3 million birds from 82 different families were marked. A total of 7,000 bands from 255 species were recovered, providing significant new information on migration routes.

The Interwader programme (now operated within the Asian Wetland Bureau) has gathered data on migrant waterbirds, especially shorebirds, using coastal wetlands in East Asia. As part of the programme, coordinated surveys of migratory waterbirds have been organized in 15 Asian countries. The key results relating to shorebirds have been published in a summary report (Howes & Parish 1989). The Asian Waterfowl Census, initiated by International Waterfowl and Wetland Research Bureau (IWRB) and now jointly organized by IWRB and the Asian Wetland Bureau, involves coordinated counts of migrant waterbirds in January each year. In 1989, counts were submitted by 500 observers from over 1,300 wetlands in 20 countries (Scott & Rose 1989).

The Royal Australasian Ornithologists Union (RAOU) has been instrumental in the last fifteen years in gathering and publishing information about the distribution, movements and status of birds in Australia. Two projects in particular have generated much-needed new data. The *Atlas of Australian Birds* project was conducted from 1977-1981 and produced distribution maps for all species on a one degree latitude/longitude grid (Blakers, Davies & Reilly 1984). The *Wader Studies Programme* ran from 1981-1985 with the aim of determining the distribution, abundance and movements of Australia's waders (Charadrii). The results were published in book form (Lane 1987) and showed the main non-breeding sites for all species of migratory wader visiting Australia and for most of the resident species. Little research on bird migration has been conducted in New Zealand. An important exception is the national counts of shorebirds, in November and December and June each year, organized by the Ornithological Society of New Zealand (Sagar, in prep.).

Geography of the region

The geographical setting for the Asian–Australasian migration system comprises the land masses of eastern Asia and Australia, and the vast western Pacific Ocean. In the tropical part of the region, these large features are broken up by the Philippine and Indonesian archipelagos and by a series of Pacific Island chains through Micronesia and Melanesia. *Figure 1* shows the region and the distribution of vegetation types within it.

Potential obstacles to the migration of most birds occur in the form of long sea crossings (except for seabirds), deserts or high mountain ranges. These probably do not stop migration as birds have been recorded making ocean and desert crossings and flying at considerable heights (Melville 1980; Lane & Jessop 1985; Lane 1987). The significance of these obstacles is that they require the evolution of strategies to overcome them. Long migrations require the capacity to accumulate fat reserves sufficient for a non-stop flight of hundreds or thousands of kilometres, and suitable habitat and food resources at the beginning and end of the migration to enable this to occur. Potential corridors in the region consist mostly of long archipelagoes such as the Aleutian Islands, Indonesia and Melanesia, or of river valleys such as the Lena, Amur and Mekong. The region resembles more the American migration system than the West Palearctic–African migration system where the Sahara and nearby deserts represent a substantial obstacle.

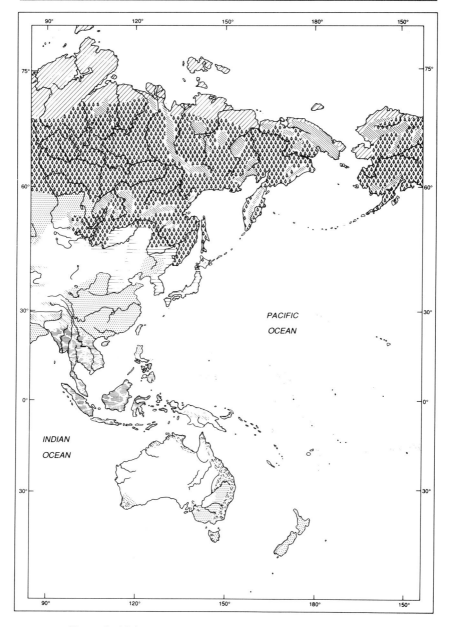

Figure 1: Major vegetation types of the Asian–Australasian region.

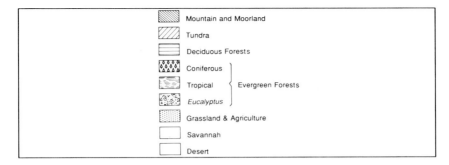

Mountain and Moorland

Tundra

Deciduous Forests

Coniferous ⎫
Tropical   ⎬ Evergreen Forests
Eucalyptus ⎭

Grassland & Agriculture

Savannah

Desert

Figure 1 also shows the broad distribution of vegetation types in the region. Tundra and coniferous forest dominate in the north, grassy steppes and desert in the central regions, deciduous forests in Ussuriland, Japan and eastern China, and tropical forests in Southern China and most of South-East Asia. Northern Australia consists of tropical woodland and savanna, grading to semi-arid shrubland, grassland and desert farther south. The south-western and eastern coastal areas of Australia consist of evergreen *Eucalyptus* forest, and the predominant vegetation types of New Zealand are agricultural land and alpine moorland. Human activities have substantially disrupted the natural pattern of vegetation distribution throughout the region.

Eastern Asia lacks the large area of northern hemisphere tropical savanna so important to migratory passerines in the world's other migration systems (see *Figure 1*). The savannas of northern Australia, although of considerable extent, are not exploited by northern hemisphere migrants. The migration of almost all northern hemisphere terrestrial birds in the flyway reaches its southernmost extent in the region's tropical rainforests and tropical agricultural areas (McClure 1974; Medway & Wells 1976). East Asia and Australasia have vast coastlines and many areas of coastal plains where large areas of wetland exist. These provide migration stop-overs and non-breeding habitats for large numbers of migratory waterbirds.

The geographical complexity of the flyway provides a wide range of options for migrating birds. This, combined with the limited amount of research compared with that on other migration systems, has made the task of determining migration routes, staging areas and destinations very difficult. A more complete understanding of bird migration in the region is still many years away.

Major migration routes

The paucity of precise information makes it impossible to identify how many of the potential corridors in the region are used by migrating birds, or to what extent. It is likely that much migration occurs on broad fronts as there is evidence of passage from many parts of the region at appropriate times of year (Mcclure 1974; Medway & Wells 1976; Simpson 1983; Ash 1984).

Bird migration in the U.S.S.R. has been dealt with in detail in a series of monographs produced by the U.S.S.R. Academy of Sciences (1985) although details are lacking for much of the far eastern U.S.S.R. Many eastern Palearctic breeding birds migrate through Korea and Japan (McClure 1974) but the details of their migration in nearby parts of the U.S.S.R. and China remain unclear. Birds passing through these countries breed in Russia and China and migrate as far south as the Philippines and the Greater Sundas (McClure 1974). McClure identified two major concentrations of migrating birds in the tropical region of the flyway:

Luzon–Palawan, in the Philippines; and the Malay Peninsula. Medway & Wells (1976) discussed the latter in detail.

In the Philippines, a major bird banding project was undertaken during MAPS in the 1960s and early 1970s. From recoveries, McClure (1974) identified a major bird migration route passing through Dalton Pass on Luzon. Both aquatic and terrestrial birds were involved, and included species from the eastern and northern Palearctic as well as those from within the tropics. Recoveries indicated that some of these species were passing through Japan, Korea and possibly north-eastern China and that they continued southwards to the Greater Sundas via Palawan rather than south-eastwards (McClure 1974).

China did not participate in MAPS so it is uncertain to what extent birds migrate from mainland China to the Philippines and beyond. It seems unlikely that long-distance migrants would fly from China to the Philippines then south-westwards to the greater Sundas. Melville (1980), in a radar study of migration over Hong Kong, found that migration of birds was south-westwards in the northern autumn and north-eastwards in the northern spring, indicating a more direct route for many birds between South-East Asia and mainland China. More recent studies of shorebirds have shown that the east coast of China is an important migration route for these birds (Victorian and Australasian Wader Study Groups, pers. comm.; Tianhiou & Sixian 1989).

On the Malay Peninsula, many birds were banded during MAPS. The following account is based on Medway & Wells (1976) who described the findings of this work in detail. Migrating birds pass southwards through the peninsula mainly between late September and late November, although the shorebirds start moving through about a month earlier than this (Parish & Wells 1984). Of the diurnal migrants, raptors are particularly conspicuous at this time in lowland areas near the west coast, and as many as 180,000 have been estimated to use this route in a season. Evidence of substantial raptor migration into Bali, in the Lesser Sundas (Ash 1984) indicates that raptors migrating through the Malay Peninsula may be moving a considerable distance eastwards in the Indonesian archipelago. Other birds, such as swifts, swallows and bee-eaters also use the west coastal regions of the Malay Peninsula at this time. Smaller but significant numbers of these birds use the plains along the east coast of the peninsula during migration. Trapping at night using nets and strong spotlights at Fraser's Hill, in the main mountain range north of Kuala Lumpur, has revealed that considerable nocturnal migration of birds, from many families, including passerines, occurs in this area. Among the birds caught in this way are many tropical species, such as pigeons, kingfishers and pittas, as well as Palearctic-breeding passerines, indicating an intratropical component to bird migration in East Asia.

Northward passage on the Malay Peninsula starts in February and continues until May. Less is known about the northward migration of birds on the peninsula. However, raptors, bee-eaters and other diurnal migrants have been observed migrating northwards in west coastal regions of the peninsula at this time.

Bird migration is little understood in the Greater and Lesser Sundas as information on bird occurrence and abundance is sketchy. Suffice is to say that it is likely that a substantial proportion of the populations of some migratory species are likely to occur in this part of the region. White and Bruce (1986) recently undertook a review of bird migration in the Lesser Sundas. Of the Palearctic and northern-tropical breeding species, 82 occur in this region, compared with 127 in Borneo (including 25 probable vagrants) and less than 50 in New Guinea and Australia (mostly shorebirds). They suggested that the many small islands of the Lesser Sundas may limit the range of niches for resident terrestrial birds. Consequently, residents have broad niches and could competitively exclude migrants. In this way, the Lesser Sundas may be acting as a screen against the spread of Palearctic migrants to New Guinea and Australia. The shorebirds were an exception however and they noted that there were few resident species of this group in the islands.

Bird migration in Australia is better understood than in many parts of the flyway, although the picture is still far from complete. Many species migrate up to 3,000 km within Australia but only those species in Australia that cross international borders are considered here. The largest group of international migrants on the continent is the shorebirds (Charadrii). Two major migration corridors have been identified for shorebirds entering Australia, based on distribution patterns and limited data from band recoveries. One enters Australia via the north-west coast and the other enters via the north-east coast (Parish *et al.* 1987). The north-western corridor is used by more species and greater numbers of shorebirds, and includes birds that breed in central and eastern Siberia. The north-eastern corridor is used by birds that breed in far eastern Siberia and Alaska and which migrate down the east coast of Asia and/or across the Pacific Ocean.

Among the other groups, small numbers of Palearctic-breeding birds occur in the non-breeding months in coastal parts of northern Australia and as vagrants elsewhere. Examples include Barn Swallow (*Hirundo rustica*) in hundreds at some sites, Yellow Wagtail (*Motacilla flava*) in tens and Garganey (*Anas querquedula*) in tens. Several species of terns and skuas, as well as two species of swift, migrate to Australia in substantial numbers from Palearctic breeding grounds. One species of tern and one shorebird migrate regularly and in large numbers from New Zealand breeding grounds to spend the southern winter in Australia.

Another group of international migrants breeds in Australia and migrates northwards to New Guinea and nearby parts of Indonesia. These include a pigeon, cuckoos (2 species), a nightjar, kingfishers (2 species), a bee-eater, the Dollar Bird (*Eurystomus orientalis*), pittas (2 species), a martin, cuckoo-shrikes (2 species), flycatchers (Muscicapidae, 5 species) and a drongo. Torres Strait is a major migration corridor between Australia and New Guinea for these species (Draffan *et al.* 1983) and smaller numbers of these migrants pass through the Darwin region and possibly other northern parts of the Northern Territory (Blakers *et al.* 1984).

In addition to the above true migrants, several waterbirds which breed in Australia occur occasionally in small numbers in New Guinea, New Zealand, the lesser Sundas and on some south-west Pacific islands. These irruptive movements can occur at any time of year after major breeding events following floods in the Australian hinterland. Examples of species that behave in this manner include the Australian Pelican (*Pelecanus conspicillatus*) and the Grey Teal (*Anas gibberifrons*).

THE IMPORTANCE OF THE REGION FOR MIGRATORY BIRDS

This section of the paper examines the significance of the region for migrating birds. The populations of migratory birds, where known, are considered first. This is followed by an account of the important migratory bird habitats in the region.

Populations of migratory birds

Very little information is available on the sizes of the populations of migratory birds in the region. The best information is available on shorebirds and some other waterbirds and then only for some parts of the region. Parish (1989) summarized

Table 1: Approximate numbers of migratory shorebirds in Australia and New Zealand during the non-breeding period. (*Source:* Lane 1987; Sagar, in prep.)

Population size range (number of individuals)	Species
> 200,000	Red-necked Stint (*Calidris ruficollis*)
	Great Knot (*C. tenuirostris*)
	Bar-tailed Godwit (*Limosa lapponica*)
100,000–200,000	Red Knot (*Calidris canutus*)
	Sharp-tailed Sandpiper (*C. acuminata*)
	Curlew Sandpiper (*C. ferruginea*)
	Little Curlew (*Numenius minuta*)
30,000–100,000	Large Sand Plover (*Charadrius leschenaultii*)
	Oriental Plover (*C. veredus*)
	Black-tailed Godwit (*Limosa limosa*)
	Oriental Pratincole (*Glareola maldivarum*)
10,000–30,000	Mongolian Plover (*Charadrius mongolus*)
	Double-banded Plover (*C. bicinctus*)
	Ruddy Turnstone (*Arenaria interpres*)
	Eastern Curlew (*Numenius madagascariensis*)
	Whimbrel (*N. phaeopus*)
	Grey-tailed Tattler (*Tringa brevipes*)
	Greenshank (*T. nebularia*)
	Terek Sandpiper (*T. terek*)
	Latham's Snipe (*Gallinago hardwickii*)
< 10,000	Grey Plover (*Pluvialis squatarola*)
	Lesser Golden Plover (*P. fulva*)
	Wood Sandpiper (*Tringa glareola*)
	Wandering Tattler (*T. incana*)
	Common Sandpiper (*T. hypoleucos*)
	Marsh Sandpiper (*T. stagnatilis*)
	Asian Dowitcher (*Limnodromus semipalmatus*)
	Sanderling (*Calidris alba*)
	Broad-billed Sandpiper (*Limicola falcinellus*)

known information on the population sizes of waterbirds in the region. Comprehensive data are not yet available, and estimates of total numbers of birds are not yet possible.

The number of shorebirds using coastal habitats in the region has been estimated at between 4 and 6 million (Parish 1989), although this is based on limited information. About 1.7 million of these reach Australia and New Zealand (Lane 1987). The number using the Pacific islands is not known. *Table 1* lists species of shorebird that migrate to Australia and New Zealand, with estimates of population sizes by order of magnitude of this part of the migration system. Data are not yet comprehensive enough to enable accurate population estimates for other species or areas in the region.

Among other migratory waterbirds, precise population estimates are not possible for most species. The total number of ducks and geese in the region has been estimated at between 15 and 22 million (Parish 1989). Estimates have been made for some rare species of waterbird, but these have been considerably revised in recent years, both upwards and downwards, as a result of the increasing number of surveys.

No estimates have been made for other groups of migrants.

Important habitats

Migratory birds breed across Asia in generally low densities and it is not possible to identify any discrete, critical sites for them. It is possible to identify important habitats for some colonially breeding species, such as egrets, terns or the Asian Dowitcher (*Limnodromus semipalmatus*), but data are generally lacking. Some species of migrants in the region have very restricted breeding ranges, for example: Nordmann's Greenshank (*Tringa guttifer*), breeding in coastal larch forests mainly on Sakhalin Island, north of Japan (Johnsgard 1981); Latham's Snipe (*Gallinago hardwickii*), mostly in open habitats, including agricultural land, on the Japanese island of Hokkaido (Naarding 1986); Chinese Egret (*Egretta eulophotes*), breeding primarily on a few rocky islands in the Yellow Sea (Long *et al.* 1988); and Ijima's Warbler (*Phylloscopus ijimae*), on the Izu Islands off the south coast of Japan (Wild Bird Society of Japan 1982).

On migration, most bird populations become more restricted in distribution as they follow migration corridors or stop at staging areas. Two broad habitat classes used by birds during migration can be defined: wetland and terrestrial habitats. These are considered separately below:

Wetlands. During migration, waterbirds concentrate on rich feeding grounds, which enable them to accumulate the fat reserves needed for long-distance flights. The number of islands in the region and the intricacy of the Asian and Australasian coasts give them a vast array of coastal and near-coastal wetland habitats. The best feeding areas are rich intertidal mudflats, shallow lakes and marshlands. In tropical and subtropical areas (from 27°N to 38°S), mangroves are an important feature of intertidal wetlands. They play a critical role in the biological productivity of habitats for waterbirds in the region. Extensive areas of intertidal mudflat and mangrove occur in most countries in the region. Howes & Parish (1989) identified 29 key wetlands for shorebirds in South-East Asia, and Lane (1987) noted 27 key sites for this group in Australia. There are four principal sites in New Zealand for migratory shorebirds (Sagar, in prep.). These sites are listed in *Table 2*.

In addition to intertidal wetlands, some shorebirds also use the extensive non-tidal wetlands that occur in Asia and Australia. In Asia, wet ricefields and other freshwater wetlands are important habitats for species such as Wood Sandpipers (*Tringa glareola*), snipes (*Gallinago* spp.) and Oriental and Australian Pratincoles (*Glareola maldivarum* and *Stiltia isabela*). In Australia, inland salt lakes, when they hold water, and non-tidal freshwater wetlands are especially important for coastal shorebirds during southward migration and as a non-breeding habitat for Latham's Snipe, Swinhoe's Snipe (*Gallinago megala*), Greenshanks (*Tringa nebularia*), Marsh Sandpipers (*T. stagnatilis*) and Sharp-tailed Sandpipers (*Calidris acuminata*) (Lane 1987). These habitats are less important however during northward migration, with the exception of the vast plains on parts of the northern Australian coast, flooded during the monsoon season (December–March) (Lane 1987).

Many of the sites used by significant numbers of shorebirds in Asia are also used by other migratory waterbirds, although data are less complete. Most ducks and geese generally spend the non-breeding season farther north in Asia than do

Table 2: Key sites for migratory shorebirds in the Asian–Australasian migration system discovered in the 1980s.

Country	Site	Numbers counted
Thailand	Samut Sakhon[1]	3,000
	Pattani Bay	10,000+
	Ko Libong[2]	3,700
Malaysia	Matang Forest Reserve	14,300
	North Selangor coast[2]	17,000
	Pulau Tengah	14,173
	Pulau Bruit (Sarawak)[1]	16,000
Indonesia	Tanjun Datuk, Tanjung Bakung, Riau (Sumatra)	20,000
	Pantai Timor, Jambi (Sumatra)[1/2]	20,000
	Tanjung Jabung & Berbak Game Reserve (Sumatra)[1]	15,000
	Banyuasin Delta (Sumatra)[1]	80,000
	Karang Mulya (West Java)	19,000
	Cirebon – Indramayu (Central Java)	80,000
	Brantas/Solo Deltas (East Java)[1]	25,000
	Kupang (Timor)	50,000
	Kupang Bay (Timor)[4]	7,500
	South-east Irian Jaya	22,000
Philippines	Manila Bay	55,000
	Olango Island[1]	20,000
Viet Nam	Red River Delta	10,000+
China	Hangzhou Bay (Shanghai)[2/3]	-
	Chong Ming Island (Shanghai)[2/3]	-
	Poyang Lake (Jiangxi)	6,500
South Korea	South Kanghwa Island[2/4]	16,200+
	South Yong Jong[2]	22,500
	Namyang Bay[2/3]	34,000
	Asan Bay[2/4]	30,000
Australia	Eighty Mile Beach (W.A.)	337,500
	South-east Gulf of Carpentaria (Qld.)[4]	250,000
	The Coorong (S.A.)	236,000
	Roebuck Bay (W.A.)[1/4]	170,900
	North-east Arnhem Land (N.T.)[4]	79,000
	Port Hedland Saltworks (W.A.)[1]	66,800
	Port Phillip Bay (Vic.)[4]	64,100
	St Vincent Gulf (S.A.)	64,000
	Lake Macleod (W.A.)	54,000
	Shark Bay (W.A.)	50,000
	Corner Inlet – Nooramunga (Vic.)[4]	46,200
	Spencer Gulf (S.A.)	37,000
	Cape Keraudren – Port Hedland (W.A.)	30,000
	La Grange Bay (W.A.)	23,800
	Peel Inlet (W.A.)	23,300
	South-west Gulf of Carpentaria (N.T.)	21,900
	Darwin region (N.T.)	20,900
	West coast Eyre Peninsula (S.A.)	19,900

(*continued*)

Table 2: Continued

Australia (*continued*)	Moreton Bay (Qld.)[4]	18,200
	Western District lakes (Vic.)	17,600
	Horsham region lakes (Vic.)	16,700
	Kangaroo Island (S.A.)	13,900
	Hervey Bay – Great Sandy Strait (Qld.)[4]	13,600
	Kerang – Swan Hill region (Vic.)	13,400
	South coast Gulf of Carpentaria (N.T.)	12,700
	Swan coastal plain (W.A.)	12,500
	Westernport Bay (Vic.)[4]	11,200
	Pilbara coast (W.A.)	11,100
New Zealand	Manukau Harbour	27,500
	Farewell Spit	22,500
	Kaipara Harbour	15,500
	Firth of Thames	11,500

Notes: Sites holding more than 10,000 shorebirds are listed, except where significant numbers of rare shorebirds occur as indicated. 1 = Asian Dowitcher (*Limnodromus semipalmatus*); 2 = Nordmann's Greenshank (*Tringa guttifer*); 3 = Spoon-billed Sandpiper (*Eurynorhynchus pygmaeus*); 4 = Eastern Curlew (*Numenius madagascariensis.*) These counts are not additive as they were conducted either during the migration season *or* during the non-breeding period.

Sources: Howes & Parish 1989; Lane 1987.

the shorebirds. They occur in coastal wetlands and unfrozen freshwater wetlands in southern China and the northern parts of South-East Asia.

Scott & Poole (1989), in a review of the status of Asia's wetlands, estimated that there were over 120 million hectares of wetlands in the Asian part of the migration system. Some 947 sites have been included in the Directory of Asian Wetlands (Scott 1989), representing 73 million hectares. A total of 734 of these sites is considered to be of international significance (Scott & Poole 1989). Of these, Bangladash, Burma, China, India, Indonesia, Papua-New Guinea and Vietnam hold the largest areas of wetland in the region.

Terrestrial habitats. Identifying important sites for migratory terrestrial birds in the region is difficult as these species tend not to concentrate to the same degree as the waterbirds, and data are therefore scarce. The following account will consider only the broad habitat types used by these species in the flyway.

In many cases, more than one habitat is important for migratory terrestrial birds. For example, many of the migratory passerines breed in the coniferous forests of northern Asia and migrate to the tropical rainforests of South-East Asia. Wells (1989) has reviewed the occurrence of migratory birds in forested habitats in the Sunda Region of South-East Asia. About a third of the bird species migrating to the Sunda Region of South-East Asia spend the non-breeding season in treed habitats. About 25 per cent of the total occur in original forest and 17 per cent are dependent on it during this period. The habitat of greatest importance within the forested areas available, at least in peninsular Malaysia, is lowland inland forest, which also holds the richest resident bird community (Wells 1989). Wells (1986, 1989) has pointed out that more species of migratory bird spend the non-breeding period in the tropical forests of the Sunda Region than do so in Africa or South America. Secondary forest and remnant treed patches in agricultural areas also hold non-breeding migrants (D. Wells, pers. comm.).

Considerable numbers of raptors migrate through South-East Asia. Many raptors need to follow land bridges, such as peninsular Thailand and Malaysia and the nearby archipelago of western Indonesia. Here, they rely on thermal lift to gain height for their soaring migratory flights. On the Malay Peninsula, raptors, notably Crested Honey Buzzard (*Pernis ptilorhyncus*), were found to migrate in greatest numbers over cleared and semi-cleared coastal plains as thermal activity was strongest in such areas (Medway & Wells 1976). Other species (e.g. Japanese Sparrowhawk *Accipiter gularis*) have been seen migrating over the South China Sea (Simpson 1983), indicating that not all raptors require land bridges in order to migrate. The final destination of raptors that migrate through South-East Asia is not known, but it is thought to be the savannas of the Lesser Sundas and the southern Philippines (McClure 1974). Considerable numbers of raptors have been recorded migrating into north-western Bali (Ash 1984). None of the South-East Asian migratory raptors reach the savannas of Australia.

Most of the terrestrial birds that migrate from Australia to nearby countries do so in evergreen *Eucalyptus* forests and woodlands along the Great Dividing Range which runs the length of Australia's east coast. Some species, such as Rainbow Bee-eater (*Merops ornatus*), migrate across relatively arid areas. Most Australian-breeding international migrants move into the northern tropical savanna before continuing to similar habitat, rather than to the rainforests, in New Guinea and eastern Indonesia (Blakers *et al.* 1984).

THREATS TO MIGRATORY BIRDS IN THE REGION

In common with the situation in other parts of the world, migratory birds in Asia and Australasia face a number of threats, including two principal ones: hunting and habitat loss. These are considered separately below.

Hunting

Details of the hunting of migratory waterbirds in east Asia are given by Parish and Howes (1990) and little detail will be given here. They believe that hunting has contributed to significant declines in populations of some waterbird species in the region. Hunting of birds is widespread in the region but little detailed information is available on its impact on populations.

Shorebirds and other waterbirds are hunted extensively, primarily for food. Hunting of other migratory species, such as raptors and passerines, also occurs, but less information is available on its occurrence or on the numbers of birds taken. Alonzo–Pasicolan (in press) gives details on the hunting of migratory birds at Dalton Pass in the Philippines. This is one example of the tendency for hunters in the region to concentrate on species that become concentrated into small, workable areas during migration.

Habitat destruction

One of the most serious threats to migratory birds is the destruction of the habitats on which they rely during the migration and non-breeding periods. The two habitats under most threat are the tropical forests and the wetlands and these are discussed below.

Apart from endangering the resident birds, the destruction of tropical forests is particularly critical in East Asia where they are an important destination of migratory terrestrial birds. Almost all lowland tropical forests in East Asia are under threat from logging operations, most of which are conducted on an unsustainable basis. Following logging, many areas are clear-felled for major agricultural development schemes while others are subject to continued degradation from shifting cultivators who gain access to these areas along logging roads. The amount of tropical forest cover remaining in South-East Asian countries ranges from 15 per cent in the Philippines to 60 per cent in Malaysia; and the amount of pristine, unlogged forest remaining is considerably less than this (Mackinnon & Mackinnon 1986).

The other important but threatened habitat for migratory birds in the region is the wetlands. Many coastal wetlands (mangrove, saltmarsh and tidal flats) have been reclaimed for agriculture, aquaculture, salt production or urban and industrial development. In the coming 20 years, the South Korean Government plans to reclaim 400,000 ha of intertidal land, including 155 estuaries, on its west coast (Long et al. 1988). In mid-1989, the Malaysian Government unveiled plans to reclaim all intertidal lands on the west coast of peninsular Malaysia (Asian Wetland Bureau data). The Korean and Malaysian schemes would together remove habitat for a significant proportion of the migratory shorebirds in the region, and for a number of endangered and rare species of waterbirds. Currently, only 14.8 per cent of the area of wetland in the region is under partial or complete legal protection, and almost half of the wetlands identified as being of international significance are threatened with destruction or serious degradation (Scott & Poole 1989).

The East Asian–Australasian migration system is probably the most threatened of all the world's migration systems. The region has some of the highest human population densities outside the developed world (56 per cent of the world's population in 14 per cent of its land area), and a population that is growing by about 55 million per year (Scott & Poole 1989). As well, the region is experiencing the fastest economic growth rates of any regional group of countries. For these reasons, it is imperative that appropriate environmental protection be incorporated urgently into national development programmes or many populations and species of migratory birds may be lost.

CONSERVATION MEASURES IN THE REGION

This section reviews migratory bird conservation measures in the region. Firstly, international treaties are considered, together with an assessment of their value in one country in the region: Australia. This is followed by an account of national programmes for migratory bird conservation. No country has a coordinated conservation programme specifically for migratory birds, but in some, considerable efforts are being made to protect them through existing instruments and agencies. Examples of reserves and habitat management in Asia and Australasia are then discussed, highlighting some of the problems that exist throughout the region and illustrating the approaches that have been adopted to achieve the successful establishment and management of reserves for migratory birds. The gaps in knowledge and needs for research on migratory birds in the region are then considered. Finally, some general recommendations are made for the conservation of migratory birds in the region.

International treaties
In East Asia, bilateral migratory birds agreements exist between Japan and China, the Soviet Union and the United States of America. Furthermore, Japan, Vietnam and Hong Kong are signatories to the multilateral Convention on the Protection of Wetlands of International Significance, Especially as Waterfowl Habitat (the

"Ramsar" Convention). The Philippines is a signatory of the Bonn Convention for the protection of migratory birds.

Australia illustrates well the benefits which may flow to migratory bird conservation from treaties. It is a signatory to three treaties covering migratory waterbirds: the Ramsar Convention and two bilateral treaties, the Japan-Australia Migratory Birds Agreement and the China-Australia Migratory Birds Agreement.

The federal government of Australia can nominate wetlands under the Ramsar Convention only on recommendations from the seven state/territory governments which have responsibility for environmental protection. Following ratification of the treaty, some Australian states nominated wetlands, often consulting non-government organizations such as the Royal Australasian Ornithologists Union for advice before finalizing a list of sites. Only the state of Queensland has yet to nominate wetlands under the convention.

All state governments have supported the objectives of the treaties and have enacted legislation which reflects this. Most state governments have declared reserves for migratory birds or are in the process of doing so, on the basis of the treaties, although some reserves were in place before the treaties were ever an issue. Thus, a positive influence of the treaties has been to provide an impetus to a coordinated national approach to migratory birds conservation and to encourage the protection of habitat. In Australia's federal-state system of government, a national approach to migratory bird conservation was lacking before the treaties were ratified.

Research on the status and distribution of migratory birds has been funded by the federal government as part of its obligations under the treaties. This has facilitated state measures to protect migratory birds effectively, by identifying the best habitats for protection in the states' reserve systems.

Finally, treaties give great credibility to the case for the protection of habitat. Non-government environment groups frequently quote the treaties as important reasons why governments should protect areas. In one case, in Victoria, the state government has argued successfully on the basis of the treaties for the protection of migratory bird habitat subject to a development proposal by a federal government agency!

In Australia, international treaties have significantly altered the approach to the conservation of migratory birds and their habitats. In the context of Australia's democratic, federal-state system, treaties have been the driving force behind a dynamic and evolving approach to the protection of migratory birds in the country. Future developments in East Asia will reveal if treaties are as effective in different social and political settings.

National programmes

East Asia. The following Asian countries are most active in studying bird migration: China, India, Indonesia, Japan, Malaysia, the Philippines, Taiwan and the Soviet Union. In addition, each of these countries, with the exception of Indonesia, has its own bird banding scheme. In cooperation with a number of international non-government groups, such as the Asian Wetland Bureau and the International Waterfowl and Wetland Research Bureau, most Asian countries are now involved in counts and surveys of migratory waterbirds. These investigations, together with banding studies, will be vital in identifying key migration stop-overs and non-breeding areas. Some examples of national programmes are presented below.

Japan has one of the most active bird-banding schemes in the region, run by the Bird Migration Research Centre of the Yamashina Institute for Ornithology. The scheme marks in excess of 100,000 birds each year (Anon 1989) over 10 per cent of which are repeated, retrapped or recovered. Between 1975 and 1982, the Wild Bird Society of Japan organized national counts of shorebirds at over 500 sites during the northward and southward migrations. In addition, in January each year, it conducted counts of waterfowl at over 1,000 sites. Research projects are also being conducted on ducks, raptors, cranes and shorebirds. Migrants, especially ducks, are still hunted in Japan but under the close control of the government's Environment Agency.

In the Philippines, the Department of Environment and Natural Resources (DENR) is the main government agency responsible for migratory birds conservation. The study and protection of migratory birds is a priority of the department as the country is one of the few signatories in the region to the Bonn Convention. The Philippines has been active in migratory bird research through MAPS, and during this programme 156,000 birds were banded up to 1972. Following training workshops in 1984, 1988 and 1989, conducted by the Asian Wetland Bureau, the Wild Bird Society of Japan and the Yamashina Institute for Ornithology, the banding programme has been revived and a national scheme has become operational in 1990. Coordinated counts of migratory waterbirds have also been conducted in the Philippines by staff of the Asian Wetland Bureau and DENR. An inventory of key wetlands in the country, used by migratory birds, has been prepared (Davies *et al.* 1990) and an Integrated Protected Area System to safeguard principal sites for migratory waterbirds will be developed in the coming year.

Australia. In Australia, where the responsibility for wildlife conservation rests with the states, the federal government plays a coordinating role. Because of the treaties, the federal government is more involved with migratory bird conservation than with some other wildlife conservation issues. Through the Australian National Parks and Wildlife Service, it regularly funds research on the status and distribution of migratory shorebirds and other birds covered by the treaties. It was a major supporter of the Royal Australasian Ornithologists Union Wader Studies Programme and of the research and training programmes of the Interwader Project (within the Asian Wetland Bureau). It has provided support to some of the wader research expeditions to north-western Australia organized by the Australasian Wader Studies Group (AWSG) and to the RAOU to review the status of migratory non-passerines, other than shorebirds.

Most state governments are also sympathetic to the needs of migratory birds, as demonstrated by the declaration of coastal and inland reserves for migratory waterbirds, especially those covered by international treaties (see under **International treaties**). The reserve network does not yet adequately cover all significant sites for such species. To remedy this situation, the AWSG, with funding from World Wide Fund for Nature, Australia, is currently preparing a management plan for Australian shorebirds. This aims to assess the adequacy of the current reserve system for protecting shorebird populations, to determine the nature and location of threats to their populations, and to recommend improvements to the reserve system and to wetland management on a state-by-state basis. This should provide a detailed blueprint for the effective protection of migratory shorebirds in every state and territory of Australia and will provide governments with the advice and direction they need to fulfil their obligations under international treaties.

Reserves and habitat management

Because of the high population density of East Asia, the needs of people and their impact on natural ecosystems must be considered in the creation of reserves. There follow two examples of wetland reserves that illustrate the problems of protecting migratory birds in East Asia. The experiences are equally applicable to terrestrial situations. This is followed by two examples from Australia, which although having one of the lowest human population densities in the world, is nevertheless subject to environmental degradation resulting from a high living standard and the resource demands this creates.

Serangoon Estuary, Singapore. Serangoon Estuary was the most important wetland in the Republic of Singapore. In the past, it supported up to 20,000 waterbirds, mostly migrants, including the rare Chinese Egret and the Asian Dowitcher. Shorebird banding demonstrated that some species migrated between Serangoon and wetlands in north-western and south-eastern Australia. In 1984, the Singapore Government initiated a plan to reclaim the entire estuary, primarily to create parkland in which residents could enjoy nature and the environment. All pleas and protests by conservation organizations were ignored. Few waterbirds now remain. Fortunately, the Singapore Government has changed its approach, with the creation of a new reserve at Sungai Buloh. This represents an important part of the five per cent of coastal wetlands that now remain on the island.

Olango Island, the Philippines. Olango Island, in the central Philippines, is a small coral atoll about 10 km long and 3 km wide, supporting seven separate sandy islands inhabited by about 17,000 people. It supports 10,000-20,000 shorebirds, including Asian Dowitchers and up to 100 Chinese Egrets. Its importance was discovered during surveys by the Asian Wetland Bureau in 1987. The most important part of Olango for shorebirds is the southern sandy island, where there is a large intertidal flat, partly covered with mangrove. The area is currently being gazetted as a reserve.

The first proposal for this reserve, in 1988, elicited considerable opposition from local people, who feared they might be evicted from the island. Through the development of an innovative and appropriate reserve management programme, this opposition has now turned to support. The intertidal flats around the sand islands have been zoned for a number of uses. A sanctuary covers 950 ha, another 300 ha have been zoned for mangrove replanting, and 200 ha have been set aside for livelihood projects. These projects have been developed for the local community in exchange for restricted access and harvesting in the sanctuary zone. They include fish cage culture, clam culturing and a tourist guide service. Support has also been given to the local fishermen's association for improved fish traps and it has been required to control dynamite fishing. Reserve management and local community development are managed by a committee comprising members from the local City Council, Asian Wetland Bureau, Department of Environment and Natural Resources, Philippine Tourism Authority and the Department of Agriculture.

The Nerang Estuary, Queensland, Australia. The Nerang Estuary in southern Queensland was once a large intertidal wetland comprising mudflats, sandy barriers, saltmarshes and extensive mangrove woodlands. In the 1950s, its nearby beaches became a popular holiday destination and ever since, the area has been subject to a real estate boom. Without proper planning measures, free market forces were given free reign. Now, little remains of the estuary's original character and almost all areas of intertidal land, including the extensive mangrove woodlands, have been "reclaimed" for canal-based housing development. The human population of the area has grown from a few thousand to almost 200,000 people in the intervening period.

Unfortunately, no systematic monitoring of the environmental effects of this development has been conducted so it is not possible to quantify accurately its impact on the estuary's wetlands and the migratory birds that inhabit them. Estuaries of similar size to the north and south hold several thousand migratory shorebirds, as well as many other birds. Today, the Nerang holds less than 100 shorebirds.

Most Australian people live on or near the east coast and the pressures for development there are greater than in any other part of the continent. Increasing affluence and leisure time, and the growth of tourism, will increase the pressures for similar developments on the Australian coast. The Nerang Estuary is an example of development incompatible with the protection of the natural environment and the conservation of migratory birds. Species such as Eastern Curlew and Lesser Golden Plover (*Pluvialis fulva*) occur in Australia in largest numbers on the east coast (Lane 1987). For their survival, it is essential that the type of uncoordinated development seen on the Nerang is not allowed to proliferate in other important coastal waterways. The knowledge and opportunity now exist to plan such development to allow for the needs of wildlife.

Corner Inlet and Nooramunga Wildlife and Marine Reserves, Victoria. These reserves, declared in 1984, were created to protect the largest intertidal wetlands in south-eastern Australia (33,000 ha). The area lies on the south coast of Victoria, 180 km south-east of Melbourne. A strong motivation for creating these reserves was provided by counts coordinated by volunteer birdwatchers from the Victorian Wader Study Group in the early 1980s, which showed for the first time how significant the area was for migratory shorebirds. The area is now listed under the Ramsar Convention, and holds up to 48,000 migratory and resident shorebirds as well as thousands of local waterbirds and several seabird colonies. It is a fish breeding and nursery area of great commercial importance.

After consultation with wildlife biologists, conservation groups, commercial and amateur fishing bodies, other government departments and the general public, a management plan was developed for the reserves. The area was zoned, higher protection being given to areas of greatest wildlife conservation and landscape value. A port development corridor was established in the least sensitive part of the area and this was excluded from the reserve. Any development in this corridor must be subject to an investigation leading to the publication of an environment effects statement subject to public review. The zoning plan and the objectives of each zone are shown in *Figure 2*.

Provided adequate resources are made available and the provisions of the management plan are implemented, this area should continue to provide a safe, high-quality habitat for the thousands of migratory waterbirds that occur there.

The above examples illustrate the conflicts inherent in efforts to protect migratory birds. Success depends not just on knowledge of the needs of migratory birds, but also on coordination and direction from governments. As the Philippines and Victorian examples show, by involving all interest groups in the planning and subsequent management of protected areas, many of the impediments to the creation and effective management of reserves for migratory birds can be overcome.

Research

Research on migratory birds in the region has played and will continue to play a crucial role in their conservation. This section briefly describes future research projects in the flyway and identifies gaps in knowledge which remain to be filled.

East Asia. For the shorebirds and some other groups of migratory waterbirds, more information now exists on important staging and non-breeding sites, and on the threats to these, than for any other group of migratory birds in the region. However, further research and surveys are needed to complete the picture. Countries where coverage could be improved include Vietnam, Kampuchea, Myanmar and the southern parts of China. Parts of Indonesia and Papua New Guinea still remain to be surveyed.

For other groups of birds, much less is known and a major research effort is required, especially in the developing countries of the region, to gather more information on migration routes and staging areas. Priorities include the clarification of staging areas and non-breeding habitats for migratory terrestrial birds as well as the location of the non-breeding areas of the migratory raptors. Much remains to be discovered about the migration of birds that breed within the tropical part of the region: both the geographical extent of their movements and the habitats on which they rely at different times of year.

Given the huge pressures on the natural environment in Asia, there is an urgent need for research on the specific requirements of migratory birds in particularly threatened areas and habitats as a basis for developing appropriate conservation and community development programmes. Furthermore, little is known of the precise effects of hunting on migratory birds in East Asia, and further investigations are needed to determine a sustainable level of hunting.

More research needs people with appropriate expertise. Currently, most countries in the region lack the expertise for studying migratory birds. Training programmes for local wildlife biologists and others are therefore vital if important questions about bird migration in the region are to be answered.

Australasia. Most research on migratory birds in Australasia has focused on the shorebirds. The RAOU Wader Studies Programme (1981-1985) and the Ornithological Society of New Zealand National Wader Counts have identified the key sites for shorebirds. The AWSG management plan described earlier will apply the results of this research to the question of habitat protection and management in Australia. Since 1986, the AWSG has conducted a number of research projects on shorebirds. Its Population Monitoring Project aims to document trends in shorebird populations. This involves twice-yearly counts at 23 selected coastal habitats. Sites were selected to represent disturbed and comparatively pristine habitats so that local, possibly human-induced changes in population levels could be distinguished from more widespread changes. Lying at the southern end of the migration system, Australia and New Zealand are best placed to monitor population changes. In 1991, it is proposed to analyse the first ten years of data. The continuation of this monitoring is considered to be a very high priority.

More shorebirds are banded in Australia than in any other part of the flyway. The involvement of volunteers in this activity and the existence of a strong bird banding scheme within the Australian National Parks and Wildlife Service make

Figure 2: Corner inlet and Nooramunga Wildlife and Marine Reserves with draft management zones. (*After* Victoria Department of Conservation, Forests and Lands; Australia.)

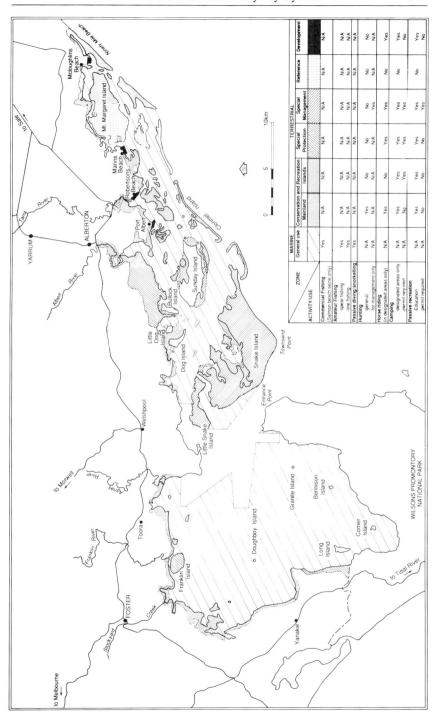

further research on the migration routes of shorebirds in the region feasible. A colour-flagging programme for shorebirds in Australia and New Zealand is currently being investigated. Colour-flagging, as it relies only on resightings, removes the need for complementary banding programmes elsewhere in the migration system and expedites the generation of information on bird movements. There is an urgent need for up-to-date information on the status of other international migratory birds in Australasia. Until this is available, it is not possible to determine whether they are being affected by environmental change in the region.

Conservation recommendations

Apart from the research needed to assist the effective conservation of migratory birds in the region, there are a number of priority areas for conservation action. The following recommendations are necessarily general, as each problem will require more detailed consideration and the development of programmes appropriate to particular circumstances in each country.

Habitat destruction and modification are the greatest threats to migratory birds in the region and are continuing at an alarming rate. It is essential for the future survival of migratory birds in the region that adequate areas of staging and non-breeding habitat be protected. Given the extreme economic pressures on the human populations in most Asian countries, the needs of local communities as well as the requirements for effective conservation will need to be considered in the planning and management of reserves. International aid agencies need to acknowledge the crucial role they can play in promoting the goals of sustainable and balanced development in many Asian countries. National and international non-government groups in developed, democratic countries need to encourage their assistance agencies to pursue appropriate programmes. International non-government conservation agencies need to continue to expand their efforts in East Asia to provide moral and technical support to the government agencies in each country, since it is these agencies that have the difficult task of achieving the effective conservation of migratory birds.

Greater impetus to habitat protection for migratory birds in the region could be achieved through a companion reserve network, similar to that operating for shorebirds in the New World (Myers *et al.* 1987). This need not be formalized in a treaty, which could take years to negotiate and ratify, but could remain an informal arrangement between states or agencies to link habitat protection measures for migratory birds in their respective areas. This could have the advantage of bringing together both developing and developed countries in the region, thus making money from richer countries available for specific habitat protection projects. International non-government conservation agencies could play a leading role in encouraging such a system.

ACKNOWLEDGEMENTS

We are very grateful to ICBP for the opportunity to contribute to this volume and thank Tobias Salathé for his patience during the preparation of this paper. We also thank David Wells, Roger Jaensch and Angus Martin for commenting on the draft.

REFERENCES

ALONZO-PASICOLAN, S. (1990) *Survey of hunting pressure on waterbirds in Luzon, The Philippines.* Kuala Lumpur: Asian Wetland Bureau (Rep. 36).

ASH, J. S. (1984) Bird observations on Bali. *Bull. Brit. Orn. Club.* **104**: 24-33.

ANONYMOUS. (1989) *Annual report of the Bird Migration Research Centre.* Tokyo: Yamashina Institute for Ornithology.

BLAKERS, M., DAVIES, S. J. J. F. & REILLY, P. N. (1984) *The atlas of Australian birds.* Melbourne: Melbourne University Press.

CLOSE, D. H. & NEWMAN, O. M. G. (1984) The decline of the Eastern Curlew in south-eastern Australia. *Emu* **84**: 38-40.

DAVIES, J., MAGSALAY, P., RIGOR, R., GONZALES, H. & MAPALO, A. (1990) *A directory of Philippine wetlands.* Cebu City and Kuala Lumpur: Asian Wetland Bureau.

DRAFFAN, R. D. W., GARNETT, S. T. & MALONE, G. (1983) Birds of the Torres Strait. *Emu* **83**: 207-234.

HOWES, J. & PARISH, D. (1989) *New information on Asian shorebirds.* Kuala Lumpur: Asian Wetland Bureau.

JOHNSGARD, P. A. (1981) *The plovers, sandpipers and snipes of the world.* Lincoln: University of Nebraska Press.

LANE, B. A. (1987) *Shorebirds in Australia.* Nelson, Melbourne.

LANE, B. A. & JESSOP, A. E. (1985) Tracking of migrating waders in north-western Australia using meteorological radar. *Stilt.* **6**: 17-28.

LONG, A. J. POOLE, C. M., ELDRIDGE, M. I., WON, P. O. & LEE, K. S. (1988) *A survey of coastal wetlands and shorebirds in South Korea, spring 1988.* Kuala Lumpur: Asian Wetland Bureau.

MACKINNON, J. & MACKINNON, K. (1986) *Review of the protected areas system in the Indo-Malayan realm.* Gland: International Union for the Conservation of Nature and Natural Resources.

McCLURE, H. E. (1974) *Migration and survival of the birds of Asia.* Bangkok, Thailand: U.S. Army Medical Component, SEATO Medical Project.

MEDWAY, LORD & WELLS, D. R. (1976) *The birds of the Malay Peninsula, Vol. 5: Conclusion and survey of every species.* London: Witherby.

MELVILLE, D. S. (1980) *Birds at Kai Tak airport, Hong Kong.* Hong Kong: Agriculture and Fisheries Department.

MYERS, J. P., McLAIN, P. D., MORRISON, R. I. G., ANTAS, P. Z., CANEVARI, P., HARRINGTON, B. A., LOVEJOY, T. E., PULIDO, V., SALLABERRY, M. & SENER, S. E. (1987) The western hemisphere shorebird reserve network. Pp. 122-124 in N. C. Davidson & M. W. Pienkowski, eds. *The conservation of international flyway population of waders.* Slimbridge, U.K.: Wader Study Group (Bull. 49, Suppl.)/International Waterfowl and Wetlands Research Bureau (Spec. Publ. 7).

NAARDING, J. A. (1986) Latham's Snipe in Australia and Japan. *RAOU Report* **24**.

PARISH, D. (1989) Population estimates of water birds using the East Asian/Australasian flyway. Pp. 8-13 in H. Boyd & J.-Y. Pirot, eds. *Flyways and reserve networks for waterbirds.* Slimbridge, U.K.: International Waterfowl and Wetlands Research Bureau (Spec. Publ. 9).

PARISH, D. & HOWES, J. R. (1990) Waterbird hunting and management in S.E. Asia. Pp. 128-131 in G. V. T. Matthews, ed. *Managing waterfowl populations.* Slimbridge, U.K.: International Waterfowl and Wetlands Research Bureau.

PARISH, D., LANE, B., SAGAR, P. & TOMKOVICH, P. (1987) Wader migration systems in east Asia and Australasia. Pp. 4-14 in N. C. Davidson & M. W. Pienkowski, eds. *The conservation of international flyway population of waders.* Slimbridge, U.K.: Wader Study Group (Bull. 49, Suppl.)/International Waterfowl and Wetlands Research Bureau (Spec. Publ. 7).

PARISH, D. & WELLS, D. R., eds. (1983) *Interwader '83 Report.* Kuala Lumpur: Interwader (Publ. 1).

SAGAR, P. M. (in prep.) Results of national wader counts in New Zealand, 1981 to 1985. *Notornis.*

SCOTT, D. A., ed. (1989) *A directory of Asian wetlands.* Cambridge, U.K. and Gland: International Union for the Conservation of Nature and Natural Resources.

SCOTT, D. A. & POOLE, C. M. (1989) *A status overview of Asian wetlands.* Kuala Lumpur: Asian Wetland Bureau.

SCOTT, D. A. & ROSE, P. M. (1989) *Asian waterfowl census, 1989.* Slimbridge, U.K.: International Waterfowl and Wetlands Research Bureau.

SIMPSON, D. M. (1983) Autumn migration of land birds off north Borneo in 1981. *Sea Swallow* **32**: 48-53.

TIANHOU, W. & SIXIAN, T. (1989) Report of the 1989 East China banding training course and expedition. *Newsl. East China Waterb. Stud. Grp.* **1**.

U.S.S.R. ACADEMY OF SCIENCES (1985) *Bird migration in eastern Europe and northern Asia: Gruiformes to Charadriiformes.* Moscow: Nauka.

WELLS, D. R. (1986) Dependence of northern migrants on evergreen forest in peninsular Malaysia. *Ibis* **128**: 173.

WELLS, D. R. (1989) Migratory birds and tropical forest in the Sunda region. In *Biogeography and ecology of forest bird communities.* The Hague: SPB Academic Publishing.

WHITE, C. M. N. & BRUCE, M. D. (1986) *The birds of Wallacea (Sulawesi, the Moluccas and Lesser Sunda Islands, Indonesia): an annotated check-list.* London: British Ornithologists' Union (Check-list 7).

WILD BIRD SOCIETY OF JAPAN. (1982) *A field guide to the birds of Japan.* Tokyo: Wild Bird Society of Japan.

PART IV
FUTURE DIRECTIONS

The structure of this volume is programmatic: after an overview of the conservation activities ICBP has undertaken for migratory birds (PART I), a brief reminder of the problems migratory birds face (PART II), and the presentation of exemplary case studies (PART III), this final part proposes future directions designed to achieve lasting conservation goals. Nature conservation is a complex subject, and migratory birds and their habitats form but part of it. Although historically pioneered by scientists in the field of natural history, many of the current problems are not solely of a biological and environmental nature as they are embedded in the context of human sociology, economics and law (McNeely *et al.* 1990). Such interrelationships must be taken into account if we are to address successfully the underlying causes of the conservation problems faced by migrants. Some suggestions on how to go about this are presented in PART IV by conservationists reflecting the points of view of organisations with which ICBP collaborates closely for the conservation of migratory birds (IUCN *et al.* 1984).

PART IV starts with an overview of international conservation regulations for migratory birds along the West Palearctic–African flyways, presented by an environmental lawyer (Biber-Klemm). This is intended to provide a useful guide to ornithologists, who are seldom expert in legal matters, and to help non-governmental organisations and local groups to lobby for their cause. The Convention on the Conservation of Migratory Species (CMS or Bonn Convention) contains species-oriented regulations, and provides good flexibility on how to agree on international conservation measures. Boere proposes in his contribution that a number of specific agreements for migratory birds should be established under this convention. The site- and habitat-specific conservation approach for migrants is provided for by other international treaties covered by Biber-Klemm and Moser in their respective contributions. Wetlands and waterbirds are of outstanding importance in migratory birds conservation, both for the importance and value wetlands represent and for the economic and recreational interests that exist in the exploitation of migratory waterfowl. Moser summarises this in his contribution about the International Waterfowl and Wetlands Research Bureau (IWRB) and the Convention on Wetlands of International Importance especially as Waterfowl Habitats (Ramsar Convention). A proposal on how to plan specific activities for migrants within the broader framework of conservation projects for sustainable socio-economic development of human populations sharing the migrants' habitats is provided by Dugan. The final paper attempts to summarise all of this by providing a strategy for migratory bird conservation in the nineties, in the form of a Forward Plan for the West Palearctic–African flyways. I hope that this regional bias, which exists for no other reason than the history outlined in the opening paper, will not upset the reader, but rather promote increased activities in areas not yet adequately covered.

T. Salathé

REFERENCES

IUCN, ICBP & IWRB. (1984) A programme for the conservation of migratory birds. Report prepared for WWF Pp. 103. Gland: International Union for the Conservation of Nature and Natural Resources.

McNEELY, J. A., MILLER, K. R., REID, W. V., MITTERMEIER, R. A. & WERNER, T. B. (1990) *Conserving the world's biological diversity.* Gland, Switzerland and Washington, D.C.: IUCN, WRI, CI, WWF-U.S., World Bank.

ICBP Technical Publication No. 12, 1991

INTERNATIONAL LEGAL INSTRUMENTS FOR THE PROTECTION OF MIGRATORY BIRDS: AN OVERVIEW FOR THE WEST PALEARCTIC–AFRICAN FLYWAYS

SUSETTE BIBER–KLEMM

*Theophil–Roniger Strasse 15,
CH–4310 Rheinfelden, Switzerland*

ABSTRACT

Several international instruments designed to protect the natural environment contain, explicitly or implicitly, regulations which admit or demand the protection of migratory birds from excessive hunting and commercialization and/or degradation of their habitats. An analysis of the substantial regulations of the legal instruments of importance for the West Palearctic and Africa (the African Convention; the conventions of Ramsar, Berne and Bonn; the World Heritage Convention, and the European Economic Community (EEC) Directive on the Conservation of Wild Birds) shows that quite a lot of the protection needs of migratory birds are covered by these instruments. Therefore the problem lies not so much in the content of the regulations as in their incomplete geographical coverage and in a lack of implementation of the contractual obligations they contain.

The reason for the lax implementation of these instruments lies on one hand in the problem of finding the necessary consensus for the wording and/or interpretation of the regulations by the contracting parties, which results in vague formulations that are difficult to implement. On the other hand, due to the fact that the obligations of the conventions have to be fulfilled within the territory of the contracting parties, direct inter-party control of implementation is not possible. In both respects, NGOs as independent bodies can make valuable contributions to improving the situation, at international level as well as at the national level, provided that they are properly informed about the substantial content of the conventions and the rules of international public law.

INTRODUCTION

Since the United Nations Conference on the Human Environment in 1972 ("Stockholm Conference"), important nature conservation treaties have been ratified by many countries, which are therefore committed to implement the regulations of these treaties by their national legal, administrative and jurisdictional means.

As will be shown in the second part of this paper, Non-Governmental Organizations (NGOs) play (or ought to play) an important role in the implementation of these international nature conservation treaties. To be able to take over this role it is important for them to be informed about the content, obligations, structure, procedure and functioning of these international treaties. Therefore, in the first part of the paper an overview of the obligations of the parties will be given, with special emphasis on the prescriptions concerning migratory birds. As the Ramsar and Bonn conventions are treated in separate articles (see Moser and Boere, this volume), the main stress will be put on the other existing conventions and on a comparison of the different treaties.

In the second part I would like to give some background information on the problems of implementation. In particular I would like to try to answer the following questions:

- Why do some treaties work better than others?
- What means does an international NGO have at its disposal to activate the working of the conventions' organs and control mechanisms?
- What can an NGO do at international or national level to improve the implementation of existing treaties at the national level?

CONSERVATION CONVENTIONS OF RELEVANCE TO THE WEST PALEARCTIC AND AFRICA

Worldwide, there are many international legal instruments dealing with the protection of nature in general or with the protection of migratory birds in particular (IUCN 1986; Lyster 1985). In this article only the treaties of relevance to the West Palearctic and Africa will be treated. Furthermore I shall exclude four conventions. The Convention on Birds useful to Agriculture (Paris 1902) and its revised follower, the International Convention for the Protection of Birds (Paris 1950), both formally still in force but only of historical and methodological interest; the Benelux Convention on Hunting and Protection of Birds (Brussels 1970) and its amendments, and the Benelux Convention on Nature Conservation and Landscape Protection (1982) between Belgium, Luxembourg and the Netherlands, as they only cover a small part of the West Palearctic.

Two more regional conventions will not be treated here because the relevant material was not available in time. These are the "Convention for the Protection of the Mediterranean Sea against Pollution, Barcelona 1976" (Barcelona Convention), of importance in the present context mainly for its "Protocol Concerning Mediterranean Specially Protected Areas, Geneva 1982"; and the "Convention for the Protection, Management and Development of the Marine and Coastal Environment of the Eastern African Region, Nairobi 1985"; of importance in the present context mainly for its "Protocol Concerning Protected Areas and Wild Fauna and Flora in the Eastern African Region" (Nairobi 1985). Furthermore, I would like to stress that the EEC Council Directive on the Conservation of Wild Birds is taken into consideration and usually included in the statements, even if not always specifically mentioned. The EEC Directive is Community Law, based on the international convention founding the Community and its amendments[1]. Finally I should like to stress, that the treaties will be discussed mainly in view of the legal instruments they offer for the protection of birds, and especially migratory birds. Some of the conventions mentioned cover wider issues (e.g. the African, Berne and Bonn conventions, see *Table 1*) and most of them also contain obligations to promote research, education and information, which are very important conditions for their implementation (e.g. for the Bonn Convention: Boere, this volume). These delimitations bring us to the list of conventions taken into consideration as shown in *Table 1*.

Table 1: An overview of the main features of the conventions discussed in the text.

African Convention on the Conservation of Nature and Natural Resources (African Convention) (1968/1969)[1]

- Prepared under the auspices of the Organization of African Unity
- Possible coverage: Africa
- Aim: Individual and joint action for the conservation, utilization and development of soil, water, flora and faunal resources by establishing and maintaining their rational utilization for the present and future welfare of mankind.
- Appendices: – List of protected species: class A
              – List of protected species: class B

Convention on Wetlands of International Importance Especially as Waterfowl Habitat (Ramsar Convention) (1971/1975)

- Prepared by UNESCO
- Possible coverage: worldwide
- Aim: Conservation of wetlands and their flora and fauna by farsighted national politics and coordinated international action
- Amendments:
    - Article 10 bis by "Protocol to amend the Convention on Wetlands of International Importance especially as Waterfowl Habitat", Paris 1982 (1986)
    - Articles 6 and 7 by the Extraordinary Conference of the Contracting Parties, Regina Sakatchewan, Canada, 1987[2]

Convention Concerning the Protection of the World Cultural and Natural Heritage (World Heritage Convention) (1972/1975)

- Prepared under the auspices of UNESCO
- Possible coverage: worldwide
- Aim: On the basis of the idea of a "Common Heritage of Mankind", the protection of natural and cultural areas of "outstanding universal value" as duty of the international community as a whole, by granting collective assistance.

Convention on the Conservation of Migratory Species of Wild Animals (Bonn Convention) (1979/1983)

- Initiated by the UN Conference on the Human Environment, Stockholm 1972, prepared by the Federal Republic of Germany
- Possible coverage: worldwide
- Objectives: Conservation and effective management of migratory species of wild animals
- Appendices:
    I: Endangered Migratory Species
    II: – Migratory species which have an unfavourable conservation status and which require international agreements for their conservation and management
        – Migratory species which have a conservation status which would significantly benefit from the international co-operation
- Amendments: Appendices in 1985 and 1988

Convention on the Conservation of European Wildlife and Natural Habitats (Berne Convention) (1979/1982)

- Initiated by the Council of Europe
- Possible coverage: Member States of Council of Europe and non-member States which participated in its elaboration. Other non-member States upon invitation by the Committee of Ministers
- Objectives: To conserve wild flora and fauna and their natural habitats, giving particular emphasis to endangered and vulnerable species, including endangered and vulnerable migratory species, and to promote cooperation between the countries

(*continued*)

Convention on the Conservation of European Wildlife and Natural Habitats (Berne Convention) (1979/1982) *(continued)*

– Appendices:
    I: Strictly protected flora species
    II: Strictly protected fauna species
    III: Protected fauna species
    IV: Prohibited means and methods of killing, capture and other forms of exploitation; (Mammals, Birds)
– Amendments: 1987: Annex II and III; inclusion of freshwater fish and invertebrates and addition of some mammals

EEC Council Directive on the Conservation of Wild Birds (79/409/EEC)

– Coverage: EC Member States: Belgium, Denmark, France, Germany, Greece, Ireland, Italy, Luxembourg, Netherlands, Portugal, Spain, United Kingdom
– Objectives: To maintain bird populations at a level which corresponds to ecological, scientific and cultural requirements
– Appendices:
    I: Species being the subject of special conservation measures concerning their habitat
    II: Species which may be hunted under national legislation (II/1: entire sea and land area; II/2: only in member states indicated)
    III: Species which under certain restrictions are exempt of the prohibition of commercialization
    IV: Prohibited means and methods of killing
    V: Research subjects on which special attention is to be paid
– Amendments: Council Directive 81/854/EEC, 19 October 1981
             (Entry of Greece into EEC; adaption of Annexes)
             Council Directive 85/411/EEC, 25 July 1985
             (Revision Annex I: "Habitat-protection-species")
             Council Directive 86/122/EEC, 8 April 1986
             (Entry of Spain and Portugal into EEC; translation of Annex)

Notes: 1 Date of signature and date of entry into force; 2 Not yet in force; cf. "Resolution on Provisional Implementation of the Amendments to the Convention" of the Third Meeting of the Conference of the Contracting Parties, Regina 1987.

An overview of the treaties' Substantial Provisions concerning the protection of species and habitats

Modern nature conservation conventions operate in two different ways to protect species of wild animals. First there is the traditional method of species protection through regulation or interdiction of hunting and commercialization, and additionally, in a more recent way, through what is called "sustainable use" ("wise use") of the species concerned. Secondly there is species protection in a broader sense, effected by protection of habitats, including the traditional approach of establishing nature conservation areas. More recent conventions include regulations concerning sustainable use of habitats and the problem of their indirect degradation by different forms of pollution. *Table 2* provides an overview of the provisions of the conventions, and these are discussed in more detail below.

Table 2: An overview of the main provisions of the conventions discussed. (See text for further elaboration.)

	Africa 1968	Ramsar 1971	Heritage 1972	Bonn 1979	Berne 1979	EEC 1979
A) Species Protection						
Lists	App. A/B Art. 8	–	–	App. I/II Art. 3/4	App. I-III Art. 5-7	App. I-III Art. 4.1/6.2-4 7.1-2
Criteria	–	–	–	Definit. Art. 1	–	Art. 4.1a-d for App. I
Hunting/ taking	Art. 7.2/ 8.1 i/ii	–	–	Art. 3.5/ 5.5j/k	Art. 6-9 App. IV	Art. 7-9 App. IV
Commercial transp.	Art. 9	–	–	–	Art. 6.e Art. 7.3c	Art. 6
"Wise use"	Art. 7	–	–	–	Art. 7.2 i.c. Art. 2	Art. 7.4 i.c. Art. 2
Migratory	–	–	–	Entire Conv.	Art. 10	Art. 7.4
B) Habitat Protection						
Species/ habitats	Art. 10.1	(i)	Art. 2	Art. 3.4a Art. 5.5e-g	Art. 4.1	Art. 4.1/5b
Migratory	–	Art. 2.6 (i)	(i)	Art. 4a/b Art. 5e-h	Art. 4.3	Art. 4.2
Network	–	(i)	(i)	Art. 4/5 AGREEMENTS	–	Art. 4.3
"Wise use"	Art. 4-7	(i)	–	–	–	–
Represent. ecosyst.	Art. 10.1	(i)	Art. 2	–	–	–
Endangered biotopes	–	entire Conv.	–	–	Art. 4.1 Art. 5b	–
Indirect	Art. 4-6	–	–	Art. 5i	Art. 4.2	Art. 4.4

Key: App.= Appendix
i.c. = In combination with
(i) = By interpretation

Explanation Table 2: Part A

LISTS: Lists specifying which species get special protection are usually placed in appendices to the conventions. Usually there are different categories of appendices, according to the different needs of protection (cf. *Table 1*). The purpose of this technique is to facilitate amendment of the appendices, e.g. by requiring smaller majorities or no ratification procedure as is required for the amendment of the text of the convention itself. This allows the system to be more flexible, by adapting the species lists to the actual needs of protection (compare Berne, Article 17, 2/3; Bonn, Article XI).

CRITERIA: These indicate whether or not the convention gives detailed criteria for the selection of species for the different appendices, as one of the problems of this system is that the choice of species is often not scientifically based but politically motivated, or that the appendices are not differentiated enough (e.g. Appendix III of the Berne Convention).

HUNTING: The hunting regulations are usually differentiated in accordance with the protection needs specified by the annexes. The level of protection ranges from total prohibition of hunting to prohibition during certain seasons and prescription of sustainable use of the populations. The Berne Convention and the EEC Directive have both included the prohibition of non-selective methods, in particular of those listed in the respective appendices (Appendix IV).

WISE USE OF SPECIES: For the meaning of the term "wise use" or "sustainable use" no general juridical definition has yet been established. The EEC Directive mentions the principle of wise use in its Article 7. 4, treating the practice of hunting without explicitly giving an interpretation. It refers mainly to Article 2, which states that member states are to take:

> "...requisite measures to maintain the population of the species referred to in Article 1 [all species of naturally occurring birds in the wild state in the European territory of the Member States to which the Treaty applies] at a level which corresponds in particular to ecological, scientific and cultural requirements, while taking account of economic and recreational requirements."

This wording is taken almost literally from the Berne Convention (Article 2), which itself does not explicitly speak of "wise use" but asks that exploitation (if permitted) be regulated in order to keep populations out of danger (Article 7. 2).

The African Convention mentions wise use of faunal resources in its Article VII:

> "Management [of faunal resources] shall be carried out in accordance with plans based on scientific principles. ...To that end the Contracting States shall...manage exploitable wildlife populations...for an optimum sustained yield, compatible with and complementary to other land uses."

As, especially for conservation activities in African countries, the strategy of wise use seems to be a practicable one, it could be important to work out a common definition for the exploitation of species' populations, as Ramsar tries to formulate for wetlands (see below). Compare also the definition given by the World Conservation Strategy for "Conservation for sustainable development":

> "Conservation is...the management for human use for the biosphere so that it may yield the greatest sustainable benefit to present generations while maintaining its potential to meet the needs and aspirations of future generations" (IUCN/UNEP/WWF 1980, Introduction, No. 4).

MIGRATORY: This indicates whether or not there are special provisions in the instrument concerning migratory species.

Explanation Table 2: Part B
SPECIES HABITATS: Indicates whether a treaty obliges the signatories to protect habitats of (certain) species, as distinct from the protection of "endangered

habitats". The species falling under these habitat protection regulations are usually defined in the appendices.

MIGRATORY: Indicates whether there are special provisions for the protection of habitats according to the different stages of migration.

NETWORK: This item denotes consideration of the need to link important habitats occurring over the length of the entire flyway.

WISE USE OF HABITATS: This criterion is mentioned as distinct from the traditional protection of habitats by means of conservation areas. The Regina Conference of the Ramsar Convention has given a definition of "wise use of wetlands" which can easily be generalized for all types of habitat:

> "The wise use of wetlands is their sustainable utilization for the benefit of humankind in a way compatible with the maintenance of the natural properties of the ecosystem."

"Sustainable utilization" is defined as:

> "...human use of a wetland so that it may yield the greatest continuous benefit to present generations while maintaining its potential to meet the needs and aspirations of future generations,"

and "natural properties of the ecosystem" are defined as:

> "...those physical, biological or chemical components, such as soil, water, plants, animals and nutrients, and the interactions between them" (Ramsar, Report of third meeting of the Parties, 1987, Annex to Recommendations, 2 and 3).

REPRESENTATIVE ECOSYSTEMS/ENDANGERED BIOTOPES: These have been added to give an overview of existing tendencies and the various possible ways of tackling the problem of habitat protection. Habitats that are to be protected can also be defined by their own characteristics (e.g. representative for a defined geographical range, endangered in a certain region), regardless of the species they may contain. This is in order to safeguard whole communities of species, together with the ecological relationships that exist between them.

INDIRECT: This criterion indicates whether measures against indirect degradation of habitats through pollution or other emissions are provided for in the conventions.

Geographical range of the conventions in relation to the flyways of West Palearctic birds

The indications given above and in *Table 2* do not tell us a great deal unless we also know which countries are parties to which conventions.

In *Figure 2* a comprehensive overview is given of the range of all conventions in the area discussed. The first impression of a fairly complete coverage by at least one convention is modified by the information that the hatched parties occurring mainly in central and eastern Africa are covered "only" by the African Convention and/or the World Heritage Convention, which for different reasons are less important for nature conservation and the protection of migratory birds. To

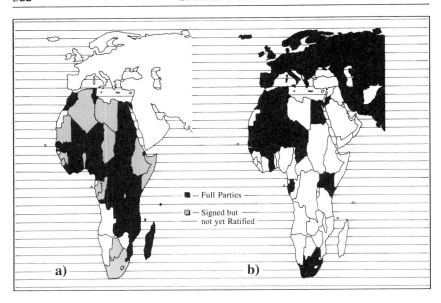

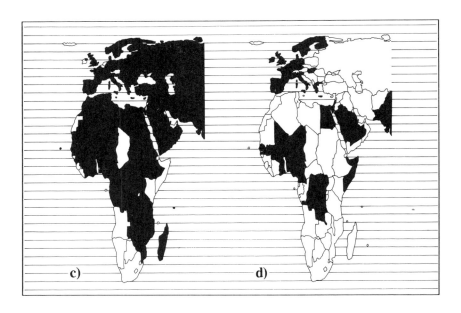

Figure 1: Contracting parties in the Western Palearctic and Africa to conventions discussed in the text: (a) African Convention on the Conservation of Nature and Natural Resources (as in 1985); (b) Convention on Wetlands of International Importance Especially as Waterfowl Habitat (as at May 1991); (c) Convention Concerning the Protection of the World Cultural and Natural Heritage (as at November 1990); (d) Convention on the Conservation of Migratory Species of Wild Animals (as at February 1991); (e) Convention on the

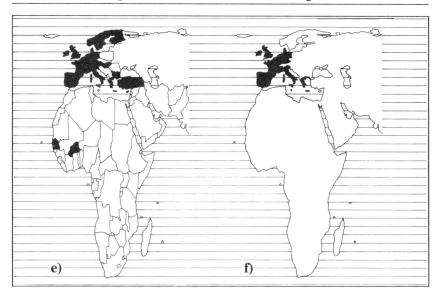

Conservation of European Wildlife and Natural Habitats (as at February 1991); (f) EEC Council Directive on the Conservation of Wild Birds.

complete the overview, in *Table 3* the membership figures are given in relation to the entire range of the conventions.

Characterization of Conventions
Combining the information given above, the differences between the conventions become quite obvious. There are two general nature protection conventions which cover more or less the whole range of conservation needs, i.e. hunting and commercial exploitation as well as habitat protection. These are the African Convention and the Berne Convention. Both are relatively restricted in their intended geographical range. In our context it is important to know that the Berne Convention is, according to the practice of the Council of Europe, what is called an "open convention". This means that non-member states of the Council of Europe can also sign/accede to the convention at the invitation of the Committee of Ministers (Article 20). The Standing Committee has the right to make recommendations to the Committee of Ministers concerning non-member states of the Council of Europe to be invited to accede to the convention (Article 14). These regulations have always been justified by the necessity to cover the whole range of migratory species, including at least northern Africa and most of the eastern European countries including the Soviet Union (Imbert 1979, p. 735).

The African Convention, which is what I would like to call a very elegant and modern one unfortunately is apparently a "sleeping convention". I think there are two reasons for this. First the convention does not provide for compulsory control measures, but probably the main reason lies in the enormous socio-economic problems of most of the member states, which are taking up most of the governments' time and efforts.

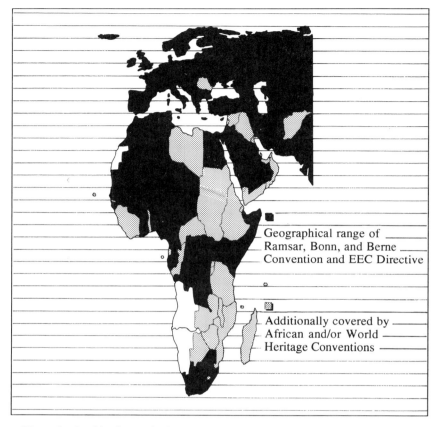

Figure 2: Combined range in the West Palearctic and Africa of all treaties discussed.

Further, there are two conventions that concentrate on the protection of certain habitats: Ramsar and World Heritage. Ramsar aims to protect wetlands; World Heritage to conserve objects/sites of "outstanding universal value", being a part of the natural and cultural heritage of the world. Both conventions are remarkable for their success: Ramsar because of the enormous efforts that have been made to improve what in a critical publication of the late seventies was called "the painless convention" (Environmental Policy and Law 1, 1975, p. 131); World Heritage for the broad adherence it has found. (In December 1988 there were 315 properties/sites on the list, of which 73 were natural sites and 12 were mixed sites.) Important for the success of this convention is the World Heritage Fund which offers poorer countries financial and technical assistance to secure the protection of important sites. The Bonn Convention is *the* convention concerning migratory birds, and will be treated together with the regulations on migratory birds of other conventions.

The EEC Directive is considered to be a detailed transcription of the Ramsar and Berne conventions into European Community (EC) law (restricted to birds). The European Community is a member of the Berne Convention and of the Bonn Convention.

Table 3: An overview of the membership of the various conventions.

	Possible range	Total member states[1]	Europe, Middle East	Africa	Rest
African Conv. (state 1985)	R	42	–	42	–
Ramsar (state 30.5.91)	W	62	29	16	17
World Heritage (state 21.11.90)	W	115	39	32	44
Bonn (state February 1991)	W	35	18	12	5
Berne (state 12.2.91)	R	24	22	2	–

Note: 1 Having deposited an instrument of ratification, acceptance or accession.

Key: R = Intended regional range
       W = Intended worldwide range

To summarize this overview I would like to state that each convention has its own emphasis and its own character; and that the conventions give a quite complete coverage of the needs of conservation in the area discussed. The problem lies rather in participation and implementation.

REGULATIONS CONCERNING MIGRATORY BIRDS

Definition of the term "migratory"

The Bonn Convention is the only one to give detailed definitions of the terms used, e.g. "range", "range state", "habitat", etc. (compare Article I. 1a–k, but see also the recent interpretative resolution of the Standing Committee of the Berne Convention, R. No. 1, 1989). The Bonn Convention's definition of "migratory species" is as follows:

> "Migratory species means the entire population or any geographically separate part of the population of any species or lower taxon of wild animals, a significant portion of whose members cyclically and predictably cross one or more national jurisdictional boundaries" (Article I. 1a).

This definition is interesting in several points:

– The fact that geographically separate populations of a species may be considered makes it possible to afford different levels of protection according to the species' conservation needs, which may differ between member states. That means that for a species endangered and in need of absolute protection in one member state, limited exploitation may be possible in another state where it is not endangered.

– The criterion of the "significant portion" allows the inclusion of relatively sedentary species in the appendices, namely species of which the post-breeding dispersal of young must regularly involve crossing of national frontiers.
– "Cyclically and predictably" seems to be interpreted in a broad sense in order to include species living in border areas, which might be relatively sedentary but which nevertheless wander back and forth across national frontiers on a regular basis (Lyster 1985, p. 281).

Thus, the definition given by the Bonn Convention is much broader than that which is classically understood by focusing on strictly long-distance migrants only. Whether this could prove useful e.g. for the protection of birds with overlapping breeding and wintering areas (partial migrants) is up to the ornithologists to decide. From the legal point of view the question is one of how the term "migratory" is going to be interpreted for other conventions; that is whether they adopt a narrow definition or, by interpretation, will take over the Bonn solution.

Regulatory systems concerning migratory species

Migratory birds listed in the appendices to international agreements get the protection foreseen for all species in the respective appendices, which is defined by the text of the convention. Besides that there are special regulations for migratory species which are mentioned in the appendices (Berne, Article 10) or – additionally – for all other migratory species not mentioned in the appendices (EEC Article 4. 2). In the following, mainly these articles will be treated.

The system of the Bonn Convention

The Bonn Convention, which aims uniquely at the conservation of migratory species, has two quite distinct sub-objectives. The first is to provide strict protection for migratory species listed in Appendix I, which consists of migratory species in danger of extinction throughout all or a significant portion of their range. The convention imposes strict conservation obligations on parties that are "Range States" (Article III). The second sub-objective is to oblige parties that are Range States, to endeavour to conclude "AGREEMENTS" or "agreements" (Article IV. 2 and 3) for the conservation and management of Appendix II species[2]. (For the meaning of "AGREEMENT" vs. "agreement" see Boere, this volume). Thus the convention does not impose direct obligations on the parties to protect Appendix II species – it merely encourages them to conclude further agreements for their protection, either among themselves or with Range States that are not parties to the convention. It also establishes guidelines as to what these agreements should contain (Articles IV and V). It is important to know that a species does not need to be threatened or potentially threatened in order to qualify for Appendix II. It is sufficient that a species would benefit from the international cooperation that an agreement would bring (Lyster 1985, p. 279/280). I think this system is very original. Obviously its basic idea is that it is easier to get a relatively restricted number of member states to find a consensus concerning the protection of one or a few species; and secondly that such regulations can be much more differentiated and adapted to the effective protection needs of this species or species group.

Protection of migratory birds through hunting and trade regulations

As shown in *Table 2*, regulations concerning hunting and commercial exploitation are contained in the African, Bonn and Berne conventions and in the EEC Directive, but not in the two conventions treating habitat protection (Ramsar and World Heritage).

The Bonn Convention prohibits all taking of Appendix I species (Article III. 5). "Taking" is defined in Article 1. i as:

> "Taking, hunting, fishing, capturing, harassing, deliberate killing, or attempting to engage in any such conduct."

Detailed regulations for species listed in Appendix II are delegated to the AGREEMENTS, which, where "appropriate and feasible", should provide for:

– Measures based on sound ecological principles to control and manage the taking of the migratory species.
– Procedures for coordinating action to suppress illegal taking (Article 5. j/k).

The Berne Convention and the EEC Directive principally protect *all* species of wild flora and fauna, including wild birds. Therefore both instruments provide a list of birds which can be hunted and exploited under certain conditions. (Berne, Article 7, Appendix III; EEC Article 7, Appendix II). As a rule, the populations are to be kept out of danger, which requires some sort of control/authorization system governing the taking. Additionally, as already mentioned, all indiscriminate means of capture and killing, and the use of all means capable of causing local disappearance of, or serious disturbance to, populations are prohibited. (Compare Berne, Articles 7 and 8, Appendix 4; EEC, Articles 7 and 8, Appendix IV).

For migratory birds that may be hunted under the quoted regulations, there are special restrictions. The Berne Convention prescribes that:

> "...the closed seasons and/or other procedures regulating the exploitation of these birds must be "adequate and appropriately disposed to meet the requirements of the migratory species specified in Appendix III" (Article 10. 2).

This prescription is implemented in the EEC Directive as follows:

> "In the case of migratory species, [Member States] shall see in particular that the species to which hunting regulations apply are not hunted during their period of reproduction or during their return to their rearing grounds" (Article 7. 4).

Appendix II of the Berne Convention, which enumerates species that are to be strictly protected (compare Article 6) also includes migratory birds. The EEC Directive prescribes strict protection for *all* species of wild birds (EEC Article 5). Thus, quite a few migratory species are totally protected by the two instruments.

The African Convention includes similar and equivalent prescriptions, with the exception that there is no general protection of all wild species of flora and fauna, and that there are no special prescriptions for migratory birds.

Protection of migratory birds by protection of habitat
The problem of habitat protection in general. As shown in *Table 2*, all six instruments discussed in this paper contain provisions for the protection of species' habitats, and five include special regulations concerning the habitats of migratory species. This is an indication that at least the significance of the problem has been recognized at the international level. It also becomes clear from the legal point of view that habitat protection is the main problem for the protection of species, and will increasingly be so.

The following facts make habitat protection a complex issue from the political and legal point of view:

– Habitat degradation is an insidious long term problem.
– Habitat degradation is caused by a great variety of human activities, and therefore...
– Habitat protection regulations can be dispersed in many different statutes and ought to be considered in many different decision-making processes.
– Habitat protection offers rewards only on a long-term basis, often probably only for future generations. Therefore a great deal of understanding and imagination is needed to be able to see the true value of the exercise. Therefore...
– Habitat protection as a matter of public interest (equal, for example, to economic interest) is a fact often forgotten by authorities and denied by certain politicians.

These problems are also reflected in the formulation of the regulations concerning the protection of habitats and their management. Both give the impression that everybody recognizes the need for protection but is rather helpless as to how this is to be brought about. This phenomenon becomes even worse, where migratory birds are concerned. It manifests itself in vague, generalized formulations of the regulations, and great difficulties in finding a way of interpreting them that is acceptable to all parties to the convention.

I discern two main reasons for this phenomenon. On one side, the need for habitat protection on a large scale is a very recent problem, on the other side it concerns questions of the free disposition of landed property, which is politically often very difficult to restrict.

The individual regulations

As *Table 2* shows, there are two instruments that concentrate on habitat protection: Ramsar and World Heritage:

Ramsar concentrates on one type of habitat, the wetlands. Each contracting party is obliged to designate "suitable wetlands within its territory" for inclusion in the "List of Wetlands of International Importance", including at least one at the time it signs, ratifies or accedes to the convention. The inclusion in the list obliges the parties to "formulate and implement their planning so as to promote the conservation of the wetlands" (Article 3. 1).

Migratory birds are explicitly mentioned in Article 2. 6 of the convention:

"Each contracting party shall consider its international responsibilities for the conservation, management and wise use of migratory stock of waterfowl, both, when designating entries for the List and when exercising its right to change entries in the List relating to wetlands within its territory."

In addition, the more general criteria for the selection of these wetlands in Article 2. 2 also take account of migratory birds:

"Wetlands should be selected for the List on account of their international significance in terms of ecology, botany, zoology, limnology or hydrology. In the first instance, wetlands of international importance to waterfowl at any season should be included."

As already mentioned, since the very beginning, the conference of the contracting parties to the Ramsar Convention was engaged in elaborating more specific selection criteria by which to judge the international importance of individual wetlands, and it is in these efforts that migratory birds are mainly considered. So, one criterion for using plants or animals to identify wetlands of importance is whether the wetland is of special value as the habitat of plants or animals at a critical stage of their biological cycles, a criterion which I think could easily be more clearly formulated in favour of migratory birds (Regina Recommendations, Annex 2c). Furthermore, the Regina Recommendation on the "Need for further studies of flyways", concerned about the "recent and severe decline in numbers of waders (shorebirds) in the Western Hemisphere", "emphasizes the need to establish reserves at wetlands linked by migratory birds" (Recommendation C.3.2.).

The World Heritage Convention is in the first place not a nature conservation convention, but one intended to conserve objects of "outstanding universal value", being a part of the natural and cultural heritage of the world. Its value for wildlife will always be limited because only the world's most select natural (and cultural) areas are to be protected under this convention.

So are considered as "Natural Heritage" only:

"...geological and physiographical formations and precisely delineated areas which constitute the habitat of threatened species of animals and plants of outstanding universal value from the point of view of science or conservation" (Article 2. II).

It is also important to know, that, in contrast to the Ramsar Convention, sites cannot be designated unilaterally by the contracting parties but are selected by the World Heritage Committee from propositions made by the parties in whose territories the sites are situated. However, migratory species are mentioned in the criteria for the inclusion of natural properties in the World Heritage List. Sites, in order to be eligible as "Natural Heritage Sites" must, among other things, fulfil the "condition of integrity". In the case of sites selected for their importance for species protection, this means that they:

"...should be of sufficient size and contain necessary habitat requirements for the survival of the species, and should have adequate long-term legislative, regulatory or institutional protection."
"In the case of migratory species, seasonable sites necessary for their survival, wherever they are located, should be adequately protected. Agreements made in this connection, either through adherence to international conventions or in the form of other multilateral or bilateral agreements, would provide this assurance" (UNESCO 1988, No. 36b. (iv) (v)).

To be of "outstanding universal value", sites that are to be selected for species protection have further to:

"...contain the most important and significant natural habitats where threatened species of animals or plants of outstanding universal value from the point of view of science or conservation still survive" (UNESCO 1988, No. 36/36 a (iv)).

Even if applicable only to outstanding cases as defined above, the possible usefulness of this instrument, for birds in general and for migratory birds in particular (e.g. in combination with an AGREEMENT of the Bonn Convention) is quite obvious. The broad adherence as shown in *Figure 1* and *Table 3*, and the financial assistance that can be granted to poorer countries, could prove useful especially for cooperation with African countries. (For details see Lyster 1985, p. 229.ff and the Operational Guidelines, UNESCO 1988). Yet it escapes my knowledge whether an application has ever been made for the inclusion of a pure "species-protection-site" in the World Heritage List as could be imagined, for example, for important habitats of the Bald Ibis (*Geronticus emerita*) or the Slender-billed Curlew (*Numenius tenuirostris*) in Africa.

Of the three comprehensive conventions treated here – Berne, the EEC-Directive and the African Convention – only the latter contains no special regulations concerning the conservation of migratory species' habitats. However its requirements for habitat protection are very detailed and in many ways exemplary, and are certainly worthy of consideration here. On the one hand the convention emphasises the need to establish "conservation areas", and it defines several different categories ("strict nature reserve", "national park", "special reserve"; compare Article III. 4) corresponding to different conservation needs. Amongst other aims, these are designed to:

> "...ensure the conservation of all species, and more particularly those listed or which may be listed in the annexes to this Convention" (Article X. 1 (i)).

This is a remarkable obligation as, literally interpreted, it means that each party is required to conserve enough habitat to ensure the survival of each species living in its territory. On the other hand the African Convention also puts great weight on the protection of habitats outside the protected areas, by prescribing sustainable use of all natural resources: soil, water, flora and faunal resources (Articles IV-VII). The "Fundamental Principle" of the convention is that:

> "Contracting States shall undertake to adopt measures to ensure conservation, utilization and development of soil, water, flora and faunal resources in accordance with scientific principles and with due regard to the best interests of the people" (Article II).

It is possible that such an ideal wording of the obligations of the convention was only accepted because of the rather programmatic character of the convention, and the fact that no measures to control implementation were provided for. But under those premises the African Convention is certainly worthy of being taken into consideration.

The Berne Convention in its article concerning habitat protection (Article 4) obliges contracting parties, with regard to migratory birds, to:

> "...undertake to give special attention to the protection of areas that are of importance for the migratory species specified in Appendices I and III and which are appropriately situated in relation to migration routes, as wintering, staging, feeding, breeding or moulting areas (Article 4. 3).

In addition contracting parties are generally obliged to:

> "...coordinate their efforts for the protection of the migratory species specified in Appendices II and III whose range extends into their territories" (Article 10.1).

In order to fullfil these provisions, the contracting parties are obliged to:

"...take appropriate and necessary legislative and administrative measures to ensure the conservation of [these] habitats" (Article 4. 1). "They shall have regard in their planning and development policies to the conservation requirements of the areas protected" (Article 4. 2).

A more concrete prescription concerning a single problem of habitat protection is contained in Article 6 b, which prohibits – for the Appendix II species – "the deliberate damage or destruction of breeding or resting sites".

It is clear that the prescriptions of Article 4 are expressed in rather general terms. This is true also for the part not concerning migratory species. "It is clear that the intention of the negotiators was to provide for a general framework within which specific implementation measures could be taken in the future (de Klemm 1988). The Explanatory Report concerning the convention emphasizes that, "the experts felt that this article should not be too explicit in order to keep it open for developing cooperation between the contracting parties (paragraph 23 of the Explanatory Report) (compare also below).

The EEC Directive on the conservation of wild birds is considered a more detailed interpretation of the Berne Convention concerning wild birds (cf. Muntingh's report to the European Parliament 1988). Being a formalization of Berne Convention and Community Law, the Directive is more explicit in regard to the measures to be taken. These include the creation of protected areas; upkeep and management in accordance with the ecological needs of habitats inside and outside the protected zones; re-establishment of destroyed biotopes; and creation of biotopes (Article 3. 2 a-d). Article 6 b of the Berne Convention on destruction of nests and eggs is repeated verbatim in the Directive (Article 5 b).

The Directive also provides for, "special conservation measures concerning [the birds'] habitat, in order to ensure their survival and reproduction in their area of distribution" for all birds mentioned in Annex I (144 species) selected according to the criteria listed in Article 4. 1 a-d. Furthermore, of particular importance in the present context is the requirement that:

"Member States shall take similar measures for regularly ocurring migratory species not listed in Annex I, bearing in mind their need for protection in the geographical sea and land area where this Directive applies...as regards their breeding, moulting and wintering areas and staging posts along their migration routes..."

It is obvious, that the EEC Directive, being – at least theoretically and formally – more compelling than the conventions, is the ideal instrument by which to create networks for migratory birds within its geographical range. This idea is taken into account in Article 4. 3:

"Member States shall send the Commission all relevant information so that it may take appropriate initiatives with a view to the coordination necessary to ensure that the areas provided for in paragraphs 1 and 2 above form a coherent whole which meets the protection requirements of these species in the geographical sea and land area where this Directive applies."

Outlook: The efforts of the Standing Committee of the Berne Convention and of the Commission of the EC

The main question in the problem of habitat protection is how and to what extent habitats are to be protected; for the problem with the respective articles, especially in the Berne Convention and probably also in the EEC Directive is, as de Klemm (1988) formulates it for the Berne Convention, "that these articles seem to have been understood as requiring the conservation of all the habitats of wild flora and fauna species. As this is obviously impossible, contracting parties and the Standing Committee have tended to disregard this provision, or at least to consider it as an unrealistic expression of an ideal conservation target which was impossible to attain". This is clearly a problem of interpretation. The Standing Committee of the Berne Convention has tried to find a solution to this problem for as long as it has existed, but for many years without success despite some quite good background work by the Council of Europe. Finally, in an extraordinary meeting of the Standing Committee in June 1989, an interpretative resolution and three recommendations concerning the protection of habitat were accepted. Interesting in this context is that it was IUCN (the World Conservation Union) as an NGO who in 1987 initiated this finally successful attempt by criticizing the lack of implementation of the Berne Convention, especially of the habitat protection regulations. Subsequently, IUCN was given the mandate to work out propositions for the solution to the problem.

The resolution provides interpretations of the most important terms of Article 4 of the Berne Convention – notably those concerning the protection of habitats, such as "habitat of a species", "necessary measures", "appropriate measures", "conservation".

Of particular interest in our context is the interpretation of "areas that are of importance for migratory birds":

> "Areas of importance for the migratory species specified in Appendices II and III" means the critical sites, wherever situated, of those migratory species that have been identified by the Standing Committee, on the basis of scientific evidence, as requiring specific habitat conservation measures."

In Recommendation 14 (1989) of the "Standing Committee to the Contracting Parties on Species Habitat Conservation and on Conservation of Endangered Natural Habitats", the Standing Committee recommends that the contracting parties:

> "...identify in the areas within their jurisdiction...migratory species requiring specific habitat conservation measures;
> ...species of which the breeding and/or resting sites require protection, and the breeding and/or resting site types requiring protection;
> and for each of these categories to indicate as far as possible their sites...
> [and] ensure that appropriate and necessary measures of conservation are taken for the species, habitats and sites identified..." (1. c, d; 4).

Also important in our context is Recommendation 16 (1989) on "Areas of Special Conservation Interest", which recommends contracting parties to:

> "...take steps to designate areas of special conservation interest to ensure that necessary and appropriate conservation measures are taken for each area situated within its territory or under its responsibility where that area fits one or several of the following conditions."

Amongst others, the criteria are that the area:

> "...contributes substantially to the survival of threatened species, endemic species, or any species listed in Appendices I and II of the convention;
> ...represents an important area for one or more migratory species."

Further measures relating to the management, supervision and conservation of these areas are also recommended.

I think these recommendations are good and valuable instruments for the protection of important migratory bird habitats (e.g. bottle-neck areas) once they are identified. That ICBP, with its *Important Bird Areas in Europe* (Grimmett & Jones 1989) could provide important information is obvious; indeed the organization has already made an important contribution by preparing a shadow list of sites for the Ramsar convention (Langeveld & Grimmett 1990).

At this point it has to be mentioned that efforts are also being made in the EC to improve the protection of habitat. The Commission has worked out a proposal for a Council Directive on the protection of natural and semi-natural habitats and of wild fauna and flora (COM (88) 381 final). "The fundamental aim of the proposal is to establish...a comprehensive network of protected areas aimed at ensuring the maintenance of threatened species and threatened types of habitats in all the regions of the Community where they occur, thus achieving more effective implementation within the Community of the Berne Convention on the conservation of European wildlife and natural habitats as well as other complementary measures appropriate to the Community framework".

Two main reasons are given for the necessity of such a directive. The first is to promote the "sharing of knowledge at European level and the coordination of management and conservation strategies, in particular for species that are endangered in one or more Member States or whose natural range extends across several Member States". The second is "to avoid threats to national or regional wildlife resources by Community actions... . This is a vital issue, for many of the main pressures for agricultural intensification and expansion, tourism, transport and industrial development come from the Community's own sectoral policies" (COM (88) 381, 1 and 2).

A critical view of these regulations

Setting aside the problem of geographical coverage, the substantial content of the conventions discussed seems at first sight quite appropriate to the needs of migratory birds.   However we are still faced with the well-known and often-mentioned weaknesses of international public law in general and of international nature conservation law in particular.

I will try to give a short summary of those criticisms.

– Concerning wording and content of the conventions:
  • the text is too vague
  • the text expresses only the lowest common denominator
  • too many exceptions and reservations are possible.

– Concerning international jurisdiction:
  • there is no compulsory jurisdiction of international courts
  • and therefore there is no institution capable of giving an authoritative interpretation of regulations needing such clarification.

– Concerning implementation:
  • contracting parties generally do not implement their obligations

- on ratifying the contract, they have made reservations which counteract seriously the aims of the convention.

- Finally the general impression is that the conference of the parties does not really contribute much to resolving these problems.

In the next section I shall give some reasons for these difficulties and subsequently try to show how NGOs can help to improve the situation.

IMPLEMENTATION PROBLEMS CONSIDERED UNDER SOME GENERAL ASPECTS OF INTERNATIONAL PUBLIC LAW

The implications of the sovereignty of states; consensus and its problems

One of the basic principles of public international law is the recognition of the sovereignty of states. Legally, all this means is that a state is independent. That is to say, a sovereign state is able to take any action it thinks fit which is not prohibited by international law and as long as it does not interfere with the rights of other states. In particular, in our context concerning the problem of habitat protection, a sovereign state has complete freedom to deal with its own territory.

The term sovereignty also includes the notion that a state is free to renounce, for example by treaty, at least some of its sovereign rights. But, and this is a central point in this context, this is valid only if done at the state's own free will. That means that in principle, decisions on international matters can be taken only by unanimous decision of the states involved and never by decision of the majority. In practical terms this means that disagreements must be resolved by discussion and compromise. The effects of this on the content of multilateral contracts are largely known and often criticized. The result is the lowest common denominator in the substantive content of the contract and the provisions regulating control measures, and the well-known phenomenon of ambiguous or vague formulation of what are – from the point of view of nature protection – the most interesting parts of the conventions.

These observations lead us to two conclusions. Obviously, the greater the socio-cultural diversity of prospective contracting parties, the more difficult it is to achieve a consensus. That means that, at least theoretically, regional conventions ought to have a better chance of being effective than conventions that are meant to have a worldwide coverage. Equally obvious is the conclusion that conventions treating only one or a restricted number of objectives have a greater chance of being widely accepted than conventions covering widely differing aims.

Viewed in this light, various questions about the content and intended geographical range of the conventions become clear; e.g. why the two comprehensive conventions, African and Berne, aim at a regional coverage and not at a worldwide one, and why the worldwide conventions, Ramsar and World Heritage, treat only a restricted number of objectives. It also becomes clear why some conventions cover an even smaller geographical range, and split up the content in different protocols which can be negotiated and accepted individually, rather than attempt to work out one comprehensive text, which would make consensus so much more difficult to obtain. So, for example, we have the Convention for the Protection of the Mediterranean Sea against Pollution (Barcelona Convention 1976) with its four protocols, the last concerning Mediterranean Specially Protected Areas, and the Convention for the Protection, Management and Development of the Marine and Coastal Environment of the Eastern African Region and its Protocol concerning Protected Areas and Wild

Fauna and Flora in the Eastern African Region (1985). And, of course, the system incorporated in the Bonn Convention is also meant to facilitate consensus between the parties of an AGREEMENT. It is going to be very interesting to observe whether this idea will work. For migratory birds there is the obvious difficulty that quite a few AGREEMENTS ought to be concluded between European and African countries, and the existing huge socio-cultural and socio-economic gaps between the two continents could make consensus very difficult to obtain.

In the context of this consensus problem it must be mentioned that the practice of concluding equivocal or vague agreements is an acknowledged diplomatic technique. In a monograph about "Managing the risks of international agreements", Bilder (1981 p. 37ff) states that "ambiguity can also be used as a conscious technique, clearly understood and recognized by the parties, for dealing with risks they perceive. Views differ as to the usefulness of this technique. Some commentators believe that equivocal or ambiguous international agreements are wholly illusory and not at all useful, giving the appearance of genuine agreement and shared understandings when in fact there are none. Others argue that deliberate equivocality or ambiguity often serves a useful function. Even where the parties cannot reach common understandings on issues central to their agreement, ambiguous or equivocal language permits them at least to commit themselves to cooperative approaches to the problem. Moreover, simply having a written agreement may promote an improvement in attitudes and establish an institutional framework and negotiating parameters in which a more genuine agreement can, over time, be more easily achieved."

As is mentioned in this quotation, in cases of ambiguous formulation the problem is obviously not resolved by the conclusion of the convention. For these, critical yet obscure formulations have to be somehow rendered applicable by interpretation. It is true that primarily the legislative, administrative or jurisdictional institutions of the contracting parties themselves have to interpret the conventions in order that they can be put into effect. But for other contracting parties, these unilateral interpretations cannot be binding – unless, at the time, they have been accepted by all member states as what is called a "quasi-authentic interpretation". An interpretation of the convention which *is* binding for all contracting parties (a so called "authentic interpretation") has also to be agreed upon by all member states. That means that any questions not resolved in the convention invariably reappear later on. This permanent and patient work on the perfection of the conventions must not be perceived as negative: the processes involved can have the advantage of contributing significantly to an effective evolution of problem-conciousness within the member states. Two examples are especially appropriate as illustrations of this fact. One is the history of the habitat protection article of the Berne convention. In its explanatory report it is stated that, "the experts felt that this article should not be too explicit in order to keep [the matter] open for developing cooperation between the contracting parties". This statement, seen in the context of the information given above, appears in quite a different light and the results of the last conference of the contracting parties, which managed to make an important step to clarify this regulation supports this thesis.

The other example is the well-known evolution of the Ramsar Convention. Since its signature in 1971 it developed from a rather programmatic and weak instrument to a very mature convention with a broad adherence. Worthy of note here are the continuous efforts made in developing and clarifying the criteria for the selection of wetlands, and mainly the adoption of the Paris Protocol in 1982, which allows the parties to amend the convention, and subsequently the adoption of the Regina Amendments which established a regular "Conference of the Parties" with expanded competences and a financial budget which finally permits the conference to have its own bureau.

It seems to me to be very significant that in both cases NGOs played an important or even initiating role in the further evolution of the conventions. The development of Ramsar is due mainly to the initiatives taken and the efforts made by IUCN and IWRB (the former in its function as temporary and unpaid secretariat until the revision of 1987 entered into force), the success in interpreting Article 4 of the Berne Convention and the initiative taken and the background work done by IUCN.

In this context I think it is important to note two facts. The first is that consensus must not be seen as a static phenomenon, definitively fixed by the conclusion of the convention, but rather as a dynamic process involving the parties to the contract. This process includes the development and raising of awareness, and the re-evaluation of opinions on the part of all the contracting parties, a result which I think is very important. Secondly it is of great importance for conservation NGOs to recognize that, as shown in the examples above, this process can be influenced. That means that not only is the substantial content of the written text of a convention of importance, but just as important are the opportunities for communication, discussion, negotiation and innovation it offers. For the NGOs of course it is essential that they are given the opportunity to introduce themselves into this process.

Summing up, the following statements can be made. The shortcomings in the wording and the content of the conventions are due mainly to the difficulties of finding a consensus. As consensus is not a static fact, but rather a dynamic process, it is important for the improvement of the convention that contracting parties are kept active, that regular meetings are provided for, and that NGOs have the opportunity to take part in these meetings.

The peculiarities of Conservation Conventions and their effect on implementation and traditional control systems

The problems of consensus are not the only handicap affecting implementation of our contracts. Another complication lies in the so-called "non-reciprocity" of the nature conservation conventions.

In the "classic" international treaty, for example a trade agreement, the contracting parties commit themselves respectively to a certain performance and counter-performance (basic example: merchandise in return for payment). If in these conventions one party does not fulfill its obligation, for example by failing to deliver the merchandise, the payment will not be made. Thus, in these classic treaties, control of performance is automatically inherent as they are based on a system of reciprocal fulfilment. Not so the obligations of the nature conservation conventions discussed here. Certainly the obligation to honour the treaty exists between the parties; but the actual fulfilment is to take place within the territory of each of the contracting parties (so called "non-reciprocity"). Non-implementation hardly has any direct effect upon neighbouring states or other contracting parties, and so cannot be directly controlled or sanctioned. There seems even to be a contrary effect. Parties often will not react to poor implementation by other members for fear of being caught themselves not duly performing their duty.

Further, the last means of enforcing the fulfilment of a contractual obligation is generally to bring about a juridical decision. The international equivalent of "going to court" is recourse to international arbitration or to the International Court of Justice at the Hague. But in either event – and in contrast with national legal systems – proceedings cannot take place without the consent of the prospective defendant. Anyway, cases brought before an international court are extremly rare and have up to now never taken place for the conventions discussed here. States are reluctant to take each other to the international court, partly because it is seen as a politically unfriendly act, to be avoided if possible (Lyster 1985, p. 11).

Obvious exceptions in this context are the experiences with the EEC Directive, which is the only international instrument that can be enforced by an ordinary judicial procedure. Several judgements have been rendered by the court of the EC against member countries whose legislation did not comply with the provisions of the directive. However, it seems that this fact did not really improve the situation. A report for the European Parliament on the implementation of the "Birds Directive" enumerates more or less the same difficulties as mentioned above for other conventions (Muntingh, Document A2-0181/88). In short, the problem of non-implementation is (at least partly) due to the non-reciprocity of the contracts. Traditional devices such as inter-party controls or going to court do not work, as this is considered an unfriendly act. But even in the EC, where an ordinary judicial procedure exists, the situation seems not to be significantly better.

Problems in controlling the implementation of conventions, and strategies aimed at resolving them

Simplified, it could be stated that the whole problem is rather like writing a paper: without outside pressure of any kind, nothing (or very little) is going to happen, and so little action is taken to implement the conventions discussed. This fact is apt to provoke two main reactions, neither of which is very helpful in resolving the problems. The first is the attitude that "international law is useless anyway; that efforts to change the actions of governments are doomed to failure; and that there is no point in trying. This view leaves lawless governments with the freedom they desire to remain lawless and to scoff at the efforts of international bodies which barely continue to exist with the minimal resources and personnel they possess". There are others, moreover, who construct visionary plans for international courts and world governments, who fail to see the real limitations which the national state has placed upon nearly all international bodies, and who, in short, provide support for the majority who believe that there is no point in trying" (Weissbrodt 1977).

For us it is important to realize that the specific problems of these "non-reciprocal" treaties are not new. They are well known from the treaties on human rights which also concern events occurring within the territory of the contracting parties. And both human rights treaties and nature conservation treaties have to deal with the historical fact that any controlling powers over the territory of a state, and its inhabitants, are by definition attributes of the sovereignty of a state and part of the so-called "domaine réservé", with which no one has any right to interfere. It is in the domain of the human rights treaties that "devices to secure compliance" have been developed, described and studied. As the NGOs in my opinion play an important role in these control measures, it is important that they are informed about these possibilities.

Control strategies at international level. International strategies to control the implementation of human rights and conservation conventions are based on the following main factors. First, that conventions that are not always kept at the forefront of the parties' attention are bound to be forgotten, to become "sleeping treaties" which are formally still in force but are not applied any more and are really more or less forgotten (e.g. the International Convention for the Protection of Birds, Paris 1902, revised 1950; and the African Convention). In this respect it is very important that the parties are kept active by a system of administration to monitor and oversee the convention's enforcement.

Secondly, that "states have a definite interest in prestige and are therefore highly sensitive to public opinion, both abroad and at home. Violations of international law may cause considerable loss of prestige. ...This is... the reason for the practical importance of non-governmental actors denouncing violations" (Bothe 1981, p. 105). Continuing, Bothe makes a statement that is very true and important: "Public pressure, however, is not the only form of inducing compliance, and it is not necessarily more effective than more discrete forms of influence. The International Committee of the Red Cross relies instead on a non-public approach to bring about compliance with international law... thus allowing a state to change an unlawful attitude or practice without losing face".

Thirdly, that under some conventions the control measures are based on the fact that non-implementation is best objected to by the individual aggrieved by it. Therefore one of the most effective (sometimes *the* most effective) means of control in the human rights treaties is the right of complaint of the individual as, for example, is possible under the European Human Rights Convention (Article 25). Some authors even believe that "there can be no prospect of success unless the system of control can be put into operation not only pursuant to governmental action but also by the alleged victim of a violation... or by a non-governmental institution..." (Golsong 1963, p. 141). Transferred to the implementation of nature conservation conventions that would mean that NGOs ought to be assigned the right to complain to an independent body, as is already realized in part, and with good success, at national level (cf. for Switzerland, Matter 1981, and for the principal foundation Gündling 1980).

Control measures provided for in the treaties discussed. In *Table 4* I have tried to give an overview of the measures to resolve the implementation problem provided for in the treaties discussed.

TRADITIONAL: The means of going to court is hardly ever applied. Neither are conflicts resolved by negotiation in a classical sense between two concerned parties but rather by general discussion in the meeting of the parties. This latter aspect is listed under **Communication**.

BASIC: Before implementation of contracts can be controlled, it must of course be clear to all parties what this implementation ought to consist of. Therefore, under **Basic** are listed those means (among other) that are the basis for clarifying interpretation. The example of Ramsar has clearly shown how important it is to be able to amend a convention. And the example of the interpretation of the Berne habitat protection regulation shows the importance of the competence of the Parties Committee to issue recommendations. This importance is also illustrated by the Ramsar Amendments, which give the Conference of the Contracting Parties, *inter alia*, the competence to "adopt other recommendations or resolutions to promote the functioning of this Convention" (Article 6, paragraph 2f).

"NON-JUDICIAL MEANS": Under this heading are listed the "devices to secure compliance" (Bothe 1981) as provided for in the treaties discussed. Under **Communication** are listed the means which I think important for promoting the consensus process as described above. Of course the parties' meetings are also extremely important to keep the conventions in the attention of the parties, especially if at these meetings reports are discussed. The importance of the admittance of NGO observers is obvious. As described above it is often they who provide new input and contribute topics for discussion and so further the development process.

Table 4: Principal means of securing compliance under the various treaties.

	Africa	Ramsar	Heritage	Bonn	Berne	EC
I. TRADITIONAL						
Negotiation Arbitration	Art. 18	–	–	–	Art. 13	Art. 13
Int. Court	–	–	–	–	–	
II. BASIC						
Amendment	Art. 19	R	Art. 37	Art. 10	Art. 16	Art. 15-17
Interpret. Definitions	Art. 3	Art. 1	Art. 1/2/i	Art. 1	(i)	
Recommend.		Art. 6/R	(i)	Art. 5e	Art. 14	
III. NON-JUDICIAL MEANS						
A) Communication						
Parties meet.	Art. 16.3	Art. 6.1/R		Art. 7	Art. 13-15	
Committee			Art. 8.1			
NGO Observer	–	R /i	Art. 8.3	Art. 7.9	Art. 13	
B) Organisation						
Secretariat		Art. 8	Art. 14.1	Art. 9		
	OAU	IUCN	UNESCO		CoE	
Scientific C.	–	–		Art. 8		
Consultative			Art. 10.3		Art. 14.2	
Finances	OAU	R 6.5/6	Art. 15-18	Art. 8.4	CoE	
C) Member States						
Reporting	Art. 16	Art. 3.2/I	Art. 29	Art. 6	Art. 9/i	Art. 9.3
Inspections	–	–	–	–	i	–
Financial Incentives	–	–	Art. 15	–	–	–

Key: R = Introduced by revision of the convention
    i = By interpretation

The importance of the means listed here under **Organisation** is illustrated by the history of the Ramsar Convention. The tremenduous contribution of the Ramsar "Bureau", in spite of its restricted competences and finances, to the working and implementation of the convention is undenied. Also it is significant that the amendments accepted concern, *inter alia*, competences of the secretariat and the financing of the convention, and that these items were directly taken up by the conference of the contracting parties in resolutions "on Secretariat Matters" and "on Financial and Budgetary Matters" to provide for respective intermediary measures until the coming into force of the Regina amendments.

Under **Member States** are listed the means employed to keep contracting parties active. In this respect reporting duties prove to be extremely useful. "If parties have to submit regular reports on what they have done to enforce a treaty, they may prefer to comply with the treaty rather than have to report that they have done nothing. Reporting requirements work especially well if reports have to be submitted to a formal meeting of the parties – and are even more effective if that meeting is open to non-governmental conservation organizations, which are quick to publicize poor enforcement and to bring the weight of public opinion to bear on transgressor states" (Lyster 1985, p. 13).

Inspections "on the scene" are obviously a rather problematic form of control measure, and only possible with the consent of the party concerned.

The function of NGOs in control strategies. At an international colloquium on human rights, the role of NGOs in the implementation of human rights agreements at the United Nations (UN) has been characterized as follows:

> "The NGO has several roles; it functions as a pressure group and fulfils supervising and criticizing functions and acts as an intermediate and bridge with two lanes between the UN and the outside world. It supplies information in the domain of its competence and detects those domains needing special vigilance. Its means are restricted. Its power is based on persuasion as well as on the weight of public opinion.
>
> In the UN, the role of the NGOs as supervisor, as watchdog and independent critic, is primordial. The role requires that the NGOs are independent and outside the process of decision-making. They must therefore avoid becoming involved in negotiations and compromises between governments on subjects which, for the NGOs, do not support any compromises" (Picken 1986).

Taking into account the similarities between human rights and conservation conventions, such statements can very well be generalized and applied also to NGOs concerned with nature protection. I should like to emphasize especially the importance of the ornithological NGOs. As widely ramified independent bodies involved, very often, in serious scientific research, these NGOs are able to obtain – at international level – widespread and detailed information that no governmental or international agency is able to gather (except perhaps at least theoretically the EC) (e.g. the International Waterfowl Census, Moser this volume; or the inventory of Important Bird Areas in Europe, Grimmett & Jones 1989). The NGOs are therefore able to give valuable input and sound and constructive criticism to the work done (or not done) by governments to implement the obligations of the conventions.

It is important to realize that the function NGOs ought to take over, according to the statement quoted above, is also an eminently political one. Nature conservation NGOs are still too often consulted for technical advice only, and often do not even consider themselves as having (potential) political influence. Some statements made in 1974 about the role of NGOs in UN environmental politics, based on research made in the context of the Stockholm Conference and the establishment of the UN Environmental Programme, may illustrate this opinion:

- "Many transnational associations regard themselves as 'non-political'.
- Contacts among technical specialists in international non-governmental organizations (INGOs), international governmental organizations (IGOs) and governments are likely to be close, important and not very visible.
- IGOs are more likely to be influenced by those INGOs that can be used in implementing the IGOs programmes than by those which cannot.

- IGOs may ask INGOs to carry out programmes or implement resolutions that the IGO or member states are themselves unable or unwilling to undertake.
- It is difficult to achieve concerted action by groups of INGOs because of the diversity of their interests and positions on a wide range of subjects" (Thompson Feraru 1974, p. 31-55).

In this context it must also be clearly stated that contracting parties are not always very keen on this kind of political engagement and easily tend to regard NGOs as intruders in their domestic affairs. Therefore considerable delicacy and diplomatic skill is needed to find the best way to achieve the purpose of improving the implementation of international conventions. On the other hand, in this context it is interesting to note that the report to the EC Council (Muntingh 1988) asks for more openness in matters concerning the Directive on the Protection of Wild Birds, and to this end – *inter alia* – proposes the integration of NGOs into the control mechanisms.

Strategies at national level. It is obvious that statements made about the possible engagement of the NGOs at the national level must remain very general. But two facts are quite certain. First, that treaties alone are not (generally) directly applicable but must normally be implemented by national legislation. This is important, because national law is easier to enforce than international law. Secondly, that the principles mentioned above for the control strategies at international level also hold good for the work done within the states. As on the national level too, obligations concerning the protection of nature tend either to be forgotten in the decision-making process, or not to be duly considered in the weighing of interests, if they are not regularly brought forward. And what is of great importance on the regional and local level, no administration official, even if he has an abundance of goodwill, is able to know as well as the members of regional and local NGOs, which natural sites are of value for nature protection. Therefore NGOs, and especially the ornithological NGOs, which at least in my country have a branch in nearly every village, bear much of the burden of responsibility of bringing forward this knowledge in order to defend the interests of nature.

The following is a rough overview of the different possible and/or necessary steps for the application of the conventions on the national level, with indications of where political or technical influence or perhaps even judicial steps to secure the implementation of the conventions could be possible or indicated (*Table 5*).

Legislation. The implementation of the conventions' obligations by national legislation is the necessary foundation and pre-condition for their implementation at national level. It is important that not only are concrete measures and behaviour regulated by legislation, but also that the procedural regulations make interventions from the private sector possible. As discussed above in this respect, the ideal target is the granting of a right of complaint or the capacity to sue for annulment of illegal administrative decisions, for (certain) non-governmental organizations. The introduction of environmental assessment procedures which encompass nature protection issues can also prove useful. It is important that regulations concerning nature protection are not only concentrated on (for example) nature conservation and hunting legislations, but that regulations about nature protection are also taken into consideration in other fields, for example, legislation regulating the utilization of soil and watercourses, land-use planning, forestry, agriculture, traffic planning, etc. The examples illustrate at what degree the concern of nature protection can become politically contested.

Table 5: Possible influences at national level.

A. LEGISLATION

Governmental action	NGO campaigning
initiation	education information political initiative
drafting and editing	technical advice
acceptance	political lobbying

B. IMPLEMENTATION

Governmental action	NGO campaigning
	information of adminstrative body
administrative measures in general	technical advice political influence, pressure legal control if possible
administrative planning and authorization procedures (land use planning, building licence)	legal means (objections) political influence

Implementation. The problem is that administrative officials usually do not have the same knowledge as many members of NGOs. Therefore information exchange and technical advice can be an important input by NGOs. However, it is also quite common for existing laws not to be applied, or to be incompletely applied. At this point lies the most crucial and hardest work of the NGOs on national, regional and local level: to make sure that the nature conservation legislation is properly enforced, by administrative actions in general and especially by those concerning authorizations and planning measures. This often requires extreme awareness, a lot of patience, and a thick skin.

This overview claims neither completeness nor an applicability in all its steps in all countries. However, I think it does show that in many domains nature conservation organizations are the only ones with the knowledge and independence to defend the interests of nature, by taking a course similar to the individual complaint in the human rights procedures. However, in this context I want to state explicitly that without the work done to increase public information and education, even the best conventions would be worthless.

CONCLUSION

In conclusion I want to make clear that my aim was not to criticize or minimize the present involvement of the NGOs but to provide information that might encourage these organizations (e.g. ICBP) to intensify their work, particularly on the juridico-political side of nature protection. I wanted to stress the fact that not only is it very important to cooperate with governments in giving technical advice, but that it is also important to know and make use of all possible legal means available and to act on the political front at all levels. Political action is a very delicate matter needing much diplomatic skill and realism. But I am persuaded that it is worthwhile, for it is the NGOs who acquire a large amount of information that nobody else is able to collect. It is they who are independent of political forces and thus relatively free to identify and criticize omissions by contracting parties. And last but not least, they are the only lobby that nature has.

ACKNOWLEDGEMENTS

First I should like to thank ICBP for their invitation to present this paper at the 17th European Continental Section Conference in Adana in May 1989. I consider interdisciplinary exchange of information in nature protection as being very important, and hope to have succeeded in finding a base of communication. Further I should like to thank the Matthieu-Foundation of Basle University for covering the entire cost of my participation in the Adana Conference. Important support for my work on habitat protection in international instruments, and the problems inherent in its implementation, which is partly anticipated in this paper, is granted by the Council of Europe, through Dr Jean-Pierre Ribaut and his staff of the Environment Conservation and Management Division of the Council of Europe (administering the Berne Convention) by their open and generous information policy. My thanks go also to everybody else who kindly procured valuable information for this paper, especially to Dr Tobias Salathé at the ICBP Secretariat. Last but not least a lot of thanks to Jean-Pierre and to Nicolas and Alison for their patience and understanding in sometimes stressed times.

FOOTNOTES

1 Environment and nature protection issues were originally based on Art. 100 and 235 of the treaty establishing the European Economic Community, 25 March 1957 (Treaty of Rome), since the acceptance of the 1986 "Single European Act" they are based on the new articles 130 r-t under the heading VII: Protection of the Environment.

2 There is an intended difference between "AGREEMENT" and "agreement." The published text of the Bonn Convention contains an important and apparently often reproduced misprint because it prints "agreements" in Article IV. 4 as "AGREEMENTS". This misprint was acknowledged in a 'Note Verbale' from the Ministry of Foreign Affairs of the Federal Republic of Germany to signatory governments dated 28 January 1982 (Lyster 1985, p. 291, note 42); cf. also Boere, this volume).

REFERENCES

BILDER, R. B. (1981) Managing the risks of international agreements. Madison: University of Wisconsin Press.

BOTHE, M. (1981) International Obligations: means to secure performance. Pp. 105 in R. Bernhardt, ed. *Encyclopedia of Public International Law, Vol. 1.*

GOLSONG, H. (1963) International Protection of Human Rights. Pp. 141 in *Académie de Droit International.* Recueil des Cours 1963 III.

GRIMMETT, R. F. A. & JONES, T. A. (1989) *Important bird areas in Europe.* Cambridge, U.K.: International Council for Bird Preservation (Techn. Publ. 9).

GÜNDLING, L. (1980) Public participation in environmental decision-making. Pp. 131-153 in Bothe, M., ed. *Trends in environmental policy and law.* Gland: International Union for the Conservation of Nature and Natural Resources.

IMBERT, P. H. (1979) La convention relative à la conservation de la vie sauvage et du milieu naturel de l'Europe, exception ou étape? Pp. 726 in *Annuaire français du droit international 1979.*

IUCN. (1986) *Migratory species in international instruments: an overview.* Gland: International Union for the Conservation of Nature and Natural Resources (Env. Policy and Law Occas. Pap. no. 2).

IUCN, UNEP & WWF. (1980) *World Conservation Strategy.* Gland: International Union for the Conservation of Nature and Natural Resources.

DE KLEMM, C. (1988) An interpretation of the provisions relating to the conservation of habitats in the Convention on the Conservation of European Wildlife and Natural Habitats, Part I. Council of Europe: Convention on the Conservation of European Wildlife and Natural Habitats (Doc. T-PVS (88) 30).

LYSTER, S. (1985) *International wildlife law.* Cambridge: Grotius Publications.

MATTER, F. (1981) Die Verbandsbeschwerde im schweizerischen Umweltschutzrecht. *Zeitschrift für Schweizerisches Recht, Neue Folge* 100I: 445-470.

MUNTINGH, M. H. J. (1988) Rapport fait au nom de la commission de l'environnement, de la santé publique et de la protection des consommateurs sur l'application dans la communauté européenne de la directive concernant la conservation des oiseaux sauvages. Parlement Européen, Document de Séance A2-0181/88.

PICKEN, M. (1986) Rôle des organisations non gouvernementales en matière de mise en oeuvre des droits de l'homme dans le cadre des Nations Unies. Pp. 137-149 in M. Bettati, *Les ONG et le Droit International.*

THOMPSON FERARU, A. (1974) Transnational political interest and the global environment. *Int. Org.* 28: 31-55.

WEISSBRODT, D. (1977) The role of international non-governmental organizations in the implementation of human rights. *Texas Int. Law J.* 12: 293-320.

THE BONN CONVENTION AND THE CONSERVATION OF MIGRATORY BIRDS

GERARD C. BOERE

*Ministry of Agriculture, Nature Management, and
Fisheries, Department of Nature Conservation,
Environmental Protection and Wildlife Management,
c/o National Forest Service, P.O. Box 1300,
3970 BH Driebergen, Netherlands*

ABSTRACT

The Convention for the Conservation of Migratory Species of Wild Animals (Bonn 1979) came into force in 1983. This young international wildlife treaty has gained much from experiences gained in the formulation of earlier treaties, and is a good instrument by which to promote close cooperation between countries that share populations of migratory animals. The protection of migratory birds forms part of the convention. The convention has three major provisions, which are discussed. For each of them examples are given of how the convention could be implemented. Coordination and stimulation of research, and monitoring of migratory bird populations, are important obligations for the parties. This provision could be used much more extensively to set up coordinated programmes, e.g. with developing countries.

Another important provision is the complete protection of 24 endangered bird species listed in Appendix I. Several examples illustrate the potential conservation power of this provision, such as complete habitat protection of critical areas, e.g. where Slender-billed Curlews (*Numenius tenuirostris*) occur, or the removal of electric power lines where these obstruct the migration routes of Dalmatian Pelicans (*Pelicanus crispus*).

The concluding of multilateral AGREEMENTS is a third provision. The convention requests Range States to work together for a species or a group of species whose conservation and management could benefit from international cooperation. Special management plans could be produced as part of an AGREEMENT. An outline is given of present work undertaken to conclude AGREEMENTS for the White Stork (*Ciconia ciconia*) and Western Palearctic Waterfowl. It is suggested that work should be started on the preparation of new AGREEMENTS for terns (Sternidae), birds of prey (Falconiformes) and cranes (Gruidea).

As a first step towards AGREEMENTS one can think of concluding agreements on a bilateral or multilateral basis, not only between governments, but also between administrative bodies of governments, and between government bodies and non-governmental organizations (NGOs). However, such agreements should never be a permanent substitute for AGREEMENTS. Throughout the paper a plea is made for a much more active policy from parties, Range States and NGOs to explore and use the provisions of this convention.

INTRODUCTION

Migratory movements of wild animals, birds in particular, may have taken place throughout the history of life on earth. Many wild birds respond to changing circumstances by searching for locations offering better living conditions. The result is an extremely complex and dynamic network of short, medium and long-distance migratory routes and movements across the earth.

Migratory birds have to cross political boundaries between nations: boundaries that have no inherent meaning for the birds, but which may have a dramatic influence on their annual life-cycles and their individual survival chances due to the large differences that exist between countries with respect to the conservation of bird populations and their habitats.

These influences are aggravated by the fact that it has long been held that migratory species legally do not fall within the jurisdiction of one particular country which could be held responsible for any harm occurring to them. However, the basis for agreements such as the Berne, Bonn and Ramsar conventions is a territorial responsibility, thus formulating obligations on the part of Range States for the conservation of species regardless of the time spent by those species within the states' borders. "Range State" means any state that exercises jurisdiction over any part of the range of a migratory species, e.g. all areas of land and water that a migratory species inhabits permanently or temporarily, crosses or overflies, etc. (see also Article I. f and h).

The notion that only the area where a species reproduces represents that species' distribution area does not make much sense from an ecological point of view. The negative effect of this idea has been that those countries in which a species occurs only during migration and in winter sometimes tend to feel less responsible for the conservation of such species (cf. Erz 1979). In my personal contacts with people and organizations from West African countries I have experienced a similar attitude towards Palearctic migrants in Africa. These are considered to be a European responsibility in the first place, and many African countries feel that they should focus their extremely limited resources on Afrotropical species only. From a biological perspective this approach is obviously not valid, considering that many Palearctic species spend so much time in their wintering areas that they could just as well be considered African species that only move north to breed (Mead 1983).

As a consequence of the establishment of an unnatural political segregation of the birds' distribution area, we do need legal instruments such as international conventions. These provide a platform on which governments can discuss the problems of migratory birds, and a framework for practical measures to use and manage bird populations wisely on the basis of a shared responsibility.

The Convention for the Conservation of Migratory Species of Wild Animals, known as the Bonn Convention (1979), is one such relatively young international legal instrument. It is, among other nature conservation conventions and treaties, intended to be used for the benefit of migratory birds, and it should be used for this purpose (*Figure 1*).

A BRIEF HISTORICAL OVERVIEW

The Bonn Convention is certainly not the first or only international agreement aiming at the conservation of migratory birds. An overview of historical and existing instruments has been published by Lyster (1985).

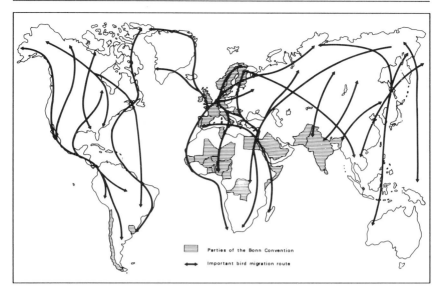

Figure 1: Parties to the Bonn Convention, and most important bird migration routes.

A first attempt to protect birds by international agreement was made by the Paris Convention (1902) (Convention for the Protection of Birds Useful to Agriculture), but it did not mention migratory birds specifically. This happened for the first time with the Convention for the Protection of Migratory Birds (1916) concluded by Canada and the U.S.A. and supplemented by the Convention for the Protection of Migratory Birds and Game Animals (1936) between the U.S.A. and Mexico.

The Migratory Bird Act between Canada and the U.S.A. is often referred to as an excellent example of close cooperation on the conservation of migratory birds. It has given birth to concrete action plans such as the North American Waterfowl Management Plan (1986), the establishment of flyway committees, the drafting of detailed management plans for individual species of waterfowl, and the Western Hemisphere Shorebird Reserve Network (see Hunter *et al.*, this volume).

Within the Old World, species of migratory birds were mentioned for the first time specifically in the second International Convention for the Protection of Birds (Paris 1950), substituting the 1902 Convention of Paris. The seventies brought a whole series of new international conventions concerning the conservation and management of wildlife. It was the period of inspired international nature conservation movements before, during and after the United Nations Conference on the Human Environment (Stockholm 1972). Many of these new international treaties included migratory birds (see Biber-Klemm, this volume). Some, however, exclusively concerned birds, such as the Benelux Convention on Hunting and Protection of Birds (1970); the Directive of the Council of the European Economic Community on the Conservation of Wild Birds (1979), and a number of bilateral conventions, e.g. between Japan and the U.S.A. (1972), the U.S.S.R. and Japan (1973), Japan and Australia (1974) and the U.S.S.R. and U.S.A. (1976). A similar bilateral convention on the conservation of migratory birds was also concluded between the U.S.S.R. and India in 1984, and several more are in preparation, e.g. U.S.S.R. and Australia and U.S.S.R. and China.

In 1983, IUCN published a very thorough study on a West Palearctic Migratory Wild Animals AGREEMENT. This IUCN study provides an excellent overview of all the legal aspects involved in such an AGREEMENT. The extensive text is often considered as a convention in its own right, but it is never adopted officially (IUCN 1983).

Lyster (1985) published a detailed overview with background information for each of these international treaties, and he describes their advantages and disadvantages. The earlier multilateral conventions for the protection of birds are mainly weak as far as their regulations are concerned. They do not require a regular meeting of the parties and do not have an appropriate administration or secretariat (the EEC Bird Directive is an exception). The bilateral conventions have by definition a restricted suitability for the protection of migratory birds because these species also pass through many countries in which the conventions do not apply. It is therefore not too surprising that, in spite of these existing conventions, a new worldwide convention has been drafted to deal with these problems. This new convention became the Bonn Convention for the conservation of *all* migratory animals: not only migratory birds.

What is an AGREEMENT?

AGREEMENTS are formal international legal documents under the Bonn Convention (Article IV. 1, 2, 3) to be drafted for Appendix II species with priority for species having an unfavourable conservation status. Range States can participate in such AGREEMENTS *without* being parties to the Bonn Convention.

Article V gives a whole series of guidelines for AGREEMENTS. Most important is that the object of AGREEMENTS shall be to restore a migratory species or group of species to a favourable conservation status, or to maintain it in such a status.

The Bonn Convention encourages parties also to conclude "agreements" for the conservation of other migratory species. (See p. 354)

THE BONN CONVENTION: GENERAL ASPECTS

Recommendation 32 of the United Nations Conference on the Human Environment (Stockholm 1972) asked governments to undertake actions to protect by international legislation migratory species that cross international boundaries. Work towards such legislation was undertaken by the Federal Republic of Germany in close consultation with the IUCN Environmental Law Centre, and was concluded in 1979 with the signing of the Convention for the Conservation of Migratory Species of Wild Animals, the "Bonn Convention".

The Bonn Convention came into force in 1983 after ratification by 15 parties, and convened its first meeting of the Conference of the Parties in 1985, also in Bonn. A second meeting was convened in Geneva in October 1988. In May 1991 the number of parties to the Bonn Convention was 35 (*Table 1*). It is a basic nature conservation convention aiming to conserve migratory wild animals, including birds, regardless of the origin and nature of the threats they are facing, as clearly stated in the Fundamental Principles (Article II. 2).

The broad approach of the Bonn Convention means that in principle all kinds of conservation issues can be addressed in an integrated way, such as pollution,

Table 1: Parties to the Bonn Convention (situation on 1 May 1991).

Belgium	Hungary	Panama
Benin	India	Portugal
Burkina Faso	Ireland	Saudi Arabia
Cameroon	Israel	Senegal
Chile	Italy	Somalia
Denmark	Luxembourg	Spain
Egypt	Mali	Sri Lanka
European Economic	Netherlands	Sweden
Community	Niger	Tunisia
Finland	Nigeria	United Kingdom
Germany	Norway	Uruguay
Ghana	Pakistan	Zaire

habitat protection, exploitation (including hunting), land use management, recreation, etc. providing these are important for the well-being of an animal population. Conservation measures may vary between Range States because the nature of the threats can differ considerably. Illegal hunting may be a threat in one Range State whereas pollution may be the major problem for the same population in another Range State.

SPECIFIC PROVISIONS OF THE BONN CONVENTION

The Bonn Convention has three major provisions by which to implement the fundamental principles of conserving migratory species (as described in Article II). These are that:

– Parties should promote, coordinate and support research relating to migratory species.
– Parties shall endeavour to provide immediate protection for migratory species included in Appendix I (*Table 2*).
– Parties shall endeavour to conclude AGREEMENTS covering the conservation and management of migratory species included in Appendix II (*Table 3*).

These are quite strongly formulated provisions, and the possible consequences of their implementation are discussed below.

Research
It is not surprising that a major provision of the convention is concerned with research, since the obligations to be included in future AGREEMENTS must be based on a sound knowledge of the migration patterns and behaviour of the species involved.

Despite increasing efforts in this field, many aspects of bird migration are still not well known. These need to be clarified before conservation and management measures can be allocated to certain Range States. It is also an important provision to stimulate research projects to close the gap in knowledge between north and south, both in the New World and in the Old. Developing countries may wish to use this provision to stimulate the exchange of existing knowledge or to stimulate the establishment of regional centres to study migratory birds in Africa, South America and Asia. The project "Save the seashore-birds" in Ghana (see

Table 2: Bird species on Appendix I of the Bonn Convention. An asterisk (*) indicates that the species, or a separate population of that species, or a higher taxon which includes that species, is included in Appendix II.

Procellariiformes
    Diomedeidae   *Diomedea albatrus*
    Procellariidae   *Pterodroma cahow*
                    P. phaeopygia

Pelecaniformes
    Pelecanidae   *Pelecanus crispus* *
                    P. onocrotalus (only Palearctic populations)

Ciconiiformes
    Ardeidae   *Egretta eulophotes*
    Ciconiidae   *Ciconia boyciana*
    Threskiornithidae *Geronticus eremita*

Anseriformes
    Anatidae   *Cloephaga rubidiceps* *

Falconiformes
    Accipitridae   *Haliaeetus albicilla* *
                    H. pelagicus *

Gruiformes
    Gruidae   *Grus japonensis* *
                    G. leucogeranus *
                    G. nigricollis *
    Otididae   *Chlamydotis undulata* * (only North-west African populations)

Charadriiformes
    Scolopacidae   *Numenius borealis* *
                    N. tenuirostris *
    Laridae   *Larus audouinii*
                    L. leucophthalmus
                    L. relictus
                    L. saundersi
    Alcidae   *Synthliboramphus wumizusume*

Passeriformes
    Parulidae   *Dendroica kirtlandii*
    Fringillidae   *Serinus syriacus*

Ntiamoa-Baidu, this volume) is a good example of such an integrated approach to research, information exchange and the stimulation of local nature conservation. Non-governmental organizations would have a much greater potential to ask their governments for financial assistance for research projects on migratory species in their own country and/or elsewhere along the flyway, if those governments were parties to the convention. I have seen many research-project applications on migratory birds, but very few refer to this provision of the Bonn Convention. There is, of course, no doubt that many other criteria are involved in making a final decision on a research application, but this obligation could be used much more.

This provision of the convention might also be important as a means of enabling Range States to work together to implement long-term research programmes aiming at the monitoring of migratory birds as a parameter of changes in their

Table 3: Bird species on Appendix II of the Bonn Convention. The abbreviation "spp." is used to denote all *migratory* species within that Family or Genus. An asterisk (*) indicates that the species, or a separate population of that species, or a higher taxon which includes that species, is included in Appendix I.

Pelecaniformes
  Pelecanidae   *Pelecanus crispus* *

Ciconiiformes
  Ciconiidae   *Ciconia ciconia*
                              C. nigra
  Threskiornithidae   *Platalea leucorodia*
                              Plegadis falcinellus

  Phoenicopteridae   *Ph.* spp.

Anseriformes
  Anatidae   *A.* spp. *

Falconiformes
  Cathartidae   *C.* spp.
  Pandionidae   *Pandion haliaetus*
  Accipitridae   *A.* spp. *
  Falconidae   *F.* spp.

Galliformes
  Phasianidae   *Coturnix coturnix coturnix*

Gruiformes
  Gruidae   *Grus* spp. *
                              Anthropoides virgo
  Otididae   *Chlamydotis undulata* * (only Asian population)
                              Otis tarda

Charadriiformes
  Charadriidae   *C.* spp.
  Scolopacidae   *S.* spp. *
  Recurvirostridae   *R.* spp.
  Phalaropodidae   *P.* spp.
  Burhinidae   *Burhinus oedicnemus*
  Glareolidae   *Glareola pratincola*
                              G. nordmanni

Coraciiformes
  Meropidae   *Merops apiaster*
  Caraciidae   *Coracias garrulus*

Passeriformes
  Muscicapidae   *M.* (s.l.) spp.

populations. It also clearly forces the parties to work together either using their own administrations (bilateral projects) or, which in my opinion is much more efficient, through existing international organizations active in the field of bird research (multilateral projects), such as the International Waterfowl and Wetland Research Bureau (IWRB) and the International Council for Bird Preservation (ICBP).

Species in Appendix I

Species in Appendix I are listed in *Table 2*. To be listed in Appendix I, a species should be endangered on the basis of "reliable evidence, including the best scientific evidence available" (Article III. 2). Parties shall endeavour to provide immediate protection for species in Appendix I. It must be clearly understood that the convention speaks about "endangered" and not "threatened" species because there are many more bird species threatened than endangered (definitions of these terms according to IUCN 1988).

Parties that are a Range States for these species "shall endeavour" to implement a series of actions (Article III. 4), including the following (which summarizes the original more extensive text).

To conserve and even restore the habitat of a species if this is important in order to remove the species from the danger of extinction. This means that Range States such as Hungary and Tunisia, which are also parties to the Bonn Convention, could be asked to give maximum protection to sites where a few of the remaining Slender-billed Curlews (*Numenius tenuirostris*; estimated total population 100-400) have been observed (Gretton 1991). It also provides a basis on which to request Israel to do more to protect or restore (e.g. by planting cedars) the habitat of the Syrian Serin (*Serinus syriacus*).

To prevent, remove, compensate for and minimize the effects of activities that seriously impede or prevent the migration of an endangered species. In principle this may be used as an international legal tool to undertake actions against electric power lines being a death trap for, e.g. pelicans (*Pelecanus crispus* and *P. onocrotalus*) in Greece (see Crivelli *et al.*, this volume).

To reduce or control factors (including introduced species) that are endangering a listed species. This may be used in a very broad sense, but it is extremely important as a tool to protect isolated islands with breeding colonies of seabirds and albatrosses, several species of which are listed in Appendix I, against feral cats, goats and rats.

It is prohibited to take individuals of listed species, but there are some exceptions such as scientific research and traditional subsistence use. This article (Article III. 5) provides for complete protection of all individuals of species in Appendix I. This applies also to the Slender-billed Curlew, of which some of the few remaining individuals have been shot because they have been mis-identified as Common Curlews (*Numenius arquatus*) or Whimbrels (*Numenius phaeopus*). In this case it would be very interesting to explore the possibility of solving this problem by concluding an AGREEMENT as proposed for Appendix II species (cf. below).

(Appendix II lists the Charadriiformes, which includes all curlew species. The "look-alike" principle could be a method for improving protection of the remaining Slender-billed Curlews by providing complete protection at least for the Whimbrel. However, it must be said that the Bonn Convention has no formal provisions for the protection of "look-alike" species as is the case with the CITES convention. This could, however, be changed.)

While discussing the species in Appendix I it is also important to note that within the Scientific Council of the Bonn Convention the view has arisen that all species in Appendix I should also be included in Appendix II. This is because one can argue that if a species is endangered, it is beneficial to have international cooperation as required for Appendix II species.

Many more examples could be given from the relatively small list of bird species in Appendix I, for countries that are not parties to the convention at this moment. Lyster (1985) has already drawn attention to the problems of the Northern Bald Ibis (*Geronticus eremita*) with probably only one truly wild individual left in Turkey in spring 1989 (Hirsch 1989). However, none of the Ranges States such as Turkey, Morocco (other breeding colonies) or Yemen and Ethiopia (supposed winter areas) are parties to the convention.

All these practical conservation actions and management measures should be taken by parties immediately, as is clearly stated in the text of the convention (Article II. 2). The potential conservation impact of this part of the convention should be explored intensively and used much more by governmental and non-governmental organizations to protect the species in Appendix I. Such protection often provides a similar protection for closely related species or many other forms of wildlife occurring in the same area or habitat.

At the moment only 24 bird species are listed in Appendix I. Recent publications provide information on 1,029 bird species now considered to be globally threatened (Collar c.s. 1988). Clearly a choice has been made in the past to include only a restricted number of endangered species on the basis of ecological and probably also political criteria. The Scientific Council is now giving consideration to additional candidate species for both appendices, although no change from the criterion "endangered" is envisaged (Secretariat, pers. comm.). It could be a standard procedure to review regularly the status of every migratory bird on the world list of threatened species. On the basis of such a review the Scientific Council of the Bonn Convention could consider the inclusion of new species in Appendix I and could, through one of the parties, make recommendations to every Meeting of the Conference of the Parties of the Bonn Convention. NGOs such as ICBP could play a vital role by providing the Scientific Council and the meetings of the conference parties with updated scientific information on every species on the list, and with well-documented proposals to include or remove species from the appendices.

In my opinion there are at the moment a few species whose inclusion in Appendix I could be considered. These are the Piping Plover (*Charadrius melodus*), Black-faced Spoonbill (*Platalea minor*), Spotted Greenshank (*Tringa guttifer*) and Aquatic Warbler (*Acrocephalus paludicola*). It is of course much better to take actions much earlier, as required from parties under Article II. 2 of the convention, and thus prevent a migratory species from becoming an endangered species. In such cases listing it in Appendix II could be a solution providing that international cooperation is beneficial for the species (see below).

Every party to the convention can make proposals to amend the appendices, to the meeting of the Conference of the Parties at least 150 days before the next meeting. Such meetings are convened every three years.

Species in Appendix II

Another important objective of the Bonn Convention is the concluding of AGREEMENTS between Range States to improve the situation of species that have an unfavourable conservation status and could benefit from international cooperation (Article IV. 3) (cf. before).

Every country, even if not a party to the convention but only a Range State for that particular species or species group, shall have the right of accession to such an AGREEMENT. This is very important because the experience with other international wildlife treaties has shown that it is not realistic to expect that the

Bonn Convention will soon have a hundred or more parties. This excellent provision makes it possible for many countries to be involved in the practical conservation and management of one species without having to wait for time-consuming formal ratification procedures. This can also provide an opportunity for countries to be involved in a positive way even if they are unable, at that time, to meet all the provisions of the convention itself.

As mentioned before, the Bonn Convention also provides for the conclusion of "agreements" of a more simple form (Article IV. 4).

What is an agreement?

An agreement is an International Memorandum of Understanding, in a simple form for a single species or to cover a particular regional problem. It may be concluded between administrative bodies of governments (as opposed to the governments themselves) or even between non-governmental organizations (NGOs). (See p. 348)

The latest Meeting of the Conference of the Parties (1988) underlined the need to conclude more of these "agreements", such as Memoranda of Understanding, under the Bonn Convention and not to focus entirely on the concluding of more formal AGREEMENTS between governments, which takes much more time. This is a very useful and positive approach because there are different views regarding the extent to which such an AGREEMENT has to be concluded by a ratification procedure.

On the other hand, the provision of concluding agreements should *never be used as an excuse not to conclude AGREEMENTS*. The concluding of agreements should also be seen as a first step towards the concluding of AGREEMENTS, which are the real international legal provisions for the conservation of migratory species. It is therefore necessary that such agreements always include the whole range of a species or a group of species and that they will be open for accession by other parties or Range States.

PRESENT WORK ON AGREEMENTS

At this moment, work is being undertaken on the preparation of two AGREEMENTS specifically related to birds: one for the European White Stork (*Ciconia ciconia*) (see Goriup & Schulz, this volume) and one for Western Palearctic Waterfowl. This decision was made by the First Meeting of the Conference of the Parties (Bonn 1985), and amended by the Second Meeting (Geneva 1988). The amendment concerned the Western Palearctic Waterfowl Agreement which should include all waterfowl and not Anatidae only. It was meant to be a start for the convention, together with the preparation of AGREEMENTS for European bats and small cetacea of the North and Baltic seas. These four AGREEMENTS are extremely biased towards Europe, but it should be very clear that the Bonn Convention is a worldwide convention.

The decision to select these four species/species groups as subjects of AGREEMENTS was taken in the knowledge that sufficient scientific data would be available to conclude the AGREEMENTS and that the Range States concerned already had enough resources to draft a management plan and implement it. They should also be considered as pilot projects to test the effectiveness and potential of the convention, its interpretation and its practical implementation. For both AGREEMENTS on bird species about 60-70 Range States are involved. Therefore the AGREEMENTS should be drafted in such a way that in principle all the Range States involved could accept the proposed conservation and management measures. This applies also if a management plan is to be prepared as an Annex to the AGREEMENT. Management plans are not compulsory under the convention, but are in general much more suitable than AGREEMENTS as a means of formulating in detail the necessary steps to be taken by individual Range States and/or groups of Range States in order to bring a population into a favourable conservation status or maintain the stability of a species already in a favourable conservation status. The AGREEMENT may then contain provisions to amend the management plan without the need to re-negotiate the whole AGREEMENT.

A management plan for the White Stork AGREEMENT has been prepared by ICBP under contract with the EC, and a draft of an AGREEMENT for the White Stork has been prepared by the Secretariat of the Convention. Further progress seems to be slow, and it is not known when the AGREEMENT will be finalized and available for accession by Range States. The AGREEMENT and management plan for Western Palearctic Waterfowl (with an action plan for Anatidae) is currently being prepared by the Netherlands Government on behalf of the EC and in consultation with the Secretariat and the Scientific Council of the Bonn Convention. Both are expected to be ready at the end of 1991, after which formal consultation with parties and Range States can be started.

These are the only two projects for birds currently in progress, and both are biased towards Europe. In my opinion much more should, and could, be done in particular through the conclusion of agreements on a smaller and less formal scale, and preferably in parts of the world other than the Palearctic. Recently, discussions have started on AGREEMENTS for the Houbara Bustard (*Chlamydotis undulata*) and for waterfowl of the Central Palearctic–Asian and Eastern Palearctic flyways.

Birds listed in Appendix II include many more species and groups of species in need of international cooperation and management. This is even true when considering that within the families listed, many species are not migratory at all. The Muscicapidae s.l. comprise about 1,200 species and an estimated 50-60 per cent of them are residents. Many are tropical forest species for which nothing or only very little is known of their migratory movements. A preliminary identification of the migratory status of all the c.1,800 bird species included in Appendix II, aimed at resolving this problem, has been prepared by the Secretariat and is under review by the Scientific Council.

Furthermore, it must be noted that in 1978 the need for AGREEMENTS covering important flyways and many species groups at once had already been recognized (Conference Documents, Preparatory Experts Meeting 18-21 July 1978). So far, however, Range States and other parties have not been active in taking initiatives towards the concluding of AGREEMENTS or agreements under the Bonn Convention. The following suggestions are therefore also meant to be a little more precise, although the general proposals made in 1978 are still valid and urgently require follow-up work.

These proposals will hopefully stimulate parties, Range States and NGOs to prepare draft AGREEMENTS and/or agreements and liaise with the Secretariat about procedures necessary to move them towards their conclusion.

SOME SUGGESTIONS FOR FURTHER WORK ON
AGREEMENTS/agreements

The following examples have been selected because of their potential spin-off effects on other bird species and habitats.

– **Scarlet Ibis** (*Eudocimus ruber*) in North America and the Caribbean. Coastal populations in particular are declining, and birds are being exploited for their feathers, which are used for decorations (Scott & Carbonell 1986; Spaans, pers. comm.).

– **Cranes** (Gruidae). Some are common and can be hunted, but several species are among the rarest birds in the world. Habitat destruction and illegal shooting are the main problems.

– **Raptors** (Falconiformes). Many species all over the world are long-distance migrants, concentrating during migration at well-known places. Although raptors are generally all protected, there is intensive illegal shooting. An AGREEMENT could in the first place focus on the protection of sites where mass concentrations occur, and as a second goal promote joint efforts to stop the illegal shooting and killing of species (education programmes, assistance with law enforcement, etc.).
Migration routes and threats are again very well known within the West Palearctic, but concentrated migration of raptors is also known from several places in Asia (Himalaya Region) and the preparation of an AGREEMENT for Asian migratory raptors has already been suggested (in 1978).

– **Albatrosses** (Diomedeidae). Vulnerable because of restricted breeding areas, extended incubation time and problems with introduced predators on some breeding sites. Also threatened by marine pollution.

– **Terns** (Sternidae). These birds are not listed in Appendix II, but it is a species group worthy of being listed because there are many threats to their populations. Major problems are the declining number of breeding sites, and the large numbers that are trapped, in particular Palearctic species along the African coast. Furthermore there is an increasing level of disturbance by tourism at the breeding islands, together with the introduction of predators. These problems occur in particular with the large colonies of tropical species. Finally there are potential problems in foraging areas because of growing over-exploitation of coastal fish resources. This latter aspect needs further research. Better conservation of other seabird species, particularly outside their breeding seasons, is above all needed. This is because unpredictably present oil, chemicals and oil spills affect seabird populations severely. Large numbers of birds are also killed because of drowning in fish nets. An AGREEMENT under the Bonn Convention could be a very useful means of achieving a better conservation status and of providing the framework for concerted actions and coordinated management.

– **Flamingos** (Phoenicopteridae). All species are vulnerable because of food specialization and concentration into large breeding colonies and wintering areas. Priority should be given to the South American species, but the Old World species, *Phoenicopterus ruber roseus*, might be a good candidate as well.

- **Passerine species** (Passeriformes). A group of species many of which concentrate during migration and are thus vulnerable to exploitation and mass trapping. Many species have a dispersed distribution during breeding and wintering and are therefore difficult to protect by creating protected areas.

  Recent expeditions to West Africa have found evidence that some passerine species such as Reed Warbler (*Acrocephalus scirpaceus*) and Grasshopper Warbler (*Locustella naevi*) together with species like Olivaceous Warbler (*Hippolais pallida*), Melodious Warbler (*H. polyglotta*) and Willow Warbler (*Phylloscopus trochilus*), winter in large numbers in stretches of mangrove forest along the coast and in reedbeds in coastal lagoons and marshes. These densities can sometimes be compared to those of waterfowl and waders wintering in estuaries and tidal areas. Having noticed the drastic and continuous decline of mangrove forests, it is necessary and extremely worthwhile to investigate the possibility of concluding AGREEMENTS/agreements under the Bonn Convention for such species and habitats.

  This may be an additional argument for the protection of mangrove forests, beside the many other well-known arguments, such as their importance as recruitment areas for many commercially important marine animals. Stop-over sites in the Mediterranean show similar densities and high turn-over rates. Work towards such an AGREEMENT could also be important as an experiment to investigate possibilities and gain valuable experience with a view to concluding AGREEMENTS on passerine birds in the Palearctic–African Flyway (for a start) and for passerine birds in other flyways in other parts of the world.

- **Migratory birds within Africa.** These occur in many families listed in Appendix II. Habitat destruction is a major problem for the whole of Africa and is threatening many species within the continent.

GENERAL ASPECTS OF AGREEMENTS/agreements

An active policy towards the concluding of AGREEMENTS/agreements can also provide a legal framework within which to provide assistance to developing countries if these are Range States and if they do not have the resources to give high priority to the conservation and management of migratory birds. The content and structure of such assistance can differ from species to species and between countries, but could include direct financial help in the management of protected areas, improvement of law enforcement, provision of training and study facilities, etc. It could also provide for education programmes and joint fieldwork projects.

AGREEMENTS are very suitable provisions under which to coordinate such activities, including, for example, the production of educational materials in countries along the whole migration route. One can also think of creating a foster system under an AGREEMENT between countries that are closely linked because they share a major part of the populations of a migratory species. Alternatively one can think of a twinning project between important staging and wintering sites. To give an example: the Netherlands Government is actually preparing a similar approach in its Forward Plan on international nature conservation policy for West Africa. The connection between The Netherlands and West Africa has a solid basis because some million birds migrate between the two regions.

Some of the bilateral conventions mentioned above can be considered as "agreements", but most of them were concluded before the Bonn Convention came into force. It may be an interesting thought to bring these bilateral agreements under the umbrella of the Bonn Convention, if such is possible from a legal point of view. A problem may arise because the Bonn Convention requires that agreements cover the whole range of the species and be open to all Range States, which is definitely not the case with most of these bilateral conventions. Clearly, in the longer term they must become multilateral in order to provide a real platform for cooperation to conserve migratory birds, and then they may fall within the terms of concluding an AGREEMENT pursuant to Article IV. 3 and Article V of the Bonn Convention.

During the last few years another kind of agreement, with no relation at all to the Bonn Convention, has been concluded and proved successful. The International Council for Bird Preservation acts mainly as a co-contracting party for these agreements between governments and non-governmental organizations involved with the conservation of migratory birds. Examples are the agreements between the Royal Society for the Protection of Birds (U.K.). and the Government of Ghana on seashore birds, and the draft memorandum between the Deutscher Bund für Vogelschutz and the Government of Sudan on migratory birds in general. There are certainly many more.

Personally I hold the opinion that the conclusion of such bilateral agreements should be part of the overall policy to implement the Bonn Convention. It is within the framework of such cooperations that real conservation work comes into practice and meets the ultimate goals for which the convention was originally drafted. That is to say, it involves the active participation of local people, communities and organizations, thus promoting concrete involvement with the conservation of species and their habitats. Participants, whether parties to the convention or not, and including the NGOs, etc., could be encouraged to "register" such agreements under the Bonn Convention and to deposit a copy of the agreement and a report of its implementation and progress with the Secretariat pursuant to Article VI. 3 of the convention. However, such agreements are not and cannot be legal agreements as described by Article IV. 4.

Regular overview publications of such bilateral or multilateral agreements and associated reports by the Secretariat or organizations like IWRB and ICBP could stimulate other parties, Range States, and non-governmental organizations, both national and international, to conclude similar agreements and thus promote direct action in line with the meaning of the Bonn Convention.

Again it must be clearly stated that such agreements *should not weaken or undermine the necessity and the willingness to conclude AGREEMENTS.* That would be a poor contribution indeed to the conservation of migratory birds, since the spirit of the convention requests cooperation between *all* Range States covering the range of a species and not just two or three of them. This problem could be partly overcome if countries involved in the concluding of these bilateral agreements became parties to the convention.

CONCLUSIONS

The Bonn Convention happens to be one of the most recently concluded in a series of international wildlife treaties. Its structure has therefore gained considerably from the experiences of those involved in the implementation of other international treaties. It has a number of articles forcing parties to work together, to report, to have regular meetings and to establish further cooperation by concluding AGREEMENTS/agreements. It provides for a Secretariat; it has a financial regime, and it has a Standing Committee (established by the Conference of the Parties). It provides for an exceptionally broad and strong conservation regime for species in Appendix I, which should be used much more than has been the case so far. More than in any other treaty the system of concluding AGREEMENTS provides an excellent mechanism for parties and Range States to work together on a larger number of species. The provision that Range States can have access to an AGREEMENT without necessarily being parties to the convention is a unique construction enabling countries to be involved in conservation measures without a formal ratification of the convention. It has many potentials, which can be used in action programmes of NGOs to convince their governments, once they are parties, to undertake a series of actions towards research, conservation and management of migratory birds.

The fundamental principle that all parties "acknowledge the need to take action to avoid any migratory species becoming endangered" (Article 11. 2) also justifies spending time and resources on those migratory birds and other migratory animals that still have good populations, albeit under great pressure. It is complementary to many of the other existing conventions and it should be used in that way and not be treated as redundant. The only real barrier to the realization of its full conservation potential is that due to the nature of migration it needs a large number of parties to be effective from a legal point of view. In other words it is not very realistic to think that an AGREEMENT can be implemented in an effective way unless a large portion of the Range States for that AGREEMENT are also parties to the Bonn Convention (Lyster 1985). Parties to the convention, and the Secretariat, should therefore follow an active policy to stimulate countries to become full parties, to conclude (as soon as possible) AGREEMENTS and additionally, and as a first step to AGREEMENTS, stimulate the conclusion of agreements between governments and between non-governmental organizations and governments. Non-governmental organizations should do the same by acknowledging the potential good effect the convention could have on the conservation of wild birds by stimulating the strongest possible cooperation between countries. The status of species listed as globally threatened should be reviewed regularly for their possible inclusion in Appendix I.

The Bonn Convention is not only a young convention, it has also had a difficult start. There has been a rapid turn-over of coordinators at the Secretariat, and at times there has been no coordinator at all. Present staff is small – three people – and while the budget may appear good on paper, it fails to be sufficient in practice because many parties do not pay their contributions. This situation may reflect a poor level of commitment to the convention on the part of many countries. If so, this represents a very unfortunate attitude towards an international treaty that has considerable potential. It does not stimulate an active promotion of the convention by other countries, or in general. This is a pity, because the Bonn Convention deserves a much more positive attitude from everybody interested in migration, and in migratory birds in particular.

For more information on the Bonn Convention please contact:

> The Coordinator
> UNEP/CMS Convention
> Ahrstrasse 45
> D-5300 Bonn 2
> Federal Republic of Germany

For information on the Western Palearctic Waterfowl AGREEMENT please contact the author.

ACKNOWLEDGEMENT

Sincere thanks to Judith C. Johnson, Coordinator of the Secretariat of the Bonn Convention, for her constructive and very useful comments on the first draft. I thank my colleagues of the Dutch support group for the Waterfowl AGREEMENT: Andri Binsbergen, Jan Wattel, Pieter van Heynsbergen, Jos den Hollander. Thanks also to Coert van Hasselt for reading the draft and providing valuable suggestions on matters of substance. My friend Jan Hoeve was extremely helpful in spending time of improving the English text. I would like to thank Drs. Chris Kalden, Deputy Director of Nature Conservation, Environmental Protection and Wildlife Management, for providing an opportunity to work for several years on what is my lifetime interest: migratory birds and their research, management and conservation.

Monique Metz and Johanna de Wit typed the various drafts and survived my handwriting! Mr Snel prepared the map.

REFERENCES

BODSWORTH, F. ((1954) 1955) 1966. *Last of the curlews*. London: Longmans, Green and Co. Ltd.

COLLAR, N. J. & ANDREW, P. (1988) *Birds to watch: the ICBP world checklist of threatened birds*. Cambridge, U.K.: International Council for Bird Preservation (Techn. Publ. 8).

ERZ, W. (1979) Schutz wandernder Tierarten zwischen Motiven, psychologischen Problemen und lokalen Hemmnissen. *Natur und Landschaft* 54: 181-185.

GOLLOP, J. B., BARRY, T. W. & IVERSEN, E. H. (1986) *Eskimo Curlew: a vanishing species?* Regina: Saskatchewan Natural History Society (Spec. Publ. 17).

GRETTON, A. (1991) The ecology and conservation of the Slender-billed Curlew (*Numenius tenuirostris*). Cambridge, U.K.: International Council for Bird Preservation (Monogr. 6).

HIRSCH, U. (1989) Lecture ICBP/ECS Conference Adana, Turkey, May 1989.

IUCN. (1983) *Elements of an AGREEMENT on the conservation of Western Palearctic migratory species of wild animals*. Gland: International Union for the Conservation of Nature and Natural Resources (Env. Policy and Law Occas. Pap. no. 2).

IUCN. (1986) *Migratory species in international instruments: an overview*. Gland: International Union for the Conservation of Nature and Natural Resources (Env. Policy and Law Occas. Pap. no. 2).

IUCN. (1988) *The 1988 IUCN Red List of Threatened Animals*. Cambridge, U.K.: International Union for the Conservation of Nature and Natural Resources.

LYSTER, S. (1985) *International wildlife law*. Cambridge: Grotius Publications.

MEAD, C. (1983) *Bird Migration*. Country Life Books. Rushden, U.K.: The Hamlyn Publishing Group.

SCOTT, D. A. & CARBONELL, M. (1986) *A directory of Neotropical wetlands*. Cambridge, U.K.: International Union for the Conservation of Nature and Natural Resources; Slimbridge, U.K.: International Waterfowl and Wetlands Research Bureau.

PRIORITIES FOR THE CONSERVATION OF MIGRATORY WATERFOWL

MICHAEL E. MOSER

*International Waterfowl and Wetlands Research Bureau
(IWRB), Slimbridge, Gloucester GL2 7BX, U.K.*

ABSTRACT

Migratory waterfowl depend on networks of wetlands throughout their range in order to complete their annual cycle. The degradation and loss of wetlands as result of human activities is the major threat to migratory waterfowl, and is to a large extent irreversible. In addition, waterfowl are exploited by hunters, and regulation of such activities is required to ensure that exploitation is sustainable. International cooperation is a prerequisite for effective conservation of migratory waterfowl and their wetland habitats. Expertise and funding are generally unevenly distributed along flyways which may comprise numerous Range States with different languages and legal frameworks. The greatest challenge for the conservation of migratory waterfowl is to design and implement, at flyway level, realistic management plans that take account of habitat requirements and which regulate over-exploitation by hunting. Increasing awareness of wetland values and development of the non-consumptive use and appreciation of migratory waterfowl give some cause for optimism over future conservation efforts.

INTRODUCTION

Migratory waterfowl show a number of life history characteristics that have a great influence on the measures that must be taken for their effective conservation (see also Myers *et al.* 1986). Although they are often dispersed at low densities on their breeding grounds, they concentrate at high densities on relatively small areas of wetland habitat during the non-breeding season. Also, many species are long-distance migrants with high energy requirements at specific times of year. These two characteristics mean that during the non-breeding season (and also during the breeding season for colonial waterbirds), migratory waterfowl depend on a specific network of wetlands throughout their flyway for feeding, moulting and resting in order to complete their annual cycle. Additionally, many waterfowl, for example the flamingos and pelicans, have relatively high adult survivorship and relatively low, unpredictable reproductive rates. These characteristics mean that their populations are more sensitive to changes that affect their adult survivorship, than to short-term variations in breeding output. Finally, many species of waterfowl, but particularly the migratory ducks, geese, swans, coots and some shorebirds, are much prized quarry of hunters. Special measures are therefore needed to regulate hunting throughout the flyways, so as to ensure a sustainable exploitation of the population.

It was this special need for international cooperation to identify and safeguard networks of important wetlands, and to ensure the sustainable exploitation of migratory waterfowl populations, that stimulated ICBP to create, in 1954, the International Wildfowl Research Bureau – now the International Waterfowl and Wetlands Research Bureau (IWRB). This paper describes some of the threats to migratory waterfowl, the contribution that IWRB has made to their conservation, and identifies priority actions for the future.

Waterfowl are defined as birds that are ecologically dependent on wetlands, and are here taken to include Gaviiformes, Podicipediformes, Pelecaniformes, Ciconiiformes, Phoenicopteriformes, Anseriformes, Gruiformes, Ralliformes and Charadriformes.

Wetlands are defined, following the Ramsar Convention, as areas of marsh, fen, peatland or water, whether natural or artificial, permanent or temporary, with water that is static or flowing, fresh, brackish or salt, including areas of marine water the depth of which at low tide does not exceed six metres.

THREATS TO MIGRATORY WATERFOWL

Threats to migratory waterfowl consist principally of changes brought about by human activities which might negatively affect their abundance or preferred distribution. Two major types of threat can be identified: (i) the effects of loss and degradation of habitat; and (ii) the effects of hunting and disturbance.

Loss and degradation of habitat

Wetlands are a valuable resource for people (Maltby 1986; Dugan, this volume) as well as for migratory waterfowl. In developing countries, the dependence of large numbers of people on wetland products (fish, reeds, water, etc.) has often contributed to the conservation and sustainable use of these valuable habitats. However, the combination of good water supply, rich soils and flat land that is often associated with wetlands, together with a desire for rapid economic growth, is leading increasingly to the conversion of wetlands to agricultural, urban, industrial or recreational use. Rates of wetland loss have generally been most severe in the more economically developed countries of temperate regions. However, in arid and semi-arid regions, where water is a scarce and valuable resource, the exploitation of groundwater and rivers for irrigation and other purposes has degraded many wetlands. In such cases, wetlands that were previously of great importance for migratory waterfowl may become increasingly temporary, saline, or may even disappear, with severe consequences for their natural functions and for their value as waterfowl habitat.

In Asian countries, such as China and the Philippines, Parish (1989) estimated that over 50 per cent of the waterfowl habitat had been destroyed or severely degraded. In North America, a persistent decline in migratory duck populations to a current level that is less than half that of the 1950s has been attributed to conversion of wetlands to agricultural and other uses (*Figure 1*). This, coupled with a drought through the 1980s, has seriously curtailed duck production (Bartonek 1989). In the Mediterranean region, where rates of wetland loss as high as 94 per cent for certain types of wetland have been reported (Psilovikos 1988), comparison of waterfowl surveys from the 1970s and the 1980s in both Greece (Athanassiou 1987) and Turkey (Dijksen & Blomert 1988) show species declines of 30-90 per cent suggesting an extremely serious situation.

Global warming may lead to further desiccation of wetlands in already arid and semi-arid regions, while any increase in sea level is likely to affect dramatically intertidal wetlands and low-lying delta areas. In addition long-term changes in temperature may bring about substantial changes in the distribution of waterfowl, particularly in the Arctic where many species breed.

Hunting, persecution and disturbance

People have hunted waterfowl for many centuries, and the fact that waterfowl and hunters still coexist on wetlands throughout the world demonstrates that exploitation by hunting can be sustainable. However, hunting can be a threat to waterfowl populations either through the direct effects of hunting mortality, or through disturbance, which may also be caused by many other human activities.

Hunting can kill waterfowl in three ways: (i) through the instant mortality of shot birds; (ii) through crippling losses (birds hit by gunfire and either not retrieved, or retrieved and discarded (Nieman *et al.* 1987)); and (iii) through the ingestion of toxic lead shot resulting in subsequent poisoning (Sanderson & Bellrose 1986; Pain 1990). Any measure of the direct impact of hunting on waterfowl populations must take account of the summed effects of all three sources of mortality.

The impact of hunting mortality on population levels of waterfowl depends on whether it replaces natural causes of mortality (i.e. it is compensatory) or whether it adds to natural causes of mortality (i.e. it is additive). If compensatory, changes in hunting regulations would not be expected to influence long-term population trends. This topic has been the centre of great debate and much research, particularly in North America (Brace *et al.* 1987). While evidence both for compensatory (e.g. Nichols *et al.* 1984; Burnham & Anderson 1984) and for additive (e.g. Ebbinge 1991) mortality has been described, Anderson & Burnham (1976) point out that hunting above a certain threshold level for a species will always become additive. Patterson (1979) pointed out that threshold levels would probably be species-specific and related to the annual rate of productivity of each species. For declining species, there must become a point below which all mortality becomes additive.

Forms of persecution other than hunting, both deliberate and unintentional, may also threaten waterfowl populations. For example, Crivelli *et al.* (this volume) cite collision with high-tension cables as a major source of mortality in pelicans, while Sears (1988) identified lead poisoning from discarded anglers' weights as a major cause of mortality in Mute Swans (*Cygnus olor*) in the Thames area, England.

Disturbance through hunting (Meltofte 1982) and other human activities, such as water-based recreation (Tuite *et al.* 1984), can affect waterfowl behaviour, ecology, distribution and survival. Meltofte (1982) estimated that in West Jutland (Denmark) 90 per cent of the ducks occur on the 20 per cent of the area of shallow water that is protected from shooting. Estimation of the impact of such disturbances at population level is extremely complex, although the possibility that such effects may be as great as those of direct hunting mortality has been raised (Wilkes 1977). The mechanism by which disturbance from hunting and other

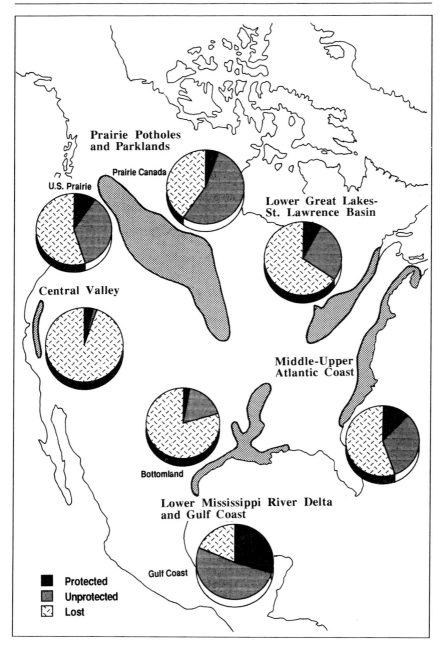

Figure 1: Status of waterfowl habitat in priority breeding and wintering areas of Canada and the United States. (*After* U.S. Department of the Interior and Environment Canada.)

sources affects waterfowl populations is likely to be similar to that of habitat loss, since disturbance creates a (usually temporary) exclusion zone around its origin, of habitat that can no longer be used. If the birds formerly occupying this area are unable to feed and rest as efficiently elsewhere, then this will reduce the number of bird days that the area can support.

ACHIEVEMENTS AND PRIORITY ACTIVITIES FOR IWRB

The conservation of migratory waterfowl depends on the safeguarding of networks of wetlands and the regulation of excessive hunting mortality throughout their flyways. For success, both measures require a high degree of international cooperation in research, monitoring and conservation action. Inevitably, the need for such activities increases with the number of countries on each flyway. The relative ease of coordinating waterfowl research, monitoring and conservation programmes in North America contrasts with the difficulties arising in Africa, Europe, Asia and Latin America, where flyways traverse many countries, with different languages and legal systems. The facilitation of such international cooperation is a major objective of IWRB, and is achieved through the activities of an international network comprising governmental and non-governmental delegates, members of research groups and large networks of collaborators in the field. This blend of experts brought together at a long series of international meetings, has provided a unique forum for the development and implementation of international cooperation for the conservation of migratory waterfowl. The programme is stimulated and coordinated through a small headquarters secretariat at Slimbridge, in England.

At present, IWRB has research groups representing various waterfowl taxonomic groups and related subjects such as Hunting Harvest and Impact, Waterfowl Ecology and Wetland Management (*Table 1*). Each research group has an international coordinator and comprises from a few tens to several hundred collaborators. International coordination of research and monitoring programmes is achieved through collaborative projects, newsletters, databases, workshops and symposia; advice on conservation management is given through publications, training courses and consultancies.

The following section details some of the key areas in which IWRB has contributed to the conservation of migratory waterfowl, and identifies the direction of IWRB's programme for the future.

Identifying networks of key wetlands
For many parts of the world, particularly where no detailed waterfowl surveys have been undertaken, one of the first steps in the development of an effective conservation programme for migratory waterfowl has been to compile an inventory of the most important wetlands. This process usually involves a regional, rapid evaluation based on existing material to identify those wetlands that meet the criteria of international importance under the Ramsar Convention (see Appendix 1). IWRB (often in association with ICBP, IUCN and WWF) has played a major role in the completion of a number of standardized wetland inventories, covering Europe and north-west Africa (Scott 1980), Europe (Grimmett & Jones 1989), the Neotropics (Scott & Carbonell 1986), and Asia (Scott 1989). Inventories of the African wetlands have been made by Burgis & Symoens (1987) and IUCN (in prep.). IWRB is currently collaborating in the production of an inventory of the

Table 1: List of IWRB Research Groups. Note that those marked with an asterisk are joint IWRB Research/ICBP Specialist Groups.

Taxonomic Groups:	Duck RG (includes Nordic–Baltic Survey)
	Flamingo RG *
	Goose RG
	Grebe RG *
	Heron RG *
	Pelican RG *
	Storks, Ibises and Spoonbills RG *
	Swan RG
	Wader RG
	Woodcock and Snipe RG
Subject Groups:	Waterfowl Ecology RG
	Hunting Harvest RG (includes Wing Survey)
	Hunting Impact RG
	Wetland Management Group

wetlands of Oceania and Australasia. In addition, Canada, the U.S.A. and the U.S.S.R. have all either begun or have completed their own national wetland inventories. The remaining part of the globe to be covered by these regional inventories is the Middle East, and IWRB plans to initiate an inventory of wetlands in this region in 1992. While these regional inventories of 'internationally' important wetlands provide an invaluable baseline for setting conservation priorities (e.g. listing under the Ramsar Convention), future attention must focus on monitoring rates of wetland loss and on setting targets, such as the 'No Net Loss' policy of the U.S.A. Severe damage has occurred to wetlands in Mediterranean countries, and this will be a priority region for IWRB during the 1990s.

The regional inventories provide a crude listing of the most important wetlands for migratory waterfowl. However, in order to determine the requirements of individual species, more detailed information on their patterns of distribution and abundance is required. Through the International Waterfowl Census, a programme of coordinated waterfowl surveys, IWRB has played a major role in determining the conservation requirements of migratory waterfowl wintering in Europe, North and West Africa, and Asia. The census is restricted to a single midwinter count each year, coordinated simultaneously on as many wetlands as possible throughout the flyway. It is undertaken largely by volunteers. The aims of the census are: (i) to determine population estimates for each species; (ii) to determine the non-breeding season distribution of each species and to identify the relative importance of sites within that distribution; (iii) to monitor trends in numbers of each species at site and population level; and (iv) to encourage a greater awareness of wetland and waterfowl conservation among governments, non-governmental organizations and individuals. Information from the census has often been complemented by studies of inter-site movements from ringing (banding) programmes, to give more precise knowledge of the importance of linkages between wetlands, and of the turnover of birds on individual sites.

The International Waterfowl Census was launched by IWRB in the Western Palearctic in 1967; results for this region have been published for swans, ducks and Coot (*Fulica atra*) (Monval & Pirot 1989), geese (Madsen 1991) and waders (Smit & Piersma 1989). In addition, an analysis of the importance of West African wetlands for waterfowl was published in 1991 (Perennou 1991). In 1987, the project was extended to Asia and now covers approximately 1,500 wetlands in 29

Asian countries. Further extensions of the Census into eastern and southern Africa and Latin America began in 1990. Detailed surveys of Nearctic shorebird species have already been undertaken on coastal habitats in this latter region (Morrison & Ross 1989). Monitoring programmes are also carried out by separate agencies in North America, Australia, New Zealand and the U.S.S.R.

The focus of the International Waterfowl Census on to a single midwinter count has a number of major advantages and disadvantages. On the positive side, it generates data that can be used for long-term monitoring and for comparison between regions. It also enables coverage by volunteers on a scale that would be impossible for paid counters. However, a major drawback is that it does not provide data on the sites that are of importance for breeding, moult or migration. This is less of a problem for the breeding areas, because the birds are often very dispersed on habitats that are, at present, relatively little threatened (e.g. Arctic tundra). However, the distribution of moulting and migration staging areas is a more serious problem, although in some cases these are also important wintering areas.

Monitoring waterfowl populations

Population size is the single most important variable to monitor in order to make management recommendations for the conservation of migratory waterfowl. Population changes at the level of whole flyways can be the stimulus for adjustments in hunting regulations, the launch of wetland conservation initiatives or of special recovery plans for threatened species. Population changes at the level of individual sites can be important indicators of ecological change and are therefore a stimulus for management action.

Because of the great mobility of migratory waterfowl, effective monitoring requires simultaneous surveys along entire flyways. The midwinter count of the International Waterfowl Census provides a major tool for monitoring waterfowl populations. In North America, monitoring on the breeding areas has been preferred, but this is more costly and must often by carried out over vast areas with few resident ornithologists.

Waterfowl counts are subject to many errors (e.g. Rappoldt *et al.* 1985). There can also be substantial difficulties in using data for monitoring unless consistent coverage can be achieved for a large sample of wetlands over many years. These problems, and those of selecting a satisfactory method of evaluating population changes, have recently been reviewed by Underhill (1989).

Impact of hunting

IWRB's objective in stimulating research into, and monitoring of, the hunting of migratory waterfowl, is to develop conservation recommendations to ensure: (i) that exploitation is sustainable for each species; (ii) that the hunting methods minimize the losses incurred through crippling and lead poisoning; and (iii) that the effect of hunting (and other sources of) disturbance on the carrying capacity of wetlands for waterfowl is minimized.

Any measure of hunting harvest that is to be used to determine whether or not exploitation is sustainable must account for shot and retrieved birds, plus crippling losses, plus birds subsequently dying from the ingestion of toxic lead shot. While some efforts have been made, through IWRB's Hunting Harvest Research Group (Lampio 1983) and many national programmes, to collect statistics on hunting seasons and number of hunters, few countries have good information on actual bags, and there has been little international coordination, except in North America. This is largely due to the sampling problems associated with gathering reliable data from hunters (Tautin *et al.* 1989). Furthermore, measures of the effects of crippling losses or lead poisoning are limited to the results of a few specialist studies. These have shown that crippling losses often account for as many as one-third of the birds that are shot (see refs. in Nieman *et al.* 1987), with a study in Denmark recording a rate of almost 50 per cent (Meltofte 1978). Lead poisoning has also been found to cause very significant mortality in ducks, both because lead-poisoned birds are more likely to be killed by hunters and because of additional non-hunting mortality (Sanderson & Bellrose 1986).

The priority activities for IWRB's Hunting Impact Research Group are clear. First, national agencies responsible for the conservation and management of migratory waterfowl need to be given information on hunting practices that are consistent with "wise use" (sensu the Ramsar Convention). Initially, this should focus on disseminating information on lead poisoning with a view to eliminating the use of toxic shot, and on hunting methods that will minimize crippling losses and disturbance.

The latter will require guidelines on zonation and the establishment of refuges from hunting and other forms of disturbance. Many studies of these subjects have been undertaken independently in Europe and North America, and a further priority for IWRB will be to synthesize the results and to identify gaps for future research. IWRB's Hunting Harvest Research Group should develop a manual to encourage the collection of standardized bag data at international level. In order to understand better the impact of hunting at population level there is a need to review and disseminate the results of studies on compensatory/additive mortality and give guidance on sustainable exploitation of waterfowl stocks.

International agreements

While IWRB can provide management guidelines for the conservation of migratory waterfowl, international agreements signed and honoured by Range States are needed to ensure that those recommendations are implemented. The most binding agreements are through intergovernmental conventions. There are four modern global conventions on nature conservation of which, at present, the Convention on Wetlands of International Importance Especially as Waterfowl Habitat (the Ramsar Convention) and the Convention on the Conservation of Migratory Species of Wild Animals (the Bonn Convention) are the most relevant to migratory waterfowl (Smart 1987). Both are intergovernmental agreements signed by countries only after approval by their highest legislative authority (usually Parliament). The Bonn Convention has been described elsewhere in some detail (Boere, this volume), and will not be covered here, except to note that IWRB is providing technical assistance to the development of a Western Palearctic Waterfowl Agreement. Until this is approved and adopted, the only measure that the Bonn Convention has for the conservation of migratory waterfowl is through an Appendix listing endangered species, for which immediate action should be taken, without needing the conclusion of an AGREEMENT.

IWRB played a crucial role in the development of the Ramsar Convention, and has continued to provide that convention with technical support through many of the activities listed above. Although specifically mentioning waterfowl, the Ramsar Convention is concerned with wetland habitat. The two principal obligations accepted by contracting parties when joining the convention are to designate at least one wetland of international importance to the convention list, and to make "wise use" of their wetlands in general. The criteria used for selecting sites for the convention list are shown in Appendix 1, and it can be seen that although some are specifically relevant to waterfowl, others relate to the wider values of wetlands. However, it must be said that a great many of the Ramsar sites have been listed on account of their waterfowl populations. At 30 May 1991, 62 contracting parties had designated 527 wetlands of international importance to the list, representing 31,933,543 ha of wetland habitat (Appendix 1). While the distribution of contracting parties is still biased towards the more developed countries, increasing emphasis on the "wise use" obligation is attracting more developing countries.

An early criticism of the Ramsar Convention was that many of the listed wetlands were already protected as National Parks or reserves, and that the convention had little additional conservation impact. However, this situation is now changing as more new sites are added, and as guidelines for the wise use of wetlands are developed. Indeed, in Denmark, several wetlands have been designated as Ramsar sites prior to their designation as reserves. While no site has ever been de-listed, many have been degraded while on the list. The success of the Ramsar Convention depends on an effective 'Monitoring Procedure'. While the contracting parties can in no way be obliged to halt degrading activities, the increasing status of this convention provides a powerful moral force for wetland conservation. In the event of the unavoidable degradation of a Ramsar site, contracting parties are obliged to list another wetland within their territory, to replace the area that has been degraded or lost.

There are many regional agreements of relevance to the conservation of migratory waterfowl, such as the EC Directive on the Conservation of Wild Birds, the Berne Convention (Batten 1987) and the African Convention (Hepburn 1987). Of particular interest is the Western Hemisphere Shorebird Reserve Network, a voluntary system of sites important to the conservation of migratory shorebirds, which is described in detail by Hunter *et al.* (this volume). Through the further development of monitoring and research programmes, IWRB will increase its technical support to these various initiatives.

The North American Waterfowl Management Plan has been signed by the United States and Canada, and is the most comprehensive and ambitious plan of its kind. It has been spurred on by the collapse of duck populations in North America, largely as a result of loss of wetlands to agricultural development. The Plan has four components: (i) it establishes principles for the cooperative conservation and use of North American waterfowl; (ii) it establishes population objectives; (iii) it identifies and costs the habitat, research and management initiatives required to obtain those population objectives; and (iv) it defines new administrative arrangements to oversee the plan's implementation. One of the great achievements of the plan, to date, has been to set goals towards which conservation agencies can pool their resources and, already, millions of dollars have been committed. The plan is now high on the North American political agenda, having made a timely entry as agricultural policies focus increasingly on sustainable development.

CONCLUSIONS AND FUTURE PRIORITIES

While the non-sustainable exploitation of migratory waterfowl by hunting is generally reversible through restrictive hunting regulations, wetland loss is not. The costs of restoring degraded wetlands or creating new wetlands are so prohibitively high as to be irrelevant for most countries. Conservation efforts for migratory waterfowl must therefore focus primarily on halting further destruction of the remaining wetlands (Dugan 1988) with the regulation of exploitation by hunting being a second priority, except where a species or population is known to be under threat from non-sustainable hunting.

The conservation of wetlands requires different approaches in different parts of the world, to provide solutions to different problems. Migratory waterfowl have already played a vital role in international efforts to conserve wetlands by linking countries and providing a vehicle for the exchange of conservation funds and expertise. IWRB is only one of a number of international organizations contributing to the conservation of migratory waterfowl. IWRB's goal in this arena is clear: to stimulate international cooperation in research and monitoring, and to transmit the results to waterfowl and wetland conservationists and managers for conservation action. No organization alone can tackle the immense challenges of the coming decades, and IWRB places great emphasis on seeking partnerships to provide the most effective solution to each problem.

The successful conservation of migratory waterfowl depends on international cooperation. The destruction of wetlands or unregulated hunting in a single, critical Range State could jeopardize entire flyway populations. The challenge, therefore, is to implement integrated management plans at flyway level. Such plans must take account of the uneven distribution of funding and expertise in different Range States, and should cover diverse topics including monitoring, research, habitat conservation, hunting regulation, training, education and awareness. This will require a coordinated approach by governments and non-governmental organizations, scientists and administrators working in partnership for a common goal. The North American Waterfowl Management Plan is the first example of such a plan in action, but it is atypical because of the high level of expertise and funding available, and because for most species the flyway is restricted to two countries speaking a common language and using similar legal frameworks. The development of flyway management plans to cover Europe, Asia, Africa and Latin America will pose a much greater challenge, requiring the careful integration of conservation objectives with the sustainable exploitation of wetland resources. The potential success for such an approach hangs in the balance. The degradation of habitat has never been greater, and the implications for migratory waterfowl never so severe. Yet, there is growing awareness of the valuable functions that wetlands provide. Furthermore, interest in the "non-consumptive uses" of waterfowl, such as birdwatching, education, tourism and research, have never been greater. The outcome of these opposing trends during the coming decades will determine the future prospects for migratory waterfowl.

ACKNOWLEDGEMENTS

This paper is based on the work of thousands of waterfowl scientists and enthusiasts who have contributed, often in a voluntary capacity, to the conservation of migratory waterfowl and their wetland habitats. The conservation of migratory waterfowl depends on their continued support. I am particularly grateful to the national coordinators of IWRB's International Waterfowl Census, and to the coordinators (past and present) of IWRB's Research Groups, who have made an inestimable contribution to the achievements of our organization. I would like to thank Myrfyn Owen and Geoffrey Matthews for their comments on this paper.

APPENDIX 1

CONTRACTING PARTIES TO THE RAMSAR CONVENTION (30.05.91)

		Date Convention came into force	1982 Paris Protocol Instrument deposited UNESCO	1987 Regina Amendments accepted UNESCO	Number of wetlands designated	Area of wetlands (hectares)
1.	Australia	21.12.75	12.8.83	25.07.90	40	4,477,862
2.	Finland	21.12.75	15.05.84	27.03.90	11	101,343
3.	Norway	21.12.75	3.12.82	20.01.89	14	16,256
4.	Sweden	21.12.75	3.05.84	6.04.89	30	382,750
5.	South Africa	21.12.75	25.05.83		7	208,044
6.	Islamic Rep. Iran	21.12.75	29.04.86		18	1,087,550
7.	Greece	21.12.75	2.06.88		11	107,400
8.	Bulgaria	24.01.76	27.02.86	21.06.90	4	2,097
9.	U.K.	5.05.76	19.04.84	27.06.90	46	210,652
10.	Switzerland	16.05.76	30.05.84	8.06.89	8	7,049
11.	F.R. Germany	26.06.76	13.01.83	21.06.90	29	360,894
12.	Pakistan	23.11.76	13.08.85	20.09.88	9	20,990
13.	New Zealand	13.12.76	9.02.87		5	38,099
14.	U.S.S.R.	11.02.77			12	2,987,185
15.	Italy	14.04.77	27.07.87		46	56,950
16.	Jordan	10.05.77	15.03.84		1	7,372
17.	Yugoslavia	28.07.77			2	18,094
18.	Senegal	11.11.77	15.05.85		4	99,720
19.	Denmark	2.01.78	3.12.82		38	1,778.968
20.	Poland	22.03.78	8.02.84		5	7,090
21.	Iceland	2.04.78	11.06.86		2	57,500
22.	Hungary	11.08.79	28.08.86	20.09.90	13	110,389
23.	Netherlands	23.09.80	12.10.83		17	308,358
24.	Japan	17.10.80	26.06.87	2.06.88	3	9,892
25.	Morocco	20.10.80	3.10.85		4	10,580
26.	Tunisia	24.03.81	15.05.87		1	12,600
27.	Portugal	24.03.81	18.12.84		2	30,563
28.	Canada	15.05.81	2.06.83	8.11.88	30	12,937,549
29.	Chile	27.11.81	14.02.85		1	4,877
30.	India	1.02.82	9.03.84		6	192,973
31.	Spain	4.09.82	27.05.87		17	98,887
32.	Mauritania	22.02.83	31.05.89		1	1,173,000
33.	Austria	16.04.83			5	102,369
34.	Algeria	4.03.84			2	4,900
35.	Uruguay	22.09.84			1	200,000
36.	Ireland	15.03.85	15.11.84	28.08.90	21	12,562
37.	Suriname	18.07.85			1	12,000
38.	Belgium	4.07.86			6	9,607
39.	France	1.10.86	26.07.84		8	422,585
40.	Mexico	4.11.86	4.07.86		1	47,480
41.	U.S.A.	18.04.87	18.12.86		9	1,128,691
42.	Gabon	30.04.87	30.12.86		3	1,080,000
43.	Niger	30.08.87	30.04.87		1	220,000
44.	Mali	25.09.87	25.05.87		3	162,000
45.	Nepal	17.04.88	17.12.87		1	17,500

(continued)

APPENDIX 2: Continued

		1982 Paris Protocol Instrument deposited UNESCO	1987 Regina Amendments accepted UNESCO	Number of wetlands designated	Area of wetlands (hectares)
	Date Convention came into force				
46. Ghana	22.06.88	22.02.88		1	7,260
47. Uganda	4.07.88	4.03.88		1	15,000
48. Egypt	9.09.88	9.09.88		2	105,700
49. Venezuela	23.11.88	23.11.88		1	9,968
50. Viet Nam	20.01.89	20.09.88		1	12,000
51. Malta	30.01.89	30.09.88		1	11
52. Guinea–Bissau	9.05.90	9.05.90		1	39,098
53. Kenya	5.10.90	5.06.90		1	18,800
54. Chad	13.10.90	13.06.90		1	195,000
55. Sri Lanka	15.10.90	15.06.90		1	6,216
56. Guatemala	26.10.90	26.06.90		1	45,000 *
57. Bolivia	27.10.90	27.06.90		1	5,240
58. Burkina Faso	27.10.90	27.06.90		3	296,300 *
59. Czech and Slovak F.R.	2.11.90	2.07.90		8	16,958
60. Panama	26.11.90	26.11.90		1	80,765
61. Ecuador	7.01.91	7.09.90		2	90,000
62. Romania	21.09.91	21.05.91		1	647,000
				527	31,933,543 *

Note: * = area yet to be confirmed officially

REFERENCES

ANDERSON, D. R. & BURNHAM, K. P. (1976) *Population ecology of the mallard, Vol. VI: The effect of exploitation on survival.* Washington, D.C.: U.S. Fish and Wildlife Service (Resrce. Publ. 128).

ANSTEY, S. G. (1989) *The status and conservation of the White-headed Duck Oxyura leucocephala.* Slimbridge, U.K.: International Waterfowl and Wetlands Research Bureau (Spec. Publ. 10).

ATHANASSIOU, H. (1987) Past and present importance of the Greek wetlands for wintering waterfowl. Slimbridge, U.K.: International Waterfowl and Wetlands Research Bureau. Unpubl. report.

BARTONEK, J. C. (1989) Status of waterfowl, cranes and other water birds in North America. Pp. 64-67 in H. Boyd & J.-Y. Pirot, eds. *Flyways and reserve networks for waterbirds.* Slimbridge, U.K.: International Waterfowl and Wetlands Research Bureau (Spec. Publ. 9).

BATTEN, L. (1987) The effectiveness of European agreements for wader conservation. Pp. 118-121 in N. C. Davidson & M. W. Pienkowski, eds. *The conservation of international flyway population of waders.* Slimbridge, U.K.: Wader Study Goup (Bull. 49, Suppl.)/International Waterfowl and Wetlands Research Bureau (Spec. Publ. 7).

BRACE, R. K., POSPAHALA, R. S. & JESSEN, R. L. (1987) Background and objectives on stablised duck hunting regulations: Canadian and U.S. perspectives. *Trans. N. Amer. Wildl. & Nat. Res. Conf.* **52**: 233-245.

BURNHAM, K. P. & ANDERSON, D. R. (1984) Tests of compensatory vs. additive hypotheses of mortality in Mallards. *Ecology* **65(1)**: 105-112.

BURGIS, M. J. & SYMOENS, J. J., eds. (1987) *African wetlands and shallow waterbodies.* Paris, France: Institut Français de Recherche Scientifique pour le Développement en Coopération.

DIJKSEN, L. J. & BLOMERT, A.-M. C. (1988) *Midwinter waterfowl census in Turkey.* January 1988. Zeist: WIWO (Rep. 21).

DUGAN, P. J. (1988) Wetlands restoration and creation – is it relevant to the developing world? In J. Zelazny & J. S. Feierabend, eds. *Increasing our wetland resources.* Washington D.C.

EBBINGE, B.S. (1991) The impact of hunting on the survival rates and spatial distribution of geese wintering in the western Palearctic. *Ardea* **79**: 197-210.

GRIMMETT, R. F. A. & JONES, T. A. (1989) *Important bird areas in Europe.* Cambridge, U.K.: International Council for Bird Preservation (Techn. Publ. 9).

HEPBURN, I. R. (1987) Conservation of wader habitats in coastal West Africa. Pp. 125-127 in N. C. Davidson & M. W. Pienkowski, eds. *The conservation of international flyway population of waders.* Slimbridge, U.K.: Wader Study Group (Bull. 49, Suppl.)/International Waterfowl and Wetlands Research Bureau (Spec. Publ. 7).

LAMPIO, T. (1983) *Waterfowl hunting in Europe, North America and some African and Asian countries in 1980-81.* Slimbridge, U.K.: International Waterfowl and Wetlands Research Bureau (Spec. Publ. 3).

MADSEN, J. (1991) Status and trends of goose populations in western Europe in the 1980s. Proceedings of the International Symposium on Western Palearctic Geese, Kleve, FRG. *Ardea* **79**: 113-122.

MALTBY, E. (1986) *Waterlogged wealth.* London and Washington, D.C.: International Institute for Environment and Development.

MELTOFTE, H. (1978) Skudeffektivitet ved intensiv kystfuglejagt i Danmark. *Dansk Orn. Tidsskr.* **72**: 217-221.

MELTOFTE, H. (1982) Shooting disturbance of waterfowl. (In Danish with an English summary.) *Dansk Orn. Foren. Tidsskr.* **76**: 21-35.

MONVAL, J.-Y. & PIROT J.-Y., compilers (1989) *Results of the IWRB International Waterfowl Census 1967-1986.* Slimbridge, U.K.: International Waterfowl and Wetlands Research Bureau (Spec. Publ. 8).

MORRISON, R. I. G. & ROSS, R. K. (1989) *Atlas of Nearctic Shorebirds on the coast of South America.* Ottawa: Canadian Wildlife Service (Spec. Pub.).

MYERS, J. P., MORRISON, R. I. G., ANTAS, P. A., HARRINGTON, B. A., LOVEJOY, T. E., SALLABERRY, M., SENNER, S. E. & TARAK, A. (1987) Conservation strategy for migratory species. *Amer. Sci.* **75**: 19-26.

NICHOLS, J. D., CONROY, M. J., ANDERSON, D. R. & BURNHAM, K. P. (1984) Compensatory mortality in waterfowl populations: a review of the evidence and implications for research and management. *Trans. N. Amer. Wildl. & Nat. Res. Conf.* **49**: 535-554.

NIEMAN, D. J., HOCHBAUM, G. S., CASWELL, F. D. & TURNER, B. C. (1987) Monitoring hunter performance in Prairie Canada. *Trans. N. Amer. Wildl. & Nat. Res. Conf.* **52**: 233-245.

PAIN, D. (1990) Lead poisoning of waterfowl: a review. Pp. 172-181 in G. V. T. Matthews, ed. *Managing waterfowl populations.* Slimbridge, U.K.: International Waterfowl and Wetlands Research Bureau (Spec. Publ. 12).

PARISH, D. (1989) Population estimates of waterbirds using the East Asian/Australasian flyway. Pp. 8-13 in H. Boyd & J.-Y. Pirot, eds. *Flyways and reserve networks for waterbirds.* Slimbridge, U.K.: International Waterfowl and Wetlands Research Bureau (Spec. Publ. 9).

PATTERSON, J. H. (1979) Experiences in Canada. *Trans. N. Amer. Wildl. & Nat. Res. Conf.* **49**: 114-126.

PERENNOU, C., ROSE, P. M. & POOLE, C. (1990) Asian Waterfowl Census 1990. Slimbridge, U.K.: International Waterfowl and Wetlands Research Bureau.

PERENNOU, C. (1991) Les recensements internationaux d'oiseaux d'eau en Afrique tropicale. Slimbridge, U.K.: International Waterfowl and Wetlands Research Bureau (Spec. Publ. 15).

PSILOVIKOS, A. (1988) Changes in Greek wetlands during the twentieth century: the cases of the Macedonian inland waters and of the river deltas of the Aegean and Ionian coasts. University of Thessaloniki. Unpubl. report.

RAPPOLDT, C., KERSTEN, M. & SMIT, C. (1989) Errors in large-scale shorebird counts. *Ardea* **73**: 13-24.

SANDERSON, G. C. & BELLROSE, F. C. (1986) *A review of the problem of lead poisoning in waterfowl.* Illinois: Nat. Hist. Surv. (Spec. Publ. 4).

SCOTT, D. A. (1980) *A preliminary inventory of wetlands of international importance for waterfowl in West Europe and Northwest Africa.* Slimbridge, U.K.: International Waterfowl and Wetlands Research Bureau (Spec. Publ. 2).

SCOTT, D. A., ed. (1989) *A directory of Asian wetlands.* Cambridge, U.K. and Gland: International Union for the Conservation of Nature and Natural Resources.

SCOTT, D. A. & CARBONELL, M. (1986) *A directory of Neotropical wetlands.* Cambridge, U.K.: International Union for the Conservation of Nature and Natural Resources; Slimbridge, U.K.: International Waterfowl and Wetlands Research Bureau.

SEARS, J. (1988) Regional and seasonal variations in lead poisoning in the Mute Swan *Cygnus olor* in relation to the distribution of lead and lead weights in the Thames area, England. *Biol. Conserv.* **46**: 115-134.

SMART, M. (1987) International conventions. Pp. 114-117 in N. C. Davidson & M. W. Pienkowski, eds. *The conservation of international flyway population of waders.* Slimbridge, U.K.: Wader Study Group (Bull. 49, Suppl.)/International Waterfowl and Wetlands Research Bureau (Spec. Publ. 7).

SMIT, C. J. & PIERSMA, T. (1989) Numbers, midwinter distribution, and migration of wader populations using the East Atlantic flyway. Pp. 24-63 in H. Boyd & J.-Y. Pirot, eds. *Flyways and reserve networks for waterbirds.* Slimbridge, U.K.: International Waterfowl and Wetlands Research Bureau (Spec. Publ. 9).

TAUTIN, J., CARNEY, S. M. & BORTNER, B. J. (1989) A national migratory gamebird harvest survey: a continuing need. *Trans. N. Amer. Wildl. & Nat. Res. Conf.* **54**: 545-551.

TUITE, C. H., HANSON, P. R. & OWEN, M. (1984) Some ecological factors affecting wintering wildfowl distribution on inland waters in England and Wales, and some influences of water-based recreation. *J. Appl. Ecol.* **21**: 41-61.

UNDERHILL, L. G. (1989) Indices for waterbird populations. Tring: British Trust for Ornithology. Unpubl. report (no. 52) to IWRB.

WILKES, B. (1977) The myth of the non-consumptive user. *Can. Field-Nat.* **91**(4): 343-349.

CONSERVATION AND SUSTAINABLE DEVELOPMENT: HOW IT CAN HELP MIGRATORY BIRDS

PATRICK J. DUGAN

Wetland Programme Coordinator, IUCN,
The World Conservation Union, Avenue du
Mont–Blanc, CH–1196 Gland, Switzerland

ABSTRACT

Concern for migratory birds has been one of the main forces driving European interest in conservation in Africa. But in order to build upon this concern and achieve effective conservation action, the conservation community must take due account of the particular socio-economic context within which conservation efforts must be pursued in Africa. The message of this paper is that conservation of migratory birds in Africa can be achieved only through a broad-based approach to management of the natural habitats upon which they depend. Rather than focus directly on the problems facing individual species of migratory birds, conservation efforts may therefore be made more effective by addressing the diverse social and economic problems which are putting pressure on those natural ecosystems upon which migratory birds depend. It is argued that activities of the Migratory Birds Action Plan should be designed to support such an approach, and specific suggestions are provided cn the form such activities might take.

INTRODUCTION

Birds have been a driving force for conservation over much of the industrialized world in the past 100 years. And today, as concern over the threats faced by the bird populations of the tropics has intensified, ICBP and its member organizations are playing a central role. In this work the bird conservation community is doing much to pursue the species goals of the World Conservation Strategy, and will certainly continue to do so in future. Yet, while there is reason to be positive, it is perhaps time to ask whether steps might now be taken that would not only increase the contribution made to implementing the WCS through bird conservation initiatives, but also increase the effectiveness of that action in conserving migratory birds. The purpose of this paper is to explore these questions and consider ways through which this desired integration can be achieved.

A STRATEGY TO CONSERVE MIGRATORY BIRDS

As understanding of the Palearctic–African bird migration system has grown, and data on the population dynamics of European breeding species have improved, so has appreciation of the linkages between wintering conditions in sub-Saharan Africa and breeding population size in Europe. Thus, as drought and dam construction have led to decreased river flood over much of the African continent, the bird species that use these flood-plain ecosystems have been obliged to use a smaller area or move elsewhere, often to less favourable habitats (van der Linden 1988). As a result, European breeding populations of many wetland-dependent species, most noticeably herons, have fluctuated in synchrony with the annual river flood in the Sahel (Den Held 1981).

Also the savanna habitats upon which many passerine migrants depend have been seriously degraded, mostly as a result of increasing grazing pressure (Timberlake 1985) and woodlands have been lost as a result of the growing demand for firewood. These gradual but measurable changes have in turn led to the decline in population levels of several species of migrant passerines (Morel 1973). As a result, there is today a call for greater investment in conservation action in these wintering areas, rather than in the European breeding areas where most past investment has been focused.

In turning towards the wintering areas, the attention of the international bird conservation community has focused initially upon those sites where several species of migratory birds are known to concentrate during certain months of the European winter. Wetlands in particular have received considerable attention in view of the role they play in supporting large concentrations of waterbirds (Roux & Jarry 1984). Yet, these species are the exception rather than the rule. For the greater part of the winter most migrants are relatively widely dispersed across the African landscape. Thus, while protected areas may be effective in maintaining a few critical sites, maintenance of European breeding populations of most species of migratory birds at, or close to, present levels will require management of a much broader landscape in sub-Saharan Africa. While protected areas may therefore play a central role in any such strategy, the conservation community must pursue action in a wider context if it is to have a real impact on the long-term future of our migratory birds. Indeed, without action to address this broader issue it is likely that protected areas will become isolated, and hence ultimately condemned, islands in a degraded landscape unable to support existing patterns of human use.

Pursuit of a broad-based approach to migratory bird conservation will therefore require study not only of the ecological problems, but also of the socio-economic conditions which drive degradation (Dugan 1987). Measures designed to manage natural habitats more effectively will in most cases need to draw upon this understanding of socio-economic issues, at both local and national level.

THE SOCIO-ECONOMIC CONTEXT

For many people, the image that migratory birds first bring to mind is of the great ecological changes these species experience in moving from their European breeding areas to Africa and back during the course of the year. Yet, as our attention focuses more sharply on how to manage their habitats on a long-term basis, rather than on further refining our understanding of where the birds go, more

Figure 1: Little Egrets (*Egretta garzetta*) wintering in the Inner Niger delta mingle with fishermen.   By saving wetlands to meet human needs we will also save the birds.
(*Photo:* WWF/J. Skinner)

attention needs to be focused on the economic contrasts rather than the ecological ones.

In moving from Europe to Africa, migratory birds move from countries with strong national economies where governments and private foundations make major investments in nature conservation, to comparatively weak agrarian economies where governments are forced to allocate their meagre resources to improving food security and increasing economic output rather than to nature conservation.   If governments are to invest in nature management we therefore need to do much more to emphasize the linkages between conservation of the natural environment, food security, and sustainable economic development.

Second, the birds move from where farmers are often amongst the wealthiest members of society, to rural communities that are often amongst the poorest of the poor, and where individuals have been obliged to degrade natural resources in search of today's meal.

Third, in Europe nature conservation is increasingly pursued as an integrated component of farming activities while in Africa conservation is still too often seen as distinct from effective use of the renewable natural resource base.   Conservation in these countries is therefore invariably still considered as being in opposition to development, and is often seen by local populations as something that is of little help to them.

Fourth, in moving south in autumn, migratory birds move from countries where, because conservation is accepted as a legitimate subject for government investment, much is to be gained by using birds as a focus for environmental awareness activities, to areas where birds are invariably regarded as pests, or as an additional food resource.   In these countries, awareness activities that focus on birds, and do not emphasize the broader context, may in the end be counterproductive and damage the conservation case.

The message of this analysis is that conservation of migratory birds in sub-Saharan Africa can be achieved only through a broad-based approach to management of the natural habitats upon which they depend. Thus, rather than focus on the problems facing migratory birds, we may be more effective by addressing the diverse social and economic problems facing these natural ecosystems and the birds that use them.

Such a broad-based approach is clearly not possible for every institution. But even more traditional conservation activities should be based upon awareness of this reality. Activities carried out through the Migratory Birds Programme should be designed to support such an approach.

HOW MIGRATORY BIRDS CAN SUPPORT IMPROVED MANAGEMENT OF AFRICA'S NATURAL RESOURCES

It is of course easy to argue for an integrated approach to conservation of migratory birds; but what action should the bird conservation community support in order to contribute to such integration in sub-Saharan Africa? Certainly, if efforts to conserve migratory birds are to be successfully linked with broader investment in management of natural ecosystems, considerable care will be required in using the limited funds available for that purpose. Among the many concerns, three issues merit particular attention.

Influencing international investment in conservation and development assistance

Throughout Africa there are very limited funds available for bird conservation. In considering how migratory bird conservation efforts in Europe might therefore contribute to the conservation of these species and their habitats in Africa, it is possible that the most effective use of these funds would be to invest in building greater awareness among the Ministries of Environment in Europe so that they invest much greater time and effort in seeking ways through which our European governments can assist migratory bird conservation in the tropics.

In short, if the Migratory Bird Programme were to succeed in persuading European Ministries of Environment to spend more of their own money in assisting African nations to conserve migratory birds and their habitats, and in turn to urge Ministries of Development Assistance to pursue development projects that improve environmental management in the countries of concern, it would take a most significant step towards conservation of these migratory species. Thus, while there is no doubt that this is a difficult task – possibly the reason why it has not yet been addressed adequately – it should now be moved to the top of the agenda.

Improving the design of field projects

If the bird conservation community is to spend less on activities in the field, and more on influencing decision-makers, the choice of projects to fund becomes even more important than in the past. In particular, care should be taken to support activities that can act as catalysts for more substantive action by other institutions, in particular the development assistance community, and that can address habitats critical for migratory birds.

In considering how to develop such a catalytic approach, it is important to note that much habitat of value to migratory birds is being lost today because of a poor understanding of the value of these habitats, and of the ways through which they can be managed to improve human well-being. Accordingly, migratory bird conservation efforts should identify those habitat types that are critical for migratory birds, and either pursue directly, or promote, projects that can help demonstrate how to manage these habitat types in a sustainable manner.

This is, of course, a major challenge, and we need to be realistic in considering how much can be done by any one institution. Also, while successful demonstration of the value of these ecosystems will constitute a major advance in migratory bird conservation, failure will severely damage the credibility of our argument. The migratory bird conservation community should therefore seek to implement two or three projects well, and in doing so work where necessary with others to achieve this result.

In selecting demonstration projects great care will be needed. Although many critical sites are known and are certainly in need of improved management, many are not representative of those critical savanna habitats which are widely distributed throughout Africa and where migratory birds are thinly distributed, but nevertheless present in much greater numbers.

Building environmental awareness

Over much of their annual range, migratory birds are still shot or captured for human consumption or because they are perceived to be pests. Conservation of migratory birds therefore requires that in addition to improved habitat management, direct human pressure upon these species must be controlled. However, particular care needs to be exercised here. Where people harvest birds or regard them as pests, for example in many of the wetland areas of the Sahel, it may not be a good long-term strategy to initiate conservation efforts by emphasizing migratory birds. Such an approach invariably means that conservation becomes synonymous with bird protection, and the local populations come to view other elements of a more broad-based conservation programme as a cosmetic attempt by expatriates to win local support for action that is in the European, rather than local, interest. The resulting lack of trust between expatriates and the local populations who are in the end those whose support is most critical, can do irreparable harm to even the best projects, and render major investments worthless.

In view of these concerns, great care should be exercised in designing the overall strategy for the conservation of critical sites and critical habitats. Specifically, such a strategy should focus first on the importance of these ecosystems for people, and only at a later stage should migratory bird concerns be introduced. A pilot migratory bird conservation project should therefore focus upon issues that are of concern to the people who use these critical sites and critical habitats. Such projects might address the reduced quality of pasture and of cattle herds; the decline in fish populations and the resulting fish catch; limited fuelwood resources; declining agricultural production, and other similar problems. By addressing these issues, improving the well-being of the local populations who use these resources, and so contributing to the improved management of the natural ecosystems upon which their production systems depend, pilot projects of this nature will contribute significantly to the conservation of migratory birds without necessarily having to raise this as being an issue of concern.

IMPLICATIONS FOR THE MIGRATORY BIRD
FORWARD PLAN

In short, if migratory bird conservation is to be successful, it has to be pursued as part of a broad-based initiative. Thus, while in Europe there is no doubt that migratory birds appeal to many people, and their problems have generated much public interest, conserving these species will require great care in translating this enthusiasm into action on the ground over much of their wintering range.

Specifically, careful attention must be paid to the severe human problems faced by the African continent, and we must recognize that, in the long term, conservation of migratory birds will be possible only if the underlying issues of rural poverty and natural resource degradation can be resolved. These are difficult problems, and any easy answers are probably the wrong ones. However, by working with other institutions involved in these issues ICBP can play a catalytic role and, in time, help redress the current decline in populations of migratory birds and their habitats.

Within the framework provided by the above analysis, the Migratory Bird Action Plan should act as a catalyst by operating at a number of levels.

Policy. In promoting investment by European governments in the conservation of migratory birds, the Action Plan can help lay the basis for long-term investment in actions specifically designed to contribute to migratory bird conservation in Africa. Similarly, by stimulating dialogue with the development assistance community, the Action Plan can do much to encourage investment by these institutions in activities that contribute to improved management of those natural ecosystems upon which migratory birds depend.

Critical habitat management. By helping to identify those habitats that are of particular importance for migratory birds, and by working with others to demonstrate how to manage these more effectively, the Action Plan can help develop an agenda for action to build upon these examples over the next five to ten years. However, to complement this work, especially careful consideration should be given to the choice of sites where ICBP will pursue field action of its own. For example, while the largest areas of concern are south of the Sahara, there is today considerable conservation investment there. In contrast, in the much smaller but equally critical sites distributed through the Sahara and along the coastal migration routes, there is comparatively little investment. Consideration should therefore be given to whether the Plan should invest more in these areas.

Training. By contributing funds to training personnel in natural resource management, and in particular by promoting integration of conservation and development, the Action Plan can do much to stimulate improved action by the government agencies responsible for migratory bird conservation in Africa. By emphasizing that such training should focus upon broader issues of habitat management, such activities can better equip conservation personnel to enter into a dialogue with other government departments concerned with rural development planning.

Building awareness. The Action Plan should help build awareness of the links between people and the natural environment. However, in doing so it will not always be necessary or advisable to stress birds. In Europe, a similarly broad-based approach to building awareness of migratory bird problems is necessary.

Specifically, much more is needed to build awareness that major changes are still required in development assistance policies before European governments begin to have a net positive impact upon migratory bird conservation in Africa.

Research. The Action Plan should promote research on issues that will help improve our ability to pursue work under the previous four categories. For example, while much is said about the role of migratory birds in controlling insect pests, there are currently few specific data that describe the economic importance of these predator species. Yet it is clear that a detailed economic analysis of the role of bird species in regulating the abundance of such pests could have a major impact on the conservation policies of individual governments and development assistance agencies. Similarly, more work is needed to determine the levels at which individual species can be harvested by local people.

ACKNOWLEDGEMENTS

I thank Delmar Blasco, Martin Holdgate, Jeffrey McNeely and Simon Stuart for their comments on an earlier draft of this paper.

REFERENCES

DEN HELD, J. J. (1981) Population changes in the Purple Heron in relation to drought in the wintering area. *Ardea* **69**: 185-191.

DUGAN, P. J. (1983) The conservation of herons during migration and in the wintering areas: a review of present understanding and requirements for future research. Pp. 141-154 in P. R. Evans, H. Hafner & P. L'Hermite, eds. *Shorebirds and large waterbirds conservation*. Brussels: Commission of the European Communities, Directorate-General for Science, Research and Development.

DUGAN, P. J. (1987) Socio-economic considerations in protecting shorebird sites in the developing world: some priorities and implications for the direction of future research. Pp. 146-148 in N. C. Davidson & M. W. Pienkowski, eds. *The conservation of international flyway population of waders*. Slimbridge, U.K.: Wader Study Goup (Bull. 49, Suppl.)/International Waterfowl and Wetlands Research Bureau (Spec. Publ. 7).

VAN DER LINDEN, J. (1988) The importance of Sahel wetlands for Palearctic migratory birds. Draft report to ICBP, Cambridge, U.K.

MONVAL, J.-Y., PIROT, J.-Y. & SMART, M. (1987) *Recensements d'Anatidés et de foulques hivernant en Afrique du nord et de l'ouest: Janvier 1984, 1985 et 1986*. Slimbridge, U.K.: International Waterfowl and Wetlands Research Bureau.

MOREL, G. (1973) The Sahel zone as an environment for Palearctic migrants. *Ibis* **115**: 413-417.

ROUX, F. & JARRY, G. (1984) Numbers, composition and distribution of populations of Anatidae wintering in West Africa. *Wildfowl* **35**: 48-60.

TIMBERLAKE, L. (1985) *Africa in crisis*. London: Earthscan.

FORWARD PLAN FOR THE ICBP MIGRATORY BIRDS PROGRAMME 1991-1994 (WEST PALEARCTIC–AFRICAN FLYWAYS)

TOBIAS SALATHÉ

International Council for Bird Preservation,
32 Cambridge Road, Girton, Cambridge CB3 0PJ, U.K.

INTRODUCTION

This Forward Plan defines the tasks for migratory bird conservation along the West Palearctic–African flyways which ICBP will address within the framework of its Strategy for the years 1991-1994. It builds on the results and experiences of activities undertaken since 1978, directed first by the European Committee for the Prevention of Mass Destruction of Migratory Birds, then by the ICBP Secretariat, and in collaboration with IUCN, IWRB and WWF.

THE CHALLENGE

Migratory birds are the common responsibility of many nations, and they are extremely valuable in establishing bonds of interest between countries. Because they often follow set routes, concentrate in conspicuous numbers in specific areas, or fill spring with their melodious dawn chorus, they attract the general birdwatching public and the scientific community, and also hunting and other exploitative pursuits.

Although only a few of the West Palearctic migratory bird species are yet threatened with global extinction, populations of many of the most conspicuous among them are markedly declining as a result of major losses of habitat available for breeding, refuelling on migration and wintering, the side-effects of pesticides used over large areas in both Europe and Africa, or heavy persecution by man at migration stop-over sites.

These birds therefore require conservation at a succession of sites, ideally through the centralized coordination of the activities of different interest groups. This work is valuable not only for its own sake, but also for the educational and institutional value it brings to countries developing their nature conservation infrastructure, and for the establishment of bonds between countries in the South and North which should lead to productive common involvement for conservation.

ICBP'S RESPONSE

Objectives and activities

The ICBP Migratory Birds Programme (MBP) covers specific activities which fall under the four categories of ICBP's main objectives: *Research, Field Actions, Advocacy and Policy, Strengthening the Conservation Movement* (cf. below). The activities can be divided into the following six fields:

Data gathering and analysis. To monitor the conservation status of important bird areas; to detect population trends of selected migratory bird species; to establish the ecological cause of changes detected in migratory bird populations, and to monitor the mass killing of migratory birds in relevant countries.

Education and training. To increase awareness of the link between environmentally sound management for migratory birds and the well-being of human populations which also depend upon their ecosystems; to provide training in habitat management, scientific monitoring of populations, sustainable wildlife utilization, and environmental education for technical staff in developing countries, and to make available and promote the wide dissemination of simple educational materials.

Species and habitat management. To promote the improved management of important bird habitats and sites by assisting the establishment or expansion of protected areas; to provide advice and assistance with the drawing up and implementation of management plans, and to assist with the development of regional management plans for threatened migratory species.

Network building. To develop a network of organizations and individuals promoting the conservation of birds and their habitats at local, national and international levels, and to foster the formation and development of organizations devoted to the study and conservation of birds.

International cooperation. To induce the provision of financial and technical assistance to countries where local expertise and funds are scarce; to advise governments on appropriate national wildlife legislation, and to promote the signing and ratification of relevant international wildlife conventions and their proper implementation.

Conservation counselling. To advise the conservation and development communities on how domestic subsidies (national or at EC level) and development-assistance policies affect migratory birds and their habitats; to recommend policy changes among the development-assistance agencies, and to specify action which these agencies should take to help the conservation of migratory birds rather than to hinder it.

Operation

The MBP has identified a clear niche to fit into the multitude of ongoing international conservation activities. The required actions are different for each region along the West Palearctic–African flyways:

In **North-western Europe** the MBP needs to build broad public awareness of the linkages between the conservation of migratory birds, tax payers' money and the environmental impacts of national subsidies within countries and bilateral and international development assistance to other countries along the flyways. ICBP member organizations in Western European countries have to play an important role in documenting these links, spreading the information, and building up the awareness of the general public. They are best suited to undertake national campaigns to increase awareness, raise funds, and conserve key habitats and sites in their own countries.

In the **Mediterranean** (i.e. southern Europe, the Mediterranean islands and North Africa), **Eastern Europe** and the **Near and Middle East,** the MBP has to focus on field projects to increase environmental awareness, conserve key habitats and sites, and reduce indiscriminate human persecution of migratory birds. Due to the links already established with many local organizations, ICBP is in a good position to focus its field actions on this region. Nevertheless, focal countries and regions will have to be selected carefully in order to ensure that ICBP activities are efficient, that they do not overlap, and that they complement the actions of sister organizations.

In **sub-Saharan Africa** (including the Sahelian countries) the MBP has to liaise and collaborate closely with other conservation and aid organizations already active in the region to ensure that planned and ongoing development and conservation projects cover adequately the problems and needs of migratory birds. Due to the existing heavy involvement of development assistance agencies and fund donors the MBP must either address gaps in specific countries not adequately covered by such agencies or add migratory bird related components to ongoing larger projects.

Thus it follows that the MBP can only be successful, and have the anticipated lasting impact on the conservation of migratory birds and their habitats, if it remains a joint effort by many partners (*Figure 1*).

The MBP needs coordination and direction of the different activities at the ICBP Secretariat. The Secretariat and ICBP member organizations must be seen as and act as one, promoting the overall aim of the MBP. The tasks outlined in the following chapters will be supervised by the ICBP Programme Department, and in particular by officers responsible for field actions in Europe and Africa, the projects on *Important Bird Areas in Europe* and *Dispersed Species in Europe.*

The MBP also needs careful coordination and collaboration with international sister organizations such as IUCN, WWF, IWRB, and others (Ramsar Convention Bureau, Bonn Convention Secretariat, etc). It needs support from European conservation, hunting and animal welfare organizations. It is the ICBP Secretariat's duty to solicit such support and ensure fruitful collaboration.

The role that national and local ICBP member organizations have to play to make the MBP a success is paramount. Some of the larger European ones (like the Royal Society for the Protection of Birds, U.K.; Vogelbescherming, Netherlands; Schweizer Vogelschutz, Switzerland; Dansk Ornitologisk Forening, Denmark; Deutscher Bund für Vogelschutz [now Naturschutzbund Deutschland], Germany and others) have been regular supporters in the past: others should be persuaded to join on a regular basis. It is these member organizations that are best suited to disseminate the information widely, to raise public awareness and concern, and have the local intelligence and infrastructure for effective campaigning and public fundraising.

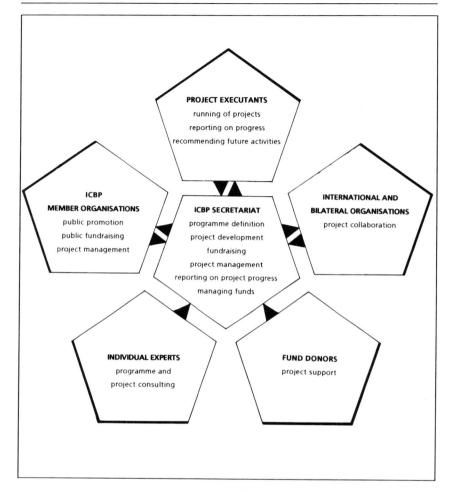

Figure 1: The functioning of the Migratory Birds Programme.

Funding needs and fundraising

Much of the MBP's success will depend on the availability of sufficient funds to carry out the tasks outlined below. Of utmost importance is the availability of sufficient funding for the core activities of the MBP which needs to cover the following staff time and related overhead costs of the Programme Department at the ICBP Secretariat: coordination (100 per cent), advocacy and policy (50 per cent), fundraising (50 per cent) and project administration/secretarial duties (50 per cent). It is anticipated that ICBP member organizations already involved with the MBP will provide these funds.

As a guideline, funds for field actions will have to be raised in three (complementary but not exclusive) ways: (1) smaller one-off projects will continue to be funded through public fundraising campaigns by ICBP member organizations (some having set up specific migratory birds committees), (2) funds for main field

Figure 2: Logo of the ICBP Migratory Birds Programme for the West Palearctic–African flyways. It illustrates the global connection of environmental problems through the Barn Swallow (*Hirundo rustica*) circulating regularly around the globe.

actions in the Mediterranean, Eastern Europe and the Middle East will need to be raised from aid and development agencies, conservation support organizations, ICBP World Environment Partners (corporate members), and other potential sources, and through special appeals by member organizations to their public, and (3) funds for specific conservation issues related to migratory birds will need to be incorporated in, and provided for, by development-assistance projects in sub-Saharan Africa; it is the coordinator's task to negotiate such agreements with the agencies involved.

RESEARCH

ICBP has undertaken various research and data-compiling projects to elucidate the threats to migratory birds in Europe and Africa. Analysis of the impact of human persecution, and the preparation of recovery plans for species and species-groups, are ongoing. Furthermore, continued interest is being shown by academic institutions in the fundamental questions of migration physiology and ecology. ICBP maintains close contact and a continuing exchange of ideas and information with organizations active in the field, and is dependent on information provided by long-term and large-scale monitoring programmes of migratory bird populations.

For the period 1991-1994, research priorities for the MBP will cover the following tasks if specific external funds can be found:

Task 1: To document, update and assess the status, distribution, ecology and conservation needs of migratory birds.

The MBP has been involved in the preparation of species recovery plans and discussions of large-scale monitoring programmes for trans-Saharan passerine migrants with different organizations in Europe. ICBP is therefore in a good position to continue to play a coordinating role for such activities. The research projects on *Dispersed Species in Europe* (funded by the Royal Society for the Protection of Birds) and on *Species of Particular Concern in Europe* (for the expert group of the U.N. Economic Commission for Europe on flora, fauna and habitats) currently undertaken by ICBP's European Programme are likely to provide further substantial data on which to proceed with targets A and B.

Target A: To prepare recovery plans for globally threatened species (*sensu* Collar & Andrew 1988) or vulnerable species groups of migratory birds (*sensu* Grimmett & Jones 1989) including habitat and site management recommendations.

Target B: To coordinate the setting-up of a European monitoring programme for populations of migrants that are currently thought to be declining or that can serve as environmental indicators.

Target C: To identify and monitor key habitats for wintering passerines in the Sahel through coordinated field surveys in carefully selected regions.

Task 2: To document and assess the impact of large-scale human persecution of migratory birds.

The MBP pioneered the first Mediterranean-wide overview on bird killing and has since continued to carry out regional assessments in the area. More recently the MBP instigated the first continent-wide ringing recovery analysis of 20 raptor and passerine species subject to heavy hunting pressure during migration (undertaken by the British Trust for Ornithology). ICBP is therefore willing to direct and coordinate future research and monitoring activities.

Target A: To follow up and expand preliminary ring-recoveries analysis undertaken by the British Trust for Ornithology in cooperation with ICBP and the Royal Society for the Protection of Birds (RSPB) (Tucker *et al.* 1990). Further work would cover a more comprehensive range of species and intensive studies of populations subject to different levels of hunting in different parts of their range.

Target B: To follow up, update and expand earlier field investigations undertaken by the MBP (Woldhek 1980) and the RSPB (Gutierrez 1990; Lambertini & Tallone 1990) in specific target areas in the Mediterranean.

FIELD ACTIONS

Field projects have constituted the main activities of the MBP in the past. Due to the substantial costs involved in carrying out field projects (which need to be set up in such a way that they will have a lasting impact for conservation in the areas concerned) it is crucial that the strongest emphasis is placed on the catalytic capacities of such undertakings, which depend in turn on the receptiveness of local people and the administration concerned. Realistically it will only be possible to carry out a very limited number of carefully selected projects in key countries.

Task 3: To conserve key wetlands and other habitats in which migratory birds concentrate and are at risk.

Wetlands hold great concentrations of migratory birds. This holds not only for birds directly linked to the presence of water, but also for migrant landbirds refuelling at stop-over sites which provide abundant food supplies. The most important habitat in this context is Mediterranean *maquis* with a diverse vegetation structure the best parts of which often remain close to natural wetlands. Being extremely fertile and having much scenic value, such areas inevitably attract dense human populations (both resident and tourist) which often destroy these resources through pollution, development and unsustainable use (overfishing, overgrazing, over-use of firewood, excessive disturbance, etc.).

The MBP aims to make a major contribution to the conservation and sustainable development of wetlands and habitats important for migrants in key areas that are not adequately covered by its partner organizations (but in close cooperation with them) in the Mediterranean, Eastern Europe and the Middle East.

Target A: Conservation and sustainable development of coastal wetlands in Egypt. Priority: *Lake Bardawil*; other target areas include wetlands of the Nile Delta, the Red Sea islands and Lake Nasser reservoir.

Target B: Conservation and sustainable development of coastal wetlands in Morocco. Priority: *Merja Zerga*; other target areas include Sidi Boughaba Lake, Massa River mouth, and Khnifiss lagoon.

Target C: Conservation and sustainable development of wetlands in Turkey. Priorities: *Menderes Delta, Camalti Tuzlasi*, and others.

Target D: Conservation and sustainable development of coastal wetlands in Algeria. Priority: *El Kala* wetlands.

Target E: Conservation and sustainable development of the *Danube Delta* in Romania.

Target F: Conservation and sustainable development of key areas in Yugoslavia. Priorities: *Neretva Delta, Deliblatsca pescara* area.

Target G: Conservation and sustainable development of key areas in Cyprus. Priorities: *Kanliköy and Gönyeli Reservoirs*, Akrotiri Peninsula, Karpas Peninsula, and others.

In sub-Saharan Africa, the MBP is currently involved in conservation activities at a number of wetlands. The future involvement of ICBP in these projects needs careful evaluation of the specific and complementary impact the MBP can have on such projects in the light of current and planned activities of sister organizations.

Target H: Re-evaluation of the specific need for ICBP's involvement in current wetland conservation projects in Ghana, Guinea, Nigeria and Senegal.

Target I: Evaluation of the specific need for future ICBP involvement in conservation projects at Abijatta-Shalla Lakes (Ethiopia), Rift Valley lakes (Kenya, Tanzania), Kafue Flats (Zambia), Okavango Delta (Botswana) and Walvis Bay (Namibia).

ADVOCACY AND POLICY

Much of the information ICBP gathers will result in effective conservation improvements only if it is made available to (and acted upon by) the appropriate authorities.

The first step in this process is to prepare the relevant information for wide dissemination, followed by campaigns to influence public opinion and to lobby decision-makers. With such broad support, better regulations and their enforcement can be obtained from the relevant authorities. So far the MBP has not adequately addressed the requirements for efficient advocacy in favour of improved migratory bird conservation; a greater part of the programme activities will therefore be directed towards these aims.

Task 4: To promote the ratification and proper implementation of international conservation conventions and directives.

During the execution of field actions many opportunities arise in contacts with national authorities and NGOs to promote the ratification of international conventions beneficial to migratory bird conservation by states that are not yet members, or to argue for better implementation of such treaties in member states where adequate enforcement is lacking.

Target A: To promote adequate implementation of the EEC Directive on the Conservation of Wild Birds in contacts with officials in EC member states and through public statements; to advise the Commission of the EC on improvements of the species-lists in the annexes of the directive; and to further the establishment of a forceful EC Directive on the Conservation of Natural and Semi-natural Habitats with an appropriate financial budget to support the implementation of its objectives.

Target B: To promote the ratification of the Ramsar Convention in states that are not yet members; to establish a shadow list of sites important for migratory birds not yet listed under the Ramsar Convention (for member states and others), and where necessary to call for the monitoring procedure foreseen under the convention for sites where the ecological character is changing.

Target C: To promote the ratification of the Bonn Convention; to promote the preparation and enforcement of agreements for threatened migratory bird species, and to advise the convention Secretariat and Scientific Council on the completion of species lists in the annexes of the convention.

The conservation of migratory birds has increasingly to be addressed in an integrated way, which recognizes the interrelations of ecological and socio-economic factors influencing the population dynamics of target species and species-groups. Such realities of today's global environment will have to be addressed under tasks 5 and 6. It is a field of expertise mainly outside the immediate experience of ICBP staff. Much effort has therefore to be devoted to establishing the most efficient contacts and working relations with external specialists. Additional funding for documentation and research work under these tasks should be sought by the Secretariat in order to provide the necessary basis for fruitful work.

Task 5: To document the production, trade and use of pesticides with harmful effects on migratory birds and their habitats, and to promote environmentally safe solutions.

Target A: To establish a collaboration with pesticide specialists in order to identify potentially hazardous products, their harmful side-effects and their range and methods of use, and to prepare a shortlist of the products and applications of most damaging effect to migratory birds and their habitats.

Target B: To investigate the trade and trade regulations governing these products; to recommend improvements for the sake of migratory birds affected by the side-effects of the use of these products, and to lobby the relevant authorities to implement the measures recommended.

Task 6: To document the environmental impact of EC structural funds, international (EC, World Bank and other development banks) and bilateral development aid on migratory birds and their habitats and promote environmentally safe alternatives.

Target A: To provide ICBP member organizations with guidelines on how to screen bilateral development-assistance projects of their national authorities and of development aid NGOs for significant side-effects for migratory birds and their habitats; to collect and publicise such data, and to lobby the relevant authorities, together with national member organizations, for environmentally sound solutions.

Task 7: To undertake campaigns in favour of improved conservation of migratory birds and their habitats.

Target A: To prepare and initiate publicity and media campaigns on the aims and activities of the MBP for adaptation and execution by ICBP member organizations in their respective countries; to raise public awareness of and concern for migratory bird conservation problems, and to raise additional funds for the MBP.

STRENGTHENING THE CONSERVATION MOVEMENT

To conserve migratory birds and their habitats in the long term, a strong and active network of non-governmental conservation organizations is needed. ICBP with its multitude of existing member organizations (from local to international level), is in a unique position to further the establishment of new groups and the development of existing organizations, and will ultimately benefit from the increased local expertise and intelligence of such groups for its own conservation work.

Task 8: To support local conservation organizations working for the conservation of migratory birds and their habitats.

The following targets list the priority countries and organizations at the time of writing. Due to the very nature of such support it has nevertheless to remain flexible and include regions and organizations other than those mentioned, if and when the political situation requires it. In particular the support and development of strong bird conservation NGOs in Eastern Europe is a priority that falls in part within the remit of the MBP.

Target A: To continue the support of and undertake joint ventures with the Malta Ornithological Society, the Ornithological Union of Yugoslavia, the Romanian Ornithological Society and the North Cyprus Society for Bird Protection.

Target B: To continue the low-level support of and undertake joint ventures with the Lega Italiana Protezzione Uccelli (LIPU), the Ligue Française pour la Protection des Oiseaux (LPO), the Sociedad Española de Ornitología (SEO), the Cyprus Ornithological Societies (1957/1970), Friends of the Earth Cyprus and the Turkish Society for the Protection of Nature (DHKD).

Target C: To encourage and support the development of strong bird conservation NGOs in Greece, Poland, Morocco, Tunisia and Egypt.

ACKNOWLEDGEMENTS

This Forward Plan is the result of many fruitful discussions at the ICBP Secretariat, during and after the workshop on the MBP held on 20 May 1989 during the 17th Conference of the European Continental Section of ICBP in Adana, Turkey, and with colleagues of sister organizations. The editor would like to thank particularly Alfred Baldacchino, Pat Dugan, John Fanshawe, Alistair Gammell, Paul Goriup, Adam Gretton, Richard Grimmett, Fritz Hirt, Christoph Imboden, Miriam Langeveld, Hans Meltofte, Günther Mitlacher, Mike Parr, Mike Rands, Joe Sultana, Shunji Usui and Siegfried Woldhek for their most valuable contributions.

REFERENCES

COLLAR, N. J. & ANDREW, P. (1988) *Birds to watch: the ICBP world checklist of threatened birds.* Cambridge, U.K.: International Council for Bird Preservation (Techn. Publ. 8).
FANSHAWE, J. & GRETTON, A. (1989) Africa Action Plan: priorities for the ICBP conservation programme. Cambridge, U.K.: International Council For Bird Preservation. Internal report.
GRIMMETT, R. F. A. & JONES, T. A. (1989) *Important bird areas in Europe.* Cambridge, U.K.: International Council for Bird Preservation (Techn. Publ. 9).
GUTIERREZ, J. E. (1990) *La caza de passeriformes en España.* Madrid: Sociedad Española de Ornitología (Report).

LAMBERTINI, M. & TALLONE, G. (1990) *Bird killing in Italy.* Parma: Lega Italiana per la Protezione degli Uccelli (Report).

TUCKER, G. M., MCCULLOCH, M. N. & BAILLIE, S. R. (1990) *Review of the importance of losses incurred to migratory birds during migration.* Tring, U.K.: British Trust for Ornithology (Resrch. Rep. 58).

WOLDHEK, S. (1980) *Bird killing in the Mediterranean.* Second edition. Zeist: European Committee for the Prevention of Mass Destruction of Migratory Birds.

INTERNATIONAL COUNCIL FOR BIRD PRESERVATION

PUBLICATIONS

RED DATA BOOK

Threatened Birds of Africa and Related Islands: the ICBP/IUCN Red Data Book, Part 1 (third edition). N. J. Collar and S. N. Stuart (1985). 795 pp. £24.00.

ICBP TECHNICAL PUBLICATIONS SERIES

No. 1 *Conservation of New World Parrots.* Proceedings of ICBP Parrot Working Group meeting, St Lucia, 1980. Ed. R. Pasquier (1981). 498 pp. <u>Only</u> available from <u>Smithsonian Institution Press</u>, Washington, DC 20560, U.S.A. <u>or I.B.D. Ltd</u>, 66 Wood Lane End, Hemel Hempstead, Herts HP2 4RG, U.K.

No. 2 *Status and Conservation of the World's Seabirds* – **out of print**.

No. 3 *Conservation of Island Birds.* Proceedings of ICBP Island management Symposium, Cambridge, 1982. Ed. P. J. Moors (1985). 281 pp. £16.50.

No. 4 *Conservation of Tropical Forest Birds.* Proceedings of ICBP Tropical Forest Birds Symposium, Cambridge, 1982. Ed. A. W. Diamond and T. E. Lovejoy (1985). 330 pp. £16.50.

No. 5 *Conservation Studies on Raptors.* Proceedings of ICBP 2nd World Conference on Birds of Prey, Thessaloniki, Greece, 1982. Ed. I. Newton, R. D. Chancellor (1985). 494 pp. £19.50.

No. 6 *The Value of Birds.* Proceedings of ICBP Symposium on Birds as Socio-Economic Resources, Kingston, Canada, 1986. Ed. A. W. Diamond, F. L. Filion (1987). 275 pp. £12.50.

No. 7 *Ecology and Conservation of Grassland Birds.* Proceedings of ICBP Symposium held at the 1986 World Conference, Kingston, Canada. Ed. P. D. Goriup (1988). 256 pp. £16.50.

No. 8 *Birds to Watch: the ICBP World Checklist of Threatened Birds.* N. J. Collar and P. Andrew (1988). 320 pp. £12.50.

No. 9 *Important Bird Areas in Europe.* R. F. A. Grimmett and T. A. Jones (1989). 906 pp. £21.50.

No. 10 *Disease and Threatened Birds.* Proceedings of ICBP XIX World Conference Symposium, Ontario, Canada, 1986. Ed. J. E. Cooper (1989). 210 pp. £16.50.

No. 11 *Seabirds Status and Conservation: a supplement.* Ed. J. P. Croxall (1991). 316 pp. £17.50.

No. 12 *Conserving Migratory Birds.* Ed. T. Salathé (1991). 405 pp. £19.50.

ICBP MONOGRAPHS

No. 1 *Biodiversity and Conservation in the Caribbean: profiles of selected islands.* T. H. Johnson (1988). 162 pp. £8.00.

No. 2 *Resident Forest Birds in Thailand: their status and conservation.* P. D. Round (1988). 225 pp. £8.00.

No. 3 *Key Forests for Threatened Birds in Africa.* N. J. Collar and S. N. Stuart (1988). 109 pp. £7.00.

No. 4 *Nepal's Forest Birds: their status and conservation.* Carol Inskipp (1989). 199 pp. £9.00.

No. 5 *Livre Rouge des Oiseaux Menacés des Régions Françaises d'Outre-Mer.* Eds. J.-C. Thibault et I. Guyot (1989). 258 pp. £25.00

No. 6 *The Ecology and Conservation of the Slender-billed Curlew* (Numenius tenuirostris). A. Gretton (1991). Available soon.